PRAISE FOR *HAITI WILL NOT PERISH*

'Deibert's exhaustive reportage gets an edge from his righteous anger on behalf of a people with whom he has a deep and abiding connection. An invaluable sourcebook for the period, and also a riveting read.'
– Madison Smartt Bell, author of *All Souls' Rising: A Novel of Haiti*

'Deibert brings his journalistic eye and deep affection for Haiti to an unflinching and urgently needed work, documenting the political corruption, culture of impunity and international meddling that have plagued this nation over the past two decades.'
– Carrie Gibson, author of *Empire's Crossroads: A History of the Caribbean*

'An engrossing tour through Haiti's extraordinary history of survival. Its great strength is Deibert's sharp ear for Haiti's many voices, for too long muted by a jaundiced media.'
– Matthew J. Smith, University of the West Indies

PRAISE FOR MICHAEL DEIBERT'S PREVIOUS BOOK
THE DEMOCRATIC REPUBLIC OF CONGO

'Scrupulously researched… compassion impels [Deibert's] curiosity'
– *The Guardian*

'Michael Deibert's work is the very model of what strong independent journalism can accomplish. His Congo book is no ordinary achievement. It bulges with both the grand sweep of history and a rich variety of voices gathered through enterprising, on the ground reporting.'
– Howard W. French, author of *China's Second Continent*

ABOUT THE AUTHOR

Michael Deibert's writing has appeared in *The Guardian, The Washington Post, The Wall Street Journal, The Miami Herald, Le Monde Diplomatique, Folha de São Paulo* and the *World Policy Journal,* among other venues. He has been a featured commentator on international affairs on the BBC, Al Jazeera, Channel 4, France 24, National Public Radio, WNYC New York Public Radio and KPFK Pacifica Radio. He is the author of *In the Shadow of Saint Death: The Gulf Cartel and the Price of America's Drug War in Mexico* (2014), *The Democratic Republic of Congo: Between Hope and Despair* (2013) and *Notes from the Last Testament: The Struggle for Haiti* (2005).

HAITI WILL NOT PERISH

A RECENT HISTORY

MICHAEL DEIBERT

ZED
Zed Books
LONDON

Haiti Will Not Perish: A Recent History was first published in 2017
by Zed Books Ltd, The Foundry, 17 Oval Way, London SE11 5RR, UK.

www.zedbooks.net

Typeset in Adobe Garammond Pro by seagulls.net
Index by John Barker
Cover design by Alice Marwick
Cover photo © Chantal Regnault

A catalogue record for this book is available from the British Library.

ISBN 978-1-78360-863-8 hb
ISBN 978-1-78360-798-3 pb
ISBN 978-1-78360-799-0 pdf
ISBN 978-1-78360-800-3 epub
ISBN 978-1-78360-801-0 mobi

Printed and bound by CPI Group (UK) Ltd, Croydon, CR0 4YY

Fuata nyuki ukafe zingani (Follow the bee and die in the hive)

– Swahili proverb

CONTENTS

Acknowledgments   ix

Abbreviations   xi

Map of Haiti   xvii

Prologue: Storm Clouds   1

1. *Istwa* (History)   11
2. *Les Blancs Débarquent*   45
3. Operation Baghdad   54
4. Deceptions and Delusions   84
5. The Return   95
6. Give Us Peace or Rest in Peace   108
7. Uneasy Neighbors   129
8. *Lavi Chè*   148
9. Plots and Revelations   159
10. *Douze Janvier*   182
11. The Republic of NGOs   202
12. Plague   217
13. Tèt Kale   239
14. In the Kingdom of Impunity   259
15. Open for Business   277
16. A Disaster Foretold   298
17. When They Are President, They Will Understand Me   321

Epilogue   337

Notes   345

Bibliography   442

Index   445

ACKNOWLEDGMENTS

During the 20 years I have been involved with the extraordinary nation of Haiti, my work there and my attempts to understand the place have been inestimably helped – and my spirit so often revived – by so many people.

Among the sons and daughters of Ayiti Cherie itself, I was aided in decoding the complexities of the country by the wisdom of Marilyn B. Allien, Jean-Claude and Sylvie Bajeux, Lolo and Mimerose Beaubrun, Russell Behrmann, Thony Belizaire, Angie Bell, Alice Blanchet, Richard Boncy, Patrick Brun, Gertrude Celidon, Clotilde Charlot, Adrien Demes, Michèle Duvivier Pierre-Louis, André Elizée, Pierre Espérance, Emmanuelle Gilles, Laënnec Hurbon, Bazelais Jean-Baptiste, Naomie Labaty, Frantz and Tacha Large, Fidji Lemoine, Jean-Claude Louis, Lorraine Mangonès, Charles Manus, Louis-Henri Mars, Alain Maximilien, Herby Metellus, Daniel Morel, Guy Noel, Raoul Peck, James Petit-Frere, Luxama Pierre-Richard, Louino Robillard, Jacques Roche, Angela Salellas, Marc Steed, Claude Sterling, Michael Stitt, Wendell Theodore, Brunette Tondreau, Hans Tippenhauer and Alexandre Viard.

Other foreigners also heard the call of the *lwa* and could not resist it, and I have been grateful for their friendship and advice: Philippe Allouard, Nadège Bellande Robertson, Peter Christopher, Katherine Coder, David Doherty, Anna Ferdinand, Ben Fountain, Anne Fuller, Carrie Gibson, Gerry Hadden, Javier Hernández Valencia, Jessica Hsu, Bahare Khodabande, Amy King, Jacqualine Labrom, Reynald Lally, Eirin Mobekk, Patrick Moynihan, Laura Parker, Jane Regan, Chantal Regnault, Thos Robinson, Sarah Sandsted, Alex Smailes, Michael Tarr, the Trimble family, Manuel Vazquez Boidard, Jan Voordouw and Amber Walsh.

Thank you also to my far-flung friends who stood by me through the years of poverty and adversity it took to write this book: Justin Cappiello, Natasha Del Toro, Anna Edgerton, Sasha Elliott, Melanie Erker, Meghan Feeks, Daniela Guzmán Peña, Andrew McConnell, Fernando Peinado Alcaraz, Natalia Pizzatti, Nomi Prins, Francesca Romeo, Pedro Rodriguez, Claudia Scalise, Philip Schnell, Laura Shafferman, Sutton Stokes, Claire Sturm and Hilary Wallis.

Thanks to Zed Books and my editor there, Kika Sroka-Miller.

This book is also a tribute to the memory of my mother, Jann Marie Deibert, that of my maternal grandmother, Leah Breon, and that of my paternal grandparents, Joseph and Elizabeth Deibert. To my grandfather, James Breon, my father, Caleb Deibert, and my brothers, Benjamin and Christopher, thank you for your support along the way.

Michael Deibert
Miami, April 2017

ABBREVIATIONS

AAA – Ayiti An Aksyon

ADIH – Association des Industries d'Haïti

AFP – Agence France-Presse

AJH – Association des Journalistes Haïtiens

ANAMAH – Association Nationale des Magistrats Haïtiens

ANC – African National Congress

APC – Armored personnel carrier

APROSIFA – Association pour la Santé Intégrale de la Famille

ASEC – Assemblées des sections communales

AVIGES – Association des Victimes du Génocide de la Scierie

BCED – Bureau du Contentieux Électoral Départemental

BLTS – Bureau de Lutte contre le Trafic des Stupéfiants

BNRH – Banque Nationale de la République d'Haïti

BOID – Brigade d'Opération et d'Intervention Départementale

BRH – Banque de la République d'Haïti

BRI – Brigade d'Intervention Rapide

CAED – Coordination de l'Aide Externe au Développement

CAMEP – Centrale Autonome Métropolitaine d'Eau Potable

CARICOM – Caribbean Community

CARLI – Comité des Avocats pour le Respect des Libertés Individuelles

CASEC – *Conseils d'administration des sections communales*

CCIH – Chambre du Commerce et d'Industrie d'Haïti

CEA – Commission d'Enquête Administrative

CEDH – Centre Œcuménique des Droits Humains

CEP – Conseil Électoral Provisoire

CEPR – Center for Economic and Policy Research

CIAPEAJ – Commission Indépendante d'Appui aux Enquêtes Relatives aux Assassinats des Journalistes Haïtiens

CICIG – Comisión Internacional Contra la Impunidad en Guatemala

CIDA – Canadian International Development Agency

CIEVE – Commission Indépendante d'Évaluation et de Vérification Électorale

CIMO – Corps d'Intervention et de Maintien de l'Ordre

CIVPOL – Civilian Police

CLED – Centre pour la Libre Entreprise et la Démocratie

CNDDR – Commission Nationale de Désarmement Démantèlement et Réinsertion

CNE – Centre National des Equipements

CNG – Conseil National de Gouvernement

CNMP – Commission Nationale des Marchés Publics

CNO – Conseil National d'Observation Électorale

CONASOVIC – Coordination des Sociétaires Victimes des Coopératives

CONATEL – Conseil National des Télécommunications

CONHANE – Conseil Haïtien des Acteurs Non Étatiques

CONOCS – Colectif des Notables de Cité Soleil

CRESFED – Centre de Recherche et de Formation Économique et Sociale pour le Développement

CSPJ – Conseil Supérieur du Pouvoir Judiciaire

CSPN – Conseil Superieur de la Police Nationale d'Haïti

DCPJ – Direction Centrale de la Police Judiciaire d'Haïti

DEA – Drug Enforcement Agency

DGI – Direction Générale des Impôts

DNCD – Dirección Nacional de Control de Drogas

DPKO – Department of Peacekeeping Operations

DV – *Délégués de ville*

ESKANP – Efò ak Solidarite pou konstui yon Altènativ Nasyonal Popilè

FADH – Forces Armées d'Haïti

FARA – Foreign Agents Registration Act

FARH – Forces Armées Révolutionnaires d'Haïti

FCC – Federal Communications Commission

FLRN – Front de Résistance pour la Libération et la Reconstruction Nationales

FNCD – Front National pour le Changement et la Démocratie

FOKAL – Fondasyon Konesans Ak Libète

FOPARK – Fos Patriyotik pou Respe Konstitisyon

FRAPH – Front pour l'Avancement et le Progrès Haïtien

FRN – Front pour la Reconstruction Nationale

FUNGLODE – Fundación Global Democracia y Desarrollo

GARR – Groupe d'Appui aux Rapatriés et Réfugiés

GHESKIO – Groupe Haïtien d'Étude du Sarcome de Kaposi et des Infections Opportunistes

GRAMIR – Groupe de Recherche et d'Appui au Milieu Rural

IACHR – Inter-American Commission on Human Rights

IADB – Inter-American Development Bank

IHRC – Interim Haiti Recovery Commission

IMF – International Monetary Fund

IOM – International Organization for Migration

IRI – International Republican Institute

JILAP – Commission Épiscopale Nationale Justice et Paix

KID – Konvansyon Inite Demokratik

KOFAVIV – Komisyon Fanm Viktim pou Viktim

KONAKOM – Komité National du Kongrés des Mouvements Démocratiques

KOREGA – Kòdinasyon Rezistans Grandans

KOZEPEP – Komite Zafè Elektoral Peyizan pou Eleksyon Pwop

LAA – Latibonit Ann Aksyon

LAPEH – Ligue Alternative pour le Progrès et l'Émancipation Haïtienne

LFHH – La Fondation Héritage pour Haïti

MIDH – Mouvement pour l'Instauration de la Démocratie en Haïti

MINUSTAH – Mission des Nations Unies pour la Stabilisation en Haïti

MOCHRENA – Mouvement Chrétien pour une Nouvelle Haïti

MOP – Mouvement des Ouvriers et Paysans

MOPOD – Mouvement Patriotique de l'Opposition Démocratique

MOREPLA – Mouvement de Revendications des Paysans de l'Artibonite

MPNKP – Mouvman Peyizan Nasyonal Kongre Papay

MPP – Mouvman Peyizan Papay

MRN – Mouvement pour la Reconstruction Nationale

MUDHA – El Movimiento de Mujeres Dominico-Haitianas

NCHR – National Coalition for Haitian Rights

NDI – National Democratic Institute

OAS – Organization of American States

OCHA – Office for the Coordination of Humanitarian Affairs

OCID – Observatoire Citoyen pour l'Institutionnalisation de la Démocratie

ODVA – Organisme de Développement de l'Artibonite

ONA – Office National d'Assurance-vieillesse

OPL – Òganizasyon Politik Lavalas

PADF – Pan American Development Foundation

PANPRA – Parti Nationaliste Progressiste et Révolutionnaire Haïtien

PAPDA – Plateforme Haïtienne de Plaidoyer pour un Développement Alternatif

PCH – Parti Communiste Haïtien

PDCH – Parti Démocrate-Chrétien Haïtien

PDNA – Post Disaster Needs Assessment

PEPADEP – Program for the Eradication of Porcine Swine Fever and Development of Pig-Raising

PHTK – Parti Haïtien Tèt Kale

PLANOPA – Plate-forme Nationale des Organisations Paysannes Haïtiennes

PLASMAGRA – Plate-forme des Secteurs Motivés pour l'Avancement de Grand Ravine

PLB – Parti Louvri Baryè

PLD – Partido de la Liberación

PNDPH – Parti National Démocratique Progressiste d'Haïti

PNH – Police Nationale d'Haïti

POHDH – Plateforme des Organisations Haïtiennes de Défense des Droits Humains

PPN – Parti Populaire National

PRD – Partido Revolucionario Dominicano

PRN – Parti de la Rénovation Nationale

PRSC – Partido Reformista Social Cristiano

PSP – Parlementaires pour la Stabilité et le Progrès

PUN – Parti Unité Nationale

RACPABA – Réseau des Associations Coopératives du Commerce et de Production Agricole du Bas-Artibonite

RAMICOSM – Rassemblement des Militants Conséquents de Saint-Marc

RDNP – Rassemblement des Démocrates Nationaux Progressistes

RNDDH – Réseau National de Défense des Droits Humains

SAKALA – Sant Kominote Altènatif Ak Lapè

SHADA – Société Haitiano-Américaine de Dévelopment Agricole

SME – Small and medium enterprise

SOCABANK – Société Caribéenne de Banque S.A.

SOFA – Solidarite Fanm Ayisyèn

SONAPI – Société Nationale des Parcs Industriels

SOUTHCOM – United States Southern Command

TKL – Ti Kominote Legliz

UCADDE – Union de Citoyens Haïtiens Démocrates pour le Développement et l'Education

UCREF – Unite Centrale de Renseignements Financiers

UDMO – Unité Départementale de Maintien d'Ordre

UEH – Université d'État d'Haïti

ULCC – Unité de Lutte Contre la Corruption

UN – United Nations

UNASUR – Unión de Naciones Suramericanas

UNDP – United Nations Development Program

UNESCO – United Nations Educational, Scientific and Cultural Organization

UNOPS – United Nations Office for Project Services

UNPOL – United Nations Police

USAID – United States Agency for International Development

USGPN – Unité de Sécurité de la Garde du Palais National

VSN – Volontaires de la Sécurité Nationale

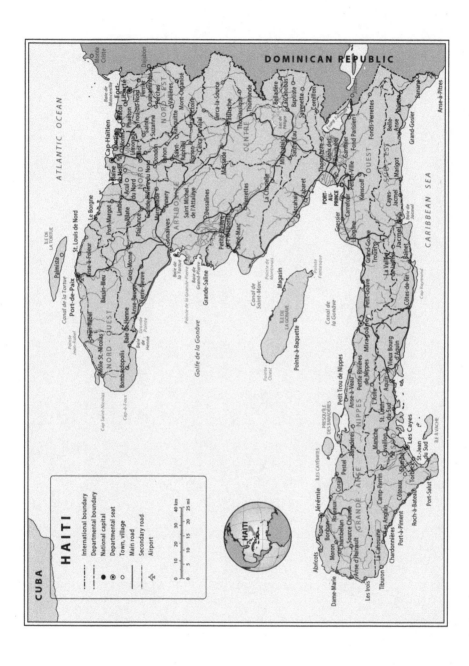

To the people of Haiti, who have taught me so much.

PROLOGUE
STORM CLOUDS

We stood in the shadow of mist-shrouded mountains stripped bare of trees, at a clutch of tarp-covered market stands pitched beside an immense, flat field. A series of boulders lay at rest like pairs of dice tossed by an indifferent divine hand. Two women sat, side by side, stirring a pot of boiling *marinade* patties.

"About midnight, the water started rushing in," one of the women told me, as a persistent, drizzling rain descended onto the valley. "Our houses were taken, almost everything we had was swept away. Everyone was running, but they had no idea where they would go. My daughter was 16 years old and she drowned."

The woman's name was Elise Rousseau, and I met her near the village of Fonds-Verrettes in the mountains near Haiti's border with the Dominican Republic. In the village of Thoman, a rough 30-minute drive down a trickling stream bed from Fonds-Verrettes, I found a 67-year-old farmer named Louis Cantel surveying a field of corn cut through at various points by a similar violent swathe of rocks and stones.

"Many people died," he told me. "From here all the way to the frontier, those who didn't die, their goats, cows and chickens were all washed away."

"We know it's dangerous to live here, because we know that the water could always come back," another Thoman farmer told me as he eyed the clouds from beneath a straw peasant's hat. "But we don't have any money to move anywhere else."

I found myself here, among the *gouverneurs de la rosée*, or masters of the dew, as the great Haitian author Jacques Roumain had once described the country's peasantry, at a pivotal time in Haiti's long struggle for liberation. Liberation from the collective trauma of slavery and occupation, from an economic system that had led the country to ruin and from the tyranny of its own leaders.

In the early morning hours of 29 February 2004, Haiti's president, Jean-Bertrand Aristide, a democratic icon who had decided years before he was not beholden to the rules of democracy, had fled the country into exile. He left

1

behind him a nation devastated by sectarian political warfare, environmental crises, and its treasury virtually bare due to years of corruption and theft.

The unraveling of the Aristide government was a uniquely painful chapter in the history of Haiti, a country that had also been deeply scarred by the 29-year family dictatorship of François Duvalier and his son, Jean-Claude Duvalier, who collectively ruled from 1957 until 1986.

I had first visited Haiti in 1997, returned a number of times, and lived there for a majority of the time between 2001 and 2004. It was an extraordinarily seductive and challenging place. The sinuous *konpa* and driving *rasin* music that pumped out of the ebulliently decorated public *camionettes* (known as tap-taps), the beautiful poetry of the country's national Creole language, the good humor and gentleness of its people living in circumstances of grinding deprivation, the byzantine pantheon of vodou spirits (called *lwa*) and their significance, the glittering output of the country's literary and visual arts. Even in the ramshackle and often squalid capital of Port-au-Prince, so different in many ways than the rather more sedate and scenic climes of areas along the coast such as Jacmel or the agrarian life of the Plateau Central, one could detect a certain appeal around a certain hour. Jacques Stéphen Alexis, one of Haiti's greatest writers, described Port-au-Prince in his 1955 book *Compère Général Soleil* as a place where:

> Towards three o'clock in the afternoon the wind picked up suddenly, galloping and roaring through the city. The pelicans over the port whirled endlessly. The sea put on its fancy green dress and donned shawls of lace foam.[1]

Gradually, my Creole improved, helped in no small measure by the fact that my modest retainer from Reuters, where I worked for a time, made purchasing a vehicle a luxury I couldn't afford. Thus obliged to do so, I traversed the streets of the capital in shared taxis, and, in between cities in jauntily colored tap-taps, people were curious to talk with this *blan* who chose to travel in the same manner they did. It was in the great patience and forbearance of the people I would chat with on a thousand such rides that I began to fully appreciate the mercurial political pulse of the country and the extraordinary battle against financial collapse and despair most Haitians had to fight against just to get from one day to the next.

* * *

Haiti was born in the fires of the infernal machine of slavery. Following the arrival of Columbus near Môle-Saint-Nicolas on the island we now call Hispaniola in 1492, the indigenous Arawak were quickly enslaved and worked to death by the Spanish, and, by way of replacement, by the mid-1500s there were over 30,000 African slaves on the island, only a foretaste of what was to come. When the Treaty of Ryswick granted the western third of Hispaniola to the French in 1697, that swathe of land was renamed Saint-Domingue, and sugar cultivation became the touchstone of its economy. By the end of the 1700s, Saint-Domingue supplied three-fourths of the world's sugar, and its economy was generating more income than that of all 13 original North American colonies combined. It quickly became France's wealthiest colony, but one where a population of 40,000 whites lorded over 30,000 mulattos and free blacks and 500,000 slaves in conditions of nightmarish brutality.

On the evening of 3 June 1770, as residents sought relief from the heat with an evening stroll under a starry cloudless sky, Port-au-Prince was struck by a horrific earthquake. At first, the earth issued a terrible, cacophonous groan that sent terrified citizens fleeing into the street, and then the mountains around the bay buckled, structures elegant and modest collapsed upon their owners and virtually every public building between Port-au-Prince and Petit-Goâve tumbled to earth. A two-month-old infant named Alexandre Pétion, the son of a wealthy French father and a mulatto mother, miraculously escaped death when gathered up into the arms of an aunt running into the street before the house his family lived in collapsed into rubble with a "frightful roar." The capital was leveled, and dazed survivors stumbled to and fro, their ears met with the terrible sounds of the dead and dying, of loved ones trapped and slowly expiring under piles of rubble, unable to be saved. It is believed over 200 people died. Following the calamity, as the sun beat down relentlessly and the dead were interred into mass graves, the Conseil de Port-au-Prince, as the city's colonial administration was known, was seemingly torn with indecision as to how to proceed as they met under a great tent. A quarter of the remaining buildings had to be torn down, largely replaced with wooden structures, the materials for which were provided by the forests around Gonaïves, Île de la Gonâve and Baradères. This would be the beginning of a parasitic and destructive relationship between Haiti's cities and its countryside.[2]

Then, on the night of 14 August 1791, a towering black overseer brought from Jamaica named Boukman conducted a long, complex vodou ceremony at Bwa Cayman (The Woods of the Crocodile) amid a dramatic tropical storm during which the attending slaves pledged to rise up against their masters, which they did, a week later, across the Plaine du Cap.[3] By August 1793, the former Toussaint Bréda (thus named for the Bréda Plantation on which he served as a coachman) announced himself as Toussaint Louverture in a proclamation in which he stated:

> I have undertaken vengeance. I want liberty and equality to reign in Saint-Domingue. I am working to make that happen. Unite yourself to us, brothers, and fight with us for the same cause.[4]

Toussaint had taught himself to read and write and was such an outstanding horseman that he became known as the *centaure de la Savanne*. He was joined in rebellion by a series of extraordinary personalities. There was Jean-Jacques Dessalines, a former slave from a plantation on the Plaine-du-Nord who, like Louverture, had held the position of foreman before he joined the cause. There was Henri Christophe, an English-speaking former slave believed to be originally from Grenada who as a very young man was thought to have fought with French forces during the Siege of Savannah during the U.S. War of Independence. There was Alexandre Pétion, whose white and mulatto parentage made him a *gens de couleur* (free man of color) and who had been educated in France before returning to Saint-Domingue. Though Pétion took some time to warm to the nationalist cause, he became one of its most valuable military commanders.

As to be expected in a battle between people who had suffered every degradation slavery had to offer and a colonial force that regarded them as subhuman, the carnage was terrible. In 1796, Toussaint declared himself "governor for life," and announced a willingness to allow Haiti to remain a colonial state – with slavery abolished – attached to France. Sectarianism soon became the order of the day, with the color issue – black versus mulatto – rearing its head in a 1799 rebellion by dissident general André Rigaud, aided by Alexandre Pétion and Jean-Pierre Boyer, in a conflict that became known as the *Guerre des couteaux* (War of Knives) and ended with Rigaud's defeat and exile. By 1800, Toussaint had doled out abandoned plantations to officers in the new revolutionary army who instituted the *fermage* system, itself little more than indentured servitude. The following year, Toussaint seized the eastern portion of the island. But with the Treaty of Amiens giving a pause in the European theater of war, France's Napoleon Bonaparte promptly sent some 40,000 troops under the command of his brother-in-law General Charles Leclerc back to Cap-Français (Napoleon's sister, Pauline, and André Rigaud would arrive with him) to crush the rebellion once and for all. Haiti's founding fathers showed their aptitude for betrayal as Christophe and Pétion defected to Leclerc's side and forced Louverture to accept an "honorable" surrender to Leclerc in May 1802 for himself and his generals. Toussaint retired to a plantation at Ennery, but a short time later was arrested and taken to France, where he died in a lonely cell at Fort de Joux in the Jura Mountains. Leclerc himself would never leave Hispaniola, succumbing there to yellow fever in 1802.

Once it became apparent that the French intended to re-establish slavery, and with Leclerc replaced by even-more brutal Jean-Baptiste Rochambeau, the former rebels, both black and mulatto, put aside their differences and united under Dessalines's cry of *Koupe tèt, boule kay* (Cut off their heads and burn down their houses) under a goal of complete independence from France. Rochambeau's response was to hold an elegant ball in Port-au-Prince for the most rarefied women in the *ville*, revealing only at the end of the evening in a coffin-lined room that he had slaughtered their husbands while they danced.[5] Finally, on 18 November 1803, at the Battle of Vertières near Cap-Français, the Haitian rebels under the command of François Capois definitively defeated Rochambeau's forces. Cap-Français would subsequently be renamed Cap-Haïtien, though it is often colloquially referred to as Au Cap.

As the new year beckoned, it was in the northern city of Gonaïves that the rebels would take a fateful step for the history of the world. There, Haiti's Declaration of Independence, written in the name of Dessalines but likely authored by Louis Boisrond-Tonnerre, Dessalines' mulatto, Paris-educated secretary, was proclaimed. The text still cries out from across the centuries:

> It is not enough to have expelled the barbarians who have bloodied our land for two centuries ... We must, with one last act of national authority, forever assure the empire of liberty in the country of our birth; we must take any hope of re-enslaving us away from the inhuman government that for so long kept us in the most humiliating torpor ... We must live independent or die. Independence or death, let these sacred words unite us and be the signal of battle and of our reunion.[6]

Thirty-four of Haiti's revolutionary leaders – including Dessalines, Christophe and Pétion – would sign the document (Toussaint, of course, was long dead), but perhaps almost as remembered as the words themselves was the impassioned declaration of Boisrond-Tonnerre, who told the assemblage that to "say what we really feel" the declaration should "have the skin of a white man for parchment, his skull for an inkwell, his blood for ink and a bayonet for a pen."[7]

Dessalines announced that Saint-Dominique would heretofore be known as Haiti, its original indigenous name. As Toussaint had done, Dessalines named himself Governor for Life, but by September he had done away with any pretense of democracy and named himself Emperor. Dessalines' first act, between February and April 1804, was to order the slaughter of almost every remaining white inhabitant under his rule, riding throughout his kingdom and personally supervising the killing. He succeeded in ridding Haiti of its hated and distrusted French population, but, in addition to the moral question of such an act, he robbed the new country of a vital reservoir of expertise in agriculture, commerce and government and left it in the hands of a military dictatorship with its own bent towards tyranny.

Though slavery's advocates and apologists were "fond of comparing the lush French colony before the revolution and the faltering decrepit black republic of Haiti,"[8] the Haitians saw things rather differently. Boisrond-Tonnerre described "the desecration of the land, widespread bloodshed, rape and murder of the *hommes de couleur* and the slaves by the colonists" as the "true scenery of the colonial period," a sanguinary dystopia where a new vocabulary was coined so that "drowning 200 individuals was a national glory; to hang someone meant to obtain a promotion; to be eaten by dogs was to descend into the arena, to shoot someone was to put him into a heavy sleep."[9]

It is difficult to overstate the impact Haiti's revolution had on neighboring slave-economy islands such as Jamaica (which in 1760 had seen Tacky's Rebellion, an uprising of Akan slaves) and the United States, which, in the prelude to its own civil war, would witness uprisings led by figures such as Denmark Vesey in South Carolina in 1822 and Nat Turner in Virginia in 1831, the former undertaken with the express purpose of sailing to Haiti and to freedom.[10] Between 1791 and 1797, the population of New Orleans went from 4,446 to 8,056, many of whom were arrivals fleeing from Saint-Domingue, and between May and August 1809, another wave of an estimated 6,000 would arrive after having transited through Cuba.[11] The U.S. would be the last Atlantic nation to recognize Haiti (in 1862), though its four-year ban on trade with Haiti (from 1806 to 1810) was an edict that many American merchants simply ignored.[12]

Setting up a lavish imperial court at the village of Marchand in the Artibonite Valley, Dessalines launched a pair of disastrous invasions of Santo Domingo before being murdered in October 1806 – allegedly at Pont-Rouge near the present-day slum of La Saline – in circumstances that still remain murky (his loyal deputy Boisrond-Tonnerre was killed around the same time). It would be the first of many spectacular assassinations – almost all of them unpunished – that would scar Haiti's history from the post-colonial period to its present day. To this day, some in Haiti believe that Dessalines was the victim of a mulatto conspiracy specifically directed by Pétion. Upon his death, Haiti's black and mulatto tensions exploded again, with Henri Christophe controlling the north and becoming first president of the "State of Haiti" in 1807, then crowning himself King Henry I in March 1811. Christophe created Haiti's currency, the gourde (the term is still used today), oversaw a plantation system of agriculture, and built an extraordinary palace, Sans-Souci, modeled on Versailles, and a massive fort, Citadelle Laferrière, from which to survey the entirety of the northern plains. In the south, Pétion ruled a mulatto-dominated government of a less imperial nature than Christophe's that oversaw subsistence farming and gave shelter in the southern city of Jacmel to South American revolutionary Simón Bolívar as the latter plotted his campaign to liberate his own region from Spanish colonial rule. When Pétion died in 1818, he was succeeded by another general, Jean-Pierre Boyer, who launched a concerted effort to reunite the country under a single government, an effort that led to Christophe's suicide when facing near-certain defeat in October 1820. Boyer invaded and occupied Santo Domingo, but in 1825, menaced with re-invasion by the French, had to agree to pay a 150 million franc "indemnity" for Haiti's intemperance at abolishing slavery and declaring its independence (the sum was later lowered to 90 million francs).[13] Boyer would be overthrown and exiled in 1843, and the Dominican Republic would declare its independence from Haiti a year later. Haiti would then settle in to 70 years as an independent republic, albeit one buffeted by foreign threats at every turn and undermined from within by endless internecine political plotting.

* * *

Those many years later, as I stood in that field, it was a strange time in Haiti. An extraordinarily diverse cast of characters had coalesced in their opposition to Aristide. There was the economist Gérard Pierre-Charles, a former Communist who had authored *Radiographie d'une dictature*, one of the most important analyses of the Duvalier regime, and his wife, the historian Suzy Castor, who had founded the Centre de Recherche et de Formation Économique et Sociale pour le Développement (CRESFED) and authored a vitally important history of Haiti's two-decade occupation by the United States. There was Micha Gaillard, a biologist and university professor who was the son of one of Haiti's most famous historians and who would greet me at his home in the middle-class district of Turgeau with his charming wife, Kathie. There was Jean-Claude Bajeux, a former priest and human rights activist who, along with his wife, Sylvie, had founded the Centre Œcuménique des Droits Humains (CEDH), and both of whom had fought against (and lost family members to) the Duvalier family dictatorship as well as the violent anarcho-populism with which Aristide attempted to rule the country. There were peasant leaders in Haiti's fertile Artibonite Valley region and its mountainous Plateau Central, among them Chavannes Jean-Baptiste, perhaps Haiti's most important rural advocate and one of the founders of the Mouvman Peyizan Papay (MPP, named after a town in central Haiti) and later the Mouvman Peyizan Nasyonal Kongre Papay (MPNKP), a 200,000-member national peasant union. There were intellectuals such as Laënnec Hurbon, the country's most eminent sociologist who penned incisive studies of both Haitian society and how it was perceived abroad, and Theodore "Lolo" Beaubrun, the tall, dreadlocked son of a famous Haitian comedian, who had, in his earlier life, gained renown as the comic character "Barnaby" on Haitian television but now, along with his wife Mimerose, formed the core of the Haitian vodou-rock band Boukman Eksperyans. There were groups of the left such as the Plateforme Haïtienne de Plaidoyer pour un Développement Alternatif (PAPDA), the Groupe d'Appui aux Rapatriés et Réfugiés (GARR), EnfoFanm and Solidarite Fanm Ayisyèn (SOFA), as well as of the right such as the Association des Industries d'Haïti (ADIH). The armed rebellion itself had begun among a group that had been previously allied to Aristide and was then joined by dissident members of the military he had disbanded almost a decade earlier, many themselves with horrific human rights records. Many in the country, such as the students, peasant groups, human rights organizations and journalists (to say nothing of the elite who always hated him), were happy to see the thuggish president gone. However, among the most desperate strata of society – such as the thousands of disenfranchised young men (many of whom were armed) who formed the irregular support of Aristide's government in the *bidonvilles* (slums) of the capital and elsewhere – the president still had his partisans, and there was still a sense of suspended animation in the capital and its environs, a feeling that, however low they had been brought, Aristide and his supporters had not played their final card yet.

As I departed Haiti in June 2004 for Rio de Janeiro, there was hope among some that, following the sanguinary Aristide years, there would be some reconciliation between the classes of Haiti; between the poor majority who lived in hovels in cities like Port-au-Prince and Gonaïves and the peasants who tried to eke out a living from the fickle earth, and the thin stratum of society that lorded over them, those based in the hills above the capital who made their money largely through importing products that Haitians needed or oversaw Haiti's minuscule industrial sector. Amid this mix there were also those in between – a struggling middle class of educated doctors, lawyers, journalists, small business entrepreneurs and others and, of course, Haiti's opportunistic politicians, for whom the general good of the people seemed to be little more than an afterthought to their own grandiose political ambitions. During the protests that, along with the armed rebellion, drove Aristide from power, a broad-based opposition coalition, the Group of 184, had toured Haiti with what it called a *Caravane de l'Espoir* (Caravan of Hope) to forge "a new social contract" that would "get rid of historical hindrances that have kept the Haitian people from making its national unity, and thus, have impeded the development of our country." With their longtime nemesis gone, now was the time to make good on their promise.

I thought of all of this as I stood in the field beneath the gathering storm.

"It's not just the floods only," a 34-year-old pastor, Destine Charles, told me near the market stands, as we watched a steady gurgling stream of water increasing in the field and the clouds descending low over the valley. "People don't have proper access to water, nor hospitals. We have a lot of children that don't have access to schools. We want to ameliorate our situation, but we need help. It's so hard, but we continue on. What else can we do?"

The citizens of rural Haiti had, for as long as anyone could remember, a system of communal work known as the *konbit*, where everyone would pitch in to clear a field, build a road, construct a house and so forth. It spoke of a deep

9

sense of shared struggle and a communalist spirit quite the opposite of what I had seen in the country's political culture. As we finished talking, I looked up and saw that a group of peasant farmers had gathered around us, some leaning against their bicycles, some on foot. In frayed T-shirts and shoes, some wearing broad-brimmed straw peasant hats, some had obviously just come from the field, their machetes hanging at their sides. Several young children had also gathered. As they saw the pastor and I had finished speaking, they came towards me. In their hands they carried mangoes, jackfruit and a bushel of bananas.

"Take these with you," said an elderly man in a straw hat and mud-spattered sandals, picking up the cornucopia of fruit and pushing it into my arms. "It will give you something to remember us by. Don't forget us."

CHAPTER ONE
ISTWA (HISTORY)

Lanne pase toujou pi bon (Past years are always better) – Haitian proverb

Following the 25-year rule of Boyer, Haiti saw four different presidents in as many years before Faustin Soulouque, an army officer hailing from Petit-Goâve, took the reins of the nation in 1847. In addition to his support from within the military, Soulouque was backed by thousands of irregular armed partisans referred to as *zinglin*. Though initially viewed as something of a malleable stand-in (a mistake Haiti's political class would make time and again), Soulouque proved himself to be anything but, surrounding himself with gifted advisors such as Lysius Salomon, a young black lawyer from Les Cayes, and massacring a host of enemies, almost all of them mulattoes, shortly after taking power.[1] Two invasions of Santo Domingo ended in retreat, and in 1849 Soulouque crowned himself Emperor. So violent was Soulouque's reign that one observer of his iron-fisted communiqués opined that all seemed to begin with the word *Quiconque* (Whosoever) and ended with the words *sera fusillé* (will be shot).[2] Soulouque was an enthusiastic *vodouisant*, but the *lwa*, as the vast pantheon of vodou spirits are referred to, were not on the Emperor's side to prevent his overthrow by mulatto forces in December 1858, Soulouque's exile reinforcing the pattern of coup, exile and black–mulatto tension that would be repeated throughout the country's history. During the presidential tenure of Soulouque's former advisor Lysius Salomon from 1879 to 1888, salutary efforts to reform the country's educational system were overshadowed by a rebellion by the president's enemies to which he responded in September 1883 with merciless fury, putting the capital's main business district to the torch and unleashing soldiers and paramilitary supporters, killing an estimated 1,000 people, a pillage that stopped only after foreign diplomats threatened an invasion.[3]

At the turn of the century, one of Haiti's more promising political leaders, the anthropologist and journalist Anténor Firmin – his prescient 1885 work *De l'égalité des races humaines* argued the then revolutionary concept that "the races are equal" – saw his presidential ambitions undermined by yet another military officer, the ancient Pierre Nord Alexis. Known as Tonton Nord, Alexis was backed by Germany (who would engage in a triangulated struggle for influence over Haiti with France and the United States) and seized power in December 1902. Nord's ascent was marked by an extraordinary final act of defiance by Admiral Hammerton Killick, chief of Haiti's navy, who boarded the navy's flagship, *La Crête-à-Pierrot*, draped himself in the Haitian flag and, accompanied only by the ship's surgeon, touched his cigar to a fuse and blew up the vessel in the Bay of Gonaïves rather than let the Germans seize her. Thus Killick became another in the long list of Haiti's tragic martyrs.[4] One of Tonton Nord's successors, Cincinnatus Leconte, showed great promise, appointing competent officials and repairing roads and telegraph wires and demonstrating, by all accounts, a genuine drive to lift Haiti out of the squalor in which it had so long dwelled. Leconte's full potential will never be known, as, one steamy morning in August 1912, the presidential palace in which he dwelt was blown to smithereens when arms stored within its walls ignited, killing Leconte and some 300 soldiers.[5]

Leconte departed a country whose sovereignty was rapidly evaporating. By 1910, American interests had a 50 percent stake in the creation of a new Banque Nationale de la République d'Haïti (BNRH), with the Haitian government in effect ceding control of its own fiscal policy to bankers in New York. Although French and German financial actors were also involved, by this point the dominant role of the United States could hardly have been clearer.[6]

Squeezed and plotted against from the outside, and violently factionalized on the inside (its warring political factions periodically recruiting *cacos* – little more than guns-for-hire brigands tempted by the promise of a day or two's looting), in 1904 Haiti greeted the centenary of its independence from France with the Haitian writer and diplomat Frédéric Marcelin looking around and chiding his fellow politicians that it was "madness" to celebrate the date. He went on to demand of them:

> What have you done that you can boast of? Show us the civilization you have created. What will you present to the tribunal of history? Where is the work, which is the idea that you have attached to your name? Is it our civil strife, our fratricidal killings, our social miseries, our economic ignorance or our idolatrous militarism that you will glorify?

And he then added poignantly:

> We glorify an ideal that despite all of this, allowed a small nation to remain free and independent, an ideal which we are sure, embraces the soul of our citizens from first to last in cities as well as in the countryside, it endures a century but is still young; Freedom or death.[7]

A decade later, even that ideal would be taken away.

* * *

By July 1915, Vilbrun Guillaume Sam had been in office for four months. A ceaselessly intriguing military commander from a prominent black family from the north, he had led the revolt against President Oreste Zamor and subsequently assumed the office himself, thus becoming the fifth president in a five-year span (Sam's cousin, Tirésias Simon Sam, had served as president for nearly six years at the turn of the century). One of Sam's first acts was to round up and imprison various, mostly mulatto, politicians he believed might be plotting against him in league with Rosalvo Bobo, a mulatto physician from Cap-Haïtien. These included his predecessor Oreste Zamor and at least 200 scions from the most prominent families in the capital and elsewhere, including the Prévals, the Polynices and the Péraltes. They were imprisoned in the capital's old prison under the questionable mercies of a Sam loyalist, Charles Oscar Etienne, known as *Le terrible*. Even as he did so, though, Bobo's forces succeeded in taking Au Cap, Fort-Liberté, and several other towns, only to be forced out of the former by the landing of French troops from the cruiser *Descartes*, joined soon thereafter by American troops from the USS *Washington*.

In the capital, on the night of 26 July, Sam's enemies launched an attempted putsch, peppering the palace with gunfire as a wounded Sam and his family fled to the nearby French legation. Down at the jail, Etienne slaughtered almost all the prisoners and subsequently fled to the Dominican Embassy, where Edmond Polynice, the patriarch of his family, paid him a visit and shot him dead where he stood. After several unsuccessful attempts to breach the walls and locate Sam, after burying their dead, at least 80 men stormed the French legation and dragged Sam outside, where he was hacked to pieces. The telegrams sent by Robert Beale Davis, the junior chargé d'affaires at the U.S. Embassy during this period, go from worried ("French legation threatened and a forcible entry") to surreal ("Mob invaded French legation, took out president killed and dismembered him"). With the grotesque public murder of Guillaume Sam, and the subsequent landing of the marines from the USS *Washington* at Bizoton early in the evening of 28 July, the U.S. occupation of Haiti began.[8]

* * *

That the United States only hazily understood the country it was to rule, and the corrosive racism that would inform that governance, was testified by the startled reaction of Woodrow Wilson's secretary of state William Jennings Bryan upon being briefed at the time of the invasion, whereupon he exclaimed: "Think of it! Niggers speaking French!"[9]

Under the command of U.S. Navy Rear Admiral William B. Caperton, the Americans seized Haitian government funds and put them into an account under Navy control, and they would continue to control customs and the Haitian budget through domination of the central bank, as they had done before the invasion. The bank's entire gold reserve – around $500,000 worth – was spirited away to the vaults of City Bank in New York.[10] Under intense U.S. pressure, Philippe Sudré Dartiguenave, the mulatto head of Haiti's senate, was elected president and shortly thereafter the government was forced to sign, virtually at gunpoint, the so-called Haitian–American Convention, a treaty affirming the U.S. right to choose a customs director and customs employees, form a new security force, develop the country's natural resources and exert total discretion when it came to deciding Haitian affairs of state. The terms were a humiliation which caused a predictable uproar and resulted in the imposition of martial law at the beginning of September 1915. That autumn, the Marines decimated Bobo's *caco* loyalists at the battles of Fort Dipitie and Fort Rivière (Bobo himself fled the country) and perhaps thought, naively, that armed resistance to the occupation was at an end.

Coming from a nation where violent white supremacy was still the rule of the day, that mindset infected the interactions of the Americans with their new colonial subjects, and when Caperton was replaced as the occupation's face by Colonel Littleton Waller in May 1916, things grew worse still. Waller's chief concern appeared to be what the people of his native Virginia "would say if they saw me bowing and scraping to these coons,"[11] and he and aids such as Smedley Butler were remembered in Haiti as "torturers without scruple."[12] The virulent racism of the occupiers came as a shock to the country's high-born mulatto elite.

14

"The Americans have taught us a lot of things," Ernest Chauvet, the publisher of the Haitian daily *Le Nouvelliste*, told the American author William Seabrook during the latter's visit to Haiti at the height of the occupation. "Among other things they have taught us that we are niggers. You see, we really didn't know that before. We thought we were negroes ... You can't pick an army of occupation from the social register or drill them with salad forks ... But if they generally regarded us as human beings ... there wouldn't be all this added, unnecessary mess."[13]

Though Waller's tenure was relatively brief – he was replaced in 1917 by Colonel John H. Russell, a far less abrasive character – the changes wrought on Haiti were deep and long-lasting. The U.S. drafted a new constitution which eliminated the bar on foreign ownership of land that Dessalines had initiated, and saw it approved in a questionable plebiscite in June 1918. The U.S. also established the Gendarmerie d'Haïti, which would eventually form the core of the re-born Haitian army, the Forces Armées d'Haïti or FADH. During the course of the occupation, the U.S. would oversee the construction of over 1,000 miles of roads, over 200 bridges and airfields in all departmental capitals and would revive the nation's moribund telephone system.

Declaring Port-au-Prince "one of the most attractive" towns in the Antilles, the British author Alec Waugh wrote when he visited the country in 1929 that "Haiti is one of the world's pleasant places," before going on to wonder "will history repeat itself? Will the road across the arid valley of Gonaïves crumble into a bridle path? Will the peasant be afraid to come down into Port-au-Prince? Will the green lawns of the Champ de Mars straggle on to the puddled and untended roads?"[14]

How were these fine projects enacted? In July 1916, the Marines brought back the hated *corvée* system, last practiced during the time of Henri Christophe, which consisted of compulsory labor on public works projects. Often, the gang-pressed nature of the *corvée* seemed little different than slavery, and the system generated particular animosity in the Plateau Central, where the peasants had been living a simple but, for their needs, adequate life in relative isolation from the tumult of the capital. They now suddenly found themselves worked like beasts of burden by American and Haitian overseers.[15] At Post Chabert, the U.S. Marines built a despised plantation-like complex where, 1922 U.S. senate hearings stated, "a prison farm is in operation."[16]

Charlemagne Péralte, a military official from a part-Dominican family resident in Hinche in the Plateau Central, had been arrested there for his alleged part in a raid and put into a corvée in Au Cap charged with sweeping the streets. As an educated man of means with links to Bobo, Péralte naturally could not accept such a fate and, shortly after being transferred to Cap, broke free and launched a rebellion. For more than a year, Péralte and his deputy Benoît Batraville would lead their bands of rebels across the north, the Artibonite and the Plateau Central. Péralte would be betrayed and killed by a U.S. Marine in November 1919, his body displayed and photographed in a kind of Haitian *pietà* in Cap afterwards. Batraville met the same fate the following year.

The main voice of civil opposition was the Union Patriotique, a cadre of Port-au-Prince intellectuals and opportunistic politicians. A series of mulatto presidents succeeded one another – Dartiguenave was followed by former foreigner minister Louis Borno and former Port-au-Prince mayor (and Union Patriotique member) Sténio Vincent – but, as is often the case in Haiti, events in the halls of power of the capital were overtaken by events in the provinces. In December 1929, at the village of Marchaterre, near Les Cayes, students, coffee farmers and dock workers took to the streets to denounce the occupation amid cries of "Down with misery!" They were soon joined by hundreds of peasants from nearby Torbeck.[17] During the protest, U.S. troops opened fire on the crowd, killing a dozen and wounding 23. It was the nadir of the U.S. occupation in Haiti, and by 1934 the foreign troops were gone.

* * *

The reverberations continued to echo, though. As the historian Matthew Smith notes, the American occupation proved a catalyst for both "black consciousness and an intense cross-class nationalism [and] produced a rare opportunity for lasting political change."[18]

That opportunity would crash on the rocks of Haiti's age-old color divide, though. In one of the many ironies found in Haiti's history, in the Haiti of the 1930s the appeal of Communism was chiefly to the country's foreign-educated elite, who returned home determined to try to change the medieval iniquity that they still found all around them. The author Jacques Roumain, whose 1943 novel *Gouverneurs de la Rosée* remains one of the most moving portraits of Haitian peasant life, despite his own bourgeois background became a committed Communist during this time, co-founding the Parti Communiste Haïtien (PCH) in 1934 under the slogan "Color is nothing, class is everything." Cutting through facile appeals to patriotism, the PCH's first national program, *L'analyse schematique*, dismissed such discourse by concluding that "the arrival to power of the Nationalists [i.e., Sténio Vincent] began the process of decomposition of nationalism," going on to witheringly characterize Haiti's bourgeois politicians as "valets of imperialism and cruel exploiters of the workers and peasants."[19]

Drawing from an altogether different well for inspiration in the person of writer and ethnologist Jean Price-Mars, whose 1928 book *Ainsi parla l'oncle* was a landmark in the *négritude* movement in the French-speaking Caribbean, a group of black intellectuals referred to themselves as the Griots, after the traditional storytellers of West Africa. Rather than seeking European social-political models, they instead looked to the country's African traditions, especially vodou, as a way to counter the exploitation of the black majority by the privileged mulatto elite. Among the Griots' number was a young doctor named François Duvalier whom Price-Mars had taught as a student years before, and who, along with others, would eventually transform *négritude* into *noirisme*, an ethos of black power.

When Sténio Vincent – whose tenure was marked by a ghastly 1937 pogrom against Haitians living in the Dominican Republic – was succeeded in 1941 by Élie Lescot, a consummate political survivor and opportunist, the mulatto elite's grip on the nation's political and economic mechanisms was thrown into the starkest relief since the end of the occupation. Lescot had served under the occupation-era government of Louis Borno as well as that of Vincent, often in politically sensitive posts such as minister of the interior, ambassador to the Dominican Republic, and ambassador to the United States, but nevertheless appears to have placed too much faith in the ability of his powerful friends to save what soon became an explicitly colorist dictatorship. In a precursor of other half-baked schemes decades later, the United States sponsored the Société Haitiano-Américaine de Développement Agricole (SHADA) in an ill-fated attempt to cultivate rubber in Haiti in an effort that ended up alienating the very peasants it was designed to help.

The overthrow of Lescot – the Revolution of 1946 – was an extraordinarily significant moment. The movement to oust him was spearheaded by young Marxist intellectuals in the capital, including the authors Jacques Stephen Alexis and René Depestre, and Gérald Bloncourt, who would go on to become a renowned painter, in a group that would coalesce around a revolutionary weekly called *La Ruche* (*The Beehive*). The movement also drew from a perhaps surprising source: a series of lectures that the French surrealist André Breton gave in Port-au-Prince at the end of 1945, during which he inveighed on behalf of personal freedom, railed against dictatorship and pointedly refused to shake hands with Lescot.[20]

After a brief military regime, Dumarsais Estimé, the first black president Haiti had seen for 30 years, was sworn in as the head of state. Estimé was a former schoolteacher who had risen up the ladder of Haiti's political establishment to serve in the Chamber of Deputies and, eventually, in the Vincent government. Voted into the executive by Haiti's parliament, though not exactly a *noiriste* himself, Estimé drew his political base from the country's disenfranchised black majority and sought to ameliorate their suffering by raising Haiti's minimum wage, expanding schools and social services, and creating a series of public works projects for the chronically unemployed Haitian labor force. Existing as he did outside of Haiti's traditional political structures – representing the black underclass without being a *noiriste*, speaking for the disenfranchised while shunning the radical left, at odds with the military and the country's economic elite – Estimé could never have expected an easy ride while in office and did not get one. With members of the black intelligentsia (including Duvalier) filling virtually every cabinet post in his government, Estimé seemed to at least try to come to terms with the desperate needs of Haiti's citizens. His attempts to reassert Haiti's control over its own economy in the face of U.S. economic interests met with a predictably vitriolic response at a time when Washington seemed unable to differentiate any labor or social movement from Communism, a particular irony in Haiti, since Estimé would go so far as to outlaw the PCH in 1948.

Representative though it was, Estimé's government also proved shortsighted on some key matters. Gestures such as the nationalization of Haiti's banana industry in 1947 were so badly managed that United Fruit, the company that had dominated Haiti's banana industry prior to that time, was back at the helm by 1949, with Haitian banana shipments being used to pay off the massive debt accrued over the two years of state control. Estimé also had the questionable claim to fame of bringing François Duvalier, whose years as a doctor ministering to the country's rural poor earned him the nickname Papa Doc, to the center of political power for the first time as his undersecretary for labor, even though Duvalier was technically an official with Port-au-Prince politician Daniel Fignolé's Mouvement des Ouvriers et Paysans (MOP). Duvalier served as Estimé's director of public health, and continued on in the government after Fignolé, his ostensible boss, resigned.

As was their wont, the Americans mistook Fignolé's fiery oratory for that of a Communist, and were fearful of the MOP's considerable organizational capacity (when desiring to make a point, Fignolé would summon his *rouleau compresseur* or steamroller – mobs that would descend from the hilly slum of Bel-Air and demonstrate, sometimes violently, in his support). Hand in hand with oppressing the MOP and attacking the PCH, Estimé's attempt to institute constitutional revisions that would allow him to succeed himself as president in the summer of 1949 provoked a violent student and labor strike, the likes of which had helped topple Lescot. He was ousted by the army the following year. The American choreographer and anthropologist Katherine Dunham, an observer of Haiti of great insight who had spent many years visiting the country and had been Estimé's lover for a time, wrote a reflection on the man that could serve as an epitaph for so many of the country's leaders to come:

> At his highest point of power, he seems to have changed from his early principles. I have often wondered about his support of mass violence … Did he believe too much in or expect too much too soon from the people to whom he had offered the real benefits of health, education, freedom from serfdom? Perhaps he saw in this act of destruction an opportunity for a people of 'self-expression' and 'political maturity' and could not foresee the outcome.[21]

After yet another military interregnum, Estimé was succeeded by Paul Magloire, a *bon vivant* black military officer who had warm relations with the elite and ushered in a period that observers sometimes nostalgically reminisce as a "golden age" for Haiti of mass tourism and economic growth, a characterization that overlooks the deep sense of bitterness and betrayal that Estimé's supporters nursed while ruled by a military dictatorship viewed by many as little more than a tool of the bourgeoisie. Magloire was quite willing to use violence to crush dissent, and, far from creating a sense of détente between Haiti's competing political factions, tensions between them continued to fester, culminating after Magloire's own ouster in December 1956.[22]

The following year Haiti saw no fewer than four interim presidents, including Fignolé, who lasted a mere 19 days. After a violence-wracked ballot on 22 September 1957, François Duvalier, the quiet doctor and Estimé partisan, was elected president (Duvalier had a strange, mystical obsession with the number "22"), and ascended to the office the following month. Since the fall of Lescot, the *noiristes* and the Communists/Marxists had stood eying one another, daggers drawn. The left, many of them of more comfortable backgrounds than those of the *noiristes* themselves, viewed *noirisme* as little more than a cover by which the black middle class could seize power, and the movement's leaders as reactionary demagogues with fascist tendencies, while the *noiristes* depicted Haiti's radical left as bourgeois usurpers.

Much has been written of the long night that Haiti endured during the Duvalier years, from the systematic terror of the state and the limitless capacity for brutality of Duvalier's security forces to the fact that none of Haiti's neighbors lifted a finger to stop it. But it is wrong to suggest, as some have, that there was no resistance to Duvalier, as, over the years, a series of quixotic and largely disastrous forays took place as anguished citizens attempted to wrest control of the country from the mad tyrant.

In July 1958, less than a year after Duvalier assumed power, a gifted young military officer named Alix Pasquet led two other Haitians – Philippe Dominique (the elder brother of journalist Jean Dominique) and Henri Perpignan – and five Americans aboard a tiny ship that landed on the Côte des Arcadins in a first foray to drive the new president from power. Their plan went catastrophically wrong almost from the beginning when one of their number was wounded in a firefight with Haitian soldiers and, after seizing the Casernes Dessalines behind the palace, all eight invaders were subsequently killed.[23]

Although he had already been involved with death squads (known in the early days as *cagoulards*), the Pasquet attack solidified Duvalier's determination to form a counterbalance to the army that had ousted so many of his predecessors and, with the aid of Clément Barbot, a former Saint-Marc schoolteacher, he created the Tonton Macoute, a group of denim-clad loyalists whose named translated into "Uncle Knapsack" and evoked a mythical Haitian bogeyman (they were later to be given the rather grander title of Volontaires de la Sécurité Nationale or VSN).[24] The Macoutes would indeed become the bogeymen (and women) of Haiti's long Duvalierist nightmare, as Duvalier – habitually garbed in black as a kind of living personification of Baron Samedi, the vodou *lwa* of the cemetery – savvily empowered the dregs of society to do his dirty work. In the capital this would mean men like Pétionville mayor Paul Vericain and

Rosalie Bosquet (better known after her marriage as Madame Max Adolphe), who became the head of the Macoute women's branch, *Fillettes Laleau*, and later the warden of the Duvalier death prison of Fort Dimanche. In Gonaïves, local vodou priest Zachary Delva would join, while in Jérémie, on the lush Grand Anse peninsula, it would be the alcoholic Saint-Ange Bontemps and the petty thief Sanète Balmir. Haiti produced social resentment in plentiful supply, and Duvalier – like Aristide later – was an expert at manipulating it. And though Fort Dimanche was the most famous prison in Duvalier's ghastly gulag, it was far from the only such locale, with the Pénitencier National and Casernes Dessalines also doing their part to snuff out the lives of a wide range of prisoners, along with torture chambers that existed at police headquarters and within the National Palace itself.[25]

Ironically, it was Clément Barbot, one of the regime's most feared enforcers, who provided the next spark of rebellion when, after having been imprisoned and tortured by Duvalier, upon his release launched a spectacular April 1963 attack that killed the chauffeur and two bodyguards of Duvalier's children, Jean-Claude and Simone, as they arrived at school.[26] This sent Duvalier into a frenzy that claimed the lives of dozens of people, including virtually the entire family of former army sharpshooter François Benoît, whom he suspected (wrongly) might be involved in the attack.[27] Barbot himself would be killed by Duvalier's forces that July. The same month Barbot died, young Hector Riobé, whose father, a Léogâne sugarcane planter, had been kidnapped and murdered by Macoutes who then confiscated virtually everything the family owned, attempted an invasion with several compatriots. After killing a number of soldiers and Macoutes in Pétionville and Kenscoff, Riobé was eventually cornered in a cave above the capital that the group had previously stocked with weapons and food in anticipation of a siege; this went on for days, at the cost of what was believed to have been the lives of at least 40 soldiers and Macoutes. Finally, outnumbered and running low on ammunition, Riobé, the last survivor, committed suicide rather than surrender.[28] Duvalier subsequently had the area bombed flat to prevent it from becoming a place of pilgrimage.

Perhaps the most tragic chapter in the anti-Duvalier struggle, though, was the story of Jeune Haiti (Young Haiti),[29] 13 young Haitians – among them Jacques Wadestrandt, Sylvie Bajeux's 31-year-old then husband – who landed on the Grand Anse in August 1964 with the intention of starting a guerrilla insurgency à la Cuba and ousting Duvalier.[30]

The group arrived with the expectation that a second front would be opened – that of Dominican Republic-based rebel Fred Baptiste's Forces Armées Révolutionnaires d'Haïti (FARH) – and Wadestrandt even went to Santo Domingo to discuss strategy with Baptiste's supporters, who never let on that Baptiste had in fact slipped back into the country from Haiti some time previously.[31] By late October, all but two of Jeune Haiti's members had been killed. Duvalier displayed the putrefying corpse of rebel Yvon Laraque at an intersection in Port-au-Prince under a sign that read "Welcome to Haiti!"[32] and the last two surviving rebels – Louis Drouin and Marcel Numa – were captured and taken to Port-au-Prince and executed against the wall of the National Cemetery in front of a crowd of thousands, including schoolchildren who had been forced to attend. What happened in Jérémie itself, though, the town from which most of Jeune Haiti hailed, was far grimmer still. Entire families – the Drouins, the Villedrouins, the Sansaricqs and others – were massacred from oldest to youngest members, and dozens of others connected to the town disappeared to face torture and death, among them Jean-Claude Bajeux's mother, two brothers and two sisters. Ghastly as it was, it was only one of a series of massacres that Duvalier would commit, including those around the towns of Mapou, Thiotte, Grand-Gosier and Belle-Anse during the summer of 1964 and one in the Artibonite village of Cazale in early 1969.[33]

Attempts to overthrow Duvalier continued throughout his reign – most notably with Fred Baptiste's FARH (Baptiste was eventually captured and died in Fort Dimanche) and the mutiny led by Coast Guard Colonel Octave Cayard in April 1970, when 118 members of the Coast Guard took Haiti's three patrol ships and bombarded the palace from the bay in an effort to force Duvalier's resignation.[34] The dictator died in office a year later, handing the country – and his "presidency for life" – to his son, Jean-Claude. The younger Duvalier – a morbidly obese 19-year-old often referred to as "Baskethead" because of his immense girth and "Baby Doc" after his father's nickname – in the words of Jean-Claude Bajeux "inherited a system of government that was based on killing people ... He was not aware of the monstrosity of what he was doing every day. To him, killing people and torturing people was normal life."[35] Influenced at first by his mother and sister, and later by his wife and Duvalierist officials such as Macoute leader Roger Lafontant, Duvalier *fils* initially had more of the reputation of a thoughtless playboy than that of an iron-willed dictator as his father had, but the machinery of repression continued without pause.

The younger Duvalier would grow into the role soon enough. In October 1977 – the twentieth anniversary of his father's assumption of the presidency – Duvalier gave a speech in which he heralded the advent of Jean-Claudisme, supposedly a liberalizing trend in Duvalierism that would foster economic development. The near-fatal beating of a prominent government critic, Pastor Luc Nerée, only weeks later gave a flavor of how limited that liberalization would be. Reinforcing that message, a human rights conference in the capital in November 1979 would be violently broken up by regime partisans.[36] Political prisoners continued to perish in Fort Dimanche, journalists continued to be driven into exile, and the Macoutes continued to enjoy the power of life and death over their fellow citizens, strutting terror in black sunglasses and blue denim. In May 1980, Duvalier married Michèle Bennett, an acquisitive divorcée who, ironically, had once been married to the son of Alix Pasquet, who had attempted to oust Duvalier's father more than two decades earlier. Their wedding marked a turning point for the 29-year-old dictator, as the government's corruption seemed only to swell, as their fellow countrymen fell deeper into poverty despite the fact that, by the early 1980s, Haiti was experiencing something of a farming boom and was producing over 80 percent of its own food.[37] However, a joint U.S.–Canadian endeavor to halt the spread of African swine fever – the Program for the Eradication of Porcine Swine Fever and Development of Pig-Raising or PEPADEP – killed 1.2 million Creole pigs in the early 1980s, and only haphazardly replaced them, dealing a nearly mortal blow to the peasant economy. Throughout the early 1980s, opposition to the regime spread across a wide range of Haitian society and, finally, after months of protests, the dictator fled into exile on 7 February 1986.

* * *

The years immediately following Duvalier's overthrow were one of the moments during which Haiti lost its way in a manner significant enough for the impact to be felt until this day. The dictator was gone, but the apparatus he had presided over – as typified by a highly militarized and unaccountable state reflexively accustomed to resorting to violence when challenged – endured.

Immediately following the tyrant's flight, it was announced that the country would be governed by a Conseil National de Gouvernement (CNG), a curious military–civilian hybrid headed by FADH General Henri Namphy as provisional president. Tasked with overseeing a democratic transition that many in the upper echelons of the FADH were actively hostile to, the CNG presided over the official dissolution of the Tontons Macoutes and the restoration of Haiti's blue and red flag (replacing Duvalier's red and black) before falling apart, with Ligue Haïtienne des Droits Humains leader Gérard Gourgue resigning.[38]

As it headed toward a November 1987 election date that few of those holding weapons in the country wanted, and with Gourgue – whom many in the military hierarchy viewed as a traitor at best and a possible Communist at worst – running as a candidate for president and standing a strong chance of winning, *le pouvoir* and its civilian supporters responded by killing so many people on election day that the vote was canceled. The most notable attack was on voters waiting patiently at the École Nationale Argentine Bellegarde off the capital's Ruelle Vaillant, where at least 20 were slain.[39]

In many ways, the same powers who were responsible for the final decision that it was time for Duvalier to leave – Haiti's army, its economic elite (which by this point consisted of about 100,000 people – including 200 millionaires – in a country of then a little over 6 million[40]), the U.S. government – sent a very clear message to Haiti's politicians and its people: "He's gone, please don't bother us with things like truth commissions, now is not the time." Once Duvalier was out of the picture, the Americans decided that their logical partner was not the social democratic sector, but the Haitian army. It was the mistake of Haiti's political parties to accept that deal, and it is a mistake that the country rues to this day. When pressure resulted in the 1987 constitution and a quasi-independent electoral body – and it appeared that the elections might result in a Gourgue presidency – the army quite literally killed the process.

* * *

After the Ruelle Vaillant massacre, a farcical ballot was held in January 1988 which resulted in the "election" of Leslie Manigat, a historian and candidate for the Rassemblement des Démocrates Nationaux Progressistes (RDNP). Manigat was in office for a mere four months, forever staining his name by cooperating with the junta, before being ousted by Namphy, who presided over a series of increasingly appalling abuses, culminating in a 11 September 1988 attack on St. Jean Bosco, a church on the edge of the capital's La Saline slum where a radical Salesian priest, Jean-Bertrand Aristide, had been inveighing against the Macoute system since his return from abroad in January 1985. At least a dozen people were killed and the church set ablaze, but, miraculously, Aristide (who by that point had already survived several attempts on his life) and some of his closest confidants – including an agronomist-turned-baker named René Préval and the peasant leader Chavannes Jean-Baptiste – survived.[41] Far from being supported by the church, only months later Aristide would be expelled from the Salesian order, leaving him quite literally a priest without a parish.[42] Namphy himself was then overthrown a week after the massacre by his former comrade-in-arms Prosper Avril, the latter initially backed by a group of noncommissioned officers calling themselves the *Ti Soldats* (Little Soldiers).[43] That autumn, three of the country's best-known democratic activists – including former journalist and playwright Evans Paul – were arrested, tortured and paraded battered on television.[44] Avril himself was finally ousted in March 1990, replaced by Supreme Court Justice Ertha Pascal-Trouillot, who, against all odds, succeeded in helping to organize democratic elections, nearly four years after Duvalier's fall.

In the 1990 vote, Jean-Bertrand Aristide ran as the presidential candidate of the Front National pour le Changement et la Démocratie (FNCD), a broad-based left-of-center coalition whose member parties included the Konvansyon Inite Demokratik (KID) of Evans Paul (now Aristide's campaign manager), the Komité National du Kongrés des Mouvements Démocratiques (KONAKOM), which had been formed by, among others, veteran political activist Victor Benoît and Jean-Claude Bajeux,[45] and buttressed by the progressive *Ti Legliz* (Little Church) strain of the Catholic Church that Aristide affiliated with and peasant movements such as Chavannes Jean-Baptiste's MPP.

Aristide trounced his opponents in the general election, chief among them former World Bank economist Marc Bazin, who ran at the head of the Mouvement pour l'Instauration de la Démocratie en Haïti (MIDH),[46] while Evans Paul was elected as mayor of Port-au-Prince. Even before the new government took office, however, the nation had to face down a Duvalierist coup attempt. The failed coup was followed by some grotesque reprisals by Aristide partisans, including the burning of the city's old cathedral (dating from 1771 and one of the oldest buildings in the Caribbean) as an act of revenge against the Duvalierist Bishop François-Wolff Ligondé,[47] and the murder of the pregnant young wife of an FADH officer named Louis-Jodel Chamblain.

At his February 1991 inauguration, Aristide had quoted from the Book of Isaiah ("to proclaim the acceptable year of the Lord, and the day of vengeance of our God") before issuing a Creole proverb that some interpreted as a threat – *wòch nan dlo ap konnen doule wòch nan solèy* (the rocks in the water will know the suffering of the rocks in the sun) – and saying that his goal was to lift Haitians from misery to "poverty with dignity."[48] He chose René Préval as his prime minister, the latter viewed as so close to the president he was often called Aristide's *marassa* (twin). In the brief interim that followed, despite positive steps, such as a literacy program and attempting to rein in the country's unaccountable military, the frequent use of mob pressure – as during a threatened parliamentary no-confidence vote against Préval – worried many, including Aristide's coalition partners. In September 1991, Aristide was apprised of a plot to overthrow him, paid for by some of Haiti's wealthiest families. Speaking to thousands of supporters, he told the bourgeoisie that they had earned their money "in thievery" (as many of them certainly had) and that "it's only chance that you'll get" to change, before going on in what many took as an obvious reference to necklacing, as death by burning tire around one's neck was called:

> If you catch a thief … don't hesitate to give him what he deserves … Your tool in hand, your instrument in hand, your constitution in hand! Don't hesitate to give him what he deserves … The Macoute isn't in this game … What a beautiful tool! What a beautiful instrument! What a beautiful piece of equipment! It's beautiful, yes it's beautiful, it has a good smell, wherever you go you want to inhale it. Since the law of the country says Macoute isn't in the game, whatever happens to him he deserves, he came looking for trouble.[49]

Three days later, Aristide was overthrown in a coup whose driving forces were Port-au-Prince police chief Michel François and FADH generals Philippe Biamby and Raoul Cédras.[50] After nearly being lynched by angry soldiers, Aristide was spirited away, first to Venezuela, then to Washington, where he spent three years in exile as thousands of his most loyal supporters were murdered. In addition to official military terror, Louis-Jodel Chamblain, who had lost his wife to a pro-Aristide mob, would help found a ruthless paramilitary organization, the Front pour l'Avancement et le Progrès Haïtien (FRAPH) with Emmanuel "Toto" Constant, the son of François Duvalier's army chief of staff. While FRAPH was going about targeting Haiti's democratic sector, Constant was being paid about $500 a month by the Central Intelligence Agency for providing them with "information."[51] Civilian thugs known as *attaché* ("attached" in French, so called because they were "attached" to the security forces) would join the various armed groups in their bloody business. A U.S.-orchestrated economic embargo designed to pressure Haiti's coup leaders also had the desultory effect of helping to utterly wreck the Haitian economy, with the more than 100,000 assembly jobs that existed in the capital before its implementation spiraling down to about 20,000 little more than a decade later.[52]

* * *

Along with the military-managed post-Duvalier transition period, the 1991 coup remains one of the great tragedies of Haitian history. Whatever he became later, in 1990 the Haitian people had emphatically chosen Aristide as the representative of their collective aspirations, and they were robbed of the chance to see the results of that choice and to evaluate it. That brutal interruption of the democratic process led to total confusion, not only about the immediate fate of the country, but also about the value of the democratic process itself.

After three years of slaughter, Aristide was returned to Haiti in October 1994 by the U.S.-launched Operation Uphold Democracy.[53] His return was greeted with immense hope among his supporters and deep skepticism among his enemies. Shortly thereafter, there were signs that perhaps all was not as it appeared. Having had virtually unfettered access to Haiti's state treasury for three years and developed a noticeable taste for sharp suits and other luxuries, shortly after his return, Aristide formally resigned from the priesthood.[54] The coalition that had helped overthrow Duvalier and win the 1990 elections splintered bitterly. First Aristide broke with Evans Paul, insinuating that Paul had been party to the coup rather than its victim (while Aristide spent his exile in the United States, Paul had remained in Haiti and was tortured for his trouble).[55] Aristide formed a new party, the Òganizasyon Politik Lavalas (OPL), with Gérard Pierre-Charles, the longtime Duvalier opponent who had spent two decades living in Mexico with his wife, the historian Suzy Castor. Less than two years later, Aristide would also fall out with Pierre-Charles, forming a new political party, Fanmi Lavalas (Lavalas Family), in January 1997 (OPL would keep its initials but rename itself the Organisation du Peuple en Lutte).[56]

Other signals were on the horizon as well. In March 1995, three days before U.S. President Bill Clinton was to arrive in Haiti, Mireille Durocher Bertin, a young lawyer who had acted as a spokesperson for the coup leaders, was gunned down while driving in the capital in a plot that American and Haitian security officials believed traced back to Interior Minister Mondesir Beaubrun, one of

Aristide's closest confidents in the cabinet.[57] Seven months later, FADH general Max Mayard was slain in a similar fashion.[58] The same year, Aristide disbanded the army, an act that was illegal without a constitutional amendment as the body was enshrined in Article IX of Haiti's 1987 constitution, but, given its dismal reputation, few Haitians save the soldiers themselves were sad to see it go.[59] The army would be replaced by a national police force, the Police Nationale d'Haïti (PNH). In the *bidonville* of Cité Soleil, longtime visitors such as Lolo Beaubrun watched in dismay as local activists died violently only to be replaced by ever younger cadres,[60] while Marie-Christine Jeune, a young PNH recruit who had criticized the government's rapprochement with armed gangs, was kidnapped and found raped and murdered.[61] When a November 1995 attack killed one deputy (Aristide's cousin Jean-Hubert Feuillé) and grievously wounded another (Gabriel Fortuné), Aristide's response was an incendiary speech at Feuillé's funeral in which he exhorted his followers to "go to the neighborhoods where there are big houses and heavy weapons" to disarm his opponents and demand "I want it and I can have it." At least seven people were killed and dozens of homes looted in the ensuing violence.[62] Though Aristide had been coy about whether or not he wanted to "recover" the three years he lost while in exile (and surrounding himself with loyalists given to screaming "Aristide or death!"),[63] he eventually endorsed René Préval with the rather ambiguous phrase "people *used* to call us marassa," and elections were held in December 1995, with Préval winning almost 88 percent of the vote in a poorly attended ballot.[64] By this point, Aristide had married Mildred Trouillot, a Haitian-American attorney he had met while in exile,[65] and together they would return to Aristide's mansion in the suburb of Tabarre.

Préval's five years in office were marked by fitful attempts to aid Haiti's peasantry and consolidate some of the country's institutions, all the while undermined both by an opposition-dominated parliament and by Aristide himself. After the brief premiership of Rosny Smarth, the parliament blocked a replacement for nearly two years until Préval unilaterally appointed educator Jacques-Édouard Alexis to fill the empty prime minister's seat. The streets of the capital were frequently disrupted by violent protesters, praising Aristide and attacking Préval for his supposed neoliberal intentions, even though Aristide himself had signed a draconian World Bank-sponsored structural adjustment program of austerity and privatization as a condition to his own return.[66] The agreements Aristide signed included reducing the tariff on rice imported to Haiti from 50 percent to 3 percent, with much of that rice imported from Arkansas, the home state of Bill Clinton. Haiti, once self-sufficient in rice production, became the fifth largest importer of American rice in the world.[67] Following the near destruction of the Creole pig a decade before, Haiti's farmers had suffered another blow. In one of his habitual public mea culpas, Clinton would later admit that the policy "may have been good for some of my farmers in Arkansas, but it has not worked, it was a mistake ... I have to live everyday with the consequences of the loss of capacity to produce a rice crop in Haiti to feed those people because of what I did; nobody else."[68]

In addition to parliamentary maneuvers and street protesters, there were also less subtle messages. When a small dog belonging to Préval's then wife was found with its spine shattered by a machete, many in Préval's circle took it as a direct threat from Aristide, who was believed to lay claim to the loyalty of many among the palace guard.[69] Eventually, Préval would replace a number of presidential and National Palace security guards, including Aristide loyalist Milien Romage.[70]

Through it all, Préval's closest councilor was the crusading journalist Jean Léopold Dominique, who, along with his wife, Michèle Montas, ran Radio Haiti Inter, the country's foremost investigative radio station that exposed the shady business dealings of the country's elite as well as the machinations of its new political class. Over the years, Radio Haiti had been a laboratory of journalistic talent, with broadcasters such as Richard Brisson (killed in an ill-fated attempt to overthrow Jean-Claude Duvalier in 1982), Marvel Dandin, Liliane Pierre-Paul, Anthony Pascal (known as Konpè Filo) and Marcus Garcia all passing through its employ. Dominique had been imprisoned by François Duvalier, exiled, and his station looted by Jean-Claude Duvalier's government, and he had to seek exile yet again after the 1991 coup. At the very beginning of Préval's term, Dominique subjected Aristide to a ferocious on-air grilling about the corruption surrounding a series of programs during his tenure known as the *Petits Projets de la Presidence*, to which Aristide responded only with bland platitudes. After that encounter, the relationship between Dominique and Aristide "cooled off tremendously," Michèle Montas would later say.[71] When Préval and parliament could not agree on a formula to hold elections and the country lapsed into rule-by-decree in January 1999, Dominique was there to provide council to what Préval often said was "a lonely job."[72] At the same time, Dominique fell foul of another powerful Aristide crony, a former FADH officer named Dany

Toussaint, during a bitter and violent struggle for the control of Haiti's newly formed police force.[73] Like Préval, Dominique was an agronomist by training, and he maintained close links with the country's peasant organizations, especially the Komite Zafè Elektoral Peyizan pou Eleksyon Pwop (KOZEPEP), led by a peasant activist from the Artibonite Valley named Charles Suffrard.

In addition to political infighting, Préval's term was marked by a series of spectacular assassinations: the activist priest Père Jean Pierre-Louis in August 1998, OPL senator Yvon Toussaint in March 1999, former army colonel Jean Lamy (thought to be a likely candidate to head the PNH) in October 1999, and, finally, in April 2000, a month before long-delayed parliamentary elections were to be held, Jean Dominique himself, slain in the courtyard of Radio Haiti along with the station's caretaker, Jean-Claude Louissaint. The killing shocked the country to its core, and perhaps the enduring image of Préval's first presidency was that of Haiti's leader openly weeping over the casket of his dead friend as Aristide sat stone-faced nearby.

The elections of May 2000 were a disaster. Préval confidant Robert "Bob" Manuel, then secretary of state for public security, fled the country after a face-to-face meeting with Aristide where the latter demanded that Manuel guarantee the coming vote "went well" for Fanmi Lavalas.[74] In the run-up to the vote, far from being able to campaign openly, opposition parties lived in fear lest they meet the fate of Mouvement Chrétien pour une Nouvelle Haïti (MOCHRENA) candidate Merilus Deus, hacked to death in front of his daughter in the northern town of Savanette in April,[75] or of 70-year-old Ducertain Armand of the Parti Démocrate-Chrétien Haïtien (PDCH), beheaded that same month.[76] After relatively calm voting on 21 May with strong turnout, Conseil Électoral Provisoire (CEP) President Leon Manus wrote of how "ballot boxes were stolen and replaced with stuffed substitute boxes ... full of ballots in favor of former President Aristide's party, Fanmi Lavalas ... The night of the elections was one of fraud, with the goal of ensuring the absolute success of the Fanmi Lavalas party." Refusing to sign off on the disputed results, Manus was called to the National Palace where, he later wrote, both Préval and Aristide "threatened me with death if I did not publish the manipulated results," though he "refused to commit such infamy against the Haitian people."[77] Manus fled into exile in the United States.

The situation in the countryside was even worse. In a November 2000 attack on a meeting of Chavannes Jean Baptiste's MPP peasant group in the Plateau

Central town of Hinche, Lavalas gunmen – including, witnesses said, Willot Joseph, the mayor of the nearby town of Maïssade – shot at least five people, including Chavannes' brother Dieugrand, who nearly died, and burned homes and vehicles associated with the group.[78] Aristide won sparsely attended presidential elections that same month. By this point, continuing a policy dating from disputed 1997 parliamentary elections, the United States, the European Community and other sources were withholding foreign aid to Haiti to the tune of $500 million.[79]

With Aristide back in office, a respected young judge named Claudy Gassant was assigned to the Dominique case but was mocked by Senate President Yvon Neptune as "an insignificant little judge."[80] In January 2001, Gassant encountered Milien Romage, the presidential security agent fired by Préval and now a Lavalas deputy, who threatened to shoot him if he continued with his investigation.[81] When the government withdrew his bodyguards in January 2002, Gassant fled the country and, from exile, said that Aristide had "done everything to block any effort to find who was involved in [the] killing [of] Jean Dominique."[82] In a March 2002 editorial, Michèle Montas spoke of how "all the resources, logistical, technical, and financial made available in this judicial case by the [Préval] government have been canceled."[83] From exile months later, Mario Andrésol, widely regarded as an honest PNH official who had also fled, told Radio Signal FM that "under the current government … there will be no progress in the Dominique case."[84] Eventually, Judge Bernard Saint-Vil would issue a 33-page indictment naming six individuals – among them, two then-incarcerated gang leaders, Dymsley "Ti Lou" Millien and Jeudi "Guimy" Jean Daniel – but not the intellectual authors of the crime, as if the thugs had simply "killed Jean for the hell of it," as Michèle Montas later exclaimed to me.

But thuggery, both tolerated and encouraged, had certainly become part of the government's strategy. Between 2001 and 2004, I spent many hours in the sprawling Port-au-Prince slum of Cité Soleil, and I counted some of the president's most fervent supporters there among my friends. A huge expanse blighted by poverty between the airport road and the bay, the vast majority of Cité Soleil residents I found to be new or first-generation arrivals from the countryside – honest, hardworking people scrambling to keep afloat in the economic shipwreck that was Haiti. However, since the late 1990s, the neighborhood had been ruled by armed factions led by young men claiming loyalty to Aristide and the Lavalas party. Though they were often described as such in the Haitian and foreign press, these men for the most part did not view themselves as gangsters or criminals, but rather as political activists and community leaders, and they referred to themselves as the *baz*, or base, of their neighborhoods. They would eventually become known by the name *chimere*, after a mythical, fire-breathing demon, appearing at a moment's notice and then disappearing, ghost-like, back into the slums which were their kingdoms but also their prisons. Robinson Thomas (known as Labanye, or Banner), backed up by his deputies Rodson "Kolobri" Lemaire and Evens "Ti Kouto" Jeune, controlled the Boston area, just at the entrance to Cité Soleil from Route Nationale 1. On the other side of Route Nationale 1, Simon Pelé was run by William "Ti Blan" Baptiste, a near-mulatto who was rumored to be the illegitimate offspring of the troubled scion of a prominent Haitian family. Emmanuel Wilmé (known as Dread Wilmé) ran the Droulliard/Bwa Neuf area, within which the Ti Ayiti district was ruled by Jean "Blade Nasson" Torchon. The area of Bélékou was run by Amaral Duclona along with his brother Raymond "Che" Duclona and Junior "Yoyo Piman" Acdhély. Soleil 19, down near the water, was controlled by Winston Jean-Bart (known as Tupac) and, after Tupac's arrest, by his younger half-brother, James Petit-Frere, alternately know as Billy or Kason Fè – Iron Pants – the latter a reference to Haiti's former military leader Paul Magloire. After Tupac – a rarity in that he frankly described himself as "a gangster" – had fallen foul of the authorities and ended up in prison,[85] it fell upon James' shoulders to provide for and protect his area of the slum, and so a young man who had once dreamed of being a reggae singer or a policeman, and who would carry foreign journalists' cameras for them when he was still a boy, had to pick up a gun. He became a dear friend, and as we walked through Soleil 19 together, a tattoo on his bicep reading "Don't Trust No One" often visible, he would tell me how he and the other *baz* leaders wanted to extricate the *bidonville* from violence and "concentrate on community projects, to help our country, teaching people how to read, how to speak English." At other times he would seem near despair and confess that "one day, man, I'd like to be able to give up this politics. If not, I'll die and I couldn't do anything for myself or my little son."

Beyond the capital, in the town of Saint-Marc, Lavalas deputy Amanus Mayette led a group called Bale Wouze (Clean Sweep), most of whom would have referred to themselves as an association of unemployed young people. In Gonaïves, Amiot "Cubaine" Métayer, a former law student, led the Armée Cannibale (Cannibal Army) from the seaside slum of Raboteau, including among its number many of those who worked in the city's port. In Petit-Goâve, the group Domi nan Bwa (Sleeps in the Woods) was responsible for the December 2001 machete slaying of journalist Brignol Lindor.[86]

Many of the young men leading the groups in Cité Soleil had grown up within the orbit of Lafanmi Selavi (The Family is Life), the home for street children that Aristide had been instrumental in founding while still a Catholic priest. All, for a time at least, believed that Aristide was the only chance that Haiti had to dynamite itself out of its feudal backwardness and brutal inequality, the latter of which the people of Cité Soleil felt as sharply as anyone. They became one of the windows through which I finally glimpsed how far the government had strayed, as I talked with them at length, visited with their families, attended the periodic press conferences they would hold downtown, and rode with them in rented tap-taps as they took their communities to the public beach to have a day of respite from grinding poverty and political wars. Although I believe I spent more time among the armed groups of Cité Soleil than any other foreign journalist, I was hardly the only one to report either on how heavily armed they were or on their connections to the government. The National Public Radio journalist Gerry Hadden[87] and Steven Dudley,[88] then writing for the *Boston Globe*, also conducted interviews with the chimere where they made plain their links to Aristide. The French filmmaker Charles Najman and the Danish filmmaker Asger Leth likewise documented the lives of the gangs there in their respective films, *La fin des chimères?* (2004) and *Ghosts of Cité Soleil* (2006).

For the young gunmen in Cité Soleil and other poor neighborhoods such as Bel-Air – and, indeed, around the country – supporting the government meant regular (if meagre) paychecks for supposed work at state entities such as Teleco, the state telephone company, despite the fact that they had never set foot there,[89] or at the Centrale Autonome Métropolitaine d'Eau Potable (CAMEP), the state water company, which doled out checks for no-show jobs.[90] For others, it was work at the capital's port, or the ports at Gonaïves or Saint-Marc or Petit-Goâve.[91] It was naked, cynical patronage and corruption, to be sure, but it was also an opening of the spigot of state money to a sector of society that had heretofore been largely denied it, and it was the only rope keeping them from falling off the cliff of economic disaster. The young men would march praising the president and disrupt opposition demonstrations, and for this they were assured their exceedingly meagre pay. The *baz* leaders told me they were in regular contact with representatives of Aristide's government, such as National Palace security chief Oriel Jean, PNH director for the West Department Hermione Leonard, Minister of Interior Jocelerme Privert and, indeed, Aristide himself, who would host them at his home at Tabarre and at the National Palace. The meetings at the latter were sometimes broadcast and the young men presented as "community leaders."

"It was after 1994 that the politicians started to use young, marginalized people and to pay them for politics, and that's when the young people started to pick up guns in the community and when you started hearing the word chimère," a friend of mine who had grown up in Cité Soleil told me. "Those guys were very close to Lavalas and Aristide ... [But] you had guns coming from Lavalas, former Macoutes, from the private sector ... Some young guys even stole some guns from a U.S. military base near Cité Soleil."[92]

* * *

But fairly early on there were signs that Aristide's relationship with the children was not entirely benevolent. An American photographer who had worked in Haiti for years and knew Aristide fairly well told the story of a dog brought to Lafanmi Selavi, yet which Aristide insisted be allowed to starve to death to teach the children that, in Haiti, there was not enough food for people, let alone animals.[93] As the children grew into the bosses of their areas, some leaders of armed groups who stepped out of line, such as Tupac, were summarily jailed without trial,[94] while others, such as Felix "Don Féfé" Bien-Aimé, who hailed from the hillside slum of Grand Ravine and scored a patronage job as head of the National Cemetery, were picked up by the police and never seen again.[95] As early as August 2002, Labanye told me: "We are losing more people here in Cité Soleil under Aristide than we lost under the coup d'état. The difference with the Macoutes is if you were a militant Macoute, when the Macoutes were in power, at least you had some protection. But we are the militant base of Aristide and now we have no protection, we can be shot any time."[96] When Aristide attempted to jail the man who was arguably the country's most powerful pro-Lavalas gang leader, Amiot "Cubaine" Métayer, his partisans responded by demolishing the jail and "liberating" him. Soon enough, Métayer was coaxed back into the Lavalas fold.

The groups engaged in some acts of spectacular violence. When an attack on the National Palace occurred in the wee hours of the morning of 17 December

2001, the cells were activated throughout the country (the *baz* leaders of Cité Soleil later gave me a blow-by-blow account of the day), and I personally watched thousands of heavily armed young men storm through the streets of Port-au-Prince under police escort, burning the offices of opposition political parties, Suzy Castor's CRESFED center (a frequent center of study for grassroots groups and impoverished students) and the home Castor shared with Gérard Pierre-Charles. At the latter, Pierre-Charles would write of losing hundreds of priceless books on Africa, Marxism and Cuba and manuscripts.[97] In Gonaïves, the Armée Cannibale torched the home of MOCHRENA leader Luc Messadieu and burned his bodyguard, Ramy Daran, alive in the street.[98] The palace attack was said to have been spearheaded by Guy Philippe, a former army officer and policeman who had fled to the Dominican Republic during the tenure of René Préval when the U.S. Embassy warned Préval that he was planning a coup. It was a name that Haitians would get to know very well in the coming years.

By the time he returned to office, Aristide had also collected a strange assortment of people around him. There was René Civil, a Lavalas activist and leader of the Jeunesse Pouvoir Populaire who had come up through the progressive Protestant movement ("They share God's word but the daily bread they keep for themselves," he told me once, referring to the church) but now was ostensibly an employee at the capital's port and roamed the city in a new SUV guarded by National Palace security personnel.[99] There was Paul Raymond, a divinity school dropout who was the public face of a group calling itself the Ti Kominote Legliz (TKL), who could be spied morosely drinking beer in his office at Teleco when not evoking Boisrond-Tonnerre and threatening to use the opposition's "skulls as the inkwells."[100] There were Ronald and Franco Camille, brothers reported to be involved in organized crime in the La Saline slum who opted for the more descriptive moniker *kadav* (dead body) rather than their own surnames.[101] And there was Annette "Sò Anne" (Sister Anne) Auguste, a vodou mambo and sometime folk singer to whom dark rumors clung in connection to the February 2000 disappearance of the newborn baby of Nanoune Myrthil from the capital's Hôpital Général, an incident that was reported by Radio Haiti Inter on at least two occasions[102] and to which two dissident Lavalas members, *baz* leader Johnny Occilius and former deputy mayor of Port-au-Prince Jean-Michard Mercier, both repeatedly linked Auguste.[103] Showing that ideology was no bar to someone versed in brutality, Aristide went as far as naming Fritz Joseph, one of the most feared FRAPH *attachés* from the 1990s, as mayor of Cité Soleil in 2002.

But Aristide's faith in his young acolytes had its limits. Not trusting his own countrymen, since 1998 Aristide had been protected by employees of the San Francisco-based Steele Foundation, to a large degree staffed by former U.S. military personnel.[104] Both Haitian and U.S. government officials said the contract fell somewhere between $6 million to $9 million per year for around 60 bodyguards, with additional provisions for weapons just shy of $1 million.[105] He also spent lavishly on foreign lobbyists to improve his government's image, with the United States Department of Justice Foreign Agent Registration Act filings listing payments to the law firm of Miami attorney Ira Kurzban and the firm of former U.S. congressman Ron Dellums totaling nearly $5 million and $1 million between 2001 and 2004 respectively (to name just two).[106]

By this point, government loyalist thugs also held more sway within the PNH than properly vetted officers. Among them was René "Grenn Sonnen" Jean Anthony, a former member of Duvalier's Léopards battalion now attached to the Delmas 33 police station, which for a time was commanded by Camille Marcellus, brother of Lavalas parliamentarian Nawoon Marcellus.[107] After Aristide loyalists such as Jean Nesly Lucien and Jean-Claude Jean Baptiste cycled through the PNH's top job, a more independent personality, Jean Robert Faveur, took the post, resigning only weeks later and fleeing the country.[108] In his resignation letter, Faveur detailed how he was ordered to sign off on illegal promotions within the police, and demanded to integrate chimere and *attaché* into the force from without, concluding that he "chose exile instead of letting myself be corrupted and enslaved," and warning that "the situation is not good within the PNH and misery rages in the country ... Many people who get rich around you are afraid to tell you how bad things are."[109]

Those who criticized the government, from former military ruler Prosper Avril[110] to Rosemond Jean, whose Coordination des Sociétaires Victimes des Coopératives (CONASOVIC) organization was agitating for restitution for the tens of thousands who had lost their money in a government-endorsed pyramid scheme[111], were thrown into jail without trial. Students and others who attempted to demonstrate – Aristide had inflamed student ire by trying to seize control of the state university system, as Duvalier had done years before – were routinely and savagely attacked by government loyalists. (The university students would eventually adopt the moniker *grenn nan bouda* – literally "balls in the ass" or colloquially "we've got balls," or GNB – and became perhaps the most radicalized element in the civil opposition.) Others, such as the feminist and educator Danielle Lustin[112] and the student leader Maxime Desulmond, turned up dead.[113]

But there was also outside, structural violence being committed against Haiti's people. By this point, Haiti's economy was the most "liberalized" in the Caribbean. As the tariff on imported rice to Haiti was slashed, the U.S. was lavishly subsidizing its own farmers and the percentage of Haiti's food coming from imports rose from 21 percent in 1995–96 to 32 percent in 2000–01, reaching 50 percent by mid-decade.[114] Between 2000 and 2005, the agricultural sector accounted for only 2.5 percent of the development aid Haiti received.[115] A United States Agency for International Development (USAID) study would conclude that Haiti was experiencing what it termed "premature urbanization," a state in which the agricultural sector was not productive and yet urban areas – where 40 percent of Haiti's population now lived – were not generating economic growth.[116] This phenomenon was the direct result of international – and specifically American – economic policies towards Haiti.

* * *

To be sure, there were other hands at work against Aristide as well as his own brutal stupidity. U.S. government-funded entities such as USAID, the National Democratic Institute (NDI) and the International Republican Institute (IRI) poured hundreds of thousands of dollars into trying to make Haiti's endlessly quarrelsome political class see the value of presenting a united front, ferrying them to Washington to meet with U.S. politicians and to Santo Domingo to powwow with one another.[117] The political opposition would eventually come together under an umbrella coalition calling itself the Convergence Démocratique (Democratic Convergence). In the IRI's case, it was believed that some of its representatives encouraged the opposition not to negotiate with the government, undermining official U.S. policy at the time.[118] The choice of Santo Domingo as locale was especially significant, as dissident members of Haiti's disbanded military such as Guy Philippe and Rémissainthe Ravix launched deadly raids into Haiti from their bases there (Philippe was quite open about the fact that representatives of Haiti's political class were meeting with him). The U.S. ambassador in Port-au-Prince at the time, the Clinton-era appointee Brian Dean Curran, grew so frustrated that, at a speech before the Haitian-American Chamber of Commerce, he denounced "the chimere of Washington," noting that "there were many in Haiti who preferred not to listen to me ... but rather listened to their own friends, the sirens of the extremists."[119]

* * *

And then there were the drugs. One of the most notorious drug traffickers in Haiti at the turn of the millennium was Beaudoin "Jacques" Ketant, who had got his start smuggling cocaine with the military. In March 1997, Ketant and 12 others had been indicted on drug trafficking and money laundering charges in the United States, but Ketant fled the U.S. on a Haiti-bound flight disguised as a woman. Back in Haiti, his drug business flourished to the point of his amassing a yearly income of somewhere around $13 million, buying an $8 million mansion in the hills above Port-au-Prince, expensive art and a fleet of expensive cars.[120] That Aristide and Ketant were well known to one another seemed beyond dispute. In 2001, Ketant had reportedly thrown a lavish christening party for one of Aristide's daughters at which the entire top command of the PNH, a roomful of Lavalas officials and Aristide himself were present, and he had also become godfather to the girl.[121] Ketant had also reportedly been a regular big money contributor to the Aristide Foundation for Democracy through a high-ranking member of the organization.[122] (Among the Foundation's U.S. board of advisors during the late 1990s and early 2000s had sat a long list of U.S. political players, including California politicians Ron Dellums and Maxine Waters, Representative Joseph P. Kennedy II, TransAfrica founder Randall Robinson and University of Miami law professor Irwin P. Stotzky.)

But by February 2003, when Ketant's brother and business partner were snatched off a busy Pétionville street by masked men wearing uniforms bearing PNH Brigade d'Intervention Rapide (BRI) insignias, taken to a home in the capital's Peguyville suburb and executed, the relationship had clearly soured. Ketant was finally arrested and bundled onto a Drug Enforcement Agency (DEA) flight to Miami. As he was sentenced to 27 years in a U.S. prison, Ketant told a Miami courtroom that Aristide was "a drug lord" who "controlled the drug trade in Haiti" and "turned the country into a narco-country ... You either pay [Aristide] or you die."[123] Ketant would tell U.S. authorities that he personally delivered $500,000 a month to Aristide at the latter's home in Tabarre in a suitcase with the lock combination 7-7-7, Aristide's favorite number.[124]

That during Aristide's second term in office virtually the entire top command of the PNH, as well as other Lavalas officials, were neck deep in the drug trade was also beyond dispute. Former PNH chief Jean Nesly Lucien[125] and BRI chief Rudy Therassan (who was also the husband on PNH West Department director Hermione Leonard, herself one of the key links between the National Palace and the chimere) would eventually be sentenced to five years and 15 years in U.S. prisons, respectively, for providing protection to Colombian traffickers shipping cocaine to the United States through Haiti and then laundering the profits. The men were also forced to forfeit nearly $2 million in assets.[126, 127] Fourel Célestin, Lavalas grandee and Haiti's former senate president, would eventually be taken into custody in Haiti and then extradited to the U.S. charged with drug trafficking offenses as well.[128] Cooperating witnesses and law enforcement officials in other drug investigations would later say that Aristide had instructed Célestin to solicit donations from drug traffickers for Fanmi Lavalas.[129] One of those traffickers who funneled money to Célestin was Jacmel's Jean Salim "Johnny" Batrony, who was subsequently arrested and extradited to the United States,[130] where, by some accounts, he became a U.S. informant.[131]

But perhaps no one's revelations would be as startling as those of Aristide's National Palace security chief and longtime confidant Oriel Jean, who counted among his circle another major drug lord in Haiti, the *borlette* patriarch Serge Édouard, who would eventually be convicted in Miami of importing tons of cocaine into the United States and paying hundreds of thousands of dollars in bribes.[132] Jean said that he had been introduced to Édouard by Hermione Leonard,[133] when, between 1998 and 2004, Édouard ran one of Haiti's most expansive drug trafficking networks.[134] After his own arrest, Jean would tell investigators that during his second term in office, Aristide approved a National Palace security badge for Édouard, which allowed him to travel freely through Haiti without fear of being searched by the police, and that Édouard gave unspecified amounts of money to the Aristide Foundation for Democracy.[135] At Édouard's trial, Jean would state that Leonard told him that Aristide was "aware that she [had] contacts" with major drug traffickers in Haiti.[136] When Jean and Édouard encountered one another at Miami Federal Detention Center after their arrests, Édouard had reportedly threatened to kill Jean's family if he continued to testify.[137] After agreeing to cooperate with U.S. authorities, Jean would plead guilty in Miami to drug-related money laundering charges, for which he could have faced 20 years in prison.[138] Instead, in recognition of his help, Jean would be sentenced to only three years in prison. The sentencing judge even went so far as to praise Jean's "good work" in providing information to investigators.[139]

A Miami jury would convict Serge Édouard of all 12 counts against him of conspiring to import cocaine to the United States and of money laundering.[140]

Defendants cooperating in a federal drug trafficking investigation of Aristide in the United States would eventually tell authorities that, upon taking office in 2001, Aristide had held a meeting at Tabarre with top security personnel to discuss the structure that would be used to acquire funds from Haitian and Colombian drug traffickers operating into the country. These arrangements, the defendants said, included payments of hundreds of thousands of dollars, some of which went to buy weapons for the PNH and the chimere.[141] Despite the suspicious transactions outlined by Haitian bank documents, investigators found definitive bank records backing up the claims of the defendants maddeningly hard to come by.[142]

* * *

As I watched what the second Aristide government had become, I was reminded of the words of Thucydides in his *History of the Peloponnesian War*, in which he discussed a reinvention of vocabulary for the civil war in Corcyra that certainly suited Haiti in the early 2000s and which Boisrond-Tonnerre might have found very familiar:

> What used to be described as a thoughtless act of aggression was now regarded as the courage one would expect to find in a party member; to think of the future was merely another way of saying one was a coward; any idea of moderation was just an attempt to disguise one's unmanly character; ability to understand a question from all sides meant one was totally unfitted for action.[143]

The end came quickly enough. With the Organization of American States (OAS) clamoring for Amiot Métayer's arrest for the December 2001 violence in Gonaïves, the government made several entreaties for the gang leader to return to jail in exchange for money. Métayer refused, and threatened to "tell everything" should he be incarcerated.[144] On 21 September 2003, Métayer drove off from his base in the Raboteau slum in the company of Odonel Paul, a Gonaïves politico who had been employed in the Ministry of the Interior. The following day, Métayer's body was found, his heart and eyes carved out, by the roadside of Bas Gros Morne near Saint-Marc.[145] Outraged at their leader's death, Armée

Cannibale members called the National Palace seeking help, only to be told that Odonel Paul was there, leading the gang to conclude that Aristide himself had ordered the strongman's demise (Odonel Paul subsequently disappeared and is believed dead). They immediately took to the airwaves to announce that "Amiot Métayer was murdered by the regime." [146] Mass demonstrations erupted in Gonaïves, only to be brutally dispersed by government forces.[147] During Métayer's funeral, hundreds of protesters chanted "Down with Aristide!" and clashed violently with police.[148] A 2 October raid on Raboteau and nearby Jubilé led by the PNH"s Camille Marcellus killed at least 15 people.[149] Returning to Gonaïves from Florida, where he lived, Métayer's brother, Buteur Métayer, said that he was taking control of the Armée Cannibale and that the group would force Aristide's resignation "at all costs."[150] The Armée Cannibale thus transformed into the Front de Résistance des Gonaïves.[151]

As the violence in Gonaïves flared, huge protests – including the political opposition, students, intellectuals, peasants and others – rocked all of Haiti's major cities. A breaking point occurred on 5 December 2003, when armed government partisans under police protection stormed Haiti's State University, brutalized dozens of students and beat the rector with iron bars until they crippled him,[152] an attack described in detail by the staff of Haiti's Fondasyon Konesans Ak Libète (FOKAL), who witnessed it from the windows of their building next door,[153] and footage of which is featured in Haitian filmmaker Arnold Antonin's *GNB Kont Attila*.

If the murder of Métayer put the coffin lid on the legacy of the Aristide regime, the university attack hammered in the final nail. Half a dozen high-ranking government officials resigned in protest. Brawling competing demonstrations continued throughout the country and the formerly pro-Aristide Cité Soleil gang leader Labanye, alarmed by the murder of his deputy Colibri at the hands, he said, of a joint operation by Dread Wilmé's gang and the zone's former FRAPH (now Lavalas) mayor, Fritz Joseph, publicly broke with the regime.[154]

"That is the way the Lavalas government is," Labanye told Radio Métropole. "The Lavalas authorities want to trample on the people's blood in order to celebrate 2004. The way things are now, Aristide is willing even to give away his own children."[155]

Labanye would quickly find his skills, such as they were, embraced by Haiti's private sector, specifically the businessman Andy Apaid, a fierce Aristide foe who operated a factory in the Cité Soleil area.

By early February, Guy Philippe, former FRAPH co-founder Louis Jodel Chamblain and others flooded across the Dominican border to link up with the rebels in Gonaïves and seize the northern half of the country. The joined forces of the two groups would name themselves the Front de Résistance pour la Libération et la Reconstruction Nationales (FLRN). As it sputtered to its inevitable dénouement, the regime committed some sickening crimes, the worst of which occurred in the northern city of Saint-Marc.

An armed anti-Aristide group, the Rassemblement des Militants Conséquents de Saint-Marc (RAMICOSM), based in the neighborhood of La Scierie, attempted to drive government forces from the town on 7 February 2004, seizing the local police station, which they set on fire. Two days later, the combined forces of the PNH, the Unité de Sécurité de la Garde du Palais National (USGPN) – a unit directly responsible for the president's personal security – and the local pro-government paramilitary organization Bale Wouze retook much of the city. By 11 February, Bale Wouze – headed by Lavalas former deputy Amanus Mayette – had commenced the battle to retake La Scierie. At Mayette's side was a government employee named Ronald Dauphin, known to residents as "Black Ronald," often garbed in a police uniform even though he was in no way officially employed by the police. Other members included Figaro Désir, Biron Odigé and a man known as Somoza.[156] After government forces retook the town – and after a press conference there by Yvon Neptune,[157] at the time Aristide's prime minister and also the head of the Conseil Superieur de la Police Nationale d'Haïti (CSPN) – a textbook series of war crimes took place. Residents told me of how Kenol St. Gilles, a carpenter with no political affiliation, was shot in each thigh, beaten unconscious by Bale Wouze members and thrown into a burning cement depot, where he died. Unarmed RAMICOSM member Leroy Joseph was decapitated, while RAMICOSM second-in-command Nixon François was shot. In the ruins of the burned-out commissariat, Bale Wouze members gang-raped a 21-year-old woman, while other residents were gunned down by police and armed civilians firing from a helicopter as they tried to flee over a nearby mountain.[158]

When the photojournalist Alex Smailes and I arrived in the town, we found the USGPN and Bale Wouze patrolling Saint-Marc as a single armed unit. Speaking to residents there – against a surreal backdrop of burned buildings, the stench of human decay, drunken gang members threatening our lives with firearms and a terrified population – we soon realized that something awful had happened in Saint-Marc.

"These people don't make arrests, they kill," a local priest, Père Arnal Métayer, told me at the time.[159]

Alex and I were not the only journalists to document what was happening. *The Miami Herald*'s Marika Lynch wrote of how the town was "under a terrifying lockdown by the police and a gang of armed pro-Aristide civilians" and that "the two forces are so intertwined that when [Bale Wouze's] head of security walks by, Haitian police officers salute him and call him commandant."[160] Gary Marx of the *Chicago Tribune* wrote of how "residents saw piles of corpses burning in an opposition neighborhood and watched as pro-Aristide forces fired at people scurrying up a hillside to flee."[161]

According to Anne Fuller, a Haiti veteran and fluent Creole speaker and a member of a Human Rights Watch delegation that visited Saint-Marc a month after the killings, at least 27 people were murdered there between 11 February and 29 February.[162] Her conclusion was supported by the reporting of the respected Haitian journalist Nancy Roc (who wrote at the time "if justice is not rendered in the case of the La Scierie Massacre, we can fear the worst for the future"[163]) and by the research of the National Coalition for Haitian Rights (NCHR), a Haitian human rights organization.[164]

On 29 February, with his enemies closing in, Aristide and his family fled the country, leaving behind partisans at the mercy of the rebels and the multifaceted forces that had ousted him, and, in a final gesture of contempt, $350,000 in rotting U.S. currency found by looters in a safe behind a concrete wall at his mansion in Tabarre.[165] A shipment of arms from the government of South African President Thabo Mbeki, routed through Jamaica with the connivance of Jamaican Prime Minister P. J. Patterson, appeared too late to save him.[166] It is believed that the looting that took place around Port-au-Prince following Aristide's departure resulted in damage somewhere in the neighborhood of $200 million.[167] Aristide himself first landed – improbably – in Bangui, the war-ravaged capital of the Central Africa Republic, and then would fly to Jamaica in mid-March where he stayed until the end of May, at which point he and his family moved to South Africa.

What were the circumstances of Aristide's flight, many wondered? The version given to me in Port-au-Prince by Luis Moreno, the deputy chief of mission to the U.S. Embassy in Haiti, only weeks after Aristide had fled, was that, after halting negotiations with United States Ambassador James Foley, Aristide had requested American assistance in fleeing Haiti, which the U.S.

provided, with Moreno accompanying Aristide to the airport (where he had ironically been on hand to see Aristide arrive back in Haiti in 1994 during a previous stint in the country).[168] A number of the armed groups in Cité Soleil also appeared aware that Aristide was planning to leave the country.[169]

Shortly after he left, Aristide himself spoke to the American radio host Amy Goodman, whose *Democracy Now!* program, long on righteous bluster but short on on-the-ground reporting from Haiti, had long acted as an uncritical conveyer belt for the views of Aristide, his party and the lobbyists he paid so handsomely in the United States. Aristide told Goodman that he would "not go into details" about his flight from Haiti, but that it was a "kidnapping … part of the global plan … to kidnap me," and that on the flight to Bangui there were "19 American agents from [the] Steele Foundation" along with U.S. military personnel who changed into civilian clothes once airborne. Aristide pilot Frantz Gabriel elaborated on the same program that Luis Moreno had arrived at Tabarre at around 5am and told Aristide that they were going to have a "press conference" at the U.S. Embassy, only to divert the convoy to the airport and hustle the assembled group – including the year-old baby of a Steele Foundation employee – onto the waiting plane where they all "just sat there and waited" until the plane took off.[170]

An unlikely story perhaps, made even more so by the comments of the Steele Foundation's CEO, Kenneth Kurtz, on the same program only a few days earlier, when he said that "we were with the president when he left the country … We took direction directly – and only – from the president … The mission of our company is to protect the head of state from assassination, kidnapping, and embarrassment, and that's what we did."[171] Kurtz's version of events was supported by National Palace security agent Casimir Chariot, who said that the men who escorted Aristide to the airport "were security officers dressed like us, with earpieces … These were not people who came with handcuffs to handcuff the president. These were men who came to assure the security of the delegation … It was all done very calmly."[172] Even Aristide's former prime minister, Yvon Neptune, like so many officials of the government left in the lurch by the president's quick exit, told Radio Kiskeya that Aristide had indeed resigned and that the president's letter of resignation "was genuine."[173] Neptune would also say that he had been "used" by Aristide, and characterized the former president as someone who allowed "no democracy" even within Fanmi Lavalas itself, and that the party was run by "manipulators" disguised as "apostles of change and inclusion of the poor majority."[174]

CHAPTER TWO
LES BLANCS DÉBARQUENT

The capital from which Haiti's yet-to-be-formed new government and the multi-national force would now attempt to rule the country was a city of 3 million where thousands of anarchically built cement block houses in areas such as Carrefour and Delmas shared space with the zinc-roofed lean-tos of the truly desperate in slums like Cité Soleil and La Saline, which teetered at times directly over canals of raw sewage. Over the broad swathe of the Champ de Mars square and the ornate National Palace – gleaming white under the Caribbean sun – rose the slum of Bel-Air, which had once been a stronghold of the populist Fignolé, and which had produced some of the nation's greatest makes of *drapo vodou* (beautiful vodou-inspired "flags" festooned with intricate sequins) and had become inhabited by some of the capital's most feared *baz*. Heading east and uphill from the bay, one would enter Turgeau and pass the lovely old Église du Sacré-Cœur, the street in front of which had witnessed the theft of the coffin of Duvalier opponent Clément Jumelle in 1959, the murder of Aristide's justice minister Guy Malary and the execution of his most important backer among the elite, the Palestinian-Haitian businessman Antoine Izméry, both in 1993. Beyond that site of ill fame, the leafy recesses of neighborhoods like Pacot (my old neighborhood, where I watched Aristide's government unravel from a little pink house) and Bois Verna surprised one with sublime examples of gingerbread architecture. Further up, towards the hills that brooded, sometimes swathed with a garland of clouds, one passed Musseau, which had once been so remote from the city it served as the rural setting for the famous Haitian novel *La Bête de Musseau* (translated into English as *The Beast of the Haitian Hills*) by the brothers Philippe Thoby-Marcelin and Pierre Marcelin. Beyond that, Pétionville had once been a posh mountain suburb but had long ago been overrun with migrants from the countryside, their hopes clinging to the mountains like the neighborhoods such as Jalousie, with residents venturing down to Place Boyer and Place Saint-Pierre to look for work. If one drove up the hill even further, one would climb into the cooler temperatures of Laboule, Thomassin and Fermathe, past the distillery for Haiti's Barbancourt rum (its *réserve spéciale* considered by many to be the finest in the world) and a gravel quarry before reaching the town of Kenscoff, where market vendors braced themselves against the alpine cold in second-hand jackets and where perhaps the country's best *tafia* (raw rum) was made. One could hike over the mountains and eventually make one's way down to the dazzling colonial town of Jacmel on the island's southern coast, sparkling like a seashell under the sun, where Simón Bolívar had once been given shelter. Beyond unfurled the Grand Anse, like the outstretched arm of a sleeping bather in the sand, dotted with picturesque towns such as Port Salut, Dame-Marie and Jérémie, the last of these the birthplace of Thomas-Alexandre Dumas, a famous mixed-race French general and the father of the novelist Alexandre Dumas.

If one turned north from Port-au-Prince, the degraded, potholed Route Nationale 1 would take one past the somnolent beach resorts along the Côte des Arcadins, where Haiti once boasted its own Club Med and where Jean-Claude Duvalier once had his beach house, through Saint-Marc – a bastion of one of Haiti's slavery-era *sociétés secrètes*, Bizango – and then the sun-blasted, treeless port town of Gonaïves, where Haiti had declared its independence from the French 200 years before and where the rebellion against Aristide began. And beyond, forking west and east respectively, towns such as Jean-Rabel and Bombardopolis and the seaside city of Môle-Saint-Nicolas, where forts built by three colonial powers – French, Spanish and British – lay decaying under the tropical sun. Or to Haiti's second largest city – proud, defiant Cap-Haïtien – outside of which Christophe's Sans-Souci palace and Citadelle Laferrière still rose, proclaiming the nation's independence to the world.

Now, for the third time in less than a century, foreign troops were strolling the streets of Haiti's cities, not just at any time but, to pour salt in the wound, during its bicentennial year. Although it would not be officially constituted until June, the new United Nations mission in Haiti – the Mission des Nations Unies pour la Stabilisation en Haïti (MINUSTAH) – would become the seventh UN mission in Haiti since 1997.[1] Its peacekeeping forces would be largely Latin American in composition, with the lead taken by Brazil, at the time governed by moderately leftist President Luiz Inácio Lula da Silva of the Partido dos Trabalhadores, and eager to increase its regional footprint.

To lead the UN mission in Haiti, UN Secretary-General Kofi Annan selected former Chilean foreign minister and career diplomat Juan Gabriel Valdés, at the time serving as Chile's ambassador to Argentina. The scion of a political family, Valdés had spent part of the years of the dictatorship of Augusto Pinochet in exile in Mexico, where he met and became friends with Gérard Pierre-Charles and Suzy Castor.

The security situation when MINUSTAH first took over was so unstable that, when U.S. Ambassador James Foley visited Valdés for an afternoon meeting at the hillside Hotel Montana shortly after the latter's arrival, the American diplomat was surprised by the amount of armed UN troops milling about the compound. The men, it turned out, were not UN forces at all, but the troops of the anti-Aristide rebel leader Rémissainthe Ravix, who was holding a meeting in the hotel at the same time.[2]

Following Aristide's overthrow and the appointment of Boniface Alexandre, the head of Haiti's Supreme Court, as interim president, a tripartite commission was formed consisting of the OPL's Paul Denis as a representative of the opposition, former government minister Leslie Voltaire as a representative of Lavalas and Adama Guendo, the resident head of the United Nations Development Program (UNDP) in Haiti, as a representative of the international community. This commission selected a Conseil des Sages (Council of Elders) to facilitate Haiti's political transition and select a new prime minister. The council included among its members the feminist activist Danielle Magloire, representatives of the Catholic and Protestant churches and politician Ariel Henry. Notably absent were any members of Lavalas.

It was announced that the new head of the PNH would be Léon Charles, up until then the head of Haiti's Coast Guard, and that Carlo Lochard, a former PNH commander in Jacmel and a man who doted on his aging mother despite having a brutal reputation, would be made director of West Department, which included Port-au-Prince. Upon his ascent to head the PNH in early March, the NCHR human rights group sent Charles a letter advising him that "the police as an institution today are not seen as a state institution but as a private militia in the service of a man, of a political party" and that a dramatic housecleaning was needed in order to restore public faith in the organization.[3]

On 12 March, the council announced that it had selected as interim prime minister Gérard Latortue, an economist from Gonaïves who had briefly served as foreign minister during the presidency of Leslie Manigat. Latortue had taught at a university in Puerto Rico before cycling through a series of United Nations posts and retiring to Florida. He was the first cousin once removed of

Youri Latortue, a former Haitian army officer who had previously served on Aristide's security detail. Described as "erudite and engaging"[4] by foreign diplomatic observers, and clearly extremely ambitious, Youri Latortue nevertheless had something of a mixed reputation among Haitians, and the Americans kept him at arm's length.

"My only mission was to organize elections," Latortue told me one day at his home in Florida. "I wanted to make the case that free elections were possible in Haiti. But many Haitians don't believe in free elections. They think it is a football club, they want to select someone, not elect someone."[5]

None of Latortue's 18 ministers or secretaries of state had particularly close ties to either Haiti's opposition or Lavalas (though three had served under either Aristide or Préval). Though he may have hoped this would lead to the appearance of a technocratic, nonpartisan cabinet, for its part, Haiti's civilian opposition felt rather under-appreciated, with Micha Gaillard telling U.S. Ambassador Foley that "after all the risks we took, suddenly we have nothing." From the beginning, the relationship between Latortue and Alexandre was one of mutual suspicion, with Latortue concerned that Alexandre might try to usurp his powers (given Haiti's history, not a baseless concern).[6] One of the key appointments, which in coming months would have significant ramifications in the country, was that of Bernard Gousse, a French-educated lawyer and bitter Lavalas foe, as minister of justice.

"The situation was extremely fragile, characterized by a lot of street violence and the very public activity of different gangs and former soldiers of the Haitian army," Valdés later told me. "It was characterized by a very weak civilian authority, because the president was a person without any real experience and far away from decision making. The prime minister was practically as new as I was, he had been out of the country for years, and members of the bourgeoisie and the political class were very unhappy with how everything had developed."[7]

One of the first moves of the interim government was to summarily fire many of the thousands of loyalists with whom Aristide had bloated the payroll of the state companies. This move, perhaps more than any other, engendered early on the enmity of not only those dismissed but also the large extended families for whom any paycheck meant successfully balancing on the cliff of economic disaster. There was also a desire, both in Haiti and among some in the international community, to exact a kind of revenge on the loyalists of the *ancien régime*, with some comparing Lavalassians to Nazis and advocating that the group be legally forbidden.[8] Lists of Lavalas partisans – some criminal, some not – to be arrested soon appeared on the walls of Haitian police stations and MINUSTAH bases.[9] Over dinner one night, one well-known representative of the private sector advised the new MINUSTAH chief that *Monsieur Valdés, la terreur est la seule méthode* (Mr. Valdés, terror is the only method).[10]

A slew of former Lavalas supporters were sent to prison. Two people whose names had frequently been mentioned in connection with the Jean Dominique killing – former assistant mayor of Port-au-Prince Harold Sévère and Annette Auguste – were arrested, the latter ostensibly for involvement in a host of malfeasance from the Dominique murder to the December university attack to the disappearance of the Nanoune Myrthil infant.[11] Another individual whose name repeatedly came up in the Dominique investigation, Franco Camille, walked free from the Pétionville prison.[12] A short time later, two more men believed to have been involved in the crime were recaptured with Dymsley "Ti Lou" Millien, seized in Port-au-Prince, and Jeudi Jean-Daniel was arrested in Jacmel.[13] Radio Vision 2000, a private radio station that had been co-founded and was owned by Réginald Boulos, a wealthy businessman and Aristide foe,[14] aired a startling confessional discourse by the Cité Soleil gang leader Labanye in which he spoke of the close links between Aristide's security chief Oriel Jean, Interior Minister Jocelerme Privert and PNH commander Hermione Leonard with the chimere, before going on to give a chillingly specific account of the Dominique murder that implicated Harold Sévère, Annette Auguste and the Camille brothers (one of whom, Ronald, had by this point died in prison).[15]

There was, perhaps, a chance for real accountability for the crimes of the regime. Survivors of the La Scierie massacre and relatives of the victims formed a solidarity organization, the Association des Victimes du Génocide de la Scierie (AVIGES), to petition the new government for justice. During the first half of 2004, both Yvon Neptune and Jocelerme Privert were arrested for their alleged roles in the La Scierie killings, although, in a demonstration of just how fractured the interim government was, Latortue only heard news of the latter's arrest while attending a church service.[16] Two investigatory bodies, the Unite Centrale de Renseignements Financiers (UCREF) and the Commission d'Enquête Administrative (CEA), were tasked with investigating the departed government's corruption. Across the ocean in South Africa, not everyone was overjoyed at Aristide's sudden appearance in the country. The fact that the Mbeki government had tried to send weapons to the Aristide regime during its last sanguinary days had provoked a furious domestic political row.[17] The columnist Rhoda Kadalie, herself the granddaughter of the nation's first black trade union leader, wrote that "Aristide left behind an almost irreparable mess, while he will enjoy the fat of our land at our expense" and wondered why Thabo Mbeki would "tarnish SA's years of struggle for democracy" by lauding the man.[18] Haitian journalist Nancy Roc also warned that "although the dictator has left, all of his repressive machine, human and financial, is still alive," and if a true disarmament program was not implemented, "citizens will be subject to the barbaric criminality of the gangs and the partisans of the former regime."[19]

Before South Africa, Aristide had briefly retuned to the Caribbean, specifically to Jamaica at the invitation of Prime Minister P. J. Patterson. Following Aristide's arrival, Latortue angrily recalled Haiti's ambassador from Kingston and suspended Haiti's relations with the Caribbean Community (CARICOM), of which Haiti had become the most populous member in 2002. Patterson himself led the CARICOM call for an investigation into the circumstances of Aristide's departure (though not into the abuses of his regime).[20] CARICOM responded by suspending Haiti's participation in its meetings.[21] With dripping condescension, St. Vincent and the Grenadines Prime Minister Ralph Gonsalves, who had remained silent in the face of the carnage of the previous months, sniffed that "you do not have democracy in Haiti today," while St. Lucia Prime Minister Kenny Anthony opined that CARICOM "clearly [outlined] a path to political power based on the freedom of citizens to elect governments on their own free will."[22]

Had CARICOM leaders only listened to one of their own, they might have been better informed on how they were viewed by a large chunk of Haitian society. Since February, Réginald Dumas, a veteran Trinidadian diplomat who had served as his country's ambassador to both the United States and the OAS, had been serving as the UN's Special Advisor on Haiti. Dumas, a Haiti veteran, realized that up until Aristide's overthrow, the democratic opposition in Haiti had viewed CARICOM as "really just protecting Aristide, whereas the Haitian people had needed protection *from* Aristide," and that this reflexive solidarity was simply a case of CARICOM leaders "identifying with one of their own."[23]

That identification by some of CARICOM's members did not, alas, extend to Haiti's citizenry. When Hurricane Jeanne devastated Gonaïves, killing nearly 3,000 people and leaving nearly 200,000 homeless, CARICOM did not lift a finger to help Haiti, to the body's eternal discredit.[24] In an editorial, the

Jamaica Observer implored that: "It cannot be beyond the collective wisdom of the Community to fashion a system of limited engagement, based on humanitarian concerns."[25] A notable exception was the government of Barbados leader Owen Arthur, who provided technical assistance and an initial contribution of 1 million Barbados dollars for the purpose of providing humanitarian aid to the victims of the storm.[26]

In this strange atmosphere, the journalist and poet Jacques Roche, who served as the cultural editor of *Le Matin* and had been involved with the progressive group PAPDA, began hosting a television discussion program, *Randevou Sosyete Sivil la* (*Civil Society Rendezvous*), in which he interviewed political, civil society and cultural figures. As he had seen the *maquiladora* model exported to the north of Haiti two years earlier, with Aristide doling out good farmland on the Maribahoux Plain to the Dominican Republic company Grupo M, Roche had written a moving poem on the loss of peasant life and the loss of Haiti's rural soul called *Le Vent de Maribahoux*. Now, as he looked around at the devastation in his country, Roche wrote one of his most poignant poems, *Survivre* (*Survive*), which read in part:

Tu peux me crever les yeux	You can put out my eyes
Et les tympans	And burst my eardrums
Me couper les bras	Cut off my arms
Et les jambes	And legs
Me laisser nu en pleine rue	Leave me naked in the middle of the road
Mais tu ne peux tuer mon rêve	But you cannot kill my dream
Tu ne peux tuer l'espoir	You cannot kill hope[27]

At a donors' conference in Washington, DC on 20 July, international donors announced a \$1.08 billion pledge of aid to the country, going even beyond the \$924 million the Latortue government had requested. Latortue said the money would be used mostly for infrastructure projects, especially on Haiti's electricity system and roads.[28]

But the situation in the country remained deeply unsettled. In late July, about 50 former rebels who had been occupying the Mirebalais police station for a week finally left after a meeting with peacekeepers,[29] but on 27 August, 100 former soldiers led by Rémissainthe Ravix took over the police station in Petit-Goâve.[30] PNH officers were threatening to strike over their working conditions, with one officer telling Radio Signal FM that: "If it were a question of promises or money, the police would have stopped working about five or six years ago … You may see ten policemen in one car, whereas a police official may have three police vehicles at his home, with his wife driving one of them and his younger brother is driving another one … Many people have heavy weapons in their hands."[31]

Just how Haiti would go about providing justice for victims of past offenses was thrown into question when, in an overnight trial, former rebel leader and FRAPH co-founder Louis Jodel Chamblain and former FADH officer Jackson Joanis were acquitted for the 1993 murder of Aristide's financial backer Antoine Izméry. NCHR denounced the trial as "a mockery of justice."[32] The Conseil des Sages announced in a statement that they "deplored" the verdict in the case.[33] In a joint early September press release, three human rights organizations – NCHR, the Comité des Avocats pour le Respect des Libertés Individuelles (CARLI) and the Plateforme des Organisations Haïtiennes de Défense des Droits Humains (POHDH) – wrote that "the Aristide government's submersion in human rights violations does not excuse us from denouncing the violence of the military government, the army and FRAPH committed against the Haitian people." The release went on to denounce the Chamblain–Joanis trial as a "masquerade."[34]

If anything, the trial seemed to embolden former members of the military. On 7 September, two former rebels dressed in camouflage were killed by police at a Port-au-Prince checkpoint when they ignored a warning to thrown down their weapons, leading the dead men's comrades in Petit-Goâve to briefly hold several policemen hostage. Hours later, another former rebel was killed by MINUSTAH troops in Hinche after he allegedly opened fire on a police station there. Ravix bitterly complained about Latortue's failure to restore the army.[35] On 8 September, several hundred marchers calling for the army's restoration and ten years' back pay brawled with Aristide loyalists in Cap-Haïtien.[36]

* * *

Though it passed with little notice at the time, a late August visit to Cité Soleil by Renaud Muselier, France's secretary of state for foreign affairs, resulted in Muselier's delegation being pinned down in the slum under heavy gunfire for two hours before being extracted by MINUSTAH forces.[37] It was a warning sign, but nobody interpreted it as such in its immediate aftermath.

"The capacity of MINUSTAH to have serious intelligence was extremely weak," Valdés later admitted to me. "Therefore it was very difficult to understand exactly what was going on with the armed groups in Cité Soleil and other areas of the city."[38]

Though some of the leaders of the Cité Soleil *baz* – James, Tupac and others – had briefly gone abroad, mostly to the Dominican Republic, following Aristide's ouster, by the end of the summer they were all back in the country and back in Cité Soleil, where they joined Labanye, the latter now firmly in the employ of Haiti's private sector.

All throughout the summer of 2004, the most fervent loyalists of the *ancien régime*, the *baz* of the capital's poorest neighborhoods whom much of society scornfully referred to as chimere, watched as they, their families and their communities sank deeper and deeper into desperation and starvation, as the brutal members of the former military that had ousted Aristide, such as Ravix, operated with seeming impunity throughout a huge swathe of the country. Far from attempting to recruit them into a new democratic experiment, many elements of the interim government and the international community appeared to be driven by a spirit of revenge, and sought instead to marginalize and punish them. Given such a dynamic, it was only a matter of time before Port-au-Prince would be in flames once again.

CHAPTER THREE
OPERATION BAGHDAD

It was from desperate, seething Cité Soleil that the explosion finally came. On 30 September – a most auspicious date as it marked the anniversary of the 1991 coup against Aristide – demonstrations had been called by the pro-Lavalas factions throughout the capital. Hundreds of protesters, led by armed baz leaders such as James, Tupac, Dread Wilmé and Amaral, began marching out of Cité Soleil to join a mass rally that was planned to reach the National Palace and call for Aristide's return. As they passed the Boston section of the *quartier* – the key zone that was one of the main entrance routes to the rest of city – they were fired upon by the gunmen of the Boston gang leader Labanye and PNH forces. Several people were killed, including the gang leader Tupac, who bled to death after being wounded. Enraged, Tupac's brother, my friend James, attempted to exact revenge, only to be shot and wounded himself, dragged out of the hospital where he sought treatment, and thrown into the prison at the Pompiers commissariat downtown.

News of Tupac's murder and the wounding of James reached me in Rio de Janeiro, where I was living at the time, and set off a furious race among his friends, both Haitian and foreign, to guarantee that he was not summarily executed by the police nor die of his wounds in prison. I was able to get a Haitian doctor friend – a gentle physician from Carrefour – in to see James at Pompiers, where the jailers were so afraid of their new charge that they covered their faces lest they be recognized and subject to any sort of street revenge. The doctor examined James and found that his wound was not that serious and that, in his words, "I could see in his eyes how much he wanted to live." Many of us – myself included – wrote to various foreign diplomatic missions in Haiti and to foreign organizations such as Amnesty International apprising them of James' tenuous situation. Then came the matter of Tupac, and many of us tried to pull together the funds to supply him with a burial. With many of Tupac's foreign friends out of the country, Verdieu, the

Haitian boyfriend of one of them, agreed to act as intermediary and deliver the money to Amaral to pay for Tupac's funeral, even though, at the time, Amaral, along with Dread Wilmé, was being mentioned on the radio as "one of the most wanted killers" in Haiti. As Verdieu met two of Amaral's emissaries downtown, he was pounced upon by masked, black-uniformed PNH agents who hauled him to Pompiers, beat him and demanded to know why he was working with foreigners who gave money so the gangs of Cité Soleil could kill police officers. After being forced to attempt to lure Amaral out of Cité Soleil for a meeting (a trap that failed), Verdieu was finally able to bribe his way out of jail and fled into hiding in Jacmel. I, along with the others, was left feeling incredibly naive and stupid for putting him in such a situation in the first place.

Outside the walls of the jail, the capital was erupting. The same day Tupac was killed, three policemen were shot during a pro-Aristide demonstration near the palace.[1] After they spoke on Radio Caraïbes, the Lavalas former parliamentarians Yvon Feuillé, Gérald Gilles and Rudy Hériveaux were arrested without warrants and accused of being involved in the violence turning the city upside down, a charge all three denied.[2] "They are kidnapping me," Feuillé told reporters as he was led away.[3] Arrested along with them was a former Haitian military officer named Arnel Bélizaire, for illegally possessing a T-65 assault rifle that he claimed was to ensure their safety. The charges against him were later expanded to include murder.[4] Bélizaire claimed that the weapons were for his security business.[5]

Between 30 September and 4 October, at least 20 people were slain in the capital, including a dozen policemen (several of whom were beheaded) and a former soldier killed in Bel-Air.[6] On 3 October, gunfire rang out in La Saline as gunmen robbed market vendors and set tires aflame to block the streets.[7] One resident of La Saline told a reporter that "every night the gangs are out shooting. No one wants to leave their homes ... The police are out but the gangs are better armed than they are."[8] In a statement, Valdés called "upon the Haitian population to avoid being drawn into a vicious cycle of revenge and violence and to follow the path of dialogue, reconciliation and peace ... There is still time to resume dialogue."[9]

As violence wracked the capital, at a dinner sponsored by the Haitian-American Chamber of Commerce, Justice Minister Bernard Gousse called for a lifting of the arms embargo in Haiti, saying that "you cannot ask us to fight unarmed against well-armed bandits."[10] Speaking on Radio Métropole, Andy Apaid called for "a broad mobilization" against the violence, asked the population to support the work of the PNH, and criticized the perceived passivity of MINUSTAH.[11] Students at the Université d'État d'Haïti (UEH), who had been at the forefront of the anti-Aristide movement only months before, criticized MINUSTAH's perceived lack of action, saying that "supporters of Aristide are merely putting into action the macabre plans they had announced after the departure of their leader."[12] At a 7 October joint press conference, Buteur Métayer and Guy Philippe announced that men under their command were prepared to take part in any action against the chimere, with Métayer adding that "we have the necessary means to confront them and are just waiting for a signal from the government."[13] More recruits arrived at Rémissainthe Ravix's base in mid-October, with Ravix promising to "arrest" those responsible for the violence, even though he had no legal authority to do so.[14] The pro-Aristide factions announced that they were dubbing the uprising "Operation Baghdad" after the insurgent attacks against U.S. forces following the occupation of Iraq, and, in an October 2004 report, National Public Radio correspondent Lourdes Garcia-Navarro, confronted by a group of hostile, armed young men when attempting to enter Bel-Air, recorded one of them saying: "We call it Operation Baghdad to prove to the interim prime minister that we are angry at what is going on." Leaving, Garcia-Navarro was followed to the border of Bel-Air by two young men, "their handguns held high in the air."[15] A Lavalas priest, Gérard Jean-Juste, was detained by Haitian police at his church, the Église Saint Claire at Petite Place Cazeau, on 13 October, with Minister of Justice Bernard Gousse accusing him of "organizing meetings in his home with gang leaders."[16] He would be released several weeks later.

On 15 October, youthful gunmen terrorized the neighborhood of Poste-Marchand near the palace, shooting in the air and setting cars on fire, while violence around the capital's port prevented the unloading of containers containing relief food for victims of Hurricane Jeanne around Gonaïves.[17] Four days later, some two dozen men walked through Bel-Air firing their guns in the air, sending residents scrambling for cover.[18] Weber Adrien, an activist with the left-wing Mouvement pour la Reconstruction Nationale (MRN) who had been active in the street protests that helped drive Aristide from power and recently had been appointed to oversee the capital's markets, was kidnapped, shot, decapitated and his corpse set on fire a few blocks away from where

MINUSTAH soldiers were stationed in Bel-Air.[19] Beyond those who had clear political convictions for joining the uprising, as a study by Norway's Fafo Research Foundation pointed out, "some of the children and youth ... joined the armed *baz* because they felt they had no choice, not even the alternative of not joining. The fear of being killed as a traitor was overwhelming."[20]

In late October, MINUSTAH and PNH forces occupied a three-story building in Bel-Air as they carried out an operation in the area that gang members would later say killed at least 15 of their number. The building housed a church and school run by an 81-year-old minister, Joseph Dantica, who happened to be the uncle of the Haitian-American author Edwidge Danticat. When the peacekeepers and police pulled out, gang members arrived at the building to tell the clergyman, who had known some of them since they were little boys, that he must pay for the burials of their number who had fallen or he, too, would die. For good measure, they looted the church and burned a life-time of memories. After hiding in a neighbor's house for several days, Dantica fled to the United States. Telling an immigration official at Miami International Airport that he would be seeking asylum, he was promptly imprisoned in the dreaded Krome Detention Center, where he died a few days later after being denied access to medicine he had brought with him to treat various medical conditions.[21] The reverend's sad fate summed up the despair that many in Haiti felt about both the violence that was enveloping Port-au-Prince and the glacial indifference of U.S. politicians to the suffering that their immigration policies might cause.[22] Just how powerful the gangs were was vividly illustrated when 11 Argentine MINUSTAH soldiers traveling out of uniform through Cité Soleil in a UN-marked vehicle were robbed and stripped at gunpoint by a group of gang members before being set free.[23]

One line of thinking in the government was summed up when Port-au-Prince assistant mayor Jean-Philippe Sassine told a visiting journalist that he supported a policy of "shoot them and ask questions later" when it came to the gangs.[24] Actual or suspected gang members who were wounded in the course of police actions, and often simply those caught in the wrong place at the wrong time, were kept in squalid conditions in the capital's Hôpital Général or various police commissariats without legal recourse or medical attention.[25] A 1 December prison rebellion in the Pénitencier National resulted in the death of at least ten prisoners and injuries to nearly 50 when rebellious detainees attacked other prisoners and guards and Corps d'Intervention et de Maintien de l'Ordre

(CIMO) riot police forces responded by raiding the jail, shooting "in all directions at anything that moved."[26]

* * *

Some in and out of Haiti thought they knew where the violence was coming from. Writing in South Africa's *Mail & Guardian* that December, the Haitian filmmaker Raoul Peck, himself a former minister of culture, wrote that "for those who know him, the chain of violence that has marred Haiti reflects Aristide's leadership style and his documented recklessness."[27] That same month, the *Boston Globe* quoted an unnamed diplomat saying that "there is a serious, concerted, well-armed, and well-financed campaign to spread terror and destabilize the interim government, led by Aristide supporters."[28] France's Minister of Cooperation Xavier Darcos told a UNESCO meeting in Brasilia that Aristide's return "would not be a good idea," even though the French government supported the participation of all parties in dialogue.[29] Returning from South Africa, where he had visited Aristide, Gérard Jean-Juste (one of several Haitian political figures who paid multiple visits to Aristide in exile) conveyed the message that if Aristide did not return to Haiti, peace wouldn't either.[30]

* * *

The coalition that had opposed Aristide was crumbling. In early December, Buteur Métayer, who had taken up the mantle of rebellion after the murder of his brother, was detained by the U.S. Department of Homeland Security in Miami and subsequently expelled for having remained too long outside the U.S., thus losing his residency permit.[31] By mid-December, Rémissainthe Ravix's contingent of former soldiers had descended from Pétionville and were squatting in the shell of Aristide's former mansion in Tabarre a few blocks from the base of Brazilian peacekeepers, painting the residence's ornate pillars FADH yellow.[32] Shortly thereafter, MINUSTAH troops and PNH forcibly evicted them. Ravix, who had claimed to be their public face, was nowhere to be found.[33] His credibility thus demolished, he would descend into naked apolitical banditry. On occasion, Ravix's new ally, the former police officer René "Grenn Sonnen" Jean Anthony, would call in to Haitian radio shows where he would threaten to rape and murder PNH spokeswoman Gessy Coicou.[34] As the government attempted to get a grip on the shifting allegiances of the capital's various armed groups, an article in *Le Figaro* noted that Prime Minister

Latortue was paying Youri Latortue the equivalent of €20,000 a month to maintain an intelligence service on behalf of the government, which presumably included paying off informants.[35] In his defense, the elder Latortue noted that "no one" knew how much foreign embassies in the country were paying for their information.[36]

When Bel-Air gang leader Dread Mackenzie – whom Boukman Eksperyans singer Lolo Beaubrun had once confided to me had been tasked with his assassination[37] – was killed by rival gang members,[38] Mackenzie's funeral, held in Bel-Air on 16 December (the date of Aristide's first election as president), featured heavily armed gang members displaying pictures of Aristide as they fired in the air and pledged allegiance to the ousted leader.[39] Ascending to replace Mackenzie would be Augudson Nicolas, better known as General Toutou. Two reporters from Le Nouvelliste who made the mistake of wandering into the neighborhood were beaten and had their equipment stolen before being sent away with the warning not to come back or "the next time you will lose your skins."[40] Eventually, the area would be carved up into zones of influence, with General Toutou running the center of Bel-Air, while Beckner "Ti Yabout" Desrosiers ran Solino, and a gang leader known as "Frank" ran Delmas 2.[41]

During the first two weeks of 2005, the Médecins Sans Frontières hospital in Cité Soleil received 47 gunshot victims, four of whom died; this number did not take into account the gunshot victims received at the Haitian Red Cross emergency center in the neighborhood. The MSF hospital near the capital's downtown treated 122 gunshot victims. Visitors to Cité Soleil would regularly see armed men and children.[42] By early 2005, it was estimated that there were at least 600 children in the ranks of the main armed groups in Port-au-Prince.[43]

* * *

As if to mark the passing of an era in Haiti, three of the most storied personalities of an earlier time – the journalist and gadfly Aubelin Jolicoeur, the musician and art dealer Issa L. Saieh and the meteorologist Renan Jean Louis, who had given generations of Haitians their weather as Capitaine Météo on television – all passed away within a few weeks of one another at the beginning of 2005. Nearly 20 years before, as a 23-year-old on my first visit to Haiti, I climbed steep Avenue du Chile to visit Saieh's gallery and bought my first ever Haitian painting, one by Dieuseul Paul of the famous Saint-Soleil school of Haitian painting. At the gallery, I listened as Saieh, a witty Syrian-Haitian who had lived for years in the United States and spoke nearly unaccented English, regaled me with stories of his time playing jazz with Dizzy Gillespie in Batista-era Cuba.

* * *

On the last day of January 2005, Haiti's electoral body, the CEP, announced that elections would be held on 9 October for local and regional posts and on 13 November for the president and parliament.[44] No doubt with their eye on the coming vote, several ancient former Duvalier officials organized a political meeting at the capital's Visa Lodge.[45] Also positioning for the vote, the veteran politician Serge Gilles announced that three political parties – KONAKOM, the Parti Nationaliste Progressiste et Révolutionnaire Haïtien (PANPRA) and Ayiti Kapab – would be merging into a new coalition, the Fusion des Sociaux-Démocrates Haïtiens (Fusion), and that he would serve as their presidential candidate in the upcoming elections.[46]

The situation heading toward the elections was further destabilized when armed men attacked the Pénitencier National on 19 February in a coordinated raid that saw hundreds of prisoners freed. Some of the most dangerous criminals in the country flooded out into the streets and fanned out to the four winds. Accused Jean Dominique assassins Dymsley "Ti Lou" Millien and Jeudi "Guimy" Jean Daniel fled to Martissant, while Arnel Bélizaire and Jean Claude Louis Jean (an influential member of Guy Philippe's group believed to have been involved in kidnapping) fled to the Dominican Republic. Bale Wouze's Ronald "Black Ronald" Dauphin made the short jaunt to Bel-Air where he reportedly took an active role in the gang wars raging there.[47] After being "liberated" and surveying such an atmosphere as existed on the streets, Yvon Neptune and Jocelerme Privert prudently returned to custody of their own accord. As for my friend James, I heard many stories. Some said he had fled to the Dominican Republic, others that he was back in Cité Soleil and working with Dread Wilmé, still others that he had traveled north and been captured by the PNH and might be in prison in the town of Arcahaie. Maddeningly, no one seemed to know for sure.

Gunmen greeted February by firing in the air and setting several houses on fire in the Nazon district.[48] A few days later, four police officers were slain near the airport by men dressed in the uniforms of Haiti's disbanded army.[49] A February attack in the capital's Village de Dieu by what residents said were "Lavalas chimere" – among their number some who allegedly had escaped from the peni-tentiary – left at least 18 dead and 24 injured.[50] Many of the dead were members of the local *brigade de vigilence*, whose surviving family members continued to be threatened.[51] In the same slum, the journalist Abdias Jean was also killed, allegedly by the PNH.[52] Speaking to reporters at Johannesburg's University of the Witwatersrand, Aristide claimed that the PNH and MINUSTAH had "killed more than 10,000 people in one year" and that "I will return." He also claimed that he was not in direct contact with protesters in Haiti.[53] For Latortue's part, his job setting up elections had become one where he "spent months and months going to the funerals of policemen who had been killed."[54]

On 30 March, the clever, duplicitous Cité Soleil gang leader Labanye met his inevitable fate and was killed by his deputy, Evens "Ti Kouto" (Little Knife) Jeune – more ruthless, less educated and believed by some to be more or less nonpolitical.[55] Evens had worked in collusion with Dread Wilmé to plan the attack,[56] after which Labanye's body was dismembered and placed next to that of a dead dog,[57] with some residents claiming that parts of it had also been consumed by the killers.[58]

* * *

When MINUSTAH troops tried to evict a contingent of ex-military from the Petit-Goâve police station just before dawn on 20 March, a gun battle erupted that left two former soldiers and one MINUSTAH peacekeeper dead. UN forces eventually succeeded in removing the soldiers,[59] but the home of Justice Minister Gousse was assaulted by gunmen two nights later in an attack that claimed the life of a policeman who had been guarding the house.[60] Despite many clam-oring for MINUSTAH to go into Cité Soleil and "crush" the chimere, Valdés admitted to me that "there was nothing more difficult than Cité Soleil – any operation could produce an enormous amount of civilian casualties, due to the lodgings there. The amount of people who were inside the zone led to enormous restrictions in terms of what the military could do."[61] In late March, an unseen hand hurled a grenade at the door of the CEP headquarters in Port-au-Prince. Three days later, two truckloads of armed men strafed its outer perimeter with automatic weapons fire, damaging an electricity transformer.[62] As a result, MINUSTAH began providing 24-hour protection of the building, and began conducting foot patrols in the area.[63] In a late March interview with Radio Solidarité, Grenn Sonnen promised to kill PNH and MINUSTAH personnel, as well as Youri Latortue.[64] On 28 March, an attack by multiple gunmen on Rue Bonamy in Delmas killed three people, including two policemen, and set the vehicle of the latter ablaze with the bodies still inside. The following day, several thousand Aristide supporters chanted "No Aristide, no peace!" as they marched through Port-au-Prince.[65]

By March 2005, an obvious split had developed among the Lavalas factions remaining in Haiti, with Gérard Jean-Juste the most visible member of the more militant and vocal section, while former Lavalas officials such as Yvon Feuillé, Gérald Gilles and Rudy Hériveaux were more open to working within the electoral process and encouraging voters to obtain national identity cards and to register. Some spoke of forming a possible coalition with Marc Bazin's MIDH.[66] Many in Haiti believed that Jean-Juste's opposition to the vote was a mere feint, and that he intended to run as a candidate for president himself.[67]

And there was a split within the *baz* itself. In early 2005, Wench Luc, the leader of the Baz Frustrée from Martissant, outlined in an interview with Radio Métropole the details of a meeting he said had taken place at the Aristide Foundation for Democracy in Tabarre on 25 September the previous year. During the meeting, Luc said Aristide loyalists Leslie Fareau, Leslie Gustave, Jean Marie Samedi and Dismy César, working in consort with former government spokesman Jonas Petit and former senator and foundation head Mirlande Libérus (both at that point in exile in Florida), had planned the initial outbreak of Operation Baghdad. He also claimed that they continued to be in regular communication with Aristide in South Africa and with gang leaders such as Dread Wilmé in Cité Soleil. Luc said that Lavalas was divided between those who opted for violence and those willing to participate in elections.[68] Luc's words were echoed by those of another Lavalas *baz* leader, Destiné Wilson, who urged militants to lay down their arms and reject violence.[69] In discussion, a high-ranking PNH official who was privy to all the intelligence regarding the armed groups in the capital from early 2005 onward described to me a system whereby several well-known personalities in Haiti's political scene would visit Aristide in South Africa and return to Haiti with messages to be delivered directly to the armed groups in Port-au-Prince.[70] By mid-2005, Dread Wilmé was believed to have emerged as the most powerful *baz* leader in Cité Soleil, working in close collaboration with Amaral and Evens, and some in the PNH believed that they had evidence that Wilmé remained in regular contact with Aristide.[71] Some in the poor quarters of Port-au-Prince, such as Bel-Air, plainly said that what had begun as a movement to press for Aristide's return quickly degenerated into "a movement of thieves."[72] Even former Lavalas senator Gérald Gilles confessed in early April that "no intelligent person would hold a public meeting in Cité Soleil or Bel-Air" due to the fact that the areas were dominated by "extremists."[73] One source of the ammunition flowing to Haiti was allegedly via the Dominican Republic, where arms were purchased on the black market and then smuggled via the Ouanaminthe border crossing "hidden in cartons of tomato sauce and other produce."[74]

On 9 April, Rémissainthe Ravix, the rogue former FADH sergeant and rebel leader, was killed by PNH forces in the area of Delmas 30 in a clash in which MINUSTAH forces also participated.[75] At least two of his men died with him.[76] A day later, the former Aristide enforcer turned freelance bandit René "Grenn Sonnen" Jean Anthony was slain along with three of his men during an intense gun battle in Delmas. The fact that Anthony had first been reported wounded, only to turn up dead, raised some eyebrows, but few mourned the bandit's passing.[77] After Ravix and Anthony died, Gousse quipped that criminals had to realize that "the police are not game to be hunted, much less are they meat for the cook pot."[78] Speaking in Jacmel after Ravix was killed, former rebel leader turned politician Guy Philippe, who had formed a political party, the Front pour la Reconstruction Nationale (FRN), issued a call for his former comrades to lay down their arms.[79] After Ravix and Anthony fell, some residents of popular quarters voiced hope that MINUSTAH and the PNH would head to Bel-Air and Cité Soleil and "finish the job."[80] When MINUSTAH and PNH forces raided a hotel in Hinche that had been occupied by the former military in late April, three were wounded by gunfire;[81] however, the dominant group of former FADH members in the Plateau Central, led by former Sergeant Joseph Jean-Baptiste (who had been a confidant of Ravix), announced afterward that they were laying down their weapons out of a "desire to contribute to a climate of peace in the country."[82] Many thought the aging rebels saw the writing on the wall after Ravix's violent end.

By this point, the violence often went beyond political motivations and overlapped with simple criminality. In late April, a 27-year-old employee of the Rasanbleman Medya Pou Aksyon Kominotè media NGO was kidnapped and held for 11 days, raped and abused by her kidnappers. Although her family paid a ransom, she would die two months after her release. Another victim, this one only 16, was kidnapped twice before being found dead on the capital's Rue

Lamarre.[83] One of the worst kidnappers was said to be a gang leader named Emmanuel Coriolan, known as *Dom Laj*.[84]

* * *

As April dragged on, Jocelerme Privert was taken without incident from the Port-au-Prince hospital, where he was recovering from a hunger strike, to Saint-Marc to be questioned about the La Scierie killings.[85] Yvon Neptune was moved to a palatial house in Pacot – referred to on Haitian radio as "a golden prison" – where he was to await trial. The government said the villa had been created to house "dangerous prisoners or those whose cases require special protection."[86] By late April, after Neptune had begun a hunger strike to protest against his detention, the director of Haiti's Direction de l'Administration Pénitentiaire was describing Neptune's health as "extremely precarious" and preparations were being made to evacuate him to the Dominican Republic for medical treatment. Neptune, however, refused to go unless he was unconditionally freed, and thus he remained in Haiti.[87] By early May, Neptune had been called four times to answer questions from the judge at Saint-Marc and each time he had refused and restarted his fast.[88] Earlier in the year, in a moment of distressing myopia, NCHR's New York parent group, which in fact had been little more than a website for several years while the Haiti group did all the heavy lifting, released a statement assailing Pierre Espérance and NCHR's Haiti staff for having "draped itself in nationalist flags to protest the decision by UN and Haitian authorities" regarding Neptune's case.[89] Others would attack the group for having received a one-off grant from the Canadian International Development Agency (CIDA), even though it received most of its funding from organizations such as Christian Aid, the Mennonite Central Committee and Lutheran World Federation. Pierre Espérance, Marie Yolene Gilles and the rest of the Haiti staff would bravely soldier on, adopting the new name Réseau National de Défense des Droits Humains (National Network of Human Rights Defenders or RNDDH), while the New York branch would cease to exist. As they provided legal counsel for the Saint-Marc massacre victims, as well as material and financial aid,[90] by mid-2005, with admirable understatement, RNDDH was asserting that "many of those aligned with the [pro-Aristide] campaign [abroad] do not clearly understand the complex reality in Haiti while many others fully understand yet continue to fuel the movement." The group went on to explain that "unfounded messages purporting subjective beliefs, presenting half truths as solid facts and sadly misrepresenting the situation in Haiti are being widely circulated."[91] Though they did not name it, RNDDH was clearly referring to the Institute for Justice and Democracy in Haiti (IJDH), an ostensible human rights body co-founded by Aristide's Miami attorney Ira Kurzban (who also served as the first president of its board of directors), which often seemed to exist solely to advance the interests of Aristide and the wing of Lavalas most closely connected to him. Writing for the CEDH on 5 May, Jean-Claude Bajeux asked the government to "exert the greatest diligence so that those responsible for those murders [in Saint-Marc] be prosecuted fairly and properly."[92] That same day, as prison authorities attempted to physically compel Yvon Neptune to go to Saint-Marc to respond to the judge's questions there, Neptune, no doubt terrified of the fate that might await him, bit one female prison guard, punched another and had to be wrestled to the ground.[93]

On 27 April, gun battles between police and armed Aristide supporters demonstrating in the capital's Christ-Roi neighborhood left at least five dead, with residents telling Radio Signal FM that the demonstrators were "violent" and had robbed bystanders as they marched.[94] Although PNH spokeswoman Gessy Coicou said the event was "not a protest … but rather a raid by bandits,"[95] one witness said that masked police opened fire when protesters began chanting "hostile" slogans at them.[96] The demonstration was viewed as an attempt to broaden the scope of Lavalas influence beyond such strongholds as Bel-Air. Some within the PNH believed that former PNH commander Camille Marcellus (who had escaped during the 19 February jailbreak) was among the "operational strategists seeking to create conditions that might lead to Aristide's return."[97] As the police and the gangs battled in the street, a prolonged blackout plunged much of the capital into darkness for days at a time, further amplifying the feeling of vulnerability.[98] Speaking at a May press conference from his gilded exile in South Africa, Aristide claimed that France and the United States were committing "a black holocaust" in Haiti, that "more than 10,000" of his supporters had been killed (a charge for which no evidence existed) and that his political movement had been "for peace, not violence,"[99] and then cast himself as a "Nelson Mandela" whom Haiti's people "wanted back."[100]

In Haiti itself, meanwhile, dozens of armed youths marched on the Marché Tête-Bœuf at Portail St. Joseph, firing their weapons and apparently attempting to set the market aflame before being driven off by MINUSTAH and PNH forces.[101] PNH chief Léon Charles denounced what he alleged was the "hypocrisy"

of the international community toward Haiti in its embargo on arms and ammunition and the inaction of MINUSTAH, saying "give me a third of the capacity
of MINUSTAH in Haiti and I will restore peace."[102]

As Haiti burned, the African National Congress (ANC) in South Africa
– seemingly detached from reality – announced via its newsletter that "the
remnants of Haiti's military past are allowed by the international community
to continue with their programme to silence the voices of the Haitian people."
Apparently without irony, the ANC suggested that CARICOM, from which
Haiti had been suspended and which had lost all credibility in the eyes of many
Haitians, might be a proper venue through which Haiti could work out its problems, which it seemed to think could mostly be solved by Aristide's return.[103]

Speaking in front of the Chambre du Commerce et d'Industrie d'Haïti
(CCIH), Léon Charles said that the capital faced "a situation of war" caused
by a "destabilization movement," and revealed that up to 50 percent of PNH
officers did not possess a weapon, and that 48 officers had been murdered in
Port-au-Prince alone since the previous March.[104] During the same event, the
CCIH's president, Réginald Boulos, requested that the government permit
business owners to possess automatic weapons to, he said, defend their properties and livelihoods.[105] Business owners around Cité Soleil said openly that
from their perspective Labanye had done a better job of policing the zone than
MINUSTAH – a public admission of the private sector's links with the dead
warlord's gang. It was common knowledge by this point that some business
owners had already begun purchasing high-caliber weapons from the street
and had given them to various PNH officers in exchange for "protection" and
regular patrols.[106] To the north of the capital, under a heavy MINUSTAH
and PNH escort, Yvon Neptune finally appeared before Judge Clunie Pierre
Louis in Saint-Marc to answer questions during a four-hour meeting. Pierre
Louis had previously interviewed both Jocelerme Privert and Bale Wouze's
Amanus Mayette. Both POHDH and RNDDH voiced their satisfaction with
Neptune having finally appeared, with the former saying "the reign of justice
begins to settle and we think it is on track," a statement that would prove
rather too optimistic.[107] CARICOM, which had not seen fit to rouse itself to
comment on the Saint-Marc killings themselves, issued a statement in which it
criticized Neptune's prolonged detention without trial.[108] Not to be outdone,
two days later in a letter sent to the administration of U.S. President George
W. Bush – co-signed by, among others, Maxine Waters (the shrillest of Aris-

tide's defenders in the U.S. Congress), Charles Rangel, Barbara Lee, Sherrod Brown, Dennis Kucinich and William Delahunt – the august congressional leaders denounced the "unjust imprisonment" of Neptune while, naturally, omitting any mention of the people slain in Saint-Marc.[109] Another letter, this one authored by Delahunt, bemoaned the loss of Aristide's "democratically elected government" and again took up the gauntlet on behalf of Neptune (no mention of the victims here, either).[110] In response to these moves, on 14 June the CEDH sent a letter to U.S. Secretary of State Condoleezza Rice in which the organization decried the fact that the U.S. legislators and the international community in general, instead of seeking to "accelerate the investigation and trial on the case of the multiple murders" in Saint-Marc, sought instead to give "carte blanche" to Neptune and Privert, "prior to any investigation and any judgment." Such a stance was, the letter concluded, "a formula used perversely to humiliate the government and people of Haiti."[111] A few weeks later, despite a letter distributed by Waters claiming that Neptune was slipping "in and out of consciousness, his internal organs are deteriorating, and his life is in grave danger,"[112] when *The Los Angeles Times* found Neptune, they reported that the former prime minister, "though thin and frail, the sole inmate at the $5,000-a-month villa paid for and guarded by the U.N. peacekeeping mission did not appear near death."[113]

* * *

At this time I returned to Haiti, disturbed by the reports of ongoing violence and wondering when, if at all, elections were going to be held. As usual, alighting from the capital's airport, I hailed a taxi from one of the throng of drivers trying to solicit business immediately beyond its gates. We immediately were caught in a traffic snarl as my driver, who told me he lived in the Fort National slum, explained that whole areas of the capital that cars used to traverse were now considered off-limits because of the insecurity roiling the city.

"It's like you're in prison," he told me. "I wish I could go outside with my kids. I leave at 6 in the morning to go to work and go home at 6 in the evening. After 7pm we stay indoors and don't leave." I asked him who was committing the violence. "Chimere Lavalas," was his response.

When I met with Pastor Enoch Joseph and Jean-Renald Registre from the Colectif des Notables de Cité Soleil (CONOCS) at a hotel just off Champ de Mars, they painted an alarming picture of what was taking place.

"We've never seen such violence in Cité Soleil," Pastor Enoch told me. "Every day there are bodies. They [the armed groups] have dug trenches all around the neighborhood; it's very hard to get in or out."

His companion agreed.

"After last year, it became all the other gangs against Labanye," said Jean-Renald Registre. "And when they attacked the French diplomat is when the trouble really began."

When I spoke to David Beer, the Canadian commissioner of MINUSTAH's Civilian Police (CIVPOL) contingent, he gave me some idea of the difficulty of reforming and reconstituting the PNH in a situation where only $220 million of some $1.08 billion pledged to rebuild the country had yet been disbursed.

"There was huge progress in the 1990s that stemmed from some stability in a five-year period during the Préval presidency," Beer told me, as he chain-smoked Dunhills. "A large number of the people in executive positions remained in place; there was some continuity in the organization. Upon the election of the Aristide government, virtually the entire executive of the organization was wiped out, either fired or quit. The destruction of the senior management, parallel entry without proper qualifications, and politicization was the start of big problems with criminality, all of which have served to demoralize the organization."[114]

The hurdles were still substantial. CIVPOL estimated that, for some 8,000 PNH checks issued every month, there were in fact only 4,500 PNH officers actually working. In an atmosphere in which a PNH officer had been killed every five days since the end of September 2004, merely putting on the uniform was an act of extreme courage.

"There is a core of people in the organization that are extremely committed to their job," Beer told me. "They work 12 hours a day, six days a week; they travel by *camionette* to start their week, they find places to sleep here, they don't make a whole lot of money. We, the international community, have to be prepared to be here with the resources necessary to get this done and stay here long enough to make sure it's a sustainable program, unlike last time."

The RNDDH's Pierre Espérance told me he had also seen the flickerings of improvement, but only just.

"If you ask me if the police are still involved in human rights violations, I would say, yes, a lot," Espérance told me when we met at the group's headquarters on Rue Rivière. "The change we have right now is that this government doesn't use gangs or civilians to persecute those who criticize it, but that's all.

When police are involved in human rights violations, there is no effort by the government to punish them."

Aside from physical security, one wondered how Haiti's economy was holding up under such prolonged crisis. By this point, the investigatory body UCREF was reporting that, based on its examinations, during his tenure in office Aristide had siphoned off $21 million of Haiti's resources to fictitious companies and his charities, the latter of which, as earlier noted, were tangled up with some of his most vocal defenders in the United States. $6 million, for example, UCREF claimed, was filtered through the Aristide Foundation for Democracy, the Lafanmi Selavi orphanage and other entities. Two fictitious enterprises, VJLS Computer Services and Accessories and Quisqueya Store, collectively received nearly $17 million. A straight-faced Ira Kurzban, Aristide's Miami lawyer, told *The Miami Herald* that he "heard" Quisqueya "bought bulk quantities of rice and sold it to the poor."[115]

Wanting to know in more detail the allegations, and interested in how the country was holding up economically in the face of such grinding violence in the capital, I went to meet with Philippe Lahens, at the time the Banque de la République d'Haïti's (BRH's) deputy governor. The bank's headquarters, on the capital's Rue des Miracles and near the now-shuttered parliament, was in an area usually bustling with activity in its fume-choked lanes, but today the street vendors who usually clogged its sidewalks had moved away in fear of the running gun battles between the police and gangs.

"The central bank was in very bad shape after Aristide," Lahens told me in the air-conditioned confines of his office. "Haiti had no net international reserves ... The public deficit was 3 percent of Haiti's GDP and the government had defaulted on two separate contracts designed to provide the country with electricity, totaling $12 million ... I think the unique challenge for the central bank in Haiti is to obtain autonomy from the government. With this independence, we will be more at ease to provide transparency and more at ease with the government in terms of the everyday running of the bank, in terms of the interest rate, the rate of exchange and depreciation of the gourde and other areas."[116]

As if to illustrate his point, Lahens then presented me with several binders laying out, in meticulous detail, payments the BRH said had been made from its coffers between 2001 and 2004. There were dozens of payments to Quisqueya Store ($800,000 in March 2003, $500,000 in October 2003, to name but two). To Digitek, a company owned by Lesly Lavelanet, the brother-in-law of Aristide's wife, there was a payment of $200,500 in October 2003. To some-thing called "Alpha Co-Op," there were payments of over $4 million between June and August 2003. To Oriel Jean, payments via the National Palace totaling nearly half a million dollars between June and December 2001 alone.

* * *

Where did Haiti's money go? One clue may have been provided by looking at what happened to Teleco, Haiti's state telephone company and one of the country's few sources of hard income, and the story of a politically connected U.S.-based telecoms company called IDT.

IDT, whose CEO was former Republican Congressman Jim Courter (who would later be a major fundraiser in the 2008 presidential campaign of Arizona senator John McCain), had included among its board members over the years "former congressman and vice presidential nominee Jack Kemp, former U.S. ambassador to the U.N. Jeane Kirkpatrick, former Virginia Governor Jim Gilmore, former Minnesota senator Rudy Boschwitz, and former Washington senator Slade Gorton."[117]

In November 2003, IDT fired its vice president for the Caribbean, D. Michael Jewett. Four months later, Jewett sued the company for wrongful dismissal in a federal court in New Jersey, charging that he had been sent packing because he had opposed the company's practices, specifically in Haiti. Those practices were, to put it mildly, highly unusual.[118] The carrier services agreement between IDT and Teleco – signed by IDT's CFO Norman Rosen-berg and both Teleco's Director General Alphonse Inevil and Director of International Affairs Jean René Duperval – called for fees (at far below market rates) to be sent not to Teleco itself, but to a Turks and Caicos-incorporated shell company called Mont Salem.[119]

In his suit, Jewett claimed that IDT referred to Mont Salem as "Aristide's bank account," a charge the firm denied.[120] Evidence that backed up Jewett's claims included a contract signed by IDT and Teleco that called for payments lower than those the major U.S. telecoms were paying and for fees to be sent to Mount Salem, the owner of which Jewett was blocked by Federal Judge Stanley R. Chesler from finding out.[121] In an interview with *Barron's* magazine, IDT founder Howard Jonas admitted that Aristide had personally met with company officials, and admitted that IDT had made payments to Mont Salem, which he said the firm believed was a "legitimate agent."[122] Alice Fisher, a partner at

IDT's law firm, Latham & Watkins, reviewed the company's arrangement with Teleco and declared it legal, neglecting to mention, though, that IDT was not sending payments to Teleco itself.[123] In his lawsuit, Jewett charged that IDT had won a 9 cents per minute rate to terminate calls to Haiti over the official 23 cents per minute.[124] The deal, Jewett alleged, was hammered out in Haiti in August 2003 during a meeting between Aristide and IDT Executive Vice President for International Business Development Jack Lerer. Haitian government documents showed that, for the minutes it billed IDT, Mont Salem was paying Teleco 6 cents per minute, leaving 3 cents unaccounted for. In the words of financial observers, Mont Salem, incorporated with only $5,000 in capital, "fit the model of a classic offshore shell company designed to receive and launder money, rather than that of a real firm."[125]

In written responses to IDT's attorneys, Jewett wrote that he had been told by Lerner that the latter had "negotiated a deal with the President of Haiti … to forward telephone traffic to Haiti for 9.5 cents a minute. IDT Telecom would deposit the settlement dollars for terminating traffic in Haiti through Teleco to an offshore account set up on behalf of President Aristide called Mount Salem Management … [Lerner] replied it was the private bank account of the president of Haiti, Jean-Bertrand Aristide."[126] The Montreal company Skyytel also admitted that its 2003 agreement with Haiti saw the firm paying 9 cents a minute to Mont Salem, which was ostensibly operating as Teleco's agent.[127]

In a 74-page civil action filed against Aristide and eight other defendants in a U.S. district court in southern Florida in early November 2005, Haiti's interim government would charge that "Aristide and his accomplices demanded and received substantial bribes and kickbacks from U.S. telecommunications carriers, which were wire transferred from U.S. banks." In addition to IDT, the suit also named Fusion Telecom, which had as its CEO former Democratic Party finance chairman Marvin Rosen. Former Congressman Joseph P. Kennedy II also served on Fusion's board, as had Clinton chum Thomas "Mack" McLarty. The suit alleged that Mont Salem was in fact an apparatus whereby Aristide et al. received and distributed kickbacks. The payments were ordered, the lawsuit alleged, by Teleco's counsel. Both companies denied their role in any corruption.[128] The interim government's lawsuit went on to allege that "at Aristide's direction, [Teleco Director General] Inevil, [and] [Director of International Affairs] Duperval … directed … IDT and Skyytel, to make their payments for Teleco's services to Mont Salem. At Aristide's direction, Teleco's then counsel also caused Teleco to request at least one other Class B carrier, Fusion, to make payments through Mont Salem."[129]

The stumbling block of the Haitian government's lawsuit was who would pay for it. One attorney involved in the case told me that "the interim government promised to pay the local counsel but never did."[130] The interim government sought to use some of the $2.9 million seized by the U.S. from Haitian drug dealers (with the Haitian government's cooperation) to help pursue its lawsuit against Aristide and other officials, as cooperating countries often receive a cut of such illicit profits. In this case, however, it did not happen.[131] Given the lack of funding, the Haitian treasury being depleted, the case was withdrawn in June 2006, pending reinstatement should there be a change.[132]

Did the Bush administration have any appetite for investigating potential wrongdoing among some major Republican figures? It appeared not. Individuals closely connected to IDT – including 17 who worked directly for the company – were among the major contributors to the successful 2009 gubernatorial campaign of New Jersey's Chris Christie, who, while U.S. attorney for New Jersey, declined to pursue an investigation into the company's practices.[133] Alice Fisher, the Latham & Watkins lawyer who had signed off on IDT's dealings with Teleco, was appointed Assistant Attorney General (Criminal Division) at the Department of Justice in a recess appointment by Bush in August 2005.[134] In a December 2006 email, the Federal Communications Commission (FCC) stated that its "Haiti file" – its record of whether or not U.S. telecoms doing business with Aristide's government had submitted their contracts to the FCC as required by U.S. law – had gone missing.[135] Nevertheless, the FCC would eventually level a $1.3 million fine against IDT for "willfully and repeatedly failing to file with the commission" vis-à-vis its contracts with Teleco between 2003 and 2004.[136] (The long fight between J. Michael Jewett and IDT over his firing would finally end with a whimper in January 2011, with both sides dropping their claims and counterclaims, generally a sign that an agreement had been reached.[137])

Beyond IDT and Fusion, between November 2001 and March 2005, Joel Esquenazi and Carlos Rodriguez, the president and vice president of Miami's Terra Telecommunications Corp., paid more than $890,000 in bribes to a shell company to guarantee Terra preferred rates in Haiti, a reduction in minutes charged and the continuance of the company's contract with Teleco. The pair would subsequently be sentenced to 15 years in prison, the longest term ever issued in a foreign bribery case in the United States.[138] Antonio Pérez, Terra's former controller, and J. D. Locator Services owner Juan Diaz conspired with Teleco's Director of International Affairs Robert Antoine to make over $1 million in payments to Haitian government officials via a system that involved "wiring money to shell companies and mislabeling invoices, checks and ledgers."[139] The two were subsequently convicted of their role in the bribery system and sent to prison.[140] Antoine also went to prison for his role in the scheme,[141] as did Jean Fourcand, the president of an eponymous company that acted as a conduit for the money.[142] Jean René Duperval, the head of Teleco's international business under Aristide after Antoine's departure, would also be sentenced to nine years in prison for laundering bribes paid to the company during his tenure.[143]

For their part, Miami's Cinergy Telecommunications and Uniplex Telecom Technologies paid more than $1.4 million to shell companies used for bribes to Teleco officials, including Director General Patrick Joseph, who, as it happens, was the son of the head of the BRH, Venel Joseph.[144] Investigators in the United States soon began to zero in on how the BRH had been used to distribute bribes and illicit payments.[145] With the government's lawsuit at a standstill, many saw investigations in the U.S. itself as the last, best chance for Haiti to recover some of its money.

* * *

One day, I found myself in a lovely home on the capital's Montaigne Noir, with hanging plants and flowers rustling in the breeze as thunderstorms rumbled just beyond the nearby mountains. I sat across from a grey-haired, patrician man who had worked for Teleco, first on its technical side and then on its board of directors, for nearly 30 years. When he saw what had been done to one of the most profitable sources of revenue for his beleaguered country, by both local and foreign actors, he was filled with scorn.

"As far as making money was concerned, they weren't Republicans or Democrats," he told me, as he shook his head in seeming disbelief. "The idea was to destroy the institution and make it profitable for others. The theft of the Duvalier years was nothing compared to what those Lavalas people did. There was $60 million in the Teleco account in New York in 1991, and by the time they came back to Haiti it was almost empty. They realized they could take the money first, and then they realized they could take more money from the international calls."

He leaned forward and took a sip from a glass of mango juice, the ice in it rapidly melting in the tropical heat. The thunder began to boom ever more loudly as it approached, and a cat hopped over a nearby wall as if to escape the coming deluge.

"You know, Michael," he told me. "I had colleagues who had been working for Teleco for 25 years, and they fired them and put 3,000 chimere on the payroll. Venel Joseph was running the central bank and Patrick Joseph, his son, was running Teleco. You're telling me that's a normal arrangement? Thousands of good people lost their jobs and everyone in Haiti and outside just shut their mouths and didn't say anything."

Of more immediate moment, though, the question of whether or not elections could be held in such an atmosphere as existed in Haiti dogged MINUSTAH. Curiously, one of those who had begun to advocate for a re-engagement with the electoral process was the fiercely Lavalassian former Milot mayor Moïse Jean-Charles, now in regular contact with MINUSTAH officials in nearby Cap-Haïtien, and having developed a reputation among some as "a smart guy who makes bad political choices."[146] I decided to go pay him a visit.

I boarded a Chilean army helicopter early one morning in Port-au-Prince and, along with my fellow travelers – Canadian, Jordanian and Chilean police and military – looked down as we broke through the cloud cover en route to Au Cap. Below, the mountains were bare and denuded, with every curve of the spine of the land exposed. At first stripped bare of trees as far as the eye could see, the land grew greener and had noticeably more trees the further north we went. The brown Artibonite River snaked through the countryside, dictating its own logic as it went along. Once in Cap, I rendezvoused with Javier Hernández, the Peruvian regional head of MINUSTAH and an old friend of mine from my days reporting in Guatemala, and we agreed to pay Moïse a visit the following day. That evening, we ate dinner on Javier's veranda, overlooking the curving bay of Cap down below, the sunset reaching narcotic shades of orange, red and purple amid a lather of humidity, and mosquitos buzzing infernally in our ears.

The next morning, we motored through a driving rain past lush, fecund fields to Milot, where a glorious stone cathedral built by Henri Christopher abutted the ruins of Sans-Souci and, above it, the Citadelle Laferrière. We were supposed to meet Moïse at the home of a local religious leader but, because of the rain, two young men waiting there flagged us down and led us through several winding lanes around the village until we came to a path off the roadside which had turned into a gurgling brown stream. We picked our way through it, wedging our boots between the rocks until we arrived at a humble pink stucco structure with a tin roof and chest-high cacti growing in the yard. Moïse was standing outside, in a T-shirt and jeans, a wisp of a mustache above his lips.

"Welcome," he said to us in English. "Come in."

Moïse had a fairly grim reputation among some in the area, accused, among other acts, of opening fire (along with Nawoon Marcellus) on anti-Aristide demonstrators in Cap-Haïtien in April 2003 (one person was killed) and involvement in the slaying of Guitz "Guy" Adrien Salvant in February 2004, just days before Aristide's government collapsed.[147] However, when I spoke with him, he was all solicitous humility.

"They looted my home," this man who had once exercised such power over this town told me. "I had to go into hiding for months, and then I came back down to Au Cap for a big demonstration in August 2004."

I asked him, when so many of the self-professed spokespeople of the Lavalas movement were advocating scorning the forthcoming elections, he was encouraging people to apply for a new identity card and to register to vote.

"The national identity card represents our right to vote," he told me, explaining why he had broken with the hardline view to encourage the party's supporters to register for the card that would eventually pave the way for a ballot. "Without that, what can we do?"

I had one more interview to do, and the following day, as I trudged up the hill at Canapé Vert under the burning sun, a pickup screeched to a halt and out of the passenger window poked the head of Boukman Eksperyans singer Lolo, who offered to give me a lift. I told him I had recently been to Au Cap, and said how nice it had been to get out of the capital for a while.

"We can't let the Republic of Port-au-Prince kill us," Lolo said, shaking his head.

After Lolo dropped me off at the MINUSTAH headquarters at the Hotel Christopher, I went to chat with Gérard Le Chevallier, the top MINUSTAH official in charge of making sure the looming elections did in fact occur. Le Chevallier, a former official in the governments of Álvaro Magaña and José Napoleón Duarte in his native El Salvador, had also played a key role as a negotiator in the peace accords that ended that country's long civil war. A Haiti veteran, he had previously served as the in-country director of the NDI.[148] I found him determined, but worried.

"The disarmament program is not working because the armed groups in Haiti are not a military, they are just bands of guys," he told me. "Cité Soleil is like another country. At present, there could be no Lavalas electoral campaign in the Artibonite or Plateau Central and no non-Lavalas campaign permitted in many *quartiers populaires* in Port-au-Prince. The Brazilians took the development approach to Haiti; they thought the political conflict would go away after the arrival of the UN. Well, that didn't happen."

As I left the UN compound following my interview with Le Chevallier, while passing through the security gate, I was confronted by a wanted poster – a death list, if you will – of six faces with the words "Wanted by HNP – Recherché par la PNH" written above them. There was Rémissainthe Ravix's face with a black "X" over it. There was Grenn Sonnen's, also crossed out, as well, and also Labanye's. Dread Wilmé's and Amaral's photos were still unmarked, meaning that they were still at large. And the final face was that of my friend James, whose whereabouts I had been trying to ascertain for months. On top of his smiling visage, which I had gazed into during our long conversations over the years as he explained so much of Haiti to me, a thick "X" had been drawn. He was gone.

* * *

After I left Haiti, the situation got even worse. Traveling near Cité Soleil, Paul-Henri Mourral, the honorary consul of France in Cap-Haïtien and owner of Au Cap's lovely old Hôtel Roi-Christophe, was waylaid by gunmen, shot several times and his vehicle stolen. He died despite the frantic efforts of Médecins Sans Frontières surgeons to save his life.[149] It was charged that the gang leader Amaral Duclona was behind the murder.[150]

The same day that Mourral was killed, the capital's Marché Tèt Bœuf was attacked by armed men who locked the market's doors and sent it ablaze. At least 11 people were burned alive and two died from their injuries in hospital.[151] The massacre occurred despite the fact that the PNH had been warned several days earlier that such an assault had been planned and despite the fact that police were communicating via radio as they observed at least 100 attackers head towards the market from as far away as Cité Soleil.[152] The attackers also hurled Molotov cocktails at a nearby police commissariat. In a corollary that no one in the country believed was coincidental, 31 May was the day before the first anniversary of the deployment of MINUSTAH to Haiti.[153] With both PNH and

MINUSTAH forces arriving on the scene long after the attack had taken place, at a meeting with the U.S. Embassy only days later, Boniface Alexandre's chief of staff, Michel Brunache, said that the government had no faith in MINUSTAH (when the attack occurred, Valdés was vacationing in Rome, which did not help this impression) and appealed for the deployment of U.S. military forces. He described an alarming picture in which Aristide's armed supporters believed that "if a handful of ex-soldiers could topple the government last year, they ought to be able to do so themselves," and went on to describe a "population seething with hatred, and living in fear of more violence to come" in an atmosphere in which "everyone" was procuring weapons.[154] Between September 2004 and June 2005, at least 1,000 people had been killed in the violence, including 73 PNH officers and four MINUSTAH peacekeepers.[155] And the peacekeeping itself remained a rather piecemeal affair, with the Jordanians stationed in Cité Soleil being viewed unfavorably, and the Peruvians, a reserve force stationed in Jacmel who had nevertheless also patrolled the capital's slums, seen as highly effective despite the fact that their home government was still waiting for the UN's Department of Peacekeeping Operations (DPKO) to pay for the cost of their deployment.[156]

* * *

In early June, anonymous callers sowed panic at the Teleco headquarters downtown, saying that the entity's building on Grand Rue would be burned, causing employees to flee. The same day, businessman Jean-Paul Médina was slain and the car he was driving stolen on the airport road.[157] It was believed by some that Médina had been killed by Dread Wilmé's men.[158] During June, a menacing leaflet was distributed by various Lavalas *baz* in Cité Soleil and Bel-Air (with the politically impotent Parti Populaire National of the United States-based Haitian politician Ben Dupuy signing on for good measure) depicting a potential voter being bitten by a crab hiding in a ballot box and featuring the warnings *Nou pa pral fè kat elektoral pèlen!* (We are not going to elections). Also scrawled on the missive were the words "If you register, it's like the kidnapping of 29 February," as well as a repeat of the demand for Aristide's "physical return" to the country.[159] One who would not be returning, however – at least not without the intercession of the *lwa* – was Buteur Métayer, who had helped lead the rebellion against Aristide after the murder of his brother. Depressed at what he viewed as the failure of the rebellion as he and other members of the Armée Cannibale were marginalized, Métayer sank deeply into alcoholism, a pattern that worsened after his December run-in with immigration authorities in Miami. His kidneys finally failed him on 8 June, and he died at home in Gonaïves, the scene of both his most bitter heartbreak and greatest triumph. He was 34 years old.[160] In an echo of that struggle, Clunie Pierre Jules, the investigating judge in the Saint-Marc massacre case, deposited the results of the investigation with the court in Saint-Marc, with the victims' attorney Samuel Madistin saying that "the order will come out in a month and the trial will be held at the end of the year if neither party files an appeal."[161]

* * *

That same month, the UN Security Council voted to extend MINUSTAH's mandate until February 2006, as well as supporting "a temporary increase, during the electoral period and subsequent political transition." This would bring the military component to a total of up to 7,500 troops and up to 1,897 civilian police.[162] Though perhaps later than many Haitians would have preferred, it was good that the Security Council acted as it did, for at almost the same time as international diplomats were debating in New York, around 200 armed men (and, indeed, some were not men, only children) invaded the capital's streets at Champ de Mars, Lalue and Rue des Miracles, firing automatic weapons in the air, sowing panic and sending pedestrians running for their lives. A young girl and a merchant on Rue Montalais were wounded by gunfire.[163] There were a few bright spots in the battle to retake the streets, though. Emmanuel Coriolan, the kidnapping ring leader better known as Dom Laj, was killed by PNH in late June.[164] Several days later, Arnel Bélizaire, who had fled Haiti after the February jailbreak, was arrested in the Dominican Republic.[165] When two kidnappers tried to seize two employees of the Sans Souci travel agency in Fontamara in late June, their subsequent traffic accident attracted a crowd that promptly lynched one and turned the other over to the police.[166]

* * *

A day after Dread Wilmé was reported wounded during a joint MINUSTAH–PNH operation in Cité Soleil, the PNH base at Portail Saint-Joseph was attacked by unknown gunmen, though no casualties were reported.[167] By late June, Assistant Secretary of State for Western Hemisphere Affairs Roger Noriega said that the U.S. government believed that Aristide's "people are receiving instructions directly from his voice and indirectly through his acolytes that communicate with him personally in South Africa ... Aristide and his camp are singularly responsible for most of the violence and for the concerted nature of the violence."[168] In Paris, U.S. Ambassador to France Craig Stapleton met with the French diplomat Gilles Bienvenu, who told him that, in the latter's view, the consequences of an Aristide return to Haiti would be "catastrophic," an analysis that, in a secret cable, Stapleton said that he shared. The two then discussed at some length ways to pressure various countries, South Africa and the Dominican Republic among them, for Aristide to remain in Pretoria.[169] In late June, CCIH president Réginald Boulos went on the radio to charge that former Lavalas deputy Nawoon Marcellus had hatched a "plot" against him, and that René Civil and Paul Raymond were continuing a destabilization campaign from the Dominican Republic.[170] Relations between the bourgeoisie and the interim government remained rocky, with industrialist Charles Baker telling Radio Vision 2000 that "when the private sector goes to hold talks with the prime minister, we feel like handing him a handkerchief for him to cry in."[171]

Around 300 MINUSTAH soldiers, led by the Brazilians, raided Bel-Air on 29 June, freeing a kidnapped woman and killing six gang members who were holding her. Five other individuals were wounded and 13 detained.[172] Other reports said that a handicapped man unaffiliated with the gang was also killed.[173] By mid-July, Brazilian MINUSTAH troops, who had been raiding Bel-Air periodically since mid-June under the aegis of "Operation Thunder," succeeded in setting up a permanent 50-man base on the western edge of the district, dismantling the barricades and trenches that carved up the neighborhood.[174]

Then, at about 4.30am on the morning of 6 July, Peruvian MINUSTAH troops, backed by Argentine and Chilean helicopters and with Brazilian troops providing perimeter security, stormed Dread Wilmé's stronghold in the Bois-Neuf area of Cité Soleil. The operation quickly degenerated into a grinding hours-long battle that saw Wilmé's gunmen firing from three directions and hurling Molotov cocktails at the troops while the Peruvians fired "5,500 rounds of ammunition, grenades and mortars" and the Brazilians "fired more than 16,700 rounds of ammunition."[175] At least 27 people were wounded by gunfire, while Wilmé and several of his lieutenants and at least one young woman were killed.[176] Following the raid, a Cité Soleil resident would call Radio Métropole to complain that two children were murdered by gunmen under suspicion of having provided information to UN troops, their bodies "burned and thrown into dustbins."[177] Nine other suspected collaborators were also killed.[178] It was believed that Wilmé's successor would be one Alain Cadet, aka Pinochet.

Three days later, hundreds of mourners carried a coffin in a "funeral" for Wilmé, at which Amaral, among other Cité Soleil bosses, was present. No journalists present could ascertain whether the coffin contained an actual body or not – some said Wilmé had been buried previously at a secret location. At the funeral ceremony, which journalists in attendance said "was much more like a political rally," speakers promised to continue their mobilization for the return of Aristide from South Africa, and even played a prerecorded message from the former president in which, in typically delirious fashion, Aristide lectured his human cannon fodder in Cité Soleil that South Africa had also been Gandhi's place of refuge when "he began his struggle for the liberation of India" in 1947.[179]

* * *

As Dread Wilmé was buried, the poet, journalist and activist Jacques Roche, who had chronicled his country's struggles so movingly in verse over the years, was surrounded by gunmen in Nazon and dragged from his car, a second-hand Honda, the first vehicle he had ever been able to afford to buy and which he had paid for partly by translating for foreign journalists over the years. After he was seized, a phone call was made to his newspaper, Le Matin, demanding a $250,000 ransom. His family and friends frantically gathered $10,000 and, so they believed, had garnered more time to collect the rest.[180] The would-be conduit for the ransom was reportedly Antonio "Don Kato" Cheramy, one of the leaders of the Haitian rap band Brothers Posse, who denied any affiliation with the gang and said that he was merely trying to help Roche's friends and family.[181] But after the first payment was made, the original gang of kidnappers apparently sold Roche to another group, this one political, that apparently wanted him dead for appearing – due to his virtue of interviewing all sides in Haiti's political debate – to be sympathetic to those who had toppled Aristide the year before. On 14 July – four days after he had been kidnapped – Roche's tortured body – handcuffed, shot, burned, his tongue cut out – was found on the side of the road in the poor neighborhood of Delmas 4, one of the brightest minds of this tormented nation dumped like so much garbage in the street.[182]

The killing rocked the city back on its heels, as did the events that followed. Less than a week after Roche's body had been found (and after having been questioned by Judge Jean Pérez Paul), Gérard Jean-Juste, while denying any involvement in Roche's death, provocatively told Radio Kiskeya that *la fin de la violence d'en-bas dépend de celle d'en-haut* (the end of violence from below depends on the end of violence from above), a strange claim coming from someone disavowing any link – or a link of his political current – to the crime. He also again called for mobilization to bring Aristide back to Haiti.[183] Meanwhile, Yvon Feuillé struck a far more moderate tone, telling Radio Métropole on behalf of his wing of Lavalas that:

> We are very sorry to see the sad and inhumane circumstances in which a journalist such as Jacques Roche lost his life. We send our condolences to all the journalists, to all the sectors he belonged to and to his family in particular. In the face of this sad situation, it is time for everybody to rise up to create a chain of solidarity to say enough, for kidnapping and assassination are a cancer that is destroying the country ... May each Haitian citizen be a light to combat the forces of darkness and the evil of violence, of poverty, of exclusion, and kidnapping.[184]

MINUSTAH's Valdés said flatly that Roche's killing had "all the elements of a political murder."[185]

* * *

More than 3,000 people showed up at Jacques Roche's funeral at the Église Saint-Pierre in Pétionville, many weeping openly. Among them, though, startling the bereaved as he arrived in full priest's regalia as if to officiate the service, was none other than Father Gérard Jean-Juste.[186]

Speaking to the ever credulous Amy Goodman earlier in the day, Jean-Juste told her that "I'm on my way to attend the funeral of Jacques Roche ... Because his parents are from my town, and at a certain time, one of his relatives saved my life. I was being attacked by a mob, and then Mrs. Roche came out, saw me, and ... sheltered me at her house."[187] Later, IJDH attorney and Loyola University law professor Bill Quigley (contemptuously referred to by the Haitian press as "a foreign lawyer"[188]) would expand on the claim, writing that Jean-Juste was "a cousin of the Roche family, and members of the Roche family protected him from a mob earlier in his life."[189]

However, according to Roche's mother, Madame Victor Roche, who spoke to Radio Kiskeya shortly after the funeral, Jean-Juste and Quigley were not being truthful. The grieving mother, herself a native of Cap-Haïtien, said she had never set foot in Cavaillon (where her husband hailed from) and had never sheltered Jean-Juste (whom she said she had never met) at her "house" when he was a child (indeed, she had no house in Cavaillon to shelter him in).[190]

Even before the ceremony began, the crowd at Roche's funeral began surrounding the priest, shouting at him, and appeared on the verge of lynching him when Jean-Juste was seized by the PNH, along with MINUSTAH, and taken to the Pétionville commissariat just across the Place Saint-Pierre from the church. Secretary of State for Public Security David Bazile said "the crowd wanted to devour him, we decided to put him here to prevent the situation from degenerating."[191] For his part, the CEDH's Jean-Claude Bajeux said that "if Jean-Juste had had any decency he would never have set foot in that church."[192]

At Roche's funeral, Monsignor Pierre André Dumas told the mourners that:

> The death of Jacques, like that of all the innocent victims, is and remains
> an insult to human dignity, a cry that goes up to the sky, a crime against
> humanity that nothing can justify … This violence is a lie, it leads to
> the destruction of our city. It is an evil and, as such, is unacceptable as a
> solution to our problem … How many more innocent victims must there
> be to stop this downward spiral of an entire people? How long does it take
> a people to destroy themselves? Yes to security! Yes to love! Yes to peace! Yes
> to a unified Haiti without violence![193]

Roche's murder provoked a groundswell of revulsion among Haiti's civil society and general populace, perhaps more than any other single crime since Aristide's ouster. Speaking to Radio Métropole from exile in Canada, Nancy Roc said that "it is now clear that these pro-Lavalas activists have targeted the press … We are now in a country that has lost its name … I have lost all hope."[194] In a tribute to what they called Roche's "exemplary life" and "permanent commitment to the most vulnerable in the country," PAPDA wrote that "today we have lost a compatriot, a worthy man, an honest fighter" and went on to ask "what will happen to a country which murders its poets, its creators, its activists of hope?"[195] In an open letter to the Latortue government, PAPDA, GARR, EnfoFanm and SOFA cited Operation Baghdad (carried out by "armed gangs executing the orders of Jean-Bertrand Aristide"), the epidemic of rape in the capital's slums, the burning of the Marché Tèt Bœuf and finally Roche's killing, and called for an immediate indictment to be issued against Aristide and his proxies for what the organizations charged were his crimes against the Haitian people.[196] Within days, the letter had over 300 co-signers.[197]

But perhaps the most poignant tribute of all came from Michèle Montas, who wrote that Roche had been "confronted with savagery in that descent into hell that has become our daily lot as a people, a descent into hell that was nonetheless predictable and avoidable, a descent into hell paved with so many stones of impunity." She went on:

> Your fellow journalists will be standing at your side to say no to the unacceptable just as they said no for Jean Dominique and Brignol Lindor. The difference is that today the unacceptable has become the norm undoubtedly as a result of so many unpunished crimes ... Today you will be put to rest with belated pomp, you will hear many official promises, and many crocodile tears will be shed on your tortured body. You will hear many promises to investigate. Do not believe too much in them. Your family will demand – as we did and as the family and colleagues of Brignol Lindor did – the truth, but the investigation will continue forever because too many influential people, under an elected government as well as an interim government – *mutatis mutandis* – have an interest in protecting impunity ... In the meantime Jacques, when you see Jean, tell him about the multifaceted violence, the gangrenous corruption, the loss of references, the shoving aside of principles and values, tell him about the bitter struggle for miserable power, and these elections, planned elsewhere, to serve a purpose. Tell him about the *pays en dehors* [country on the outside] drained of blood and abandoned to its own devices. Tell him about the wind of Maribahoux ... But do not forget to tell him, Jacques, about the courage displayed daily by thousands of us, when confronted by savagery, stupidity, cowardice, the courage that you yourself displayed. Tell him about the resistance and tenacious hope. Tell him that your struggle has more than ever meaning and that no murderer can assassinate the dreams of his loved ones and your loved ones. I know that you will understand one another with few words. Dreams like people put forth new shoots and flowers. And the murderers who roam the city cannot put an end to it. And the time will come for your dream to be born again. Goodbye, my friend. We will never forget.[198]

CHAPTER FOUR
DECEPTIONS AND DELUSIONS

Following Roche's slaying, the Conseil des Sages recommended that Lavalas be banned from forthcoming elections, charging that "political groups who identify themselves with the Fanmi Lavalas Party, and particularly with Mr. Jean-Bertrand Aristide, continue to promote and tolerate violence," and urged the government to "make the bold political and beneficial decision to disqualify the [party] … from the electoral process." The CEP, however, stressed that the forthcoming election would be for "all" political parties.[1] A short time later, a gangster viewed as a key link in the Roche killing, Johnny Cicéron, would be arrested for his alleged role in the crime only to be released without explanation after several months in prison.[2]

Four days after Jacques Roche's body was found, Léon Charles submitted his resignation as head of the PNH. It was announced that he would be transferred to Haiti's embassy in Washington, DC as head of intelligence and that his replacement would be Mario Andrésol, the police official who had been driven into exile five years earlier.[3] Andrésol took over as head of the PNH the following month.[4]

Andrésol was a curious hybrid. Born to a poor family off the capital's Grand Rue in 1960, among his earliest memories were the Octave Cayard mutiny and Papa Doc's funeral. Andrésol joined the FADH in 1982 at the age of 22, spending two years in the military academy and then almost a year training at Fort Benning, Georgia. When he returned to Haiti in August 1985, he found a country in complete upheaval against the Duvalier family dynasty, the only form of government many Haitians – including himself – had ever known. Assigned as a lieutenant to head a tactical unit in Cap-Haïtien with 40 men under his command, he developed a reputation for walking up unarmed and in uniform to talk to demonstrators and try to defuse volatile situations with words rather than bullets.

Upon his arrival back in the PNH, Andrésol realized all was not as it appeared.

"There were bad guys in those [slum] areas, of course, but the elite and the politicians also used the police as a weapon against the poor people," Andrésol told me. "Probably 65 percent of what happened in Port-au-Prince in terms of criminality, the police were responsible. I came from the popular quarters downtown, I realize that this is the same scheme for 200 years, the elite using the security forces against the people. I said no."[5]

* * *

As Haiti bled and mourned its dead, as its progressive organizations and long-time opponents of dictatorship and tyranny spoke out in furious protest, what was the response of much of the international left, who one would think would have been their natural allies?

As often arises in the discussion of any tumultuous place, naturally there was the demented extreme which, given a facility for writing in English and spreading its message on the internet, in Haiti's case often attracted more notice than it deserved. Writing from the safety of Connecticut, a perennial Aristide acolyte and sometime performance artist called Marguerite Laurent (who often went by the name Ezili Danto) gloated that Roche's murder was "the fruit of a poison coup d'état-tree."[6] An article on the website of Canada-based Center for Research on Globalization – a body headed by a 9/11 conspiracy theorist who had also written defenses of North Korean dictator Kim Jong-il[7] and Libyan dictator Muammar Gaddafi[8] – attacked NCHR (now RNDDH) for "contributing to a climate of anti-Lavalas terror," despite the fact that NCHR had publicly protested against the arrests of Yvon Feuillé, Louis Gerald Gilles and Rudy Hériveaux,[9] and assailed the feminist group Enfofanm and the media entity AlterPresse – both Haitian staffed and run – for accepting grant money from the Canadian International Development Agency, as if doing so somehow discounted the years of struggle of the activists in the trenches.[10] Also hewing closely to this line of thought was the Brooklyn newspaper *Haïti Progrès*, run by a white American, Kim Ives, which acted as the mouthpiece for the political ambitions of U.S.-based Haiti political operator Ben Dupuy and his minuscule Parti Populaire National (PPN), before, in the manner of many sectarian thinkers, the two bitterly fell out.[11] Ives went on to carry the Aristide banner in a new paper, *Haiti Liberté*, which the veteran progressive Haitian activist Daniel

Simidor wrote was "a sadly irrelevant and useless newspaper … [that] doesn't matter to anyone outside the small clique that runs it."[12]

This lot might have been dismissed as outliers were it not for the fact that people far better connected and financed were saying much the same thing in an effort to exculpate the Lavalas current and its leader from assertions of its involvement in human rights violations. Perhaps the key groups in this campaign were the Haiti-based Bureau des Avocats Internationaux (BAI) and the IJDH. The BAI had been formed after Aristide's 1994 return to Haiti with the ostensible aim of prosecuting human rights violations from the 1991–94 coup period. In this, they had a notable success with the Raboteau trial in 2000, which prosecuted the perpetrators of a 1994 massacre of Aristide's supporters. Led by the Haitian attorney Mario Joseph, the BAI, whose staff of lawyers included an American attorney named Brian Concannon, became more a kind of public relations arm for the government than a neutral human rights body as the regime itself became more and more involved in gross human rights abuses. Following Aristide's February 2004 ouster, the BAI continued to defend the interests of the former president on the ground in Haiti while the newly formed IJDH, with Concannon as its public face, would do so in the United States.

The financial links between the BAI and IJDH and Aristide were extensive and long-standing. The Miami attorney Ira Kurzban, whose firm – as shown by U.S. Department of Justice Foreign Agents Registration Act (FARA) filings – received nearly $5 million from the Aristide government of behalf of its lobbying efforts,[13] continued to serve as Aristide's personal attorney in the United States even as he was listed as both the IJDH's co-founder and the chairman of its board of directors.[14] In a still-extant (as of March 2017) link on IJDH's website, donations to the organization are directed to be sent to an address in Key Biscayne, the same Florida island town where Mr. Kurzban resides.[15] The BAI's Mario Joseph served as one of Aristide's coterie of lawyers in Haiti. All the while, the two groups were claiming to advocate on behalf of the victims of human rights abuses.

The efforts of the IJDH/BAI were aided by such curiosities as a highly controversial study published by the British medical journal *The Lancet* and authored by Athena R. Kolbe, at the time a graduate student at Wayne State University, and Dr. Royce A. Hutson, a professor of social work at the school. The report stated that it had sampled 1,260 households in the Port-au-Prince area and that Lavalas partisans had committed "none" of the instances of murder or sexual assault it chronicled during the previous two years.[16] That such a conclusion flew in the face of many years of on-the-ground reporting by local human rights organizations, journalists and others was obvious (as was the difficulty of conducting research in some *quartiers populaires*, where suggestions of disloyalty to Haiti's former leader could be fatal). It was revealed later that report co-author Kolbe, under the pseudonym Lyn Duff, had in fact for many years been described as "a friend of Aristide,"[17] had written pro-Aristide tracts praising the Haitian leader as a "caring humanist"[18] who ran a "democratic government,"[19] and had actually worked at Lafanmi Selavi.[20] Despite the obvious conflict of interest – amplified by the fact that the paper contained footnotes credited to "Lyn Duff" as a background source – the pair decided not to disclose it to either *The Lancet* or their readers.[21] The report caused outrage among human rights groups, with a member of Haiti Rights Vision noting that "[what] our evidence overwhelmingly suggests is that all groups are implicated in abuse against women"[22] and the Montréal-based Rights and Democracy attacking the report's "flawed methodology."[23] A subsequent inquiry into Kolbe and Hutson's research conducted by the authors' home institution (not an independent third party) consisted of merely auditing 7 percent of the questionnaires and observing whether the handwritten records corresponded with the project's computerized database.[24]

This historical amnesia bled into the press as well. The Canadian author and activist Naomi Klein traveled to South Africa to meet Aristide and repeat his contention that it was his opposition to the "privatization" of Haiti's state industries that had led to his overthrow, an explanation Aristide no doubt cannily tailored to Klein's own anti-globalization leanings and which must have come as a surprise to those who had watched the looting of Teleco. But Klein simply repeated it, stating that "Haitians ... on the streets [are] rejecting the planned sham elections."[25] Writing in *The New York Times*, Walt Bogdanich and Jenny Nordberg opined that "an accused death squad leader helped armed rebels topple" Aristide from power and that "police fought gun battles with a gang called the Cannibal Army," with no mention of the building years of civil protest nor, astonishingly, of Amiot Métayer, his links with the government or his murder.[26]

Nor was academia spared. Before setting foot in Haiti, Peter Hallward, a Canadian academic specializing in modern French philosophy, wrote that Aristide had been "forced from office ... by people who have little in common except their opposition to his progressive policies and their refusal of the democratic process."[27] Later, having freely admitted that he had "visited Haiti only twice" and had "no special interest in the peculiarities of Haitian society" and speaking no Creole,[28] Hallward wrote a book the deified Aristide and demonized anyone who would issue the mildest criticism of the president, dismissing Jacques Roche as simply an "anti-FL journalist," with no mention of his years of work with peasant groups or his literary accomplishments.[29]

In a letter to *The Nation*, Mark Weisbrot, co-director of the Washington, DC-based Center for Economic and Policy Research (CEPR), claimed that most of the Lavalas leadership and activists in Haiti were in jail, hiding or exile, that there was little evidence that the Aristide government had actively thwarted the Jean Dominique investigation, and that the chimere–police collusion during the December 2003 university attack was "simply an allegation."[30] All of these claims were false.[31]

* * *

One aspect that foreigners who knew Haiti only by its reputation as a place of misery and political violence missed was the captivating creative resistance the country's tumultuous history had inspired within both its own creative class (of which Jacques Roche was a part) and, through example, many of the outsiders who were fortunate enough to visit it over the years. I believe the lack of appreciation for this aspect of Haiti's culture is one of the key causes for the frequent descent into shrillness and sloganeering when those from abroad write about the place.

From its earliest days, a robust debate on the nature and meaning of Haiti's revolution had been waged in the works of Haitian scholars such as Thomas Madiou and Beaubrun Ardouin, and the writing in later years of intellectuals such as Anténor Firmin and Oswald Durand further refined these theses. During and after the U.S. occupation – which had the double-edged effect of somewhat opening up the heretofore marginalized country to visits from the outside world – both Haiti's own literary scene and the influence it had on the world at large would blossom. The author, ethnographer and diplomat Jean Price-Mars, a son of Grande Rivière du Nord, in his 1928 work *Ainsi parla l'oncle* produced one of the pivotal works of *négritude*, a philosophy which sought to embrace, rather than reject, the African heritage of French-speaking people of African descent. The author Jacques Roumain, born to an affluent Port-au-Prince family and having spent much of the first 20 years of his life at schools in Belgium and

Switzerland, nevertheless in 1943 produced the timeless peasant fable *Gouverneurs de la Rosée* (*Masters of the Dew*) as well as a book of verse, *Bois d'ébène*. The latter contained a line referring to *les damnés de la terre*, which would later be appropriated by the Martinique-born author Frantz Fanon as the title for his own book of anti-colonial polemics, translated into English as *The Wretched of the Earth*. The African-American author and anthropologist Zora Neale Hurston visited Haiti in 1937, a visit that would form a large part of her book *Tell My Horse*. A decade later, the British author Malcolm Lowry, by this point a shambolic alcoholic who had nevertheless published one of the era's greatest novels, *Under the Volcano*, in 1947, arrived in Haiti and was quickly befriended by the Haitian author Philippe Thoby-Marcelin. The Ukrainian-American avant-garde filmmaker Maya Deren made many trips to Haiti in the late 1940s and early 1950s which would become the basis for her film and book *Divine Horsemen: The Living Gods of Haiti*. In the 1950s and 1960s, even as the country groaned under the tyranny of Duvalierism, the banner of Haitian literature was carried by the likes of Jacques Stephen Alexis (who would perish at the head of an unsuccessful invasion to oust Papa Doc that landed at Môle-Saint-Nicolas in 1961), Anthony Phelps and Marie Vieux Chauvet, and, in the second half of the twentieth century, Haitian writers such as René Depestre, Frankétienne and Paulette Poujol Oriol produced work of stunningly high quality. During a 1975 visit, the French author and diplomat André Malraux was seduced by the Saint Soleil school of Haitian painting, popularized by artists such as Louisiane Saint Fleurant and Dieuseul Paul.

What some foreigners failed to grasp is that Roche's murder, like the killing of Jean Dominique or the university attack, was a watershed moment in the way the political struggle was perceived in Haiti itself, a searing punctuation of a corrupting drift towards violence that had been examined for some time in books such as Gary Victor's *A l'angle des rues parallèles*,[32] in which the despotic Chosen One lords over a mad political landscape (one that eventually encompasses the murder of God), or Lionel Trouillot's *Rue des pas perdus*,[33] in which a final battle between the forces of the Prophet and those of the Deceased Dictator Forever Immortal is envisioned. The Haitian cinéaste Raoul Peck would add his own take on this narrative with his film *Moloch Tropical*, while the music of such popular groups as Boukman Eksperyans, with songs such as "Tipa Tipa" and "Nou Pa Vle Lagè," ruthlessly mocked the brutality, stupidity and rapaciousness of the country's political class.[34] In the words of Lyonel Trouillot, most Haitians realized all too well that "bloodshed isn't a virtue or a miracle, it's just plain bloodshed."[35]

* * *

The newly returned Mario Andrésol clearly had his work cut out for him. In little more than a three-week span beginning in late July, at least a dozen suspected gang members were lynched by local residents in Bel-Air.[36] These included seven presumed members of the pro-Lavalas Chaba Gang, whom residents told Radio Métropole had been murdering, raping and kidnapping the population there, with other residents stating that "we are against the chimere and we support the national police in its fight against the bandits."[37] Mirroring these actions, in Solino, five presumed bandits were lynched, and locals handed over several automatic weapons to the police after gang leaders Bibi and Beckner "Ti Yabout" Desrosiers fled to Cité Soleil. Former Delmas assistant mayor Ernst Erilus appealed to MINUSTAH and the PNH to take action in Cité Soleil, where he said the population remained at the mercy of the gangs, especially after criminals evicted by recent operations in Solino and Bel-Air had taken refuge there.[38]

When a contingent of Peruvian troops were patrolling Cité Soleil around this time, the captain noticed a skinny, bedraggled boy of seven or eight years old watching them every day as they passed. Striking up a basic conversation, the captain would give the boy some water, cookies or some other food whenever the patrol passed. One day, when passing the accustomed spot, they found the boy's disemboweled body, a sign reading *collaborateur* around his neck.[39] By early August, the capital's Saint Martin had been emptied of many of its inhabitants due to gangsterism and insecurity, with one student group estimating that 19,000 people had fled.[40] As former TKL leader Paul Raymond was arrested in the Dominican Republic and turned over to Haitian authorities,[41] business had timidly resumed in downtown Port-au-Prince, though merchants would often go hours without recording a sale. A few weeks after the Raymond arrest, Camille Marcellus, the rogue former PNH official who some believed was a conduit helping prosecute Operation Baghdad, was also arrested in the Dominican Republic.[42] At least 350 MINUSTAH troops entered Bel-Air on 8 August, not firing a shot but arresting 11 suspected gang members, with local residents saying publicly that they preferred the UN to the black-masked PNH who "come in and shoot everything on the street."[43] By this point, Haiti had registered 500,000 of its 4.5 million eligible voters according to the UN and OAS.[44]

But, as Mario Andrésol had noted, the poor were not the only ones who would become caught up in the criminal anarchy. On 2 August, Nathaël Génélus, an employee of Haiti's UNIBANK, was spirited away by police from the Delmas 62 station ostensibly for questioning on a charge that was never revealed. He was never seen again.[45] The PNH arrested Arab-Haitian businessman Stanley Handal for alleged involvement in the disappearance, alleging that Handal had been running a kidnapping ring along with Delmas 62 police officer James Bourdeau, for whom the PNH were actively searching.[46] Handal's attorney, Gilbert Léger, claimed that the charges against his client "did not exist."[47] PNH units eventually tracked Bourdeau to Camp Perrin, where he was arrested.[48] According to Haitian human rights groups, a judge would issue a warrant for four alleged kidnappers arrested in connection with the Génélus abduction, including Handal, but the file mysteriously disappeared.[49] Within a few months, Judge Jean Pérez Paul, president of the Association Nationale des Magistrats Haïtiens (ANAMAH), ordered that Handal and the three police officers be released. In response, a dissident PNH officer, Lamy Enock, took to the airwaves to denounce what he charged was "a vast and powerful criminal network involved in laundering drug money, acts of kidnapping and other illicit activities."[50] Days after making his statements to the press, the security that had been provided to him by the PNH was removed, and Enock was the victim of an assassination attempt on the airport road.[51] Handal and the other men were eventually freed, and an order dismissing the charges against him would be rendered in Handal's favor by a Haitian court.[52] For his part, Pérez Paul was widely viewed as corrupt and only given to taking a case "where money is involved,"[53] a reputation that the coming years would do nothing to diminish.

* * *

By mid-August, AVIGES head Charliénor Thomson was denouncing what he called a plan by the international community and the interim government to free Yvon Neptune.[54] With many powerful people clearly anxious to make the case go away in the interest of "elections" (the lessons of the post-Duvalier period apparently never learned), the UN Special Rapporteur for Human Rights in Haiti, Louis Joinet, caused outrage when, after meeting briefly (and only once) with survivors of the La Scierie massacre, he dismissed the killings as merely "a clash." The AVIGES criticism was echoed by RNDDH, which said that the attitude of MINUSTAH chief Valdés and Minister of Justice Henry

Dorléans to the case was "a scandal" and that, by pressuring for Neptune's release, MINUSTAH and the interim government "sought to perpetuate impunity in Haiti." Where, RNDDH asked, were such herculean efforts on behalf of finding justice for Jean Dominique, Brignol Lindor, the priest Jean Marie Vincent and others?[55] Within the interim government itself, there was something of a mini-rebellion as to what to do with Neptune, with Latortue favoring some sort of liberty but Justice Minister Gousse and others opposed, with one going so far as to threaten "let Neptune go today, there will be a mass demonstration tomorrow and I will be at the head of the demonstration."[56] In his prolonged pre-trial detention, Neptune was hardly alone. Barely 2 percent of prisoners in the Pénitencier National had ever seen a judge.[57] Soon, Clunie Pierre Jules, the judge investigating the La Scierie killings, announced that, in the court's estimation, a massacre had indeed taken place, with at least 44 killed over a series of days, perpetrated by the PNH, National Palace security services, Bale Wouze and various armed civilians from Port-au-Prince. The judge's report listed a ghastly series of beheadings, rapes and other crimes, and said that Neptune's declarations to the court and others regarding the killings revealed "glaring contradictions," and that, between 7 February and 13 February 2004, phone records from his mobile showed that Neptune had spent over nine hours on the phone to police and members of Bale Wouze in Saint-Marc. The judge concluded that sufficient evidence existed to charge 29 people, including Bale Wouze members Amanus Mayette, Biron Odigé, Roland "Black Ronald" Dauphin and Figaro Désir, former Aristide government officials such as Neptune, former PNH head Jean-Claude Jean-Baptiste, Jocelerme Privert and former Minister of Justice Calixte Delatour, and a number of others, including an American pilot, Ron Lusk, who had been working with the government. The judge said that insufficient evidence existed to charge Aristide himself, government spokesmen Mario Dupuy and Jonas Petit and a number of others.[58] In an interview with Radio Métropole, Aristide's former justice minister Calixte Delatour said flatly that the former president was directly responsible for the massacre in La Scierie, saying "everything went through Aristide, not because he was the president but because it is the tradition in Haiti; Jean-Bertrand Aristide is the main culprit of the massacre of La Scierie."[59]

Pressure continued in the provinces. In Gonaïves, a day of anti-government protests and gang clashes left at least eight wounded, with the Armée Bouteille and Armée Roche fighting in Raboteau, while armed members of

Guy Philippe's FRN clashed with MINUSTAH troops.[60] In a demonstration unreported outside Haiti, three peasant groups – the Mouvement de Revendications des Paysans de l'Artibonite (MOREPLA), the Réseau des Associations Coopératives du Commerce et de Production Agricole du Bas-Artibonite (RACPABA) and the Plate-forme Nationale des Organisations Paysannes Haïtiennes (PLANOPA) – marched through the streets of Petite Rivière de l'Artibonite to protest the fact that "farmers are excluded from the management of public affairs and their claims are ignored, while during election time, their votes are courted by politicians who have never kept their promises."[61] At a peasant conference in the northern town of Jean-Rabel to commemorate the eighteenth anniversary of military-era mass killings there, peasants bemoaned the fact that 49 percent of products consumed in Haiti came from abroad and said that "farmers have the right to find land to work."[62]

As Brazilian Lieutenant-General Urano Teixeira da Matta Bacellar replaced Augusto Heleno Ribeiro Pereira as MINUSTAH's military commander in Haiti,[63] MINUSTAH military spokesman El-Ouafi Boulbars announced that henceforth the mission's number one goal would be to "pacify" Cité Soleil.[64] In an interview with Radio Métropole, Colonel André Luis Novaes Miranda, the commander of Brazil's forces in Haiti, said that the days of Bel-Air gang leader Général Toutou "were numbered."[65] Toutou eventually fled Haiti, first to the Dominican Republic, and then to the Bahamas, where he remains today, living under an assumed name.[66]

* * *

Following the lynchings of the gang members in Bel-Air and Solino, the atmosphere was thick with tension in Martissant, which had become a redoubt of some of the most recalcitrant criminals in the city. Once one of the capital's most pleasant neighborhoods, with sweeping views of the bay, Martissant had hosted the Haitian home of Katherine Dunham, for years a jet-set hotel known as the Habitation Leclerc. When the journalist Anna Ferdinand first started visiting Martissant in 1995 (she would spend a great deal of time there over the next decade), she found in the Grand Ravine area of the district "the need for schools, infrastructure, reforestation and the need to promote a beautiful culture in a country filled with artists ... [It was] a time when there was hope that these things could now be achieved." By May 2000, however, she wrote about how former members of a theater troupe had become Lavalas "security" and were toting guns. By the time of the disappearance of gang leader Félix Bien-Aimé, it was just a question of "political mutations in an atmosphere devoid of positive development ... Idealism, ideas of justice and development were long gone, lost to gang war."[67] However, organizations such as the International Organization for Migration (IOM) and Haiti's own secretary of state for youth and sports were trying to dial down the violence by sponsoring community-building events at relatively neutral locales such as the Parc Sainte Bernadette, where a 20 August football match drew around 6,000 spectators in what residents no doubt hoped was a spirit of mutual amity. All was relatively calm when, around halftime, a curious leaflet was distributed. Titled *La Police + Pèp = Solisyon* (*The Police + The People = The Solution*), the leaflet advised local residents to "rise up" against the "killers," "rapists," "kidnappers" and "thieves" in their midst, and to give police information to help them do their job.[68]

Then, at the cry of *la police encerclé les bandits au parc!* (police surround the bandits in the park!), around 30 black-clad and masked police who had encircled the park stormed in. They were accompanied, witnesses said, by civilians carrying glinting new machetes.[69] Gunfire erupted and a man believed to be a police informant was killed. At least 13 other people were also killed, a number of them by machetes.[70] The civilians, it was said, belonged to a group called the Lame Ti Manchèt, which residents said was close to PNH commander Carlo Lochard, who had overseen the operation.[71] Mario Andrésol, who at this point had been PNH chief for only a week, first heard about the operation through news reports on television.[72] Just days later, Radio Kiskeya carried an alarming report that "inhabitants of various districts of Martissant launched an SOS to the authorities on Monday so that they would forcefully intervene in a zone infested with heavily armed gangsters. These inhabitants, the majority of them young people coming from 4th and 5th Avenue Bolosse, describe the reactivation in the district of groups from the regime of Jean Bertrand Aristide, who have taken up residence in the Grand Ravine zone of Martissant." The broadcast then went on to interview residents who said that the gangs would "rob, rape, loot and kill," that they were in possession of "weapons of war" superior to those of the police, and that Dymsley "Ti Lou" Milien, one of the suspected murderers of Jean Dominique, was among their leaders.[73]

Haiti appeared to be drowning in its own blood. When, many pleaded, would it end?

CHAPTER FIVE
THE RETURN

He had been living in the mountain town of Marmelade, working on projects to help local peasants grow bamboo, citrus and coffee with help from a grant from the Taiwanese government, and residing in a modest home that could not have stood in greater contrast to the garish mansions some politicians lived in.[1] René Préval, Haiti's ultimate political survivor, might have played at being a simple yeoman farmer, but the image hid the cagiest mind among the country's power elite. He had served as prime minister and minister of the interior, had completed his 1996 to 2001 mandate without being overthrown, and had lived through the chaos sweeping through the north in 2004 unmolested. Possessing a unique ability to embody a political figure within whom both the bourgeois and the disenfranchised could meet, Préval had been quietly gathering aides around him for the coming presidential electoral contest. Among them were Robert "Bob" Manuel, the former secretary of state for public security who had been driven into exile in Guatemala years before, who now returned to Haiti to become Préval's campaign manager. There was Charles Suffrard, the leader of the Jean Dominique-allied KOZEPEP peasant group, who had also gone into exile under Aristide and now also returned to work on the campaign. And there was Moïse Jean-Charles who, from his base in Milot, believed that participating in elections was a better option than the zero-sum game that some among the Lavalas base had advocated. On 15 September – the last day of registration – Préval arrived at the CEP headquarters in Port-au-Prince and registered to run for Haiti's presidency.[2]

When Préval launched his campaign, it was at the head of a new political platform, Lespwa (Hope), an amalgam of various political currents, including the Parti Louvri Baryè (PLB) and regional organizations such as the Efò ak Solidarite pou konstui yon Altènativ Nasyonal Popilè (ESKANP) and the Kòdinasyon Rezistans Grandans (KOREGA). Significantly, in early 2004, both ESKANP and KOREGA had called for the Aristide government's overthrow, citing the president's "desperate and reactionary violence" and policies of "letting armed gangs across the country kidnap, rape, kill, terrorize and generally mistreat anyone who does not agree with him ... smashing all the institutions ... turning the country into a cemetery where human life has no value ... [and] destroying national production by applying neoliberal economic policies."[3] Between making common cause with these parties and the return in high-profile roles of Manuel and Suffrard in the campaign, Préval was sending an unambiguous message: this time around it was to be him, not Aristide, in the driver's seat. He would be his own man. In a striking demonstration, the day before his official announcement, thousands of marchers poured out of Cité Soleil and La Saline, dancing to music from sound trucks and voicing their joy at the former president's potential return.[4] Leslie Manigat, Guy Philippe, Evans Paul and a host of others would also be in the running for the presidency. By early October, the CEP had announced its list of approved candidates for the 30 seats in the senate, with 120 approved of some 316 who applied. For the 99-seat Chamber of Deputies, 749 of the 1,123 who applied were approved. Lavalas, making an unlikely political alliance with Marc Bazin's MIDH (Bazin would run as their dual presidential candidate) would be fielding only three candidates for the senate. In the run-up to elections, the desire of MINUSTAH was "to channel the leadership of Lavalas into some sort of institutionality."[5] Préval's Lespwa, on the other hand, rapidly developed a national profile and organization, especially in the south.[6] Two other would-be presidential candidates, the Haitian-American businessman Dumarsais Siméus and the Haitian entrepreneur Samir Mourra, were revealed to be holders of U.S. passports and thus ineligible to run in Haiti's elections.[7] A former Dread Wilmé lieutenant, Louis "Ti Pa" Étienne, was arrested at the Parc Industriel when he attempted to register as a candidate.[8] On a visit to Haiti in late September, U.S. Secretary of State Condoleezza Rice said that Aristide would be under "high surveillance" in South Africa as Haiti prepared for the vote.[9]

A variety of other interesting characters would be running for seats in parliament. There was Joseph Lambert, a Jacmel native who had been close to Fourel Célestin. There was Rudy Hériveaux, representing the more moderate wing of Lavalas. And there was Rudolphe "Rudy" Boulos, running for senate from the northeast. The Boulos family – whose public faces were Rudy and his brother, the rather more right-wing Réginald – were politically active Syrian-Haitians whose great-grandfather, Simel Boulos, was a Cap-Haïtien merchant who had imported arms to help Nord Alexis seize power in 1902. When Alexis was overthrown, Simel Boulos was clapped into prison. Bribing his way out of jail, Boulos thought it prudent to decamp from Cap-Haïtien, eventually settling in Ouanaminthe, where only the trickle of the Massacre River separated the family from the safety of the Dominican Republic. Réginald and Rudy's father, Carlo Boulos, was born there, leaving Haiti to study medicine at Harvard and then becoming minister of health for Papa Doc for a year and a half at the very beginning of the elder Duvalier's reign, handing in his resignation when he realized, as he matter-of-factly told the British writer Ian Thomson, "the fellow was quite gaga."[10] Carlo Boulos later opened up the Complexe Médico-Sociale de la Cité Soleil in the slum of the same name; Labanye would later tell me that the baz had driven it out on Aristide's orders, "though nothing came to replace it."[11] The Boulos name was perhaps best known in Haiti, however, for their running of Laboratoires Pharval, which produced various medicines for local consumption, pirated versions of which (they said) had been responsible for the poisoning of at least 60 children. Although the company was strongly criticized in some quarters (including by Jean Dominique on Radio Haiti), Pharval eventually filed a joint lawsuit with some of the victims against a Netherlands-based company that had distributed the contaminated product.[12] Members of Haiti's elite wandering into politics, though, was always a charged affair.

* * *

Thousands of demonstrators marched in Port-au-Prince on 3 November to voice their support for Préval's candidacy,[13] dancing to the accompaniment of *rara* bands, the long bamboo wind instruments Haitians call *vaksin* providing the musical accompaniment for the trip to the CEP's headquarters.[14] A Gallup poll the same month showed that Préval was the most popular presidential candidate, with 32 percent of respondents preferring him, while Dumarsais Siméus (soon to be disqualified) placed second with 25 percent and Leslie Manigat third with 5 percent.[15] Despite terrible hurdles, more than 80 percent of potential voters had been successfully registered.[16]

Whoever won the forthcoming election would take over a country where the rule of law, in the capital at least, had almost disappeared. Beginning in mid-November, more than a week of clashes erupted in Martissant between armed groups in Grand Ravine and the Lame Ti Manchèt, leaving at least two dead, several injured by bullets and a number of houses set ablaze.[17] The Marché Guérite, near the capital's City Hall, was largely destroyed by a fire believed to have been arson. When firemen appeared late on the scene, pleading a lack of gas and water for their trucks, they were met with jeers from the informal traders who had lost their livelihoods, with one saying that "the government totally despises us."[18] The director of Haiti's judicial police, Michael Lucius, at least, had apparently had enough, and denounced the liberation of gang leaders from prison, saying "each time a bandit [is] behind bars, he corrupts a member of the judiciary and gains his release."[19] Two alleged leaders of Lame Ti Manchèt, Rousse Jocelin and Jinel Joseph, had been released under suspicious circumstances and reportedly then killed again only hours after they were freed.[20]

By November, Haiti's judicial police, the Direction Centrale de la Police Judiciaire (DCPJ), had compiled a 900-page report on the Martissant football killings and sent it to the state prosecutor's office in Port-au-Prince. The report pointed the figure squarely at PNH head for the West Department, Carlo Lochard, as bearing chief responsibility for the massacre, saying that the operation at the Parc Sainte Bernadette "was conducted outside of all legal boundaries." The report also found fault with commander Renan Etienne for providing Lochard with CIMO and SWAT units.[21] To the amazement of many, Lochard and Etienne were actually arrested in a move that, in the words of a confidential cable from the U.S. Embassy, Mario Andrésol had undertaken "with risk to future [PNH] professionalization efforts and an even greater risk to his own life."[22] Shortly after the arrests, dozens of protesters – many of them discharged police officers – gathered at the police station on Champ de Mars, calling for Lochard and Etienne's release and Andrésol's arrest.[23] Among many in the international community, Andrésol was viewed as a lynchpin of the country's progress, someone who "had a sense of his historical role with the police, and managed to build around himself a very important group of followers to play a role [that] was extremely positive."[24]

Impunity remained rife, though. Two years after the chimere assault on Haiti's state university, many expressed their dejection at the lack of recognition the role of the students had received, with former student leader Romane Duperval telling Radio Métropole that there "was not a formal speech or even a government statement … to salute the courage of the student martyrs who died under the Lavalas regime of Jean-Bertrand Aristide."[25] Several dozen students marched under the slogan "Never Again," with student leader Hervé Saintilus observing that "the bandits" who committed the attacks "still roam the streets."[26]

As the year ended, three OAS officials were kidnapped on the airport road.[27] Simultaneous raids around Port-au-Prince nabbed a dozen alleged kidnappers and freed a Belgian PAPDA volunteer who had been seized.[28] Three Chilean MINUSTAH peacekeepers were wounded by gunfire in the northern town of Plaisance on 16 December as they were about to visit a polling center. When the Chileans returned fire, the gunmen fled.[29] Juan Gabriel Valdés later suggested that former military may have been behind the assault.[30] On Christmas Eve, a Jordanian soldier was slain in Cité Soleil after gunmen fired on his patrol,[31] and, days later, thousands of residents left their homes in Droulliard, fleeing what they claimed were armed gangs and sexual assaults by Jordanian peacekeepers.[32] As January began, gun battles raged between the Grand Ravine and Ti Bois gangs in Martissant, and armed groups from Cité Soleil continued to make advances in the industrial areas around Droulliard "under the impassive gaze of Jordanian peacekeepers," radio reports said.[33] Soon thereafter, an arrest warrant was issued against the Cité Soleil *baz* leader Amaral Duclona and 11 others for the May 2005 murder of French consul Paul-Henri Mourral. Evens Jeune and Beckner "Ti Yabout" Desrosiers were also subject to arrest on various charges.[34]

Meanwhile, the long saga of the Lavalas priest Gérard Jean-Juste, in jail since the funeral of Jacques Roche, was nearing its final act. In a 12 January decree, investigating judge Jean Pérez Paul charged that Jean-Juste should be tried for "criminal association and illegal possession of firearms," though he dismissed other charges pending against the priest. The announcement stated that "the accused ... himself confessed that he holds three Glock 9 mm [revolvers] and two guns, property of the National Palace and its security agents." Asked who these agents were, the decree said Jean-Juste refused to answer.[35] By late January, a gravely ill Jean-Juste, who was said to be suffering from cancer,[36] turned down an offer by the interim government to free him to forgo an appeal on his pending charges and undergo a "speedy" trial, where, if convicted, the government would commute his sentence (which raised the question of why have a trial at all). In a letter read aloud to supporters in Miami, the usually pugnacious Jean-Juste struck a melancholy tone, writing: "unfortunately I will leave more work for you ... However, I believe God always arises new workers for his vineyard."[37] By the end of the month, Jean-Juste would be freed and would return to Miami, where he had spent so many years. He would die of a stroke there three years later at the age of 62, his passing and his complicated legacy receiving a circumspect reading in Haiti itself.[38]

* * *

Another figure would also exit the pre-electoral scene. On the evening of 5 January, MINUSTAH's military commander, Lieutenant-General Urano Teixeira da Matta Bacellar, attended a ceremony for the presentation of medals to Guatemala's military contingent, where he seemed to be in good spirits.[39] The following day, however, during a meeting with the Haitian-American Chamber of Commerce, Bacellar was "insulted and accused" and told by the business community that "he was no kind of military at all," insults that quite wounded and offended him.[40] That evening, at the Hotel Montana, Bacellar's neighbor, Chilean General Eduardo Aldunate, heard a single shot, left his bed, opened the door to the adjoining room and saw Bacellar with a gun in his hand, dead.[41]

Brazil promptly sent a team of investigators to Haiti to look into the death, citing that the commander did not seem in a depressed frame of mind immediately preceding his demise.[42] The improbability of a man who had been vetted by both the Brazilian government and the United Nations taking his life in such a way was somewhat diminished by the autopsy results from Brasilia, which showed that Bacellar had shot himself in the mouth and had gunpowder on his hand.[43] MINUSTAH officials also believed that there was no foul play involved.[44] Bacellar would be buried with full military honors in his native country, in a flag-draped coffin as a band played the song "Eterno Herói" ("Eternal Hero").[45]

Many muttered darkly their doubts that Bacellar's death was suicide at all but rather an assassination designed to scuttle elections, but little evidence existed to support that theory. In his yearly (and typically strange) "New Year message" to Haiti, Aristide had made what many took to be a very clear call for violence with the words *lawouze koudeta fè banda, tout tan solèy retou a poko leve* (the consequences of the coup d'état against me must continue to be felt until that sunrise comes).[46] But a Cité Soleil gang leader interviewed by the news agency EFE in January said that "everyone" there would vote for Préval in the 7 February elections, and that those in the zone who robbed and killed did so for sheer survival, saying that "we have nothing, no food, no drinking water, no electricity, no health services and no education."[47] Speaking to Radio Métropole, Préval cagily told his interlocutor that: "Aristide's return is not something that depends on me … Article 41 of the constitution says that any Haitian citizen can return to the country without a visa … It is not up to me at all if this person can just buy a ticket and come back home."[48] In an interview with Agence France-Presse (AFP) around the same time, Préval said that "the rich are cloistered in their walled villas and the poor are crammed into slums and own nothing, the gap is too big ... Weapons must be taken from the hands of children and replaced with pens and books." Asked about MINUSTAH's presence in the country, he criticized what he called the "falsely nationalist stance" of some, and said that "those that want to create instability in the country and to continue drug trafficking will be the first to demand MINUSTAH's departure. They will wave the flag to demand that they go."[49]

* * *

People held their breath and wondered how the election would come off. During January, an official with the presidential campaign of Charles Baker and a candidate for deputy from MOCHRENA were both slain, in Pétionville and Camp Perrin respectively,[50] while the Lespwa office in Saint-Marc was set ablaze by unknown arsonists.[51] There were indications of just how volatile the atmosphere remained in the provinces when a Préval campaign visit to Ouanaminthe, on the Dominican border, was punctuated by gun battles between opponents and supporters, forcing the candidate to deliver his brief speech "in the middle of a shooting range," as Radio Kiskeya put it.[52] Back in the capital, despite the outstanding arrest warrant against him, Amaral Duclona led several hundred demonstrators in Cité Soleil to call for more voting centers in the quarter for the upcoming election.[53] Two days later, three French nationals, including an 85-year-old nun, were kidnapped on the airport road and whisked away to the slum.[54] Two Jordanian peacekeepers were slain and a third wounded in Cité Soleil when gunmen attacked a checkpoint they were manning.[55] Even ordinarily placid Petite-Rivière de l'Artibonite was not spared, and in late January a local gang leader named Blanc Raymond, who had terrorized local peasants, was decapitated by a band of local farmers and his deputy – "Bin Laden" – severely wounded by their machete blows. Gang members responded by burning peasant huts and stealing livestock in the nearby hamlet of Nan Palmiste.[56]

* * *

On Sunday, 7 February 2006 – the twentieth anniversary of Jean-Claude Duvalier's flight into exile – Haiti voted again for the first time in six years. Denounced and mocked by their foreign detractors since the ballot's beginning – the CEPR's Mark Weisbrot derided the election as a "farce"[57] while the IJDH's Brian Concannon called it a "phony election" that "ninety percent of the Haitian people want nothing to do with"[58] – Haitian voters nevertheless responded to the vote with magnificent patience and forbearance, with tens of thousands waiting in line for hours and some 60 percent of eligible voters casting ballots.[59] The voting itself was, by Haitian standards, remarkably free of violence.

By the following Monday, after voters had waited more than a week for results and despite word that he had held an early lead, the CEP was announcing that, with 90 percent of the vote tabulated, Préval's share had shrunk to 48.7 percent, which still put him ahead of Manigat's 11.8 percent but not by enough to avoid a runoff.[60] With some 2.2 million ballots cast, around 125,000 ballots were declared "invalid" because of sometimes unspecified irregularities.[61] Many of those discounted were from districts thought to be sympathetic to Préval.[62]

CEP member Patrick Féquière publicly accused the body's chief, Jacques Bernard, of unilaterally releasing results, while council member Pierre Richard Duchemin said CEP members were being locked out of the tabulation process. Bernard denied the accusations.[63] Others said that Bernard had wanted to declare Préval the victor in order to calm an increasingly tense situation.[64] Manigat told reporters that "we cannot let violence guide the process, we must respect the Constitution. We must go to the second round."[65] The sentiment might have been more convincing were it not for Manigat's own illegitimate usurpation of the presidency in 1988, itself only made possible when the Ruelle Vaillant massacre had canceled elections he was all but sure to lose. The parliamentary elections, though, were marked by a dirtiness that would become commonplace in the voting process. One senatorial candidate, the ophthalmologist Frantz Large, who was running for senate in his native Jacmel, told me that, when he challenged his defeat on the basis of fraud, his attorney was told by an electoral council member that three members of the body were willing to review the case for a fee of $25,000 plus $5,000 each for a pair of lawyers to be employed.[66]

Préval flew to the capital from his northern Haiti headquarters aboard a UN helicopter, landing as his supporters set up flaming barricades around the city, threatening to "burn this country down" if final results were not released. Préval's supporters stormed into the Hotel Montana, where the CEP information center was housed, waving tree branches and Préval posters and jumping in – fully clothed – to splash about in the hotel's pool under the largely impassive gaze of UN peacekeepers. The South African Nobel Peace Prize laureate Desmond Tutu, who was staying at the hotel, came out onto his balcony to appeal for calm. Préval told reporters that he was looking for a way to "save the process," while Gérard Latortue, speaking on national radio, told listeners that "the transitional government is not stealing your vote."[67]

By the following day, Préval said that the election had been marked by "gross errors and probably gigantic fraud," but at the same time asked his supporters "to be mature, to be responsible, to be nonviolent."[68] After hours of wrangling between Préval, the CEP and a contingent of foreign diplomats, finally, at a press conference held at 3am on a Thursday morning, the CEP announced that they were subtracting enough of the blank ballots cast from the total number of votes counted in order to push Préval over the 50 percent mark.[69] Convinced that the long nightmare of Operation Baghdad might finally be over and that they might finally have a president who understood their needs and how to address them (and who would eschew the cult-of-personality syndrome that plagued so many politicians), Haitians poured into the streets to celebrate throughout the day. In Washington, the U.S. Secretary of State Condoleezza Rice said that "we are going to work with the Préval government, we want this government to succeed." Manigat denounced the CEP decision as a "Machiavellian maneuver" and an "electoral coup" during which "violence has been rewarded."[70] After victory was handed to Préval, Mirlande Manigat, with brutal indifference to those who had supported her bid, announced that she was abandoning her campaign for senate in the country's West Department out of "solidarity" with her husband. Her exit effectively handed the senate seat to Jean Hector Anacacis of Préval's Lespwa.[71]

Not everyone was convinced of the wisdom of the decision, with the historian Claude Moïse writing a bitter dissent in *La Matin* accusing the international community of simply tossing aside the democratic process in exchange for calm.[72]

* * *

After Préval won, Aristide gave an interview to South Africa's *Mail & Guardian* in which, after again comparing himself to Nelson Mandela, he asserted that "when we look at the people of Haiti, it's clear there is a love story. If they love me and express that love for the past 10 years, the way they are dying for me to be back ... They voted for my return."[73] The South African government, though, said it was "not in a hurry to ship him back to Haiti" but that "he will not reside in South Africa for life."[74]

Préval's response to his own victory, however, could not have been more different. Speaking to Cuba's Radio Havana, he told journalist Ana Kovac that "this is not a victory for René Préval. This is a victory for the Haitian people. The Haitian people did not vote for René Préval, they voted for a change, and they have given Préval the responsibility of leading this project to achieve a change in their lives. Therefore, it is not my victory; it is a victory for the people ... I think the greatest reconciliation we should strive for is the one with the starving people who need food, it is with those who are sick and who do not have access to medical services; it is for those who have no education to make sure that they have access."[75] Later, he invited the press to his sister's backyard where he sat in "dappled sunlight," and told the assembled journalists that Haiti was like a bottle (a perhaps telling metaphor given his long-rumored fondness for rum), and that a bottle must rest on its broad base to be secure, because resting on its narrow mouth it would topple over and shatter. He said his job would be to facilitate an independent parliament and judiciary, and to "put the bottle on its base, on these institutions, so everything is not concentrated in the presidency."[76]

And Gérard Latortue? He had voted for Manigat, a close personal friend of many years, and not for Préval. He was glad that the elections had been held, but as soon as Préval was in office, he would leave Haiti, returning to the United States, and not come back.

"Having lived abroad for so long, I didn't know what Haiti had become," he later told me. "Had I known I would have never accepted the position."[77]

* * *

Following his election, Préval flew to Washington to meet with U.S. President George W. Bush in a brief parlay during which Bush "congratulated president-elect Préval and noted that he was looking forward to working" with him.[78] Underlying the somewhat unique goodwill he was able to generate, Préval would also quickly make visits to both Cuban president Fidel Castro in Havana and Venezuelan president Hugo Chávez in Caracas. Préval promised that, under his government, Haiti would have a "non-politicized police force."[79] In a late April visit to Caracas, Préval announced that Haiti would be integrating into PetroCaribe, the new energy initiative launched by Chávez's government to supply oil to Caribbean nations at discounted prices and with an extended time slated for repayment.[80]

Everyone was waiting for Préval's inauguration. Two security guards from the U.S. Embassy were slain at the beginning of March.[81] A few weeks later, another embassy guard would be killed.[82] Over the weekend of 11–12 March, four policemen were slain in the capital.[83] In late March, 28 human skulls were discovered around the capital, first in Pétionville and then Canapé Vert, apparently after having been dumped by a truck that was passing through the area.[84] In the weeks before Préval took the reins of government, both Carlo Lochard and Renan Etienne, imprisoned for their alleged involvement in the August 2005 Martissant football killings, were ordered released by Judge Pérez Paul, and walked out of jail.[85]

The April runoff elections for parliament, despite sporadic violence, were "positive," according to CEP president Max Mathurin, although the turnout of voters was very low.[86] The representative of the European Union observer mission estimated that turnout was between 8 percent and 15 percent.[87] Among those elected to the senate were Youri Latortue at the head of his Latibonit Ann Aksyon (LAA) party in the Artibonite, Lespwa candidate Jean Hector Anacacis (trouncing two Lavalas-affiliated candidates) for the West Department, and the Protestant pastor Andrys Riché of the OPL in the Grand Anse.[88] The final composition of parliament would thus be instructive of both the disintegration of Lavalas and the strengthening of the left-of-center social democratic current. Lavalas gained only four seats in the senate, the same number as political parties such as Fusion and OPL. By comparison, Lespwa won 11. In the Chamber of Deputies, Lespwa garnered a total of 19 seats, the Alliance Démocratique (Alyans) took 13, the OPL ten and Lavalas only six.[89] Such results, and the palpable disgust so many in Haiti felt for the party, would not stop Reuters, for example, from running stories even years later referring to the emasculated Lavalas cadres as Haiti's "most popular political party."[90] Fusion's Micha Gaillard told a reporter that his party "was going to support the government of President Préval, there will be no obstructionism," while Evans Paul said the new president could "count upon our support in parliament. We can't demand that he share his victory with us. He is the one who won."[91]

According to a grassroots Lavalas activist, having failed to derail the elections, by mid-2006 Aristide had intensified his contact with his followers in Haiti, urging them to demonstrate for his immediate return.[92] At a late April press conference, the Lavalas radical base, including Jean-Marie Samedi, said they would launch a new round of street protests calling for Aristide to return.[93] Underlying the complex, fluid nature of the armed groups, however, in early May, General Toutou's gang was said to have executed and burned three suspected kidnappers in the slum.[94] During that same month, at least ten PNH officers would be slain in the capital.[95]

As May began, René Civil was arrested at the Jimanì/Malpasse border crossing as he attempted to return to Haiti just before Préval's inauguration.[96] The same week, public hearings finally began in Gonaïves into the La Scierie killings, but by this point AVIGES was speaking openly of a Préval "plot" to free Neptune and the other detainees.[97]

* * *

Visiting with Canadian Prime Minister Stephen Harper in Ottawa two weeks before his inauguration, Préval told reporters that "elections have taken place at the presidential level, at the legislative level, but we have to continue to support this democracy because people voted for an improvement in their lives and that takes resources. We are in a country where we have, in the capital, two hours of electricity per day. Students can't study, businesses can't work, industry can't work. We need immediate aid."[98] Canada responded by adding $48 million to its Haiti aid budget, $18 million of which was slated to help pay Haiti's debt to the Inter-American Development Bank (IADB).[99]

Haiti's Chamber of Deputies was sworn in on 8 May, with the senate following a day later, with Lespwa deputy Steven Benoît (brother of Préval's second wife) saying that the body's first challenge would be "to last four years without a coup d'état."[100] In parliament, Lespwa had two of its number, Eric Jean-Jacques and Joseph Lambert, as presidents of the Chamber of Deputies and the senate respectively.[101] The priorities of the Chamber of Deputies were illuminated by a demand – quickly granted – that each member receive between $15,000 and $25,000 towards the purchase of a new car to "improve their working conditions." Eric Jean-Jacques justified thus $2 million expenditure from Haiti's treasury by saying that officials needed a vehicle of "a certain robustness ... [to] stop arriving tired to parliament."[102]

At the Te Deum at Port-au-Prince's cathedral to mark Préval's inauguration, several noted Lavalassians, including former officials of Aristide's government, appeared to observe the new president's return.[103]

During the speech that followed, Préval asked Haitians for "peace and unity" and said that "the cooperation between the various sectors of national life that has begun must be consolidated by humility."[104] He continued that "we have to make peace, we have to have a dialogue ... Peace is the key to open doors, the door of investment to create jobs and employment, the door for tourists to come to the country, for roads, more schools, more hospitals."[105] Préval announced that Jacques-Édouard Alexis, who had served as his prime minister from 1999 to 2001, was his pick to occupy that post again, and called for a rapid approval from parliament.[106] The day of his inauguration, with Venezuelan Vice President José Vicente Rangel signing for his country, Préval inked an agreement that made Haiti's ascension into PetroCaribe his first official act as president. Venezuela committed to providing Haiti with 7,000 barrels of oil a day at a preferential rate. That same day, a Venezuelan tanker appeared in the capital's harbor, like a vision of hope, bearing 10,000 barrels.[107]

CHAPTER SIX
GIVE US PEACE
OR REST IN PEACE

Shortly after Préval's 2006 inauguration, Juan Gabriel Valdés would be replaced as the head of MINUSTAH by Edmond Mulet, a veteran Guatemala diplomat who had previously served as Guatemala's ambassador to the European Union and the United States. Mulet had only been in Haiti once before, during the brief interim of Aristide's first truncated term in 1991, and yet, strangely, the office of the MINUSTAH chief on the fifth floor of the Hotel Christopher was the exact same room where he had stayed.[1] Though the pair would have an often fractious relationship, Préval and Mulet would work together to stabilize Haiti after years of upheaval and integrate it back into the international community, the latter typified by Haiti's full readmission to CARICOM shortly after Préval took office, with CARICOM Secretary-General Edwin Carrington telling the Haitian president at a meeting in Basseterre that "the community stands ready to work with you."[2]

But there was immense work to do. Despite its new president, the capital remained gripped by a terrifying insecurity and the internecine squabbling between the country's security and political factions. To accelerate the process, Préval formed a Commission Nationale de Désarmement Démantèlement et Réinsertion (CNDDR), headed by Alix Fils-Aimé, a former political prisoner who had been tortured under Jean-Claude Duvalier.

On 19 May, Lucienne Heurtelou, the octogenarian widow of pivotal Haitian president Dumarsais Estimé, was slain during a robbery in the capital's Bois-Verna district.[3] Two of the alleged culprits were arrested, but then freed from prison in what one observer called "record time" after having presumably paid a bribe.[4] In a 25 May letter to Commissaire du Gouvernement Fredd'Herck Lény, the head of Haiti's judicial police, Michael Lucius, who had decried corruption in Haiti's judiciary, denounced what he charged was a plot against him by rival police officers, judges, lawyers, members of Martissant's Baz Pilate gang and even some members of the press. As a sign of the rot within the system, he pointed to the cases of former police officer Harold Gaspard, arrested for alleged involvement in the 2000 murder of an employee of the Fondasyon Kole Zèpòl (Fonkoze) micro-credit organization and other crimes who was released in May 2006 "without any form of trial," and the release of Robenson "Ti Ben" Bien Aimé, one of the chief suspects in the murder of Estimé's widow.[5] A Port-au-Prince judge, Napela Saintil, for her part, stated that an arrested gangster claimed he "worked" for the judicial police, and said that Lucius must explain himself.[6] Thus began a protracted tit-for-tat battle between the judiciary and the police that would last for much of the rest of the year.

A meeting to attempt to bridge the divisions within Lavalas held in Port-au-Prince on 2 June instead widened them, exposing a bitter gulf between a faction led by, among others, René Civil, which pledged eternal fealty to Aristide and wanted to continue demonstrating for his return, and another faction including former Chamber of Deputies president Rudy Hériveaux and Lavalas baz leaders such as Bel-Air's Jean-Baptiste Jean-Philippe (better known as Samba Boukman), who had become part of the CNDDR in an effort to bring peace to his community, and who was among those who wanted to engage in the electoral process. Civil, accompanied by "many chimere," attempted to disrupt the meeting, demanding that all present commit to a plan of street demonstrations. This was met with reproach from Boukman, who called it reckless with the lives of Lavalas supporters, whom Boukman said Civil had deserted when he fled Haiti. Also attended by former Lavalas senators Gérard Gilles and Yvon Feuillé and activist Lovinsky Pierre-Antoine, the meeting broke up in acrimony with the Civil faction accusing the others of being agents of the CIA and MINUSTAH.[7]

After a 7 June clash between gang members and MINUSTAH forces in Cité Soleil left at least six dead,[8] Jacques Édouard Alexis and U.S. Ambassador Janet Sanderson, who had replaced James Foley in February, announced a joint U.S.–Haitian program in Cité Soleil to help provide residents of the quarter with increased access to drinking water, with its $5 million budget funded by USAID via the IOM.[9] In late June, the Association pour la Santé Intégrale de la Famille (APROSIFA) health organization warned how the violence in Martissant was leaving mothers too afraid to bring their children to the group's nutritional centers.[10] Over a mere few days in July, 40 people would die, with

Grand Ravine and Ti Bois each blaming the other for the violence.[11] During July alone, Médecins Sans Frontières would treat more than 120 people for gunshot wounds at its clinic in Port-au-Prince.[12]

At the beginning of July, Mario Andrésol was confirmed to a renewable three-year tenure to head the PNH by Haiti's senate, with no votes against and only two senators, Joseph Lambert and Gabriel Fortuné, abstaining. In his remarks, Andrésol asked for "the grace, mercy and forgiveness of the Almighty" for the nation and "the courage, wisdom and insight" to carry out his mission.[13] Between May and June, at least a dozen policemen had been slain.[14] Préval announced that Luc-Eucher Joseph, a former inspector general of the PNH who had fled Haiti under pressure from Aristide-linked groups in 2000, would become the new secretary of state for public security.[15]

* * *

In late July, I returned to Haiti, crossing the border from the Dominican Republic aboard a bus on my thirty-third birthday after spending a lovely evening visiting with friends in Santo Domingo's salubrious Zona Colonial. I arrived in Port-au-Prince to find a city at war. I was staying at the home of an old friend near my old place in Pacot, where an extended family from the countryside had moved in and welcomed me warmly into their midst. At night, as the female members of the family cooked and washed outside in the courtyard, one of them, a young girl of about 17, would sing Creole religious songs in an achingly beautiful voice. Following my usual routine of shared taxi cabs and moto taxis, at one point I found myself sharing one with a uniformed PNH officer and we started chatting about the security situation, at which point he told me of a ten-year-old he had arrested who had told him he was going to "put a bullet" in the police officer's head. "And then, at the station, we had this electronic keyboard in a corner, and he went over to it and started playing it and starting to sing," he told me, shaking his head.

When I met Lionel Delatour, vice president of the Centre pour la Libre Entreprise et la Démocratie (CLED), for a drink at the Hotel Montana, its veranda overlooking the sweep of Haiti's coast as it curved north beneath bare mountains, he appeared concerned.

"President Préval's honeymoon was a short one, and there is no doubt that there are forces that want him to fail," he told me. "The election brought a lull, but by June some sectors in Lavalas realized that Préval's first priority was not to bring Aristide back ... And Andrésol is doing some cleaning up in the PNH and there are some forces saying 'Over my dead body.'"

When the American photographer Thos Robinson, Radio Métropole reporter Amos Charles and I visited Martissant the following day, we found plenty of death to contemplate. A ghostly silence wrapped itself around scores of burned tin shacks, concrete hovels gutted and scorched black by flames, and jagged rocks spattered with blood that formed the paths of the hillside slum. Dozens of people scurried down the zone's Avenue Bolosse, their belongings piled on their heads. I found over 300 people taking refuge in a nearby Baptist mission. Some women and young children were sitting on the open ground under palm trees, while others were sleeping on the concrete floor of a steaming conference hall, trying to shelter from the summer rains.

"They were shooting a lot of people and everybody had to run," Marie Julien, who fled Grand Ravine with her six children and now sat under the blazing sun in the mission's parking lot, told me. "They burned our house. I don't know why they are doing this."

"We can't sleep; we are very hungry because we have nothing to eat," said Avile Pierre, an elderly woman, as she sat among the exhausted refugees at the mission. "Our homes are gone, and we don't have any money to go anywhere else."

When Thos, Amos and I climbed up a ladder and over a wall that brought us into Grand Ravine (the usual entrances were more or less free-fire zones), we found almost no one on the street of the usually bustling quarter.

"Go down there and you can see for yourself," Bruner Esterne, a silver-haired local activist told me as he came out to greet us and lifted his orange T-shirt to reveal a fresh bullet wound in his side. "There is nothing but death in this neighborhood, no life at all."

He motioned toward a dirt path surrounded on all sides with still-smoldering shacks, shell casings littering the ground, and scorched animals lying among the ruins.

In front of a shuttered *borlette* (lottery bank), we found a group of fierce-looking young men, pistols bulging from underneath their shirts, swilling rum from champagne glasses. Sitting at their center was Wilkens "Chien Chaud" Pierre, the leader of one of Grand Ravine's armed *baz*.

"You can see what the gangs from Ti Bois have done," said Wilkens, dressed in a New York Knicks basketball jersey and a baseball cap pulled down over a scar that crisscrossed one eyebrow. "They have killed people, burned down their houses, some police are giving them weapons."

Wilkens went on to talk of how rogue elements within the PNH were involved in the killings, specifically charging that Carlo Lochard was financing and organizing the Lame Ti Manchèt. Heading into Ti Bois, we saw dozens of people carrying belongings down Route des Dalles, and encountered more burned houses, shell casings strewn about the thoroughfare and a few stray goats baying mournfully. We were approached by a group of rough-looking young men inquiring as to our purpose in the neighborhood. Engaging them in conversation, one of them left and came back with photos of burned houses and mutilated corpses, including one of a pregnant woman, that they said came from massacres the Grand Ravine gangs had committed in the neighborhood in October 2001, May 2005 and November 2005.

"The latest killings, this was Wilkens and Ti Lou," one of the men said, mentioning the suspected assassin of Jean Dominique now believed to be based in Grand Ravine.

As we spoke, the Lycée Jean Dominique, a high school built in tribute to the journalist and straddling the border between Grand Ravine and Ti Bois, sat within view, now abandoned and riddled with bullet holes, as if in mute testament that the violence which felled the reporter was still a part of daily life.

"We are suffering. They burn houses, they kill people with guns and machetes," said a young man in a group loitering at a small, abandoned band-shell further up the path, marking the apex of a hill covered with gutted homes. He threw a blue tank-top over his head to shield himself from the blazing sun. His leg sported a recently healed bullet wound.

Further down the path we spoke to a local man who told us of a secret grave in a coconut palm grove where the gangs dumped their victims' bodies, which we looked for but were unable to find. We did, however, find a UN post in the heart of the zone, manned by three Sri Lankan soldiers who could speak neither English nor French nor Creole nor Spanish nor Portuguese (all of which I attempted to engage them in). We saw no sign of the PNH.

"We have children and we are very afraid," said Ti Bois resident Destine Jocelyn as she nervously peered out from a square, concrete home on an other-wise largely deserted path. "Those gangs from Grand Ravine come to kill us."

The following day, I met with Edmond Mulet at his office in the Hotel Christopher.

"We cannot prevent what is going on in Martissant," Mulet told me, going on to say that Andrésol only had "about 600 policemen" he could really count on. "We are here to support the government and we don't have an executive mandate. I have to wait for the government to request that. We always have to go in accompanying or supporting PNH actions."

"If you take a picture of Haiti today, the overall security situation is appalling, it's really bad," Mulet went on. "But if you compare this picture of today with the one of six months ago, or a year ago, or the situation two years ago, I think there's been an incredible positive evolution. We think Andrésol is an excellent professional. He knows what he wants, he's a decent person and he's very committed to fight against corruption within the police force at large and in Haiti overall. And Préval and Alexis have given him instructions to never, ever accept any kind of political pressure for anything."

Mulet knew something about pressure himself. If anything, he had been greeted with even more hostility than Valdés in certain quarters. An initial attempt to reform a justice system in which 92 percent of incarcerated inmates had never seen a judge was greeted with banners courtesy of the ANAMAH reading *Edmond Mulet est un âne têtu* (Edmond Mulet is a stubborn donkey) strung around the capital. He told me that MINUSTAH was requesting additional reinforcement by specialized units, anti-kidnapping and SWAT units so the mission was better prepared to support the PNH.

"The mandate for MINUSTAH is to stabilize the country, and the ones who are destabilizing the country are the kidnappers, the gang leaders, supported by political interests, by drug traffickers, by people who would prefer to have impunity here and who benefit from the lack of rule of law ... [But] Préval formed his government with all the major political parties and kept up a dialogue with the private sector, civil society groups, human rights groups, and they really want this government to succeed. I think people are tired of going round and round in this cycle of violence and confrontation, and nothing positive coming out of it. They recognize that this is a legitimate government, it's a five-year mandate."

As we concluded our chat, Mulet spoke of what he said he hoped was the finite nature of the peacekeeping mission itself.

"How many times has the international community had to intervene in Haiti in the last 20 to 25 years?," he asked, somewhat rhetorically. "When you see the amount of not millions but billions of dollars that has been poured into this country and there's nothing on the ground to show for it, now we have to learn from those lessons. We have to have an exit strategy. The international community at some point has to leave Haiti, we can't be here forever, and in order to do that we have to leave behind institutions ... The basic thing here is to establish the rule of law, because without that you will have nothing."

The following day I watched Préval greet UN Secretary-General Kofi Annan at the National Palace, its perimeter ringed by heavily armed Jordanian peacekeepers.

"We have achieved a lot together in our partnership, but much more needs to be done," Annan told the assembled press, adding that he was proposing that the UN Security Council extend MINUSTAH's mission for 12 months as opposed to the standard six months, and that he would ask for additional police trainers to aid the PNH. "We are determined to work with the government to end the problem of insecurity. You are off to a good start and you can count on us."

When Préval, slight and elegant as I remembered him, his wispy grey beard neatly trimmed, stepped to the microphone, he spoke only briefly, as befitted his reputation as a man of few words.

"The Haitian people are very pleased to welcome the Secretary-General," said Préval, addressing the audience of foreign dignitaries, government officials and journalists in Creole. "The situation is not easy, but with the support of the United Nations, we will move forward. Of all our problems, the problem of security, from which everyone suffers, is paramount."

When the men finished, I walked across the Champ de Mars and bought some chicken from a woman grilling it on the roadside, washed down with an ice-cold Prestige. In front of me, I saw the slums of Bel-Air rising. I had been coming to Haiti for nearly a decade by this point, and so little had seemed to change. Actually, it had gotten worse. I was depressed. I decided to go and visit an old friend.

The Haitian industrialist Patrick Brun was a decade older than me, but we had bonded during the final days of Aristide, when the country seemed to be off to a more hopeful future, and he was among the vanguard of those I would describe as the enlightened elite, advocating a concept of "social entrepreneurship" that acknowledged that the country could not move forward on the model it had before.

Patrick's business, with its factory located in the red zone of the Complexe Bâtimat, was a hardware and building material company that had been founded by his father in 1971. After studying finance and marketing at the University of Miami, Patrick had returned to Haiti with his Guyanese wife and taken over family business.

It had not been easy. Since 2003, he had been the victim of three kidnapping attempts, including one where his car flipped over and he ended up upside down as he fled his assailants, who left him for dead. The factory, which once had 250 employees, had been forced to scale back to 200, then to 160, and then finally to 120, and was probably going to have to cut down again. The factory's workers occasionally needed a MINUSTAH escort to get to and from the plant, and gangs broke into the factory one night and left a message saying that they were going to come back and destroy it. One deaf factory worker had been robbed of his $30 pay and had the bicycle he got to work on stolen. When I took a moto taxi out to the building, gunfire was audible from the nearby *bidonville* of Simon Pelé.

"We are having to make very serious business decisions in order to stay in operation," Patrick told me as he smoked a cigarette as we stood outside the factory.

"But we keep on," he said. "It's more than investing and getting a return, it's more than creating wealth. You have to be able to create wealth *and* value. You cannot create wealth while you are destroying and exploiting the values of your community because nothing is left after that. Polarization is mainly what put us where we are today, and I hope the government will support a private sector that shows indications of wanting to try and resolve these problems. If these young kids slip into criminality two or three times, it's very hard for them to go back to normal life."

The following day, Patrick and I drove up to a cottage that he had in the mountains of Belot above the city. The contrast to the horror in Martissant was profound. The air smelled fragrantly of coffee beans, and leek plantations dotted the hillsides. One could see local peasant farmers growing strawberries, apples and artichokes, planting bamboo to stop soil erosion (as bamboo makes a sturdy "net" of roots), as well as elephant grass, whose root system holds dirt well. At Patrick's cabin, overlooking a broad valley, the air was thick with the smell of pine and the buzz of bees. The sounds of *rara* band from a village below were filtering up the mountainside.

"We have to grow, but our environment has to grow also. We need to incorporate into the core of our businesses the impact we are going to need to have in our environment, so everything around us can grow as we are growing. We have to realize this is all interconnected."

That night, Thos and I went to a concert by Chill, the new band of the famous Haitian singer Jude Jean, at a club in the Bois Verna neighborhood, which was, in fact, little more than a palm-lined dancefloor. As the sensual rhythms of *konpa* unfurled like an elastic band of sound, the middle-class couples danced groin to groin in a tight embrace, their eyes closed, in a brief moment of ecstasy and respite under Haiti's nighttime stars.

* * *

On the weekend of 22–23 July, Ronald "Black Ronald" Dauphin, the former Bale Wouze member and one of the accused perpetrators of the La Scierie massacre almost two years earlier, was rearrested in the Port-au-Prince suburb of Pernier by the PNH in the course of an operation against a kidnapping ring (a recently kidnapped doctor was freed during the course of the raid).[16] Ronald had been among those who escaped during the mass February 2005 jailbreak from the Pénitencier National. Earlier in the summer, Haiti's struggle against impunity had suffered a blow when former Minister of the Interior Jocelerme Privert, who had been in office during some of the Aristide regime's worst excesses, walked out of prison a free man. He had been in jail for a little over two years.[17] By the end of July, former Prime Minister Yvon Neptune, who had been head of the CSPN at the time of the killings, was also free. Neither man had ever faced trial. Weighing in on the release of Neptune and Privert, Human Rights Watch noted that "the La Scierie case was never fully investigated and the atrocities that the two men allegedly committed remain unpunished."[18]

The international community apparently had bigger fish to fry than worrying about justice for the victims of La Scierie, though. At a late July gathering in Port-au-Prince, international donors pledged $750 million to Haiti, more than the $540 million Préval had requested.[19] During the conference, Mulet met with Ambassador Sanderson and Assistant Secretary Thomas Shannon to tell them that he had information that Aristide was manipulating "agents" and "instigators" who had "stoked public fear and warned of a new round of violence" in the capital. Mulet also told them that, at his request, Kofi Annan had met with South African President Mbeki during the previous month's African Union summit "to ensure that Aristide remained in South Africa."[20]

By this point, it was believed that Evens Jeune had brokered a truce between gang factions in Cité Soleil,[21] but between early June and early August at least 100 people were slain in Port-au-Prince.[22] As automatic weapons fire crackled around the capital's international airport on 31 July, two armed thieves were shot down by police on the corner of the capital's Rue du Centre and Rue des Fronts Forts, one of them still grasping the paper money he had stolen from market women in his hand as he lay dying.[23] On 2 August, the owner of Place Boyer's beloved Boulangerie Mont Carmel and his two-year-old son were shot and killed by bandits and his wife wounded just after he had closed up shop for the day.[24] Days later, gunmen firing around the airport road wounded at least two people, and gunfire was heard throughout Nazon, Christ-Roi and Delmas that night.[25] The same day, two died during a joint MINUSTAH–PNH operation in Cité Militaire.[26] An Italian businessman was killed and his wife kidnapped during the course of a robbery.[27] The bodies of two men and a woman, dead from gunshot wounds, were found on Rue Lamarre on 10 August.[28]

During a visit to the Village Solidarité *bidonville* near the airport, Préval told reporters that "the holders of illegal weapons in the country are faced with a single alternative: surrender the weapons by integrating into the CNDDR program of the United Nations and the Haitian government or die when you are disarmed by force."[29] He said his government's strategy would be "to combine strength with dialogue."[30] Others familiar with his thinking said that, through interlocutors, Préval had given a stark ultimatum to the gang leaders who were destabilizing his government: give us peace or rest in peace. Sensing the public mood perhaps even better than his boss, Jacques-Édouard Alexis said in early August to the gangs that "you surrender your weapons and enter the CNDDR program. If you refuse, you'll be killed."[31] Speaking to Radio Métropole, Senate President Joseph Lambert said he was against any negotiation with "bandits," and charged that Préval seemed willing to "continue dialogue with armed groups until they take control of all areas of Port-au-Prince and even the National Palace."[32]

* * *

On 14 August, several thousand protesters – the Cité Soleil gang leaders Amaral Duclona and Evens Jeune among them – rallied at the ruins of St. Jean Bosco before marching to the National Palace, demanding the return of Aristide and chanting that *Préval ak asayan se marasa* (Préval and the assailants are twins, a reference to Préval's old nickname vis-à-vis Aristide). Led by, among others,

117

Lavalas militants Jean-Marie Samedi, Lovinsky Pierre Antoine and Deshomme Présengloir, the marchers also chanted slogans against Réginald Boulos, Andy Apaid, Charles Baker and Evans Paul, accusing them of forming gangs (an ironic charge, given the personages at the march's start). The demonstration marked one of the first large-scale public protests against Préval and a rather stark reminder of the delicate balancing act he was performing.[33] The same day, following a farcical trial "announced at the last minute" and conducted without a jury, and during which only witnesses for the defense appeared (some of the accused represented by BAI's Mario Joseph), Judge Fritzner Fils-Aimé released Lavalassians Annette Auguste, Paul Raymond, Yvon Antoine and Georges Honoré, citing a "lack of evidence" to prove their involvement in the December 2003 university attack.[34] At this point, of the Lavalassian grandees accused of dire crimes, only Amanus Mayette was left in prison. After their release, the former prisoners held a press conference, attended by Mario Joseph, where they announced that they would continue mobilization to force Aristide's return from South Africa, with Antoine strongly criticizing Préval for calling on the gangs to disarm.[35] After the freeing of the prisoners, students at the UEH, some of whom had suffered through the December 2003 attack, protested, with one student telling local media that the releases were "a political decision to appease the political and security climate ... Freeing people who had participated in wrongdoing against the university, it is a proof that the Préval–Alexis government gives no importance to the fight against injustice and impunity."[36] Around the same time, the former Lavalas deputy Nawoon Marcellus, who had been in exile for two years, returned to his base near Cap-Haïtien.[37] In a written response to parliamentary questions, South African Foreign Minister Nkosazana Dlamini-Zuma stated that Aristide would be treated "as a guest of the South African government for as long as is necessary."[38]

***

Given such a set of circumstances, it was perhaps unsurprising that the UN Security Council renewed MINUSTAH's mandate for an additional six months.[39] Some in Haiti, however, were pushing for what they said was a more permanent solution to the country's ills. In August, the Senate Committee on Defense, Justice and Security, chaired by Youri Latortue, recommended that Préval reconstitute a new Haitian army, saying that the PNH were "facing difficulties and deficiencies of all kinds."[40] Latortue himself would go even further, suggesting, in his capacity as the head of the senate's security committee, that specialized PNH units made up of former soldiers be tasked to deal with the capital's gang problem.[41] A few weeks later, Marc Elie Saint Hillien, the departmental delegate for the Artibonite (he had been appointed to the position by the Alexandre/Latortue government to serve as the government's representative in the department the previous year), shared his own views of Latortue with the U.S. Embassy, charging that Latortue had become the "mafia boss" of Gonaïves, and that he had deep connections with the Armée Cannibale of Raboteau, as well as with the gangs in the Jubilé and Des Cahos areas of the city.[42] (Latortue would later successfully sue Saint Hillien for defamation and win compensation.)

In late August, Rodney Alcide, a representative from Préval's Lespwa party in the Chamber of Deputies for the north's Plaisance, was kidnapped along with a bodyguard and driver while driving through Carrefour. He was released after several days.[43] Days later, a raid by gunmen on the wharf in Gonaïves left two policemen wounded.[44] In a move that was welcomed by many, on 18 August, Préval announced that he was naming Claudy Gassant, the former investigating judge in the Jean Dominique case, as *commissaire du gouvernement* for the West Department, including Port-au-Prince, a district attorney-like appointment that came with broad powers for investigation.[45] One of Gassant's first moves was to oversee the re-arrest of René Civil, stopped by police in Pétionville riding in a stolen car (and in the company of a PNH deserter), in a move that police said was "related strictly to banditry."[46] Gassant promptly ordered him to be held in the Pénitencier National while his lawyer, the BAI's Mario Joseph, alleged that the arrest was certainly political.[47] Another former apparatchik of the *ancien régime*, former National Palace security chief Oriel Jean, would be released in the U.S. that September after serving a little over two years on drug trafficking charges (a sentence greatly reduced by his cooperation with authorities) and would get a job as a parking lot attendant at Fort Lauderdale International Airport.

* * *

According to the Commission Épiscopale Nationale Justice et Paix (JILAP), 228 people had been slain in and around the capital between June and September, including at least 11 policemen.[48] In early September, another wave of violence hit the capital, with at least three killed in Solino, a former diplomat who had served in the Dominican Republic murdered in Delmas, and a policeman killed in Pétionville, all in the space of a few hours.[49] Just outside my favorite Pétionville restaurant, Anba Tonel, a young couple, Véronique Valmé and Carl Lubin Zounon, were slain by thieves.[50] On the evening of 14 September, former FADH Colonel Guy François was gunned down in Pétionville (he had been jailed without trial for over two years for suspected but unproven involvement in the December 2001 attack on the National Palace).[51] Leaving a wedding in Delmas, Robenson Casséus was kidnapped and shot eight times by abductors when they realized that his family was too poor to pay a ransom. He feigned death on the ground for hours, shooing off a pig that tried to devour his bleeding left arm. Miraculously, he survived.[52] In mid-September, the head of Haiti's civil aviation authority was kidnapped.[53]

The nature of the violence remained complex, however. Speaking to Radio Kiskeya from his bastion of Simon Pelé in September, the gang leader William "Ti Blan" Baptiste said: "We are not criminals or armed gangs. We are political combatants, and this situation requires political negotiations."[54] As insecurity spiraled, chaos erupted within the PNH, with a judge, Napela Saintil, issuing an arrest warrant against judicial police chief Michael Lucius, who said the judge wanted him in jail so he could be assassinated.[55]

* * *

On 21 September, Bruner Esterne, the community activist from Grand Ravine whom I had interviewed in the neighborhood little more than a month earlier, was murdered by gunmen while returning from a meeting concerning the July 2005 soccer massacre.[56] Residents of Martissant demonstrated before parliament, charging that the Lavalas deputy from the area, Jean Clédor Méril, had "allowed armed gangs to evolve with impunity" in the neighborhood.[57] In an early October broadcast, Radio Kiskeya lamented that "armed gangs openly controlled areas of the Haitian capital and the population is terrorized."[58] The U.S. Embassy in Port-au-Prince announced that it was partially lifting the arms embargo in place on Haiti since the 1991 coup, allowing the government to purchase firearms, body armor and other items for the police in order to "fight against rampant criminal and gang activity."[59] As students from the UEH launched a protest against the MINUSTAH presence in the country, setting up burning barricades and hurling bottles and stones that broke the windshields of passing cars,[60] in an echo of Haiti's dark past, on 22 October, several Duvalierists

– including Jean-Claude's partner Véronique Roy and Rony Gilot – gathered in Port-au-Prince to "celebrate" the forty-ninth anniversary of Papa Doc's ascension to power and announce the creation of an eponymous foundation to "celebrate the achievements of Duvalierism."[61]

* * *

By late October, Lavalas *organisation populaire* (OP) leader Hilaire Prophète was threatening to launch Opération Pa Ka Tan-n (Operation Can't Wait), which he said would be a successor to Operation Baghdad if the government did not reintegrate Aristide loyalists who had been booted off the state's payroll after his ouster. Prophète told Radio Métropole that "we'll start another stage in our movement as we used Operation Baghdad."[62] It would appear that Prophète's words were not an idle threat, as self-described Lavalas militants erected flaming barricades in Bel-Air days after his declaration.[63] In Martissant, gunmen killed one and wounded several, telling Radio Métropole that they were ready to face down PNH and MINUSTAH forces and would sow panic until Lavalas activists were reinstated in their jobs in government enterprises.[64]

Throughout October and November 2006 the gangs had been advancing, seizing areas and occupying roads to the point where they had virtually surrounded the airport. Two Jordanian MINUSTAH peacekeepers were ambushed and killed in Cité Soleil on 11 November, only steps away from the main fortified UN position there.[65] Even Fred Joseph, Préval's finance minister from his first term, was kidnapped, as was former senator Schubert Alexis.[66] Although Haiti's political class spoke out in protest at the violence, it seemed unwilling or unable to put an end to it.[67] The work of MINUSTAH troops and PNH was further complicated by Préval's somewhat ambiguous relationships with the armed actors in the capital's slums. When the PNH and UN soldiers would stage a raid, Préval would sometimes call them, furious, telling them they had arrested some of "his" people.[68]

In November, two crimes would shock the nation and force the president to act. First, it was six-year-old Carl Rubens Francillon's turn to be kidnapped. Though his parents paid the ransom demanded by his captors, the boy's putrefying corpse was found more than two weeks later in Cap-Haïtien.[69] At the boy's funeral, the child's father told reporters: "The situation cannot remain like this, something must be done. If society does not rise up there will be nothing left of this country."[70] Then, less than two weeks later, the young student Farah Natacha Kerbie Dessources was kidnapped from the capital's suburb of Santo and savagely tortured before being murdered and dumped in the street two days later. Dessources' mother and brother both had to eventually flee Haiti after receiving repeated death threats, and they did so saying that neither the police nor the judiciary had contacted them regarding the investigation into the young woman's death.[71] Before they left, however, the girl's funeral turned into a spontaneous demonstration against insecurity and the Préval administration, with hundreds of angry protesters shouting slogans against the government.[72] Two of Dessources' alleged killers, Pierre Leger and Millet Jean Elie aka Ti Elie, were arrested months later, in the capital[73] and in the Grande Anse town of Pestel[74] respectively. Another assailant, this one only 15 years old, was arrested later still.[75]

Compelled by dozens of gunmen circulating among the crowd, hundreds of residents from Decartes and Ti Bois blocked the Carrefour road at the start of the working week on 13 November, demanding the release of various gang members and threatening to scuttle the upcoming local elections.[76] Over the night of 19–20 November, gunmen opened fire on a public market in Grand Ravine, killing at least six and wounding seven others.[77] Beginning on 20 November, gun battles raged as armed groups from Ti Bois and Descartes attacked Grand Ravine during a cultural presentation designed to promote peace between the warring gangs there. At least five people, including Wilkens "Chien Chaud" Pierre, the gang leader I had interviewed the previous summer there, were killed.[78] The Ti Bois gangs denied their involvement in the attack, but few were convinced, with Radio Kiskeya contemptuously referring to them as "posing as altar boys."[79] In mid-November, the pastor of an Adventist church in Cité Soleil accused MINUSTAH soldiers of repeatedly firing on the building and wounding his parishioners.[80]

At the end of November, despite a growing public outcry following the Dessources and Francillon killings, Jacques Édouard Alexis announced that the government would "continue to negotiate with the bandits."[81] At the same time, he said, of the $750 million pledged to Haiti at the July meeting in Port-au-Prince, "99 percent of this money has not really been disbursed."[82] Days after Alexis spoke, a 30-year-old man and a six-year-old child were killed during the course of a car-jacking on Rue Macajoux.[83] In early December, another "jail-break" occurred at the capital's Pénitencier National, during which, mysteriously, at least 30 prisoners managed to escape despite not a single shot being fired.[84]

Surveying the situation, one report concluded that "if MINUSTAH [is not] willing and able to confront the gang threat, the likely consequences [will be] the collapse of the Préval administration and the failure of the UN mission."[85]

In December, local voting began in a feeble, disorderly, but relatively peaceful fashion in the capital, except in Delmas 33 and Martissant, where bursts of automatic weapons fire discouraged voters from heading to the polls.[86] The voting was to fill 1,420 posts of the *conseils communaux*, the *conseils d'administration des sections communales* (CASEC), the *assemblées des sections communales* (ASEC) and *délégués de ville* (DV), plus a handful of parliamentary seats.[87] At Limonade, in the north, however, a Molotov cocktail was thrown into a voting station, exploding and killing one.[88] Nevertheless, CEP president Max Mathurin pronounced himself "satisfied" and said the voters "showed maturity throughout the election day."[89] The round of voting saw the election of wealthy businessman Rudolph Boulos to the senate as the representative of Fusion for the Northeast Department, as well as his Fusion colleague Judnel Jean to represent the same area.[90]

Later on the day of voting, PNH officer André Jean Noël was shot and killed at his residence in Martissant, an act that would have fateful consequences.[91] On the night of 3 December, four people were slain in the Bolosse area of Martissant in what was believed to be a revenge attack for Noël's killing, with two found in a Nissan burned so thoroughly that "the violence of the flames almost reduced the two bodies to ashes." The perpetrators were allegedly from Baz Pilate, who had considered Noël an ally. Intense gunfire continued in the zone throughout the following day.[92] Only a few days later, Martissant was again rocked with violence, with Radio Métropole reporting that Grand Ravine gangs from the Baz Pilate had attempted to invade the La Foi, Descartes and Martissant 1 areas of the zone, leaving at least two dead and several wounded. Grand Ravine residents said an attack by the Lame Ti Manchèt had also left two dead. Some residents interviewed also claimed that UN soldiers had aided the Baz Pilate in killing and burning the body of one of the victims.[93]

By mid-December, a wide and growing outcry was building at the government's attitude towards the gangs, which some saw as ineffectualness and others as outright collaboration.[94] Following the kidnapping of a schoolgirl and shooting of her father in the heart of the busy Turgeau district, Radio Kiskeya bemoaned that "the civilian population feels terribly alone in its fight against the scourge of insecurity."[95] As the month drew on, two busloads of students were kidnapped to the north of Port-au-Prince.[96] Days later, two more buses – these regular *camionettes* – were seized by gunmen who posed as passengers before drawing their weapons. They were driven to Cité Soleil.[97] Even a sitting senator, the OPL's Andrys Riché, was kidnapped – it was believed by the gang of Belony Pierre – and taken to Cité Soleil but escaped, spending a night traversing alleys and hiding in bushes before running into a police convoy at dawn.[98] Lespwa senator Kelly Bastien said that the country was living under "terrorism" from the armed groups.[99] Mario Andrésol announced his intention to purge the PNH of corrupt officers, explaining that 60 police officers were already in custody and some 200 had been fired.[100]

Préval's attempts to coax all the gangs into the CNDDR program, some of which were made personally to gang leaders at the National Palace, failed.[101] At a tense meeting on the morning of 15 December, Mulet told Préval at the National Palace that a "revolution" was coming as people could no longer accept the level of insecurity, and that the government and MINUSTAH needed to act quickly. After a long discussion, Préval assented to a series of large-scale operations in the capital's slums.[102] In advance of the raids, Haiti's Secretary of State for Public Security Luc-Eucher Joseph announced that the PNH would be adopting new security arrangements, which included a ban on cars with tinted windows, forbidding more than two people traveling on a moto, and an increase in roadblocks and vehicle searches.[103]

The raids began on 22 December and would last for nearly two months, usually beginning in the wee hours of the morning, with ground forces bolstered by Chilean helicopters with night vision capability. Mulet would wake up every morning at 1am, go to the MINUSTAH base and closely follow the operations. The first salvo was a MINUSTAH operation against the baz of Evens Jeune, Belony and Amaral in Cité Soleil, during which technical problems forced MINUSTAH to abandon an armored personnel carrier (APC) outfitted with two Russian machine guns, a sniper rifle, 1,400 rounds of ammunition and four percussion grenades. The truck was eventually recovered without the weapons and ammunition.[104] They largely succeeded, however, in destroying Belony's base of operations. It was believed the raid left at least nine dead and over 30 injured.[105] Before Christmas, as they tried to stop another attempted lynching of suspected kidnappers, this one at Delmas 62, MINUSTAH troops actually fired on those attempting to exact what they viewed as justice, further enraging residents, who threw stones and bottles at the peacekeepers.[106]

In his Christmas message from South Africa that year, Aristide gave a typically bizarre, rambling response to the country's agony. In the recording – which did not once mention Préval's name – Aristide told listeners of the "presidential kidnapping" he claimed he had suffered, and that *fidelite patriyotik akouche ewo, pwazon trayizon akouche zewo* (patriotic fidelity generates heroes, the poison of treason generates zeroes). The term "treason" was mentioned several times.[107] As Haiti continued to bleed, Aristide and his family were enjoying something of the high life in South Africa, with the former president driven by a chauffeur in a white Mercedes (with security guards in a BMW in tow) to his office at the University of South Africa in Pretoria, and having all his expenses paid for by the South African government at a cost "similar to the cost normally incurred for a South African cabinet minister."[108] Education Minister Naledi Pandor told a skeptical parliamentary opposition that Aristide was "earning his keep" by publishing such papers as "Theology of Love" and "The Psychology of Ubuntu" at the university.[109] Gabriel Fortuné, the Union senator (himself a survivor of the November 1995 attack that killed Aristide's cousin Jean-Hubert Feuillé) claimed that the orders to kidnap children were coming "directly from South Africa," and that former police officers now resident in Martissant could be involved.[110] Between October and December 2006, JILAP announced, 539 people had been killed in the Port-au-Prince metropolitan area, with 445 of those killed by firearms. Citing the "political" aspect to the kidnapping phenomenon, JILAP observed that "some groups use it to achieve a political objective, either the departure of the government, or to force it to some changes, or force it to adopt certain decisions."[111]

As if to underline the challenges that Haiti faced, when Préval attempted to deliver the traditional Independence Day message on New Year's Day 2007 in Gonaïves, a series of power failures forced him to abandon it. The last words the public heard from him that day denounced "enemies of democracy, the forces opposed to peace and equality between Haitians."[112] As the new year began, MINUSTAH's Mulet said that operations would "intensify" and that "the days of the bandits are numbered."[113] Voicing support for the policy, Préval nevertheless left the door ajar for those with guns "wanting to integrate into the disarmament" program.[114] In early January, two policemen died during an anti-kidnapping operation in Martissant,[115] only days after two others had been slain on Rue des Césars.[116]

An early January break-in at a Port-au-Prince courthouse resulted in the theft of the files of 93 cases and at least 52 firearms.[117] Claudy Gassant's office was completely emptied of files. Several days later, Minister of Justice René

Magloire, Luc-Eucher Joseph and Mario Andrésol made a surprise visit to the courthouse, after which Magloire curiously said that "at first glance ... there had been no burglary."[118] Furious, Gassant temporarily quit his duties. In January, Senator Gabriel Fortuné claimed that his colleagues had been bribed to pass a resolution favoring the private Société Caribéenne de Banque S.A. (SOCABANK), charging that "members of the 48th legislature have committed themselves in the business of consolidating a genuine financial mafia in Haiti."[119] According to Fortuné, Franck Ciné, the CEO of the mobile phone company Haïtel and a major SOCABANK shareholder, had bribed several senators.[120] In subsequent senate hearings into corruption, Lavalas senator Rudy Hériveaux denied receiving such a bribe while Youri Latortue used the hearings to deny long-rumored ties to drug traffickers.[121] In the coming weeks, Fortuné would amplify his claims, calling for an investigation of the senate by the UCREF and the Unité de Lutte Contre la Corruption (ULCC) anti-corruption body and saying that drugs had been transported from Haiti's southern coast in official senate vehicles.[122] A March resolution by the senate decided that the accusations against it in the SOCABANK scandal did not warrant further investigation, a decision that the anti-corruption organization Le Fondation Héritage pour Haïti (Haiti's branch of Transparency International, known as LFHH) said robbed the body of a chance to strengthen its credibility.[123]

By 19 January, Radio Kiskeya was reporting that "a wild war has been underway for several months among gangs called Baz Pilate and Lame Ti Manchèt, which imposes the law of the jungle on Bolosse, Grand Ravine and Ste-Bernadette." One young man was shot and killed in the Bolosse section,[124] and, after that day, freelance journalist Jean-Rémy Badio was shot and killed in Martissant after having been threatened by the gangs there. Badio had worked for a variety of news outlets, photographing the gang wars in the area and selling the photos to publications such as Le Matin, an extraordinarily brave and risky endeavor.[125] A few days after Badio's murder, Jacques Édouard Alexis announced that there would be an intensification of MINUSTAH and PNH operations in Martissant, saying that residents there were "hostages" to bandits.[126]

One bright spot in January occurred when Haiti won football's Caribbean Cup after defeating Trinidad and Tobago 2–1 in the final, which was Haiti's best result in the tournament's 18-year history. Thousands of deliriously happy fans swarmed the team as they landed at Haiti's Toussaint Louverture Airport in Port-au-Prince.[127]

MINUSTAH forces again raided Cité Soleil in the early morning hours of 24 January, sparking clashes that left at least five dead and a dozen wounded.[128] The raid, however, did not prevent unknown assailants from killing yet another policeman on the Carrefour road the following day.[129] Two more policemen were killed in Martissant in separate incidents hours later.[130] As February began, the United States announced that it would be supervising a $20 million grant slated for development projects in Cité Soleil.[131] On 9 February, 700 MINUSTAH soldiers launched an assault on Evens Jeune's base in Cité Soleil,[132] which resulted in one killed and four wounded, including two UN soldiers.[133] In the coming days, several more people would be killed and Evens' home base would be captured; it contained identity documents of dozens of people believed to have been kidnapping victims. After MINUSTAH troops searched the building, it was looted by local residents.[134] Following the raid, Evens fled Cité Soleil.[135] Journalists were later taken on a tour of the building, which housed, among other accoutrements, an artificial pool and expensive ceramic tiles.[136] MINUSTAH's Brazilian contingent would transform the structure into a medical clinic.[137] One of Evens' main deputies, Johnny "Ti Bazil" Pierre-Louis, would be arrested,[138] and 6,000 rounds of ammunition seized.[139] By mid-February, MINUSTAH said they had arrested 16 members of the Lame Ti Manchèt.[140]

In a 12 February letter to Jacques Édouard Alexis, Youri Latortue, in his role as head of the senate commission for justice and security, wrote that the body was "deeply concerned by the rise of organized crime that takes unexpected forms and unfortunately continues to sow grief and desolation in Haitian families" and that "the difficulty of diplomatic negotiations at each renewal of the mandate of MINUSTAH should make us aware of the urgent need to give our country the means of its sovereignty in military matters." Latortue continued that "the Commission remains puzzled by the slow pace of your government in taking appropriate action, if only to start the process of reflection on the formation of the new Haitian army."[141] By mid-February, Lavalas senator Rudy Hériveaux, while denouncing what he charged was the brutality of the MINUSTAH interventions in Cité Soleil, was telling his supporters that "the population must take its distance from individuals involved in criminal acts … We cannot build a democratic state if we do not respect the law and the constitution."[142]

By the end of February, MINUSTAH forces had seized Amaral Duclona's home in Cité Soleil. Duclona himself, however, was nowhere to be found.[143] Amaral's brother, a fierce dreadlocked gangster named Raymond Duclona but who went by the sobriquet Che, had fled and somehow managed to get a visa to Jamaica, where he began a new life. MINUSTAH and the PNH were soon announcing that Amaral's Cité Soleil zone of Bélékou had also been "liberated" from the gangs, and that "his" criminal network "was dissolving."[144] On 27 February, Mulet walked into Cité Soleil accompanied by security personnel and painted over a mural of a Kalashnikov with white paint. However, as February drew to an end, kidnappings continued to plague the capital, with at least a dozen recorded in a three-day span, and the body of a well-known businessman who had been seized was found decomposing in a water tank in Tabarre.[145] A gun battle between rival gangs in Bel-Air on 19 March left at least seven dead,[146] and three days later five died in La Saline.[147] Nevertheless, in a gesture of regional solidarity, when Venezuelan President Hugo Chávez arrived in Port-au-Prince on 12 March, the mastermind of PetroCaribe was reportedly shocked by the poverty he saw, and told thousands of cheering acolytes that "the Haitian people are an heroic people; so heroic but so downtrodden" and that he "came here to confirm our affection and our commitment to Haiti."[148]

* * *

Only weeks after his Cité Soleil bastion was seized by MINUSTAH, Evens Jeune was discovered and arrested by police in the southern city of Les Cayes.[149] Commenting on Jeune's arrest, Préval said that his government "chose to give a chance to those" who were members of gangs but Jeune had rejected it.[150] Jeune would languish in the Pénitencier National for more than two years before finally succumbing to a "long-term illness" which many assumed to be AIDS.[151] In early April, Alain Cadet aka Pinochet, the number two of the Cité Soleil gang leader Belony, was arrested in a joint MINUSTAH–PNH operation near his hideout near the PNH academy in Frères.[152] Then, Simon-Pelé gang leader William "Ti Blan" Baptiste was arrested at a Delmas market on 5 April.[153] Baptiste would eventually be sentenced to 14 years in prison, convicted of "criminal association and armed robbery" in a trial during which the judge casually noted that, during Baptiste's reign, "official vehicles regularly went to Simon Pelé" for negotiations with the gang leader.[154]

Amidst it all, Préval and Alexis launched Haiti's carnival at the National Palace with a colorful, hopeful *bal* (party) that was attended by, among others, the renowned painter Levoy Exil and the musicians Michel "Sweet Micky" Martelly and Lenord "Azor" Fortuné. The theme was *Solèy Leve* (Sunrise).[155]

CHAPTER SEVEN
UNEASY NEIGHBORS

In 1953, Jean-Price Mars left his job at Haiti's Ministry of External Relations to open a new Haitian diplomatic mission in the Dominican Republic's Ciudad Trujillo (as Santo Domingo was then called) on behalf of the Estimé government, spending two years working in the city that then bore the name of one of the hemisphere's great tyrants.[1] After a year at his post, he published *La République d'Haïti et la République Dominicaine*, a key work in the study of how the nations of Hispaniola viewed one another, and in which he depicted their fraught relations, existing under the shadow of the grim possibility of the "destruction of one or the other nationalities by one or the other community fascinated by the doctrines of racial, class or cultural superiority."[2]

Since Haiti declared its independence from France, the peoples on each side of the Massacre River had gazed at one another with a mixture of awe and fear, and the situation of Haitians living in the Dominican Republic had been a frequent topic for Haitian authors, from Jacques Stephen Alexis's *Compère Général Soleil* to René Philoctète's *Le Peuple des Terres Mêlées* to Edwidge Danticat's *The Farming of Bones*. Dominicans, for their part, found their national identity often defined in opposition to Haiti, a self-conception with deep historical roots and which would only be amplified as Haiti's political wars continued throughout the beginning of the twenty-first century.

* * *

In 1838, Dominicans desiring independence from Haiti formed a secret society known as La Trinitaria (The Trinity), whose founding members included the liberal thinker Juan Pablo Duarte (the organization was so-named because members operated in clandestine cells of three). Taking advantage of the unrest in Haiti following the overthrow of Boyer, La Trinitaria and its allies launched a rebellion, and in 1844 the Dominican Republic was born, ending 22 years of Haitian rule. Significantly, though, Duarte – himself an avowed anti-racist[3] –

was outpaced in the quest for political power by Pedro Santana, a totalitarian figure who installed himself as dictator and enthusiastically persecuted those advocating for a more open political process. These two traditions were locked in relentless struggle with one another until May 1916, when a coup provided the pretext for a U.S. invasion that saw the country occupied for the next eight years. When the Americans did leave – just as they would do in Haiti – they left a new armed force populated by local Dominican soldiers.

Rafael Trujillo was one of the "native" officers raised up under the occupation, his former penchant for criminality (reportedly including forgery and rape) serving as no bar for his matriculation into the armed forces, and he assumed the presidency in 1930. Under Trujillo, *antihaitianismo* became ever more codified as an official ideology, despite the fact that Trujillo's own family contained Haitian blood.[4] At a speech in Dajabón on 2 October 1937, Trujillo made clear his intention to eradicate the Haitian presence in his country once and for all, and, with this signal, one of the hemisphere's great massacres began.[5] For weeks, Trujillo's forces slaughtered Haitians wherever they found them, often trying to identify them by forcing them to pronounce the Spanish word for "parsley" (*perejil*), which led the pogrom to become known as "The Parsley Massacre" (it was also called El Corte, or The Cutting). Although they were fully aware of what was happening, the governments of Haitian President Sténio Vincent and U.S. President Franklin Roosevelt did virtually nothing to stop it. Precise figures remain elusive, but it is generally accepted that no fewer than 10,000 and perhaps up to 20,000 Haitians died during the weeks-long paroxysm of genocidal rage.[6] Trujillo continued on in power for the next 24 years before being shot to death by a group of conspirators in May 1961, an assassination at the very least tacitly approved by the United States.[7]

The dominant politician after Trujillo was Joaquín Balaguer, who actually served his first term as a puppet president when Trujillo was still alive. For a brief seven-month interim in 1963, Juan Bosch of the left-wing Partido Revolucionario Dominicano (PRD) served as president after winning democratic elections by a wide margin, only to be overthrown by a military coup that September. By April 1965, pro- and anti-Bosch forces were engaged in a civil war, which precipitated the landing of thousands of U.S. troops in the country. The following year, Balaguer was president again, having formed the Partido Reformista Social Cristiano (PRSC) in 1963 with a large degree of American support. He would hold the presidency until 1978, and again from 1986 to 1996.

Balaguer's imprint – of economic development coupled with an authoritarian political model and pervasive corruption – in some ways marked the Dominican Republic as profoundly as the Duvalier years marked Haiti.

Standing in opposition to Balaguer was José Francisco Peña Gómez, the black son of Haitian immigrants born the year of the Parsley Massacre and raised by a Dominican peasant family. Peña Gómez had been a Bosch supporter and became one of the key figures in the PRD. A brilliant intellect, he studied political science and law at the Sorbonne and then at Harvard.[8] However, by 1973, Bosch had drifted away from the party he founded and formed the Partido de la Liberación (PLD), while Peña Gómez continued with the PRD. Peña Gómez proved an adept politician, and was elected mayor of Santo Domingo in 1982.

During the 1994 election, Peña Gómez ran against an aging Balaguer in a ballot that foreign observers characterized as "outrageously corrupt," ahead of which commercials depicted Peña Gómez in grotesque racist caricatures as the dictator of a united Haiti and Dominican Republic (a standard paranoid fantasy of the Dominican right), and during which as many as 200,000 PRD voters were prevented from casting their ballots.[9] Rather than choose conflict – one wonders how such a scenario would have played out in Haiti – Peña Gómez chose negotiation, which led to another presidential election in May 1996 in which Balaguer would not be a candidate. To defeat Peña Gómez, Juan Bosch, then 87 years old and infirm, made a devil's bargain with the forces of Balaguer, by that point 89, and the PLD made common cause with Balaguer's PRSC. The two announced a pact designed to keep Peña Gómez from office and assure the success of the PLD's candidate, Leonel Fernández, a 42-year-old attorney who had grown up largely in the (heavily Dominican) New York City neighborhood of Washington Heights.

Any moral authority Bosch and the PLD may have ever had evaporated in the nakedly racist campaign that followed, with Balaguer telling voters "we must prevent the government from falling into the hands of those who are not truly Dominican."[10] A number of prominent Dominican intellectuals put themselves at the service of the campaign against Peña Gómez, including the academic Bruno Rosario Candelier, who warned voters that Peña Gómez was "culturally Haitian and ... subordinated to a pattern of ancestral behavior."[11] Following a steady diet of such ethnic calumny, Fernández won the second round with 51 percent of the vote, at the same time having earned a reputation for being willing to use "the Haitian issue" for political gain – a reputation that the succeeding years would do nothing to diminish.[12] Though he would lose the presidency to the PRD's Hipólito Mejía from 2000 to 2004, Fernández would return to power that year, ruling until 2012 and presiding over the transformation of the Dominican Republic into a virtual one-party state in the process.

By the time Préval returned to office in May 2006, he and Fernández – and Haiti and the Dominican Republic – were facing one another again, bringing with them decades of accumulated suspicions, hostilities and fears. The Haitian presence on Dominican soil increased in direct proportion to how chaotic the geopolitical and economic situation was in Haiti itself, and the preceding years had been as tumultuous as one could possibly imagine. Although Haitians had first headed to the Dominican Republic largely to work in the agricultural industry, cutting cane on vast plantations known as *bateyes*,[13] by this point they were also essential – though vulnerable and exploited – components of the country's construction and tourism industries, and their presence in cities such as Santo Domingo and Santiago was impossible to miss. By some estimates, a million Haitians lived and worked in the Dominican Republic. For the economic sector, which depended on cheap Haitian labor, and the Dominican right – obsessed with ideas of racial purity – this created a thorny problem. Article 11 of the nation's constitution guaranteed the right to Dominican nationality to anyone born on Dominican soil unless they were the offspring of diplomats or those born to persons "in transit," a case that would have been hard to make for Haitian families who had lived there for decades. By September 2005, the Inter-American Court of Human Rights had ruled the Dominican Republic in violation of the American Convention on Human Rights (to which it was a signatory) and of its own constitution by refusing citizenship to two Dominican girls of Haitian descent.[14] The Fernández government and the PLD were closely linked to wealthy business interests in the country who had a direct interest in the marginalization of Haitians and Dominicans of Haitian descent. These forces included the Vicini family, a Dominican family of Italian origin, one of whose members, Juan Bautista Vicini Burgos, served as president from 1922 until 1924 during the U.S. occupation, and who, by the twenty-first century, in addition to sugar, had expanded into other endeavors, including ownership of the *Diario Libre* newspaper.[15] To help shape its public image, Grupo Vicini retained the services of Newlink, a Miami-based public relations and consulting firm co-founded and run by former television journalist Sergio Roitberg and

Florida International University professor Eduardo Gamarra, whose other clients included the country's Policia National and the PLD itself.[16]

* * *

In May 2005, a year before Préval returned to power and a year after Fernández had done so, I found myself standing at the Massacre River in Ouanaminthe, watching Haitians strolling back and forth across the knee-deep channel under the watchful eyes of Dominican soldiers at Dajabón, where Trujillo's 1937 speech had kicked off the Parsley Massacre. After the murder of a Dominican business-woman in the city of Hatillo Palma, for which Haitian immigrants were blamed, Dominican authorities had carried out a mass expulsion of Haitians and Domin-icans of Haitian descent, resulting in what Javier Hernández, MINUSTAH's regional head in Cap-Haïtien, told me was a "massive and unexpected influx" of humanity.[17] Many had been transported on buses under military guard and taken by armed soldiers to the Dajabón border crossing. In a press release, Chris-tian Aid wrote of how people had been expelled "without verifying their legal status, basing [the decision] solely on the colour of their skin," with "many dark-skinned Dominicans ... being expelled from their own country."[18]

As I wandered around Ouanaminthe, a bustling market town, I was trailed by more than a dozen schoolchildren who would squeal in delight when I spoke to them in Creole. I would eventually make my way to the Soeurs St.-Jean Evangeliste convent, where I met Sister Yolande Duverger, who told me some of what had taken place.

"People arrived, children without their mothers and their fathers, parents without their children," said Sister Yolande. "I think it was around 2,000 who were expelled, and they slept in and around the Notre-Dame church."

"There were men who said their wives had been killed, women who said their husbands had been killed," she continued. "The Dominican army tore up many people's papers at the border. A lot of people looked like they had been beaten up."

Louis Amelice, the caretaker at her church, concurred, telling me that those expelled "said the army had destroyed their documents so they couldn't return."

As I strolled through the town, its streets muddy from recent rain, I spoke with Lissaint Antoine, director of Ouanaminthe's Service Jésuite aux Migrants.

"We heard what was happening in Hatillo Palma," he told me. "The popu-lation had begun revolting against the presence of the Haitians there, and the provincial governor ordered the expulsion of 400 living in the zone. Refugees began coming on May 11th, but the flood really started on the 13th when eight buses arrived at the border full of Haitians."

Haitians also were forced from the La Vega, Monte Christi and Santiago districts, Antoine said.

"We had a woman who stayed for three days here who said that her husband had been killed." Separately, two brothers, 13 and 14, told the Jesuit mission official that Dominican civilians armed with machetes had killed their parents.

The story of one Haitian cane-cutter, Sedwàn Louis, was typical, as he spoke of how, while working 15 hours a day in the *bateyes* for 26 years, he was "almost a slave, almost free." Finally expelled to Haiti when the *batey* owner no longer needed his services, he returned to his village of Belle Fontaine to find that his brother, his only immediate relative, had recently died. Eventually his extended family took him in.[19]

Walking across the bridge to Dajabón, I chatted with a Dominican immigration officer who told me that, although Dominican authorities did not intentionally expel Haitians with Dominican papers, when the Haitians "saw what was going on in Hatillo Palma, they fled back to their country." Another officer chimed in with "we have too many Haitians in the Dominican Republic." A few weeks later, more than 2,000 more people would be summarily expelled, in expulsions that GARR characterized as "based on the color of their skin."[20]

Speaking in late June 2005 at an event at the Fundación Global Democracia y Desarrollo (FUNGLODE) he had founded, Fernández frankly admitted that the expulsions "certainly" violated the rights of Haitians.[21] Though he often had the perfect social democratic speech, Fernández chose Carlos Morales Troncoso to head his foreign relations team, a man who had served as Balaguer's vice president and his ambassador to the United States. Morales Troncoso was a pure product of the Dominican Republic's sugar oligarchy, an industry that for decades had benefited from the disenfranchisement and marginalization of Haitians in the Dominican Republic and their Dominican-born offspring. He had served for years as the president and one of the most important shareholders of Central Romana Corporation, the Dominican Republic's major producer by volume of raw and refined sugars, had founded the CBI Sugar Group, and had served as director of the state-owned consortium of sugar mills, the Consejo Estatal del Azúcar.[22] It was the *consejo* that officially began recruiting Haitian workers to work in the *bateyes* in the 1960s.[23] Other principals in Central Romana included the Cuban-American sugar barons Alfonso and Pepe Fanjul, who had built a family fortune importing cheap immigrant laborers to toil in the sugarcane fields of South Florida, becoming major power brokers in Tallahassee and Washington while benefiting from a system activists charged was little better than "modern-day slavery." The power of the Fanjuls in U.S. politics was such that then U.S. President Bill Clinton interrupted one of his trysts with Monica Lewinsky to take a call from Alfonso.[24] Along with the Vicinis, the Fanjuls represented some of the most powerful interests benefiting from cheap Haitian labor in the Dominican Republic.

The PLD government, its supporters among the Dominican elite and sectors of the press, such as the virulently racist television host Consuelo Despradel, had anyone who spoke out in defense of Haitians and Dominicans of Haitian descent firmly in their sights.

* * *

One such individual was Christopher Hartley, a Spanish-British Catholic priest who had spent years working with Mother Teresa in Calcutta and in the South Bronx in New York before arriving in the Dominican Republic in 1997. Assigned to the parish of San Jose de los Llanos in the province of San Pedro de Macoris, he had no idea of what a *batey* was or their role in Dominican society. The first *bateyes* Hartley began working in – Canipa, Savanatosa and Contador – belonged to the Vicini family. Gradually, Hartley expanded his ministry further into the sugarcane fields.

"I was absolutely appalled at the living and working conditions of the sugarcane cutters, the Haitian migrant workers that were smuggled into the Dominican Republic at the beginning of every migrant season," Hartley later told me. "There were no sanitary conditions, no toilets or latrines, no running water, no proper drinking water, no electricity, no access to education for children, no healthcare services. People were living basically as animals, in very harsh conditions and in extreme poverty."[25]

Hartley set up feeding centers in Batey Gautier, Batey Contador and Batey Paloma, feeding close to 400 children one meal a day, and, with the help of a courageous Dominican lawyer, Noemí Méndez, he began educating *batey* workers on human and labor rights. For the following nine years – and especially after Hartley delivered an incendiary January 2000 address in the presence of Leonel Fernández at Batey Gautier, where he told the president that the country's sugarcane had been "fertilized with the blood of Haitian men at the threshold of hell" – Hartley was the subject of a sustained and organized campaign of character assassination and death threats, not only against him, but against those who worked with him.[26] He was finally expelled from the Dominican Republic in October 2006.

"Everything [Hartley] said about those conditions, he didn't need to say it," a reporter for a major South Florida daily newspaper told me. "When you walked around in the *bateyes*, you could see that people were living in bad conditions, were defeated, it was a miserable life. You didn't need words to explain it, it was there."[27]

Another such figure was the Belgian priest Pierre Ruquoy, who arrived in the Dominican Republic in November 1975 and, from his base in Barahona, played an enormously influential role over the next 30 years advocating for Haitians, Dominicans of Haitian descent and the downtrodden in general. Ministering to 15 *bateyes*, he organized the Sant Pon/Centro Puente to attempt to bridge the gulf of misunderstanding between communities, founded Radio Enriquillo (eventually banned by Balaguer), wrote extensively about conditions in the *bateyes*, and would even take his Creole ministry to Haitians harvesting oranges and coffee in the remote Bahoruco mountains.[28] A tireless defender of the right of black Dominicans to be registered as Dominicans and of Haitians to have decent working conditions, Ruquoy attracted the ire of the Dominican ultra-nationalists which, by late 2004, had increased to include physical assaults and a threat by an army colonel that he was "just waiting for the signal" from a local plantation owner to kill him.[29] In November 2005, Ruquoy was forced to leave the Dominican Republic.

(It is worth noting that Hartley's and Ruquoy's stances sometimes put them in conflict with the Dominican clergy, including Nicolás de Jesús Cardenal López Rodríguez, the notoriously reactionary archbishop of Santo Domingo.[30])

But the person who became the defining symbol of the struggle for equality by Haitians and Dominicans of Haitian descent was a child of the *bateyes* herself. Sonia Pierre had been raised in a dirt-floor shack in a *batey*, one of the 12 children of a Haitian migrant worker,[31] and by 1976, at the age of 13, was arrested for helping to organize a protest of cane-cutters agitating for better working conditions.[32]

In 1983, at 20, she founded El Movimiento de Mujeres Dominico-Haitianas (MUDHA), an organization dedicated to improving the lives of vulnerable communities, especially women and children, and addressing the intersectional legacies of oppression such as class, gender and race. A striking, tall woman who spoke fluid native Spanish, Pierre had been one of the petitioners in the case before the Inter-American Commission on Human Rights (IACHR) that found the Dominican Republic guilty of violating of its own constitution, and the following year was awarded the Robert F. Kennedy Human Rights Award, praised as "a driving force for change and a leader in the movement to end human rights violations."[33] Living up to his pedigree as a slave of the nation's elite, Carlos Morales Troncoso lashed out at Pierre after the award, claiming that it was "divorced from the realities on the island of Hispaniola and lamentably ill-informed about the consequences of Ms. Pierre's work,"[34] and later that unspecified international organizations were involved in a "vile and irresponsible … smear campaign … designed to force the Dominican government to grant citizenship to Haitians."[35] He would lead a campaign to suggest that Pierre was not Dominican, but rather Haitian, based on a clerical error on her Dominican birth certificate.[36] Fernández's administrative secretary, Luis Manuel Bonetti, struck a paranoid tone, suggesting that there was an international "campaign against the country" and that a national movement should be formed to "confront" those besmirching the national atmosphere.[37] Perhaps unsurprisingly, Bonetti's family were among the wealthiest on the island and ran Grupo SID which owned, among other companies, Agrocítricos (which maintained vast orange plantations) and the Induspalma agribusiness.[38]

An October 2006 cable from the U.S. Embassy in Santo Domingo said that "unfulfilled promises, nationalistic rebuffs and outright distortions continue to characterize the Dominican response to international concerns over the country's treatment of its largely undocumented Haitian minority." The cable went on to detail the Dominican Republic's refusal to comply with the Inter-American Court of Human Rights ruling and concluded that "discrimination, mistreatment and arbitrary deportations targeting individuals of Haitian ancestry are commonplace," affecting "even Dominican-born persons who have never set foot in Haiti."[39]

However much Haiti's politicians saw a modus vivendi between the governments of the two countries on points of mutual interest, by the time of his second turn in office Fernández had become something of a hate figure among many in Haiti, and reports of Haitian immigrants slain in the country became a weekly occurrence. This being the state of affairs, it was perhaps not surprising when, as Fernàndez arrived in Port-au-Prince for an official state visit on 12 December 2006, he was greeted by hundreds of enraged protesters, a large contingent of whom were university students, who clashed with PNH and MINUSTAH forces along the Champ de Mars and in front of the National Palace. The protesters burned photos of Fernàndez, waved photos of the victims of racial attacks across the border, and were briefly joined by Guy Philippe and some of his partisans. As Fernàndez drove away, protesters threw rocks at his motorcade.[40] At least three protesters were wounded by gunfire, though MINUSTAH denied having fired at any point.[41] In an illustration of the reciprocity of hostility, after the violence, threatening leaflets were left outside the apartments of Haitian students studying at the Universidad Tecnológica de Santiago.[42] During the first three weeks of 2007, more than 4,000 people would be expelled to Haiti from the Dominican Republic.[43]

But if the tangled issue of Haitians living in the Dominican Republic and Dominicans of Haitian descent often seemed to be one in which the Haitian state was utterly disengaged, this was because, regardless of stated ideology or personnel, it largely *was* disengaged. One former politician told me of a conversation he had had with a high-ranking official in the Préval government in early 2007 where the politician asked "Don't you think it's about time we sign something with the Dominicans?" regarding the status of Haitians there.

"Yes," came the reply.

"OK, let's do it."

"But we don't want it."

"Why not?"

"Because we don't want it."

"It was then," the politician later told me, "that I realized for them solving a problem is not the end. Keeping the problem alive is the end."[44]

* * *

But what Haiti's politicians seemed to fail to grasp was that, beyond the inhumanity visited upon their brothers and sisters there, by keeping the Dominican Republic as a glittering talisman before their people, half refuge and half purgatory, the danger by no means remained a one-way street. Before the 2006 elections, the Dominican army had intercepted an enormous cache of ammunition and arms that was heading to Haiti via Barahona.[45]

Meanwhile, in Haiti itself, Hugues Saint-Pierre, the president of the Gonaïves court of appeal and head of the faculty of law and economics in the city, was killed in Delmas in April 2007 when he was struck by a bus while waiting at a tap-tap stand, an event that would have a profound impact on those seeking justice for the La Scierie massacre. Unlike the perfumed, SUV-riding cadres in parliament, Saint-Pierre, by all accounts a rare honest and humble judge, had never been able to afford a car and usually traveled by either bicycle or public transportation.[46] Saint-Pierre had been summoned to the capital by judicial authorities, including Justice Minister René Magloire, who were preparing to make a final decision on the La Scierie case.[47] (Magloire later denied having summoned him.) Samuel Madistin, one of the attorneys for the victims in Saint-Marc, openly called Saint-Pierre's death "suspicious."[48]

In one of the most shameful episodes of Haitian justice, days after Saint-Pierre's death, Bale Wouze founder Amanus Mayette walked out of prison a free man, liberated by Saint-Marc judicial official Ramon Guillaume under questionable circumstances.[49] RNDDH denounced the release as "arbitrary" and a move that would "strengthen corruption" and "allow the executioners of La Scierie to enjoy impunity,"[50] asserting that "the government is trying to prevent the trial for the massacre of La Scierie."[51] Relatives of those who had been killed staged a sit-in in front of the Palais de Justice in Saint-Marc, calling for an explanation of Saint-Pierre's death and the removal of Ramon Guillaume and government commissioner Worky Pierre (no relation), who they charged with subverting their quest for justice.[52] Although Préval stressed the decision was neither his nor "a political decision," many of those in Saint-Marc believed Préval had a hand in Mayette's release.[53] Hugues Saint-Pierre's funeral in Gonaïves was marked by violent outbursts, with students from the law faculty that Saint-Pierre once headed demonstrating in front of the cathedral and calling for the arrest of René Magloire, who was in attendance. Mourners also hurled stones at the vehicles of government officials in attendance, including Jacques-Édouard Alexis.[54]

Following Hugues Saint-Pierre's death, in a heart-rending open letter to UN Special Rapporteur for Haiti Louis Joinet, AVIGES coordinator Charliénor Thomson asked the judge "Who cares about our case?" before going on to recount some of the horrors that had been visited upon Saint-Marc in February 2004 and continuing:

> The victims of these horrors live under the constant threat of criminals who were all released under pressure, in particular, from some agencies of international civil society … Today, what justice should we expect? Who can testify freely while the assassins are free and can circulate with

impunity? The majority of inhabitants in Saint-Marc are afraid. Even those who have been direct victims of acts mentioned above are scared. The victims want to flee the city and the witnesses to hide. When will the state allow us to have the benefit of the justice we ask for? In the current circumstances, in what form does it come?[55]

But Joinet was already halfway out the door on his way to a comfortable retirement back in France, and as the citizens of Saint-Marc fought their uphill battle for justice, rather than supported, they were actively undermined by some in the international human rights community. This was especially true of the so-called human rights organizations with deep financial and personal links to the Aristide regime such as the IJDH, who wrote fawningly of Ronald Dauphin as "a Haitian grassroots activist, customs worker and political prisoner," and talked of the work of the BAI's Mario Joseph as Dauphin's attorney in a "legal analysis" of the case.[56]

* * *

At a late April meeting of the Rio Group of Latin American nations in Santo Domingo, the European Union pledged €233 million in aid to Haiti, saying it would increase the grant by 25 percent if the country improved its governability.[57] Whether or not it could do so was somewhat questioned by the fact that, by early May, Gabriel Fortuné was suggesting putting the ULCC under control of the executive branch and parliament,[58] a suggestion that Marilyn B. Allien of the anti-corruption group LFHH spoke out strongly against.[59] Addressing the nation on Haiti's Flag Day on 18 May, Préval declared that 2007 would be "the year of the war against corruption" and that those who engaged in corrupt practices were "traitors."[60] Many spoke out in support of Préval's speech, including Senator Rudy Boulos, who told Radio Métropole that Haiti had been run "as a plantation" since its founding.[61] Perhaps as a precursor, SOCABANK grandee Franck Ciné had been briefly detained in Port-au-Prince.[62] A short time later, Claudy Gassant would order Ciné's arrest, as well as that of three other members of the bank's board.[63]

* * *

During late April and early May, nearly 30 suspected gang members were arrested,[64] including Jean "Blade Nasson" Torchon, the leader of the *baz* in the

Ti Ayiti section of Cité Soleil.[65] The arrests were not enough to save Radio-Télé Provinciale director Alix Joseph, who was slain on 16 May. One of his suspected killers, the gang leader Adecla Saint-Juste, was subsequently tracked to Anse-Rouge and killed there, though exactly by whom remained something of a mystery.[66] In a crime that shocked even crime-hardened Port-au-Prince, the celebrated Haitian actor and radio personality François Latour was kidnapped and slain on 22 May, his lifeless body found under driving rain dumped on Rue Bâtimat.[67]

On 12 June, the Cité Soleil gang leader Junior "Yoyo Piman" Acdhély, believed to be the number two of Amaral Duclona, was killed during a gun battle with Brazilian peacekeepers in that quarter's Bélékou district. He had reportedly only recently returned to the capital from Les Cayes after a relative with whom he had been hiding there threatened to turn him in to the police.[68] Another gangster, Evens Jeune's former second-in-command Bazile "Ti Bazile" Soifette, was nabbed by PNH forces a few weeks later along the airport road.[69] Speaking to Radio Métropole to mark the twentieth anniversary of the PNH's founding in mid-June, Mario Andrésol talked of how "until 2001" (the year Aristide had returned to power) the PNH had functioned well and that there had never been a conflict between the police and the judiciary under his watch but rather "differences of opinion between members of the two institutions."[70] A survey by a Catholic human rights organization saw a welcome decrease in criminality around the capital.[71]

* * *

On 18 June, Youri Latortue met with a representative of the U.S. Embassy and offered "unprompted" that "some people believe [I am] a drug trafficker," but stated that these were claims made by his "uncle's" political enemies. He said that he had denied invitations by Cuban and Venezuelan officials to parlay and that he had "always been, and will continue to be, a friend of the United States." The embassy was unmoved, calling him in a secret cable "the poster-boy for political corruption in Haiti" while admitting that "Latortue's influence makes it increasingly difficult for [the] post to shun him completely, but we will maintain our policy of keeping him at arm's length."[72] Days later, and taking many by surprise, Haiti saw a flurry of anti-drug operations. In Cap-Haïtien, PNH and DEA officers arrested two suspected drug traffickers, one of them a former army officer, while in Gonaïves businessman Lavaud François was arrested and quickly spirited away to the United States.[73] Most spectacularly, on 16 July, U.S. and Haitian forces launched a joint operation from Guantánamo Bay Naval Base in Cuba, complete with Black Hawk helicopters, swooping down on Les Cayes and its environs to try to capture former anti-Aristide rebel leader Guy Philippe, wanted on a November 2005 indictment for conspiring to import cocaine into the United States stemming from his time with the PNH. The ever wily Philippe heard the approaching roar, however, and escaped.[74] Philippe would settle into a kind of *marronage* throughout the Grand Anse, occasionally phoning in to Haitian radio stations such as Radio Caraïbes, where he denied any drug ties and claimed that "clearly this is a political game that is happening … They're trying to destroy me, they're trying to eliminate me … These people did not come to arrest me. They came to assassinate me."[75] In the following weeks, several others, including the owner of a Jacmel morgue called *La clé du paradis* (The Key to Paradise), would also be arrested.[76] The businessman Fritz Brandt and his son David Brandt were also arrested and sent to the Pénitencier National as the result of suspected customs violations.[77] Somewhat unsurprisingly, the CCIH was soon calling for the "provisional release" of the members of their clan.[78] A few weeks later, Gassant summoned Réginald Boulos, majority shareholder of *Le Matin*, Radio Vision 2000, Safari Motors and other concerns, to address allegations of corruption.[79]

* * *

At the end of July it was announced that Edmond Mulet would be replaced by Hédi Annabi, a Tunisian diplomat who was serving as UN assistant secretary-general for peacekeeping operations, a job that Mulet would now assume.[80] A 30-year UN veteran, Annabi had worked for many years in Southeast Asia, particularly in Cambodia.[81] He had spoken of seeing the Haiti mission as "one more throw of the dice" before his retirement in a few years' time.[82] Under Annabi, the Brazilian diplomat Luiz Carlos da Costa, who had assumed his role the previous year, would continue serving as MINUSTAH's deputy special representative.[83] A few weeks earlier, Da Costa told the Spanish news agency EFE that he believed it would take at least four more years – at least until 2011 – until Haiti was sufficiently "stabilized" to permit the withdrawal of UN troops.[84] On his first visit to Haiti in early August, the UN's new secretary-general, Ban Ki-moon, praised Préval and said that the international community "must not step aside and let spoilers jeopardize Haiti's progress."[85] Days earlier, several dozen greying former FADH soldiers marched through the capital while a band played patriotic music, gamely trying to exhibit an exercise regime before onlookers as they called for the re-establishment of the army and 13 months of salary they said they were owed.[86]

In mid-August, Préval announced that he was forming an "independent" body – the Commission Indépendante d'Appui aux Enquêtes Relatives aux Assassinats des Journalistes Haïtiens (CIAPEAJ) – to look into the cases of journalists murdered since 2000, including Jean Dominique. Michèle Montas, René Magloire, Luc-Eucher Joseph, Claudy Gassant and Mario Andrésol were all present at the announcement. Préval said that the commission would be headed by Guy Delva, who had succeeded me as Reuters correspondent in Haiti, and would also include Radio Vision 2000's Valéry Numa, Radio Ibo's Marie Nic Marcelin and Radio Solidarité's Anne Marguerite Auguste, among others.[87] That same month, former senator and Aristide ally-turned-foe Dany Toussaint was summoned before Judge Fritzner Fils-Aimé to answer questions in the Dominique case, after which he reiterated to reporters that he "was not involved either closely or distantly" with the crime.[88] As August ended, two individuals, 22-year-old Alby Joseph and 16-year-old Chéry Beaubrun, were found guilty of involvement in the kidnapping and murder of Jacques Roche two years earlier and condemned to life "at hard labor." Three others linked to the case – François "Bibi" Daniel, Dérosiers "Ti Yabout" Beckner and one known only as "Gaetan" – were already in prison. Roche's former colleagues in the press called on the government to also pursue the "intellectual authors" of the crime.[89] Before year's end, two members of the Lavalas OP Domi nan Bwa would be convicted and sentenced to life for their role in the December 2001 murder of Radio Echo 2000's Brignol Lindor in Petit-Goâve.[90]

* * *

By the middle of August, pursued by MINUSTAH and PNH forces to the Descartes quarter of Martissant, Lame Ti Manchèt leader Rudy Kernisant, one of the believed perpetrators of the August 2005 soccer killings, was said to "commit suicide" by shooting himself.[91] On the night of 12 August, Lavalas activist and head of Fondation 30 Septembre, Lovinsky Pierre-Antoine, disappeared while en route to his home in Delmas 31. Police eventually found the vehicle he was driving – abandoned – and a ransom call was made to his family some 48 hours after he had disappeared.[92] A few weeks later, former DCPJ chief Michael Lucius was shot and wounded by unknown gunmen in Freres.[93] Between early July and early August, Claudy Gassant would release around 200 prisoners for "humanitarian reasons,"[94] and in late August, Gassant met with Lespwa senator Jean Hector Anacacis and FUSION senator Michel Clérié after he refused to heed the by-now usual parliamentary summons regarding his anti-corruption investigations and the increased number of people in pre-trial detention.[95] With René Magloire present, Gassant finally agreed to meet privately with three members of the senate's justice committee.[96] Departing MINUSTAH chief Mulet enigmatically blamed the fracas on "ill-intentioned individuals" in parliament.[97] As far as Gassant was concerned, however, peace was not a long prospect, and he almost immediately stumbled into a war with the CEP, summoning its president, Max Mathurin, secretary-general Rosemond Pradel and treasurer François Benoît to answer questions about alleged corruption – a summons they collectively refused, saying that Gassant had no authority to call them, and with Benoît denouncing "a gestating dictatorship."[98] Speaking from his French exile later in September, Jean-Claude Duvalier, an actual former dictator, said in a recorded message to the tiny, Duvalierist Parti Unité Nationale, that "if, during my presidential mandate, the government caused any physical, moral or economic wrongs to others, I solemnly take the historical responsibility ... to request forgiveness from the people and ask for the impartial judgment of history." He went on to describe himself as "broken by 20 years of exile."[99]

* * *

An early September MINUSTAH report hailed the "major progress" seen within the PNH, which now numbered 8,000 officers.[100] A visit that same month to the Pénitencier National, however, left members of the senate's Commission on Justice and Security with the conclusion that the conditions of incarceration in Haiti were "inhumane," citing 160 people "jailed" in a space of 4 square meters as an example. Youri Latortue said he would propose a body of judges and government officials to review cases of prolonged detention.[101]

Also in September, a strange occurrence happened in Jacmel that made many wonder what exactly was going on in the usually somnolent southern town. Ten people aboard a damaged yacht near Tiburon were detained when police concluded that they might be involved in the drug trade. Following this, Pierre Lambert, the father of senate president and Jacmel native Joseph Lambert, passed away at the family's home. At the elder Lambert's funeral – attended by, among others, Jacques-Édouard Alexis and MINUSTAH deputy Luiz Carlos da Costa – Lambert accused an unnamed "Jacmel politician" of causing his father's death due to stress caused by "unfounded" rumors of his involvement in drug trafficking and that the boat was in fact his.[102] Lambert would later produce customs slips in parliament which he claimed showed that the boat was in fact registered to someone else, and lay blame on deputy Jean Délouis Félix, a member of Fusion from the south, as the source of the "rumors."[103]

In late November, amid reports that gang leaders had been using cell phones to talk to their remaining cadres in Cité Soleil, Senator Gabriel Fortuné advocated bringing back the death penalty for kidnappers. Fortuné's statement also came after Claudy Gassant's decision to release Martissant gangster Lafortune "Kadafi" François – a decision that many found inexplicable.[104] Another well-known Martissant criminal, Pierre Richard Mulus, was also freed by Gassant – not once but twice – after being arrested,[105] and yet another, Patrick Jean François, a lieutenant in Amaral's gang, was released and later implicated in the kidnapping and shooting of a well-known Haitian musician.[106] Around the same time, Gassant had arrested (and later had to release) PAPDA-affiliated agronomist Franck Saint-Jean and his wife after the car they were in did not clear the way for Gassant's convoy fast enough for his liking.[107] By this point, relations between Alexis, Andrésol and Gassant had deteriorated to the point that Alexis was threatening legal sanctions against the latter two; it was unclear whether he had the legal power to enforce this.[108] Meanwhile, Fortuné spoke of "a deep malaise" between the prosecutor and the PNH.[109]

* * *

And yet there were bright spots. During 2007, Haiti's GDP even managed to grow by around 4 percent, while inflation fell from above 40 percent to below 10 percent and the gourde remained relatively stable.[110] There was also the sense that Haiti might, after all, present some opportunity. After entering the country in May 2006, by August 2007 the Irish mobile phone operator Digicel had spent $260 million, the largest foreign investment in Haiti for years, and had garnered 1.4 million customers.[111] Groups such as the left-wing PLANOPA, though, warned that "misery and hunger are killing the people" and that the government was "implementing neoliberal policies, bowing to meet imperialist interests at the expense of the masses." Meanwhile, the release said, parliament "did nothing."[112]

By this point, the political personality of Préval 2.0 was becoming more apparent, an outline that was met with cautious approval by some while disturbing and alarming others. In early December, Préval surprised many by unilaterally dissolving the CEP and replacing it with a new, nine-member CEP to organize parliamentary and local elections.[113] Some saw the move as a way for the executive to exert more control over the council going forward. To replace Max Mathurin, Frantz Verret, the representative of the Catholic Church on the council, was selected, with Rodol Pierre, viewed as close to Lavalas, selected as vice president.[114] As the director general of the new CEP, Préval would eventually tap Pierre-Louis Opont, who had served as the ULCC's director of operations and also worked for the Boulos family while in the private sector.[115] By late 2007, Préval began floating the idea of amending Haiti's 1987 constitution, saying during an address at the National Palace that, among other changes, presidents should be allowed to serve their two terms consecutively, that the president should have the power to hire and dismiss the prime minister without parliamentary oversight, and that all elections, both local and national, should be held on a single day every five years.[116] Earlier in the year, Préval's former adversary Leslie Manigat had announced that he would be retiring from politics and that his wife, Mirlande, would be succeeding him as the head of the RDNP.[117] As the year wound up, rumors also began to circulate about the alleged U.S. citizenship of Senator Rudolph Boulos, with Joseph Lambert and Youri Latortue charging that it was up to the accusers to "prove" such accusations.[118]

In the traditional New Year's speech in Gonaïves, this one marking the two hundred and fourth anniversary of Haiti's independence, Préval declared that, in the coming year, his priority would be to fight against the high cost of living in Haiti, saying that "any increase in the world market has consequences on prices in Haiti" and that the country "must create jobs" for its citizens by strengthening national production, particularly in agribusiness.[119] Préval told his audience that there would "be no miracle" but that *piti piti, wazo fe nich-li* (little by little, the bird builds its nest).[120]

"He drove me crazy, but I always felt until the day I left he really cared about Haiti," said a foreign diplomat who worked closely with Préval for several years during his second mandate. "He had some personality traits that did not make him a great leader, but of the people I met in the political class, with one or two exceptions, he cared the most about where the country was going."[121]

Another foreign diplomat, though, described Préval as "an anarchist" who would only fleetingly pay attention to issues at the margins,[122] while a Haitian senator who dealt with him extensively thought of him as "a nihilist" who behaved out of "purely political and egocentric" rather than financial motives, and who "put us all in his pocket, the whole country."[123]

In a break with the often garish opulence of some of his predecessors, though, in late January Préval made a low-key tour of the Plateau Central, arriving at the border town of Belladère on the back of a moto taxi to the delight of residents.

"Peace," he told those who turned out to speak with him. "We need to preserve the climate of peace we now enjoy in order to attract investment and promote the development of the country."[124]

CHAPTER EIGHT
LAVI CHÈ

As 2008 began and he took over the role of the senate presidency from Joseph Lambert, Lespwa senator Kelly Bastien reminded his often absentee colleagues that "you have deadlines to meet."[1] Fusion's Rudolph Boulos was elected as the body's vice president, to which Senator Gabriel Fortuné responded by charging that "everyone knows" that Boulos had two passports, one Haitian and one American, in violation of Haiti's 1987 constitution.[2] For his part, Boulos claimed that he was the victim of a plot by Préval, and said he had never denied that he was a U.S. citizen, but had given up his U.S. passport for a Haitian one before running for office.[3]

As if to underline how fragile was the peace Préval had spoken of in Belladère, within a few days of one another, as the year began, two small children near the capital were kidnapped and killed, an employee of the BRH was slain in Tabarre and a former FADH colonel and his wife were kidnapped in Pétionville.[4] The feared La Saline gang leader Ti Likou, a native of Ti Bois, was slain by a deportee in the quarter.[5] A short time later, a joint operation of the PNH's Bureau de Lutte contre le Trafic des Stupéfiants (BLTS) and the DEA to try to snatch up Guy Philippe near his base in the Grand Anse again came up short, the resourceful former rebel leader once more outwitting his erstwhile pursuers.[6] Residents of Pestel, where the raid was centered, complained of being handcuffed, tied up and otherwise mistreated by the commandos.[7] Speaking by phone to Radio Kiskeya after the raid, Philippe promised to run for senate in the coming elections.[8]

After being summoned in to answer some of his comments regarding kidnapping by the imperious Claudy Gassant, CNDDR chairman Alix Fils-Aimé had apparently had enough, noting in a letter to Jacques Édouard Alexis that "the abusive use, repeated and illegal, of the office of government commissioner is a destabilizing factor in the state, especially for the PNH."[9] By this time, many observers were commenting on Gassant's "dark, unpredictable side

... fueled by ego as much as by his sense of impunity as an appointee of the Executive."[10] Though Gassant would stay on for the time being, it was soon announced that Préval had chosen former judge Jean Ostrict Hercule, who had been in charge of the Jean Dominique dossier, to take over as director general of the anti-corruption body UCREF from the departing Jean Yves Noël. It was a choice that many found disheartening, noting the lack of progress in the Dominique case. RNDDH weighed in that Hercule was "severely lacking in the credibility necessary to direct an agency such as UCREF ... Lacking, that is, unless the powers that be are not truly interested in fighting corruption and impunity."[11] In late February, Prime Minister Alexis received a large vote of support in the Chamber of Deputies, with 63 voting against a measure to censure his government as opposed to eight voting in favor and 13 abstaining.[12] However, there were signs that things might be amiss. By mid-March, Youri Latortue was bitterly attacking Préval's Minister of Public Works Frantz Véréla, saying that the latter had been lavishing sweetheart deals on the Dominican construction company Estrella at the expense of Haitian firms, and charging that corruption was rife at the Centre National des Equipements (CNE), the state's construction entity. Véréla said that all contracts were made through the IADB.[13] The CNE's co-founder and its chief since 2005 was a little-known Haitian engineer named Jude Célestin, who had purchased a $1 million home in suburban Broward County only a year after becoming head of the agency, one of three homes he purchased in South Florida (two were subsequently fore-closed on).[14] Célestin's uncle, Rony Gilot, had served as minister of information under Jean-Claude Duvalier.[15]

Parliament itself seemed to be in little better shape. As claims and counterclaims regarding his citizenship swirled, Rudolph Boulos made a "verbal declaration" before colleagues that he was resigning the senate, only to reverse two days later and announce, via radio from Ouanaminthe, that "according to the wishes" of the people of his district, he would in fact serve until 2012.[16] In a letter Boulos subsequently sent to Senate President Kelly Bastien, he wrote that he had been the victim of "a political lynching" and that he would "seize every legal means to defend my rights and those of my constituents who are currently denied in the most shameless manner."[17] Within a few days, however, Boulos had crossed into the Dominican Republic and was describing himself as a "senator in exile" and saying that he would petition the IACHR to hear his case.[18] Showing in the meantime that they were always committed to leading by example, on 1 April – April Fool's Day – one member of the Chamber of Deputies, Isidore Mercier, from Jérémie, drew his revolver (many deputies were habitually armed) and shot at Léogâne's representative Anthony Dumont. RDNP members both, the men were arguing not about some great affair of state but rather over who would get to use the office of missing deputy Maxo Balthazar, who had appeared at parliament only a few times since being elected. Mercier missed Dumont and instead wounded a parliamentary employee.[19]

* * *

As Haiti's politicians continued with their ceaseless intriguing, protests began erupting in the south. Between Friday and Saturday (4–5 April) at least four people were killed during demonstrations in Les Cayes (other sources put the number of dead at closer to 15) during which MINUSTAH troops and PNH officers were attacked.[20] In subsequent violence, protesters would attempt to burn down a hotel owned by Gabriel Fortuné, at which point security guards fired on the crowd, killing one. The mob then moved on to loot a store they believed belonged to Fortuné's wife.[21] During the same period, a police patrol on the capital's Avenue Christophe was shot at and one policeman wounded.[22] In the wake of the violence, Pierre Léger, the president of the Chamber of Commerce for the South Department, called on Préval and Alexis to resign, accusing them of "resounding failure."[23] The protesters said they were demonstrating against the rising cost of living in Haiti – *lavi chè*, as it was known in Creole – but many believed they were backed by Préval's opponents, including drug traffickers. Some thought they might even be backed by Préval himself.

Peacekeepers formed a security perimeter around the National Palace after an unsuccessful attempt to storm it, and shot at protesters who attempted to breach it, wounding several people, including a *Le Matin* journalist. Demonstrators were also seen in the capital's Delmas, Nazon and Canapé Vert neighborhoods.[24] Motorists who attempted to traverse roads near Martissant were met with hurled bottles and rocks, while in Jérémie dueling protesters carried placards praising both Aristide and Guy Philippe.[25] Only hours later, a worried Hédi Annabi addressed the UN Security Council in New York, telling them that "the growing public discontent has the clear potential to undermine efforts at stabilization."[26]

Throughout the chaos, allies and adversaries were mystified by Préval's silence, with Youri Latortue telling the *Miami Herald* that "when people are destroying other people's property, you can't just sit and say nothing."[27] According to Haitian and international diplomats in the country at the time, during the height of the riots, Préval simply "went to ground" and "disappeared" to the point where no foreign embassy nor even officials in his own government could get hold of him.[28] As noted, this led some to speculate that Préval himself had a hand in the protests.[29]

By Wednesday, panic began to spread in certain parts of the capital as looters attacked businesses and private homes.[30] Thousands of protesters, characterized by Radio Métropole as "very violent," marched to the Palace, breaking windshields and setting a number of cars, including MINUSTAH vehicles, on fire and promising to "burn the city."[31] At least 18 people were wounded by gunfire and the MINUSTAH base in Petit-Goâve was attacked.[32] In Limbé, someone set fire to the elections bureau and protesters attempted to block Route National 1 with flaming tires at Frecineau, near Saint-Marc.[33]

Finally, on Wednesday, Préval addressed the nation, saying: "I'm giving you orders to stop."[34] He went on to promise fertilizer subsidies for farmers and other agricultural measures, saying that he understood the "problems" and the "despair" of the protesters and that the nation must "get back on the road of peace and work together."[35] Appearing to undercut Préval, though, on the same day Chamber of Deputies President Pierre Eric Jean Jacques (himself a Lespwa member) declared the protests "legitimate," although he called on protesters to respect private property.[36]

Only hours after Préval's address, 16 of the 27 senators sent a letter to Jacques Édouard Alexis demanding that he resign, its signatories including Youri Latortue, Rudy Hériveaux, Edmonde Supplice Beauzile, Michel Clérié and Gabriel Fortuné.[37] Hériveaux said that the demand for the resignation was "irrevocable."[38] By 12 April, parliament – which had so often been lax and desultory in its duties – voted to oust Alexis, who was present in the chamber for the ballot and said he was "at peace" with his conscience. As they did so, a handful of Lavalas supporters shouted "Aristide or death" outside. Blocks away, a Nigerian riot control officer was gunned down while out to run an errand. Shortly before the vote, Préval had announced that new government subsidies would lower the price of a 50-pound sack of rice from $51 to $43. A $10 million emergency grant from the World Bank was also announced.[39] After the vote, Senator Evalière Beauplan alleged that those who had voted for Alexis's departure had been the subject of death threats.[40] For his part, Préval publicly called the decision to oust Alexis "unjust."[41]

The riots would also eventually bring to the surface the schizophrenic side of Préval's political personality. It is tempting to view Préval as a docile agronomist, committed democrat and reluctant politician. It would not, however, be accurate. Probably the country's most capable and wily political operator, Préval was neither an ardent champion nor a staunch foe of the democratic process in Haiti, a process that, though it brought him to office twice, also habitually introduced opportunists, thieves and murderers into the public sphere who showed none of his interest in ameliorating the misery in which so many Haitians existed. There was also a pronounced dark side to Préval – Machiavellian, given to intriguing against his rivals and even his allies, deeply distrustful (with reason) of Haiti's political class even as he tried to open up its political system, and sometimes as resentful of those he viewed as outshining him as he was at ease working with international institutions. Looking at Haiti's elections, which time and again failed to put people in power who were committed to addressing the country's chronic issues, one can understand his skepticism. Far from being a marassa of Aristide as he was once viewed, he was a Janus-like figure with one face looking forward to develop Haiti's future and another face stubbornly looking back to practices of the past. Préval was, in fact, a marassa of himself.

* * *

Nearly two weeks after Alexis's divestment, Préval announced that he was selecting 63-year-old IADB economist Ericq Pierre as his next nominee for prime minister. Pierre had been nominated – and rejected by parliament – 11 years earlier during Préval's first term in office after the resignation of Rosny Smarth.[42] Haiti's senate voted to support Pierre as prime minister,[43] but the Chamber of Deputies rejected the nomination because, among other reasons, the black, Creole-speaking Pierre could not prove "that he was descended from native-born Haitians."[44] Pierre thus had the distinction of being the only person in Haitian history rejected as prime minister not once but twice.

Following Pierre's rejection, Préval announced that his new choice for prime minister would be the former chief of his re-election campaign and former Secretary of State for Public Security Bob Manuel. How Manuel, who had for a number of years been living in Guatemala working for the United Nations mission there, planned to skirt the five-year residency requirement for the post was unclear. After a glacially slow debate, the parliament was said to be "divided" on the issue, with Luther King Marcadieu pointing out that Préval himself had not been resident in the country for five continuous years when he was elected president during his first mandate in 1996 (he had been in exile for a time during the de facto government).[45] Nevertheless, the Chamber of Deputies rejected Manuel, charging that he didn't own property in Haiti and was not registered to vote.[46]

* * *

Following the failure of yet another choice as prime minister, Préval reached back into his own past to tap Michèle Duvivier Pierre-Louis, a respected civil society figure and the head of the organization FOKAL.

Pierre-Louis had been born in the southern city of Jérémie in 1947, and had left the town with her family in 1964 following the pogrom by François Duvalier against his perceived enemies there. Studying in the United States and France before returning to Haiti in 1977, she worked in a variety of roles before taking a management job at the capital's airport, where she hired Préval. After Frantz Bennett, the brother of Jean-Claude Duvalier's wife, was arrested trafficking cocaine in Puerto Rico in 1982,[47] the regime summarily fired all the airport staff when the director there was deemed insufficiently supportive of the jailed scion. Shortly thereafter, Pierre-Louis and Préval opened a bakery together devoted to serving the capital's poor, and, in that context, while delivering bread to the Saint Jean Bosco church on the edge of the La Saline slum, both first met a young priest named Jean-Bertrand Aristide.[48] Pierre-Louis served in Aristide's private cabinet during his truncated first seven months in office, and was one of the first people to denounce the 1991 coup against him, in an interview with Radio France Internationale. As with so many, Pierre-Louis' relationship with Aristide disintegrated once the latter had returned from exile, and was severed altogether following the August 1998 murder of her brother-in-law, the activist priest Père Jean Pierre Louis, whose funeral was disrupted by a mob shouting pro-Aristide slogans. In the meantime, she opened FOKAL with the support of businessman and philanthropist George Soros's Open Society Institute. In the coming years, FOKAL would be responsible for opening a network of community libraries throughout Haiti, a cultural center for economically disadvantaged youths in the capital, a debate program for young people and an initiative to supply running water to those who did not have regular access to it.

Announced shortly after Manuel's rejection, the reaction of Haiti's parliament was to stall, and to make no move towards assessing the Pierre-Louis appointment for over a week.[49] But finally, on the last day of July, more than three months after the collapse of the Alexis government, the senate followed the Chamber of Deputies and approved Michèle Pierre-Louis as Haiti's new prime minister.[50] Pierre-Louis thus became Haiti's second female prime minister, the first having been Claudette Werleigh, who served as Aristide's prime minister for less than a year after he returned from exile during his first term.

* * *

As Pierre-Louis entered public service, another figure was leaving it. The public unraveling of Claudy Gassant, a man who had once inspired so much hope in Haiti, was now nearly complete. At a July music festival, Gassant reportedly assaulted one member of Métro Sécurité, the group providing security for the event, after asking if his men were "Mario's [i.e. Andrésol's] boys," menaced others with a gun, destroyed the equipment of a journalist whose camera had documented his behavior, and arrested Métro Sécurité's chief, Fahed Esper. Days later, when police stopped a vehicle in Delmas they suspected of being involved in kidnappings and the occupants fled, it was later revealed that the vehicle belonged to Préval spokesman Assad Volcy, a friend of Gassant's, who the latter was drinking with in Pétionville at the time, and that the men who fled were Volcy's bodyguard and driver. Gassant arrived on the scene and engaged in a furious argument with Pétionville PNH commander Frantz Georges, finally ordering the car be driven to his office.[51] Later still, Gassant reportedly had a conflagration with Georges at a concert by the band T-Vice at the posh seaside Club Indigo on the Côte des Arcadins.[52] This public outburst proved the final straw, and, after a tenure that had been marked by chaos and recrimination, Gassant tendered his resignation after a meeting with Préval, René Magloire and Mario Andrésol.[53] The Haitian system had claimed another scalp.

* * *

As Haiti's eternal political crisis appeared to be edging towards a truce, disaster of a different sort was visited on the country in the form of no fewer than four immense storms – Tropical Storm Fay, Hurricane Gustave, Hurricane Hanna and Hurricane Ike – that made landfall in Haiti between mid-August and mid-September. By Ike's end, the Haitian government was saying that more than 120,000 people were in shelters throughout the Artibonite. One journalist visiting Gonaïves after Ike's floodwaters had receded described "a stinking mud bath and homes … carpeted with muck and encrusted pots, pans and laundry."[54] The storms had killed at least 793 people and wiped out more than half of the year's harvest.[55] On 13 September, Michèle Pierre-Louis led a government delegation that included Youri Latortue and local deputy Arsène Dieujuste to Gonaïves aboard a UN helicopter. Flying over a seemingly endless expanse of flooded land and arriving in the stricken city, a visibly moved Pierre-Louis said that Gonaïves had been "ravaged to the core" and looked as if it had "suffered all the horrors of war." Residents trudged through waist-deep fetid water to hear Pierre-Louis speak atop a MINUSTAH truck in front of city hall, where she told them that they "had to mobilize and be unified … because we must rebuild this city!"[56]

"It's really hard to overestimate the impact the year of the hurricanes had on the government's agenda falling apart," said one international diplomat in Haiti at the time. "It really blew everything out of the water."[57]

Despite the devastation wrought by the hurricanes, during a mid-October visit to the country, World Bank president Robert Zoellick said there were no plans for the body to forgo demanding payments on the share of the $1.7 billion foreign debt Haiti was in hock for. Haiti was at the time making payments in the neighborhood of $1 million per week.[58] The UN Security Council, on the other hand, voted unanimously to renew MINUSTAH's mandate for another year, though pointedly ignoring the Haitian government's request that the mission's focus be shifted from security to economic development.[59] A contemporaneous study by Canada's Rights & Democracy and Haiti's Groupe de Recherche et d'Appui au Milieu Rural (GRAMIR) noted that Haiti ranked among the top three countries with the highest deficit in daily caloric intake per inhabitant, with 46 percent of women and 61 percent of children under the age of five suffering from anemia.[60]

* * *

After the wrenching succession of hurricanes, I found myself sitting in a modest home in Brooklyn talking to someone who had, for decades, been working to reverse Haiti's environmental death spiral. I had first met the peasant leader Chavannes Jean-Baptiste in Haiti's Plateau Central after a November 2000 attempt on his life. The head of Haiti's MPP and MPNKP peasant unions, Chavannes was the son of illiterate peasants and had been a Catholic lay worker before helping to found the MPP in 1973. I had gone back to Papay to visit him several times since then, inevitably sitting in the passenger seat of a tap-tap next to the driver, as we climbed up the alarmingly crumbling road up Mon Kabrit, *konpa* music pumping on the sound system as the rhythm of conversation and laughter came behind us. Two years before our meeting in Brooklyn, Chavannes had been awarded the Goldman Environmental Prize, the world's largest prize for grassroots environmentalists.

"The economic situation of the peasantry is very difficult, we have witnessed the degradation of the entire environment," Chavannes told me. "There is less agricultural production, and people are migrating to the cities, creating slums such as those we see in Port-au-Prince. This adds to the urban population and to the demand for wood charcoal."

"We've planted 20,000 trees around the country over the last 20 years, but over the same time period some 50,000 trees have been cut down. We can say that we have never had a government in Haiti that ever changed the problems of the peasantry. We need to create environmental protection and work together, at the same time, in a national framework. There has been a lot of demagoguery, because none of the politicians have had a program to help the peasants. The politicians and the government are working to implement a neoliberal program, and the parliamentarians have one preoccupation: to remain in parliament."

As we got ready to go to a talk that he was giving at a local branch of the Brooklyn Public Library, he had a message he wanted to convey.

"What seems clear now is that Haiti is going from catastrophe to catastrophe, and they are getting worse as we go along. And that is a direct result of the destruction of the environment. We need to change this pattern. Now."

* * *

And there was another warning. In Pétionville, on the morning of 7 November, the La Promesse school collapsed due to its shoddy construction, killing at least 90 people – mostly children – and grievously injuring many more. As rescuers, including teams from the United States and Martinique, searched for the dead and extracted the injured and the stench of decay began to fill the air, hysterical relatives of the missing clawed at the raw debris with their bare hands. Ugly scenes of PNH and MINUSTAH driving off the intruders at baton-point soon developed.

Visiting the site, Préval said that "what we need is political stability" and that, although building codes already existed in Haiti, they were rarely followed.

Stephen Benoît, the community's representative in the Chamber of Deputies warned that, with such chaotic construction rife, the collapse was "one catastrophe but we have many more to come."[61]

* * *

But who exactly, one wondered, was in a position to enforce such an order? After the tortured body of Monique Pierre, the girlfriend of the popular Gonaïves police commissioner Ernst Bouquet Dorfeuille, was found just north of Port-au-Prince, Senate President Kelly Bastien made the extraordinary revelation that the license plate of a grey Nissan Patrol used in the murder – Officiel 00332 – was in fact in the employ of Joseph Lambert, who in return denied any involvement in the case and claimed that his license plate may have been "tampered" with.[62] He later said that he had been using the vehicle with the license plate in question "to distribute seeds and food" to farmers in his home district in the southeast of the country.[63] It was later revealed that Pierre's real name was Monique Antoine, and that she had been arrested in New York in 1995 for possession of narcotics, serving nearly two years before being released and deported back to Haiti. After her return, she became a wealthy woman who owned properties throughout the country, including some that she rented to MINUSTAH.[64] According to the PNH, her connections with the narco underworld continued after her return.[65] After initially eliciting sympathy – including a visit from Préval – Dorfeuille was subsequently arrested and charged with Pierre's murder, and would spend two and a half years in prison before being released and returning to Gonaïves.[66] Although the senator himself was never arrested, several of those subsequently arrested for Pierre's murder were current or former PNH officers with personal links to Lambert.[67] And the troubles for the PNH were not over, as one agent was stoned and lynched by a mob in Cité Soleil on 4 December, allegedly on the orders of a local crime boss.[68] On 16 December – the eighteenth anniversary of the elections that first brought Aristide to power – several thousand Lavalas partisans demonstrated in Port-au-Prince to call for his return (an event they said Préval had "promised"), among them René Civil, Yvon Feuillé and Jacques Mathelier.[69] Also among the protesters were two wanted criminals, Mercius "Ti Wilson" Fénel and Riccardo "Kiki" Pyram, who claimed that he was a "distinguished rapist" who would "rape his own mother" if the opportunity arose. The men were pointed out and arrested after they attempted to rob onlookers watching the demonstration.[70]

As 2008 drew to a close, Préval and Pierre-Louis announced that long-delayed legislative elections would be held during the coming year, with the first and second rounds on 19 April and 7 June respectively.[71] The *jwèt elektoral* (electoral game), as some called it, was soon to begin again.

CHAPTER NINE
PLOTS AND REVELATIONS

After the tribulations of 2008, it was a grim-faced Préval who addressed the nation at the traditional 1 January independence commemoration in Gonaïves, the damage from flooding still visible throughout the city.

"Haiti will suffer in 2009," Préval told the country's citizens, joined by Michèle Pierre-Louis and others members of the government, citing how the global economic crisis, the storms that had battered the country the previous year and Haiti's political instability "shook" the nation. He went on to say that, during 2009, the government's objectives would be the construction of a "national road network" and "peace-building," singling out for praise the work that Jude Célestin's CNE had done in the former department.[1] A few weeks later, a confidential cable from the U.S. Embassy in Port-au-Prince seemed more concerned with Haiti's internal, rather than external, threats, concluding that "investigation and prosecution of corruption under President Préval is haphazard and has failed to bring a single major case to trial." It went on to state that Gassant's office had "acted as an overzealous policeman, conducting spectacular raids and hauling in suspects for questioning, but the prosecutor and examining magistrates have failed to build prosecutable cases." The cable continued that "although President Préval does not use his office to enrich himself, many of his aides and other government leaders do," before concluding that "what passes for the Government of Haiti's anti-corruption campaign displays the central penchant of the Haitian President: bursts of energy for policy initiatives that peter out for lack of follow-up."[2]

That corruption would figure at the heart of one of the darkest chapters of Préval's second term in office, an incident that, while in no way implicating the president and passing almost without comment by the international community, vividly demonstrated the impunity and ruthlessness with which those pulling the threads of the webs of corruption in Haiti could act when they felt their interests were threatened.

It was said that during the reign of Jean-Jacques Dessalines a certain level of corruption was tolerated and dismissed with the phrase *plumez la poule, mais ne la laissez pas crier* (pluck the chicken, but make sure it doesn't squawk). That tradition of corruption had been a woeful constant in Haiti's political life since Dessalines was assassinated over 200 years previously. As 2009 began, Joseph François Robert Marcello was the coordinator for Haiti's Commission Nationale des Marchés Publics (CNMP), a body that had been extant since late 2004 to guarantee fair public bidding on all government contracts and to maximize the efficient use of Haiti's meagre public funds in a country where 78 percent of the population still lived on $2 or less per day.[3] Given its mandate, the CNMP had close dealings with the CNE that Préval had heaped praise on in Gonaïves. Formerly an employee of Haiti's Banque Nationale de Crédit, the 65-year-old Marcello was, by all accounts, an honest and competent public servant, exactly the kind of person who, if the Haitian government was serious about its stated desire to combat corruption, would serve as one of its prime foot soldiers.

It was exactly that competence and honesty, however, that may have led to Marcello receiving a series of increasingly dire telephone threats in late 2008 and early 2009, threats his family said he had informed the Préval government about, and the dates and times of which he recorded on a small index card that would eventually find its way into the hands of the DCPJ.[4] And it was that honesty and competence, many also believe, that led to his kidnapping by a car full of gunmen while out walking near his Delmas home on 12 January. From her home in Canada, his daughter, Rose, bemoaned "the indifference of the police and the government since the beginning of this case."[5] Préval, for his part, maintained a stony silence, so much so that the Marcello family, again through the pen of daughter Rose, wrote an open letter they said was "an appeal to the entire Haitian population."

She wrote:

Beyond those who ordered the kidnapping or those who rejoice or benefit from it, we want to reach the neighbors of the place where he is detained, those who have seen or heard him, or those who may have a mere suspicion ... [Our father] treated his employees and collaborators, most modest, and the inhabitants of the vast slum that stretches not far from our own neighborhood, with as much consideration as himself ... If he can be reproached, despite his legendary pragmatism, it can be that he was too naive for the Haitian government, believed too much in the decency of others; believed, sometimes even beyond all of the proof otherwise, that another Haiti is possible … We will fight, we will cry out until we have an outcome.[6]

And no doubt the family meant every word, and desperately wanted to believe that their collective will, and the will of a nation, would have an effect. But Robert Marcello, it appeared, was destined to join Haiti's long list of the unavenged.

* * *

On 22 January, Lavalas, by this point headed in Haiti by sitting senator Rudy Hériveaux and the physician Maryse Narcisse, announced that it would be fielding candidates for the upcoming election with what they said was Aristide's consultation and blessing. These candidates would include Nawoon Marcellus, Gérald Gilles and Jacques Mathelier, and Bale Wouze's ex-chieftain Amanus Mayette.[7] To anyone wondering whether or not Lavalas was interested in distancing itself from its sanguinary past, surveying such a rogue's gallery, the answer was a definite "no." However, the announcement also begged the question of exactly what was "Lavalas" in the present context, as yet another political grouping – led by Yvon Neptune, Jocelerme Privert, Annette Auguste and former deputy Yves Cristalin – also claimed the Lavalas banner and were running their own slate of candidates.[8] One of the most recognizable faces of Lavalas, former Milot mayor turned Préval advisor Moïse Jean-Charles, had jumped ship some time ago and was running for senate under Préval's Lespwa banner. Moïse's presence in the president's camp was not without controversy, as Limonade deputy Hugues Célestin, also Lespwa, charged that it was "no secret" that the would-be senator was "accused of murder" and that he could not understand how the party could make such a choice.[9] Among the others registering was wanted man Guy Philippe, who was escorted by PNH officials as he put his name in the running for senate in Jérémie.[10]

In early February, the CEP announced that, among others (40 in all of 105 prospective candidates), all candidates from Aristide's Fanmi Lavalas party and Guy Philippe would be barred from contesting the upcoming election. The reason given for excluding Lavalas was that the party had failed to produce a definitive attestation from an official party leader (Aristide) as to which of the two competing Lavalas branches was the legitimate one.[11] The attorneys for the two competing branches of Lavalas promptly took to the airwaves warning of dire legal consequences for their "illegitimate" rivals.[12] On 11 February, the CEP announced that Maryse Narcisse had 48 hours during which to produce a "genuine mandate" from Aristide regarding the legitimacy of her wing of the Lavalas party, "notarized and registered by the consular services of Haiti" (presumably in South Africa).[13] A day later, several of the banned candidates from the Narcisse wing of the party (Nawoon Marcellus, Amanus Mayette and Gérald Gilles among them) went to the offices of the CEP to plead for their reintegration into elections.[14] When neither faction of Lavalas was able to produce what the CEP viewed as an "authentic" attestation from the head of the party, they were granted yet another extension, this one lasting 72 hours.[15] A day after that deadline passed, the CEP announced that the slate was definitively rejected.[16] The fact that CEP councilors were reportedly threatened with physical harm if they did not approve the Lavalas candidates and that CEP president Verret allegedly grumbled that the group were "criminals" probably did not help their case.[17] Lavalas announced that it would launch a *porte fermée* (closed door) protest for the day of the elections.[18] A subsequent article in South Africa's *Sunday Independent* reminded readers that Aristide continued to live a "multimillion-rand lifestyle [with a] protection package here bankrolled by taxpayers."[19]

* * *

As Haiti's perpetual political squabbles churned, another vision for the country was being promoted by the powerful forces who had exercised such influence over it in recent years. With the positive growth of 2.5 percent displayed by Haiti's economy for 2008–09 due at least in part to public investment, the government announced that in the coming year it would concentrate on attracting private investment to Haiti, and would use public money to do so.[20] At the behest of the United Nations, the Oxford University economist Paul Collier released a report titled "Haiti: From Natural Catastrophe to Economic Security" at the beginning of the year, a report that, to a great degree, would serve as a lens through which foreign powers would view the country's potential.

The report stated that, despite the shocks to Haiti caused by the *lavi chè* riots and the storms, the potential for its economic development was in fact "far more favourable than those of the 'fragile states' with which it is habitually grouped." It continued that Haiti was "in a prosperous and peaceful neighborhood" and did not "have the intractable structural sociopolitical problems that beset most other fragile states," such as ethnic divides or "an armed and organized political group ready to launch rebellion," a conclusion that seemed to largely ignore Haiti's previous two decades, to say nothing of its previous 200 years. The report was full of praise for the commitment of Préval and Pierre-Louis to "the maintenance of social peace," Haiti's skilled diaspora, and the "massive economic opportunity in the form of HOPE II," a reference to the Haitian Hemispheric Opportunity through Partnership Encouragement Act, which established unlimited duty-free treatment for some clothing and textiles. Haiti's future, the report suggested, would be in such sectors as the garment industry and the construction of various "export zones," while granting that coordinating garment exports would require "international private sector convening power such as might be appropriate for the Clinton Global Initiative," as an ancillary of the Clinton Foundation nonprofit set up by former U.S. president Bill Clinton was known. In terms of agriculture, the report suggested a "food-for-work" program but nowhere suggested revisiting the draconian free-trade policies that had so devastated Haiti's peasantry.[21] In early March, UN Secretary-General Ban Ki-moon, Bill Clinton himself and Haitian-American musician Wyclef Jean visited Haiti aboard a U.S. government plane to lend their support to Collier's plan, and to show, in Clinton's words, "people back in America and throughout the world ... that Haiti's worth supporting."[22]

Despite his popularity with Haiti's youth and his presence on the Clinton mission, though, questions dogged Wyclef Jean about his charity, Yéle Haiti, which he had founded several years previously, and which had been surrounded by controversy ever since its inception. Only months after its creation, Yéle's executive director had resigned over alleged misuse of funds.[23]

Following a donor's conference in Washington that brought the total U.S. commitment to Haiti to $302 million for 2009 (thanks, in large part, to the efforts of Michèle Pierre-Louis), during a brief stopover in Port-au-Prince, U.S. Secretary of State Hillary Clinton (representing the newly inaugurated president Barack Obama) said that, after a meeting with Préval, she believed the president's great hope was to "see progress begun and finished to give the future back to the people of Haiti."[24] Soon thereafter, Ban Ki-moon would announce that he was naming Bill Clinton as the body's special envoy to Haiti, a perhaps somewhat confusing decision as Hédi Annabi was already in the country on behalf of the UN heading up MINUSTAH. Clinton told *The Miami Herald* upon his appointment that "Haiti's government and people have the determination and ability to 'build back better,' not just to repair the damage done but to lay the foundations for the long-term sustainable development that has eluded them for so long."[25] Despite the boosterism, however, earlier in the year a European study had pointedly warned that "many development projects fail or do not prove sustainable because donors do not listen to the voices of the people, and the Haitian government is not necessarily fulfilling its role as an agent to represent their interests."[26]

* * *

In late February, Préval announced that two new commissions would be formed by presidential decree. One, focusing on proposed changes to the 1987 constitution, would include, among others, Jean-Claude Bajeux, Yves Cristalin, Charles Suffrard and Daniel Supplice, while the other, focused on reform of the justice system, would include Sylvie Bajeux, Micha Gaillard and Thierry Mayard-Paul.[27] Such extra-parliamentary analysis was perhaps well-founded as parliament itself was again the scene of violence when Fusion's Emmanuel Fritz Gérald Bourjolly assaulted Chamber of Deputies president Levaillant Louis-Jeune after not being granted the floor to address the body during a discussion on the use of emergency funds. In the wake of the fracas, Michèle Pierre-Louis and several members of her government were escorted, under armed guard, from the chamber.[28] Levaillant subsequently sent a letter to the government apologizing for Bourjolly's actions.[29] Two days later, Sandro Joseph, the former director of Haiti's Office National d'Assurance-vieillesse (ONA), was arrested and charged with embezzling and misappropriating funds, charges that stemmed directly from a ULCC investigation into the body dating from the previous year and alleging that monies were siphoned from pension funds to pay for the 2007 carnival.[30] Joseph, a former journalist and Teleco official, was taken to the Pénitencier National.[31] In a rare success for Haiti's justice system, Joseph would actually be tried and convicted for his role in the scheme.[32] Several parliamentarians named in the ULCC's report, however, escaped sanction.

Another Préval creation, the CIAPEAJ, marked the ninth anniversary of the murders of Jean Dominique and Jean-Claude Louissaint with dozens of journalists demonstrating in Port-au-Prince over the lack of progress in the investigation, and with CIAPEAJ president Guy Delva noting that "nine judges, each more clever than the last, have succeeded in producing no results after nine years of investigation." The body announced a new reward for information in the case.[33] And the shadow of impunity also fell elsewhere, with *Le Nouvelliste*'s Roberson Alphonse demanding on the three-month anniversary of Roberto Marcello's disappearance "Where is Marcello?,"[34] while DCPJ chief Frantz Thermilus said, rather too placidly for some, that "the investigation is progressing."[35] Even as Thermilus spoke, Préval advisor and law professor Enex Jean-Charles was kidnapped in Delmas but, unlike Marcello, managed to escape his captors after 48 hours.[36] By mid-April, masked, armed men in PNH uniforms again appeared in Pestel, allegedly looking for Guy Philippe.[37] Despite these high-profile incidents, however, the UN Office on Drugs and Crime would note that Haiti was not even among the top ten most dangerous countries in Latin America and the Caribbean.[38]

* * *

The April parliamentary elections – many months late – were marked by participation characterized as "timid," though voting centers largely opened on time and remained so for the rare voter who would amble by.[39] Though Lavalas attempted to claim credit for the abstention due to their *porte fermée* protest, there is little evidence this was the case. In Mirebalais some gunmen stole ballots,[40] while another set of armed men, reported to be traveling in vehicles belonging to Senator Jacques Jean Wilbert from Préval's Lespwa, forcibly shut other voting centers.[41] Willot Joseph, the former Lavalas mayor of Maïssade mentioned in connection with the 2000 attempt on the life of Chavannes Jean-Baptiste, now affiliated with the Union de Citoyens Haïtiens Démocrates pour le Développement et l'Education (UCADDE), was also reported circulating around the region threatening people with a Galil rifle.[42] A dispute between two of Joseph's "close collaborators" would eventually result in the death of one by firearm.[43] A report by RNDDH would later say that Joseph and his cadre were "the main perpetrators of violence" in the region during the election.[44] Given such an atmosphere, as the day progressed, the CEP would eventually call off elections in the Plateau Central.[45] At least three candidates withdrew due to what they said were insurmountable hurdles in the process.[46] MINUSTAH issued a statement praising the "good technical organization of the elections" while criticizing the incidents in the Plateau Central.[47] Official turnout was later estimated at 11 percent.[48] In addition to general skepticism, an official ban on public transportation and motorcycles was also thought to have depressed the vote.[49] Despite initial reports that there were no winners in the first round for the 11 vacant senate seats,[50] by 6 May the Bureau du

Contentieux Électoral Départemental (BCED) in the North Department was announcing that Préval ally Moïse Jean-Charles had won 51 percent in his senate race.[51] Questions arose as to how Lespwa candidate John Joël Joseph managed to garner 6,266 votes in his native Cité Soleil when only 44,000 people voted in the entire metropolitan area of Port-au-Prince.[52] Senate Vice President (and OPL member) Andrys Riché called for the vote tabulation to be called off to avoid "a major political crisis."[53] A later elections-related clash in Cayes-Jacmel between supporters of Joseph Lambert and those of OPL's Ricard Pierre would leave one dead.[54] Speaking in Gonaïves, Préval told his audience that "I am neither a member of Lespwa nor Lavalas. I have never been a member of any political party."[55] Members of OPL, Lavalas and MOCHRENA promptly lambasted the president for what they charged was his lack of results after three years in power.[56]

* * *

An explosive debate about Haiti's minimum wage had also erupted, with some parliamentarians, led by Pétionville deputy Stephen Benoît, urging it be raised to 200 gourdes per day. The ADIH funded a study that claimed that the average salary for garment sector workers was already 173 gourdes a day and claiming that raising the daily wage to 200 gourdes would result in the loss of 10,000 jobs.[57] Préval sent a letter to the senate and Chamber of Deputies asking that the bodies "consider the impact [higher wages] would have on employment and the overall investment climate in Haiti."[58] The U.S. Embassy was vocally and openly hostile to the move, and supported Préval's position opposing it.[59]

* * *

In mid-May 2009, over the border in the Dominican Republic, Carlo Mérilus from the Artibonite's Verrettes was decapitated in front of a braying crowd in Santo Domingo when it was believed he had been involved in an earlier killing.[60] When news of the Mérilus killing reached Haiti, about 150 protesters gathered outside the Dominican Embassy and Consulate in Pétionville, tearing down a sign and breaking a window at the former.[61] Mérilus' funeral in Verrettes became an occasion for airing grievances against successive governments that had done so little to ameliorate the plight of Haiti's citizens and forced them to look for a new life across the Massacre River.[62] Days later, at the opening of the joint committee that Préval and Fernández had set up for Haitian–Dominican affairs,

Michèle Pierre-Louis said that "recent events" had obliged her to address "the repeated attacks, wanton killings, harassment, nuisance repatriation, border incidents suffered by our fellow citizens" in the Dominican Republic and that the situation "has lasted too long."[63] The Dominican government responded with a statement in which it said that "only the unwillingness of the Haitian government could jeopardize relations" between the two countries, and that it was "regrettable that the leader of the Haitian government did not mention the speed with which Dominican authorities have responded" to the incidents of violence in its country.[64] Shortly thereafter, the Dominicans suspended their participation in the body, and later said they were going to be moving thousands of soldiers and their families to the southwestern province of Pedernales to counter what they saw as an invasion of Haitians in the area, though the entire scenario the government painted was one some local observers dismissed as "a farce."[65]

* * *

The security climate, while vastly improved since the dark days of Operation Baghdad, was still hardly ideal, as was demonstrated when PNH officer Accelesse Laîné, a known opponent of the capital's gangs, was slain while driving through Martissant's Cité l'Eternel area.[66] Residents said they had been warning MINUSTAH for weeks about the return of various criminal elements to the zone.[67] A few days later, an attempted kidnapping in Cité Soleil left three dead.[68] Michèle Pierre-Louis said that the government was determined to prevent a return of the insecurity that had plagued the capital in past years.[69] By this point, Haiti could boast 9,247 police officers in a force that, under the leadership of Mario Andrésol and others, had become as professional and effective as it had ever been.[70] In a few weeks' time, a large cache of weapons – M14s, M1s, shotguns and a vast amount of ammunition – would be seized in La Saline in a joint operation by the CNDDR and the PNH.[71]

On 3 June, the first day of a university student mobilization in favor of raising Haiti's paltry minimum wage, individuals inside the Faculté des Sciences Humaines showered stones down on FOKAL, terrorizing the young students present, leading other cultural institutions to "condemn these acts of violence which can only lock us in the cycle of destruction … [and] say forcefully that culture is what saves us from barbarism."[72] On the second day of the action, a confrontation with the PNH along Avenue Christophe saw a rain of hurled stones, liberal lashings of tear gas and a student hit in the head by a rubber bullet.[73] A similarly chaotic confrontation happened the following day; however, this time several journalists were attacked by protesters claiming to be students and their vehicles damaged.[74] The mood of the students and their alleged allies had been growing increasingly ugly, with a pair of filmmakers assaulted when they attempted to film at the Faculté des Sciences Humaines.[75] The situation escalated still further when a student was slain under unclear circumstances near the UEH during clashes between the PNH and protesters, several of whom were found to be armed.[76] As June dragged on, a United Nations Police (UNPOL) vehicle was burned, its occupants forced to flee, a bus set aflame near the École Normale Supérieure and "hundreds" of car windshields broken by hurled rocks, turmoil that was only stopped by Haiti's heavy summer rains.[77] Although Steven Benoît, referred to as the "father" of the minimum wage dispute, called for dialogue between Préval and the students,[78] the president refused to budge.[79]

Amid such turmoil in the capital, the dissident priest Gérard Jean-Juste, whose name in Haiti evoked rather more conflicted emotions than it did among his acolytes abroad, died in Miami. At Jean-Juste's funeral at the National Cathedral in Port-au-Prince on 19 June, there was a large outpouring of grief from the sectors of *le lumpen* who believed he had been their champion,[80] with some mourners waving Aristide banners[81] and yet others chanting pro-Aristide slogans as a *rara* band played.[82] Other mourners chanted slogans hostile to, among others, Radio Kiskeya journalist Liliane Pierre-Paul.[83] During subsequent clashes with MINUSTAH troops, at least one person was killed.[84] Jean-Juste was laid to rest as he lived, surrounded by violence and recrimination.

* * *

Despite all the churning unrest, there were signs on multiple fronts that Haiti was beginning to inch forward. I found evidence of this when I returned to Haiti in June 2009 after an extended absence. Flying into Port-au-Prince, I looked down at the blue Caribbean again and was deeply happy to see it. Though there were the same tin shacks, the same dirt roads, the same bald, brown mountains, and, on Champ de Mars, still the seemingly idle-yet-searching multitudes, as I traveled throughout the capital there was a mood of calm and a guarded optimism that I was pleasantly surprised to encounter. An airport previously staffed by political cronies, where passengers sweated in boiling halls, was now a model of air-conditioned efficiency. Streets once deserted after sunset now teemed with life, with upper-class restaurants in Pétionville district and the kerosene-lit roadside stands of the *ti machann* (vendors) downtown luring customers late into the evening, something unthinkable only a few years earlier. At the beginning of 2009, Préval had created the Groupe de Travail sur la Compétitivité, a body designed to increase Haiti's competitiveness in attracting global businesses.

One of my first meetings was with Hédi Annabi, the Tunisian diplomat who had taken over as the head of MINUSTAH in September 2007. I passed through the security gates at the Hotel Christopher, where I had seen the death list on which my friend James and others had appeared years before, and was shown into Annabi's office. His manner seemed cool, almost bloodless, a contrast to Mulet, who could often exude a chess player's intelligence that could suggest ruthlessness.

"The capacity of the police has improved quite significantly, and the image of the police has begun to change within the society," Annabi told me. "The level of respect for basic freedoms, such as freedom of the press, is at a historically remarkable level."

According to Annabi, the number of kidnappings had fallen dramatically, from more than 500 in 2006 to about 50 during the first six months of 2009. A projected five-year UN-supported police reform program was in its third year of implementation.

Part of the new peace came from initiatives such as *Le Partenariat pour la Paix et la Prospérité à Saint Martin*. Formed in the volatile Port-au-Prince neighborhood of the same name, the initiative worked in cooperation with the Irish NGO Concern Worldwide, which had been in Haiti since 1994, and the Glencree Centre for Peace and Reconciliation, which had been formed during the Irish Troubles to promote reconciliation between warring Catholic and Protestant communities in Northern Ireland. Working with community members in Saint Martin – small business owners, health and education workers, the *baz* – the foreign interlocutors heard that it was not only local gangs but also "outside" forces that were having an impact on violence in the community. In a significant detail, a link existed between factory owners whose businesses resided in the area and the population of Saint Martin in the person of Louis-Henri Mars, the grandson of the Haitian diplomat and author Jean Price-Mars. A committee would eventually be formed consisting of three members of the businesses community, two members of Concern and 12 residents of Saint Martin. After the collective trauma of Operation Baghdad, the goal of the meeting was to try to get these disparate groups to find some common ground.

"The basic mistake that is made with groups here in Haiti is that they don't know each other well," Louis-Henri Mars – goateed, bespectacled and as comfortable in a dashiki as he was in a business suit – told me one day as we were stuck in traffic on the Route de Delmas, en route to Saint Martin. "They go out and want to 'do something,' then get mad at one another and it fails."

"The real question in Haiti is not health, economics or whatever," he continued. "That's a consequence. It's always been an issue of relationships, of 'are we in this together or are we separate tribes?' You have a mosaic of tribes here that don't really understand or appreciate one another, or realize they have a common humanity. And we need to make that connection."

The dialogue had been going on for two years by this point, and a recent general assembly to address community concerns had attracted nearly 150 people. Some of the bourgeoisie seemed to be reconsidering their role within the community as well.

"You can no longer put a business in a community where it is built against the community," Ralph Edmond, the president of Farmatrix, which had manufactured pharmaceutical products in the district since 1994, told me as we toured his factory. "If we are to live in this country, then we have to live differently than our fathers did before."

* * *

If Haiti truly wanted to change, one of the hurdles the country needed to overcome was the Himalayan impunity that stood between it and progress, and, with that in mind, I decided to pay a visit back to Saint-Marc. I drove there one morning with Pooja Bhatia, a journalist who was heading there to write an article about mango production. I would be heading back to La Scierie, to see what had become of the case and the victims of the February 2004 massacre.

We drove north along Route Nationale 1, through swirls of dust kicked up by the wind and passing tap-taps and skirting the gorgeous shimmering blue Caribbean. We passed Cabaret's raucous, filthy market, and Baby Doc's former mansion, now the embarkation point for ferries to Île de la Gonâve. After I hopped out and Pooja continued to her rendezvous, I waited on the roadside in the afternoon sun until AVIGES coordinator Charliénor Thomson arrived on the back of a moto. We walked into La Scierie together. Eventually, we came upon the burned-out RAMICOSM headquarters, which had been turned into something of a memorial to the victims, with an AVIGES mural, an image of a flaming torch and the words "Founded 16 March 2004." Soon we were joined by another man.

"They came here and they massacred people," 44-year-old Marc Ariel Narcisse told me. He wore a T-shirt reading "We won't forget 11 February 2004" in Creole. "A grenade thrown into my mother's house exploded, and the house caught fire. My cousin, Bob Narcisse, was killed there."

I wandered over to visit Amazil Jean-Baptiste, whose 23-year-old son, Kenol St. Gilles, had been shot, beaten unconscious and then thrown into a burning cement depot, where he was incinerated, by Bale Wouze members. In contrast to the air-conditioned luxury in which most foreign human rights "experts" existed in Haiti during their trips there of a few days, Jean-Baptiste lived in a dilapidated structure without running water. She was 49 but looked at least a decade older, wearing a threadbare skirt, a T-shirt and sandals.

"They killed my boy and burned my boy," she told me, as we stood in the half-finished entrance of the building. "And I am still suffering. We need justice, we demand justice, because we have never had it. I just want justice for my son."

The next day, back in Port-au-Prince, I sat discussing the case with RNDDH's Pierre Espérance in the group's Port-au-Prince office. While international groups had all but ignored the La Scierie massacre – more concerned with the accused held in jail without trial than with justice for the victims of the massacre itself – RNDDH had been pushing for justice for five years, with little to show for their efforts. Finally, during a lull in our conversation, Espérance looked off into space as if deep in thought and then spoke.

"In our system, the criminal becomes a victim because the system doesn't work."

* * *

Late one afternoon, I went to visit Jean-Claude and Sylvie Bajeux for dinner. On the back of a moto taxi, I drove up through Peguyville to Jean-Claude and Sylvie's home in a light rain just as the sun was setting, the streets looking delicate and glittering. En route, I passed in front of the house of the *konpa* singer Michel Martelly, its front gate unexpectedly open and its lush grounds dripping with greenery.

Jean-Claude and Sylvia greeted me warmly, and Jean-Claude doled out some of his own homemade rum punch, the best I had ever tasted.

"We are working hard, but the country doesn't seem to be going anywhere in terms of really reforming its institutions," Jean-Claude told me.

The couple seemed depressed about the continuing corruption and pointless political battles, about the continued disenfranchisement of the vote by violence and bribery, about the squalid conditions in which so many of their fellow citizens continued to live. They were exactly the kind of people the country needed, but I sensed that perhaps they wondered what 30-plus years of struggle had been for.

"Do those people realize they're there to make laws?" Sylvie asked at one point, referring to parliament.

As we talked, the rain picked up, until finally it was a torrential downpour and we sat on their porch, furniture pushed under an awning against the rain, as if to shield the more delicate things in life from the destructive downpour of the reality of Haiti.

* * *

A few days before the runoff parliamentary elections were scheduled, I ran into Steven Benoît at a Pétionville voting station, where he was checking on preparations for the day to come.

"In the first round we had a lot of violence, and you had a bunch of candidates who paid to get elected," he told me. "The candidates are not that popular, you have ex-drug dealers and criminals, and no one wants to vote for them."

I asked him about the minimum wage battle.

"I left Haiti and went to New York in 1983. The minimum wage then was $3 a day, now it's $1.80. What can someone do with that? Nothing."

When I wandered into the Faculté de Médecine downtown, nexus of some of the most bitter protests surrounding the wage dispute, I found a handful of students milling about, two of them wearing Che Guevara T-shirts. I started chatting with one student, who wore an ivory necklace that spelled out the word "Kill" in the middle. He told me his name was Beneche Martial.

"They chose not to listen to us," Martial told me. "We were obligated to mobilize about our concerns."

When election day itself dawned, I found market women still selling fried bananas and patties on the street, church services still blasting their messages of hope of redemption, and *borlette* lottery banks still open. The voting station in Pétionville's Place Saint Pierre was filled with dutiful poll workers and electoral observers, but precious few voted, and the Brazil–Italy football match seemed to generate more enthusiasm than the vote, with the Brazilian flag still draped on the walls of poor neighborhoods.

As it turned out, very few participated, and Préval himself, at the Lycée Marie-Jeanne in the capital (where he was virtually the only voter), said that "the political class should question this abstention, because when the people want to vote, it is expressed." In the Grand Anse, a Fusion supporter was lynched during a clash with Lespwa supporters,[85] while in Jacmel, Raymond Lambert, the brother of Lespwa senator Joseph Lambert, and another brother, Wencesclas Lambert (also a candidate), were arrested in possession of several firearms as OPL candidate Ricard Pierre denounced armed raids by Lespwa supporters on voting stations. Assaults by Lespwa supporters were reported in Miragoâne as well.[86] Perhaps unsurprisingly, Lespwa thus won five of the 11 senate seats at stake, with Moïse Jean-Charles, John Joël Joseph and Wencesclas Lambert all ascending to the body, while other seats went to Miragoâne's Jean William Jeanty (a Muslim, a rarity for parliament) and Fusion's Jean Rodolphe Joazile, among others.[87] The discord was not limited to the politicians, however. In an open letter to CEP president Frantz Verret, the body's vice president, Rodol Pierre, claimed that the announced results of the June elections "do not reflect reality" and cited what he charged was blatant fraud, especially in the South Department.[88] To this, Verret – joined by the other members of the CEP – responded with his own open letter, in which he expressed "shock and outrage at the appalling and insulting letter" before going on to inquire "Were you lucid, counsellor, while writing?"[89]

* * *

Before I left Haiti, I went to meet Michèle Pierre-Louis at the official prime minister's residence, an elegant villa off Avenue Pan American. We talked and drank coffee as the sun set in the bay of Port-au-Prince, wind rustling through the palms.

"My involvement started very early because I was involved in youth groups against Duvalier, which at the time was very dangerous," she told me. "There were lots of groups that were fighting clandestinely against the dictatorship, and I lost a lot of friends who disappeared. One day you would hear that the government got them and put them in jail and you would never hear from them again. So I was marked by this situation, and even when I went to study abroad, Haiti was always in my mind."

Those years after Duvalier were "very exhilarating," she said. "Everybody in the world was saying finally Haiti is going to come out, finally democracy is going to be built ... When the 1991 coup occurred, I was probably the first person to give an interview and say, no matter what, the coup was unjustified. Aristide was our president and he was elected democratically and we're going to fight for him to stay in power."

"Those were very long years, and something happened to the country and to the president. When he came back, things got really rough, we really started going down the drain. Somehow, something very deep happened in the mind of this country, and we have not really put our finger specifically on it."

"For a long time, a lot of the elite would say that Haiti was not ready for democracy, and I was totally against that. It's not because people are poor and they are illiterate that they are not ready for democracy. When you go to the people at the bottom, I have a deep feeling that these people really want things to change, and they are waiting for the leadership that will not bring miracles but will show them the way and not lie to them."

As we prepared to finish the interview, the sun was almost gone, with just the faintest glow of orange tropical twilight filtering into the room from between the palms. But first, Pierre-Louis had a final observation.

"All the elites – the mulatto elites, the university elites, the union elites, the peasant elites – are like a huge elephant sitting on this country and you cannot move it, because there is no political class, because there are no political parties, and everyone becomes corrupted and perverted. If you can't go into that system, the system rejects you. And so far we have not found the wrench that will move this thing."[90]

* * *

After visiting Haiti in late June, a bipartisan U.S. congressional delegation, including Florida's Kendrick Meek, Debbie Wasserman Schultz and Ileana Ros-Lehtinen, called for granting temporary protected status to the estimated 30,000 undocumented Haitians living in the United States and also for the State Department to tone down its often blood-curdling travel warning, with Lincoln Díaz-Balart saying that Haiti was "a beautiful country ... with an extraordinary history and one of the ways in which they are going to lift themselves up from poverty is with tourism."[91] Shortly thereafter, the World Bank, the International Monetary Fund (IMF) and the IADB announced that they would collectively cancel $1.2 billion of Haiti's debt, effectively wiping away almost two-thirds of the country's outstanding debt. Haiti had previously been making monthly debt payments in the neighborhood of $1.6 million.[92] By late June, even the student protests showed signed of slackening, with some students and faculty returning to class.[93] Several other organizations, however, reaffirmed that they would continue pushing for the 200 gourde daily wage.[94] Haiti's parliament finally voted for the increase after rock-throwing protesters were dispersed by police tear gas before the building.[95] By 18 August, the Chamber of Deputies had voted to grant Préval his objections to the new minimum wage, thus raising it to 125 gourdes per day in the textile sector and 200 per day in the industrial and commercial sectors.[96] When the new senate was installed on 4 September, it was packed with Préval allies to the point where Préval loyalists now controlled around two-thirds of the body.

* * *

As the bruising minimum wage fight concluded, Haiti also got a new U.S. ambassador, with the departing Janet Sanderson replaced by veteran diplomat Kenneth H. Merten, who had done two previous stints in Haiti in 1988–89 and 1998–2000. Despite the political battles, Merten arrived to find, in his view, that "Haiti was on a gentle, upward swing" and that the "institutions of the state seemed to be working."[97] Around the same time, I participated in a conference in Miami sponsored by Florida International University assessing Haiti's road ahead. The conference also included MINUSTAH's political affairs chief Gérard Le Chevallier, the sociologist Laënnec Hurbon and the Jamaican historian Matthew Smith, among others. Most attendees, myself included, were cautiously optimistic about Haiti's future prospects for the coming year, which we all hoped would be one of increasing stability and reinforcement of democratic institutions. As the conference broke up, I shared a quiet drink with Le Chevallier at the hotel bar, and we discussed our hope that the coming year's elections would go off relatively smoothly. As we parted, I told him I would see him soon, whenever I next visited the country.

* * *

Across Haiti's border, the long-sought Cité Soleil *baz* leader Amaral Duclona was finally arrested in the Dominican Republic's plush Casa De Campo resort, where he had been working under the name Jolicoeur Berthony.[98] Duclona was transferred to the headquarters of the Dirección Nacional de Control de Drogas (DNCD) in Santo Domingo, and France let it be known that they would seek his extradition for the May 2005 murder of Cap-Haïtien consul Paul-Henri Moural (Duclona had also been linked to the killing of the Franco-Haitian businessman Claude Bernard Lauture during Aristide's last days).[99] It was reported that, with the aim of obtaining more favorable treatment upon his extradition to France, Duclona made a series of startling revelations to DNCD investigators and others, among them that he personally kidnapped and killed CNMP coordinator Robert Marcello, who had disappeared the previous January, on the orders of CNE director Jude Célestin, who he said believed that Marcello was opposed to awarding the CNE a lucrative contract to rebuild areas damaged during Haiti's disastrous year of hurricanes.[100] After several months of negotiations, Duclona would be extradited to France to stand trial.[101] He would be convicted for the murders of Claude Bernard Lauture and Paul-Henri Moural, and then acquitted on appeal due to the lack of response the court was able to secure from key witnesses.[102]

* * *

During a two-day visit to Haiti in late September, French foreign minister Bernard Kouchner said that MINUSTAH's mandate should be renewed the following month, and that the mission should stay in the country through the following year's presidential elections.[103] At its annual conference in New York, the Clinton Global Initiative announced that it would be spearheading $258 million worth of aid projects in Haiti in the coming years, with USAID and Habitat for Humanity pledging $4.5 million to repair 1,500 hurricane-wrecked homes and actor Matt Damon's Water.org pledging $2 million to improve water and sanitation access.[104] Beyond aid, in early October, Haiti's WIN Group, a conglomerate privately held by the Mevs family, and the Soros Economic Development Fund announced plans to build a $45 million, 1.2 million square foot industrial park in Cité Soleil, with an expected benefit of 25,000 jobs.[105] Still later in the year, the World Bank announced a $24.5 million grant to support the government's efforts to rebuild the electricity sector, "contribute to more transparent and cost-effective public expenditure," and aid the rehabilitation of key roads and bridges.[106] The road from Carrefour-Feuillés to Fort-Mercredi had already been rehabilitated, its reconstruction financed largely by the U.S. government.[107] The American chain Choice Hotels also announced its intention to build two new hotels in Jacmel.[108] In October, as expected, the UN Security Council renewed MINUSTAH's mandate for another year,[109] and that same month Préval was unexpectedly awarded the title of "Hero of the Hemisphere" by the Pan-American Development Foundation.[110]

Speaking in Marchand Dessalines on the two hundred and third anniversary of the death of Jean-Jacques Dessalines, Préval told the assembled crowd that "MINUSTAH is not an occupation force ... Those who demand its departure are irresponsible," and went on to detail Haiti's history of "coups, disorder" and "the lack of unity" between "the sons of the soil." With Michèle Pierre-Louis present, local political leaders praised the work of the team in working to repair the Saint Michel de l'Attalaye–Marchand Dessalines road and the town's century-old Catholic church and initiating the construction of a new courthouse.[111] The previous day, a march of peasants toward the headquarters of the Organisme de Développement de l'Artibonite (ODVA) in Pont Sondé was dispersed after a violent clash with a group of counter-protesters.[112] Meanwhile, the leadership of the CEP to oversee forthcoming elections would change hands, with Gaillot Dorsainvil assuming its presidency.[113]

* * *

Haiti looked to be enjoying a heretofore unexpected upswing, with a democratically elected president and an honest and committed prime minister at the head of a competent team. But the idea that it might become a nation of law was apparently too much for some to bear. Government insiders spoke darkly about millions of dollars in aid money being siphoned off via the CNE, and about the machinations of the Groupe de Bourdon, a cabal of allegedly corrupt businessmen with firm roots in Haiti's elite who had the president's ear.

Making it clear from the outset that it was their intention to oust her, six senators, including Lespwa's Joseph Lambert and Jean Hector Anacacis, supported by others such as Lavalas' Yvon Buissereth, issued a demand that Michèle Pierre-Louis appear before parliament to answer charges that she had "moved too slowly" to solve Haiti's myriad of problems.

"We have to replace that woman," Anacacis told *The Miami Herald*, continuing without apparent irony to contend: "If they are accusing us of inviting a crisis, then we are inviting a crisis to avert another crisis."[114]

Craven and cowardly to the last, Haiti's senate took advantage of Pierre-Louis' absence from the country to send a letter to her office demanding her return in order to appear before parliament.[115] Over the weekend of 24–25 October, U.S. Secretary of State Hillary Clinton telephoned Préval to remind him of the support that Michèle Pierre-Louis continued to enjoy in Washington, to which Préval responded that he was "not involved" with the parliamentary drama.[116] Once Pierre-Louis returned to Haiti, she countered by demanding an audit of the $197 million of emergency funds that had been spent on recent catastrophes in the country, including by bodies such as Préval protégé Jude Célestin's CNE, an offer which the senate, packed to the gills with *gran manjè*, unsurprisingly demurred.[117] Pierre-Louis' request would be seconded by the anti-corruption organization LFHH.[118] In a pre-recorded address to the nation on 27 October, Pierre-Louis said, come what may, she would leave the government "with my head high."[119] A seemingly mystified editorial in *The Miami Herald* said that Préval had "been too quiet through this whole affair, as if it does not concern him, yet he is the head of state, and his party controls the Senate. He has a responsibility to lead, and now is the time to show it."[120]

One of the few who had the courage to speak out in Pierre-Louis' defense, OPL's Andrys Riché, charged that the "indecent and unacceptable" maneuvers of the Lespwa senators and their allies "plan to overthrow the government at this crucial time of national life."[121] Lavalas senator Rudy Hériveaux called the move to oust Pierre-Louis "illegal, unconstitutional and unfair" and noted that "it is really unjust to say Prime Minister Pierre-Louis is responsible for the problems of poverty and social inequality we have been facing for more than 200 years."[122] Smelling blood, Joseph Lambert crowed that the prime minister was like "an animal being dragged to slaughter."[123]

Summoned to the National Palace, Pierre-Louis was greeted by Préval and his political consigliere Paul Denis, with both men telling her it was her "constitutional duty to go to parliament." Pierre-Louis, who had appeared before the body many times before, this time was steadfast in her resistance and told the men "the game is over and I am not going there to be insulted and humiliated by those thugs."[124]

Instead, she sent a letter in which she wrote that "at a time when efforts are under way for Haiti to join the international community and it has possibilities of investment, national and international, to better the lives of the Haitian population … my government decides not to participate in this hearing. I leave the senators of the republic to face their responsibility in front of the nation."[125]

On 30 October, a majority of the senate voted to dismiss Pierre-Louis, with Joseph Lambert stating that she had "proved she did not have the capacity nor the leadership to meet the population's expectations and satisfy its basic needs," a strange judgment coming from such a judge.[126] The vote took place just after midnight – a traditional time for crimes high and low – and did not include Youri Latortue, Rudy Hériveaux, Evalière Beauplan, Andrys Riché or Edmonde Supplice Beauzile, all of whom left the chamber in protest,[127] with Riché calling the move "a disaster" before departing.[128]

Following the vote, the MPNKP peasant union issued a statement warning that Préval was seeking to form an omnipotent political party, and that, through "indecent and unacceptable manipulation," he was "using government resources to try to establish a dictatorship in the country." They went on to detail how government resources were made available to politically friendly farmers in the Artibonite, while in the northwest and northeast of the country, farmers went without aid.[129] Many in the international community felt equally despondent following this latest self-inflicted wound. One diplomat who worked closely with Préval said that the president acted "partly out of reasons of jealousy. Pierre-Louis was very much feted in Washington after her appointment and he felt he wasn't getting any credit."[130] Another diplomat who had worked closely with Pierre-Louis told me that "she was someone who did have a vision for the country, and if her hands hadn't been tied, she could have done great things."[131]

* * *

Years later, while sitting in her book-lined flat only blocks away from my own old home in Port-au-Prince's Pacot neighborhood, its streets lined with lovely gingerbread-style houses and shaded by copious amounts of tree cover, Pierre-Louis mused on the larger meaning of her ouster.

"I accepted to be prime minister for two reasons, even though several members of my family were against it," she told me. "First of all, René had been a longtime friend, and, secondly, I thought maybe, together, we could do something for the country. I never thought the betrayal could have reached the point that it did. It was extremely painful."

Rising from our seats, we walked to the balcony of her flat. From below, one could hear the sound of a child crying, a radio playing *konpa* music and the Creole conversation of the guards nearby. Beyond, before she spoke again, Pierre-Louis took in Port-au-Prince glistening under the high sun through an exhaust- and dust-tinged haze.

"Is it that anything that works here has to be killed?"[132]

* * *

Hours after the expulsion of Pierre-Louis, Préval announced that the Minister of Planning and External Cooperation Jean-Max Bellerive would be his new choice for prime minister.[133] Educated in Switzerland, France and Belgium, Bellerive had served in bureaucratic capacities under three previous prime ministers, Jean-Marie Chérestal, Yvon Neptune and Jacques-Édouard Alexis, before joining the Pierre-Louis government.[134] Perhaps just as significantly, Bellerive had more than once been described to me with the rather nasty Creole phrase *se yon ti poul ki mare nan pye tab yo*, an allusion to someone who essentially does whatever they are told, and rather an underestimation of a highly capable man. In the words of one diplomat, though, Bellerive "knew that Préval was his boss."[135] The president of the Chamber of Deputies, Levaillant Louis-Jeune, said the body would make itself available for Bellerive's rapid confirmation.[136] Joseph Lambert, leaving aside abattoir metaphors for a moment, declared Bellerive "the right man to cope with the current situation."[137] Bellerive would be confirmed in short order on 10 November.[138] It was announced that his cabinet would include the ubiquitous Paul Denis as minister of justice and former Lavalas deputy Yves Cristalin as minister of social affairs.[139] Bellerive's installation meant little to the capital's restless streets, however, as the month was marked by continuing street brawls between students and police, with every bout leading to more arrests which would in turn lead to more protests.[140]

* * *

Shortly after Bellerive was installed, at an event in the Plateau Central town of Mirebalais, it was announced that Préval was forming a new political current, Unité (INITE in Creole), which would encompass more than 300 mayors and other local and departmental officials around Haiti in advance of pending elections.[141] Among INITE's ranks would be backsliding Lavalas members such as Saurel François, as well as Marie-Denise Claude, the daughter of former Aristide rival and slain pastor Sylvio Claude.[142] By late November, 68 other political parties had registered their intention to contest the election with the CEP, including a grouping called Alternative that represented a collaboration between OPL, Fusion and KID.[143] In short order, the CEP announced that it was rejecting more than a dozen, including (again) Lavalas, Protestant pastor Chavannes Jeune's Union and the Lespwa member ESKANP.[144] In an interview with Radio Solidarité from South Africa, Aristide, who had sent a letter to CEP president Dorsainvil specifically authorizing Maryse Narcisse "to represent

Fanmi Lavalas before the Provisional Electoral Council,"[145] accused the CEP of wanting to organize "selections" not "elections," and said that if they needed to see his authorization as head of the party for it to participate, "I will bring it to them myself."[146] RNDDH later released a statement harshly criticizing the CEP's decision as "anti-democratic."[147] On 16 December, as was tradition, hundreds of Lavalas supporters demonstrated in the capital, both to mark the anniversary of Aristide's first electoral victory and to call for the dissolution of the CEP. With Préval having successfully picked the movement clean of some of its most volatile members, the demonstration passed without incident.[148] The Haitian journalist Gotson Pierre mused that the upcoming months would span "a crucial year" in Haiti's political life, "where the stakes are very high."[149] Even amid such upheaval, Préval found time for a personal milestone, his third marriage, to Élisabeth Débrosse Delatour, the widow of former minister of finance Leslie Delatour, in the airy coolness of Kenscoff.[150]

* * *

As the year ended, Préval could survey Haiti's political landscape with satisfaction at how adroitly he and his allies had triumphed over their adversaries, domestic and foreign. Lespwa and its cohorts now controlled a vast majority of parliament. A recalcitrant prime minister had been ousted and replaced with one more to the president's taste and, despite the initial grumbling of the international community over the matter of his predecessor's ouster, the "friends of Haiti" now seemed disposed to accept Bellerive. The creation of a successor to Lespwa, more thoroughly under Préval's control than the unwieldy political coalition had been, was well under way. Aristide, under whose shadow Préval had dwelled for so long, could now only fire his impotent missives from South Africa as his onetime marassa now unquestionably held the upper hand. Haiti even promised to host its most successful carnival ever in 2010. In the chess match that was Haiti's political life, René Préval, its consummate survivor and wiliest fox, appeared only one or two moves away from his definitive endgame.

CHAPTER TEN
DOUZE JANVIER

At 4.53pm on the afternoon of Tuesday 12 January 2010, the political maneuvering of Préval and his rivals, the "roll of the dice" for MINUSTAH chief Hédi Annabi and those under his command, the preparations for Haiti's carnival, the afternoon crowds, meetings, plans, trysts and studies of Port-au-Prince and every other daily task and enthusiasm were ripped violently from their foundations.

A 7.0-magnitude earthquake, the first of any significance to hit the capital since 1770, sent crashing to earth what little stability Haiti had gained in recent years, along with a huge swathe of Port-au-Prince, Léogâne, Petit-Goâve, Jacmel and the surrounding areas. In this single catastrophe, the claustrophobic squalor and desperation of Haiti's urban poor, its frivolous and venal economic elite, its rapacious political class, the dunderheaded and destructive schemes of the international community foisted on its people and the interminable multinational attempts to "fix" the country all met in a fearful symmetry of disaster.

* * *

After meetings with Hédi Annabi and U.S. Ambassador Merten earlier in the day, Préval returned to his private residence in Canapé Vert. It was late in the afternoon and he was tired. As he was alighting from his car, he saw a maid carrying his infant granddaughter. Reversing course, he turned away from the house and walked toward the woman and the child, scooping the baby into his arms and whispering entreaties to her. He rocked the baby in his arms once, twice, and on the third rock there was a sound like a factory collapsing behind him. He looked back and the house vanished before his eyes. A mile down the hill, the great white dome of the National Palace teetered and then collapsed down through the building's roof.

At the MINUSTAH headquarters at the Hotel Christopher, lives from the far corners of the world that had become unexpectedly intertwined in Haiti were suddenly brought to a halt as the long United Nations presence was reduced to buckling floorboards, crumbling plaster, collapsing stones and terrified screams. Hédi Annabi, his deputy Luiz Carlos da Costa, Deputy Special Representative and political affairs chief Gérard Le Chevallier, whom I had seen in Miami only months before, all died as the building collapsed. Along with them died a profile of figures whose diversity reflected the organization itself: Andrea Loi Valenzuela, a human rights officer from Chile; Marc Plum, the French head of MINUSTAH's electoral assistance section; international policemen from places like Guinea such as Frantoumani Kourouma; Haitian security guards such as Marie Renée Joseph; professionals such as former Radio Métropole reporter turned MINUSTAH communicator Riquet Michel; and dozens of Brazilian soldiers. All told, 101 UN employees would die, the largest one-day loss of life in the organization's history.[1]

At the Hotel Montana, it was barbecue night and just approaching happy hour when the hotel's terraced balconies and elegant rooms sheared off from the hillside and pancaked on top of one another in a smoldering pile, killing at least 80 people.[2] Among them were Chrystel Cancel, a 34-year-old French tourism consultant on assignment with USAID who had arrived in the country only days earlier; two high-ranking reverends in the Methodist Church, Sam Dixon and Clinton Rabb; Colombian contractor Sandra Liliana Rivera, who had been in Haiti to help improve the airport's security; and the six-year-old grandson of one of the hotel's owners.[3] Rudy Bennett, the younger brother of Jean-Claude Duvalier's first wife, Michele Bennett, also perished there.[4]

At Haiti's Ministry of Justice, Micha Gaillard was working on the commission to reform the justice system when the building heaved and collapsed on top of him. Pulled alive from the rubble, he died of his injuries a day later and was buried in the yard of his modest house in Bois Verna.[5] Préval confidant and Minister of Justice Paul Denis managed to escape from the same building.[6]

Standing on a balcony and surveying the landscape for a car to take him to a meeting, Port-au-Prince Archbishop Serge Miot was pitched off his feet by the force of the earthquake and died when he landed headfirst on the ground below. The Port-au-Prince cathedral itself crumbled.[7]

At the chic Caribbean Market on Delmas, where one could find such luxuries as brie, cat food and calvados, the automatic doors of the store, filled with shoppers at that hour just before the evening meal, froze shut, trapping staff and customers alike inside as the building collapsed in on itself.[8]

The great Haitian geographer Georges Anglade and his wife, the writer Mireille Neptune, were visiting the home of the noted economist Philippe Rouzier and his wife, Marilise Neptune, along with Olivier Neptune, the grandson of Jean Dominique. As they were entertaining, Marilise Neptune stepped outside for a moment to her car. The earth heaved, and the house collapsed and buried all who had remained inside.[9, 10]

When the parliament came tumbling down, two senators, Lespwa's Jacques Jean Wilbert and independent Louis Michelet, were among those killed. At the Direction Générale des Impôts (DGI – Haiti's tax office), both the body's director general, Jean Frantz Richard, and its director of operations, Murray Lustin Junior, died when the building collapsed. Citizenship and land documents – some dating back 200 years – were buried.[11] So was Lytz Elie, a young bureaucrat who had created new software to help the government fight fraud.[12]

At the UEH, hundreds of students and faculty were milling about as the change of classes approached when the structure lurched violently and collapsed, burying dozens, among them the noted Creole linguist Pierre Vernet. In the Christ-Roi neighborhood, the veteran politician Hubert Deronceray died along with his sister.[13] Carlo Lochard, the former PNH officer accused of orchestrating the August 2005 football massacre, died in his home in Carrefour-Feuillés, along with three of his children and his mother.[14] Three of Haiti's greatest feminist activists and theorists – Kay Fanm leader Magalie Marcelin, SOFA founder Anne-Marie Coriolan and Myriam Merlet, then working as chief of staff for the Ministry of the Feminine Condition – all died. When Grand Rue collapsed, it did so on scores of *ti machann*, who lay groaning in agony until death overtook them.[15] The Pénitencier National collapsed, allowing the prisoners to flee out into the street. Over 5,000 prisoners would escape when it and various other jails crumbled to earth.[16] Some 500 schools would also be destroyed.[17] During the earthquake's 30-plus seconds, 60 percent of Haiti's GDP disappeared.[18]

My friend Philippe Allouard, a Frenchman who had lived in Haiti for more than a decade, first arriving as a Dominican Order novice priest before leaving to work for various organizations in the country, was riding his motorcycle up the Canapé Vert road when all of a sudden the ground began to buckle and he was nearly thrown from his bike. All around him walls collapsed, houses caved in and the sun suddenly disappeared behind a cloud of rising debris. When the dust had cleared somewhat, he saw a young man trapped beneath a collapsed wall, the top half of his body visible as he pleaded for aid. Instinctively, Philippe rushed to him, holding his hand and trying to offer some words of comfort to the agonized figure. At one point he looked up, and down the snaking path that he knelt at the bottom of, a solid wall of water – whether from a broken water tank or a sewer main he didn't know – was rushing towards then. He ran.

At the U.S. ambassador's residence in Bourdon, Kenneth Merten and the visiting deputy commander of the United States Southern Command (SOUTHCOM), Lieutenant General Ken Keen, had just returned from visits to Cité Soleil and Martissant. The pair were about to sit down on the back veranda when the entire building began shaking. The structure, built in 1938, heaved to and fro but did not collapse. When the tremor finally stopped, Merten looked across the valley to where the Hotel Montana had stood. All he could see was a tremendous cloud of dust rising into the air.[19]

At the PNH headquarters in Pacot, the roof collapsed on PNH chief Mario Andrésol, who spent 15 minutes trapped under the rubble before being extracted by his colleagues. Once thus freed, he raced to check on Préval. The two then toured the city as darkness fell, in a swirl of dust and in a landscape of collapsed buildings and rubble, hearing the cries of the trapped and injured but powerless to help them.[20] With phones not working and radio the only form of communication, around midnight Andrésol and several other officials arrived at the U.S. ambassador's residence at Bourdon riding all-terrain vehicles. Merten was patched through to Préval, who asked if he had heard a tsunami was coming. Merten said he had not, and asked Préval how he could help. Préval asked for help getting the airport open. Merten said he would do his best.[21]

* * *

I was sitting in my apartment in the Paris suburb of Bagnolet about ready to shut down my computer for the night and lie down to sleep when the first reports started coming across the wires.

"Quake devastates Haiti, many casualties feared," the Associated Press headline read, a surreal and strange message that prompted me to stay awake and try to secure more information. What I read over the next hours filled me with dread. Staying up until 2am and powerlessly watching the news unfold online, I soon read of "thousands of collapsed buildings" and "staggering damage."[22] I awoke again a few hours later and found the news worse than I could have ever imagined. I walked around my old neighborhood of Château Rouge and made my way to a Haitian grocery story, the Saint-Marc, filled with a sense of hopelessness and loss. Later, I met a friend, Manuel Vazquez-Boidard, who had finished working at the UN's headquarters at the Hotel Christopher only days before, and we sat morosely drinking beer in Montmartre as the news continued to filter in, each update more grim and unbelievable than the last.

A little over 24 hours later, I was on a plane heading back to Haiti.

* * *

The following day, a visibly stunned Préval told journalists that thousands were likely dead and that the devastation was "unimaginable."[23] Bodies pulled from the rubble lined city streets, covered with simple sheets, often piled on top of one another.[24] At the capital's Hôpital Général and the main morgue, hundreds of bodies lay around the two buildings.[25] Writing on the Salvation Army's website, the organization's director in Haiti wrote of how "thousands of people poured out into the streets, crying, carrying bloody bodies, looking for anyone who could help them."[26]

The clinical director of Partners in Health, Louise Ivers, issued a frantic email that read in part: "Port-au-Prince is devastated, lot of deaths. SOS ... [Need] supplies, pain meds, bandages. Please help us."[27] Haiti's Red Cross said the organization believed "between 45,000 and 50,000 people have died."[28] Surveying the destruction, Jean-Max Bellerive told reporters that he believed the death toll could exceed 100,000.[29] More than 30 significant aftershocks in the hours after the quake further terrorized people.[30] A terse 13 January press release from MINUSTAH outlined the devastation:

> The earthquake has caused major damage in the Port-au-Prince area, as well as in Jacmel. The National Palace, the Cathedral, the Ministry of Justice and other important government offices have been destroyed. Hotels, hospitals, schools and the national penitentiary have all suffered extensive damage. Casualties, which are vast, can only be estimated ...[31]

Léogâne was perhaps even harder hit than the capital, with hundreds of buildings collapsing, and the local police chief estimating that 80 percent of the town had been destroyed and at least 10,000 killed.[32] Petit-Goâve and Jacmel were also devastated, with an estimated three-quarters of the buildings in the latter's downtown area damaged and some 3,000 believed dead.[33] The government would eventually estimate that 225,000 residences had been rendered inhabitable and 2.1 billion cubic feet of concrete and rubble would have to be removed from the capital alone.[34] The already-teetering electric system suffered $40 million worth of damage.[35]

Despite being an administration that would sometimes move with agonizing slowness on the foreign policy stage, the government of U.S. President Barack Obama reacted swiftly. Within hours, 2,000 Marines were dispatched from Camp Lejeune, North Carolina.[36] In a televised address from the White House, Obama said the U.S. would devote $100 million for the relief effort and that financial assistance to Haiti would increase over the coming year. Speaking "directly to the people of Haiti," Obama said: "You will not be forsaken, you will not be forgotten. In this, your hour of greatest need, America stands with you … More American search-and-rescue teams are coming. More food, more water."[37] By Friday, the U.S. navy aircraft carrier USS *Carl Vinson* appeared in the harbor of Port-au-Prince.[38] Soon, over 100 members of the 82nd Airborne had landed and were handing out food, water and medical supplies from a pair of cargo pallets outside the airport, while a duo of helicopters, one with water to distribute and one conducting reconnaissance for suitable drop zones, took off into the sky.[39] By the end of the weekend, that number of troops would grow to 3,000.[40]

By 15 January, the U.S. military controlled the airport and the U.S. Federal Aviation Administration had begun coordinating air traffic, refusing permission to land to planes without express permission to do so.[41] This did not, however, mean an end to chaos. With a reservation, almost anyone could access the airport, and reporters from CNN and the Associated Press landed in Port-au-Prince, as did Church of Scientology ministers, but five Médecins Sans Frontières planes with medical supplies and French portable hospitals were forced to land in the Dominican Republic. The balance eventually shifted to aid flights, but only after precious hours had been lost.[42]

* * *

Waiting at the airport in Paris, I began talking to the brother and daughter of the Haitian industrialist Joel Baussan, whose headquarters was right next to that of my friend, Patrick Brun, in the Complexe Bâtimat industrial park. Baussan had been in his office at the moment the quake struck and had not been heard from since. They were flying on the same plane to Miami as I was, hoping to later continue on to Haiti. Although by this point it had been nearly 72 hours without signs of life, they would not give up hope that their loved one might still be alive, a scene that I saw repeated time and again in Haiti. It was a hope that, as with so many, would alas not be borne out, as Baussan's body would be found in the ruins of his factory several days later.

Flying from Paris to Miami and then from Miami to Santo Domingo, I arrived in Haiti's eastern neighbor after dark, and spent a fitful night at the apartment of a friend in the Gazcue neighborhood. Everywhere in the Dominican capital, there were signs of solidarity for the victims in Haiti, advertising food and clothing drives. Early the next morning, I got into the car of Pan American Development Foundation (PADF) official Daniel O'Neil, who had worked in Haiti for years but was then based in the Dominican Republic. The warm Caribbean sun was rising over the mountains as we drove west.

"The world came crashing down and people were left with what they had in their pockets," O'Neil, who had already been back and forth to Haiti once since the quake, told me. "It's overwhelmed so much that it's hard to imagine getting on top of it."

As we entered the arid, cactus-dotted plain before Jimaní, we began to hit bumper to bumper traffic miles before the border. Dominican soldiers seemed to be waving through trucks bringing relief supplies to Haiti with very little fanfare. I saw a shipment of portable latrines going. As we stopped momentarily at the frontier, I spoke with Juan Pablo Fernández, a Spanish businessman based in Santo Domingo, who was driving one of his company's container trucks – full of water, condensed milk and vegetables.

"When I saw the images on TV, I started crying," he told me over a cacophony of car horns and shouting in Spanish and Creole. "I had to do this."

At Jimaní's Hospital General Melenciano, I found staff overwhelmed, with patients with grievous wounds groaning on the floor and laying on cardboard, guarded by Dominican soldiers with masks. Officials believed over 300 people had arrived at the tiny hospital thus far. Around 4,000 Haitians injured in the quake received treatment in Dominican hospitals.[43] The Dominicans – both the government and private individuals – also sent electrical workers, generators and field kitchens.[44]

Minutes away from the border, one began to see the crumbled walls of homes, until at one point it appeared, still miles from Port-au-Prince, that every third structure was partially destroyed. Campaign slogans for legislative elections, now futile, remained daubed on the walls still standing. When we entered the capital, the buildings along the Route de Delmas looked as if they had been swept aside by a giant hand, while in Pétionville collapsed buildings and rubble spilled out onto what had been its most prominent thoroughfares. Taking a brief moto taxi tour around the city, I was overwhelmed by the devastation. The Digicel building in Pétionville was destroyed, pancaked down upon itself, and the rank smell of human decay emanated from it. Houses along Avenue Pan American had tumbled down into the street, and huge sections of the once grand mountainside appeared to have been sheared off. Somehow – I forget where – I managed to get a few bags of groceries and brought them downtown to Madame Claudette, the mother of a friend of mine who had immigrated to the United States, who lived a few blocks away from the National Palace. I didn't even know if she was alive or not, and was filled with dread as I saw the partially destroyed warren of houses where she lived. But then, sitting among a group of other people on a small concrete rise, I spied her. When she saw me, she smiled wanly and shrugged her shoulders as if to say, "Can you believe this happens to us, too?" I dropped the bags of groceries at her feet and gave her a hug.

"What happened to your house?" I asked her.

"It fell in."

"Where are you going to sleep?"

"Right here."

I walked to the National Palace, through the throng of displaced people, who had already set up tents throughout the Champ de Mars and who were desperately getting water issuing forth from an untapped faucet on the side of a half-destroyed building. Thousands were camped in front of the structure, and many stared at it, half-mesmerized. There was a terrible symbolic poignancy that this place, from which so much ill fortune arose but which Haitians rightly viewed as an architectural jewel and a symbol of their national pride, lay in ruins, and, with it, the fragile vestiges of a Haitian state that had been completely engulfed by the scope of what had occurred.

"Don't look at that, look at us," Emanuel Joseph, 35, told me when our eyes met. "And give aid to the Haitian people, not the Haitian government."

Everywhere I turned someone wanted to speak to me.

"It was a terrible night," said Dickinson Moliere, who said he hailed from Bel-Air and lost three relatives in the earthquake. "MINUSTAH has distributed water to us, but no food."

A young boy wandered through the crowd, and someone told me he had lost his family in the quake.

"Every house was destroyed and we are all living in the street," said Donelus Verette, who lived in Nazon.

I had heard that the Cathédrale Sainte Trinité, which boasted stunning indigenous murals by such eminent Haitian painters as Wilson Bigaud and Philomé Obin, had collapsed, and I took a moto taxi there. When I first started traveling to Haiti in the late 1990s, I had spent hours in its cool confines, fascinated by the artwork and the peaceful ambiance. But I found it almost completely rent, and through a broken window, I spied Philomé Obin's mural of the Last Supper, fissures running through its center, a strange benediction to the horror it now overlooked.

* * *

During this trip, I would be working with Scout Tufankjian, an American photographer making her first trip to Haiti. As I was staying in a hard-to-find house off the Route de Frères, we agreed to meet the next morning at the Villa Creole hotel, which, when I arrived, I discovered had partially collapsed, its parking lot turned into an improvised triage center. Still shaken from what I had seen downtown, I started speaking to a woman standing with a little girl with a bandaged, badly scraped arm in a sling. She wanted to get to a hospital but, having heard that most hospitals had also collapsed, I told her I didn't know if there was help to be had there. Finally, I gave her a little money and walked with them to hail a cab out on the street in Pétionville. When one finally stopped, the driver demanded an exorbitant amount, at which point she reproached him with "You are *profiting* from this?" Eventually, we found a driver who was willing to take them and they went on their way. Walking back to the hotel, I saw an old acquaintance of mine, Cyril Pressoir, the owner of a well-known tour company, drive up in his truck.

"What to make of it?" Cyril asked rhetorically. "All the prisoners were set free and the judges died in their chambers."

When Scout arrived she was being shuttled by a driver taking deep swigs from a bottle of rum and driving a car that looked to be held together by tape. We decided that we would drive out of the city, towards the west, where we heard the devastation had been severe and there were not many foreign reporters to tell the story. On our way down the mountain and towards the Carrefour

Road leading out of town, we picked up my friend, the physician and former senate candidate Frantz Large.

At the Médecins Sans Frontières hospital in Carrefour, several hundred people lay on makeshift surgical tables, on benches, or sprawled on the floor. Half a dozen people groaned with severe suppurating burn wounds caused when a gas cylinder exploded during the great tremor. A nine-year-old boy lay with blood caking his face, his leg in a primitive cast and tears in his eyes.

"This is the worst situation I've ever seen," Julien Mattar, the project coordinator for the hospital, told me. "We have huge needs in terms of human resources, medical supplies, and materials."

Along the Route des Rails, almost every home seemed to have been destroyed, and, again, the intense smell of decay intensified under a glaring Caribbean sun.

"No one has even been here," said Vilaire Elise, a 38-year-old Protestant minister, as he led us and fellow residents to survey homes where his neighbors had died. "We have no water to drink, nor food to eat. We are suffering here."

Driving west to Léogâne was like awakening from one nightmare only to enter another. Along Léogâne's Grand Rue, once-stately concrete buildings lay in rubble, with only a few structures built in Haiti's distinctive wooden gingerbread style remaining, having been wrenched off their foundations, more or less intact, into the street. The putrid smell of death wafted through the lanes, helped along by an ocean breeze.

"There's a lot of corpses here," Frantz said, as we walked through the streets.

When I met Elvis Cineus, an English teacher, he described to me how he had rushed to his home after the earthquake stopped, not prepared for what awaited him. Under the remains of his home, smashed flat as if pummeled by a giant fist, lay the bodies of his wife, his nephew, his cousin and a friend, all dead. His one-year-old son was dangling from the building's jagged facade, injured but alive.

"It was a miracle," he said of the infant's survival. "But I think there are still survivors in the fallen schools, because we still hear them screaming."

At a ruined dental clinic, a woman cried when she told of how a neighbor had died after her leg was severed by falling debris and how the neighbor's child, a little girl, took off screaming down the road.

On the street, I ran into Michael "Didi" Moscoso, a local businessman with roots in the town.

"It's beyond chaos, beyond catastrophe," he told me through the window of the SUV he was driving, stopped in the middle of the street. "The losses cannot be numbered."

Late that day, with the sun setting outside Léogâne, I counted at least 1,500 townsfolk rendered homeless by the quake taking cover on a flat patch of grassy land, having constructed fragile shelters from logs, twigs, bed sheets and leaves.

"Since the disaster, everyone here has had nothing," 31-year-old Innocent Wilson told me when I stopped to talk. "No one is here to help us, so we are organizing ourselves."

* * *

By now, Belgian first-responders and Canadian military medics had set up a field hospital outside the national public health laboratory.[45] In ten days of operation, a field hospital set up by the Israel Defense Forces would treat more than 1,100 patients.[46] Medical students from Quisqueya University were helping administer what medical help they could at makeshift tent clinics next to their school's shattered buildings.[47] By 17 January, the Red Cross called for $100 million for aid to cover "emergency relief and long-term recovery assistance for 300,000 people over the next three years."[48] In a single day, Wyclef Jean's Yéle Haiti Foundation raised $1 million via text donations.[49] Soon, the total would be $2 million. The 12 nations of the Unión de Naciones Suramericanas (UNASUR) promised $100 million in aid.[50] Around 125 Marines landed outside Léogâne and set up a base in a cow pasture outside town.[51] The UN Security Council voted unanimously to approve an additional 3,500 police and soldiers.[52]

And yet, by the time he spoke from MINUSTAH's destroyed headquarters on 17 January, U.N. Secretary-General Ban Ki-moon felt compelled to say that "many people are frustrated and they are losing their patience" and sincerely appealed "to the Haitian people to be more patient." Later the same day, the caskets of Hédi Annabi and Luiz Carlos da Costa, draped with the UN's flag, accompanied him back to New York.[53] Days after the tremor, there was still no sign of any relief effort in downtown Port-au-Prince beyond a U.S. chopper hovering in the sky.[54] With neighbors frantically trying to free her for two days while listening to her cries, the lifeless body of nine-year-old Haryssa Keem Clerge was pulled from her family home. No one in any official capacity had arrived to help the neighbors who had worked to save her.[55] In Carrefour, residents were left with no choice but to burn bodies on a huge pyre next to the ocean.[56] Four days after the quake, a government official estimated that 2,000 bodies had been burned there alone.[57] In Léogâne, UN troops sat behind the walls of a base full of personnel, vehicles, food and water for days, haggling over the price of shampoo with passing salesmen as the stricken town agonized only a few minutes' walk away.[58] Two Haitian doctors, meanwhile, set up a make-shift clinic in the town's nursing hospital.[59] Some 85 residents of a municipal nursing home, little more than a mile from the airport where the rescue was being staged, awaited death in the ruined structure, no aid having yet reached them.[60] Eventually, a local gang would begin providing security to the home, and after some eight residents died, an aid group arrived to attempt to provide some sustenance.[61] At Titanyen, earth-moving vehicles buried tens of thousands of bodies in mass graves, some with their arms and legs still raised skyward as if in a desperate plea not to be forgotten.[62]

* * *

One canard that surfaced frequently after the earthquake was that of average Haitians being susceptible to becoming an out-of-control mob. On 15 January, a *New York Times* headline blared "Patience Wears Thin as Desperation Grows" and asserted that "reports of looting increased," despite granting, much further down in the article, that Port-au-Prince "remained relatively calm,"[63] while *The Guardian* warned that "looters roam Port-au-Prince."[64] Two days later, *The Wall Street Journal* wrote of how "thousands of looters played a deadly version of cat-and-mouse with police ... [who were] far outnumbered by the teeming mob."[65] A week later, it was *The Guardian* again, telling its readers that there was "rising concern over outbreaks of looting by desperate survivors and the re-emergence of notorious gang leaders who escaped when the country's prisons collapsed."[66]

But was it accurate to even describe such people as looters? In the midst of a horrendous catastrophe, with no aid coming yet in any discernible form equal to the dire need, they grabbed the basic necessities of survival to keep from dying. In a decision of simple humanity, the PNH had been given orders not to shoot people unless absolutely necessary.[67] This image of rampaging hordes in no way matched the reality that I and many others saw on the ground, though it may have helped badly skew the focus of aid coming in.

"Considering the millions of people who are in the streets because they lost their loved ones and their homes, and who peacefully pray, sing and help each other the best they can, it is a shame that once again some media persist with the image of barbarism which is so often associated with my country," Michèle Pierre-Louis told me. "Under these stressful conditions, they behave respectfully and admirably well."

And, indeed, they did.

* * *

On my third morning in Haiti, sleeping outside in the courtyard of a house, too shaken to sleep inside after a recent aftershock, I awoke to the sound of evangelical hymns and then gunshots. Hopping on a moto taxi, I sped past pleas of *Aidez nous* (Help us) scrawled on half-destroyed walls. I drove through Canapé Vert, where a laughing young boy was tossing bottles of water to a crowd from the back of a truck parked in front of the police station. Hailing an actual car, I headed south and passed people climbing aboard tap-taps and taxis out of the city, Haitians taking pictures of the rubble with their phones, as if trying to make sense of it. A huge tent city had sprung up near Admiral Killick coast guard base in Bizoton.

We were driving towards Petit-Goâve, and as we did so we had to negotiate great fissures that had opened up along the road. On either side of us as we drove were roadside funerals, with Biblical invocations and wailing mourners under the trees. At one, near Léogâne, mourners dressed in black and white stood solemnly as a young man recited Bible passages over a white-draped coffin.

"We need help," the graffiti read, in English. Then, *Necesitamos ayuda* in Spanish.

As we arrived in Petit-Goâve – a town I had visited perhaps 20 times before – I was stunned. So many buildings had collapsed that I was utterly lost, lacking a familiar landmark to orient myself by.

When I attempted to locate the town's storied Église Notre Dame, which once loomed over the city in gleaming blue-and-white relief, I found instead a crew of men working under the blazing sun, hammers and saws in hand, pulling down the last remnants of a structure that had served as the crowning jewel for this once-picturesque town. Only its foundation and the altar remained.

"This church was here for a long time, for 208 years," said 67-year-old Nathan Leger, pausing as hammers echoed in the background and men milled about wearing surgical masks to protect them from particles of dust and human decay. "It's a catastrophe. We will not have something like this again."

The church collapsed within seconds, burying market women, passers-by, and people who had paused to rest in its shade. Residents estimated that at least 350 died in the town, which was playing host to three large meetings on the day of the quake.

As well as the church, the state telephone company building, the mayor's office, a hotel and scores of houses – all with people still inside – were leveled by the tremor.

"We were injured, we were hit hard, and now we are sleeping in the street," said a white-haired woman camped out in the middle of Rue Faustin with a dozen members of her family, some of whom bore deep cuts and gashes that had yet to receive medical attention. Sitting in front of a house with half its roof collapsed, the family had strung a blanket between two trees to provide some cover. Like most people in town, she said that, other than patrols by a Sri Lankan contingent of peacekeepers, they had yet to receive any outside help.

"Only God knows why this happened," Robert Henry Etienne told me as he walked the dusty streets with a notebook in hand, carefully cataloging every ruined and damaged structure in meticulous handwriting in the hope that they might one day be rebuilt. "But we need the international community to help the Haitian people, who are sleeping on the streets. We need help, from whatever country in the world."

On our way back to the capital, in a clearing in the town of Carrefour Dufort, I found members of the 22nd Marine Expeditionary Unit, based in Camp Lejeune, North Carolina, distributing food aid by helicopter.

"It's just good to be able to be here to help," Sergeant Claude Barthold, who was born in the Haitian capital, told me. "But it's overwhelming what you see."

Later that day, Scout and I went to the ruined Justice Ministry, where hunks of white stone covered police IDs, bank account books, invitations to social events. Nearby, several bodies lay covered in flowered sheets. Graffiti indicated that "USA Team" had searched the location on 15 January, found four bodies and pulled two of the living from the wreckage. A few yards away, a man was selling beautiful wood-carved furniture. In Canapé Vert, members of the PNH supervised the distribution of food donated by private individuals in the Dominican Republic. When we made it up to the grounds of the capital's elite Pétionville Club, we found several thousand Haitians waiting patiently behind a rope barrier for food and water packets being distributed by a group from the U.S. 82nd Airborne Division.

"We are waiting to get some food and water," said Lesly Jeudy, who said that almost every structure in his Christ Roi neighborhood had collapsed. "We haven't had any food or water for two days."

We stopped at the Université de Port-au-Prince. The university complex had been full of staff members and students, with classes about to change and students angling for the best seats in always-crowded classrooms. Then the apocalypse struck, the building swayed and bounced on the shifting earth before collapsing into a chaos of screaming, dust, and blood.

We found a pile of gravel and rocks with students' papers and notebooks scattered under chunks of concrete and splays of metal bars. A body still lay pinned beneath a flattened Suzuki 4x4 SUV, and the cloyingly sweet smell of human decay and swarms of flies sent passers-by hurrying past. But a crowd of students and relatives of the missing had nevertheless gathered, both to mourn and to express the hope that miracles might transpire.

"I was there on the third floor, but I escaped," said one student, Michelet Saint-Preux, his arm bandaged and a deep gash in his chin. "I lost many friends there."

Wesley Jimmy Pierre stood in the street, his eyes fixed on the ruins. His fiancée, Sandy Fab, 24, had been a third-year science student before the quake.

"I left work and spoke to her on the phone. We were supposed to meet after her class, at 6.30pm," said Mr. Pierre. "I searched for her in the hospitals but couldn't find her."

Ms. Fab's father stood with a photograph of his daughter, tears rolling down his cheeks.

"I only have one daughter," he cried.

"They are alive," said a girl who said she had received text messages from someone trapped in the ruin. "They're alive."

That night, I found myself cruising through the city on the back of a moto taxi. Visible through the darkness, the ruined shells of destroyed buildings looked over the fragile forms of hundreds of thousands of people reduced to sleeping in the streets, while in the air mingled the corrosive smell of burning garbage and the vomitous sweet smell of uncollected human remains. Port-au-Prince had never seemed more desperate or defeated.

And yet, somehow, despite the terrible suffering that had been visited on the country, it began to dawn on me that, along the streets that I knew so well, life was going on after this terrible trauma. Next to the National Palace, market women were still frying up *marinade* and *fritay* in old steel pots. As we headed through the Pétionville market, despite the late hour and lack of electricity, goods and fried chicken were still being sold by the orange glow of kerosene lamps. By the following day, I would watch dozens of young Haitians begin sweeping with brooms in front of the ruined Cathédrale Nationale, in preparation for the Saturday funeral on its grounds of Archbishop Serge Miot.

"I've worked with this moto for my entire youth," the moto driver, a young man named Emmanuel, told me that night as we headed up Avenue Pan American, past the ruins of the MINUSTAH compound.

"*Tout moun jwenn,*" Emmanuel told me. "*Kounye-a, y'ap domi ak Jezi.*" Everyone was hit. Now they sleep with Jesus.

Only a few days after the earthquake, writing on the website of Radio Kiskeya, Harold Isaac, the station's webmaster and the son of the well-known journalist Liliane Pierre-Paul, wrote that:

> The Haiti I knew, where I grew up, died this 12 January 2010 at 4.53pm. The image of the kneeling National Palace symbolized, if need be, the bankruptcy and total decay of the Haitian state. Before we were on the brink. Now, we're right into it … Beyond the need for immediate support to the victims, it is essential to capture this momentum to bring new energy to the nation and to ensure that the holocaust did not happen for nothing.[68]

Such a call was echoed elsewhere. A former Haitian government official, who narrowly escaped death when her apartment was totally destroyed, emailed me that *malè pa gen klaksòn* (roughly, bad luck gives no warning) and continued that "rebuilding Port-au-Prince could eventually lead to the rebuilding of the country. Now is the time."[69] Speaking in Washington, IMF chief Dominique Strauss-Kahn said that Haiti needed "some kind of a Marshall Plan."[70] On 20 January, in a hushed voice, Préval told French radio that "it is through calmness [and] an even more organized solidarity that we're going to get out of this."[71] By this point, Edmond Mulet had returned to Haiti and, after a tearful reunion with Préval at MINUSTAH's logistics base near the airport, took over the reins of MINUSTAH from the deceased Hédi Annabi.

* * *

By 21 January, the Haitian government was announcing plans to settle 400,000 of the homeless in camps on the capital's outskirts.[72] Some were not waiting. A little more than a week after the earthquake, an estimated 200,000 people had fled the capital for the countryside by tap-taps, ferries or even on foot.[73] Nearly 63,000 arrived in the Artibonite alone.[74] Aided by peasant groups such as the MPP and Tèt Kole, many rural Haitians took family members and others under their wing, providing food and shelter, often with little or no help from the outside world.[75] By late January, the IOM was estimating that at least 472,000 people were living in more than 500 improvised settlements.[76] A temporary location had been set up for the Haitian senate at the PNH academy in Freres, but as only 15 senators showed up for the first meeting (three fewer than they needed for a quorum), they could not hold a formal session.[77]

Ten days after the quake, an Israeli search team had pulled a 22-year-old man from the ruins of a three-story home.[78] The following day, the Haitian government had announced that it was calling off the search for survivors.[79] Unbelievably, though, the capital's wreckage held one more surprise, and on 27 January – over two weeks after the earthquake – a French team pulled barely alive 17-year-old Darlene Etienne from beneath a collapsed house in Carrefour-Feuillés. With a barely audible pulse, she was whisked to the *Sirroco*, a French hospital ship.[80] Incredibly, Etienne, who had just left her home in the Artibonite to attend high school in the capital, survived. She made a full recovery and eventually returned to her family in Marchand Dessalines.[81]

By 24 January, the Haitian government was saying that Jude Célestin's CNE had buried more than 150,000 people, whereas the UN cited at least 112,250 confirmed deaths.[82] Haiti's government said that it believed the total number of dead was closer to 200,000.[83] In a terse mid-February announcement, the government said 170,000 bodies had been interred at Titanyen.[84] By 27 January, the government was saying that 112,392 had been killed and 196,501 injured, with anywhere from 800,000 to 1 million displaced.[85]

With thousands of bodies piling up at Titanyen, businessman Daniel Rouzier hired two backhoes, summoned a Catholic priest and dumped the corpses into a trio of long, rectangular mass graves, the priest emoting prayers and Rouzier himself sprinkling holy water on the soil.[86]

* * *

Within a few weeks, there would be 20,000 U.S. troops in Haiti.[87] Though some of Haiti's politicians and the international left stomped their feet about the "militarization" of aid, several people I spoke to in Haiti openly talked about how they wished the U.S. would "take over" the country, a sentiment echoed in the reporting of others speaking to people on the ground.[88] A field hospital set up by the U.S. Department of Health and Human Services next to the Groupe Haïtien d'Étude du Sarcome de Kaposi et des Infections Opportunistes (GHESKIO) and guarded by the U.S. Army's 82nd Airborne Division saw more than 3,000 patients in four weeks.[89] In late January, the USNS *Comfort* treated 932 patients and performed 32 surgeries.[90] A joint Stanford University–Columbia University medical relief team that arrived in Haiti less than a week after the quake later wrote that "the support of the U.S. military was unequivocally integral to the success of the medical mission ... We saw consistent professionalism, competence and compassion in the American soldiers."[91] By late January, though, the U.S. had suspended its medical evacuations from Haiti due to a dispute over who would pay for the patients' care.[92] A few days later, however, it was announced that these flights would resume.[93] The U.S. government subsequently announced that it would reimburse hospitals that treated victims of the earthquake with life-threatening injuries.[94]

And of those left alive? By the end of January, even the more than 500 people camped in a field in Tabarre – a few minutes' drive from the airport where the relief effort was based – said they had received no food.[95] For weeks, some continued to live among the shells of partially or completely destroyed structures fearful that thieves would steal their belongings should they leave.[96] By the beginning of February, the IOM was reporting that seven organized settlements had been established for 42,000 displaced people while 460,000 people remained in 315 spontaneous settlements in and around the capital.[97] One such camp of 800 people boasted a single portable toilet.[98] Makeshift schools and churches were popping up in the vast tent cities.[99, 100]

Speaking to the World Economic Forum at Davos, Switzerland, Bill Clinton told the attendees that Haiti needed cash, and that "this is an opportunity to re-imagine the future for the Haitian people."[101] At a meeting in Canada, the G7 group of countries announced that they were erasing Haiti's entire debt, and that international lenders should follow suit.[102] The Dominican Republic waved visa restrictions for Haitians seeking aid there, and helped facilitate over 300 flights.[103] Speaking to the BBC at the end of January, Edmond Mulet said that rebuilding the country was "going to take many more decades ... we will not have to start from zero but from below zero."[104]

Some measures moved rather too slowly. A joint operations tasking center to coordinate humanitarian assistance and consisting of MINUSTAH, the UN's Office for the Coordination of Humanitarian Affairs (OCHA) and the U.S. and Canadian military was not launched until 26 January, nearly two weeks after the quake had taken place.[105] By late January, UNDP had hired 12,000 people to help start carrying away debris but their efforts were a drop in the bucket in the leveled city.[106] By mid-February, reports had surfaced of a dozen Haitian hospitals charging patients for medicines they had received for free via international shipments.[107]

Once they recovered their equilibrium – as much as they could have been said to ever have had it – Haiti's politicians began calling for the scalp of Préval, whom they charged had been seen to be completely overwhelmed if not absent during the crisis. Mirlande Manigat said that, since the earthquake, Haitians had seen in the president "not a leader, but a broken man."[108] The Aristide Foundation for Democracy was soon bussing people to Titanyen to call for Préval's resignation.[109] Several political actors, including Senator Evalière Beauplan, Maryse Narcisse of Lavalas and Union's Jean Techelet Dérac, announced that they were debating plans to possibly replace the government as it had "failed" in its response to the earthquake.[110]

On the sidelines of Archbishop Serge Miot's funeral, Préval responded to the criticism by telling Reuters "in my job, we have two ways of doing things: the way politicians do, where we go to the hospital and we cry with the people. Or to sit, and to work and try to find the right way to recovery. I chose to work."[111]

Others also had a more sympathetic view.

"I find myself hard-pressed to judge him negatively," U.S. Ambassador Kenneth Merten told me. "It was a very difficult time. To see a city that he had known through much of his life leveled like those pictures of Hiroshima and Nagasaki ... And he didn't have a whole lot of people around him giving him clear advice or guidance."[112]

By the end of January, MINUSTAH was announcing that the scheduled elections "cannot take place under these circumstances."[113] Around the same time, members of the U.S. senate were openly floating the idea of putting Haiti into "some sort of receivership" of international organizations.[114] By early February, after announcing, quite reasonably, that the scheduled February vote would be postponed indefinitely, Préval was telling *The Miami Herald*, with rather significant understatement, that "it has been an extremely challenging mandate." At this point he was running the government out of a room in a police substation.[115]

* * *

On the one-month anniversary of the earthquake, tens of thousands flooded the streets of the capital in mass prayer, At exactly 4.53pm, the noisy city descended into silence for a full minute, some falling to their knees to entreat whatever deity they prayed to for succor and redemption.[116] Préval, sitting flanked by his wife and Jean-Max Bellerive, rose from his seat at the Université Notre Dame in Pacot, walked to the podium and delivered his message to the nation.

"I have no words to speak of this immense pain," he said, a black armband encircling his white shirt in mute mourning. "It is in your courage that we find the strength to continue."

"Haiti will not perish."[117]

CHAPTER ELEVEN
THE REPUBLIC OF NGOS

In 1997, the OPL politician Sauveur Pierre Etienne published his book *Haiti: L'invasion des ONG* (The Invasion of the NGOs), which looked at the double-edged sword of the role foreign organizations had played in a Haiti of rapacious economic and political elites, often supplanting rather than supporting the state. The concept had been refined in popular jargon even before the 2010 *tremblement de terre* into *la république des ONG* (the republic of NGOs), a mordant observation that at once evoked the utter failure of the state and its usurpation by outside actors. For many years a subtext in Haiti's relationship with the world, and the world's relationship to Haiti, these tensions burst out into stark relief in the immediate aftermath of the catastrophe. As Haiti's many friends would demonstrate, even among the worst disasters, there was money to be made. And, as Haiti's elites would show them, even among the worst calamities, there was politics to be done.

The IADB estimated that damage from the quake could total $14 billion.[1] Préval said he thought it would take "1,000 trucks moving rubble for 1,000 days" before the country could finally start rebuilding.[2] The clean-up would be largely managed by Jude Célestin's CNE.[3] From all over came plans, proposals and promises of aid. A plan drafted by the staff of Hillary Clinton's office called for the creation of an "Interim Haiti Recovery Commission" to oversee the country's reconstruction and a "Haitian Development Authority" to coordinate the flow of foreign aid.[4] The Canadian government said that it would spend up to $12 million to replace a series of government offices that had been destroyed.[5] President Nicolas Sarkozy became the first French leader to step on Haitian soil since Haiti's independence more than 200 years earlier, and announced that France was canceling Haiti's $56 million debt – a move not quite so magnanimous when one considered Haiti's 90 million franc payment to France for its independence – and also that France would contribute $245 million for rebuilding purposes and $54 million for the Haitian government's budget.[6] USAID announced that it was tasking Washington, D.C.-based Chemonics International and Bethesda, Maryland-based Development Alternatives Inc. with $100 million of work in Haiti, which included a cash-for-work program with contracts awarded under emergency noncompetitive task orders.[7] At a summit between Mexico and the CARICOM countries in Cancún, Préval promised not just to "rebuild, but to refound" Haiti, and to "decentralize" the country.[8]

In these efforts, Haiti's agricultural sector was again all but forgotten. At a mid-February meeting in Rome with Agriculture Minister Joanas Gue and Jacques Diouf, the director general of the UN Food and Agricultural Organization, it was announced that only 8 percent of the $23 million requested for seeds, fertilizer and tools to help Haiti's struggling farmers plant their March crops had been dispersed. The March planting season traditionally accounted for 60 percent of the yearly fruits, grains and vegetables produced in the country.[9] The international community clearly had a myriad of priorities in Haiti, but helping Haitians feed themselves was obviously not one of them.

Around the time of the one-month anniversary, early precursors of the country's rainy season began drenching the camp dwellers in their fragile structures. Only 272,000 of the up to 1.5 million people displaced had been provided with any emergency shelters.[10] The UN said that only 30 to 35 percent of the need for waterproof shelter in the country had been covered, and 25,000 toilets were still needed.[11] A total of 104,132 tents still sat in storage.[12] According to one employee of a U.S. firm involved in relief efforts, some of the tents were kept in storage so USAID could put their logo on them, as nothing went out the door until it could be properly labeled.[13] The mayor of Delmas, Wilson Jeudy, spoke of evicting the thousands of squatters who had taken over the grounds of the Saint-Louis de Gonzague high school, saying "after talking to them, we'll use force."[14] Jean-Max Bellerive spoke openly of his fear that the government might collapse,[15] and later announced that it would be commandeering private land to build temporary settlements for the displaced.[16] Several thousand people were flocking to a place that became known as Canaan, a rocky treeless expanse off Route National 1 with the sea on one side and vaulting mountains on the other. On the Route des Rails, families set up barely-there shelters between two roaring lanes of traffic.[17] The emergency coordinator in Haiti for Médecins Sans Frontières called the shelter situation "shocking."[18]

In late February, GARR issued a statement in which it voiced consternation that "Haitian leaders must stop complaining and instead assume the leadership of the situation by developing concrete proposals, by making decisions and communicating with citizens."[19] To further unnerve people, in late February the capital was rattled by a series of aftershocks, including one measuring 4.7.[20]

* * *

By mid-February, the number of U.S. troops in Haiti had decreased to around 13,000.[21] The lack of nighttime patrols by MINUSTAH (or anyone else) in the camps led to an increase in the sexual abuse of women and girls living there, and some young girls were forced to trade sex for shelter, according to evaluations by Refugees International and Human Rights Watch.[22] However, Amnesty International would conclude that "the self-organized camp management committees confirmed ... that sexual violence is not an issue and that security commissions to patrol the camps at night have been set up. Most of the women in the camps interviewed by us did not express concerns about sexual violence."[23] Little more than a month later, however, Haiti's Komisyon Fanm Viktim pou Viktim (KOFAVIV), an organization formed to seek justice for victims during the 1991–94 era and affiliated with IJDH/BAI, said that it had documented "over 200 cases" of rape since the quake.[24] RNDDH concluded that the total was closer to 30.[25]

The Post Disaster Needs Assessment (PDNA) was officially launched in mid-February, and commercial flights to Haiti also resumed a day later.[26] Speaking at the White House with Préval at his side in early March, Barack Obama called the situation in Haiti "dire" and said that "America will be your partner in the recovery and reconstruction effort."[27] Préval told *The Miami Herald* in March that "all of the millions that are coming into Haiti right now are going into the hands of NGOs."[28] Bellerive spoke openly of how his government was given little to no information about how much money had been given to the organizations operating in the country and by whom, making coordinating relief efforts on the government's part near impossible.[29] Nor did the Haitians make it easy for those who did want to help. When the Wisconsin company Briggs & Stratton sent 240 portable generators, they languished in customs for months.[30] The same fate befell 20 vehicles sent by Médecins Sans Frontières.[31]

* * *

And what did the world understand of the country it was rushing to save? Writing in *The Wall Street Journal*, Lawrence Harrison, a former director of the

USAID mission to Haiti, opined that the blame for Haiti's ills should be laid at the altar of vodou, as "its followers believe that their destinies are controlled by hundreds of capricious spirits who must be propitiated through voodoo ceremonies." Harrison further informed his readers that, following the overthrow of the French in 1804, free Haitians "were left with a value system largely shaped by African culture" and quotes the economist Sir Arthur Lewis ("himself a descendant of African slaves") as saying that Haitians "inherited the idea that work is only fit for slaves."[32] The U.S. televangelist Pat Robertson solemnly informed his viewers that the earthquake had taken place because Haitians "swore a pact to the devil" in order to free themselves from French rule (Robertson had previously blamed the devastation wrought by Hurricane Katrina on New Orleans on U.S. abortion policy).[33]

The earthquake and its aftermath were not one of the media's shining moments, either. While Haitians were still unearthing the dead and hundreds of thousands huddled against the oncoming rains, the U.S. photographer Zoriah Miller announced on his website that he had decided to offer a "workshop in Haiti focused on photographing the aftermath of the earthquake" at $4,000 per person for seven days, with participants responsible for their own expenses such as airfare and tents (which no doubt their subjects could have used rather more urgently).[34] Following an outcry on such profiteering, Miller tacked on an addendum that 50 percent of the money raised would be going to "my friends at Hospice Saint Joseph," a Port-au-Prince facility almost completely destroyed by the quake.[35] In an article for the website GOOD, Mother Jones human rights reporter Mac McClelland recounted how, as the article's title suggested, "violent sex helped ease my PTSD." The PTSD, it turned out, came from reporting in a Haiti of "ugly chaos" and "gang-raping monsters."[36] Referring almost in passing to the gang rape of a Haitian woman living in one of the tent cities, the rest of the article recounts a foreign reporter's journey of self-discovery, with McClelland, to whom nothing at all out of the ordinary happened – a rather disturbing and atypical incident with a driver aside – essentially painting the entire country as a nation of bloodthirsty, sex-mad brutes that pushed her over the edge. The article met with a response from 36 other female journalists who had worked in Haiti and who wrote that it "[made] use of stereotypes about Haiti that would be better left in an earlier century: the savage men consumed by their own lust, the omnipresent violence and chaos, the danger encoded in a black republic's DNA."[37]

Miller and McClelland may have been examples of extreme narcissism, but they were hardly alone in their failure to accurately convey the reality of the country. Viewers of cable news channels such as CNN were treated to virtually nonstop dire warnings about "looting" and "anarchy" in Haiti, none of which came to pass, but which did much to reinforce the image of Haiti as ungovernable and to distract attention from the debacle, both domestic and imported, that was taking place.

* * *

In early March, the EU released €100 million to help pay salaries and to repair roads and schools.[38] It announced that it would donate €1 billion in development aid to Haiti during the coming year.[39] The IADB said it was canceling $479 million of Haiti's foreign debt,[40] and that it would raise $70 billion in new capital for Haiti.[41] Venezuelan President Hugo Chávez canceled Haiti's $200 million debt to his country.[42]

By mid-March, heavy rains in Haiti were turning the displaced persons camps into mires of misery, swamping and terrifying residents ever mindful of Haiti's historic flash floods. The camp set up on the golf course of the capital's Pétionville Club, now said to be home to at least 45,000 people, was particularly hard hit. After meetings with donors in Washington, Préval said that the Americans "understand very well the problem and they are ready to help ... They understand the urgency to act."[43] By this point, Indiana University's Centre for Philanthropy concluded that charities had received more than $1 billion in the U.S. and $154 million in Canada.[44]

When the PDNA finally unveiled its reconstruction plan in mid-March, it outlined an $11.5 billion effort, with the money going "50 percent for the social sector, 17 percent for infrastructure including housing, and 15 percent for the environment and disaster risk management."[45] Just before the UN donors' conference, it was announced that Bill Clinton and Jean-Max Bellerive would co-chair an Interim Haiti Recovery Commission (IHRC) to coordinate projects and the flow of aid money.[46] In order to become a foreign voting member of the IHRC, an entity would have to have contributed at least $100 million in two consecutive years or to have canceled at least $200 million of Haiti's debt. The funds themselves were to be managed by the World Bank and Préval would maintain veto power over the body's decisions.[47] Until the inauguration of a new president, this is how decisions about Haiti's future would be made, by Préval and the international community. Alone.

At the late March donors' conference, countries and international organizations pledged $9.9 billion to Haiti over three years, vastly exceeding the $3.8 billion that Haiti had requested.[48] At the conference, Hillary Clinton announced a two-year U.S. commitment of $1.2 billion.[49] Bill Clinton said the goal of the money spent in Haiti should be to make the country "self-sufficient."[50] Surrounded by secret service agents, Clinton and his successor, George W. Bush, toured the Haitian capital on 22 March, with the latter asserting that "our visit will remind people that Haiti needs help."[51]

* * *

In the meantime, however, politics would go on. In April, parliament approved the creation of the IHRC and an 18-month extension of the state of emergency declared after the earthquake.[52]

Edmond Mulet said that, come what may, Haiti had to hold its scheduled elections sometime in 2010,[53] a sentiment echoed by Hillary Clinton when Préval visited Washington.[54] Speaking to AFP in mid-April, Préval reiterated his intention to hold elections in 2010 and leave office on 7 February 2011.[55] Concurring with Préval's assessment but perhaps over-optimistic given Haiti's history, Bill Clinton said that the vote "will be one of the things we don't have to worry about."[56] Speaking at a meeting of the Clinton Global Initiative in Miami, Clinton predicted that Haiti would be like "the gunfight that's going on in northern Mexico" (a reference to the narco violence there) if the international community did not remain involved in the former's reconstruction.[57] Shortly thereafter, however, Préval was proposing that he could perhaps remain in office until mid-May 2011.[58]

By mid-April, the process had begun of razing what was left of the National Palace.[59] Some students had begun returning to classes, albeit many were conducted in makeshift quarters such as tents.[60] By the middle of the month, OCHA reported that nine out of ten survivors of the earthquake had received emergency shelter, more than 1 million people.[61] But in the space of a few days, the government forcibly evicted more than 7,000 people who had been living on the grounds of the Stade Sylvio Cator, which itself had been significantly damaged.[62] By late April, there were more than 3,000 people in the Corail camp.[63] By this point, the American Red Cross had raised $430 million from donors in the name of Haiti's earthquake victims, $106 million of which was spent during the first 60 days of the crisis, but this had petered out to $5 million during the month of April.[64] By May, of the $34.4 million CARE had raised, the organization had spent only 16 percent, some $5.75 million, with $2.5 million of that, they said, on shelters.[65]

In front of the ruined National Palace on 10 May, about 1,000 protesters calling for Préval's resignation, some armed, rioted and robbed passers-by before being dispersed by the tear gas and warning shots of the PNH.[66] Many of the protesters identified themselves as Aristide partisans.[67]

With strong bipartisan support, at the outset of May, Barack Obama signed the Haiti Economic Lift Program (HELP) Act, which expanded duty-free quotas for Haiti's textile and apparel industry, which had accounted for 75 percent of Haiti's export earnings before the earthquake.[68] By mid-May, Brazil had paid $55 million into the World Bank's reconstruction fund, becoming the first nation to do so.[69] The World Bank took the further step of writing off Haiti's $36 million debt after a number of other countries stepped in to cover the shortfall.[70]

An electoral task force, consisting of representatives of the Haitian government, the UN, CARICOM, the OAS, the EU, the U.S., Canada and Brazil, met for the first time in mid-May at a rendezvous co-chaired by Préval and Edmond Mulet.[71] At Flag Day in Arcahaie, Préval told the crowd: "This is the last 18 May, I will spend with you as president … I will go and my heart will be calm."[72]

As Préval and Bellerive attempted to foment support for Haiti's rebuilding, Maryse Narcissse took the opportunity to address a group led by René Civil, at the Hotel Plaza in the capital, to call for the government's resignation and Aristide's return.[73] Almost simultaneously, opposition senators Edmonde Supplice Beauzile and Jean William Jeanty said that they, also, would lead protests to call for Préval to step down.[74]

* * *

U.S. policy towards Haiti remained, at best, confused. A late June report by the U.S. Senate Foreign Relations Committee charged that "key decisions remain in flux and critical humanitarian issues related to shelter and resettlement are not resolved," that the chaotic coordination among donors was "undercutting recovery and rebuilding," and that "Préval should take a more visible and active role." It also recommended a reconstituted CEP.[75] However, Vermont Democratic Senator Patrick Leahy moved to block funds for a judicial reform program, referencing killings that had taken place at a Les Cayes prison after the quake and saying that "no funds ... should be obligated for justice programs in Haiti until a thorough, credible and transparent investigation occurs," as if further weakening the justice sector would help.[76] Republican Senator Richard Lugar of Indiana urged Préval to hold elections and stated that the United States' "commitment [to Haiti] should not be taken for granted."[77] Asked in the magazine *Esquire* about Haiti's possibilities in July, Bill Clinton said: "I'm excited about it, enough so that after a couple of heart incidents and being sixty-three years old, I am prepared to spend three years on it."[78] At its first meeting, the Clinton-co-chaired, 26-member IHRC produced Mexican billionaire Carlos Slim and Canadian mining magnate Frank Guistra, who each pledged $10 million to a fund for small and medium enterprises (SMEs).[79] But by early July, Ban Ki-moon admitted to the BBC that not enough aid had yet reached Haiti.[80]

Following the Foreign Relations Committee report, Préval, with Pierre-Louis Opont at his side and declaring "the time of negotiations is over," announced that the first round of elections would be held on 28 November, and that there would be no change in the composition of the CEP. He dismissed the concerns of "competitors who have fallen foul of the provisions of the electoral law," a clear reference to Lavalas.[81] Préval also had a message for the Americans: "I'm not doing the CEP with international partners. I'm doing the CEP with national partners."[82] Camille Leblanc, Préval's justice minister during his first term, accused the president of wanting a "third mandate" by dominating a "puppet president."[83] Some speculated that Préval's proxy might be former prime minister Jacques Édouard Alexis.[84] With elections looming, the musician Wyclef Jean mused "after all these years, when these [elite] families have made so much money, why aren't people in schools? Why can't kids read, and why can't they write? Is this modernized slavery, in a way?"[85] Shortly thereafter, in a statement emailed to journalists, Jean wrote that his "commitment to his homeland and its youth is boundless, and he will remain its greatest supporter regardless of whether he is part of the government moving forward."[86] Many thought that Jean was planning on running for president. When the CEP published a list of several hundred candidates who would compete in the upcoming elections, Lavalas would once again be excluded.[87]

At a donors' conference his government hosted at the resort of Punta Cana in early June, Leonel Fernández told attendees that "Haiti is not alone, and never will be," while Préval told them that Haiti's rebuilding presented an "immense challenge" to the country but that it could produce "a more decentralized, fairer Haiti."[88]

In Hinche in early June, thousands of MPP-affiliated protesters marched against a move by U.S. multinational Monsanto to donate 475 tons of "hybrid" maize seeds to local farmers via the USAID initiative Project Winner.[89] The rather upside-down logic of foreign seed distribution was summed up by one USAID official, who told AFP flatly that "the goal is not self-sufficiency. We want to help increase the income of farmers and non-farmers so they will be able to buy food."[90] Speaking to the U.S. Congress in July, USAID director Ravij Shah still told the politicians that "the resources are flowing and are being spent in country" in Haiti.[91] In the north, outside of Cap, the two dozen workers of Medika Mamba, a peanut butter paste that combatted childhood malnutrition, found themselves struggling to compete with imported alternatives flooding the market, including those used by UNICEF.[92] On the twenty-third anniversary of a massacre in Jean-Rabel, hundreds of peasants gathered there to call for decentralization and a recovery of local agriculture. The meeting, though far more substantial than many of the scripted press conferences that regularly occurred in the capital, nevertheless went uncovered by the foreign press.[93] Minister of Agriculture Joanas Gué announced that the IADB had committed $200 million and the U.S. government $110 million over the next year to help rehabilitate Haiti's agricultural sector.[94]

Six months after the quake, only 28,000 of those displaced had found permanent shelter, and only a tenth of the $5.3 billion pledged had been disbursed.[95] One evening, strong winds blew down 350 of Corail's fragile tents,[96] and a statement by Haiti's Jesuit Refugee Service bemoaned the fact that "Haitian political actors are more interested in struggling for power than the humanitarian situation and the country's reconstruction process."[97] Once more, though, showing the country's capacity for creative defiance, as the summer wore on, a song emerged from the desperation that demonstrated as clearly as any politician's words the never-say-die spirit of the people of Haiti. Called "Boule Jou" ("Burn the Day") and performed by the group Vwadèzil, one of the main purveyors of Haiti's often-suggestive *raboday* electronic dance music, the song laid forth of litany of woes and married them to the advice to abandon one's worries and enjoy life, for who knows what might happen tomorrow. As much as images of wailing women and fetid tent camps, *this* was the soul of Haiti.[98]

* * *

By mid-July, JILAP was warning that the capital's criminal gangs were reforming and that this was directly reflected in a recent increase in violence,[99] while CONOCS also raised the alarm about the return of the gang phenomenon to Cité Soleil.[100] A pre-dawn joint MINUSTAH–PNH raid on the camps would net 30 suspected criminals.[101]

At the end of July, Préval and Leonel Fernàndez paid a joint visit to Limonade, outside Cap-Haïtien, to inaugurate work on a new branch of the state university there, its construction financed by the Dominican Republic. As the two toured the site, protesters, united by antipathy towards both men, marched in Au Cap.[102]

On 3 August, it was reported that INITE had nominated Jacques Édouard Alexis as their presidential candidate.[103] Then, having flown into Haiti on a private jet, Wyclef Jean strode into the CEP office ten minutes before it closed and filed his documents to run for the presidency under the Viv Ansanm political grouping. Stepping onto the back of a truck before several hundred cheering supporters, Jean told them: "America has Barack Obama and Haiti has Wyclef Jean." How Jean intended to skirt the five-year residency requirement was unclear, though he claimed his 2007 appointment by Préval as a "roving ambassador" negated the stipulation.[104]

Before he had thrown his hat into the ring, Jean had resigned from Yéle Haiti. The organization, however, had still not sorted out its highly question-able finances. There was the $31,000 in annual "rent" paid to Platinum Sound, which was co-owned by Jean and his partner Jerry Duplessis (who was also a Yéle Haiti board member). There was the $250,000 payment in 2005 for pre-purchased "advertising time" to Haiti's Telemax network, in which Jean and Duplessis owned a controlling interest. There was the $100,000 that Jean paid himself through Yéle for his "musical performance services" at a 2006 fund-raiser in Monte Carlo (it was later stated that most of this covered production costs and musicians and only a quarter went to Jean himself). At a proposed joint fundraiser between Yéle and their French charity FXB International the following year – ostensibly to finance the construction of a school in Haiti – Jean demanded an identical amount, specifying this time that it was purely the fee for his performance. And so on.[105] These transgressions seem to have had little import in Haiti, though, where Jean's candidacy had a profoundly electri-fying effect on the youth and the urban poor.

Despite having leaked word of Alexis's selection as INITE's presidential candidate, on 7 August Joseph Lambert announced that 48-year-old CNE director Jude Célestin, not Alexis, would be the party's presidential candidate. Lambert asserted that Célestin met the criteria of "youth, competence and honesty" the party sought.[106] Thus twice humiliated, Alexis would run as the presidential candidate for the Mobilisation pour le Progrès d'Haïti party of Haitian-born Miami businessman Samir Mourra, himself an unsuccessful candidate in the 2006 elections.[107]

Although Lavalas remained officially out of the running, no fewer than five candidates associated with the political current would be vying for the presidency under various groupings: Yvon Neptune (Ayisyen pou Ayiti), Yves Cristalin (Oganizasyon Lavni), Leslie Volatire (Plateforme Ansanm Nou Fò), Jean-Henry Céant (Renmen Ayiti) and Lavarice Gaudin (Veye Yo). The RDNP's Mirlande Manigat and singer Michel "Sweet Micky" Martelly would also be running, the latter under the newly formed Repons Peyizan banner. The singer Jean Renel Bruno, known as Ti Pay, himself a Cristalin supporter, told Radio Kiskeya that he knew Préval intended to "impose" Célestin on Haiti, and warned of the machinations of a "clan" surrounding the president that included John Joël Joseph, Moïse Jean-Charles and René Momplaisir.[108] Jean-Henry Céant claimed he was receiving death threats, for which he blamed Préval, whom he charged was manipulating the CEP "to designate his own successor."[109] Soon, the MPP's Chavannes Jean-Baptiste had added his voice to the calls that voters should abstain from elections and that Préval should resign.[110] RNDDH and Haiti's Conseil National d'Observation Électorale (CNO) noted that among the candidates were a number who were subject to prosecution for "criminal conspiracy, arson, the massacre at La Scierie, the prison breakout of 19 February 2005, drug trafficking, rape, theft of vehicles, etc." and noted that most people believed the CEP to be "totally dependent on the government" as opposed to being an independent entity.[111]

* * *

After a tense day that saw Wyclef Jean's supporters flooding Delmas and chanting slogans, the CEP announced late on 20 August that Jean had been barred from running in Haiti's presidential election.[112] Immediately following the ruling, Jean issued a statement that he would "respectfully accept the committee's final decision" and urged his supporters to do so "peacefully and responsibly."[113] MINUSTAH also called for calm. Later, however, he said that he would appeal the ruling, even though the CEP stated that its decision was final.[114]

Following the CEP's ruling, Préval visited Leslie and Mirlande Manigat at their home, declaring himself "neutral" in the upcoming contest.[115] He would also meet with Alexis and Yvon Neptune.[116] The joint OAS–CARICOM electoral observer mission criticized the lack of transparency behind the CEP's decision to disqualify candidates.[117]

As Haiti's politicians prepared to campaign, one of them, Fusion's Edmonde Supplice Beauzile, thought it a good idea to open a library in the Plateau Central town of Mirebalais named in honor of none another than Rosalie Bosquet, the notorious Duvalierist Macoute leader better known as Madame Max Adolphe, a development met with outrage by many of Duvalierism's still-surviving victims.[118]

An early September report by the UN warned that "the security situation ... remained generally calm but fragile,"[119] an observation brought home when Willy Etienne, a feared gang leader from Haiti's north believed involved in the kidnapping of deputy Hugues Célestin, was arrested by the PNH while at the Ministry of Finance.[120] How exactly a wanted criminal had come to be wandering the halls of a government building was unclear, though the ministry suggested, improbably, that he was there to update his tax information.[121] An extensive PNH and UNPOL operation in Cité Soleil resulted in at least 12 arrests, including that of Zacharie Occénat aka Barthold, one of the men jailed for the murder of Jacques Roche, who had escaped during the earthquake.[122] In a separate operation, seven police officers would also be arrested for alleged criminal links.[123] The possible price for such actions might have been suggested two days later when Manouchka Louis Brice, the wife of PNH's Director for the West Department Ralph Stanley Brice, was gunned down while returning home to the Vivy Mitchel district in what appeared to be a planned ambush.[124]

As Haiti prepared to vote, only 2 percent of the debris from the January earthquake had been cleared away.[125] Despite USAID director Ravij Shah's brazenly untrue claim of the efficacious use of funds before the U.S. Congress months before, by late September, none of the $1.15 billion the U.S. had promised in post-earthquake aid the previous March had in fact been dispersed, the money the victim of partisan wrangling and egomania in Washington, even as a storm killed six people (including two children) and tore apart 8,000 tents.[126] Among those blocking the aid was Republican Senator Tom Coburn of Oklahoma, who, with blithe disregard for the lives at stake, wrote that "our charity today should not come at the expense of the next generation ... additional aid we provide must be paid for with cuts to lower priority programs elsewhere."[127]

An October report by Refugees International concluded that "ten months after the January 12 earthquake, the people of Haiti are still living in a state of emergency, with a humanitarian response that appears paralyzed."[128] The IHRC, meanwhile, approved 18 new projects totaling $777 million in areas of housing reconstruction, education and the protection of women.[129]

As October began, Jacques Édouard Alexis warned at a rally in the capital that "Préval wants to retain power" and that "weapons were distributed" to this end and to guarantee a Jude Célestin victory.[130] Though several candidates – Jean-Henry Céant and Leslie Voltaire among them – expressed concern about Alexis's "revelations," Jean Hector Anacacis dismissed them.[131]

Alexis was not the only one making such charges, however. Fusion's Edmonde Supplice Beauzile alleged that weapons were being distributed to INITE supporters in Belladère and Lascahobas.[132] Youri Latortue, who had thrown his support behind Mirlande Manigat, charged that members of his party were being intimidated by INITE partisans, who he said were already openly campaigning in defiance of the 15 October opening date.[133] After the national identity office in Les Cayes was set ablaze by unseen arsonists,[134] at an INITE rally on 7 October, Paul Denis – who was still serving as Haiti's minister of justice – predicted that Jude Célestin would "be brought to power to transform the living conditions of the population."[135] This drew a strong rebuke from former senator Gabriel Fortuné, who charged that Préval was using public money to finance Célestin's campaign and noted that "in any case, ministers … cannot campaign for a party, because they must manage the environment of the elections."[136] At the official launch of his campaign in Croix-des-Bouquets in front of several thousand people, many clad in new INITE T-shirts and having been transported in state-run Dignité buses, Jude Célestin proclaimed "we have already won," and, joined on the dais by Joseph Lambert, Moïse Jean-Charles, John Joël Joseph and others, he promised "political stability to ensure the development."[137]

As the UN Security Council voted in New York to prolong MINUSTAH's mandate until October 2011,[138] outside Jean-Max Bellerive's office dozens of those displaced by the earthquake demonstrated for adequate housing, with one resident, a mother of seven from a camp near the airport, telling reporters that "the tents are infested with bugs, rats, insects, it looks like [the government] has completely forgotten us."[139]

***

Post-earthquake Haiti saw another return, as well, although this one was not in the country to campaign. Amaral Duclona's brother, Raymond "Che" Duclona, came back from exile in Jamaica looking much the same tough natty dread he had been, but having undergone a complete metamorphosis in his outlook towards the world. Arriving with his family "to help rebuild Haiti," he returned to Cité Soleil and, stripped to the waist, began cleaning out sewage canals with a simple shovel. Despite being arrested by the police again (and then quickly released), Duclona would stay in Cité Soleil, he said, to try to make it a better place, and to keep its young people from the fate that had befallen his brother and so many like him. Around the same time, a local Cité Soleil activist named Louino Robillard, who, like so many living there, had been born elsewhere (in his case, the northern town of Saint-Raphaël), began a movement in the neighborhood called Konbit Solèy Leve. Robillard had moved to Cité Soleil when he was three with his father after his mother passed away, and had grown up in the Ti Ayiti section of the neighborhood when Blade Nasson and the other chimere were at the height of their powers. Blade Nasson had returned to Ti Ayiti after fleeing the national prison when it collapsed, and was killed there only days later. But Robillard saw something different for the neighborhood's future.

"There are lots of good people here trying to stay on the good path," he told me one day as we sat in a Port-au-Prince courtyard in the cool air of a January morning, his own dreads tucked up beneath a leather cap that he habitually wore. "We wanted to give another possibility to young people that they have another choice other than the gang stuff."

The group put the *konbit* model into practice, gathering residents to clean the fetid canals and other areas of the district and trying to sow connections between the sometimes fractious different neighborhoods. The organization initiated a Cité Soleil Peace Prize to honor and encourage young people trying to make a difference in the community, and diligently worked with groups like the Sant Kominote Altènatif Ak Lapè (SAKALA) to reduce conflict and bring economic opportunity to the district.

It wasn't an easy job. Once, when a gang leader named Ti Jackson from the Bwa Neuf section of the slum was running amuck, Robillard went to talk with him, to calm him down. The gangster was unmoved.

"Listen, I have a gun, and my daughter is hungry," Ti Jackson told Robillard. "Who's going to give me food to give her? I don't like to kill, but I put her in the world and that's the only way people respect me."

When the Cité Soleil basketball team – made up of non-gang-affiliated young men – started gaining prominence and was invited to play a match downtown, some of the crowd mocked them and claimed they were hiding guns under their jerseys.

But Robillard was determined not to give up

"This violence is something that exists in Cité Soleil," he told me. "But *this* is not Cité Soleil. This is not our true face."

CHAPTER TWELVE
PLAGUE

Immediately in the aftermath of the earthquake, one of the stated great concerns of the international community in Haiti was, quite naturally, the spread of disease as a result of the grim sanitary conditions in the spontaneous settlements that sprung up in the affected areas.

"The spread of disease has become a major concern in Haiti," *The Guardian* reported days after the quake.[1] "Interruptions in basic services such as the water supply can increase the risk of waterborne disease outbreaks … Animal and human fecal matter and bodies can become sources of contamination if they're in the water supply," warned CNN.[2]

When a deadly scourge began stalking the land, however, scythe in hand to reap the harvest of yet more Haitian lives, it did not come from the camps, nor did it come from the Haitians themselves. It was brought, like a fair share of the calamity that had befallen them in their history, by those from abroad who had told them they were there to help.

In the Artibonite village of Meille, at a base set up by MINUSTAH peace-keepers from Nepal, a broken PVC pipe was pouring raw sewage into a tributary that flowed directly into the Boukan Kanni and Jenba rivers, which then flowed into the larger Artibonite River. Elsewhere at the base, pits of sewage over-flowed during frequent rainstorms and dumped their foul-smelling refuse into the community's water source, its bacteria then carried to hundreds of communities downstream.[3]

The Artibonite, the long winding life source across which Benoît Batraville and Charlemagne Péralte once crossed and into which Jean Dominique's ashes had been poured, became the artery into which the new plague flowed. Health officials expressed bewilderment at the arrival of cholera, which had been absent from Haiti for decades.[4] By late October 2010, over 200 had died and 2,000 had fallen ill, with dead and dying patients sprawled throughout the courtyard of the main hospital in Saint-Marc.[5] By early November, the United States Centers for Disease Control and Prevention said the strain of cholera devastating Haiti matched strains most often found in South Asia.[6] A few days later, the first case was confirmed in the capital.[7] Despite the mounting evidence of MINUSTAH's culpability, the mission's spokesman, Vicenzo Pugliese, continued to issue ever more improbable denials, telling reporters that "allegations the Nepalese [peace-keepers] have spilled fecal matter into the river are completely false," and adding that "the strain [of cholera from South Asia] could have reached Haiti from any point on the globe."[8] By mid-November, cholera had claimed 800 lives and sickened 11,000.[9] Soon more than 1,000 would be dead and the disease would have spread to six departments. In the space of three days, Médecins Sans Frontières saw the number of cases increase sevenfold.[10] Soon, the first case was detected in the Dominican Republic.[11]

***

As cholera spread throughout the country, worrying signs were also arriving from the campaign trail. On 26 October, gunmen attacked a bus carrying journal-ists to cover the campaign of Jacques Édouard Alexis in Cap-Haïtien, resulting in the death of one attacker and one policeman. A day later, a clash between partisans of INITE's Arodon Bien-Aimé and Groupement Solidarité's Hugue Bien-Aimé in Cerca-Carvajal left 15 injured.[12] At the beginning of November, Chavannes Jean-Baptiste said that weapons were being distributed to INITE partisans in Hinche, and by Willot Joseph in Maïssade.[13] POHDH released a statement voicing its concern about the claims.[14] Mirlande Manigat said that INITE planned to "terrorize" its opponents on the eve of the election to assure a Jude Célestin victory.[15] Jean-Henry Céant told a reporter that Préval's "plan is to stay in power with the election of Célestin."[16] Several hundred displaced people again demonstrated in front of Bellerive's office, chanting "No election under tents and tarps!" and calling for the departure of MINUSTAH.[17]

Thousands of demonstrators took to the streets of Cap-Haïtien on 15 November demanding the departure of MINUSTAH for bringing cholera to the country and throwing rocks at UN vehicles before being dispersed by tear gas and live ammunition. At least one person died.[18] A similar protest rocked Hinche, where several UN personnel were injured.[19] In an address to the nation, Préval called for calm.[20] Edmond Mulet warned of the disruption that "every second that passes can save or break thousands of lives," although he remained silent on the UN's culpability for the plague.[21] In a subsequent demonstration in front of the National Palace, protesters tore down Jude Célestin election posters.[22] At a rally in Croix-de-Bouquets, its festivities illuminated everywhere by his signature color, pink, supporters of Michel Martelly – now widely referred to as Tèt Kale (Bald Head) in recognition of his gleaming pate – chanted "cholera" against *le pouvoir*. On stage, Martelly bemoaned the dissolution of the Haitian army, which he said could have been reformed to provide jobs instead of the nation "paying a foreign army."[23]

One aspect of Haiti that is often lost on foreigners deluged by ceaseless images of poverty, violence and political turmoil is the country's tremendous capacity for ribaldry and joy, an aspect of the Haitian personality that Michel Martelly embodied perhaps as much as any single individual in the country. An encapsulation of many diverse aspects of Haiti's character, Martelly had grown up in the capital's southern suburb of Carrefour, had attended Saint-Louis de Gonzague, the high school of the elite, and entered (but dropped out of) Haiti's military academy. He was known for outrageous antics such as performing in Haiti's 1996 carnival in full drag and announcing during that era that he would perform nude atop Haiti's National Palace if ever elected to the presidency (he was already referred to as the *prezidan* – president – of *konpa*).[24] I had known him slightly, and, from time to time, I saw flickerings of a social conscience, such as during a moonlit drive he and I took through the darkened streets of Port-au-Prince one January night in 2001, when he looked out at the poverty surrounding us and told me of the country's elite: "These people, they have so much money and they wouldn't even build one fucking fountain for the people to get water from." The rise of Martelly's candidacy – which had been viewed as a joke by many only weeks before – came as a surprise to nearly all foreign observers in the country, many of whom were only dimly aware up to that point of who he was. Building on his years of playing before large audiences and his fluid, often humorous command of Creole, Martelly formed a natural gravitational orbit for disaffected youth who otherwise would have voted for Wyclef Jean. His chances were further bolstered by the presence in his campaign of the Miami-based Spanish political strategist Antonio Sola, who had played a key role in the successful 2006 presidential campaign of Mexico's Felipe Calderón. Martelly had also, suggestively, gathered around him a coterie of highly able supporters and surrogates, many of them with links to the government of Jean-Claude Duvalier. There was the former Duvalierist minister Daniel Supplice, arguably one of Haiti's savviest politicians, the brothers Gregory and Thierry

Mayard-Paul, both well-known attorneys and the sons of Duvalierist lawyer Constantin Mayard-Paul, and the dean of the capital's bar, Gervais Charles. And there was Laurent Lamothe, a U.S.-educated telecoms tycoon who had co-founded the Global Voice Group and made a small fortune in Africa.

One foreign diplomatic veteran of several Haitian missions, watching Martelly campaign, thought the singer "touched a nerve with people ... he was very much an outsider, a non-typical product of the Haitian elite, and people were very thirsty for that ... he also brought a real understanding of how to talk to the Haitian people."[25] One of the more insightful readings of Martelly's rise came from the Haitian sociologist and former ambassador to the Dominican Republic Guy Alexandre, who wrote that it was "explained by the frustration of the population and its rejection of Préval, who has not been able to manage the country after the earthquake ... [Martelly] is a right-wing populist backed by former Duvalierists and the youth of the popular classes for whom he represents a break with the traditional political system."[26]

It was a perception that Martelly's strategist Antonio Sola sought to exploit, crafting an image that saw the wild performer Sweet Micky gradually morph into the more serious Michel Martelly while at the same time highlighting the differences between Martelly and Haiti's loathed traditional political class.[27]

* * *

By mid-November the electoral campaign was heating up. An INITE-affiliated radio station in Les Cayes was attacked by stone-throwing Martelly partisans, injuring two employees, while INITE and Rasanble partisans brawled in Aquin.[28] The leader of an RDNP-affiliated union was slain in Port-au-Prince.[29] A series of chaotic rolling demonstrations in the capital on 18 November – the date of Haiti's pivotal victory over the French in Vertières in the north – saw protesters chanting slogans against Préval and MINUSTAH, hurling stones at PNH and UN vehicles, and defacing or destroying anything they could find with Jude Célestin's face on it.[30] Again in Aquin, the site of earlier disturbances, a rally by Mirlande Manigat was disrupted by armed INITE partisans waving photos of Jude Célestin. A later Manigat rally in Les Cayes was disrupted by Martelly partisans on motos carrying posters of their candidate.[31] In Beaumont, in the remote Grand Anse, Jude Célestin's campaign convoy was fired on by unknown gunmen.[32]

On the campaign trail, Martelly chided Manigat for abandoning her senate bid four years earlier, asking the crowd "Can you trust her?" and telling them that "she is everything that the public is not, I am everything that they are."[33] Manigat derided Martelly as "immoral." Then Martelly and Céant accused Manigat of having a secret pact with Préval.[34] And so on. Manigat, leading in the polls two days before the vote, said that 500,000 fraudulent ballots had been distributed to assure a Célestin victory.[35] In Plaisance, INITE supporters formed a militia called Lame Dòmi Nan Bwa (an echo of the group that killed journalist Brignol Lindor in 2001) that terrorized government opponents.[36] At the ODVA compound in Gonaïves, 20 two-wheeled tractors (*motokilti* in Creole) appeared, dangled in front of local farmers as an incentive to vote the right way.[37]

A group of Haitian organizations observing the election questioned the CEP's decision "to move many voters and to force them to fulfill their civic duty in centers distant from their place of residence" and suggested an active campaign to disenfranchise those displaced by the earthquake.[38] Two days before the election, no one in the sprawling tent city of Canaan had any idea where they would vote.[39] Announcing that the candidates were all advocating "against the interests of the Haitian people," the Tèt Kole peasant group announced that it would not be endorsing anyone in the election.[40] Even the head of Haiti's electoral registry glumly concluded that "there will be fraud everywhere."[41]

* * *

Campaigning was to end at midnight on Friday, with the vote coming the following Sunday. Mirlande Manigat addressed thousands of supporters at the Église St. Charles in Carrefour. Just down the road, Jude Célestin addressed supporters at Bizoton. Jean-Henry Céant held his final event in Bel-Air, while in Les Cayes, a planned Martelly rally was disrupted by gunfire.[42] On Saturday, thousands of people waited in lines to pick up new identity cards, with many still in line when the offices closed at the appointed hour, some making little accommodation for those still waiting.[43] The night before the vote, Willot Joseph reportedly led a group of armed men on a tour of polling centers at Boucan-Carré, "creating a psychosis of fear among the population of the voting center officers and supervisors."[44]

On election day in the capital, some voters were turned away when poll workers couldn't find their names on lists of registered voters, and at other locales young men reportedly voted multiple times, threatening journalists who tried to investigate.[45] Even Célestin, trying to vote at a Pétionville high school, had to vote by provisional ballot when the photo of him on the voter list did not match.[46] Three people were killed in a gun battle in Desdunes in the Artibonite, and in Tabarre young men stormed a voting center and dumped the ballots in the street.[47] Some reporters on the ground couldn't find a single person who admitted voting for Célestin.[48]

In Cap-Haïtien, one supporter of Nawoon Marcellus, now affiliated with INITE, displayed a purse containing "at least" 50 identity cards needed to vote.[49] Marcellus supporters descended on voting locations, including those in Grande Rivière du Nord and Milot, and stuffed ballot boxes in favor of their candidate. Willot Joseph also appeared again, this time distributing T-shirts emblazoned with Célestin's likeness, and fired in the air at a polling place in Maïssade, destroying some voting materials and carting others away as those inside fled. In Cité Soleil, armed self-described INITE supporters took one ballot box away only to return it later, filled.[50] Near Pignon, in the north, INITE paid people to vote for Célestin but they then turned around and voted for Martelly. Local politicos perceived as being insufficiently enthusiastic supporters of Célestin were threatened with guns and machetes for the poor turnout, and some were told they were marked for death.[51] In Les Cayes, in the south, intimidation at the polling places – for those who were able to vote – was said to be rife, and, in some areas, potential voters were being turned away "in droves."[52] At one point, a dog wearing a Jude Célestin yellow and green campaign T-shirt was sent running down the Kenscoff Road.[53]

Mulet, who earlier that same day had called Préval to congratulate him on the smoothness of the election, called a meeting at his residence as conditions deteriorated throughout the day. In attendance would be Mulet himself, U.S. Ambassador Merten, Colin Granderson, the Trinidadian diplomat in charge of the OAS mission, Ricardo Seitenfus, the Brazilian diplomat serving as OAS special representative to Haiti, and others. Although, in a move pregnant with symbolism, no Haitians had initially been invited, Jean-Max Bellerive called U.S. Ambassador Merten and, after being "invited" by the latter, arrived with his chief of staff to find a tense atmosphere. Mulet spoke about what he said was the fraud that was happening across the country and the violence swirling around the elections and then said: "If we don't confront this situation, the president will have to take a plane out of here, this is getting completely out of control."[54]

At this, the room froze. Seitenfus would later say that Mulet had confided in him that "an airplane would be at [Préval's] disposal to leave the country" and that the latter would "have to leave the presidency and abandon Haiti."[55] This claim was dismissed to me as "totally false" and "rubbish" by two other diplomats present at the meeting.[56] Jean-Max Bellerive, however, *did* interpret Mulet's comment to those assembled as a threat and asked why, with voting still going on at 90 percent of the polling places, the international community would call a halt to it. Then, having been told that he might have to head a transitional government, Bellerive told the diplomats that "I entered by the main door. I'm not leaving and coming back in by the window. You're talking about a coup d'état. If you want to do this, put me on the plane, too."

At this, Seitenfus stood up and said "the OAS does not support a coup d'état in Haiti" and looked at the Brazilian ambassador, Igor Kipman, who said: "Neither does Brazil."

Everyone then turned to Merten, who looked at Mulet and shook his head: "No."[57]

The crisis at Mulet's residence had passed, but the crisis outside its walls continued. Before the day's voting was over, 13 of the 18 presidential candidates – including Michel Martelly, Mirlande Manigat, Jacques Édouard Alexis, Charles Baker and Yvon Neptune – were calling for the elections to be halted, saying that Préval was in the process of stealing the vote for Célestin.[58] Their calls were soon echoed by hundreds of pro-Martelly demonstrators on the streets of Pétionville and in Saint-Marc, while Manigat supporters attacked polling stations.[59] By early evening, pro-Martelly demonstrators had flooded into the Champ de Mars and Delmas, and were clashing with INITE partisans in Cap-Haïtien, while anti-government demonstrations had erupted in Jacmel and Petit-Goâve.[60] In Aquin, at least two people were killed.[61]

When all was said and done, out of a potential electorate of nearly 5 million, only 1.1 million were able to cast their votes.[62]

* * *

On Monday morning, things were largely calm, if tense.[63] By afternoon, however, demonstrators, again a majority of them favoring Manigat, had once more reclaimed the streets of Saint-Marc, where they hurled rocks and bottles at MINUSTAH peacekeepers.[64] At least six people were injured by gunfire in the town, while, in Gonaïves, Manigat supporter Youri Latortue led a march of several thousand people.[65] In Jacmel, burning barricades were erected.[66] That afternoon, Martelly reversed his position, saying that he was against the annulation of the vote.[67] Manigat also said that she would participate in any runoff in which she was one of the two candidates.[68]

Despite all that had happened, on Monday, Colin Granderson, head of the OAS–CARICOM mission, told reporters that "these irregularities, serious as some were [do not] necessarily invalidate the process."[69] To U.S. State Department spokesman P. J. Crowley, the elections were "a significant step," while Ban Ki-moon said he wanted to move "forward to a solution to the political crisis."[70] However, on its website, MINUSTAH released a statement saying that "the United Nations and the international community expressed their deep concern at the numerous incidents that marred the voting."[71] RNDDH was far more critical, and soon issued a scathing report in which they wrote that "instead of resolving the country's political situation, [the elections] made it more complicated. Haiti has regressed in organizing and conducting the elections while the amount of money allocated today far exceeds that of previous years ... Due to the gravity, and the systematic and repetitive nature of fraud and violence ... RNDDH believes that this was a premeditated operation on the part of the executive powers."[72] The CNO criticized what it called "systematic irregularities" in the vote.[73]

Using uncommonly undiplomatic language, Mulet warned that "if the popular will is not respected, the UN and the international community are going to withdraw, and the country will not receive the benefits of political support and foreign resources for its rebuilding."[74] By Tuesday, Préval's *éminence grise* Joseph Lambert was telling reporters: "INITE is ready to accept democratic change. If we've lost the elections at the presidential level we'll go into opposition, and we can live with the party that has won the elections."[75] Around the country, calm appeared to be gradually returning.[76] Speaking at a press conference on Wednesday, Manigat declared serenely: "I will be president."[77]

* * *

By 6 December – more than a week since the vote had been held – Haiti's CNO was saying that their tabulations put Manigat in first place, with 30 percent of the vote, followed by Martelly with 25 percent, while Jude Célestin was third with 20 percent.[78] Youri Latortue warned that the country would "erupt" if Célestin was declared the winner, adding that the government had "to see that Jude doesn't have the popular vote."[79] Martelly said "we will not go in a second round with Célestin" and charged that the government was attempting to organize "a vast fraud in his favor."[80]

When election results were released around 9pm on 7 December, the CEP said that Manigat had received 31.37 percent of the vote, Célestin 22.48 percent, and Martelly 21.84 percent.[81] Several INITE candidates, such as Jacmel mayor Edwin Zenny, Saurel Jacinthe and Levaillant Louis-Jeune, won election to parliament in the first round.[82]

The response to the announced results by Martelly's supporters was immediate and furious. Roadblocks went up and gunfire was heard throughout Port-au-Prince.[83] Attackers set fire to the INITE headquarters in the capital, and protesters also hit the streets in Cap-Haïtien and Les Cayes.[84] One masked protester announced that "the people came out to vote for Martelly because Manigat and Célestin are not going to sort anything out ... We will destroy the country until Martelly is made president."[85] Another stated: "We're still living under tents and Célestin wastes money on election posters."[86] Several hundred young men brandishing clubs and other implements marched to the U.S. Embassy, and American Airlines flights in and out of the capital were suspended.[87] Some protesters went as far as to chant "Hang Préval!"[88] In Les Cayes, mobs sacked the local elections and tax offices and National Credit Bank.[89] Several supermarkets and a police station at the entrance to the town were also looted and burned, with weapons and ammunition carted away from the latter.[90] At least three people were killed there.[91] In Cap-Haïtien, clashes between Célestin and Martelly supporters left one dead.[92] Préval's appeals for calm had little effect. A statement by the U.S. Embassy in Port-au-Prince on the day the results were announced urged "efforts to thoroughly review irregularities in support of electoral results that are consistent with the will of the Haitian people expressed in their votes."[93] Thursday also saw chaos, with armed men in INITE T-shirts shooting at demonstrators on Champ de Mars.[94] Finally, later that same day, CEP president Gaillot Dorsainvil read a statement carried on Haitian radio where he said, "given the evident dissatisfaction of many voters, protests and violence that followed the publication of preliminary results," the CEP would immediately begin a recount of the votes.[95] By this point, a local team of Médecins Sans Frontières doctors had treated at least 15 victims of gunshot wounds in the capital.[96]

Friday saw some semblance of calm return to the capital and other cities, though both Martelly and several electoral observer bodies continued to voice their doubts that the recount would not also be corrupted.[97] Six of the latter co-signed a letter to the CEP warning that "the determination of the Haitian people to defend their rights is now clear and leaves no doubt to anyone."[98] Ironically, it was Jude Célestin himself who filed the first legal challenge to the vote, claiming that he had in fact won more than 50 percent in the first round, thereby forgoing a runoff.[99] Manigat denounced the recount as "a trap."[100] Some politicians and civil society leaders even called for the cancellation of elections and the forming of a "national unity" government, an idea Préval rejected.[101] Only days after a group of OAS "experts" arrived in the country to help supervise the recount, they announced that it might take weeks as "many experts are going home for Christmas to see their families."[102] In the United States, Vermont senator Patrick Leahy again called for a suspension of aid to Haiti while the recount mess simmered, a suggestion dismissed by Secretary of State Hillary Clinton.[103]

Amid the election controversy, nearly 2,000 people had died of cholera, with one clinic in Limbé alone seeing 250 patients a day.[104] An early December report submitted to France's foreign ministry concluded that the strain of cholera ravaging Haiti could be traced to the Nepalese base.[105]

* * *

As his tenure wound down, in an interview published in the Swiss newspaper *Le Temps*, the OAS ambassador Ricardo Seitenfus was quoted as saying that Haiti was "not in civil war" (he had been spared the horrors of Operation Baghdad) and that the international community had "imposed" MINUSTAH on the country and that instead it "must build roads, erect dams, participate in the organization of the state, the judicial system … Its mandate in Haiti is to maintain the peace of the cemetery." Seitenfus went on to say that the work of the international community in Haiti was a "failure," that Haiti was in a situation where aid "replaces the state in all its missions," and that "charity cannot be the engine of international relations; autonomy, sovereignty, fair trade and respect for others should be."[106] Following these statements, Seitenfus said he was told to take "a vacation."[107] Other sources, however, said he had been removed from his post.[108]

* * *

Speaking at Gonaïves again for the traditional New Year's message, Préval said that Haiti was at "a dangerous crossroads" and asked that "a legitimate president and legitimate parliament" replace the outgoing ones. As he spoke, for the first time, some in the crowd heckled him.[109] It was about this time that Préval also announced that, as he wasn't inaugurated until May 2006, he would be leaving office on 14 May – not 7 February – as the constitution stipulated. He position was somewhat bolstered by the fact that the CEP said openly that a January runoff was "not possible" given the tangle of objections to the first round.[110] A report by the OAS concluded that there had been strong evidence of fraud in the vote and that, for the vote to reflect reality, "the position of the candidate in third place [Martelly] would change to second and the candidate now in second place [Célestin] would move to third."[111]

As Haiti approached the first anniversary of the earthquake, the mood was grim. In addition to the political crisis and the cholera crisis – which by this point had killed nearly 3,500 people[112] – almost 1 million people were still living in the camps and only 5 percent of the rubble had been cleared.[113] The economist (and former nominee for prime minister) Ericq Pierre penned an essay in which he opined about the international presence in Haiti and the many planned observances by different organizations involved in the reconstruction:

> They came with too many propositions, too many resources, too many promises. They make too many decisions. They came with too much knowledge, and not enough know-how. So many embraced us that, in the end, they embarrassed us. How can that be? With the warmth of their embrace, we are almost suffocating. Do they even realize this? … I only ask them not to organize public commemorations, celebrations, or inaugurations of any kind on 12 January 2011. My suggestion is to choose any other date … Leave the 12th to the Haitians, finally to remember our dead alone. I ask our foreign friends to give us a day at least. Just one day … To mourn our dead, remember them, and reflect on what is happening to us, and how and why we got where we are today. We need to find some peace that day, alone with our own.[114]

* * *

After making the OAS wait several days, Préval assented to receive their report on the elections.[115] Célestin supporters erected flaming barricades around the capital, sparking melees in which one person died.[116] The government condemned the disturbances.[117] RNDDH denounced the armed groups sowing panic in the city.[118] Upon receiving the report, the CEP issued a statement in which it said that "the possibility of a change of position in the rankings of the second and third candidates ... will be considered."[119] Further ratcheting up the pressure, the U.S. ambassador to the United Nations, Susan Rice, told the UN Security Council that "sustained support from the international community, including the United States, will require a credible process that represents the will of the Haitian people."[120]

* * *

Three days later, another earthquake – or perhaps a plague – would arrive – or more specifically return – to the country, like the cholera that was killing them, borne to Haiti by silver wings from distant shores.

Late on the afternoon of 14 January, Jean-Claude Duvalier returned from his nearly 25-year exile aboard an Air France flight from Paris. Nearly a year before, the 59-year-old former dictator had lost a Swiss court fight to prevent a legal basis for the confiscation of some of the millions he had been accused of plundering from Haiti decades before. Swiss courts had previously found that the Duvalier empire was clearly "a criminal organization," and, at the time of the decision, a spokesman for the Swiss Department of Foreign Affairs flatly called Duvalier a "thief."[121] Nevertheless, when he landed in Port-au-Prince, it was said he kissed the ground and told stunned reporters "I've come to help."[122] Greeted by a few hundred people – some of them chanting "Long live Duvalier!"[123] – the now sallow and sickly looking former despot was driven away to the Karibe Hotel in a convoy of PNH vehicles.[124] As to what the government's position was on the return of such a notorious citizen, Jean-Max Bellerive blandly told reporters that "he is a Haitian and, as such, is free to return home."[125] With three-fifths of Haiti's population under the age of 30, disturbingly, a good chunk of the popular sentiment about Baby Doc seemed to be summed up by the comments of a 44-year-old man playing dominoes by the roadside who was interviewed by AFP's Haitian reporter Clarens Renois and mused "[Duvalier] doesn't faze me. He has a right to come back to his country. This is where he was born ... They say his government killed a lot of people, but a lot of governments after him did the same."[126]

Many of those who had suffered Duvalierism's depredations and worked in the years following his ouster to try to make Haiti a decent country, however, were aghast. Jean-Claude Bajeux, who had lost most of his family to the elder Duvalier's 1964 massacres, declared he "would not breathe the same air as Duvalier." The former football player Bobby Duval, who had endured the agonies of

Fort Dimanche for over a year in the 1970s, told *The Economist* that the Duvalier era was "a very harsh reality we thought we had passed."[127] Michele Montas, now back in Haiti after years working at the United Nations in New York, said that she was "outraged, angry and dismayed ... What bothers me the most is the fact that so many people seem to have forgotten what happened."[128]

How did Duvalier get back to Haiti? Some, such as a former UN official I spoke to, were convinced that Préval had engineered the return "for his own sake ... He could not bear the thought of leaving Haiti and living anywhere else. All former presidents should have the right to live in Haiti, and none of them were living in Haiti so he wanted to establish that precedent."[129] A U.S. official I spoke to, however, said he had the impression that Duvalier's return "was a complete surprise" to Préval.[130]

* * *

Despite conflicting reports that Duvalier had been or would be arrested shortly after his return, despite a brief round of questioning he existed more or less unmolested. Four of the Duvalier regime's former victims – Michèle Montas, Alix Fils-Aimé, Nicole Magloire and Claude Rosier – would eventually lodge complaints against the former dictator with Haiti's government.[131] Eventually, a number of organizations, including the CEDH, RNDDH, Kay Fanm and over 20 others, would form a Collectif Contre l'Impunité to pursue legal action against the former dictator.[132]

Shortly after his return, Duvalier released a statement saying that he had no political ambitions.[133] He would eventually leave his hotel and settle into a private home on Montagne Noire.[134] In brief remarks delivered in French and in a quavering voice before journalists the following day, Duvalier said:

> I return to show my solidarity in this extremely difficult period of national
> life where you are still hundreds of thousands living under the stars, amid
> the ruins ... I was expecting all sorts of persecution; but believe me, the
> desire to participate with you in this *konbit* for national reconstruction
> far exceeds the annoyances that I could be facing ... Whatever the cost,
> the main thing is for me to be here with you ... I take this opportunity to
> publicly present my condolences to my millions of partisans who, after my
> voluntary departure from Haiti to avoid bloodshed and facilitate the rapid
> conclusion of the political crisis in 1986 ... were brutally murdered ... their

goods looted, their homes burned ... I also take this opportunity to express once more my deep sadness to my compatriots who recognize, rightly, to have been victims under my government.[135]

The return of Duvalier, of course, raised the question of what would become of Haiti's other famous exiled despot, Aristide. In an email sent to supporters after Duvalier's appearance in Haiti, Aristide said that he wanted to return to the country "to contribute to serving my Haitian sisters and brothers as a simple citizen in the field of education." The IJDH's Brian Concannon, identified as "a lawyer who has represented Aristide," said Préval had not responded to the former's request for a new passport.[136] Saying that "Haiti has its hands full dealing with the current ongoing election process," U.S. State Department spokesman P. J. Crowley opined that this government did "not think that any actions by any individual at this point that can only bring divisiveness to Haitian society is helpful in helping Haiti move forward."[137] Préval told reporters that Duvalier was under "house arrest" and that, like Duvalier, Aristide was free to return.[138] Rumors and counter-rumors continued for the rest of the month, with Préval saying that Aristide was entitled to a diplomatic passport but had not yet applied for one (this was in response to a letter from Aristide's lawyer, Ira Kurzban, still doing double-duty with Aristide and the IJDH, which often amounted to the same thing),[139] and Cuba denying a persistent rumor that Aristide had arrived on the island.[140]

* * *

Haiti's electoral crisis continued to roll on. Having run out of patience with Préval and the CEP, Edmond Mulet spoke to U.S. Ambassador Merten about revoking the U.S. visas of Préval, his advisors and members of the CEP and even members of Préval's family, 36 names in all.[141] The U.S. promptly did so.[142] Among those affected were Célestin himself, Senator John Joël Joseph, Minister of Social Affairs Gérald Germain, and Préval lackeys Assad Volcy and René Momplaisir.[143] By late January, a meeting of INITE's executive board would openly be discussing the possibility of Célestin dropping out of the race.[144] Célestin was said to be resistant.[145] INITE senator and former Préval advisor Moïse Jean-Charles claimed that Célestin would have won in the first round were it not for "the international community."[146] During a one-day trip to Haiti, Hillary Clinton said that the U.S. supported "the OAS recommendations and we would like to see those acted on."[147]

What was not widely known at the time were the specifics of Clinton's meeting with Préval while she was in the country. According to Jean-Max Bellerive, who was present during it, it was a disarming performance from one of the world's great political manipulators, whose skills surpassed even those of Préval. After meeting with Martelly, Célestin and Manigat, Clinton went to meet with Préval and Bellerive at the offices behind what was left of the National Palace at around 7pm. Préval met Clinton ready to do battle with boxes of documents to "prove" to the secretary of state that Jude Célestin had won his place in the runoff election.

Clinton – unlike her husband, not known (at least publicly) for her great personal warmth – came into the office and sat next to Préval, putting her hand on his knee and not taking it off during the entirety of their conversation.

"René," she said, calling the president by his first name. "I came here to see how we can solve this mess and save the elections, but most of all to save you. Bill and I have known you for a long time, you're our friend in Haiti. But now you appear internationally like a crook who tried to steal an election to put your friend in, and I cannot save you from that. So let's work together to save what you represent in Haiti, because you are the champion of liberty in Haiti, you established freedom of the press, you stopped political arrests. Let's find a way out of this."

Préval, so prepared for a fight, was not prepared for that, and it utterly unnerved him and took him by surprise.

"It was almost too intimate," Bellerive later told me. "You almost wanted to leave."[148]

After her meeting with Préval, Clinton headed back to the airport in a U.S. Embassy car accompanied by Ambassador Merten, Clinton's Chief of Staff Cheryl Mills and Jean-Max Bellerive. After an awkward silence of several minutes as they drove, Clinton spoke.

"Jean-Max, how do you think this is going to proceed?"

"Simple. Martelly will be president."

"What???" Clinton said in apparent disbelief. "I met those three. Madame Manigat seemed a little bit crazy because immediately she was giving me orders. Michel Martelly was charming, but … In fact, the only one who talked about Haiti with me was Jude Célestin. It's a pity we never knew him before."[149]

* * *

Clinton's personal diplomacy apparently had its desired effect. Finally, early on the morning of 3 February, the CEP announced that, as per their revised electoral tallies, Manigat and Martelly would go to the second round of the presidential elections, with Célestin ejected from the race.[150] Following the announcement, Martelly told a press conference that, though Haiti had "many difficulties awaiting us ... together we can resolve them."[151] U.S. Ambassador Merten declared the day "a good day for Haiti."[152] The mood in the Célestin camp was rather different, with Célestin issuing an open letter in which he referred to the vote as a "pathetic chapter" in the country's history, accused the Préval government of having fallen into a "trap" set by international diplomats (especially the OAS "gravediggers") and complained bitterly at what he said was his betrayal by INITE. Célestin concluded by advising: "Courage, sons and daughters of Dessalines, the blackest night announces the most radiant dawn."[153]

RNDDH quite correctly expressed its concern that the international community's focus on the presidential ballot had resulted in the virtual ignoring of the legislative elections, which were arguably every bit as corrupt and where the sponsors of violence would now be "rewarded for their ingenuity" with positions in parliament.[154] On the day that Célestin was removed from the slate of runoff candidates, all the *motokilti* that had been dangled in front of local farmers to encourage them to vote for the "correct" candidate disappeared without benefiting a single farmer in the Artibonite.[155]

* * *

As Haitians cautiously awaited the next round of voting, the South Korean garment manufacturer Sae-A Trading Co. Ltd signed a deal with the Préval government to build an industrial park near Cap-Haïtien that those involved and Bill Clinton (still active in his role with the IHRC) said would provide 20,000 jobs for the region, effectively setting Sae-A Trading up to be the largest private employers in the country. The deal was negotiated even before the earthquake, and was viewed as one of the lynchpin projects for implementing the recommendations contained in the 2009 Collier report. It was a project for which the IADB was to provide $50 million of funding to help build the factories themselves, and the EU additional funds to help rehabilitate the area's roads.[156] Meanwhile, in a scene illustrative of how surreal the national body politic had become, on 7 February – exactly 25 years to the day after he had been driven from power – Jean-Claude Duvalier was cheered by thousands of people while visiting the graves of his grandparents in Léogâne, where he also laid a wreath at a memorial for those killed in the earthquake. Hundreds of people ran alongside his car chanting supportive slogans.[157] The same day, it was announced that the Préval government had issued a diplomatic passport for Aristide, valid until February 2016, and that Ira Kurzban would soon be heading to Haiti to pick it up.[158] Days after the announcement, several thousand Aristide supporters marched through Port-au-Prince demanding the exiled politician's return.[159] An Obama spokesman said the U.S. president had "deep concerns" about the former leader's potential reappearance.[160]

* * *

As the ghosts of Haiti's past flitted in and out of the national consciousness, those who would direct its future took their messages to the public. Michel Martelly toured the north, speaking to huge crowds in Cap-Haïtien and Fort-Liberté.[161] In Au Cap, Martelly was joined by Wyclef Jean, who had endorsed the candidate after his own expulsion from the race (five losing candidates would also endorse him).[162] The candidate received a similarly enthusiastic welcome in Les Cayes in the south.[163] Martelly also traveled to Santo Domingo to meet with Dominican President Leonel Fernàndez.[164] Manigat, on the other hand, addressed journalists in the grounds of what was left of the capital's Hotel Montana, telling them that the two candidates did not "resemble each other at all," a perhaps unwittingly telling assessment.[165] In Cité Soleil, Manigat appeared amenable to recruiting the help of Ronique Joseph, the wife of former FRAPH attaché and Lavalas mayor of Cité Soleil Fritz Joseph.[166] In Martissant, she was received warmly by a large crowd.[167]

At a 10 March rally by Manigat in Cap-Haïtien, the candidate's motorcade was stoned and counter-protesters brandishing Martelly posters were beaten by Manigat supporters.[168] During a 15 March rally in Mirebalais, Manigat's event was derailed by gunfire and rock-throwing and protesters carrying Martelly posters. Many were injured and Manigat was forced to flee the town under police protection.[169] A day later – following the collapse of a reviewing stand on which she was to speak in the Artibonite's Liancourt – Manigat denounced what she called the *milice rose* (pink militia), a reference to Martelly's signature color, and what she warned was the "totalitarian threat" posed by his candidacy.[170] (When asked about his tangled U.S. real estate dealings by Haitian journalist Gotson Pierre during a televised debate, Martelly appeared to threaten that "the street" might take revenge against the reporter.[171]) Three campaign workers putting up Manigat posters were arrested by a PNH patrol and later turned up dead in the capital's morgue.[172]

* * *

Two days before the second round of elections was to take place, Jean-Bertrand Aristide returned to Haiti from South Africa and from his nearly seven-year exile. As he did when traveling from the Central African Republic to Jamaica, Aristide's plane was packed to the gills with assorted groupies and acolytes. Along with the American actor Danny Glover was the journalist Amy Goodman, who continued her role as Aristide's chief public relations arm with alacrity and to whom Glover confided that he was there "to accompany my friend, President Aristide, home back to Haiti ... he is going home to be of assistance in the rebuilding of Haiti."[173] (Strangely, during Glover's many trips to Haiti, the star had never found time to meet with the victims of La Scierie.) Smithsonian Institution official James Early and the filmmaker Katherine Keane (herself the scion of a wealthy New Jersey political dynasty) were also on hand, as was Ira Kurzban.[174] During a brief address at the airport, Aristide said he was happy to be back in Haiti and criticized the exclusion of Lavalas from the elections.[175] Aristide was met at the airport by a crowd of "about 3,000" supporters[176] and then returned to the house he had fled and in which there had been left behind piles of rotting money years before. Police lavished tear gas on the crowd to clear a path through which Aristide could go to his home in Tabarre.[177]

Jean-Claude Duvalier and Jean-Bertrand Aristide, the two men whose political currents had most defined Haiti's political identity during the previous 30 years, were home.

* * *

As was by now routine, a number of polling places either opened late or waited for election materials that arrived late, but, overall, the ballot seemed far calmer than November's first round.[178] Martelly voted at the Lycée de Pétionville, traveling down a road festooned with posters and photos of himself.[179] All was not entirely peaceful, however, as fighting between partisans of INITE's Woodly Simon and Lavni's Gracia Delva left one dead and several wounded in Marchand Dessalines, and another person died in clashes between supporters of INITE's Yves Duprat and Alternative's Eloune Doréus in Mare Rouge.[180]

As Haiti awaited the results of the election, the country remained tense. A raid by gunmen firing from motorcycles left two dead and several injured at the capital's Marché Salomon.[181] Manigat's RDNP announced that they had submitted a complaint of "fraud" to the CEP regarding the vote tallies.[182] Their concerns were echoed by CEP president Gaillot Dorsinvil himself,[183] and eventually at least 1,718 of over 25,000 presidential tally sheets would be discarded.[184] By Monday, partial results showed that the wind was clearly at Martelly's back, with the singer leading in areas as diverse as Pétionville and Cité Soleil in the capital.[185] By 1 April, Martelly was already claiming victory with "69.74% of the vote" via his Twitter account.[186] One of Martelly's more dunderheaded supporters, the Haitian-American hip-hop singer Pras Michel (who in the 1990s had performed along with Wyclef Jean in The Fugees), used his own Twitter account to send out the violence-baiting message "Manchète + gasoline + matches = the will of the people."[187]

* * *

On 4 April, the CEP announced results showing that Martelly had won the presidential elections with 67.57 percent of the vote. Thousands of Martelly supporters flooded into the streets of the capital and elsewhere to celebrate the victory of Tèt Kale.[188]

"Things will change," Martelly said at a press conference the following day. "You have seen fit to entrust me with carrying the country to its destination, leaving behind the old demons and quarrels of Haitian politics … I want to work with everyone, I am the president of all Haitians."[189]

Despite making initial sounds that she would dispute Martelly's win, Manigat soon announced that she would not, in fact, contest the result.[190] At several appearances after his victory, Martelly outlined what he said were his policy goals. He proposed a levy of $1 on every $100 wire transfer to Haiti, which he said would raise $50 million a year, as well as a 5-cent levy on every telephone minute, which he said would raise $36 million a year, which he said would help fund free education for every Haitian child.[191] He also announced his intention to create "a modern army" for Haiti to replace MINUSTAH and buttress the PNH.[192]

Shortly after his victory, Martelly had what was described as "a working lunch" with Préval and Bellerive at the president's private residence in Laboule.[193] Meeting with Martelly in Washington after his election, Hillary Clinton said "we are behind him, we have a great deal of enthusiasm."[194] Martelly also announced that he was considering "an amnesty" for Duvalier and Aristide.[195]

Préval himself also made an early April visit to the United States, during which he addressed the UN Security Council and noted with characteristic understatement that it was "sad" that he was "the only president to have done a first term, then a second constitutional mandate, and also the only one in 25 years not having been in prison or exile."[196]

While the world was focused on Martelly's victory, however, Préval proved that Haiti's consummate political survivor still held cards to play. In the final tally of the parliamentary votes, without explanation, many of INITE's candidates were assessed to have won with a far larger percentage of the votes than had been first reported in the preliminary findings.[197] INITE would control the lion's share of parliament, with 46 deputies and 17 senators (Martelly's party, on the other hand, won only three seats in the Chamber of Deputies).[198] "Martelly must reckon with us," asserted the often-bellicose Joseph Lambert. "We are in a position to impose a prime minister."[199] Rumblings of discontent regarding the results of parliamentary elections continued to cost people their lives in Belladère[200] and Tiburon.[201] In Fort Liberté, supporters of an unsuccessful INITE candidate burned a community radio station, a cultural center and a library.[202] CEP member Ginette Chérubin went so far as to resign, saying that the prestige of the institution had been "irrevocably tainted."[203] The OAS–CARICOM mission called for the annulation of the victories of 19 INITE candidates who it said had won their majorities through fraud.[204] By 5 May, Martelly had issued an ultimatum to the CEP that the body was "sabotaging my efforts, all the work I have undertaken since my election to show the world the image of a country politically stable and ready to welcome foreign investment." He went on:

> The CEP must respect the vote of the people. It would be better if the CEP agreed to integrate into modern Haiti, but if it persists in clinging to the old system, justice will have to assume its responsibilities ... As of 14 May, Haiti will change. The rule of law, like it or not, will be a reality. No one, and no institution, will be above justice.[205]

Eventually, the CEP would reverse its decision on all but four of the 19 contested seats, still leaving Préval with a commanding lock on parliament.[206]

Proving that concerns about them were well-founded, parliament's first acts – after electing INITE member (and former FADH officer) Rodolphe Joazile as senate president, Jean Hector Anacacis as his deputy, and Saurel Jacinthe as president of the Chamber of Deputies[207] – were full-frontal assaults on the fragile democratic gains that Haiti had made over the last two decades. The assembly voted down Article 134.3 of Haiti's constitution, which barred consecutive presidential mandates, declared that mayors would be appointed by the president rather than elected, extra-constitutionally extended the terms of senators elected in the 2008 ballot, and reaffirmed the continued legality of Haiti maintaining an army.[208] They also got around to amending the constitutional provision forbidding dual nationality to instead allow it.[209] In an outraged editorial on Radio Kiskeya, the Haitian journalist Marvel Dandin called the moves a "parliamentary coup" and a case of *kase fèy kouvri sa* (a Creole expression for sweeping things under the rug or concealing them), accusing the parliamentarians of "contempt for public opinion, refusal of debate and dialogue, lack of transparency … subordination of the general interest to the individual interests of clans and parties … Cynical opportunism … [and] disregard of the constitution and it laws and rules."[210]

* * *

At his 14 May inauguration outside the gates of the ruined National Palace, flitting in and out of Creole, French and English, Martelly told the assembled dignitaries and spectators that "Haiti has been sleeping … Today she will wake up, stand up!"[211] He went on to say that Haiti had "the best beaches in the world, the most beautiful sun in the Caribbean and the deepest culture, diverse and authentic," but also warned that "discipline and order will rule the entire country." Along with various Haitian politicians, the audience included Dominican President Leonel Fernàndez, Suriname's President Desiré Bouterse (indicted for drug trafficking in the Netherlands) and France's Foreign Minister Alain Juppé. At several points, the audience heckled Préval, who was also present.[212] Martelly took the actual oath of office in Haiti's temporary parliament, where the power went out, an event that some saw as an unsubtle message from the INITE-ruled legislature.[213]

And Préval? As Haiti's president prepared to leave, his record appeared to be one of both hard-won successes and tragic failures. He had allowed the press to speak in total freedom, allowed the PNH to go about their work with more or less genuine independence from executive meddling, and helped to depolarize a violently divided society by presenting himself as a man whom both the bourgeois and the *pep la* could speak to and from whom neither had anything to fear. But he also turned a blind eye towards pervasive corruption by his allies, engaged in ceaseless political intrigues to oust two competent prime ministers and attempted to subvert the electoral process in the (not unfounded) belief that Haiti's politicians could not be trusted not to wreck all his accomplishments once he left power.

Surveying Préval's two terms in office, the only democratically elected president to twice hand power over to a democratically elected successor, one was tempted to remember the self-assessment of Cuban president Carlos Prío Socarrás, whose tenure was upended by Fulgencio Batista's 1952 coup.

"They say that I was a terrible president of Cuba," Prío had mused once while in exile. "That may be true. But I was the best president Cuba ever had."

For the vast majority of the previous 20 years, Haiti had been governed by two men – Jean-Bertrand Aristide and René Préval – who had come to political prominence by helping to topple the Duvalierist system. Now they would be replaced by one of that system's products, who had come to power by the ballot box, with a groundswell of popular support from ordinary Haitians.

CHAPTER THIRTEEN
TÈT KALE

Michel Martelly assumed office in a country where nearly 700,000 were still living in temporary camps.[1] Of the $4.58 billion that had been pledged in grants at the international donors' conference, only $1.74 billion had been disbursed.[2] An independent panel of experts investigating the cholera outbreak – which by this point had killed over 5,000 people – concluded that "the evidence overwhelmingly supports the conclusion that the source of the Haiti cholera outbreak was due to contamination of ... the Artibonite River with a patho-genic strain of current South Asian type ... as a result of human activity."[3] A report by a group of epidemiologists and physicians in the journal of the U.S. Centers for Disease Control and Prevention concurred, saying evidence "strongly suggests" that the cholera strain had been brought to Haiti by UN peacekeepers and spread through a faulty waste disposal system along the Arti-bonite River.[4] A report by the United Nations itself, later leaked to the press, cited sanitary failures on the part of MINUSTAH, including the dumping of raw sewage onto the open ground.[5]

A political novice surrounded by counselors with noticeably sharp elbows, Martelly faced an opposition-dominated legislature more or less publicly praying that he would fail, who even as he took the oath were embroiled in bitter, chaotic recriminations regarding the proposed constitutional amendments they had passed. As evictions of displaced people – often quite brutally carried out, partic-ularly by Delmas mayor Wilson Jeudy – became more widespread around the capital, Moïse Jean-Charles accused Martelly of being complicit in the expul-sions, a charge Martelly took strong exception to.[6] The evictions continued, however, including around the capital's Stade Sylvio Cator, with many of those driven out saying they had nowhere to go.[7] As Martelly took office, RNDDH sent out a warning about figures of "dubious morality," including former Guy Philippe deputy Gilbert Dragon and former Delmas police chief Jacky Nau, in Martelly's entourage.[8] Under intense pressure from the international community,

Martelly's head of security, Carel Alexandre, was eventually forced out, replaced by Pierre Léon Saint-Rémy, a relation of Martelly's wife, Sophia.[9] Speaking to journalist Rotchild François, Martelly said he had "found" a bag of 29 million gourdes in a government building, its provenance unknown, and brought it to the ULCC. Haiti became a signatory to two treaties, the Inter-American Convention against Corruption and the United Nations Convention against Corruption.[10] Many wondered what would become of Duvalier and Aristide, both accused of grievous crimes, under Martelly's government. In a testimony to how desperate things had grown in certain parts of the country, two swords and a bridle that adorned the monument to the Battle of Vertières in Cap-Haïtien were stolen and believed sold as scrap metal.[11]

Martelly announced that his selection for prime minister would be Daniel Gérard Rouzier, a U.S.-educated businessman, fervent Catholic, vice president of Haiti's chapter of the Christian charity Food for the Poor, and Jamaica's honorary consul in the country. Generally speaking, Rouzier had quite a good reputation for an affluent member of Haiti's often-predatory elite, and had personally tried to give the multitudes buried at Titanyen after the earthquake a proper burial. He told reporters that if ratified, he would get rid of Haiti's reconstruction panel and replace it with a new government agency.[12]

* * *

A violent fracas at the capital's airport during which Brazilian MINUSTAH troops objected to their bags being searched by Haitian customs officials suggested that the mission might be wearing out its welcome.[13] Around this time, Edmond Mulet also left Haiti, replaced on an interim basis by former Chilean Foreign Minister Mariano Fernández. Gunmen stormed the home of Guiteau Toussaint, chairman of the board of the Banque Nationale de Crédit, and executed the man credited with saving the institution from near-insolvency.[14] In the next several weeks, a number of other crimes – including the killing of university professor Yves Dorvil[15] and an attack against a downtown business that left two dead[16] – would further unsettle the capital.

On 21 June, the Chamber of Deputies rejected Daniel Rouzier's candidacy for prime minister.[17] Following Rouzier's rejection, Martelly addressed the nation, warning that "the parliament should be aware that the country cannot wait any longer and that people are tired," and saying that "this decision slowed all the possibilities that allow my promises to be changed into realities."[18] In an open letter following the fiasco, Rouzier denied a myriad of accusations against him and voiced his regrets at being prevented from serving "a population scorned, betrayed, despised by those who had promised hope, democracy and development, only to deliver unemployment, misery, beggary and insecurity," and called the country's "extreme poverty" and "underdevelopment" a "monstrous tyranny."[19] Before traveling to the United States in late June, Martelly announced that he was appointing a group of advisors – the Mayard-Paul brothers, former Gonaïves mayor Calixte Valentin and former Duvalierist official Pierre Pompée – tasked with smoothing out his relations with parliament.[20]

* * *

It was announced that Martelly's new choice for prime minister was former Minister of Justice Bernard Gousse, whose selection was greeted with a ranting denunciation by the INITE/Lavalas faction in parliament reminiscent of a Soviet-era show trial and with signatories including the Lambert brothers, Moïse Jean-Charles and John Joël Joseph.[21] Amid the uproar, Martelly left for a ten-day government trip to Europe designed, he said, to encourage investment in Haiti.[22] In an unprecedented move, 16 of 30 senators rejected Gousse's nomination "in advance" before even conducting hearings on it, with the resolution accusing Gousse of "repression, arbitrary arrests and assassinations" during Operation Baghdad, and with Moïse Jean-Charles declaring that "the prime minister-designate is politically dead, and when a person dies, there is no other choice but to bury him."[23]

Returning to the country from his foreign tour, Martelly appeared vexed when speaking to a crowd in Jacmel, telling them that it was he who assured the parliamentarians were paid every month.[24] He nevertheless met with 16 opposition senators, though the two sides emerged with no tangible results.[25] Continuing on with work despite the lack of a prime minister, in late July, Martelly asked for the recovery panel's extension for at least another year (it was slated to expire in October), naming former Ministry of Women's Affairs official Ann Valerie Timothee Milfort as interim executive director and six of his own associates as board members. By this point, the panel had secured $1.8 billion in funding for its projects, but many questioned what exactly had been done.[26] With Martelly's support, Haiti's Banque Nationale de Crédit and Banque Populaire Haïtienne launched a 4 million gourde program called *Kay Pa'm* (My Home), which provided below-market-rate loans to enable people to buy their own homes.[27] Another side of

Martelly's personality was on display a few days later when declaring at an event in Pétionville that his intention was to change Haiti's "image," and those who did not agree should "shut up" because "you have already failed."[28]

The security situation continued to be dicey. During a visit to Cap-Haïtien, while passing the traditional Lavalas stronghold of Shada, Martelly's entourage was showered with rocks and bottles.[29] A man carrying an M1 rifle was also among the attackers, though he was not believed to have fired. Martelly later characterized the incident as a foiled assassination attempt.[30] A day later, Dional Polyte, an INITE deputy from the Grand Anse, was shot to death in the southern town of Duchiti.[31] Polyte's relatives accused the fugitive Guy Philippe of planning the murder, while Philippe accused Chamber of Deputies president Sorel Jacinthe.[32] Before the summer was out, the former director of the PNH's judicial police, Jean Denis Fortin, would also be slain in the south, near the town of Torbeck.[33]

* * *

As they had threatened to do since his name was put forward, 16 senators voted against the nomination of Bernard Gousse for prime minister in a chaotic late-night ballot on 2 August.[34] In a blistering editorial, Radio Ibo's Hérold Jean François accused the senators of merely continuing Operation Baghdad through parliamentary maneuvers, suggesting that in Haiti one only need disappear from public view for a short time "before easily being recycled into the ranks of our institutions." He went on to say that:

> Our society unfortunately suffers from an amnesia as we allow former
> torturers to dress up and wear all kinds of costumes to again impose their
> law ... Intellectual perpetrators or officials of the deposed regime ... are
> now, unfortunately, the thundering voice from the top of our respectable
> institutions ... While in Argentina, Chile and elsewhere in Latin America,
> over thirty years later, the torturers of past dictatorial and military regimes
> have been caught and held accountable ... today in Haiti, without a
> decade to separates us, these protagonists are our new leaders and we find
> ourselves in a reality where the former executioners are the very ones who
> impose their law ... We are paying for our passivity as a society.[35]

Martelly, for his part, took yet another foreign trip, this time to Chile.

* * *

In the midst of this stalemate and acrimony, I went back to Haiti, both to get a read on the situation myself and to act as a guide and translator for my friend Francesca Romeo, a photographer and filmmaker who was working on a project about the country.

I arrived in the midst of Haiti's torporous summer, and as I drove around Port-au-Prince, Martelly's image gazed out at passers-by from billboards and murals affixed to walls, smiling broadly and with messages such as "*Nouvelle Haiti*" and "*Bienvenue au pouvoir*" stenciled painstakingly next to them, the murals' optimism belying Haiti's intense political struggles.

"I love President Martelly, I voted for President Martelly, so did my mother and my sister," Carlos Jean Charles, a resident in Camp Toussaint, a 2,800-person collection of fragile tents set up in front of the ruins of the National Palace, told me. "I think Martelly has a good heart. But the problem is the parliament. Those people have been doing this shit for 25 years, fighting for power. They don't give him a chance."

Up the hill, in the offices of the anti-corruption group LFHH, its director Marilyn Allien told me that "the population who voted for Martelly perceived the change he offered as drastic change, a complete rupture from the way things were done in the past."

Some things in Haiti remained constant. The ebullient Creole evangelical hymns still reverberated in the mornings from the mountainsides and ravines that crisscrossed the city, and radios still pumped out a nonstop diet of *konpa* music of the kind that first brought Martelly to prominence, along with the driving *racine* rhythms of vodou and endless political chatter.

But the hostility with which MINUSTAH was viewed by many people was palpable, and a bunker mentality appeared to have developed. In several instances, I witnessed peacekeepers patrolling with their mounted machine guns pointed down at crowds of people who appeared to pose no threat at all and were merely going about the business of trying to secure the basic necessities of survival. Staying at the Hotel Kinam, only feet away from a tent encampment where thousands sat in darkness through long evenings of pounding rain, we watched as a group of surly, well-fed men identifying themselves as Canadian police advisors with MINUSTAH drank themselves into oblivion and splashed in the hotel's pool over the course of two days under the gaze of local Haitian staff and other guests. Speaking to others in the capital, I discovered that such behavior was not an uncommon occurrence, and created the perception of a fraternity party amid an apocalypse, making the mission appear very removed from the daily struggles of the Haitians it was ostensibly there to protect.

Along the Côte des Arcadins, a sense of tragic timelessness asserted itself, with tent camps lining either side of Route Nationale 1. The Caribbean glittered blue-green, and resorts from when Haiti was once a tourist destination – now largely empty save for Haiti's wealthy and the moneyed foreigners in the country – fronted the ocean. Skiffs with canvass sails plied the channel between the mainland and the immense, isolated Île de la Gonâve in the bay. Stopping at one of the hotels for the night – at which we appeared to be the only guests – we sipped rum with our feet in the surf and watched a spectacular electrical storm miles out at sea.

During the visit, I had intended to see an old friend. But I found that Jean-Claude Bajeux was no longer able to be grasped in the material world. He had passed away, if not exactly unexpectedly then rather suddenly, days earlier from cancer at the age of 79, before I had a chance to see him. His goal of an inclusive, transparent and just political system in Haiti still remained an unrealized dream.

Shortly before he died, in a conversation with a friend, Bajeux had time enough to deliver a simple charge.

"My generation is passing away. We did all we could. Now it is up to you."

* * *

After Martelly returned from Chile, before even having a prime minister (he had been in office 100 days without one), he announced the names of "his" ministers of education and justice, the latter being Josué Pierre-Louis, a jurist with a rather suspect reputation given his behavior during the investigation of the Jean Dominique murder. After meeting U.S. Ambassador Kenneth Merten, the so-called "G-18" parliamentary opposition group published a list of ten "demands" on Martelly that needed to be met before they would approve a new prime minister, including presidential approval of the previous changes to the constitution, appointment of new judges, renewing of the IHRC and a modification of MINUSTAH's mandate.[36] It was a ransom note with the nation as its hostage. As August drew to a close, Martelly announced that his third nominee for prime minister would be Garry Conille, a U.S.-educated former United Nations official who had served as Bill Clinton's chief of staff in his role as the UN special envoy to Haiti.[37] Conille's selection was strongly supported through back channels by the Clinton Foundation.[38] Like so many of Martelly's inner circle, Conille also had familial ties to the Duvalier regime, with his father having served as Baby Doc's minister for youth and sports.[39] Martelly's relations with parliament further frayed when his close associate Roro Nelson reportedly assaulted INITE deputy Patrick Joseph in the northern town of St.-Michel de l'Atalaye, where Martelly was visiting to inaugurate a housing project, when Joseph refused to applaud the president.[40] The housing situation had stabilized somewhat, though; in early September, a spokesman for the IOM said the homeless population in Haiti had plunged 90 percent, from 300,000 to 30,000.[41]

* * *

In early September, the deterioration of MINUSTAH's reputation in Haiti continued when RNDDH announced that they had evidence that some among 900 Uruguayan peacekeepers had sexually assaulted an 18-year-old boy in Port Salut.[42] The assault had allegedly occurred weeks earlier, and an inconclusive part of it was recorded on a cell phone by one of the peacekeepers. It was described as a brutal and apparently premeditated gang rape of a young man who had been one of a number of civilians who had attached themselves to the local base. RNDDH said that the Uruguayan contingent in Port Salut had been leading "a life of debauchery" for some time, and had regularly exchanged food for sex with local women, and used illegal drugs.[43] A preliminary UN investigation found "no evidence" to support the assault claim, but Uruguay announced that its force commander in Haiti and the soldiers involved in the incident would be sent back home.[44] The Uruguayan government said it would issue an official apology to Martelly for the incident and compensate the youth who had been assaulted.[45]

Haiti had, alas, long been something of a haven for accused foreign pedophiles. Among them were Ron Voss, a defrocked Catholic priest from Indiana who in his petition to leave the priesthood recounted that "my sins are too numerous to detail, but the most grievous gather around the sexual abuse of many adolescent boys, including some minors." Despite this admission of abuse, Voss was long defended by, among others, Detroit Bishop Thomas Gumbleton and William Slavick, an activist with the Catholic antiwar group Pax Christi. An Aristide partisan, Voss acted as something of a conduit for left-wing Catholic groups visiting Haiti, running what he called a "Visitation House" at Antoine

Izméry's former home and maintaining access to youth through the center's clinic, English classes and youth sports programs.[46]

Around the same time as the Port Salut incident, Brazil announced that it was planning to begin removing peacekeepers from Haiti, though it gave no numbers or timetable.[47] A violent mid-September protest in the capital demanded the mission's ouster.[48] Martelly said he was opposed to any reduction in MINUSTAH's troop strength, stating that there was still "instability" in the country.[49]

Martelly's solution to what would take MINUSTAH's place once the mission left, however clearly articulated during his campaign, still gave many pause.

"According to the constitution, the army has never ceased to exist," Martelly observed to Radio Télé Ginen in late September, saying that he would shortly present a draft to parliament of a plan for the army's reconstitution.[50] It was estimated that such a move would cost at least $95 million.[51] Many progressive groups in Haiti, such as Tèt Kole Ti Peyizan and the workers' union Batay Ouvriye, denounced the plan.[52]

In another echo of Haiti's past, when Amnesty International attempted to present a report about abuses under Jean-Claude Duvalier's government at the capital's Plaza Hotel on 22 September – the fifty-fourth anniversary of the elder Duvalier's ascension to power – about two dozen Duvalierists, including the attorneys Reynold Georges and Osner Févry, waved the red and black Duvalierist flag and shouted them down.[53]

Amid the army furor, Martelly announced his desire, in the interest of "dialogue," to meet with all of Haiti's living former leaders still in the country: Duvalier, Leslie Manigat, Prosper Avril, Aristide, Préval and Boniface Alexandre (he had already met with Ertha Pascal Trouillot).[54] Following his meetings with Duvalier and Aristide, Martelly said that he hoped Haiti's former leaders "could unite to work for the progress of Haiti."[55]

After delaying the session for weeks, the senate finally voted on Martelly's selection of Garry Conille for prime minister, this time approving the president's choice with 17 for (including government allies Youri Latortue and Edwin Zenny), three against (including Moïse Jean-Charles) and nine abstentions.[56] Echoing Mirlande Manigat's comments during the campaign, Jean-Charles denounced what he called Martelly's "pink militia" (as Zenny sat before him in a pink shirt), and accused Martelly of plotting to have him jailed.[57] Before the vote, Conille told one foreign journalist that he wanted "to get everybody excited about what Haiti could be."[58] At Conille's inauguration, however, Martelly upstaged his new prime minister, chatting garrulously to reporters and making the rather surprising confession that his "enemy" Joseph Lambert had become his "best friend."[59] Among Conille's new ministers would be the telecoms mogul Laurent Lamothe as minister of foreign affairs, Thierry Mayard-Paul as minister of interior, Josué Pierre-Louis as minister of justice, Daniel Supplice as minister of Haitians living abroad and Stéphanie Villedrouin as minister of tourism. Products of Duvalierism like Mayard-Paul and Supplice would work alongside someone like Villedrouin, the Jérémie branch of whose family had been all but wiped out by Papa Doc in 1964. At the same time, Martelly announced that the state would be paying for the tuition of 142,000 students who would go to school – for free – for the first time, a program he said would be paid for by taxes on Haiti's telecoms sector and financial sector (specifically wire transfers) and supported by a $1.25 million donation from the Clinton Fund.[60]

* * *

When one crisis seemed to be resolving, another erupted. At a meeting with parliamentarians at the National Palace (sections of which had now been rehabilitated enough to permit the use of offices there), Martelly got into a heated exchange with several of those in attendance, including Arnel Bélizaire, who had somehow managed to get elected as deputy for Delmas, with the president allegedly warning them that "anyone who dares [attack the presidency] may not even be able to leave the National Palace, even if he enjoys immunity."[61] Martelly subsequently called for Haiti's justice system to act against "fugitives" who were "refugees" in parliament, an obvious reference to the recently imprisoned Bélizaire.[62] In late October, Martelly's government commissioner for Port-au-Prince, Félix Léger, announced that he had informed the PNH that Arnel Bélizaire was a fugitive from justice, having escaped while being held for murder and illegal possession of firearms, charges that Bélizaire, who was traveling in France, denied. An arrest warrant against Bélizaire, who ostensibly enjoyed parliamentary immunity, was subsequently issued.[63] Speaking to Radio Vision 2000, Bélizaire's lawyer said the deputy had indeed been imprisoned but had been "released" in 2010 after serving his sentence.[64]

When Bélizaire alighted from his plane at Toussaint Louverture International Airport in the capital on 27 October, he was quickly arrested.[65] Several members of parliament threatened to impeach Martelly when the body returned to work in January (they were enjoying a two-month "break") and denounced what they said was a nascent dictatorship.[66] Although it was not technically in session, the body circulated a demand by 71 of its members calling for the resignations of Josué Pierre-Louis, Thierry Mayard-Paul, Secretary of State for Foreign Affairs Michel Brunache, and government commissioner Félix Léger.[67] Airport security agents even launched a brief strike to protest what they charged had been abuse by Mayard-Paul and his security personnel during the course of Bélizaire's arrest.[68] After a day in custody, Bélizaire was released and headed directly to parliament.[69] Arriving back in Haiti from a trip to the United States (and greeted by bussed-in supporters screaming *Viv Tèt Kale!*), Martelly himself claimed he had nothing to do with the arrest.[70] A subsequent senate vote against Josué Pierre-Louis and Michel Brunache failed, and a "commission of inquiry" was established instead. Several senators, including Moïse Jean-Charles, stormed out of the chamber when the motion failed. In this showdown with the parliament, Martelly had won,[71] but Josué Pierre-Louis would eventually resign. The arrest, however, appeared to derange the already distinctly unstable Bélizaire even more, and he would become a bizarre and threatening presence both on the streets of the capital and in the halls of parliament.

Still angry over the affair, senate head Rodolphe Joazile and Chamber of Deputies chief Sorel Jacinthe rebuffed Martelly's offer to accompany him on a state visit to Cuba.[72] René Préval, however, was more receptive to Martelly's overtures, and the pair spent several hours chatting at the former's home in Laboule.[73] At a ceremony marking the Battle of Vertières, with Prosper Avril and Boniface Alexandre looking on, Martelly repeated his pledge to reform Haiti's army.[74] Days later and only miles away from where Martelly spoke, ground was broken on Bill Clinton's signature project, the $257 million Caracol industrial park, with Martelly telling the attendees that the park was "the model of investment Haitians need," and that he hoped it would employ 65,000 people.[75] It was left unmentioned that 366 farmers had been dispossessed from a fertile patch of land that had been worked by some families for generations to make way for the project in what amounted to a big and perhaps reckless gamble.[76] It was virtually the same patch of land where the U.S. Marines had run the Post Chabert prison camp during the U.S. occupation almost a century earlier.

In late November, Digicel announced that it would be building a hotel in Port-au-Prince under the Marriott Hotels brand, adding 173 rooms to a capital that at the time had only around 500. It was also said the hotel would provide 175 jobs. It was a project largely midwifed by the Clinton Foundation.[77] Commenting on the sometimes obsessive focus on Clinton, Ericq Pierre wrote that: "I still have to remind my countrymen that with or without Bill Clinton, with or without the international community, the ball of the development of our country is in our court and we are responsible for the future of our nation."[78]

As the executive and legislative branches stood at odds, a presidential security guard[79] and a PNH officer were gunned down in the capital,[80] while in Cité Soleil, gang members gunned down yet another policeman.[81] Running gun battles between gang members in Bel-Air left at least one dead,[82] and in Santo 17 another policeman was slain and his body publicly burned. At least 30 PNH officers had been killed during 2011.[83] On Rue du Centre, the car of human rights activist Kettly Julien was fired upon, wounding his son and driver.[84] The PNH announced they were launching an operation, codenamed "Dragon," aimed at reining in the city's criminal elements.[85] The human rights office of MINUSTAH and the UN's main human rights body in New York, meanwhile, released a joint statement accusing the PNH of involvement in torture and summary executions.[86] In mid-December, Brazilian MINUSTAH troops patrolling Cité Soleil assaulted three men guarding a water truck that had broken down, forcing them into the back of their vehicle and then abandoning them naked at a location near Route Neuf.[87] That autumn, JILAP released the startling figure that 6,640 people had died due to violence in the capital region over the last decade.[88]

* * *

Amid the political fight, where was Aristide? Since returning from South Africa in March, the former president had been almost completely silent, and there were some who wondered whether or not he was in earth orbit anymore. When one foreign journalist went to see him in Tabarre shortly after his return, she found the former president lauding the praises of an electroencephalogram machine in his office, to which Haiti's ex-ruler sat hooked up, occasionally playing the flute, for several hours a day, "studying the effect on brainwaves of different words, languages and music."[89] Lavalas, which had been the dominant political movement in the country less than a decade earlier, was now fractured and divided, with some of its most recognized names having left Aristide for the political currents led by Martelly and Préval. At an event to mark the twenty-first anniversary of his first election as president at the Aristide Foundation for Democracy on 16 December, Aristide was not even present; instead, the ceremony was led by such marginal figures as Lavalas spokeswoman Dr. Maryse Narcisse, the singer Farah Juste, Joël Édouard "Pacha" Vorbe and Aristide's wife, Mildred. Rodolphe Joazile and Sorel Jacinthe also attended, as did René Civil and Paul Raymond. Annette Auguste and Rudy Hériveaux did not.[90]

* * *

As 2011 ended, Sonia Pierre, one of the greatest champions of Haitians and Dominicans of Haitian descent, died of a heart attack at only 48 years old. Many charged that she had been hounded to her death by repeated death threats and attacks from the Dominican right.[91] Amid emotional tributes, she was buried in her hometown of Villa Altagracia – in death as she was in life, a daughter of the Dominican Republic.[92]

* * *

After distributing motorbikes in Mirebalais, where he was greeted by supporters chanting "Give the president a chance" and slogans hostile to the press,[93] Martelly ended the year by dissolving the Gaillot Dorsinvil-led CEP and instructing its members to return all state property in their possession. Government spokesmen said this would pave the way for new elections to be held in 2012.[94]

* * *

The new year started with the panel Martelly had formed to study the feasibility of the remobilization of Haiti's army – to the surprise of no one – recommending just that.[95] Speaking at the independence event in Gonaïves, Martelly was coy about fixing an exact date for such an undertaking.[96] In a somewhat pathetic display, a few dozen armed men occupied a disused military camp in the capital as if awaiting marching orders from the government.[97] More seriously, about 50 camouflage-clad men bearing heavy weapons appeared outside a government office in Cap-Haïtien to demand 18 years of "back pay" and announcing their willingness to "reintegrate" into the "new" army.[98]

Moïse Jean-Charles began the year by claiming on Radio Kiskeya that Martelly held U.S. and Italian citizenship (thus rendering his presidency illegitimate), that Minister of Tourism Villedrouin held a Canadian passport and that Foreign Affairs Minister Laurent Lamothe was "a Bolivian." Jean-Charles suggested that the first order of business for parliament should be to take up this matter when it returned from its long vacation.[99] As he spoke, on the second anniversary of the earthquake, over 500,00 people were still living in tent camps, and the people in camps such as Corail-Cesselesse remained nakedly vulnerable to heat, wind and rain.[100] The mandate of the IHRC had expired the previous October and parliament, busy with trying to drive Martelly from power, had refused to extend it.[101] Despite all this, Garry Conille appeared undaunted, vowing that Haiti's economy would witness 8 percent growth in the coming year and that he would renew the IHRC.[102] On 9 January, Martelly finally addressed parliament in a special session of both houses, telling them that Haiti as it presently existed was "the sum of internal strife, assassinations, kidnappings, embargo, anarchy, chaos, environmental destruction, selfishness and greed. This must change."[103] Following Martelly's address, one of his fiercest critics, Levaillant Louis-Jeune, was elected president of the Chamber of Deputies, while Simon Dieuseul Desras became president of the senate.

* * *

As the first anniversary of Jean-Claude Duvalier's return to Haiti arrived, RNDDH expressed its disappointment at the former dictator's seemingly casual reintegration into the life of the nation.[104] Noting that Duvalier was often seen at official functions and traveled with a police escort, the Collectif contre l'Impunité's Danielle Magloire noted that "despite all the complaints against him, [Duvalier] has VIP treatment in the country. The government is sending a very ambiguous signal."[105] Judge Carvès Jean issued a 20-page ruling that declared there was insufficient evidence to charge Duvalier with human rights abuses during his reign but that he could be tried for corruption.[106] Martelly was vague about what, if any, role the government would play in the deliberations, alternately saying that he would pardon Duvalier in the name of "reconciliation" and then saying he would not.[107] Shortly after the decision, the Collectif contre l'Impunité issued a statement saying that "reconciliation without the sanction of justice is unacceptable … The sad spectacle of impunity continues in this country."[108]

Duvalier was not the only one from the regime to be present in Haiti. Former FADH officer Emmanuel Orcel, who had worked closely with former Macoute leader Roger Lafontant and had a horrific reputation from his tenure at the Casernes Dessalines barracks, had returned.[109] The former head of Duvalier's presidential guard, Christophe Dardompré, was also back, as was Duvalier's chief of protocol, Claudel Gauthier.[110] Franck Romain, the notorious former Duvalierist mayor of Port-au-Prince, was quite old and had been living in quiet freedom in the capital for many years.[111]

During a brief visit to Haiti at the beginning of February, Brazilian President Dilma Rousseff said that her country intended to draw down its military presence in Haiti and switch to a more "development"-oriented approach, partially as a way to stem the exploding Haitian immigration, much of it illegal, to Brazil.[112]

* * *

Would Haiti's politics allow the type of development the country desperately needed? INITE's John Joël Joseph claimed that Martelly had arrived unexpectedly at a meeting between Garry Conille and several parliamentarians and accused them of plotting a coup, though both Conille's office and that of Joseph Lambert claimed that the meeting had passed uneventfully. Conille was said to be of a mind to comply with parliament's information requests with regards to the question of Martelly's citizenship, while Martelly was, on principle, opposed.[113] At a press conference before departing to Venezuela and Panama, Martelly said he would never cooperate with the parliamentary committee looking into his nationality and that "my passport will remain where it is – in the pocket of the President – because no institution has the authority to question me on it."[114] As Moïse Jean-Charles continued to fulminate about the issue, Joseph Lambert lost his normal poker-player-like cool and said that Jean-Charles "should stop singing like a parrot" and bring the much-referred-to "proof" of Martelly's alleged citizenship before the parliament.[115] Lambert's relations with his INITE colleagues eventually soured to the point where he was fired as party leader and then dismissed from the party altogether, accelerating his move into Martelly's camp.[116]

* * *

In this atmosphere of charges and counter-charges, Martelly appeared before a rally of students near the state university, where several hundred young men cheered him, some chanting Duvalierist-era slogans.

Finally, Garry Conille had enough. Only four months after assuming the role of prime minister, he announced that he was resigning because his government had "reached an impasse."[117] Martelly said that he "regretted" that the resignation occurred "when the country is beginning to advance," but said that he would accept it.[118] The infernal machine of Haiti's politics had struck again. Following Conille's resignation, unable to control himself (a chronic weakness among Haiti's politicians), Moïse Jean-Charles gloated that "we are only a few meters from the National Palace" and vowed that he would drive "the Italian-American" president from power.[119]

As the nation pondered Conille's departure, Radio Kiskeya reported that a file concerning "several charges" against Aristide had been submitted to an investigating judge for possible prosecution.[120] Enacted by UCREF on the government's behalf, it was later revealed that the file contained allegations of drug trafficking and abuse of public funds, some of them linked to the Aristide Foundation for Democracy. One of Aristide's cadre of lawyers, Newton Louis Saint-Juste, publicly rejected the charges.[121] In testimony to the trepidation that Aristide could still generate in some quarters in Haiti, the investigating judge promptly recused herself from the case.[122] Following the announcement, several thousand Aristide supporters, led by senators John Joël Joseph and Jean-Baptiste Bien-Aimé and deputies Arnel Bélizaire and Sorel Jacinthe, marched through the streets of the capital, tearing down posters of Martelly and vowing to protect Aristide.[123]

Martelly announced that his new choice for prime minister would be foreign affairs minister and telecoms mogul Laurent Lamothe.[124] Shortly after this declaration, Martelly, flanked by Lamothe and Thierry Mayard-Paul, addressed a news conference where he held up eight stamped Haitian passports and again stated that he had never renounced his Haitian citizenship. Seated in the audience, U.S. Ambassador Kenneth Merten confirmed that, though Martelly at one point had a green card and now had a visa, there was no record of him ever being a U.S. citizen.[125] At the same time, Haiti inaugurated its $1.9 million U.S.-funded temporary parliament, abutting the Caribbean and across the street from the ruins of the old structure. Parliamentarians promptly protested about the building because each office did not contain a private bathroom.[126]

As Lamothe's nomination was announced, another wave of insecurity hit the capital. A judge was gunned down in Croix-des-Bouquets.[127] The director of Cité Soleil's community-oriented Radio Boukman, Jean Liplète Nelson, was slain when gunmen fired on his car.[128] The celebrated Haitian-American painter Burton Chenet was killed in his Turgeau residence, his wife gravely wounded.[129] While dropping his child off at school in the capital's Delmas

95 area, the former *organisation populaire* leader and CNDDR commission member Samba Boukman was confronted by gunmen on the back of a motorcycle, who shot him as he sat in his car, ending the life of a controversial figure but one who had shown a willingness to compromise and to try to lessen the violence that had so blighted the poor neighborhoods of the capital.[130] In response, the PNH announced that they were launching another operation – Dragon 2 – to target criminals.[131]

* * *

As Haiti mulled over its new potential prime minister and worried about the capital's spiraling violence, a trial began in Miami. The inquiry was based on a federal indictment charging "four South Florida business people and two former Haitian government officials" in connection with $2.3 million of illegal payments made by Miami's Cinergy Telecommunications and Uniplex Telecom Technologies to shell companies set up by officials skimming kickbacks from what had been Teleco's long-distance business. The indictment referred to "Official A" and "Official B" as figures to whom kickbacks were passed via Digitek, a company owned by Aristide's wife's brother-in-law, Lesly Lavelanet. Among those cooperating with the investigation was former Teleco chief Patrick Joseph, the son of Venel Joseph, who had been head of Haiti's central bank during Aristide's second term. In the indictment, which detailed how the central bank was used to distribute bribes and illicit payments, the official referred to as "Official A" was the elder Joseph. "Official B," attorneys familiar with the case said, was Aristide.[132]

Had he ever been forced to give evidence by prosecutors, Venel Joseph could have perhaps provided some of the most compelling testimony on the looting of Haiti's state telephone company, a crime in which dozens of well-known personalities, both Haitian and foreign, were implicated.

But he would never have the opportunity to do so. Days after news of his son's cooperation in the Teleco case had been splashed across the pages of *The Miami Herald*, Venel Joseph was shot and killed by several gunmen as he was driving through Port-au-Prince. To this day, the killing remains unsolved.[133]

* * *

Haiti's elected officials contributed to, rather than damped down, the population's feeling of insecurity; statements by Joseph Lambert and Steven Benoît announcing likely unrest and urging people to rush home to take shelter set off a panic throughout the capital.[134] On 23 March, armed men claiming to be former military again marched through Cap-Haïtien.[135] A few days later, Guy Philippe – still a fugitive – appeared in the city, calling on Martelly to make good on his promise of restoring the army, and that, although "everybody knows I'm not a friend of Aristide," Haitians "should take to the streets" if the former president was arrested – a vivid demonstration, if one was needed, of how impunity benefited all sides in Haiti's political struggles.[136] In a strongly worded statement, Michel Brunache, now Minister of Justice and Public Security, said that "the circulation of men in uniform and sometimes armed belonging to neither MINUSTAH nor the PNH is absolutely unacceptable. The police must act with the utmost rigor to end this illegal situation that disturbs public order."[137]

As the former military marched, Mario Andrésol, while recuperating at his home from a torn ligament suffered during a football match, was paid a surprise visit by Justice Minister Brunache and Secretary of State for Public Security Réginald Delva, who both suggested to the PNH chief an "honorable exit" from the force, the fig leaf pretext being the failure of the police to clamp down on the armed protests by former members of the military, protests that Martelly's public statements had all but encouraged.[138] Andrésol's way of doing business – professional, rigorous, transparent, nonpolitical – evidently no longer had a place within the law enforcement body that he, perhaps more than any single person, had helped reform. Andrésol would hang on for several more months, but his days were clearly numbered.

"Préval never asked me to do things for him, like Martelly did," Andrésol told me later. "Préval is a fox, you never know what he has on his mind. But Martelly is more about confrontation. When Martelly came to power, they began balkanizing the police again."[139]

* * *

A little more than a week after several thousand Lavalas supporters held a rally on the Champ de Mars calling on Martelly to resign,[140] the senate voted in favor of Laurent Lamothe's ratification as Haiti's new prime minister, with only three senators (Moïse Jean-Charles, Steven Benoît and Francky Exius) voting against and one (Jean-Baptiste Bien-Aimé) abstaining.[141] When the Chamber of Deputies took up the issue, the building was surrounded by dozens of armed, uniformed men claiming to be former members of the military and ordering the chamber to approve the nomination.[142] The chamber would eventually approve Lamothe with a vote of 62 to 3. Lamothe greeted the news stoically, saying "we have a lot of work to do."[143] Lamothe's cabinet – which, in a first, included seven women – retained Martelly confidant Thierry Mayard-Paul as minister of the interior and Stéphanie Balmir Villedrouin as minister of tourism, and added former INITE senator Rodolphe Joazile as minister of defense and ex-Aristide quisling Mario Dupuy as minister of culture, among others.[144]

As Lamothe took office, Haiti's tangled relations with the Dominican Republic reared their head once more. Days after Martelly had been awarded the *Orden al Mérito de Duarte, Sánchez y Mella*, the Dominican Republic's highest honor, by Leonel Fernández, a report by the Dominican journalist Nuria Piera alleged that Félix Bautista, a businessman and senator for Fernández's ruling PLD, had been involved in illicit dealings with unnamed "Haitian political leaders."[145] When it became clear that one of the politicians that Piera was referring to was Martelly, and that she was accusing him of having received $2.5 million in bribes from Bautista and awarding $385 million in fraudulent contracts to a quartet of Bautista-controlled firms (Mirlande Manigat was also alleged to have received $250,000 on the eve of elections),[146] the Haitian leader denounced what he charged was a "media lynching" and both he and Manigat denied receiving any money.[147]

***

Between January and May 2012, at least eight policemen were slain in Port-au-Prince.[148] The chain of events that would result in the death of one of them began on the morning of 17 April, when a young officer of the traffic police, Walky Calixte, arrested one Marc Arthur Junior Charles at a roadblock for carrying illegal firearms and ammunition. Charles claimed the guns and ammunition belonged to Deputy Rodriguez Séjour, whose motorcade he had been following. Following the arrest, Séjour reportedly appeared personally at the Commissariat de Port-au-Prince and leveled threats while demanding Charles be released, which he was. Later that afternoon, Walky Calixte was gunned down.[149] It was believed that the actual triggerman in the killing was Grand Ravine gang leader Mackendy "Ti Kenken" François,[150] but many police and others were convinced that Séjour had ordered the killing. The following day, furious policemen attempted to lay siege to Radio Caraïbes, where Séjour was speaking, with some even firing into the air. The parliamentarian was only saved from being lynched due to the intervention of acting Prime Minister Garry Conille, still in office until Laurent Lamothe formally took over.[151] Relatives and friends of the slain policeman protested in Carrefour and elsewhere, calling on parliament to lift Séjour's parliamentary immunity.[152]

* * *

The Martelly–Lamothe team's attitude towards impunity was itself vividly demonstrated by the murder of a young trader, Octanol Dérissaint, in Fond Parisien that spring.

Following Martelly's inauguration, Calixte Valentin, one of the Martelly advisors tasked with smoothing relations with parliament (and failing to do so), had been visiting the border zone of Malpasse, near Fond Parisien, opening and closing the border gate and, some said, bringing sums of money from the booming border trade back to the palace. Under Valentin worked at least two dozen individuals whose precise role was not clearly defined, though sometimes they appeared to work as customs agents. When Valentin closed the border 30 minutes early on 18 April, disorder ensued, leaving merchants stranded on both sides of the frontier. Octanol Dérissaint, returning from the Dominican Republic, was forced to park his truck and wait for a moto taxi, at which point, witnesses said, Valentin's hangers-on interrogated him as to his business and place of residence, which, upon learning, Valentin for some reason denounced in vituperative terms. After firing his gun in the air, witnesses (including police) said that Valentin followed Dérissaint back to nearby Fond Parisien, where he shot him down outside the Ambassadeur du Christ boutique. Witnesses said that Valentin and his accomplices then sped away, firing in the air as they did so.[153] A policeman, Jean Garry, was among the bystanders nearly killed who later spoke on the radio of Valentin's alleged involvement in the killing.[154] Two days later, Valentin, claiming he had only "fired in the air," was arrested in Croix-des-Bouquets for Dérissaint's murder.[155] But that would not be the end of the story.

* * *

As Lamothe assumed office, the policeman Walky Calixte was laid to rest in Carrefour. The scene at the Mont-Carmel church was one of wailing family members, but also of the dignity of the fallen officer's colleagues, all spit-and-polish in their khaki PNH uniforms or dress blues, and of hundreds of mourners carrying wreaths and photos as they made their way to the cemetery.[156] Calixte's father read a Bible passage from Psalm 115, Verse 3 ("But our God is in the heavens: he hath done whatsoever he hath pleased") and recalled a recent conversation where his son had told him "to live in subhuman conditions isn't living, to die like a man isn't dying."

No high-ranking officials of either the Martelly–Lamothe government or the PNH attended.[157]

CHAPTER FOURTEEN
IN THE KINGDOM
OF IMPUNITY

Haiti's new prime minister was an interesting personality. The son of an educator and a well-known artist, like so many of Haiti's elite, he had begun his education at Saint-Louis de Gonzague before moving to Miami to pursue degrees in political science and business management. For a time a semi-professional tennis player, Lamothe had twice represented Haiti at the Davis Cup before co-founding the Global Voice Group, which rode the nascent wave of telecoms technology in developing countries, particularly in Africa, and eventually developed into a revenue assurance specialist for emerging nations. For three years, Lamothe was based in Cape Town, South Africa, an experience he said impressed him deeply as there he "saw a country that was very strong in terms of national production, that produced most of what they consumed, that had strict exchange laws in terms of protecting their currency."[1]

As someone who had flitted in and out of Haiti for years in his life as an international businessman, once in office, Lamothe began to see the harsh realities of his country with new eyes. He was stunned, for example, to visit remote Île de la Tortue off the country's north coast and find that it had "one police officer; two nurses; no gynecologist and only 13,000 out of 23,000 children in school."[2] After a meeting with Hillary Clinton in Washington, as well as with officials of the World Bank and the IMF, Lamothe told reporters that "governments of Haiti have made a lot of bad decisions in the past, the consequences of which for Haiti have us depending entirely on international aid. Today we will take very different decisions." Lamothe also said that senatorial, municipal and local elections would be held before the end of the year.[3] Shortly after Lamothe became prime minister, it was announced that INITE, the tool that Préval had used to subsume Lespwa and contest the 2010 elections (and which had seen one its most prominent members, Joseph Lambert, be ousted and defect to

Martelly), was going to be dissolved.[4] It was unclear what, if anything, would replace it.

***

When parliament reconvened, Moïse Jean-Charles went on the warpath again, this time against Venezuela ambassador Pedro Antonio Canino González, saying he had declared the diplomat "persona non grata" in Haiti (which he had no legal power to do), accusing him of colluding with Martelly to hide corruption connected to PetroCaribe.[5] Parliament and Martelly also continued a long simmering argument over the modus operandi for selecting future prime ministers, with Martelly arguing that, lacking an absolute majority of any one party in parliament, "the President of the Republic chooses the Prime Minister in consultation with the President of the Senate and of the Chamber of Deputies," while parliament itself demanded a straight up or down vote in both its houses.[6] As an illustration of how volatile even simple acts of governance could be, when the administration tried to act against the unauthorized construction of homes in the capital's Juvénat quarter in late June, the response was barricades of burning tires blocking the Canapé Vert road.[7]

But there were some riches to be had for those who knew where to look for them. By June 2012, Canada's Eurasian Minerals boasted that it controlled "over 1,100 square miles (1,770 square kilometers) of real estate" in Haiti, mostly in the north, and had partnered with the American mining company Newmont, the world's second largest. Haiti's royalty share for any gold extracted from this venture was to be only 2.5 percent per ounce, a startlingly low sum. Since he had negotiated these terms on behalf of Haiti between 2010 and 2011, former Minister of Finance Ronald Baudin had left the government and had gone to work for Newmont, telling one interviewer "I have to eat, right?"[8] It was later revealed that sitting on the advisory board of one mining company exploring northern Haiti, Delaware-based VCS Mining, was none other than Tony Rodham, the brother of Hillary Clinton (Rodham took the position after Clinton stepped down as secretary of state). Rodham claimed – and the company confirmed – that he had met VCS president and Democratic donor Angelo Viard at an event for the Clinton Global Initiative, a spinoff of the Clinton Foundation (former Prime Minister Jean-Max Bellerive sat on the board), to which Viard had paid $20,000 to become a member.[9] Parliament would eventually vote in a law that ceased the exploitation of the country's natural resources "without consulting parliament and without the knowledge of the national public opinion."[10]

* * *

After two months of accomplishing virtually nothing (not enough members had attended to reach a quorum since 8 May), Haiti's senate finally reconvened, with Senator Jean Willy Jean-Baptiste of Ayiti An Aksyon (AAA, Youri Latortue's rebranding of Latibonit Ann Aksyon, formed to contest seats across the country) imploring his colleagues to "act responsibly" given the problems confronting the nation. He all but begged them to see to the formation of a permanent electoral council and to lower the number of senators present for the body to function from 16 to 11, a move that was supported by Simon Dieuseul Desras and Steven Benoît. The suggestion was mocked by Andrys Riché and Jean-Baptiste Bien-Aimé, who preferred to use the session to inveigh against the "unacceptable interference" of the United States in Haiti's affairs because of statements by Hillary Clinton deputy Cheryl Mills that the U.S. supported the formation of such a council.[11] John Joël Joseph refused in advance to serve on any commission looking at the electoral council question, saying he "wanted to be consistent with myself."[12] He was soon joined in his categorical refusal by Jean-Baptiste Bien-Aimé.[13] A Martelly spokesman said that the new CEP would be constituted with or without parliament.[14]

* * *

Despite ongoing political and security challenges, Martelly announced that an out-of-season *carnaval des fleurs* (carnival of flowers) would be held in the capital at the end of July. The move had explicit Duvalierist overtones, as Papa Doc had first thrown his own out-of-season carnival to celebrate the creation of the Tontons Macoutes in July 1958.[15] Ever the showman attuned to the pulse of the crowd, Martelly's carnival was, in fact, a tremendous success, and Haitians were treated to an image of themselves – festive, joyful and, in a word, beautiful – that they hardly ever saw depicted either at home or abroad.[16] One who was not impressed, however, was Moïse Jean-Charles, who announced that he would lead a "popular mobilization" to prevent the formation of an electoral council. Calling Senate President Simon Dieuseul Desras a "traitor," Jean-Charles vowed to scuttle any meeting in parliament to even discuss a body to oversee forthcoming elections.[17] Martelly's response was to sign a decree unilaterally creating a new CEP, with former Minister of Justice Josué Pierre-Louis the most recognized name among six presidential and judicial appointees.[18] Outflanked by Martelly, whose move was almost certainly illegal, Simon Dieuseul Desras said parliament would now convene to name the six additional members required by the constitution.[19] By this point, with the expiration of the terms of various members, the senate had been reduced to a third of its mandated strength.[20]

* * *

The reputation of the PNH as a professional, neutral, apolitical force, one that had been painstakingly nurtured by Mario Andrésol and René Préval, was gradually being eroded. At the end of July, officers of the PNH's Unité Départementale de Maintien d'Ordre (UDMO) raided Martissant's Nan Beny and Ti Bois districts in an ostensible search for bandits, but their visit degenerated into beating people and setting fire to homes, vehicles and businesses after two of their members were wounded by gunfire.[21] During a subsequent visit to Martissant, West Department PNH head Michel-Ange Gédéon announced a reward of 10,000 gourdes each for information leading to the capture of the gang leaders Ti Kenken (Grand Ravine), Cristla Chéry (Ti Bois) and Nicodème Chéry (no relation) aka Pè Nico (Saint Martin).[22] The heavy-handedness of the government was also apparent at the Parc National La Visite, near Séguin in the hills above Jacmel, where local representatives of the Martelly administration and around 30 UDMO police violently evicted squatters who had taken up residence in the park, killing four.[23] In the same 15 August declaration in which he announced the formation of the CEP, Martelly had also announced the departure of Mario Andrésol from the PNH, to be replaced by Godson Orélus, the director of Haiti's judicial police.[24] The POHDH human rights organization asked that Orélus respect the "neutrality" that Andrésol had helped bring to the force.[25] RNDDH, POHDH and JILAP would soon issue a statement that they were concerned about "the subordination of legislative and judicial powers by the executive" and warned, prophetically, of the possible impact it might have on the planned 2013 vote.[26] RNDDH would eventually raise concerns about the illegal matriculation and promotion of officers into the force.[27]

* * *

By mid-August, Martelly announced that he was forming a new political party, the Parti Haïtien Tèt Kale (PHTK), to compete in the forthcoming elections.

Negotiations regarding the controversial CEP and what parliament's contribution to its composition would be were ongoing, with Martelly stating a tad imperiously that parliament was welcome to submit their representatives to the body "in any formula" they chose.[28] A few weeks later, opposition senator François Anick Joseph claimed that the government was planning to kill him along with Moïse Jean-Charles, Jean-Baptiste Bien-Aimé and Jean William Jeanty.[29] Martelly's close collaborator, the Jacmel senator Edwin Zenny, was accused of spitting in the faces of a judge and a political activist after he burst into the studio while the pair were being interviewed, a charge that Zenny alternately apologized for and denied.[30] At the end of September, when Martelly forced Jean Renél Sénatus out of his position as the capital's chief prosecutor (Claudy Gassant's old job), Sénatus responded by charging he had been ousted for refusing to issue arrest warrants against various opposition figures, warrants he said were sent to him by the current minister of justice, Jean Renél Sanon, and Sanon's predecessor, Josué Pierre-Louis. Sanon in turn called Sénatus a "liar" who had been suspended for "insubordination."[31]

* * *

On 12 September, several thousand people, led by Moïse Jean-Charles, protested against Martelly in Cap-Haïtien, the largest such display since Martelly came to power.[32] A general strike in Les Cayes followed, with the former senator Gabriel Fortuné playing a key role.[33] The following week, two more days of demonstrations occurred in Cap, this time with at least three injured by gunfire.[34] The genesis of such protests was hard to gauge, however, as residents of traditionally Lavalas neighborhoods claimed that Moïse Jean-Charles had distributed $50,000 in bribes to ensure that the protests would be well attended and disruptive incidents would occur.[35] On 30 September – the anniversary of the 1991 coup against Aristide and a traditional day of protest for his followers – several thousand Lavalas supporters and fellow travelers marched in the capital, among them Moïse Jean-Charles (riding on a horse) and Gérald Gilles.[36]

During September, as his opponents made their displeasure known in the streets, Martelly summoned 60 members of the Chamber of Deputies to the posh Club Indigo on the Côte des Arcadins north of the capital, where they committed to forming a new "presidential majority" bloc in parliament.[37] Several thousand pro-Martelly demonstrators paraded in Gonaïves, chanting that the president had to finish his five-year mandate.[38] Returning from a subsequent trip to the United States, Martelly landed at the capital's airport and, accompanied by Laurent Lamothe, Joseph Lambert and others, walked the nearly 7 miles to the National Palace accompanied by hundreds of supporters as well as government employees bussed in for the event, backed by DJs on sound trucks.[39] Choosing to deal with opposition by another method, security services brutally dispersed a demonstration planned to coincide with a presidential visit to Petit-Goâve, leading to the death of one octogenarian who was overcome by tear gas.[40] On a visit to the capital's Wharf Jérémie area, one of desperate poverty near La Saline, Martelly was warmly received by the residents, for whom he said he would create a vocational school.[41] In an interview with France 24, he said that, thanks to the presence of MINUSTAH, he felt "immune" to coups.[42]

* * *

Throughout October, the demonstrations continued, though. Thousands on the streets of Port-au-Prince.[43] Thousands more in Au Cap a few days later, with new personalities, such as former Justice Minister Paul Denis, former senator Turneb Delpé of the Parti National Démocratique Progressiste d'Haïti (PNDPH), deputy Sorel Jacinthe and veteran politico Evans Paul, participating along with the usual Lavalassians.[44] One of the co-sponsors of the march was the Initiative Citoyenne, which had been a strident anti-Aristide group during the latter's second tenure. One former member of the Initiative, while also writing scathingly of Martelly, wrote of his disgust that the Initiative had acted "without any thought of justice for the souls of those who fell [during the Aristide regime], or reparation for those who are still carrying the stigma of their injuries," before continuing that the opposition was made up of "an amalgam of former human-rights violators and leaders displaying a total lack of political values who are willing to associate themselves with yesterday's devil to get rid of today's fiend at the expense of justice and the rule of law."[45] When Lamothe spoke at a high school at Plaine du Nord near Au Cap, trying to drum up support for the government's *Ede Pèp* (Help the People) anti-hunger program, a rain of rocks and bottles clattered onto the roof of the building.[46] In the meantime, parliament was again postponed when the required number of senators to initiate a session once more failed to show up. Senate President Simon Dieuseul Desras felt the need to remind his colleagues that it was a *requirement* that they be present at sessions.[47]

* * *

In late October, Haiti was rocked by the arrest of Clifford Brandt, the ne'er-do-well scion of one of the country's richest families, who owned the Compagnie Haïtienne de Moteurs car dealership, for being at the head of an organized crime ring. The group had recently engineered the kidnapping of two members of another well-to-do family, the Moscosos, for a $2.5 million ransom and had held them in a vacant house in the suburb of Pernier (both were rescued).[48] Fifteen others were also arrested, among them five police officers, including Marc Arthur Phébé, head of a police unit based at the National Palace, who was moonlighting as the head of security for the Brandt family. Information gleaned from subsequent police interrogations suggested that the gang had been active for several years, had claimed at least 13 victims, and also had a lucrative side business smuggling weapons into Haiti from the United States for resale.[49] Brandt had also apparently been in possession of a National Palace security badge identifying him as an advisor to the president, a badge the Martelly government said was fake.[50] Lamothe said the arrests were "a victory for the forces of good."[51] Brandt would be housed in a spacious private cell at the prison in Croix-des-Bouquets, the most modern and secure in the country.[52] Before November was out, the scourge of kidnapping would also strike often deceptively peaceful Jacmel, where a two-year-old boy and his uncle were slain in the course of an attempt to seize the former, leading to a near riot by thousands of angry residents furious at the deterioration of the security situation in the town.[53]

*　*　*

A September 2012 review of the $53 million that had been awarded to the Washington-based Chemonics International read like a brutal, Swiftian parody of the aid world's claims of its accomplishments in Haiti.[54] The audit revealed that the company had gobbled up the funds and accounted for them by chaotic and often outright deceptive means, such as planting 700,000 jatropha seedlings and then conducting the required environmental review of the project's likely impact only afterwards.[55] The organization's cash-for-work program employed only a third of the number of Haitian workers required in its contract, and a number of its projects were evaluated based on criteria that had nothing to do with the work it was tasked to complete, such as rating the success of a program distributing school supplies on how many children returned to school.[56] Despite a contract stipulating regular evaluations of the programs – taken to mean between two and four times a year – only one evaluation had been done in the previous 16 months.[57]

Nor was Chemonics the only entity to have squandered money in Haiti's hour of great need. Wyclef Jean's Yéle charity, the subject of scandals over misappropriation of funds in the past, had eventually raised $16 million based on its earthquake appeals, but more than two years later, almost no sign of its work in the country could be found. Yéle spent $600,000 on its Haiti headquarters, put its logo on tents that fell apart, and spent over $4 million on travel, salaries and consultant fees in 2010 alone (including $630,000 to Jean's brother-in-law). Where $230,000 for "revitalizing" Cité Soleil went, no one could say.[58]

* * *

In Cité Soleil itself, at the beginning of November, gunmen from the Boston section of the neighborhood – allegedly accompanied by a police vehicle from the local commissariat – attacked Simon-Pelé in a nighttime assault that left at least four people dead. The PNH, for their part, denied any involvement in the raid.[59] Days later, several hundred residents from both neighborhoods participated in a "peace march," with security provided by both PNH and MINUSTAH and a sound truck with an MC shouting Lapè! (Peace!).[60] A few days later, Pernier commissariat chief Yves Michel Bellefleur was slain by masked men in a car with a Service de l'État license plate just after he dropped his children off at school.[61] A second policeman was killed in the city center only hours later.[62] Many believed that Bellefleur was killed to prevent him from revealing information connected to the Brandt case.[63] Now in retirement, Mario Andrésol requested additional security on the basis of unspecified threats against his life.[64]

* * *

Raymond "Che" Duclona, the brother of Amaral Duclona, the imprisoned former boss of Cité Soleil's Bélékou area, might have changed, but it appeared Haiti had not. Having returned after the 2010 earthquake to try to help his community, Duclona had found himself running up against the area's new boss, a young tough who went by the nom de guerre Iska and reportedly had connections to politicians from the Fusion party. Iska had his doubts about Duclona's intentions and Duclona, who had been in that life for many years before, could see the writing on the wall.

"I know they are planning to kill me this week," he told a friend. "I am Che, you know I can find a gun if I want one. But my youngest daughter has never seen me with a gun. I'd rather die than have her see me like that."

As Raymond Duclona sat in the passenger seat of a *camionette* waiting to leave Cité Soleil one afternoon, a young man walked up to him and shot him in the head. He died on the streets of Cité Soleil.[65]

"As far as I am concerned," Konbit Soléy Leve's Louino Robillard told me later, "he wasn't born a gangster and he didn't die a gangster. He died a social leader."

* * *

By November 2012, Calixte Valentin, the presidential advisor who had been imprisoned for his alleged role in the killing of the Fond Parisien merchant Octanol Dérissaint, had been released without trial by Judge Paul Fernaud Jude.[66] The judge, RNDDH would charge, was "a seasoned racketeer" who, in all likelihood, did not even hold a law license let alone qualify to sit on the bench.[67] On the 18 November anniversary of the victory of rebel forces over the French in the Battle of Vertières, several thousand demonstrated for Martelly's resignation in Port-au-Prince, joined this time by a relatively new pro-Lavalas current, the Fos Patriyotik pou Respe Konstitisyon (FOPARK).[68] FOPARK would in time be joined by another new political group, the Mouvement Patriotique de l'Opposition Démocratique (MOPOD), a political conglomeration founded by an ideologically promiscuous group of politicos and assorted hangers-on, including the RDNP's Mirlande Manigat, Groupe 77's André Michel, the PNDPH's Turneb Delpé, Veye Yo's Jean Simson Desanclos and the attorneys Newton Saint-Juste, Samuel Madistin and the BAI's Mario Joseph.[69]

* * *

In late November 2012, the clouds hung low over Port-au-Prince, pregnant with the threat of rain. When the deluge did issue forth, life continued irrepressibly on. Moto taxi drivers plied the streets in their jaunty raincoats, and people continued hawking anything there was to sell under any surface providing shelter. I drove through a city now festooned with solar-powered streetlights, and at regular intervals would encounter teams of workers in matching T-shirts sweeping the streets and cleaning the gutters. Working stop lights at several intersections even made a game attempt to control the traffic.

All was not calm, though. As I strolled through Pétionville's Place St. Pierre one Saturday afternoon, with clouds rumbling down from the mountainside, a group of about 200 young men commandeered the square, halting traffic and periodically hurling bottles in various directions (one of which shattered at my feet). The lads thumped their chests for about three hours before moving on. Their message was that life was too expensive for people in Haiti and that Martelly, whom they said they had previously supported, wasn't doing enough to ameliorate the situation. The fact that Martelly was winding up a long trip to Europe during which he addressed the European Parliament, attended the Ibero-American Summit in Spain and met with the Pope at the Vatican (he was even absent from Haiti during the anniversary of the Battle of Vertières) was not lost on the protesters.

"He wants to work well for the people," said a middle-aged taxi driver named Jackson plying the road near the airport as he drove me towards the MINUSTAH base. "But the problem is his entourage."

Passing the security checks into the office of Mariano Fernández, the Chilean diplomat who was then heading MINUSTAH, I was momentarily taken aback to find a framed recent picture of a sallow-faced Jean-Claude Duvalier on the wall, the former dictator sitting mournfully alone at an exquisitely made-up banquet table.

"This is how I see Duvalier," Fernández told me, before going on to assert that "a stabilization process is taking place albeit a fragile one … We continue planning to reduce and reconfigure MINUSTAH depending on the stability of the conditions."[70]

I saw first-hand the tenuousness of the stabilization process as I took a moto taxi up into the neighborhood of Saint Martin, bouncing over deeply rutted, muddy streets, and passed brightly colored murals of Haitian historical figures such as Toussaint, Dessalines and Martelly himself. Soon I was sitting sharing a beer with Nicodème Chéry, a diminutive young man whose moniker, Pè Niko ("Father Nico"), belied his youthful appearance. Pushing 30 years old but looking barely into his twenties and resplendent in a Miami Heat baseball cap, Pè Nico led the armed faction in Saint Martin, though at this moment he seemed more concerned with delicately caressing a small child with her hair in braids who approached him. It turned out to be his daughter.

"We liked Martelly and we thought he would help a lot of people," Pè Nico told me. "But this neighborhood has always been forgotten."

Pè Nico's *baz*, some armed, stood around us (MINUSTAH appeared completely absent from the zone). One was wearing a Mickey Mouse T-shirt, and a large number were wearing the T-shirts of the Irish NGO Concern. Along with Lakou Lapè, an organization that Louis-Henri Mars had helped form (its name essentially meant "Peaceful Neighborhood"), Concern had been working to lessen the cycle of violence in the quarter with a cash-for-work program, among other initiatives, measures that appeared to have largely petered out. Pè Nico said his *baz* voted – "99 percent" in his words – for Martelly, but were obviously hoping for more. For years the *baz* had warred against the Baz 117 only a few streets away; things were calmer now, but the tension remained. As I got ready to leave, the leader of Baz 117, a young man named Odonel, arrived on the back of a moto taxi. He and Pè Nico disappeared into the warren of alleys for further consultations.

I had the chance to visit with some friends while in town. The French media worker Philippe Allouard took me on the back of his moto down through the rain-slicked streets of Canapé Vert to a Thanksgiving dinner at the home of Amber Walsh, an old friend of mine who had been working for foreign and local organizations for the last 15 years. As we chatted over a good feast and many glasses of Barbancourt rum, Philippe recounted watching Martelly's "long march" from Caracol earlier in the year and concluded that "the people will continue to support their wild and eccentric president." (Along with the respected media worker Léonidas Gareau, Philippe would tragically die on the very same moto only months later when he was struck by a tap-tap while driving to Jacmel.)

Others painted a darker picture, of how Secretary of State for Public Security Réginald Delva exercised more operational control over the PNH than Minister of Justice Jean Renél Sanon, his nominal boss, and how Joseph Lambert, now firmly in Martelly's camp, also wielded influence beyond what one would expect. One friend of mine in the private sector bemoaned the way that the country had been "invaded" by foreign corporations and NGOs.

When I stopped by the offices of RNDDH to ask Pierre Espérance about the country's human rights situation, he didn't even feign surprise at the Brandt arrest.

"The bourgeois control the police with their money, and a lot of police officers also provide security for businesses and the private sector because there is no control, and they can receive more money for their work," he said, shrugging his shoulders. "Each kidnapping gang has its connection with the police."

On my last day in Haiti during the visit, purely by chance, my path over-lapped with that of Martelly.

Waiting at the airport to board my flight home, I saw Martelly's American Airlines plane fly in from Miami. As if on cue, and so apt for a showman, the cloudy gloom that had plagued the capital for days broke and rays of brilliant golden sunshine spilled out of a blue sky. Diplomats, Haitian police officers in their crisp khaki uniforms and every airport worker who could sneak away from their job were standing there to greet him. He was going to be inaugurating a new arrival hall, they told me, then this week he would be leaving again, this time for Cuba.

Martelly disembarked from the plane, his bald head and smiling visage visible among the mostly smaller Haitians.

They cheered.

* * *

Given his behavior during the Jean Dominique case a decade before, Josué Pierre-Louis was perhaps always a strange choice to be Haiti's minister of justice, and stranger still to be president of its ostensibly neutral CEP. Few might have predicted, however, the explosive scandal that erupted at the end of November when both RNDDH and SOFA accused him of having raped an assistant, only referred to as "Maylielore," at his residence on the night of 26 November.[71] In due time, the victim was identified as Marie Danielle Bernadin, and her father spoke to Radio Kiskeya of how Pierre-Louis had allegedly promised $300,000 and a "diplomatic post" should the charges be dropped.[72] RNDDH, POHDH, SOFA and Kay Fanm all signed a letter to the Conseil Supérieur du Pouvoir Judiciaire (CSPJ) shortly thereafter warning that investigating judge Joseph Jeudilien Fanfan had been the subject of serious threats by other judges and supporters of Josué Pierre-Louis.[73]

Just before Christmas, 20 young men who had been associated with Lafanmi Selavi, the Aristide-run orphanage that so many of the now-dead chimere leaders had passed through, walked into a courtroom in Port-au-Prince and filed a criminal complaint against the former president for physical violence, economic exploitation and utilization of their cases for personal gain. Among their number was Sonny "Ti Sonny" Thélusma, who years before had been one of the institute's most well-known members.[74] Thélusma told journalist Amélie Baron that he "was 6 when Aristide took me from my mother's house

… He was using me as a puppet, making us play in front of foreigners in order to raise money for his own political interest."[75] Neither the BAI, whose attorney Mario Joseph was one of Aristide's cadre of lawyers in Haiti, nor the IJDH, whose Ira Kurzban was still Aristide's lawyer in the United States, seemed moved to take the case and defend any violation of these young men's rights. Days later, CONASOVIC, the organization of victims who had lost their money in the Aristide-endorsed cooperative scheme, sued the former president and several former co-op chiefs for "fraud, breach of trust, theft and criminal conspiracy."[76] The capital's chief prosecutor, Lucmane Délile, announced that Aristide would be summoned to court in the new year to answer the charges.[77] When Aristide won a last-minute delay in the hearing, his partisans, in typical fashion, launched a chaotic, threatening demonstration in front of the courthouse that had to be dispersed with tear gas, and saw the former president's accusers evacuated under police protection.[78] The complainants in the Lafanmi Selavi suit soon began receiving threatening phone calls.[79] As a man with such a legacy would be wont to do, in addition to Kurzban and Joseph, Aristide retained a phalanx of lawyers to defend him, including former Minister of Justice Camille Leblanc and prominent Martelly critic Newton Saint-Juste.[80] Aristide's old apprentice Moïse Jean-Charles also spoke up in his defense. A third complaint was filed against Aristide by former noncommissioned officers of the FADH, accusing him of unconstitutionally disbanding the army.[81] For 30 minutes on 9 January, prosecutor Lucmane Délile questioned Aristide at the latter's home in Tabarre.[82] The POHDH human rights organization said that, by interviewing Aristide at home rather than his coming to court, set "a bad precedent."[83] The former Lavalas senator Mirlande Libérus, who had been resident in the United States since Aristide's 2004 overthrow, was also summoned to court in absentia by investigating judge Yvikel Dabrésil in connection with the Jean Dominque slaying, a move that Mario Joseph strenuously denounced as "political persecution."[84] In stark contrast to the chaos that accompanied any attempt to compel Aristide to appear before a judge, René Préval also submitted to questioning by Yvikel Dabrésil, arriving accompanied only by his wife and a few bodyguards.[85]

* * *

Martelly soldiered on, trying to sell his vision of a new Haiti. Speaking at a diaspora forum in heavily Haitian North Miami Beach, Martelly tried to convince his audience that "Haiti has changed a lot" and that "there is more that can be done by the diaspora."[86]

And it *was* changing. A United Nations report predicted that Haiti would have the fastest economic growth of any Caribbean nation in 2013.[87] But, at the same time, inflation had risen to almost 7 percent since the previous June, leading to great hardship and loss of purchasing power.[88] In December, the 128-room Royal Oasis Hotel opened in Pétionville, and a Best Western would open up a few months later.[89] Though some foreign journalists and activists sneered at such developments, both hotels provided direct and ancillary jobs for hundreds of Haitians, and were looked upon as a boon by the people working there.

But the rule of law continued to be feeble. As January rolled on, both CEP president Josué Pierre-Louis and his accuser, Marie Danielle Bernardin, answered questions before an investigating judge.[90] Then, to the surprise of many, Bernardin abandoned her complaint, issuing a statement that, although she was "reaffirming that I was beaten and raped by Josué Pierre-Louis," threats and intimidation by Pierre-Louis's supporters were forcing her hand, especially after her parents had been forced to flee the country and given that "my safety was never supported by the Haitian authorities."[91] In late January, Pè Nico, the gang leader I had interviewed in Saint Martin the previous November, was slain and decapitated by his rivals from Baz 117, a betrayal led by Odonel, the former rival who had pretended to befriend him some months before.[92] Odonel himself met the same fate a few weeks later.[93] Baz 117 would continue to terrorize the local population despite a crackdown by the PNH that resulted in 60 arrests.[94] Even Haiti's carnival, this year held in Cap-Haïtien, proved controversial, with the Brothers Posse excluded due to a song that denounced what they called the government's broken promises (a fairly usual carnival theme over the years).[95] At least one anti-government protester on the fringes of the gathering was killed.[96] Many thousands, however, still flooded the streets of Haiti's second city in what was, all told, rather joyous revelry.[97] There was much discussion of how the fête had signified the rebirth of the northern metropolis. In little more than a year, the city's airport (renamed Hugo Chávez International) would be refurbished enough to accommodate Boeing 737s, and American Airlines would add direct daily service from Miami.[98] In perhaps a move of atonement from the man who helped, as much as any, to decimate Haiti's agricultural sector, the Clinton Foundation announced that it was awarding over $700,000 to help Haiti's farmers in reforestation and coffee-growing efforts.[99] Around the same time, the Martelly government announced a reforestation program that the government hoped would "give us forest cover of 4.5%; in 10 years, it will be 8% to 10% and in 50 years we hope to be at the level of Cuba and have 29%," from the 2 percent that Haiti currently boasted.[100]

It is perhaps worth pausing here to examine how the role of Bill Clinton was viewed in Haiti itself. In my 2013 book on the Democratic Republic of Congo, I wrote scathingly of Clinton's policy towards the Great Lakes Region of Africa during the 1990s (an analysis I still stand by), and I've written for years since very critically about his role in destroying Haiti's peasant farming tradition.[101] The fact that many of his grand proposals for Haiti bore far less fruit than first promised is also beyond dispute. But talking with those who had to deal with Clinton on a regular basis in Haiti, a somewhat more nuanced picture emerges.

"He brought what we needed, he brought attention to Haiti, he brought the cameras of the world behind him, and he brought people here who would have never thought of Haiti," Jean-Max Bellerive told me one day as we chatted at his house in Port-au-Prince.

"He supported the Haitian government in global negotiations, and was fighting for Haiti in a way I would never have dared," Bellerive said. "He took the last productive years of his life and gave them to Haiti."[102]

Bellerive's assessment was echoed by that of his successor.

"He could have gone anywhere in the world, and he chose to come to Haiti," Laurent Lamothe told me. "His role is often misunderstood, but he's always been there to help Haiti, and he brought in a lot of investment. It's up to the Haitians to take his participation and make something out of it."[103]

* * *

The whirlwind of activity of the president and the prime minister continued. During a CARICOM summit held at the Royal Oasis and the Karibe Convention Center in February, Lamothe announced that a "plot" to violently disrupt the event had been foiled.[104] Heading to Caracas for the funeral of the recently deceased Venezuelan leader Hugo Chávez, both Martelly and Lamothe garbed themselves in Chavista red in tribute to the left-wing leader who had deigned to lavish PetroCaribe on Haiti.[105] But, as Martelly and parliament continued to bicker about the composition of the CEP, scandals continued to erupt in the government. In early February, a vehicle with official plates, its occupants unknown, was involved in a traffic dispute that ended with the gunning down of a tap-tap driver and his cousin on Grand Rue.[106] The same month it was revealed that an aid to First Lady Sophia Martelly had embezzled nearly $30,000 from a South Florida bank where he worked and was on the lam from U.S. justice (the employee subsequently resigned).[107] But, in fairness, Martelly's adversaries gave as good as they got. In early March, the volatile deputy Arnel Bélizaire stormed into the headquarters of the country's postal service, breaking open a locked door, interrupting a meeting and threatening staff present, apparently in the course of a mission to find "evidence" incriminating the body's former executive.[108]

* * *

And impunity continued to reign.

After having ignored two previous requests, Duvalier was ordered to appear in court on 8 February to answer the accusations against him.[109] This time, Duvalier showed up, and answered questions for about 15 minutes and left without incident, but not before contemptuously addressing his accusers by saying: "In my turn I would ask them, what have they done to my country?"[110]

In late March, Jean Wilner Morin, the judge investigating the killing of police officer Walky Calixte, called on parliament to lift the immunity of deputies Rodriguez Séjour and M'Zounaya Bellange Jean-Baptiste, based on what the judge called significant evidence of their involvement in the crime, including incriminating telephone records.[111] As per usual, however, the Chamber of Deputies could not debate, let alone vote, on the request as not enough members showed up to hold a session.[112] As the judge made his request, Marcelin Jevousaime, a police officer who witnessed Calixte's killing, was gravely wounded by unknown gunmen in the capital's southern suburb of Arcachon.[113] Days later, Jean Richard Hertz Cayo, another PNH officer who had been part of the same patrol when Calixte was shot, was gunned down by unknown assailants in Carrefour-Feuillés.[114] Hertz Cayo had been interviewed by the judge just before his murder, to whom he confided that he was afraid of being attacked.[115] Martissant itself, where Calixte had been killed, remained violent as gangs from Grand Ravine and Sainte Bernadette did battle.[116] Eventually, Calixte's mother and two brothers would testify before the parliamentary committee looking into lifting the deputies' immunity.[117] The committee, not surprisingly, decided that "there was not sufficient evidence" to lift immunity, to which one of the attorneys for Calixte's family, the fierce Martelly critic André Michel, responded by asking Judge Morin "to bring everybody before the court" and stating that the committee decision was "proof" of the involvement of Séjour and Jean-Baptiste.[118] Eventually, Haiti's Chamber of Deputies voted unanimously against lifting Séjour and Jean-Baptiste's immunity.[119]

Also in March, Michel Forst, who had served as the UN's independent expert on human rights in Haiti, resigned, firing a last blast at the Martelly government by publishing an open letter from his base in Geneva in which he specifically criticized the handling of the Calixte Valentin case and stated (perhaps a tad self-aggrandizingly) that "when I leave my office, I do not want to hide my concerns and disappointment in the developments in the field of rule of law and human rights."[120] Eventually, both Minister of Finance Marie Carmelle Jean-Marie and Minister of Communications Régine Godefroy resigned, with the latter saying she was unable to perform her functions "with rigor, honor and integrity."[121]

* * *

Cité Soleil was now on the boil as the municipal council had been dissolved and a Martelly ally, Jean Reynold Philippe, who had an unsavory reputation among some residents for alleged gang links, including with those linked to the killing of Samba Boukman, was appointed as interim executive.[122] As different gangs would fight in the coming weeks, at least three would be killed in the zone.[123] In Delmas, Georges Honorat, an associate of the politically moribund PPN and an editor at *Haïti Progrès*, would also be slain.[124] During May, police began finding executed young men dumped in formerly placid areas of the capital such as Bourdon.[125]

* * *

When it was announced that Aristide had again been summoned to appear before the judge in the Jean Dominique case, his supporters, among them Franco Camille, whose name had been consistently mentioned in connection with the crime, said they would "accompany" him to any hearing, which many took as a thinly veiled threat.[126] On the day of the summons, a few dozen Aristide supporters – senators Jean-Baptiste Bien-Aimé and John Joël Joseph among them – chanted slogans and waved photos of Aristide in front of the latter's residence in Tabarre.[127] When the object of their affection finally appeared before the judge, hundreds more behaved in the usual manner, physically assaulting Radio-Télé Ginen journalist Frantz Henry Délice and damaging the station's vehicle.[128] The Association des Médias Indépendants d'Haïti condemned the assault, with its president, Marcus Garcia, reminding the former president that "freedom of expression is one of the most valuable achievements [of] our country in our age-old struggle against tyranny and obscurantism."[129] Among the crowd at the court were several politicos, including those who had been present at Tabarre as well as Moïse Jean-Charles, Francky Exius, Yvon Feuillé and Yvon Bissereth.[130] Marching through the capital's streets, the partisans chanted "Aristide king!" and homophobic insults against Martelly as they tore down and publicly urinated on posters of the president and prime minister.[131] At a press conference the following day, Aristide told reporters that a "stronger, more powerful" Lavalas was "ready to win the next election."[132]

CHAPTER FIFTEEN
OPEN FOR BUSINESS

Shortly after Laurent Lamothe became prime minister, he gave an interview in which he emphatically stated: "Haiti is open for business."[1] It would become the recurring theme of the government he and Martelly would run. By mid-2013, there was some evidence they were succeeding in their attempts to rebrand the country as something other than a place of ceaseless misery.

At an early June mining conference in Port-au-Prince, co-organized with the World Bank and attended by representatives of such mining giants as Eurasian Minerals and Newmont Mining, Lamothe told attendees that "Haiti would like to place itself as an emerging mining country in the next 20 years" and that a "modern and precise" mining code was needed to "allow for transparent contracts with competent experts who have national interests at heart." He said he hoped such a law would be introduced before the end of the year.[2] During 2013, the 106-room Best Western – the first U.S. brand hotel to arrive in Haiti in 15 years – would open its doors in Pétionville, its walls festooned with a gorgeous mosaic of Haitian art.[3] A tourism – yes, tourism – article appeared in *The Los Angeles Times* lauding Haiti's attractions and concluding that "you'll come home with memories of a place you might not have expected."[4] When I spoke to Minister of Tourism Stéphanie Villedrouin, she told me that "the whole strategy that we put in place two and a half years ago was to reposition Haiti as a tourism destination after it was off the tourism map for the last 20 years."[5] Villedrouin and her team hoped to coax ever more visitors to what Haiti's new tourism brochures called "the soul of the Caribbean."

In addition to its long-standing economic links to the United States, Canada and the Dominican Republic and its petro-based camaraderie with Venezuela, Haiti's partnerships with other countries began to expand. Vietnam's Viettel, its largest mobile network wholly owned by its Ministry of Defense, partnered with the nearly defunct Teleco to create NATCOM, a $100 million joint venture to provide mobile phone services across the country. By 2013, there would be

$42 million of trade between the two countries.[6] Lamothe formed the Coordination de l'Aide Externe au Développement (CAED), a body tasked with coordinating external aid to Haiti and, at its first meeting in May 2013, called on the remaining 48 percent of promised post-earthquake aid that had never been dispersed to be released.[7] The same month, the UN predicted that Haiti's rice harvest would be a quarter over the previous year's, a gentle upward trend.[8] Even the slum of Jalousie, rising precariously on the hills behind Pétionville, received a new beautifying paint job, its facades splashed with exuberant psychedelic colors. Beyond the government's own efforts, in gang-plagued Martissant, FOKAL, the organization headed by Michèle Pierre-Louis and Lorraine Mangonès, succeeded in rehabilitating 17 hectares (42 acres) of land into a tranquil green space that became the Parc de Martissant, and which encompassed the historic Habitation Leclerc, the former home of Katherine Dunham that had long been rumored to have once housed Napoleon's sister, Pauline Bonaparte.[9]

As with so much in Haiti, though, attempts to develop the country were riddled with acrimony. When Lamothe announced that the picturesque Île-à-Vache near Les Cayes would be turned into a "tourist destination," the concept was greeted with fierce protest by some local residents, who were likely to be displaced by a proposed international airport and highway. In May 2012, Martelly had created, by decree, a provision by which "state possessions" were determined to be "the subject of the lease or transactions between individuals," a clear reference to the Île-à-Vache dispute."[10] A plan with Miami's Carnival Corporation to develop the beach at Pointe-Ouest on Île de la Tortue, off Haiti's northern coast – frequently described as one of the ten most beautiful in the Caribbean – was scuttled when it turned out that a Texas businessman had signed a 99-year lease agreement with François Duvalier for the beach, which his heirs were hell-bent on enforcing.[11] And the improvement in the rice harvest was barely a blip. By 2013, Haiti, a country that only three decades earlier had produced 80 percent of the food it consumed, now imported half of that food and 80 percent of its rice, with 67 percent of the population classed as being food insecure, according to government figures.[12]

* * *

By mid-year, concern was growing about the delayed elections. A "transition" CEP had been formed but for more than a year the senate had been operating at only two-thirds capacity (for those senators who bothered to show up) and for more than two years the mandates of local officials such as mayors had expired.[13] Canada's ambassador to Haiti, Henry Paul Normandin, pleaded to the country's political factions to break their impasse and hold elections before the end of the year.[14] The Trinidadian diplomat Sandra Honoré, who would take over as the head of MINUSTAH in May 2013, made similar appeals.

Haiti's body politic, though, was far from having exhausted its appetite for sensational scandals, and two that exploded in July would help push the delayed vote ever further to the sidelines.

In early July, Haiti was rocked by the allegations of one Sherlson Sanon, inevitably described in the Haitian media as a "henchman" of Joseph Lambert, which he delivered in person to RNDDH. In written testimony, Sanon charged that Lambert had recruited him into a gang of local Jacmel toughs in 1998 (when he was 11 and when, he noted, Lambert was close to Fourel Célestin), and that in the ensuing years he was party to a sordid life of drug trafficking, kidnapping and murder. He claimed that use of his services eventually expanded to include Edwin Zenny and members of a well-known Jacmel family. He said that he had grown tired of his life, and feared that the senator would have him killed, thus his visit to RNDDH.[15] Lambert and Zenny furiously rejected the accusations, saying that they had never met Sanon and criticizing RNDDH for creating a "political montage" designed to discredit them.[16]

The same month, Judge Jean Serge Joseph opened an investigation into alleged corruption by Martelly and his family, especially by the president's wife, Sophia, and son, Olivier. Joseph immediately came under strong pressure from the government – including, allegedly, at a meeting with Martelly, Lamothe and Justice Minister Jean Renél Sanon – to close the dossier (the men denied they had met the magistrate).[17] The accusations stemmed from allegations by Enold Florestal, a militant of Evans Paul's KID party.[18] Less than two weeks after news of the investigation broke, Joseph died of a stroke.[19]

A subsequent (and naturally highly politicized) senate inquiry charged Martelly, Lamothe and Sanon with "high treason" and recommended impeachment.[20] Enold Florestal was subsequently arrested – with considerable brutality – along with his brother and imprisoned for his alleged role in the 2010 killing of a young student.[21] He would be released more than a year later without charge.[22] A definitive report by the coroner in Québec, though, determined that Joseph had indeed died of "natural causes."[23]

Martelly toured the north in late July, his visit roughly coinciding with the vodou pilgrimage at Plaine du Nord, which Martelly walked to from Cap-Haïtien accompanied by a huge crowd of supporters. Plaisance deputy Renaud Jean-Baptiste charged that Moïse Jean-Charles had plotted an attempt on the president's life. Jean-Charles denied the accusations, and said that he was in the area only to lead a "peaceful protest."[24] Jean-Charles in turn accused Martelly supporters of opening fire on demonstrators, wounding three.[25] Amid another *carnaval des fleurs* in the capital, Martelly accused RDNP leader Mirlande Manigat of "leading those who want to commit a coup," and mocked what he said was his opponents' lack of popularity, claiming that "the personal security that I have does not prevent the population from trying to kill me, but from trying to kiss me."[26] The RDNP denied the charges and, in an open letter, Manigat wrote that "an ill wind blows through the presidency" and accused Martelly of presiding over "a rogue state."[27] For Martelly's carnival ramblings to have an impact on the public's view of him, however, he would have had to look at least as ridiculous as parliament, where, in a scene broadcast to the nation, deputy Jean-René Lochard punched his colleague Fritz Gérald Bourjolly in a dispute over the proposed extension of the mandates of some parliamentarians. The sight of the two portly men wrestling in such a hungry country, knocking over furniture and stomping on legal briefings, served as an apt and sad metaphor for the legislature itself.[28] Or as ridiculous as deputy Levaillant Louis-Jeune, who urged parliament to declare the presidency "vacant" because Martelly had reportedly passed a night gambling at a casino in the Bahamas.[29] (According to a confidant, Martelly was also frequently a guest of Suriname President Dési Bouterse, a former military dictator who had been sentenced in absentia for drug trafficking in the Netherlands.[30]) By mid-August, the opposition OPL, Fusion and MOPOD were refusing even to meet with Martelly to discuss the planning of the coming elections.[31] Finally, after a two-month delay, Justice Minister Sanon, accompanied by such government supporters as Youri Latortue and Joseph Lambert, deposited a draft of the new electoral law with parliament on 27 August, along with a letter from Martelly asking the body to "urgently" approve the law.[32] Eventually, Martelly would personally call on the leadership of OPL and KID at their party offices.[33]

* * *

Across the Massacre River, after August 2012, Danilo Medina, another PLD politician, had taken over as president of the Dominican Republic from Leonel Fernández. With the nearly complete neutralization of the opposition, including the once-mighty PRD, a report from the Center for Strategic and International Studies wondered aloud if Haiti's neighbor was becoming "a one-party state," noting that the PLD controlled the executive branch and held a majority both in congress and in the National Council of Magistrates, which appointed the nation's judiciary and prosecutors.[34] A number of observers saw the repeated PLD efforts to denationalize Dominicans of Haitians descent as part of a deliberate plan to strike tens of thousands of PLD-hostile voters from the rolls.[35] Such a possibility became less theoretical in late September 2013, when the Dominican Republic's Supreme Court issued a ruling that specifically targeted black Dominicans, retroactively stripping tens of thousands of people of citizenship if they could not prove that their families had lived in the country since 1929, applying the criteria of a new constitution passed in 2010 to the citizenship status of people who had been born decades earlier.[36] The court's chief justice, Mariano Germán Mejía, was Leonel Fernández's former law partner.[37]

Writing in *El País*, the Peruvian author Mario Vargas Llosa (who had written a searing depiction of the Trujillo years in *La fiesta del chivo*), minced no words and called the ruling a "legal aberration" that seemed "directly inspired by the famous Hitlerian laws of the Thirties dictated by Nazi German judges."[38] The Dominican journalist Felipe Ciprián wrote of the "strange patriots" who "blamed Haiti and Haitians for all the misfortune that befalls the Dominican Republic."[39]

* * *

In Haiti itself, legal imbroglios dominated the autumn. In mid-September, Evinx Daniel, the owner of Port Salut's Dan's Creek hotel and a well-known Martelly supporter who had served in the U.S. army during the 1990–91 invasion of Iraq, was arrested on the orders of prosecutor Jean Marie Salomon. Daniel was jailed as a result of 23 packages of marijuana he claimed to have found floating at sea. Martelly's brother-in-law, Charles "Kiko" Saint-Rémy, had called the United States DEA after discussions with Daniel to inform them of the drug load, but Salomon reportedly believed the story was a ruse to cover up a larger drug trafficking endeavor. While in prison, Daniel reportedly called Justice Minister Jean Renél Sanon and was released the next day. Salomon was suspended from his post and briefly fled the country. Shortly after Daniel's release, Martelly passed a leisurely visit at his friend's Port Salut hotel,[40] and, three months later, Evinx Daniel disappeared. A high-ranking PNH source familiar with the investigation later told me that police subsequently found a burned body near the northern town of Anse-Rouge they believed to be that of the missing hotelier, though the discovery was never made public.[41]

Also in mid-September, Judge Lamarre Bélizaire, viewed as being very close to Martelly, served legal papers to Radio Kiskeya's Liliane Pierre-Paul, who, in her broadcasts, raised questions about whether or not Bélizaire had been suspended from his judicial role as the result of misconduct.[42] It was a continuation of bitter relations between the government and the station that would accelerate the following month after Radio Kiskeya journalist Rodrigue Lalanne was brutally assaulted by Martelly's security while covering a presidential event.[43] In late October, the attorney and fierce government critic André Michel was arrested after refusing a search of his car and held for 24 hours until he was freed after hundreds of protesters shouting anti-Martelly slogans descended on the court where he was being detained.[44] Following the arrest, Senate President Simon Dieuseul Desras denounced Martelly as a *bandit légal* (legal bandit), a reference to one of Martelly's old songs.[45]

* * *

By early October, anti-Martelly protests were happening every couple of days in the capital, a number of them organized by the pro-Lavalas Mouvman Gran Bèlè, FOPARK and MOPOD. The demos sometimes took on a markedly racial character, with protesters marching toward Pétionville chanting that they were the "sons of Dessalines" on their way to "visit" with "those of Pétion."[46] When protesters attempted to approach the Champ de Mars and the ruins of the National Palace, police would lash them with tear gas.[47]

By early December, an attempted demonstration in Les Cayes – largely a Lavalas affair with the party's national coordinator Maryse Narcisse presiding, though also buttressed by the presence of Moïse Jean-Charles, André Michel and former Préval spokesman Assad Volcy – was brutally broken up by police and pro-Martelly counter-demonstrators. Significantly, however, during the event, Narcisse and Jean-Charles partisans bitterly insulted one another over who was the movement's true leader.[48] The breaking point between the two currents had come days after Jean-Charles had led a march on the U.S. Embassy, a march that had coincided with the anniversary of the 1987 massacre of voters at Ruelle

Vaillant. The march's timing conflicted directly with the "official" commemoration by the Fanmi Lavalas party at the site of the attack, but, while the Narcisse event attracted only a few hundred, Jean-Charles drew several thousand to his march, which resulted in a sharply worded rebuke from the Lavalas executive committee.[49] Moïse Jean-Charles responded by saying that the party had been taken over by a "Macoute-bourgeois group" and that he had told Aristide personally that "it is destroying the party ... the bourgeoisie will simply take it over completely and finish with it." Jean-Charles pointed out – quite correctly – that he had twice been elected mayor of Milot under the Lavalas banner and that Narcisse had no history of popular advocacy.[50]

When I asked Jean-Charles about the split, he told me: "[Aristide] has a problem with me, I don't have a problem with him. He supports the ideology of Toussaint Louverture while I support the ideology of Jean-Jacques Dessalines ... Dessalines wanted a completely autonomous nation and to take total independence for us, and that's what I want, too."[51]

One could see echoes of Jean-Charles' words when, in December, a coalition of peasant groups in the north and northeast denounced what it charged was the government's forcible expulsion of farmers from their lands for the benefit of multinational mining companies and rich landowners.[52]

* * *

With the political street theater appearing to grow ever more direct, as the year ended Chamber of Deputies president Jean Tholbert Alexis announced that the Catholic Church was willing to broker a dialogue between the president and his adversaries.[53] MOPOD, however, continued to call for Martelly's resignation and the holding of early elections.[54] At a graduation ceremony for a new class of police cadets, Martelly made the rather startling statement that the police were "the armed wing of the government."[55]

At the independence ceremony in Gonaïves as the nation greeted 2014, Martelly told the audience that: "Haiti is very sick, we need to rebuild this country of ours ... This work is not that of a single president or group. It is the job of all of us, together we will get there." He also told his audience that "peace and stability" were required "to achieve victories in the fight against ignorance, for job creation and to establish schooling and health for all."[56]

Martelly's declarations were eminently reasonable, but what startled many spectators was the presence at the ceremony of Jean-Claude Duvalier, apparently as an official guest, as well as Prosper Avril. Evans Paul, once perse-cuted by Duvalier and tortured by Avril's government, was spotted in cheery conversation with the two. Paul was the only opposition figure to accept the invitation to the ceremony and told reporters later that he had "already forgiven" the two men, and had conversed with them in the spirit of "tolerance."[57] Alix Fils-Aimé, one of those who had felt the whip end of the regime, called the dictator's presence in Gonaïves an "insult to the victims and a lack of respect for historical truth."[58] Eventually, an appeals court would recommend that legal processes against the former dictator should be resumed.[59] With typical intem-perance, Duvalier's lawyer, Reynold Georges, threatened "civil war" should the court's decision stand.[60]

The opposition OPL, Fusion and Kontrapèpla parties greeted the new year by issuing their by now more or less pro-forma calls that Martelly resign.[61] Arnel Bélizaire would again be in the news for violently "liberating" two cronies who were being questioned at a capital court in connection with a kidnapping.[62] The task of the anti-Martelly forces became more difficult when, in mid-January, the pro-Martelly Parlementaires pour la Stabilité et le Progrès (PSP) grouping gained control of Haiti's lower house of parliament, with Jacques Stevenson Thimoléon elected president of the body.[63]

* * *

The same month as Duvalier had his official coming-out, another former Haitian president also made the headlines, though in a moment of far graver import.

On 17 January, Judge Yvikel Dabrésil announced the results of his inquiry into the April 2000 murders of Jean Dominique and Jean-Claude Louissaint and said evidence indicated that Jean-Bertrand Aristide had ordered his confidants to "silence" Dominique and tasked several underlings with that task. The judge indicted nine people for the murders: former Lavalas senator and head of the Aristide Foundation for Democracy Mirlande Libérus (now living in Florida), Lavalas militant-turned-Martelly ally Annette Auguste, former Port-au-Prince deputy mayor Harold Sévère, Franco Camille, Dymsley "Ti Lou" Milien, Jeudi "Guimy" Jean-Daniel and three others.[64] One of the key witnesses in the case, it turned out, was Aristide's former security chief, Oriel Jean, who had returned to Haiti after serving his sentence for drug trafficking in the United States and had given extended testimony to Dabrésil.[65] Michèle Montas, noting that it had been a decade since she had testified in the case, called the indictments "a positive step."[66] Another suspected conspirator, Philippe Markington (who had been both a member of the Aristide Foundation for Democracy and an informant for the U.S. Embassy), would eventually be detained in Argentina and, after several months, extradited to Haiti.[67]

Many were perplexed by the failure to indict Aristide, with Guy Delva, the former head of Haiti's Association des Journalistes Haïtiens (AJH) and a former Reuters correspondent who had briefly served in Lamothe's government, questioning: "How could you indict Libérus for receiving the order to get rid of Dominique, and not the person who gave the order?"[68] Shortly after the report was released, Delva held a press conference at the capital's Hotel Plaza to denounce what he said were threats Dabrésil had been receiving since his findings had been made public.[69] Newton Saint-Juste, wearing (as would Mario Joseph), his hat as one of Aristide's lawyers, attacked Oriel Jean as "not credible."[70]

* * *

At a late January meeting between the government and the opposition brokered by the Catholic Church, several currents, including MOPOD, FOPARK and Lavalas, refused to attend, with FOPARK's Rony Timothée instead announcing demonstrations against Martelly to be held.[71] Lavalas would eventually relent, and Maryse Narcisse would attend the consultations at the Hotel El Rancho.[72] Shortly thereafter, MOPOD announced that it had become "a political group" (one wonders what it considered itself before) and said that it would work for "the seizure of power," calling on Martelly and Lamothe to resign.[73] After seven days of meetings, Haiti's cardinal, Chibly Langlois, announced that those present at the El Rancho negotiations had arrived at a formula for a provisional CEP and a constitutional amendment to create a more permanent body.[74] The agreement was delayed, however, when Senate President Simon Dieuseul Desras refused to sign off on it, ostensibly because Martelly had published only seven of ten names for the country's auditing board in *Le Moniteur*, the official government publication.[75] By late February, high-level international delegations where shuttling in and out of Port-au-Prince, pleading with Haiti's political factions to sign an accord and pave the way for a vote.[76]

Part of the political wrangling involved the creation of a hugely bloated cabinet – 23 ministers and deputy ministers and 20 secretaries of state – that saw former Lavalassian Rudy Hériveaux become minister of communication, with Jean Renél Sanon continuing as minister of justice, as did Stéphanie

Villedrouin as minister of tourism, while Réginald Delva became minister of the interior.[77] The government showed its less conciliatory side at the beginning of February, when UDMO officers violently evicted dozens of families living in the Village Mosaïque section of the post-earthquake Canaan camp north of the capital, bulldozing houses that were meant to be permanent and tear-gassing and beating residents.[78] In a further black eye for the president, one of his strongest supporters in the senate, Wencesclas Lambert, brutalized a student, leading to protests for justice in Jacmel.[79] Lambert was subsequently found not guilty of the assault in a trial human rights groups called "a public scandal."[80]

* * *

On 8 February, Daniel Dorsinvil, the director of the POHDH human rights organization, and his wife, Girldy Larêche, died in a hail of gunfire as they were driving near Canapé Vert.[81] One of the believed hitmen, who had fired from a motorcycle, was arrested at a pre-carnival party on the Champ de Mars.[82] Five people would eventually be jailed for the crime, all part of the gang then dominating Grand Ravine.[83] It was believed that Grand Ravine gang leader Mackendy "Ti Kenken" François, one of the capital's most effective assassins for hire, was involved in the killing.[84] Questions abounded about the quality of the investigation, as the motive for the murder – and its intellectual authors – remained a mystery.[85]

Following the release of a kidnapped businessman, Samy El Azi, Aristide attorney and political activist Newton Saint-Juste told reporters that there was evidence of the involvement in the crime of Woodly "Sonson La Familia" Ethéart, a Haitian businessman and close associate of Martelly's brother-in-law, Kiko Saint-Rémy.[86] RNDDH was soon calling for the dismantling of what it called the "Gang Galil," allegedly Ethéart's criminal network. A report by the group alleged that the gang had received nearly $2 million in ransom money from the families of 13 people kidnapped between 2011 and 2014, and also noted that Ethéart and Kiko Saint-Rémy were apparently co-owners of the elegant Pétionville restaurant La Souvenance, which the president was known to frequent. It claimed that, although four members of the gang had been incarcerated, the leader (Ethéart) and the number two (Renél Nelfort) remained free, with Ethéart having apparently fled as police were about to raid his home.[87] At one point, Ethéart's wife was arrested for several days and then released.[88] Her attorney was former government commissioner Claudy Gassant.[89] Ethéart would eventually be arrested after surrendering to authorities in the company of Gassant.[90] Kiko Saint-Rémy bitterly accused Lamothe of having set Ethéart up, and called on government officials to lobby for the latter's release, calls that some said veered over the line towards threats.[91]

* * *

After more than two months of talks at the El Rancho, the government and the opposition finally signed an agreement mandating a first round of elections to be held on 26 October, with opposition senator Steven Benoît and Cardinal Chibly Langlois having played pivotal roles. Having rejected negotiations previously, Lavalas, Fusion and MOPOD did not sign the accord.[92] MOPOD announced that it would not take part in elections while Martelly was in power and would organize a new round of protests to drive him from office.[93] Other opposition figures made sneering homophobic references against Martelly and Benoît, calling the pact "a deal between Pétionville boyfriends."[94] Moïse Jean-Charles said that several senators, himself included, would not recognize the agreement and called for the formation of a new electoral council consisting of members drawn from nine different sectors of national life.[95] The author Lyonel Trouillot lashed out against the "reactionary passivity of the wealthy middle class … those who had shown the same passivity in the Duvalier years, who feel that things are going well because they are not disturbed in their daily routine."[96]

* * *

That April, the Conseil National des Télécommunications (CONATEL) issued a statement vaguely attacking certain radio stations for "broadcasting false information liable to disturb public order," and containing a not-so-subtle threat that stations could be sanctioned for violating broadcasting codes. As justification, CONATEL cited the notorious 1977 Duvalierist media law, which Aristide had also attempted to revive a decade earlier.[97] The Association Nationale des Médias Haïtiens denounced the statement.[98] A few days after the CONATEL declaration, RNDDH's Pierre Espérance received an anonymous letter in the mail accusing him of trying to destabilize the Martelly government and stating, in reference to the previous attack against him, "in '99 we missed you, this time you won't escape."[99] RNDDH would later say they believed Lamothe was behind the letter, while Rudy Hériveaux, assuming his new role with gusto, accused RNDDH of publishing "packs of lies" that cause

287

"harm" to democracy in Haiti.[100] As if to venture further into the dictatorial past, on the same day as the CONATEL declaration, some 200 men, dressed in FADH uniforms and, extraordinarily, Macoute denim, appeared in Belladère to name one Lucknel Morette as the head of the newly formed Parti de la Rénovation Nationale (PRN). Lest anyone miss the symbolism, one PRN member, Bernadin Constant, who claimed affiliation with the National Palace (which denied any such link), said "this is another page of 1957."[101]

* * *

I returned to Haiti that spring, landing in the Dominican city of Santiago and spending a pleasant evening chatting and drinking beer on the street with Haitian migrants who, despite the obvious hardships they were facing, all seemed relieved to have arrived at a place where they at least had a chance. The air-conditioned bus drove through the scrubland of the northwestern Dominican Republic, and I was pleasantly surprised to find that what used to be a multi-hour ordeal passing from the Dominican border to Cap-Haïtien had instead become an hour on a good road, with newer, lovely hotels such as Auberge du Picolet and the Habitation des Lauriers joining the old standbys of the Hotel Mont Joli and the Hotel Roi Christophe (the latter boasting a melancholy framed photo of its former owner, French consul Paul-Henri Mourral, slain in 2005). On the Boulevard du Carenage, a rollicking new restaurant – Lakay – had opened and was full of Haitians and foreigners and music almost every night. I even ran into tourists who had hopped over to Haiti from the Turks and Caicos to check out the Citadelle when they found the former island "too boring." Traversing the hairpin turns out to the Cormier Plage, I found a hotel full of visitors splashing in the surf and unexpectedly ran into a group of old friends at the hotel bar.

I drove to the Caracol industrial park in the company of Max Édouard Vieux, the representative of the Société Nationale des Parcs Industriels (SONAPI). It was late afternoon and the sun was slanting in a beautiful honeyed light across Haiti's fertile northern plains.

"With improved transportation, the port has been working much better, the people in the areas around Caracol are living much better, opening their own commerce and things like that," Vieux told me. Around the park, some 400 homes were now electrified that had never had electricity before. "Things are moving here," Vieux said.

At the park itself, however, there was a curiously somnolent air. Although the previous year had seen $28 million of output, by this point it was employing only 2,700 people out of the envisioned 60,000. Employees at Caracol made 200 gourdes for a workday lasting from 7am to 4pm. That translated into roughly $5 per day for a six-day working week, or $120 per month, or $1,440 per year, near-starvation wages. But some at the plant appeared glad to have the opportunity to make even that in a region where any sort of paying work had been scare not for years but for decades.

"After the industrial park opened, it was a big thing for the area, it was a beautiful change for the area," said Wesley Joseph, a supervisor at Sae-A Trading Co. Ltd as we walked through the complex.

After another bus ride – this one making a pit stop in Gonaïves where passengers feasted on the delicious spinach-based dish *lalo* – I arrived in Port-au-Prince. I was again impressed by the functioning traffic signals, street lights powered by solar panels and armies of apron-clad workers diligently sweeping the sidewalks and gutters of what had historically been the filthy fiefdom of Haiti's warring political factions. The huge billboards around the country bearing Martelly's image (in violation of Article 7 of Haiti's constitution), though, showed that the government had by no means entirely abandoned the realpolitik of Haiti's past. As they once did for Aristide, graffiti slogans around Port-au-Prince lauded the *bèl ekip* (beautiful team) of Martelly–Lamothe.

Although MINUSTAH was cautiously hailing the elections accord, the international community was still clearly worried. When I spoke with the MINUSTAH second-in-command, Carl Alexandre, he told me that though "there are a few parties who chose not to participate, it was an open process … It is our hope that those who didn't participate initially will want to join as the process unfolds, because the alternative is unthinkable. If the elections are not held this year, in January there will not be a functioning parliament. There will be no one there."

My friends among Haiti's civil society were even less optimistic.

"Despite everything that has happened in the last 30 years, it is as if they want us to return to the situation that existed before February 7, 1986," Laënnec Hurbon said to me as we sipped coffee in the garden of his house. When I went up the hill to Peguyyille to see Sylvie Bajeux, still soldiering on with the CEDH and the Collectif contre l'Impunité after Jean-Claude Bajeux's death, her sentiment was much the same.

"We are talking about the situation of impunity that has been the rule since François Duvalier came to power, and something has to be done to stop that," she told me. "If we don't, we are going nowhere, we cannot talk about reconstruction. Jean-Claude Duvalier's case has become the symbol for the need to put an end to impunity. He's being charged with monstrous deeds. So what is going to happen? What happens with Duvalier's case is something that will affect the whole future of this country."

I was staying with a friend, a Dutch NGO worker named Jan Voordouw, and we decided to take a weekend trip to Jacmel, a town where I had passed many pleasant days but hadn't visited in a decade. Snaking through the sludge-like traffic in Carrefour, we finally started climbing up into the mountains that separate the capital from the south coast, and before too long we saw Jacmel glittering like a jewel by the sea below us. We drove through its winding streets, still scarred by the remains of houses half-destroyed by the earthquake.

In my absence, Jacmel had built a beautiful *malecón* of exquisite tile along its seafront, facing the tumbling Caribbean and the mountains sloping dramatically in the distance. The town had a melancholy air, though, overrun by noisy moto taxis and blighted by boxy modern buildings replacing those damaged in the quake.

"It is not the same town that it once was," Madame Jolicoeur, the grande dame of the guest house were staying at, told us.

Parking on Rue du Commerce one day, we went into the old Hotel Florita, where I had stayed and caroused when I was a younger man. As we entered the hotel, it seemed nearly deserted. From somewhere, soft *konpa* played: keyboard runs and an ebullient male voice at once full of joy and longing. In the old building, wreathed in dripping greenery, the fountain that had once splashed in its garden was still, and the doors to the upstairs rooms were shut tight. As I stood in the garden in the gathering dusk, a single petal from the bougainvillea above came loose, floated through the air and came to rest in silence at my feet.

* * *

Another visitor came calling to Jacmel a few weeks after I did. Potential indictment or no, Haiti's former dictator seemed not at all worried, and in late April, Jean-Claude Duvalier – along with several hundred other people – inaugurated an office of his new political party, the Parti Unité Nationale (PUN) in the town center. [102] Shortly thereafter, Senate President Simon

Dieuseul Desras said he would request Martelly's resignation if elections weren't held by the end of the year.[103] Several hundred protesters calling for Martelly's resignation, led by MOPOD's Turneb Delpé and FOPARK's Rony Timothée, marched from Bel-Air's Notre-Dame du Perpétuel church down to Delmas and then to Lalue, setting at least one car aflame and breaking the windshields of others as they did so.[104]

* * *

Marking three years in power with a speech on the Champ de Mars, Martelly exhorted the opposition "You have to go to elections!" and in front of thousands of cheering supporters shouted *Eleksyon tèt dwat!* (Elections, forward all!).[105] A few days later, Martelly marked the two-year anniversary of his *Ti Manman Cheri* program at a Delmas park, lashing out at the opposition and promising to appoint as his successor "one of the young men selflessly devoted to the cause of the country."[106] This statement led many to speculate that Martelly intended to allow Lamothe to succeed him, speculation further fueled when Senator Jean-Baptiste Bien-Aimé stated publicly that Lamothe had consulted parliamentarians about obtaining the necessary *décharge* (basically a certificate of good conduct while in government), which Bien-Aimé said the senate had already decided not to give him.[107] On 17 May, FOPARK's Rony Timothée was beaten and arrested by police in what RNDDH called an "arbitrary and brutal" arrest.[108] When an opposition delegation including Mirlande Manigat and Gérald Gilles attempted to visit Timothée in prison in Arcahaie, PNH and a contingent of MINUSTAH troops prevented them from doing so.[109] When Moïse Jean-Charles tried to visit the prison several days later, he was literally flung into the street by a penitentiary officer.[110]

On 10 June, after several hours of waiting as they tried to gather participants, a new opposition march began to descend toward the Champ de Mars from the Église Notre-Dame in Bel-Air, quickly growing to several thousand.[111] This time, however, they were led by Arnel Bélizaire, who, dressed in a white polo shirt, marched with an M4 assault rifle dangling from a strap around his neck.[112] On at least one occasion, he fired it into the air.[113] Members of MOPOD and FOPARK participated in the march, including the latter's Byron Odigé (a former henchman of Saint-Marc's Bale Wouze),[114] as did the Mouvement de Liberté, d'Egalité des Haïtiens et de la Fraternité, a movement co-founded by one-time Lavalas militant David Oxygène. As was by now standard, anti-gay slogans directed at Martelly were daubed on walls as the marchers passed.[115] The chaotic march was eventually sent scattering by wild volleys of automatic gunfire shot into the air and heavy doses of tear gas dispensed by the UDMO.[116] The march appeared to be the beginning of another out-of-control spiral for Bélizaire, who, days later, allegedly assaulted and threatened to kill Phélito Doran, Martelly's minister in charge of relations with parliament, over a dispute regarding carnival funds.[117] The government strongly protested the alleged assault, issuing a statement recounting Bélizaire's past transgressions and calling him "a multi-recidivist who repeatedly behaves contrary to the dignity of parliament."[118] Surprisingly, Bélizaire was actually punished for the Doran assault, and was ejected from parliament for two months.[119] He would subsequently launch a quixotic "hunger strike" in his parliament office to advance a number of hazy "demands" – a hunger strike that was all but ignored as yet another *carnaval des fleurs* danced outside.[120]

* * *

Grand Ravine gang leader Mackendy "Ti Kenken" François, believed implicated in the murders of PNH officer Walky Calixte and POHDH's Daniel Dorsinvil and the latter's wife, Girldy Larêche, was slain in late July by his deputy Junior Doyle, aka Doy Junior.[121] Speaking to Radio Kiskeya, Doy said that Ti Kenken "had triggered the war" in Grand Ravine and that, when an unspecified NGO gave him money to improve the district, Ti Kenken had kept it for himself, spending the money on nice clothes, stripteases and even food for his dogs, while his followers "did not even have 25 gourdes for food." Doy went on to say that Grand Ravine "wanted peace."[122] Doy Junior would then enter into a co-partnership in the running of the slum with a gang leader nicknamed, like Martelly, Tèt Kale.

* * *

In late July, Max Mathurin – the president of the 2006 CEP – was elected president of its newest incarnation. Martelly first attempted to name seven out of nine officials to the body, but relented and withdrew two after an outcry, leaving the CEP composed of various representatives of the executive, judiciary and legislative branches of government.[123] With six opposition senators continuing to use parliamentary maneuvers to keep the CEP from functioning, Lamothe spokesman Michel Brunache called the legislators "kamikazes and enemies of democracy."[124] Martelly also vented his exasperation, noting that the senate had met only nine times in the preceding eight months and that "compared to the volume of work to do and the expectations of the population, the senators are not doing their job."[125] Pro-government senator Wencesclas Lambert would eventually say that opposition parliamentarians had 15 days to vote on the electoral law or those sympathetic to Martelly would resign to force an election.[126] Speaking on local radio, INITE's Paul Denis claimed that the international community, in particular the OAS, were "accomplices" of the government as, despite Martelly's failure to hold elections, they continued to fund and praise him.[127] Civil society organizations called on the government to organize yet another round of negotiations, almost pleading that "current leaders demonstrate the political maturity and patriotism to place the interests of the nation above their personal interests."[128]

Earlier in the summer, in typically despotic fashion, Aristide anointed Maryse Narcisse as the presidential candidate for Fanmi Lavalas, even though, contrary to party statutes, she did not become coordinator by a popular vote of party members.[129] The selection of Narcisse was viewed as a final rejection of Moïse Jean-Charles, who went on the radio to announce that "it is the U.S. Embassy and USAID who imposed Maryse Narcisse … Aristide is under the control of the imperialist countries."[130] A few weeks later, Aristide was summoned to appear before Judge Lamarre Bélizaire to answer questions pertaining to an investigation into alleged "drug trafficking, embezzlement of public funds, treason, bribery and money laundering." The summons noted that if Aristide failed to appear, a warrant could be issued for his arrest. As usual, Aristide's attorneys – Mario Joseph and Ira Kurzban – rushed to defend their client in the court of public opinion.[131] Joseph took particular aim at the journalist Guy Delva, whom he charged was the source of the president's legal troubles.[132] By mid-August, an arrest warrant was reportedly issued against Aristide, though not enforced, and the former president was subsequently said to be under "house arrest."[133]

* * *

Security continued to be fragile. On 12 August, dozens of prisoners escaped from the prison in Croix-des-Bouquets due to what a police spokesman called "a conspiracy carried out inside the prison," though some residents mentioned the arrival of three cars full of armed men. Among those who absconded was the accused crime ring leader Clifford Brandt, who was captured a day later by the Dominican army after he had crossed the border and was handed back to Haitian authorities.[134] On the night of 17 August, UDMO forces ran amuck in Petit-Goâve at the close of that town's yearly festival, killing two and injuring at least 43 in a display that the CSPN condemned.[135] In Cité Soleil's Bélékou quarter, five people were slain in an attack that some residents blamed on the leader of Soleil 17's armed *baz*, Gabriel Jean-Pierre. Jean-Pierre had begun life as an ordinary young person who liked football, but, along with other residents, he had helped push out a murderous group of criminals from the area around 2011. Soon thereafter, as one of the brightest young men in the slum, residents began coming to him with more and more problems until he eventually became the leader of the *baz*. Like so many others in this role, he had a foundation, the Foundation Gabriel, set up to do charitable works. Locals from Bélékou, however, alleged that Jean-Pierre had recently met with Lamothe and was more or less acting as the government's proxy enforcer in the slum in an effort to prevent all but pro-government candidates from competing in the looming election.[136] When Jean-Pierre was arrested, several hundred people from Cité Soleil demonstrated in front of police headquarters for his release.[137]

* * *

On 5 September, the Chamber of Deputies finally voted in favor of the implementation of the El Rancho Accord.[138] Four days later, as the parliamentary session ended and the senate had still not voted, Martelly issued a terse press release in which he noted that the six abstaining senators had been invited to a new round of negotiations.[139] Speaking at the United Nations two days later, U.S. Ambassador Samantha Power told the assembly that "Haitian political leaders had worked tirelessly to seek a resolution to the impasse ... [But] six Senators [are] holding elections hostage."[140] Addressing Senate President Simon Dieuseul Desras, a letter from 15 U.S. lawmakers told the senator that "we urge you and your colleagues to quickly pass legislation to enable elections to take place."[141] The body's vice president, Andrys Riché, warned that "the nation is expecting a dénouement, as civil war is at our door."[142] Eventually, John Joël Joseph, Jean William Jeanty, Jean-Baptiste Bien-Aimé and Pierre Francky Exius would meet with Martelly, while Moïse Jean-Charles and Wesner Polycarpe would refuse, with the latter saying that his colleagues "went to the fair with [Martelly], but they did not go in my name."[143] Apparently deciding that the time was ripe to have some good fun with one of his predecessors, Martelly withdrew Aristide's

USGPN security, resulting in the appearance of dozens of Lavalas partisans at the latter's mansion at Tabarre, supposedly to "defend" the president lest anyone try to arrest him.[144] When pro-Lavalas demonstrators attempted to approach Tabarre in the annual commemoration of the 30 September coup against Aristide, they were doused with tear gas and dispersed.[145]

* * *

The wars in the capital's slums churned on. Doy Junior, the Grand Ravine gang leader who had murdered and usurped his predecessor Ti Kenken, was himself slain after a brief war of succession with the gang leader Tèt Kale. POHDH's Antonal Mortimé bemoaned the fact that, with the killings of Ti Kenken and Doy Junior, the chances of tracing the intellectual author of the killing of the organization's head, Daniel Dorsinvil, and his wife grew ever more remote.[146] In La Saline, two Lavalas activists would also be killed in unclear circumstances, leading Moïse Jean-Charles to call on mourners at the funeral to "avenge" the deaths "by any means available."[147]

As the wars in the capital continued, I found myself traveling through the north. A photographer and I were on assignment for a travel magazine (for whom I penned a story that they decided was too strange to publish) and we were driving to Môle-Saint-Nicolas, on Haiti's far northwestern coast. Amid a stunning landscape of deep valleys and peaks alternating between dry scrub and palm-dotted fecundity, we passed through small settlements and scenes of women leading goods-laden donkeys down dirt lanes, the flags of vodou *peristyles* (temples) occasionally waving in the breeze, a direct cultural link to Haiti's African past. We passed through Jean-Rabel, the scene of a terrible 1987 massacre of peasants, but which turned out today to be peaceful and lush, with the characteristically dapper Haitians standing around and chatting with one another in the late afternoon light.

Finally, just after dark, we arrived in Môle-Saint-Nicolas, and a small inn run by an expatriate Frenchman built along a fringe of beach kissed by clear, warm water. That night we dined on shark as the stars revealed themselves festooning the night sky overhead.

One of the oldest towns in Haiti, Môle-Saint-Nicolas had a storied and dramatic history including successive occupations by the French, Spanish and British that had left it with multiple ruined forts dotting its environs. Walking down a narrow path framed by the long grass the Haitians call *zeb kanno*, I arrived at the Batterie de Grasse, which dated from 1773, its stone walls still solemnly guarding the entrance to the harbor as if waiting for its soldiers to return. Now, however, only batches of yellow butterflies and goats, braying unseen and hidden somewhere in the bushes, disturb the silence.

Further towards town, the Batteries de Vallières boasted a grand entrance, while the Fort Vieux Quartier, in the town proper, had rusting cannons still lining its walls, now patrolled by spry goats and the occasional rooster. But the gem of the entire collection was the Poudrière du Môle-Saint-Nicolas, a former gunpowder storage facility dating from 1765 that lay half-ruined but still imposing and grand, mildly toxic plants now defending its grounds. As in the Citadelle, here once again one felt the vibrations of the past so strongly that it might as well not be the past at all. That feeling was reinforced when, quite by chance, I spied a mural in the town square, lovingly painted and maintained, of a somber-looking man of middle age in a dark suit and thick glasses, his arms crossed, gazing out at the world with perhaps a trace of contempt. It was François Duvalier.

* * *

One Saturday afternoon in early October, Jean-Claude Duvalier, the scion of one of the hemisphere's most brutal dictatorships who himself had held the power of life and death over millions, collapsed in his Port-au-Prince home and died of a heart attack at the age of 63.[148] The man who had taken over a country when all but a boy from his psychopathic father, who had overseen the looting of its treasury, the further codification of Macoutism, who had looked impassively at the horrors of Fort Dimanche and other such prisons, and the echoes of whose reign were felt even today, left this world at home, never having had to face trial for his multitude of crimes.

Shortly after Duvalier died, I was sitting with Sylvie Bajeux in the CEDH office in Peguyville. We were drinking coffee and discussing the country's culture of impunity, how no one ever seemed to be punished for anything, no matter how grave the transgression, and the struggles that she and Jean-Claude Bajeux had fought over the years.

"There's something I want you to see," she said to me.

She handed me a glossy Haitian publication. *Viv Magazine*, the cover said. I flipped through its high-resolution depictions of Haiti's tourist attractions and advertisements for luxury goods and shops. Then Sylvie reached over and opened it to a specific page.

There was a photo of a black-suited man from the neck down, a flaming cylinder of tobacco clutched defiantly between his index finger and thumb. "Papa Doc Cigars" the advertisement proclaimed, and, lest anyone miss the point, the number 57 (the year of François Duvalier's inauguration) was printed on the band.

I pushed the magazine to one side, deeply disturbed. From the street outside, boys playing a pickup football game called to one another in the diminishing afternoon light. I stared into my coffee, its warmth vanishing in delicate curls of steam into the air, before looking back at Sylvie, who had, I thought, a slight, sad smile on her lips as she spoke.

"It was only once Duvalier returned that we realized he had never left."

CHAPTER SIXTEEN
A DISASTER FORETOLD

Duvalier was dead, but Duvalierism – or more specifically Jean-Claudisme – and its age-old foe, anarcho-populism, lived on.

By October 2014, the UN Security Council voted unanimously to prolong MINUSTAH's mandate, while at the same time ordering that its drawdown of troops continue,[1] as Martelly met with Préval to seek his support in exiting the electoral crisis.[2] MOPOD's Turneb Delpé stoked the racial fires by comparing Martelly to Pétion, who he charged was responsible for Dessalines' murder.[3] A demonstration of several thousand people took place in the capital on 26 October, at which Rony Timothée and Biron Odigé were both arrested for "inciting violence."[4] Arrest warrants were also issued against Assad Volcy and Franco Camille.[5] Simon Dieuseul Desras predicted that Martelly would suffer the same fate as Blaise Compaoré, the recently deposed and exiled dictator of Burkina Faso.[6] During an 18 November demonstration – where much of the vitriol was directed at Lamothe rather than Martelly – the president's brother-in-law, Kiko Saint-Rémy, even made an appearance, denouncing what he claimed was Lamothe's "macabre" plan for Haiti and confirming rumors of a split with Lamothe within the presidential family itself.[7] Demonstrations continued of varying degrees of size and intensity throughout November, to the point where, by the end of the month, Martelly had formed an advisory council consisting of, among others, former senator Gabriel Fortuné and the industrialist Réginald Boulos to help him find an exit from the crisis.[8] When U.S. Ambassador Pamela White attempted to meet with Fusion party members at the group's headquarters, she encountered stone-throwing protesters waving signs that read *Aba enjerans* (Down with interference) and *Fwa sa a nou pap pran dikte nan men anbasad amerikèn* (This time we won't take dictation from the American embassy).[9]

Several thousand anti-government protesters finally succeeded in reaching the National Palace on 5 December, the first time they had managed to do so.[10]

The following day, thousands more, led by Moïse Jean-Charles, marched in Cap-Haïtien.[11] Several days later during another protest, Arnel Bélizaire, again holding an assault rifle, approached and harangued Canadian MINUSTAH peacekeepers who, miraculously, did not shoot him. With typical Canadian understatement and politesse, Canada's ambassador to Haiti noted that "such provocative actions could dampen investor interest."[12]

In early December, Martelly's advisory council came back with its recommendations: the resignations of Lamothe, the head of the Supreme Court and the members of the CEP and the release of all "political prisoners."[13] Eventually Biron Odigé, Rony Timothée[14] and the Florestal brothers would all be freed from prison.[15] In an address to the nation, Martelly said that he accepted the recommendations and would implement them quickly. "He is willing to make that sacrifice," Martelly said, as Lamothe sat feet away from him.[16] In a taped speech that aired at nearly 2am, Lamothe told the nation: "We can say today, that after 31 months, the results are there ... We are going with the sentiment that we did all we could for the country ... I leave the post of prime minister this evening, with the feeling of accomplishment."[17]

* * *

I was visiting Cap-Haïtien when Lamothe finally resigned. I was staying in the Auberge Picolet that faced the *malecón*, a melancholy drizzle blanketing the city, concealing the mountains on the other side of the bay behind a curtain of mist and reflecting the sense of a place seemingly stuck eternally in the wet, restrictive clay of its genesis and of historical forces greater than any one man.

I had been doing a brief consultancy for an international organization working in Haiti at the time. My photographer, Hilary Wallis, a local friend, Angela Salellas, and I had driven up from Port Salut, where we had risen by the sea in the early morning to watch fishermen standing in the azure surf and pulling their nets onto shore. Earlier, we had driven through nearby Camp Perrin, its lanes lined by the melancholy (but highly picturesque) above-ground tombs of departed residents under dripping vegetation. We had visited the Artibonite hamlet of Grande-Saline, turning off Route National 1 to traverse lush green fields where cows and horses munched contentedly on grass growing up through the water and a seemingly endless supply of rice was laid out to dry on tarps under the sun in front of humble shacks. In Grande-Saline itself, abutting the ocean and built among rice fields strung out under a piercing blue sky, a new Swiss-manufactured solar-powered water treatment system was generating a melodious hum, its solar panels vaulting towards the sky and residents arriving to collect drinking water in jerry cans or large plastic jugs. Residents told me that, before the water treatment system, they would have to go all the way to Saint-Marc in order to buy water, a nearly two-hour drive. Residents had formed a *komite dlo* (water committee) to manage the system, which ensured that the town's population had a personal stake in and responsibility for its maintenance. And we once more visited Caracol, which, three years after its opening, still employed only around 2,800 people of the envisioned 60,000, most of them in Sae-A Trading Co. Ltd and the Haitian painting firm Peintures Caraïbes. In nearby Limonade, one late Friday afternoon, we found residents in a party mood – men playing dominos on the street, young men and women flirting, and women frying Haitian *marinade* in great metal pots.

"We have electricity now," said Norvella Ateus, a resident of Limonade, 65 years old and dignified in a straw hat and purple blouse, as she sat on a low wall chatting with her neighbors. "They built a school. Things are getting better."

Martelly and Lamothe were far from angels. Their tenure steering Haiti's ship of state was marked by an atmosphere of nepotism and corruption, and they showed no more appetite for battling the country's gangrenous impunity than any of the leaders who had come before them. But, despite that, they made a dynamic team, and had gone farther, against all expectations, towards changing Haiti's perpetually negative image than many ever thought possible. A window of opportunity seemed to be opening for the country that I had seen only once before, during the summer of 2009 before the earthquake. They seemed to try, in their way, to at least suggest the possibility that Haiti need not forever remain what it had for so long been.

Months after Lamothe resigned, after watching him speak to a packed and enthusiastic crowd at Florida International University in Miami, I sat and chatted with him in the lobby of the building where he maintains an apartment, just off Miami Beach's Venetian Causeway. He expressed a frustration that I found familiar among those I had previously spoken to from inside Haiti's political system.

"It's cronyism and personal greed that dictates political decisions, and that's what makes the country fail at times," Lamothe told me. "Everybody lives off politics and that means you have to have the country unstable in order to be relevant. In order for someone to be relevant they have to break a car window, they have to burn a tire. But how does that help Haiti?"[18]

* * *

Rather than mollifying the opposition, Lamothe's departure seemed to embolden them to new extremes. Assad Volcy, now affiliated with a new political party, the Platfòm Pitit Desalin (Children of Dessalines), told AlterPresse: "We fight for the fall of the government [and] we are moving towards the overthrow of the regime."[19] Although Pitit Desalin was to a large degree a creation of the Lavalas defectors who had followed Moïse Jean-Charles out of the party, it would eventually also come to host individuals such as Claudy Gassant and the attorney Evel Fanfan. Separately, Maryse Narcisse told several hundred Lavalas supporters in Tabarre that the party was fighting for "free elections, fair and democratic," an ironic statement given the party's history of thwarting just such aims.[20] Martelly met with a series of political groupings – Fusion, Kontrapèpla, INITE, Ayisyen pou Ayiti, OPL – but Pitit Desalin would refuse time and again.[21]

The security situation around the capital was again deteriorating, with JILAP noting 223 people killed by gunfire between October and early December.[22] On 21 December, Joceline Pierre, briefly the head of the PNH under Aristide and former dean of the civil court, was found strangled in her home in the Vivy Mitchell neighborhood.[23] Along with many other victims of violence, her body was left to putrefy in a poorly refrigerated morgue in what *Le Nouvelliste* referred to as "an intolerable situation."[24] PNH chief Godson Orélus told reporters that he believed up to 250,000 illegal firearms were circulating in the country.[25] JILAP's Rovelson Apollon worried that the coming elections would be "a disaster foretold," and noted that each of Cité Soleil's 34 neighborhoods was dominated by a different gang leader and that much of the recent violence there was due to different political factions angling for control, a scenario the group worried was being reproduced across the country.[26] Alix Fils-Aimé, who had run Préval's disarmament program, said the country was witnessing "a struggle between political protagonists for a piece of the pie" and that the figures were "extremely worrying, because now we are starting to get closer to countries with high crime rates such as Jamaica, Venezuela and Honduras."[27]

* * *

In his waning days in power, something of a *lekol lagé* (school's out) mentality seemed to develop within Martelly and his coterie, during which excess was not only tolerated but actively encouraged. In a startling display of Baby Doc-esque cynical largess, at a pre-Christmas reception for journalists, Martelly handed out envelopes stuffed with 50,000 and 40,000 gourdes (around $800 and $700 respectively), which he classified as "a small gift."[28] The president's entourage continued to generate gossip, with both RNDDH and *Le Nouvelliste* reporting that Martelly's brother-in-law Kiko Saint-Rémy had assaulted Minister of Agriculture Fresner Dorcin in a dispute over a government contract the former wanted.[29]

With Lamothe gone, Martelly was free to pick a more pliable prime minister, and, in doing so, reached back to a perennial figure in Haitian politics. On Christmas Day, startling nearly everyone, Martelly announced that he was nominating veteran politico and opposition leader Evans Paul.[30] It was a politically adroit selection, as, with one move, Martelly appeared to be offering the opposition a plum role while at the same time elevating someone known as a bitter enemy of the fractured and divided Lavalas. It was noted that, unless he was approved before 12 January, when the mandates of all members of parliament expired, he could *automatically* become prime minister.[31]

The announcement of Paul's selection appeared to disorient the opposition. At one announced protest, only a few hundred people showed up. A scheduled 26 December demo was simply canceled for lack of interest.[32] Paul struck a moderate tone, saying: "I'm not the prime minister to make war on anyone, to fight anyone."[33] At year's end, Martelly and the parliament signed a deal agreeing that, providing a new electoral law was passed, the terms of deputies would expire in April 2015 and those of senators in September 2015, as opposed to on 12 January.[34] MINUSTAH's Sandra Honoré said she welcomed the "advances" and "gestures of goodwill" symbolized by the deal.[35]

One could have wondered how deep the reservoir of goodwill ran, however. When Martelly summoned parliament to a special session to discuss the new law, the session had to be canceled because the representatives refused to return from holiday.[36] Finally, on 7 February, Martelly met with a group of senators who had formed a special committee to negotiate an end to the legislative impasse, including Jocelerme Privert (who had been a sitting senator from the Nippes department since 2011 for Préval's INITE), Jean William Jeanty, Francisco Delacruz and Edwin Zenny.[37] Chile's ambassador to the UN, Cristián Barros (Chile was a major provider of troops to MINUSTAH) said that "the priority of the president of Haiti should be to develop a credible electoral timetable."[38] On 8 January, protesters organized by MOPOD and Pitit Desalin carried ropes through the streets of Port-au-Prince and chanted "We prefer the civil war ... the burning of the parliament ... to negotiation!"[39] Two days later, about 1,500 young men burned tires and threw rocks at police.[40]

The U.S. Embassy wrote in a statement that it "strongly supports the efforts by President Martelly to arrive at a global political consensus to resolve the political impasse in Haiti ... [But] despite the President's wide-ranging concessions, parliament has not voted an electoral law ... We urge all parties to agree on a framework for parliamentary mandates, a new Provisional Electoral Council, passage of amendments to the electoral law and the formation of a government of consensus."[41] In the last hours before the parliamentarians' terms expired, the body tried – and failed – to hold a vote. Once again, not enough senators had shown up to achieve a quorum.[42]

Bypassing parliament, Martelly met with 11 political parties – including Fusion, INITE, Kontrapèpla and AAA – at the Hotel Kinam and signed an agreement pertaining to the formation of a new government and the holding of elections.[43] After the expiration of parliament's mandate, the so-called "Core Group" (the ambassadors of Brazil, Canada, France, Spain, the U.S. and the EU, and the special representatives of MINUSTAH and the OAS) issued a press release stating that it "[deplored] the fact that the Haitian Parliament has become dysfunctional and expresses its support to the President of the Republic in the exercise of his constitutional duty," and that it welcomed the new political agreement.[44]

On the fifth anniversary of Haiti's earthquake, as he attended a ceremony at the mass grave near Titanyen, Martelly said solemnly:

> On this 12 January, there was no Lavalas, there was no Macoute, there was no deputy, there was no "my man," there was no white, there was no black ... All Haitians were victims, and all Haitians were helping one another without discrimination ... The country has enough problems already ... This [political upheaval] is too much. Let's give the country a chance in the name of all these victims.[45]

In mid-January, after several of his supporters brawled with police, some self-declared demonstrators in the camp of Moïse Jean-Charles in Milot announced that they were abandoning "peaceful" struggle for an approach of *koupe tèt, boule kay*.[46] When Ducken "Ti Blan" Monfrère, the leader of one alleged armed group, was killed in a confrontation with police, Jean-Charles distanced himself from their actions.[47] When U.S. Ambassador Pamela White visited the remaining parliamentarians at the parliament building, Pitit Desalin issued a statement accusing her of being "the project manager for Tèt Kale," who "acts as if Haiti was a state in the United States."[48]

* * *

Martelly and Paul announced the formation of the latter's government on 19 January. It was one of 18 ministers and 16 secretaries of state, with, among others, Duly Brutus as minister of foreign affairs, veteran journalist Rotchild François Jr as minister of communication, and the opposition's Victor Benoît as minister of social affairs.[49] Paul's decision to name the scandal-plagued Josué Pierre-Louis as his chief of staff met with outrage from Haitian human rights groups, with RNDDH and SOFA calling it indicative of "the trivialization of impunity."[50] Following the announcement of Benoît's participation in the government, Fusion's headquarters in the capital was attacked with rocks and bottles.[51] A Fusion activist was also subsequently murdered in Martissant.[52] The radical opposition announced that they would continue their protests, and demonstrators in the capital on 22 January robbed pedestrians and burned a state vehicle.[53] RNDDH wrote that it "deplored the fact that citizens who do not participate in these streets movements are robbed and vehicles were vandalized."[54]

Martelly announced that he had constituted a new CEP to oversee elections, headed by Pierre-Louis Opont, and including nine representatives of various sectors of Haitian society.[55] The Core Group announced its pleasure at its formation[56] and RNDDH also announced its guarded approval of the body.[57] Meeting with a delegation of the UN Security Council, Martelly again reiterated his determination to hold elections before the end of the year.[58]

An opposition-led call for a general strike, ostensibly linked to rising fuel prices, led to a split among Haiti's trade unions, with some in support and some opposed to the measure.[59] MOPOD's Turneb Delpé accused the unions of "stabbing the opposition in the back," exposing once more the gap between the politicians and the people they claimed to speak for.[60] In several parts of the capital, the strike was enforced with threats and acts of violence.[61] A subsequent protest by university students was also marked by violence, with at least two vehicles burned and the windshields of others smashed.[62] As an opposition spokesman vowed to "tighten the screws" on the government, Martelly spokesman Lucien Jura described the methods by which the stoppages were enforced as "not a strike" but rather "hostage-taking and terrorism."[63]

* * *

Despite the chaos, some signs of progress stubbornly continued. In Léogâne, Martelly inaugurated a new school and a library.[64] Work continued on a hydro-electric dam in the Artibonite, which had been commenced by the government of Jean-Claude Duvalier nearly four decades earlier and then revived under the second Préval administration, and which Lamothe had obtained funding from Brazil's BNDES to intensify work on.[65] A French group began financing the production of cacao in the north to the tune of €1.2 million over four years.[66] Venezuela's ambassador to Haiti, Pedro Antonio Canino Gonzalez, took the unusual step of stating publicly that audits had been conducted of 234 PetroCaribe projects in Haiti and that the Venezuelan government was "satisfied" with the management of the projects.[67]

Many worried that Haiti was ushering in an *année terrible* when, during carnival, a horrific electrical accident with the float of the well-known rap group Barikad Crew killed 18 and injured 78, leading to the cancellation of the nation's famous bacchanal for the first time since the earthquake.[68] It was taken as an ill omen for the days ahead.

In the northern Dominican city of Santiago, a young Haitian man, Jean Claude Jean, was found publicly hanged in mid-February, an image that brought to mind some of the most horrific moments of racial hatred in the Americas.[69] The response in Haiti itself was one of outrage, and during a march on the Dominican consulate, some protesters tore down the Dominican flag and burned it, attempting to hoist a Haitian flag in its place.[70] Foreign Minister Duly Brutus quickly condemned the act and said those who committed it "did not represent the majority of Haitians."[71] Following the incident, at a march in Santo Domingo, Dominican ultra-nationalists called for the deaths of local journalists reporting on the abuses of Haitians in the country, all of whom they charged were "traitors" and "pro-Haitian."[72]

* * *

In the middle of the afternoon of 2 March, just off Delmas 30 and in full view of dozens of witnesses, gunmen on a motorcycle mowed down Aristide's former security chief, Oriel Jean. Although Jean had cash on him, none was taken, nor was his vehicle.[73] Both SOS Journalistes and the CIAPEAJ condemned the killing of one of the key witnesses in the Jean Dominique murder, and said that for months Jean had been the target of death threats from individuals close to Aristide to such an extent that they had attempted to solicit special police protection for him. Jean, they said, had always expressed his readiness and commitment to testify before the criminal court regarding the Dominique case.[74]

Though it was not widely known, about a year before his murder, Jean had sat down with journalist Guy Delva and recorded a long interview in which he claimed how, around 1999, Aristide had launched "an offensive" against Dominique because of the latter's critical stance in regard to the corruption and violence that was taking hold in Lavalas. Haiti's radio listeners sat transfixed as the dead man's voice issued eerily from Radio Caraïbes, which broadcast part of the interview.

"President Aristide said that if Jean Dominique was not subdued, it would be a handicap to his return to power," Jean told his interlocutor, adding that it was only after Dominique's murder that he understood the meaning of those words. Jean said that Aristide had seen the rise of KOZEPEP, linked to Dominique and Préval, as a possible precursor to a Dominique presidential run, and that he had contracted Mirlande Libérus (who, Jean said, had described Dominique as "a cancer") to "silence" the journalist.[75] Delva said that by broadcasting the interview he hoped he could encourage other witnesses to come forward. Eventually, the government said it would seek the arrest and extradition of Mirlande Libérus, then resident in Florida.[76] The PNH would eventually arrest two suspects in Jean's murder outside the Pitit Desalin headquarters in Delmas.[77]

* * *

A mid-March call for a strike was so feebly adhered to that the opposition canceled a planned second day.[78] Tens of thousands of people, on the other hand, participated in a "fitness walk" the government organized for 15 March.[79]

In a communiqué, the government informed Haiti that elections would be held in two rounds, on 9 August and 25 October, with the presidential vote occurring on the second date and going to a second round, if need be, on 27 December. The release concluded by exhorting "the firm determination of the

Executive to facilitate the holding of free, credible, independent, transparent and inclusive elections, [and inviting] all citizens of voting age and holders of their national identification card to perform their civic duty and at the same time contribute to the strengthening of democracy and the rule of law."[80] MOPOD, Pitit Desalin and Lavalas were coy about whether or not they would go to the polls.[81, 82] By 19 March, however, more than 20 parties, including OPL, Fusion, INITE and Lavalas, had registered with the CEP for the upcoming vote.[83] By the time it was all over, 192 political parties had registered, proof if any was needed of the factionalized and riven nature of Haiti's political scene.[84] A total of 166 parties, including most of those most severely opposed to the government (MOPOD transformed itself from a coalition to a party, for example), would make the final cut.[85] Martelly, Préval and Aristide would all be represented in the election with Martelly having formed the PHTK to front a slate of his own candidates and the other two represented by INITE and Lavalas respectively. The CEP's Opont speculated that elections would cost somewhere in the neighborhood of $60 million.[86] Speaking to the UN Security Council in New York in late March, MINUSTAH's Sandra Honoré told attendees that Haiti was "relatively stable."[87]

If international observers weren't worried about the climate in the country as it headed towards a vote, Haitians were, with journalist Gotson Pierre asking, quite naturally, "Is it possible today, in the current institutional and security conditions, to achieve good elections in Haiti?" and CRESFED's Suzy Castor noting that "clientelism is at the heart of Haitian political practice."[88] As if to underline her point, following an April court appearance before the pro-Martelly judge Lamarre Bélizaire, accused Gang Galil leader Woodly "Sonson La Familia" Ethéart and his associate Renél "Le Recif" Nelfort were summarily released, with the judge claiming that there was "insufficient evidence" of their guilt.[89] RNDDH called the releases "outrageous" and "illegal."[90]

* * *

The slate of candidates was an eclectic and disturbing one, with Haiti's Cardinal Chibly Langlois drolly noting during a homily in Jacmel that the search for both gainful employment and the privileges that came with holding office (such as immunity) appeared to be motivating factors.[91] Extraordinarily, candidates were allowed to throw their hats into the ring without first having a letter of police clearance of criminal charges.[92]

Among those on the pro-Martelly PHTK ticket for parliament were the president's wife, Sofia (who would be disqualified by electoral authorities amid questions about her citizenship), former Lavalas militant and accused conspirator in the Jean Dominique slaying Annette Auguste, Les Cayes businessman Hervé Fourcand, who was accused of involvement in the December 2011 violence in that city[93] and of having been a former FRAPH attaché,[94] and former Maïssade mayor Willot Joseph (previously Lavalas, now PHTK), who had been linked to violence in the 2010 election and the November 2000 attack on the MPP meeting in Hinche during which five people were shot.[95] Two other parties, Youri Latortue's AAA and Bouclier, a party formed by Calixte Valentin, were closely identified as being sympathetic to PHTK and the latter would even run former Lavalas baron Nawoon Marcellus as its senate candidate in the north.[96] On the Lavalas slate, Shiller Louidor and Louis Gérald Gilles ran for senate, but, startlingly, the party seemed to think that indicted Franco Camille, also sanctioned for his alleged role in the Jean Dominique murder, would make an appealing candidate for office in Port-au-Prince. In the Lavalas spinoff Renmen Haïti, René Civil would register to run for senate. Two of the former leaders of the 2004 rebellion that toppled Aristide, DEA fugitive Guy Philippe and former FRAPH co-leader Lois Jodel Chamblain, would also run for office in the Grand Anse, for senator and deputy respectively. Arnel Bélizaire would attempt to ascend from deputy to senator, as would M'Zounaya Bellange Jean-Baptiste, accused in the Walky Calixte killing. A senate candidate for Evans Paul's KID, Alfredo Antoine, had spent three years in jail and would be arrested – and then released – on a forgery charge in the middle of the election and keep right on campaigning.[97]

The presidential field was just as crowded, and just as strange, with an initial list of 70 candidates. After shunting Lamothe aside, Martelly would eventually settle on Jovenel Moïse, a relatively unknown agribusinessman from the country's north whose cultivation of bananas quickly earned him the nickname *nèg banann* (banana man), as PHTK's presidential candidate. Moïse Jean-Charles would run as the candidate for Pitit Desalin, Samuel Madistin for MOPOD, veteran politico Sauveur Pierre Etienne for OPL, former senator Edmonde Supplice Beauzile for Fusion, Steven Benoît for Conviction, peasant leader Chavannes Jean-Baptiste for Kontrapèpla, former PNH chief Mario Andrésol as an independent, and, rounding out the crowded field, Maryse Narcisse for Lavalas and Jude Célestin as the candidate of the newly formed Ligue

Alternative pour le Progrès et l'Émancipation Haïtienne (LAPEH). To make things even more unpredictable, two of the most formidable candidates, Université Quisqueya rector Jacky Lumarque, who was running as the candidate for Préval's political platform Vérité (itself essentially of spinoff of the still-extant INITE), and Laurent Lamothe himself, who attempted to run as the candidate for the Plateforme Paysan, were ruled ineligible by the CEP due to what was said to be the lack of a positive *décharge* certificate for Lamothe's duties while minister of planning and Lumarque's time on two government commissions.[98] Most viewed the *décharge* issue as little more than a feint and an excuse to exclude both men. Many were clearly worried about Préval's continuing influence, real or imagined. Préval's own former justice minister, Camille Leblanc, now of Renmen Ayiti, and Rudy Boulos, whose second attempt at the senate was rejected by the CEP, accused the former president of "controlling" the CEP and of colluding with Martelly to "steal" the election.[99] Essentially, the vote pitted various strains of the Jean-Claudiste vision of the country (PHTK, AAA, Bouclier) against the anarcho-populist tendency as typified by Lavalas, Pitit Desalin and Renmen Ayiti, with Vérité, Fusion and OPL introducing a quasi-social democratic current. As election materials arrived from South Africa at the end of June, the CEP announced that it was holding firm to its 9 August date for the first round of elections.[100] Campaigning began on 9 July.

* * *

Around the capital, reorganization of the armed political nexus seemed to be taking place. On 14 June, Mackenson Salomon, the leader of an armed group in Cité Soleil, was killed in what MINUSTAH and the PNH characterized as an exchange of fire. The following day, gunmen attacked the police commissariat there.[101] Two days later, thousands of people in the district demonstrated against MINUSTAH, saying that Salomon had been a benefactor and protector of their community.[102] An attack by the Baz 117 in Simon Pelé near the airport left at least eight dead, according to residents.[103]

* * *

By mid-2015, a "psychosis of fear" was rife among Haitians living in the Dominican Republic.[104] In eight days in June, more than 4,000 were expelled to the Plateau Central.[105] Finally, on 3 July, at the CARICOM summit in Barbados, Martelly spoke up, decrying the fact that "Dominican authorities prefer to speak of assisted voluntary repatriation when it is often violent deportations," accusing the Dominican government of "using every trick [and] systematically refusing" to discuss their rights and responsibilities to Haitians in the Dominican Republic and Dominicans of Haitian descent, and saying that the international community "could not be silent" in the face of such abuses.[106] By November, hundreds of Haitians were living in ghastly conditions in the border community of Anse-à-Pitres, with some – especially young children – dying of diseases directly linked to poor sanitation.[107] By the following month, that number would grow to over 3,000.[108] For weeks, Haitian authorities would do virtually nothing to help them. Instead, Martelly spoke again about how he wanted to create a new Haitian army before the end of his mandate to bolster security, and, indeed, a group of trainees who were to form its nucleus were being trained by Ecuadorian advisors in Petite Rivière de l'Artibonite.[109] However, for the moment, he appeared to content himself with the creation of a new elite police unit called the Brigade d'Opération et d'Intervention Départementale (BOID), which had received training from both CIVPOL and MINUSTAH.[110]

* * *

As the capital waited to hear which candidates would compete and which would be rejected, a heavy atmosphere hung over Port-au-Prince, punctuated by burning tires and gunshots. The omens once the campaign began were not auspicious. Préval's Vérité initially seemed to bear the brunt of attacks, with three activists slain by motorcycle gunmen as they put up posters in Carrefour, another partisan killed in the Artibonite's Grande-Saline, and a candidate in Gressier attacked by unknown gunmen as he attempted to launch his campaign.[111] In Petit-Goâve, a brawl between the supporters of two rival candidates left three injured.[112] Seeing the uptick of violence, JILAP's Rovelson Apollon warned that "there are the hidden hands of politicians in the violence in the country a few weeks before the elections, and quite often politicians use violence to get elected," adding that "a mafia sector, very close to the government, is involved in the sale of weapons and ammunition."[113]

* * *

It was around this time that I found myself sitting inside a Day-Glo-colored nightclub in the hillside slum of Ti Bois, speckled with squat cement houses over a commanding view of the bay. I was chatting with Cristla Chéry, the

32-year-old leader of the Ti Bois *baz*, who pushed his baseball cap back on his head and outlined his community's problems.

"We don't have water, we don't have electricity, we don't have anything here. The state is completely absent from this neighborhood," he said, as the Caribbean winds clattered over the zinc roof. "This is a prison where we are deprived of our liberty. We would like the freedom of every person here to enter society."

The neighborhood wrapped like a necklace around the southern hills of the capital. From this remove, the city pulsed below, a nearly silent tableau of the tumbling azure ocean, curling smoke rising from burning garbage, and thousands upon thousands of cars.

Although many referred to Chéry and his compatriots as gang leaders – as with others filling his role elsewhere – they had a different perception of themselves. Chéry and his men enacted a role that fell somewhere between political pressure group, warlord and tax collector, gathering tolls from the various supply trucks that passed along the narrow lanes. He had already been in and out of prison, and had seen how politicians had used people like him and his friends. As such, he had given the order that they were not to do "political" work anymore.

"For years, the politicians would ask us to burn tires, to cause disorder … but there was no development, and we don't want that anymore," he told me.

(Chéry was not alone. Several witnesses told me that, when Arnel Bélizaire had appeared in Saint Martin to seek support for his political ambitions, he had been relieved of his weapon and his money and sent out of the neighborhood with a message not to return.)

Louis-Henri Mars' Lakou Lapè had been working with Chéry to try to bring a durable peace to Ti Bois.

"It's like three steps forward, two steps backward," Louis told me. "But we know it takes time. Change comes from positive encounters and relationships that make positive connections happen. They allow you to get a different world view to come out of the craziness you've been living in."

By this point, relations between Ti Bois and Grand Ravine were relatively calm. Just a few streets below Chery's house I entered FOKAL's beautiful Parc de Martissant, a restful space filled with dripping vegetation and bright bird of paradise flowers. There were hints of hope all around, but still so much to be done. The gang leader Dymsley "Ti Lou" Milien, the alleged killer of Jean Dominique who had broken out of jail, was still in the background, regularly

311

calling his followers among the gangsters in Grand Ravine from a foreign mobile number, as they listened, rapt, the phone held aloft to transmit his words.[114]

Later, Louis-Henri and I sat sharing a beer at a nightclub/restaurant, Yanvalou, that had opened near my old home in Pacot. Around us were painted murals of some iconic Haitian cultural figures. One of them was the great singer Toto Bissainthe. One of them was Louis' grandfather, Jean-Price Mars.

"You know," Louis said as we sipped our Prestige, so cold that ice still clung to the bottle despite the tropical heat, "my grandfather said that losing the 1930 presidential election was the best thing that ever happened to him. He told me 'I would have lost my soul'."

When I went to visit Mario Andrésol at his home, where he was hosting a meeting of young activists from Bel-Air and Cité Soleil, he had his own thoughts about what direction the country should take.

"We need to redefine ourselves as a nation, and the vision is to change a corrupted system," Andrésol told me. "We need to have institutional reinforcement. The executive, the legislative and the judiciary are supposed to be independent, but they're not. The president has too many privileges, too many prerogatives. The president needs to understand that he's the servant of the people."

* * *

There were worrying signs about the economy as well. In May it was revealed that the government was running a deficit of more than 1 billion gourdes ($16,836,070).[115] By July, BRH governor Charles Castel said the trade deficit was around $3 billon, with Haiti exporting just under $1 billion worth of goods per year (mostly from the assembly sector) while importing around $3 billion, with the gap largely covered by remittances from the diaspora.[116] And since the departure of Lamothe nine months earlier, Martelly appeared to have grown ever more bellicose and erratic.

First there had been an obscene tirade by an apparently intoxicated Martelly at a concert by the American musicians Chris Brown and Lil Wayne, only ending when he was led offstage by his son, Olivier.[117] A few days later, during a political rally in Miragoâne, Martelly, standing in front of the PHTK logo of an upraised fist, verbally attacked a woman in the audience who had complained about the lack of electricity where she lived, by essentially telling her in front of the crowd that she should go and get fucked up against a wall.[118] He later claimed that he had not used the word for whore (*bouzen*) but rather one for cousin (*kouzen*) and was in fact talking to a man in the audience.[119] Nevertheless, a chorus of outrage ensued. A group of human rights and women's organizations wrote that "this behavior reflects the president's contempt for women."[120] Members of Fusion quit Evans Paul's cabinet in protest.[121] Weeks after the Miragoâne incident, as Haiti hosted CARIFESTA, Martelly called Communications Minister Rotchild François Jr on stage and guffawed to the audience: "There is nothing easier than being minister of communication – he lies every day!"[122] A few weeks later, adding to the impression of laissez-faire corruption and drift, the government announced that it would be initiating a "financing" scheme to allow local journalists to buy automobiles, thereby reducing pollution and congestion in the capital (many saw it as an obvious bribe).[123] Later still, the government announced that 23 government ministers would get severance packages of around $50,000 each when their terms ended as well as free police protection for at least six months.[124]

* * *

An EU electoral observation mission wrote that, of the 20 rallies they observed, "only those of PHTK brought together several thousand people when others are attended by at most a few hundred participants," an observation that could be interpreted as either a measure of PHTK's support or of its skill at spreading around largesse to fill their crowds with spectators.[125] As elections approached, the situation grew ever more fraught. Two people were shot at a PHTK rally in Mirebalais, violence the government blamed on the opposition.[126] In Petit-Goâve, PHTK and Vérité supporters continued to clash sporadically.[127] PHTK supporters assaulted a pastor outside Jacmel when he protested at campaign posters being affixed to his church.[128] Violence between the camps of opposing candidates erupted in the Artibonite, leading to at least one death.[129] While the CEP took the press on a guided tour of its vote tabulation center, where it said 800 technicians would help count the vote, and said that all was on course for the first round to be held on 9 August,[130] RNDDH warned that the country was heading for "an electoral disaster" and "a post-electoral crisis" because the vote was taking place in a "climate of terror."[131]

* * *

Voting day – to select two-thirds of the senate and the entire Chamber of Deputies – began amid little traffic (public transportation had been banned), technical difficulties and the failure of many polling stations to open at the appointed hour.[132] In Savanette, three voting centers were burned, and armed, hooded men roamed the area around the town.[133] Two were slain in Mirebalais and one in Dondon,[134] and at least three voting centers in the capital region were ransacked.[135] In Arcahaie, the PHTK candidate was accused of trying to rig the vote, while in Cabaret it was the candidate for Fanmi Lavalas.[136] In Belladère and Savanette, activists of Renmen Ayiti and the Rapwoche party protested what they charged was an attempt by Fusion to rig the vote there.[137] In Mirebalais, the candidates for deputy from Pitit Desalin, Fanmi Lavalas and Vérité were all arrested for incitement to violence.[138] In Jacmel, eight were arrested.[139] The city would see seven days of violent protests between supporters of rival candidates.[140]

A network of 1,500 observers deployed by RNDDH, the CNO and the Conseil Haïtien des Acteurs Non Étatiques (CONHANE), however, reported irregularities, fraud and violence, including activists of various political parties acting as electoral observers; arbitrarily curtailed or extended hours at voting centers; inferior indelible ink to mark the fingers of voters, which allowed for multiple voting; and armed men either threatening voters or trashing voting locations in several areas.[141]

Despite the fact that 26 voting centers had to shut due to disturbances and despite the fact that electoral authorities would eventually say an astonishing 290,000 voters could not cast their ballots, the CEP declared itself largely satisfied with the results.[142] The CEP put the official voter participation at 18 percent, with an even lower rate of 10 percent for the West Department around the capital.[143] The EU observation mission called the vote "a positive step,"[144] a sentiment echoed almost word for word by the OAS observer mission.[145]

Calling the elections "the most Haitian ever" (he did not mean it as a compliment), the author Gary Victor wrote that the vote was defined by "preplanned poor organization, disorder, violence and obvious fraud, against a backdrop of a sidelined population that dare not get through the hordes of *baz*" to vote.[146]

Although no senate candidate cleared the threshold for victory in the first round, several names from Haiti's benighted past made it to the second round, including Guy Philippe, Hervé Fourcand and the Lambert brothers, Nawoon Marcellus, Willot Joseph and Antonio "Don Kato" Cheramy (running on Vérité's ticket around the capital).[147] Eight deputies were elected in the first round, including the Martelly allies Gracia Delva (like Don Kato, a well-known singer) and Cholzer Chancy.[148] A few weeks later, the CEP would summarily reverse themselves and decide that both Youri Latortue and Jean Renél Sénatus had "won" in the first round despite having received only 46 percent and 43 percent of the vote, respectively.[149] The CEP released a list of 14 candidates who would be excluded from the second round because of their behavior in the first round, including Arnel Bélizaire, whom the CEP charged had fired an automatic rifle in Cité Soleil and had "caused a general panic"; PHTK's Lionel Previlon, who was accused of stealing ballot boxes in Desdunes; PHTK's Tony Antonelly Francous, charged with sacking a polling place in Port-de-Paix; and AAA's John Altenor, charged with firing an automatic weapon and sacking a voting station in the Artibonite.[150] POHDH thought the CEP did not go far enough, and that far more candidates should have been excluded.[151]

Even given that the CEP said the vote would have to be redone in 25 constituencies, Opont estimated that only 5 percent of voters were possibly affected, and that irregularities were not enough to affect the outcome of the ballot.[152] Despite the violence and fraud of the first round, the CEP made it clear that it thought the second round should go on as scheduled.[153] U.S. Ambassador Pamela White agreed, downplaying the problems with the wild understatement that "the elections weren't perfect but we had elections."[154] The OAS also backed holding the second round as scheduled.[155] By early September, a dozen parties, including Fusion and Renmen Ayiti, were calling for Opont to resign.[156] INITE would soon add its voice to the chorus, urging unity among the parties to avert what it called "an electoral coup."[157] On 4 September, several hundred people gathered at the CEP office in Pétionville calling for the results of the August ballot to be nullified.[158] Soon, Lavalas-affiliated senators such as Jean-Baptiste Bien-Aimé and Wesner Polycarpe were calling on candidates to boycott the second round.[159] By mid-September, cabinet ministers from INITE quit the government to protest the August vote.[160] Soon, Mirlande Manigat was talking of the need for a transitional government, with herself, naturally, at its head.[161] Despite all this, Opont said he would not resign. The U.S., now boasting former ambassador Kenneth Merten as special coordinator for Haiti, threatened to suspend cooperation if the elections were postponed.[162] Amid the brewing political crisis, Haiti received a new U.S. ambassador, with career foreign service official Peter Mulrean replacing Pamela White.

* * *

A government plan to carve out a new municipality from Arcahaie in an area where Martelly owned property – thus depriving the town of much-needed revenue from the hotels, beaches and other attractions nearby – led to days of violent protests, and an even more violent security services intervention.[163] The incident was indicative of the tin ear towards public opinion that Martelly – for so long the master communicator – had developed as his last year in office wound down. Eventually, it was decided that a tripartite commission consisting of representatives of the government and residents of Arcahaie and Montrouis would be formed to seek a solution.[164] The dispute dragged on through September, however, and a Sans Souci tour bus was burned along with several motorcycles that tried to traverse Route Nationale 1.[165] After weeks of unrest, Martelly announced that he would initiate a dialogue with residents for "serene discussions."[166] With Martelly's behavior growing ever more erratic, Rotchild François Jr, the journalist turned minister of communication, submitted his resignation, saying that a "deleterious working environment" prevented him from "continuing a difficult mission with [the] professionalism and rectitude" that he had demonstrated throughout his career.[167]

* * *

As the country headed towards the presidential vote, the climate remained tense. On the afternoon of 14 September, two policemen were slain in Cité Soleil's Droulliard section.[168] Dozens of police officers would hold a protest demanding justice for these and other slain colleagues, pointing out that the police were tasked with protecting the population and yet often could not even protect themselves.[169] In late September, clashes between armed groups in the lower Artibonite around Marchand Dessalines saw at least seven killed.[170]

Both LAPEH's Jude Célestin and Vérité party militants admitted that the former had been getting support from the latter since the exclusion of Jackie Lumarque from the presidential vote.[171] Within a few weeks, both Vérité and INITE would be openly supporting Célestin's presidential bid.[172] On the twenty-fourth anniversary of the 1991 coup against him, Aristide told supporters at Tabarre that the country was experiencing "an electoral coup" and that they should respond to it by electing Maryse Narcisse president of Haiti.[173] By early October, Néhémy Joseph, the representative of the vodou sector in the CEP, resigned, saying that he was "uncomfortable' in the institution.[174] When Martelly summarily named a replacement, the vodou sector criticized him for trampling on their right to name their own representative.[175] Martelly, meanwhile, threw himself energetically into campaigning for Jovenel Moïse, telling a crowd at a rally in Carrefour in mid-October that "all the opposition offers the young people of the country is to burn tires in protests" and saying they had no concrete plan to improve the lives of citizens.[176] Jovenel Moïse himself called for people to comport themselves peacefully on election day, and for his supporters not to wear PHTK T-shirts to the polls.[177]

In mid-October, Martelly inaugurated CIMO's impressive new base in Delmas 2, a stone's throw from Cité Soleil.[178] Only days later, at least 15 people were reported killed when the BOID raided Cité Soleil's Bélékou, Boston and Fort-Dimanche sections, with journalists finding bullet-riddled corpses apparently mutilated with knives. Some residents charged Cité Soleil's acting mayor, Esaïe Beauchard, and PHTK's Wladimir Jean-Louis, with having instigated the raid for electoral purposes in order to terrorize potential opposition supporters.[179] Residents also described clashes between the gangs of Bois Neuf and Droulliard, with one acquaintance describing to me how chimere (the term he used) entered Bois Neuf, killed two pregnant women and then burned their bodies.[180] Residents told me that Iska, the gang leader running Bélékou, maintained closed links with the local deputy, Almétis Junior Saint-Fleur, and that the political divisions were sowing the seeds of violence in the neighborhood.[181]

* * *

The second round of voting opened in a largely calm atmosphere, with a strong police presence and what observers noted was apparently larger participation than in August's round.[182] Long lines of voters were noted in Cap Haïtien, Pétionville and other locales.[183] As had by now become standard, both the Plateau Central and the Artibonite were the scenes of delays and irregularities as the day wore on.[184] In Cayes, three were wounded by gunfire.[185] Police said they made 60 arrests around the country during the course of the day,[186] which ended with statements of general content by voters, electoral authorities, government officials and international observers.[187] Even Pierre Espérance of RNDDH told a journalist that "this is much better … The police are taking their responsibilities more seriously."[188] Participation was eventually put at around 30 percent.[189]

But rancor was not long in surfacing. Representatives of Jude Célestin's LAPEH accused electoral officials of expelling party observers before vote counting began and of engaging in ballot stuffing in the north.[190] Moïse Jean-Charles at first said he was "comfortable" in terms of expecting victory despite any irregularities (even as Célestin's team rather preposterously claimed a first-round win),[191] before changing his tune and denouncing "massive fraud."[192] Steven Benoît, Jean-Henry Céant, Sauveur Pierre Etienne and Mario Andrésol would also eventually accuse the government of fraud, as would a number of other presidential aspirants, with some saying that ambulances were used to transport fake ballots to polling centers.[193] At a press conference – again before the results were announced and in violation of Haiti's electoral law – Moïse Jean-Charles claimed that he had evidence that he had already "won" in five of Haiti's departments.[194] He also claimed to have found partially burned ballots supporting his candidacy in Delmas. His announcement, journalists noted, was attended by only "about three dozen backers." How the ballots were taken from the tabulation warehouse – monitored by international observers and guarded by PNH and UN troops – was not explained.[195] On 3 November, LAPEH's Jean-Hector Anacacis called for Jovenel Moïse to be excluded from the electoral race (Sauveur Pierre Etienne, Jean-Henry Céant and Steven Benoît made similar demands), and went on to threaten that Moïse's businesses would be "destroyed" if the incorrect results were published.[196] The Observatoire Citoyen pour l'Institutionnalisation de la Démocratie (OCID) noted worriedly that the CEP was breaking with past practices by not announcing on a daily basis the results of each day's vote tabulation and called for greater transparency in the process.[197]

* * *

Finally, at a press conference on the afternoon of 5 November, Pierre-Louis Opont read out the official results. In the presidential race, Jovenel Moïse had come in first with 32.81 percent of the vote, Jude Célestin second with 25.27 percent, Moïse Jean-Charles third with 14.25 percent and Maryse Narcisse fourth with 7.05 percent.[198] Ascending to the senate was Antonio "Don Kato" Cheramy, while, in the re-run of elections that had been scuttled due to violence, Nawoon Marcellus, Willot Joseph and Guy Philippe were listed as coming in first in their constituencies.[199] The PHTK-allied current appeared assured of a commanding presence in parliament.[200] Only 15 of 94 deputies retained their seats.[201] One CEP member – Jacceus Joseph of the human rights sector – had refused to sign off on the results due to lack of transparency in the tabulation process.[202] Shortly after the results were announced, Maxo Gaspard, a Pitit

Desalin activist, was slain in front of the party's headquarters in Delmas, and Moïse Jean-Charles was soon calling for a "popular mobilization," saying that if Martelly "was not involved in the drug trade and the corruption, he has nothing to fear from our government."[203] Lavalas also said it would organize protests.[204]

On 11 November, thousands of Lavalas, Pitit Desalin and LAPEH partisans marched from Bel-Air to the National Palace, protesting the election results and tearing down any pictures of Martelly and Jovenel Moïse they came across.[205] During the night, gunfire echoed throughout the capital, and the sense of crisis was deepened by statements from PHTK deputy Antoine Rodon Bien-Aimé, who alleged that the United Nations Office for Project Services (UNOPS) had been in charge of orchestrating a fraud on behalf of the party to which he belonged.[206] UNOPS strongly denied the charges, as did a PHTK spokesman.[207] Amid rumors that gangs from the Plaine-du-Cul-de-Sac were about to descend on the city, residents in poor neighborhoods set up makeshift roadblocks and formed vigilante posses that marched through the streets chanting and clanging machetes on the ground to keep their courage up and deter any potential attackers. At least one young man was killed in Pétionville when his explanation for why he was in the neighborhood was doubted.[208]

* * *

Eventually, eight candidates – Jude Célestin, Moïse Jean-Charles, Sauveur Pierre Étienne, Jean-Henry Céant, Steven Benoît, Mario Andrésol, Eric Jean-Baptiste and Samuel Madistin – would come together to form a coalition called the G8. When the coalition asked for an independent commission to look into the election results, the CEP summarily rejected the request.[209] The CEP noted that it had already disqualified more than 120,000 ballots for alleged fraud.[210] Protests continued throughout the capital, often being dispersed by tear gas before they made it halfway up Delmas. At a chaotic demo on 18 November, both Moïse Jean-Charles and Steven Benoît were struck by rubber bullets fired by police.[211] Two days later, Franco Camille marched with a group carrying posters of Aristide and Narcisse, joined by Rony Timothée, André Michel and René Civil, as marchers chanted "Down with the faggot Martelly" and the old standby "Aristide is king!"[212] The government countered with a statement criticizing what it called the marchers' increasing violence, lack of respect for agreed-upon march routes and aggression against uninvolved civilians.[213] At a Lavalas-sponsored demonstration on 20 August, marchers clashed with residents around Delmas

95, leading to at least one death and several injuries as protesters smashed car windows and glass shopfronts.[214]

The CEP released what it called the final results of the October election on 24 November, and reaffirmed that Jovenel Moïse would face off against Jude Célestin. The CEP said the final round of elections – including the presidential runoff – was scheduled for 27 December.[215] Chaotic protests began around the capital almost immediately, seeing at least two shot.[216] LAPEH's Jean-Hector Anacacis said that only Jovenel Moïse's withdrawal from the presidential race (the latter's exclusion from the contest was by now a standard opposition talking point) or the formation of a transitional government would quiet them.[217] Some demonstrators were seen armed with machetes around Carrefour Aéroport.[218] Jovenel Moïse reminded his critics that "farmers keep their machetes sharp."[219] At a 26 November demonstration, several journalists were assaulted by protesters.[220]

Having linked up with the G8, Jude Célestin was now beholden to a collective decision on whether or not he should participate in the second round. The decision finally came at the end of November, when, in a communiqué, the G8 said that "honest, free, transparent and democratic elections [could] not be held" with Martelly as president and that they were advocating for a transitional government to oversee new elections. Célestin, they said, would not be participating in the second round.[221]

As the protests against the election result had commenced, they showed that even Haiti's age-old fratricidal struggles could not forever resist the march of time and technology. Moïse Jean-Charles had sent out a Tweet in clipped French paraphrasing words that Dessalines was said to have uttered before the pivotal Battle of Crête-à-Pierrot in the Artibonite in 1802, a battle that the Haitians in fact lost, despite inflicting heavy casualties on the French:

Je ne vx garder avec moi que des braves. Que ceux qui veulent mourir en Hoes libres se rangent autour de moi. Viv yon Ayiti Lib.[222]

I only want to be surrounded by the brave. Let those who want to die as free men line up around me. Long live a free Haiti.

CHAPTER SEVENTEEN
WHEN THEY ARE PRESIDENT, THEY WILL UNDERSTAND ME

As the crisis grew, the CEP's Pierre-Louis Opont continued to resist calls for an independent evaluation commission to review the body's work, saying there was no constitutional provision for such a body.[1] Whereas G8 spokesman Samuel Madistin described the councilors as "villains," Opont in turn said the coalition was "the Group of 8 losers."[2] Jovenel Moïse labeled the demonstrators as "those who want to destroy the country" while Célestin proxy Simon Dieuseul Desras called the PHTK "drug traffickers."[3] Cracks began to appear within the G8 itself, when Jude Célestin indicated that he might, after all, participate in the 27 December vote "under certain conditions."[4] Steven Benoît, however, denied there was any disunity in the group.[5] The OCID appealed for the government, CEP and opposition parties to eschew violence and commit to dialogue.[6] That violence was a real worry was driven home when unknown gunmen fired upon Radio Kiskeya, resulting in no injuries but rattling the staff.[7]

The Martelly-created Ministry of Defense announced that its first batch of trainees to form a new military would be commencing classes at a location in Gressier, donated by the South Korean government, with Minister of Defense Lener Renaud telling reporters that "it is the responsibility of every Haitian to allow this embryo army to survive, grow and produce."[8] As went without saying, another kind of "army" already existed in areas such as Cité Soleil, where interim mayor Esaïe Beauchard told Radio Métropole that children as young as 12 were now carrying firearms in support of the various armed factions in the zone, and pleaded for the attention of the country to be focused on the situation of the slum.[9] On 8 December, a police commissioner was shot at in Grand Ravine by members of a local gang. The PNH responded by sending a contingent of BOID, UDMO and CIMO into the neighborhood, seizing two young men who were beaten, stomped on, stripped and flogged at the local substation.[10]

* * *

Rejecting any talk of a commission to verify the October election results, several thousand Lavalas demonstrators hit the streets of the capital on 16 December, calling for the fall of the Martelly government and a transitional administration to take over.[11] As protests continued, Haiti's Economics Minister Wilson Laleau spoke of the deleterious effect on the economy, noting that far fewer diaspora appeared to be returning to the island for the Christmas and New Year's holidays than in years past.[12] Lakou Lapè issued a press release bemoaning "how political conflicts and violence are spreading fear and mourning among the Haitian people," before going on to note:

> As long as the Haitian people do not sit together to listen to each other, to discover what makes us one nation, and search for a common vision and principles so that we can function as one people, we are not going anywhere … If we do not do this, we will keep on digging a hole to bury ourselves deeper. Violence brings death. Dialogue and reconciliation is the way to life. Let's sit and talk.[13]

As CEP member Jacceus Joseph renewed his criticism of his colleagues by telling reporters that he believed the popular vote "had not been respected,"[14] several members of the CEP threatened to resign as a bloc.[15] The Association Nationale des Médias Haïtiens criticized what they said was the "obstinacy and blindness" of the body.[16] Finally, giving into pressure, Martelly and Evans Paul announced the creation of an independent commission to review the conduct of the elections. The commission would be chaired by civil society leader Rosny Desroches and feature among its members the well-known Haitian folk singer Mano Charlemagne and the former Radio Haiti Inter journalist Anthony Pascal, better known as Konpè Filo.[17] After initial hesitation, Haiti's Catholic Church said that it would support the commission, and chose Bishop Patrick Aris as its representative on it.[18] Despite the across-the-board concerns about the elections, the committee announced that it would assess only the disputed presidential ballot and not the August or October parliamentary votes.[19] The commission was to report back with recommendations to the government and the CEP.[20] For the first time, Evans Paul admitted that it would be "difficult" to hold elections on 27 December as scheduled.[21] A few days later, in a terse statement, the CEP announced that the vote was postponed "until further notice."[22]

As several members of the commission had ties – direct or indirect – to the government, criticism was not long in coming, with Fusion's failed presidential candidate Edmonde Supplice Beauzile saying that the commission would "only exacerbate the post-election crisis and remove the possibility of saving the polls in 2015,"[23] and Lavalas denouncing the body as "bogus."[24] Within a few days, however, Lavalas had moderated its position, with Louis Gérald Gilles saying they were "ready to accept" the verdict of an "inclusive" commission.[25] Days later, the party's position had changed yet again, with Maryse Narcisse announcing new demonstrations.[26]

When the commission finally issued its report – after Haiti had glumly greeted the new year – their chief finding was one of chaos, sloppiness and disorganization plaguing the polling centers and tabulation of votes, which resulted in a situation where "votes were not cast by some voters even though they were eligible to do so," and more than half of the staffers at polling places had not been able to do their work properly. The commission concluded that it did not find evidence of organized, systematic fraud to benefit one of the presidential candidates, and that it was likely incompetence – rather than plotting – that led to the inconsistencies.[27] The commission recommended dialogue between the political actors and a thorough investigation to determine the extent of irregularities, and argued that more time was needed to determine the extent and nature of those irregularities.[28] The member of the commission from the human rights sector, RNDDH's Gédéon Jean (who did not sign the report), characterized the voting tabulation system as "opaque" and called for a more in-depth examination of the entire process.[29] Commission chief Rosny Desroches told the Associated Press that "unless we have people who are really qualified [at the polls] we cannot say that there was massive fraud."[30]

Although Jovenel Moïse said that he supported the commission's work,[31] Pitit Desalin criticized its hesitancy to characterize the voting as fraudulent,[32] while Lavalas rejected the commission's findings outright, called for a new CEP and announced two days of protests.[33] The G8 also rejected the commission's report, instead demanding "the resignation of the CEP and the establishment of a provisional government responsible for taking all steps" to hold elections.[34]

In a 5 January statement, the United Nations and the Core Group thanked the commission for its work and urged "all state institutions and political actors to take all measures necessary to ensure a peaceful transfer of power to a newly elected president on 7 February, according to the requirements of the Constitution."[35]

In a 4 January letter to Martelly, the CEP's Opont said that it would be "difficult or impossible" to have elections on the new date of 17 January.[36] After meeting with Opont and the other members of the CEP at the National Palace, Martelly announced that the elections would instead take place on 24 January, a statement that was blunted by the news that the representative of the Catholic Church on the CEP (also serving as the body's treasurer), Ricardo Augustin, had resigned, and that the CEP had published the names of several "winners" of legislative elections subject to ongoing disputes.[37] This caused intense debate over whether or not the newly elected members would join the ten holdovers in parliament and, if so, when. Radio Métropole worried aloud that the new parliament was destined to become "the center of confrontation between the government and the opposition."[38] The U.S. government said in a statement that it "welcomed" the announcement of the presidential decree and that it looked "forward to the completion of the electoral process."[39] During a 19-minute address to the nation on 6 January, Martelly criticized "people who don't want elections" and spoke of what he called the sacrifices his government had made "for our country, for our dear Haiti" to make the vote possible. He said that the only way forward was via elections and that he was opposed to handing power to any transitional government.[40]

On 7 January, the CEP distributed certificates of victory to those parliamentarians "elected" in the controversial August and October votes, with CEP spokesman Roudy Stanley Penn calling the move "an important step," and Acting Senate President Andrys Riché saying that the body was "ready to welcome" its new members.[41] The same day, a joint communiqué by the CNO, CONHANE, SOFA and RNDDH criticized Martelly for "sidelining" the recommendations of his own commission, publishing the results of the disputed parliamentary elections in Le Moniteur (thus making them official) and unilaterally choosing 24 January as the date for new elections, and urged "the government and political actors to measure the extent of the crisis in which the country is sinking and its impact on the lives of the Haitian people."[42] Speaking at a memorial for Maxo Gaspard, the Petit Desalin militant who had been slain in November,

Moïse Jean-Charles called again for a transitional government, a call echoed by Mirlande Manigat, Edmonde Supplice Beauzile and René Civil.[43]

On 10 January, 92 of 119 members of the Chamber of Deputies were sworn in at parliament.[44] In the chamber as it stood, PHTK had 26 representatives, while its allies in KID and AAA had seven and six respectively. In terms of opposition, the Préval-affiliated Vérité and INITE had 13 and four deputies respectively, while Lavalas had six.[45] Unsurprisingly, Martelly's allies thus won the leadership of the chamber, with AAA's Cholzer Chancy becoming president of the body.[46] After the deputies were sworn in, one of the members of the electoral commission, Armand Louis, told the press that the swearing-in of the deputies was "a serious failure" and that the recommendations of the commission "have not been respected," sentiments echoed by Rosny Desroches, who called the swearing-in "grossly unfair."[47] In testimony to how unsettled the political situation was, and to his own considerable political abilities, Jocelerme Privert, the former Aristide minister of the interior and now affiliated with Préval's INITE, succeeded in besting Martelly ally Youri Latortue to claim the presidency of the senate.[48] It was thought that Martelly had been keen to control the position in the event that an interim government had to be formed in consultation with the body. Privert's highly dubious reputation – having controlled the Interior Ministry at the height of the chimere phenomenon and during the La Scierie killings – was apparently viewed as no bar to his elevation to the role by his colleagues.

* * *

One night that January, I watched them marching in their thousands to the throb of drums and the incantatory wail of their long bamboo *vaksin*. Waving flags, dancing and chanting, the multitude began in Pétionville before marching down traffic-clogged Route de Frères, where phantasmal swirls of dust were alternately illuminated by the lights of cars and the tapering orange kerosene flames of women selling cigarettes, crackers and patties called *fritay* from gurgling metal pots.

But this was no political protest. The throng heading down the road was following one of Haiti's storied *rara* bands, street musicians whose appearance marked the run-up to the country's carnival, which was set to begin on 7 February, the same day Haiti was slated to inaugurate a new president.

Despite the parties in the street, however, now back in Haiti I found that a sense of dread and foreboding had settled on the country's political elite.

"Between now and February 7 we are on a razor's edge and anything can happen," a former Martelly advisor told me as we sipped Barbancourt one night in the cool hills above the capital.

When I went to see Mario Andrésol, even though he was firmly in the opposition's camp, he was similarly concerned.

"What the government, the opposition and the international community don't know is that right now those guys in the slums are thinking they're always the victims, and if something happens they will be victims again," he told me. "But they are not just going to stay and die in Cité Soleil and those other areas forever, and that's what we need to prevent right now. That's what the oligarchy also has to understand. Today we are in a situation that could explode at any time."

Meeting with Louino Robillard in the *lakou* (courtyard) of an NGO in the Clercine neighborhood, he seemed similarly dejected. For the first time since the organization had been formed, Solèy Leve had been unable to hold its yearly 12 January commemoration of the earthquake in Cité Soleil because of the roiling violence there.

"I didn't vote," he told me. "Vote for who? Look at all of those politicians and all of those rich people and all of those organizations here. What have they done?"

In so many words, Louino told me that, as he had become more and more visible, he had had to move out of Cité Soleil (which was the ultimate desire of virtually everyone who lived there and, as such, was not in itself surprising). He said he intended to remain committed to Solèy Leve, but was also planning on starting work on a reforestation project near his birthplace in Saint-Raphaël in the north of Haiti.

Returning to Cité Soleil itself, I was greeted by the corpse of a man lying in the middle of Route Neuf – from the looks of it freshly gunned down. Heading past Soleil 4 and towards the Brooklyn section, a local friend, Willio Deseme, and I got off the tap-tap we were traveling in and started to chat with the people milling around. One man, the 50-year-old head of a deprived primary school named Christly Jackson, took us to a schoolhouse that lacked just about everything but rough wooden benches and a blackboard.

"These children need a real school," he pleaded. "And when they become adults, they don't have jobs and our hunger continues."

The Brazilians still had their base in Cité Soleil, in the district, "for nothing," residents told me.

We walked through Soleil 21 – perhaps the most desperate area of this already desperately poor quarter – where people lived in shacks fashioned out of castaway plastic and tin, and found ourselves at the open ocean. Here, hundreds made their living by fishing the polluted waters of the bay of Port-au-Prince. Passengers boarded rickety canoes for other areas on the nearby coast and men and women sought shade from the blazing afternoon sun as they mended nets and sails. As always had been my experience, my presence as a white outsider was met with curiosity and some gentle ribbing but no hostility. In another part of the neighborhood, I ran into Phozer Louis, who had formed the hip-hop collective *Fos Lakay-Majik kleng* with some of his friends. We sat on a low wall and chatted as planes landing at the nearby airport passed low overhead with a roar.

"We would like to do an orphanage right here," Phozer said, pointing at a disused building. "But you know, when people want power, they attack Cité Soleil ... For 35 years there has been conflict between Boston and Brooklyn neighborhoods. I don't think anybody even knows why anymore. But most of us would like to see a durable development in Cité Soleil. The armed groups are a minority, the people are a majority."

A few days later, accompanied by the Iranian-Canadian photographer Bahare Khodabande, I went back to Grand Ravine as well, heading up a nearly vertical road hemmed in on either side by cement-block homes before we were greeted by about a dozen members of the neighborhood *baz*, guns stuck in many of their waistbands. Their leader, like Martelly nicknamed Tèt Kale, sat astride a motorcycle, his T-shirt revealing arms adorned with tattoos. Despite his nickname, he sported a modified afro.

"Welcome," Tèt Kale said to us, as if he were some bizarre sort of tour guide.

Up the hill from the improvised checkpoint, in a spotless office, members of the Plate-forme des Secteurs Motivés pour l'Avancement de Grand Ravine (PLASMAGRA) were meeting to try to ameliorate their community's situation.

"We have been able to put peace in this community, and would like to continue with its development," said Nicolson Joachim, a 32-year-old Grand Ravine resident who ran as a candidate for the local assembly in the elections for Lavalas. As he spoke, children played football in the street and a young artist daubed Caribbean beach scenes onto canvases in the hope of selling them later. The contrast between the charnel house I had seen a decade earlier and the scene today was striking. We strolled through the neighborhood to a new park that residents were lovingly maintaining, Bahare snapping photos at will with no sense of pressure or restriction.

When I went to speak with Moïse Jean-Charles, we met in the still-under-construction shelter of a Delmas hotel (its predecessor had been destroyed in the 2010 earthquake). My photographer and I arrived a bit early and we were left to chat with one of Jean-Charles' self-described bodyguards, who told us matter-of-factly that Martelly and Jovenel Moïse would be *dechouked*, a reference to the general destruction directed at the Duvalier regime's henchmen after its fall, if Jovenel attempted to take office. When Jean-Charles finally arrived, it was with a small entourage that included Evel Fanfan, a lawyer who had been especially active during the 2004–06 interim government.

"This is not my struggle, but the struggle of the Haitian people," Jean-Charles said, before outlining a promise to force the departure of MINUSTAH and the nullification – not merely cessation – of the mining contracts Martelly awarded while in office. "We will modify our strategy, continuing our mobilization with strikes, civil disobedience … We need good governance, political and economic stability."

Despite the obvious role Haitians themselves played in facilitating yet another crisis, many felt this particular crisis had the international community's fingerprints all over it. Writing in Haiti's *Le Nouvelliste*, Lyonel Trouillot asked those abroad: "Do you know what they are doing here in your name?"[49]

But still, even in such a grave moment, it was not all misery.

I went to a screening of a film about young Haitians deported from the United States and Canada at a cinematheque in Pétionville. As I descended from my moto taxi, a *rara* band was massing near the Pétionville market, the *vaksins* wailing, the drums pounding, and people dancing in the streets. As they began to march, one reveler unfurled a large green flag with a single Creole word written in its center: *Ayiti*.

* * *

By mid-January, Jude Célestin was announcing that he would not participate in the second round of elections due in only a few days' time.[50] Speaking to AFP, Célestin said: "It takes two to tango and this election is a one-way affair."[51] Nevertheless, the CEP said the vote would occur on 24 January as planned.[52] The majority of electoral observers – including the CNO, RNDDH, CONHANE, JILAP, POHDH and OCID – all announced that they would not be observing the elections, with the latter body saying that it regretted that the Martelly government had ignored two of the key recommendations of its own commission – a reshuffle of the CEP and political dialogue. The OCID continued that "political tensions are worsening alarmingly, acts of violence are increasing, a climate of uncertainty, fear and insecurity has settled in on the population ... The conditions do not exist for the holding of democratic elections."[53] Opposition senators said they were working on a resolution to order a halt to the elections, though it was unclear if they had the constitutional authority to do so.[54] At this point, only five of the mandated nine members of the CEP remained in their positions, with four others having resigned with varying degrees of rancor.[55]

Thousands of protesters hit the streets on the 19th – only five days before the vote was to be held – burning tires and throwing stones at police, who responded with tear gas.[56] The rhetoric of the protesters was extremely violent as well, with some chanting *Netwaye zam nou* (We are cleaning our guns),[57] while another told the crowd that "on January 24, there will not be elections; we will have our machetes and stones in hand ... Close your doors and stay inside."[58]

To no effect, Haiti's Chamber of Commerce urged the political actors to engage in dialogue.[59] Passing their threatened resolution – which in fact was just a recommendation to the CEP – Haiti's senate called for a halt to elections, although they left the question of what would happen after Martelly's scheduled departure on 7 February up in the air.[60] As the opposition announced an intensification of protests to derail the planned vote up to and including the day of balloting, Evans Paul announced that all demonstrations would be banned from that Saturday morning until voting was completed.[61] Martelly appeared unyielding, telling reporters that "from the point of view of the state, we have a responsibility to organize elections."[62]

* * *

As duplicitous as Martelly had been throughout the electoral process, the chief modus operandi of the opposition protest actions seemed to be suicidal nihilism. In Léogâne, the school that Martelly had inaugurated less than a year before was reduced to ashes by arsonists, almost certainly because it was being used as a voting center (three other voting centers were set aflame the same night).[63] On Friday, 22 January, two days before the election, a chaotic and violent opposition demonstration charged up Delmas and into Pétionville, where protesters burned tires and smashed car windshields.[64] As protests raged in the streets literally at the CEP's doorstep – with demonstrators smashing shop windows, robbing pedestrians, and beating one man who shot at them into a bloody pulp[65] – Pierre-Louis Opont blinked and announced that Sunday's vote would be canceled "due to reasons of security."[66] It was unclear whether or not the CEP had consulted with Martelly before making the announcement. After the decision, yet another CEP member – Pierre Manigat, the representative of the press – announced his resignation.[67] One who had previously excused herself, Yolette Mengual, the representative of the women's sector, would return.

Despite the announcement of the annulation of the elections, similar scenes were repeated downtown the following day, with Evel Fanfan, an attorney for Petit Desalin, calling the chaos "good violence."[68] The ADIH lashed out at the demonstrations, saying that "thieves and thugs have been able to operate with impunity, without regard to the peaceful citizens, victims of the barbaric acts committed by the protesters."[69] Despite the attempts by those close to the anarcho-populist element to sell what transpired as some sort of peaceful people's revolution – one foreign BAI attorney Tweeted that the scuttled elections were "not result of violence – result of speech and political protest – human rights in action"[70] – nothing could have been further from the truth. The electoral process, corrupt as it was, was not canceled because of the entreaties of civil society or the protests of the more enlightened in the international community. It was canceled because those charged with overseeing it feared for their lives and some in the opposition had quite explicitly threatened to slaughter voters at the polls – no idle threat in a country that had experienced Ruelle Vaillant. Carline Viergelin, the CEP representative from Haiti's vodou sector, admitted as much during an interview with Radio Métropole.[71]

Following the announcement that elections had been shelved indefinitely, the G8 issued a press release in which they denounced Opont as a "villain" but nevertheless warned "the Haitian people not to indulge in triumphalism and to remain vigilant and mobilized until the satisfaction of their key demands" – those being a new CEP and Martelly's resignation.[72]

* * *

The U.S. State Department, having apparently really believed that Martelly could carry off elections in such a context, issued a statement that said it supported "all efforts aimed at finding consensual and constructive solutions that will conclude the electoral process expeditiously with an outcome that reflects the will of the Haitian people, consistent with Haitian law and the Haitian constitution," while noting, a bit late, that "electoral intimidation, destruction of property, and violence are unacceptable, and run counter to Haiti's democratic principles and laws."[73]

As the electoral process fell apart, two of Martelly's less self-controlled associates, Jojo Lorquet and Roro Nelson, launched verbal salvos against the president's critics while speaking on Storm TV, particularly singling out for attack Radio Kiskeya and its director, the bitter Martelly foe Liliane Pierre-Paul, who had been unstinting in her criticism of Martelly and his family.[74] Rousing himself from the torpor of internal exile on the Grand Anse, Guy Philippe suggested a more direct approach, releasing an audio recording denouncing the "anarchists" in the streets of Port-au-Prince and saying that he had all the men and arms necessary to restore order and that "we are ready for war."[75]

By Monday, 25 January, things were still tense in the capital, with heavy gunfire heard in Bourdon in the early morning hours, light traffic and many parents keeping their children home from school.[76] Consensus seemed to be growing among the *classe politique* around the idea of some sort of transitional government to take the reins once Martelly's mandate expired on 7 February, and to oversee new elections. The G8 appeared supportive of the idea that, as the constitution stipulated, Jules Cantave, the president of Haiti's Supreme Court, would step in as interim president, as the Supreme Court president had done in both 1990 and 2004.[77] The Americans also seemed to be realizing – too late – that a replacement would not be seated before Martelly left office, with Kenneth Merten telling Reuters that "we may be looking at some sort of temporary solution until there is a handover to a new elected president."[78] Youri Latortue spoke out in favor of Martelly's on-time departure.[79]

With PHTK protesters in the streets of Au Cap, Port-de-Paix and Jérémie calling for a definitive date to be set for the final round of the elections,[80] a policeman was shot during a pro-government demonstration blocking the bridge at Croix-des-Missions and later died. The following day, PHTK protesters blocked the road between Limonade and the industrial park at Caracol as well as demonstrating in Miragoâne and Gonaïves.[81] At the latter location, government supporters hurled stones at the Lycée Fabre Geffrard because its students refused to join them.[82] In an interview with Radio France Internationale (RFI),

Celso Amorim, the Brazilian diplomat serving as the chief of the OAS electoral observer mission in Haiti, said that it was "up to the Haitians to decide the future of Haiti."[83] The G8 advanced its own rather low opinion of the OAS with a statement that the body suffered from "a deficit of neutrality and is an irritating factor in the search for a solution to the Haitian crisis" because of its perceived support for Martelly.[84]

* * *

Things grew more tense, however, when, during an event in Cité Soleil, Martelly told the crowd that "I will not hand over power to people who refuse to participate in elections" and invited the OAS to send a special mission to Haiti to help resolve the crisis.[85] As he spoke, thousands of PHTK partisans marched through the capital, often dancing along to Sweet Micky tunes played on a sound system, some chanting "Down with the opposition. We demand peace in the country."[86] The president's supporter Youri Latortue, however, declaring himself "a slave to the constitution," said that the president did indeed have to leave on 7 February.[87] The same day, CEP chief Opont announced that he was quitting, saying in his resignation letter that he "regretted that tragic events beyond [his] control had hindered the electoral process."[88]

With only days remaining of his mandate, Martelly began holding meetings with Senate President Jocelerme Privert and Chamber of Deputies president Cholzer Chancy as the trio tried to hammer out some sort of transition plan.[89] When an OAS delegation landed in Haiti, headed by Antiguan diplomat Sir Ronald Sanders, the G8 refused to meet with them, though both Martelly (who had requested their visit) and Jocelerme Privert did so.[90] Several other senators, including Antonio "Don Kato" Cheramy, refused to see the diplomats and muttered darkly of "conspiracies" dating back to the 2010 elections.[91] As February began, the senate announced that it was trying to concoct an agreement whereby a prime minister – likely to be initially, at least, Evans Paul – would govern the country; others, including the G8, suggested an interim president to govern until new elections could be held.[92] Although rumors of Paul's imminent resignation flew fast, they proved unfounded.

All of this took place in the run-up to carnival, and then, startlingly, Michel Martelly vanished and Sweet Micky reappeared (in fact, he had never entirely gone away). Releasing a wild *konpa* meringue titled "Bal Bannann Nan" ("Give Her the Banana"), the president savaged his critics over an ebullient musical backing, taking particular aim at the journalist Liliane Pierre-Paul, whom he mockingly referred to as "Ti Lilli" and assailed with vulgar sexual references.

"When they are president," Martelly sang over a driving beat, "they will understand me."

The song, unsurprisingly, provoked an uproar and a widespread backlash among Haiti's intelligentsia, with RNDDH saying Martelly "went too far" in attacking the "moral and physical integrity" of the journalists, before denouncing the increasing "slackness" and vulgarity of carnival music.[93]

* * *

On 2 February, thousands of pro-PHTK protesters waving photos of Jovenel Moïse and blaring "Bal Bannann Nan" again marched through Port-au-Prince calling for elections.[94] Speaking to reporters the following day, Privert told them that Martelly had assured the senate of his 7 February departure from office.[95] At the opening of both houses of parliament on 4 February, Privert told the assembled lawmakers that Haiti faced a "multidimensional crisis" and urged them in "the spirit of sacrifice and solidarity" to prevent the looming presidential vacancy.[96]

Speaking less than 48 hours before the end of his term, at the inauguration of a housing project his government had built, Martelly told the assembled crowd that "we were serious in our efforts to change the image of Haiti," and said he regretted the damage the violence in recent weeks had done to that end. "I fought for the triumph of democracy in Haiti ... Haitians must change their behavior if we want to achieve positive results. I thank all those who helped me to serve the country, it was an honor."[97] He also lifted any remaining doubt as to whether or not he would leave office the following Sunday, saying "I do not want to hold onto power one extra day."[98]

Roused briefly to notice Haiti again in yet another moment of crisis – the only kind of moment in which its attention could seem to be bothered to engage – the media in the United States performed every bit as poorly as the foreign diplomats. Although Chiara Liguori, a researcher on Haiti for Amnesty International, wrote trenchantly for Al Jazeera that Haiti's political class en masse was "choosing to hold a country hostage in this electoral crisis ... [and] playing risky games with the lives and human rights of millions of Haitians," such circumspection was the exception, not the rule.[99] In an editorial that read like it might have come from the pen of Ira Kurzban, *The Miami Herald* laid the entirety of Haiti's problems on Martelly's shoulders, opining from their offices in suburban Doral that "Haiti's people have already paid too dearly for Mr. Martelly's disrespect for constitutional order and inept management" and that his term was an "unrelieved record of failure."[100] (A Haitian friend forwarded the article to me with the subject heading "Crazy going mainstream?") *The Washington Post* sniffed about Martelly's "stage antics" and claimed that he "treated his constituents … with no more dignity or respect" before going on to advocate "a stronger U.S. diplomatic role."[101] Short of outright occupation, one wondered how much "stronger" the *Post* thought the U.S. role could be.

* * *

As the hours wound down to the end of Martelly's tenure, residents of the capital were startled to wake up to see dozens of armed men in olive green uniforms parading through the city in trucks and on motorcycles, claiming to be members of the disbanded army (though some were clearly too young to be so), pointing guns at civilians, claiming their support for Martelly and declaring "from tonight, all illegal weapons become legal."[102]

At one point a group of the armed men came within shouting range of a group of a few thousand anti-government protesters. Hurled insults turned to hurled rocks from the demonstrators towards the military supporters, who then fired their weapons in the air before driving off, realizing they were badly outnumbered, but not before one of their number – an elderly former FADH captain named Neroce Ciceron – was pulled into the swirl of a mob.[103] What followed was a repulsive display that saw a swarm of young men – some appearing to be barely teenagers – surround him and smash his head in with a paving stone, rifle through his pockets and throw his boots over a utility line.[104] They then threw a small card bearing the image of Jovenel Moïse on the corpse.[105] The images of the savage murder – the faces of the perpetrators clearly visible – quickly spread via photographs and cell phone videos around the world, in one afternoon putting the final nail in the coffin of Haiti's resurrected image, an image that the violent demonstrations had already begun to batter down.

Watching the video – aside from violating the taboo of respecting the elderly – one felt one was seeing something new and terrible in Haiti. It was not a hitman carrying out a political assassination, a policeman carrying out an extra-judicial killing, or even someone using a demonstration to settle an old score. It was random, senseless violence – someone killed because a few people felt like killing him and knew that there would be no repercussions to doing so. It was the fruit of the impunity so many in the political scene enjoyed, played out there on the street for all to see.

* * *

With less than a day to remain in office, Martelly announced that he and parliament had arrived at a deal whereby Evans Paul would remain at his post until an interim president could be elected by both chambers of parliament, an event slated to happen within days. The president's term would be limited to 120 days and he would be tasked with a single duty: to hold elections on 24 April and inaugurate a new president on 14 May. If precedent was followed, it was likely that the president of Haiti's Supreme Court, Jules Cantave, would be Martelly's successor, as had occurred previously twice before when the presidency became vacant. However, Cantave's mandate had expired weeks earlier and, among the ceaselessly intriguing politicians, talk began to center on none other than Jocelerme Privert himself, the very person who had helped hammer out the deal in the first place.[106] Privert's own extraordinarily murky history appeared to be of little import to the international community, with the OAS mission chief Ronald Sanders chirpily declaring himself "pleased that the stakeholders have all committed themselves to democracy, peace and stability."[107] The accord was signed by Martelly, Privert and Chancy that Saturday in front of parliamentarians and the full foreign diplomatic corps.[108] The G8 denounced the deal as "a parliamentary coup."[109]

"Long live democracy," Lyonel Trouillot had written nearly two decades earlier.

> Messocracy, bureaucracy, slumocracy, shamocracy, stupidocracy,
> kleptocracy, all the squalor and ineptitude, all the bigwigs and filthy
> tricks, all the civilo-military decorum, so they can feast themselves on
> our illusions and desperation. All they have to do is change the color of
> the uniforms or scrap them completely. As though painting the rope blue
> would make a hanged man feel better![110]

As he cleared his desk at the National Palace late on the night of the 6th, Martelly was trailed by a television crew from a Miami TV station that recorded him tearfully saying goodbye to an equally tearful staff, dancing with brawny security guards and, seated behind the presidential desk for the last time, telling the interviewer that "Haiti has suffered great loss because people who never wanted elections are about to get power again without elections because they forced me into a deal."[111]

The following day in parliament, introduced by a grim-faced Privert, Martelly put on the reading glasses he sometimes wore and, bedecked with the presidential sash and his bald pate gleaming, switching between French and Creole, said, in part, the following:

> Haitian people, brothers and sisters ... I am an original child of Haiti, a
> child of Dessalines, a child of Pétion, a child of Capois ... In good times
> and bad, Haiti has always been there for me ... My greatest regret is the
> deferred elections ... [But] I think the day 7 February is a special day –
> it is for every Haitian – a day that marked history. I want to use it for
> forgiveness: forgive each person who stood in the way of the development
> of Haiti; forgive each person who saw to their personal interests rather than
> the interests of Haiti; forgive each person who took pleasure in selling a
> bad image of Haiti ... Martelly will pass away, but Haiti will remain. And
> if you think it is Martelly that you hurt when you destroy, it is in fact Haiti
> that you hurt ... Today, the time comes for me to tell the Haitian people
> thank you. Thank you for your courage, thank you for your patience. May
> God bless and protect Haiti. Amen! Thank you![112]

Martelly descended from the stage, shook hands all around, and removed the red and blue presidential sash. And then, just like that, he was gone. After he left, mobs attacked the carnival stands he had built on the Champ de Mars, damaging several but not all.

In the maw of uncertainty in which it was thrust, the country was left to meditate on this strange, garrulous, mercurial, unpredictable, ebullient man who had ruled them for the last five years, and who was now leaving to be replaced by ... What?

Perhaps, people thought, before he got into that system that breaks and deforms the best of people, he was different.

Perhaps he wanted to be.

EPILOGUE

With Martelly gone, it was left to those who remained to divide up the spoils and to position themselves for the upcoming elections. Given the tenuous security situation, the first day of carnival was canceled. As Martelly departed, the World Food Programme announced that the number of food insecure people in Haiti had grown for the third straight year to 1.5 million, largely due to a drought compounded by the *El Niño* weather pattern.[1] When Yonel Previllon, a former PHTK candidate, was gunned down in Delmas 75 in close proximity to the car of Jovenel Moïse by unknown killers, the party issued a statement charging that "members of the radical opposition, supporters of violence, have never ceased to launch open and public violent threats against members and supporters of the platform."[2]

I visited friends and sources around the capital, and found the political class with its collective head spinning.

"Suddenly the international community says an elected president has to replace an elected president," Jean-Max Bellerive told me as he chain-smoked Comme Il Faut cigarettes in his living room. "But they didn't have that position when they closed the parliament, they didn't have that position when they replaced 144 mayors. They closed the senate, they closed the Chamber of Deputies, the president appointed new mayors, new local officials, and it didn't seem to bother a lot of people They accepted the destruction of the whole structure of our democracy."[3]

In front of Saint Jean Bosco, Aristide's former church in the La Saline slum, I ran into Arnel Bélizaire leading a sad demonstration of a few dozen protesters. Under a drizzling rain that turned the streets into slippery paths of grey mud, they chanted, drank *tafia* (raw rum) and waved photos of Aristide before embarking on a brief march.

"We continue our demonstrations to let the government know that we need a real negotiation," Bélizaire told me. "We've been doing this since 1986, and the people are still suffering. What parliament has done is completely illegal."

When I went to parliament, however, I found those present quite pleased with themselves.

"We reached an accord with Martelly that avoided civil war and chaos, and we're continuing to work to elect a provisional president," Jean-Baptiste Bien-Aimé, a Fanmi Lavalas senator, told me. "The parliament saved the people of Haiti."

The registration for the post of interim president was described as "feeble," in no small part due to the fact that registering alone set aspirants back nearly $10,000.[4] Among those who threw their hat into the ring for the job was Jocelerme Privert, thus competing in a process his own parliament was tasked with overseeing. Beginning on the afternoon of 13 February, a bicameral session of parliament debated the election for over 12 hours. Viewers – those who could stay awake – were greeted by the interminable sadomasochistic spectacle of black-suited senators and deputies clad in brilliant white endlessly pontificating until finally – at 3.30am and on a second ballot – they chose Privert.[5]

Privert, the man whose name would forever be linked with the chimere of Cité Soleil and with the killings in La Scierie, had succeeded in taking power in a completely extra-judicial manner. Amid pomp and popping champagne corks, he was installed as Haiti's president – with a term to last no longer than 120 days and with the single task of organizing elections – on 14 February, Valentine's Day.[6] Far from being outraged, the international community applauded, with the United States, France, the Core Group and the United Nations all saluting Privert's seizure of the reins of power.[7] Exactly what kind of government Privert envisioned was open to question: at a reception at the National Palace for Privert's investiture, Lavalas diehards swilled champagne and one such activist crowed to a visiting journalist that "Lavalas and Aristide are back in the palace. We are back in power and we won't let it go."[8]

Moïse Jean-Charles announced that Pitit Desalin would not participate in the transitional government and that his party would seek the exclusion of Jovenel Moïse from the new elections.[9] The G8 as a whole also said they would not integrate into the government.[10] Jovenel Moïse called for the interim government to "scrupulously" adhere to the agreement, which called for holding elections on 24 April.[11] Various organizations of the far left denounced the regime as "an attempt to protect the interests of imperialists and multinationals and end the popular mobilization."[12]

Although he had been tasked with setting up new elections, some of Privert's first comments concerned Haiti's economy, where the gourde had recently surpassed 60 to the dollar. This led to immediate friction between Privert and Evans Paul, who disavowed Privert's statement that Haiti's economic situation was "catastrophic," noting that the treasury's situation was in fact not notably worse than at the same time the previous year, and that lower revenue could be attributed to the uncertain political situation.[13] In mid-May, former planning minister Yves Germain Joseph charged that there were "illegal" contracts between the Paul government and various construction firms (one could fairly ask why he had remained silent while serving in government).[14]

Privert met with members of Haiti's various civil society sectors and invited them to appoint representatives to the CEP within 72 hours,[15] and reiterated that his government would do "everything it can to meet the 120-day timetable."[16] He said he bore no ill will and met with everyone from pro-Lavalas to neo-Duvalierist elements in an effort, he said, to set conditions for elections to occur.[17] Privert announced that he was nominating former BRH head and economist Fritz Jean, a Martelly foe, as prime minister and installed him in the role before parliament had even confirmed him.[18] Jean subsequently went down in defeat, only to be replaced as prime minister designate by Enex Jean-Charles, an economist who had served in both Préval's and Martelly's administrations and who parliament quickly approved.[19] It was announced that Léopold Berlanger, who had been president of the CEP during the disputed May 2000 elections, had taken over as head of the body yet again.[20]

Although it had been stipulated in the February agreement that elections were to be held no later than 24 April, three days before that date – and with no elections in sight – Privert breezily offered that "if elections are not held on April 24, as provided in the agreement, it's not the fault of the executive branch."[21] Once the deadline passed, and more than two months after he assumed the presidency, Privert made it clear that he intended for a "verification commission" to look into the October vote before any elections would occur.[22] A new electoral calendar would likely not even be published until the end of May, he said.[23] Following the announcement, thousands of PHTK partisans hit the streets of the capital to call for a vote.[24] Privert also announced that the country's financial situation was "precarious" and that the windfall from participation in Venezuela's PetroCaribe was "gone."[25] After some deputies expressed their openness for prolonging Privert's term in power,[26] Moïse Jean-Charles accused Privert of bribing parliament to extend his mandate.[27] Soon, Enex Jean-Charles was saying that it would be "impossible" to respect the February agreement.[28]

By the end of April, the Commission Indépendante d'Évaluation et de Vérification Électorale (CIEVE) was finally seated, headed by François Benoît (whose family had been wiped out by François Duvalier) and four virtual unknowns.[29] After it looked at 3,235 tally sheets (about 25 percent of the total), CIEVE declared that 29 percent of the votes it had surveyed were ascribed to "untraceable" (or, as popular discourse would have it, "zombie") voters, that a "highly centralized" production of national identity cards linked to nonexistent people had taken place, and that, taking into account other factors, only 9 percent of the votes were "valid."[30] Benoît said that some tally sheets the group had examined had multiple fingerprints that nevertheless appeared to be from a single person.[31] It recommended re-running the October elections (though, in a moment of cognitive dissonance, not the August vote).[32] When Benoît handed Privert the report before reporters, Haitians could look and see for themselves the fruits of intergenerational impunity – victim and beneficiary – standing together on the stage all these years later.

Much about Privert's actions suggested pretensions to permanence. Upon occupying the National Palace, virtually the first thing he did was to replace all the cleaning staff.[33] Soon thereafter, he replaced Godson Orélus, the Martelly-appointed head of the PNH, with Michel-Ange Gédéon, up until then the head of the police for the West Department.[34] Meeting with the visiting head of a large NGO that had operated in Haiti for many years, Privert told the official in "not so many words" that he intended to stay in office, and as such needed the organization to make some public displays of good faith in his government.[35] Eventually, after the CIEVE report, Léopold Berlanger got around to saying that the presidential elections would not be held until October. Eventually, Privert himself said that he had no intention of leaving until the following year.[36] Eventually, the U.S. said they wouldn't be paying for new elections after all.[37]

Many changes awaited Haiti in the coming months. When the elections were finally held on 20 November 2016 – seven months late and only a month after the Grand Anse had been battered by Hurricane Matthew – it came as little surprise that Jovenel Moïse – the candidate with by far the highest national profile and best-organized national network – won, but many were surprised that, against a slate with so many opponents, he pulled in 55.60 percent of the vote, easily besting Jude Célestin (19.57 percent), Moïse Jean-Charles (11.04 percent) and Maryse Narcisse (9.01 percent), thus forgoing the need for a runoff.[38] There was the usual grumbling among the losing candidates but also a sense both in Haiti and abroad that it was finally time to put the election cycle in the rearview mirror and move forward, however an unknown quantity Moïse himself might be. As for Privert, despite the grave doubts many (including the author) had for his stewardship of Haiti as interim president, perhaps another way to read the lesson of his tenure is by remembering some lines from the Czech writer Milan Kundera's 1967 novel *The Joke*, which asks the reader to consider that "to live in a world in which no one is forgiven, where all are irredeemable, is the same as living in hell."

Perhaps, some wondered, that aforementioned desire for some forward motion was behind the removal of a long hovering specter on Haiti's political scene. After years on the run and before he could be invested in his new role as senator and enjoy the privileges of parliamentary immunity, Guy Philippe was snatched up during an interview with Radio Scoop FM in Pétionville, packed onto a plane bound for Miami, and charged with drug trafficking and money laundering. The fact that Philippe had been turned over by the PNH to the Americans became a brief cause célèbre among a certain type of Haitian politico who had generally remained silent in the face of so many innocent lives lost for so long.[39]

* * *

As the year began, another shock would be visited on the country.

On 3 March 2017, only weeks after attending Jovenel Moïse's inauguration, René Préval died suddenly in the home he stayed at when in the capital in the cool hills of Laboule. As recently as a few months before, Préval, who had celebrated his seventy-fourth birthday earlier in the year, could be spotted waiting in line with the other passengers at Port-au-Prince's Toussaint Louverture International Airport, shunning the pomp of so many other of the country's politicians. Since leaving the presidency, he had spent much of his time in his ancestral home of Marmelade, where he worked on projects such as an agricultural co-operative, an education center and a juice factory.

Préval's death hit Haiti as a body blow, as, despite his two terms, there was a sense that he had not quite finished all the work he wanted to do for the country. Despite his glaring flaws, he was also an example of a democratically elected political leader who twice turned power over to a democratically elected successor after his own terms in office, and who had never had to flee into exile. Perhaps not much of an achievement in some countries, but this was Haiti.

After lying in state in the Musée du Panthéon National d'Haïti, René Préval was interred in Marmelade, in a bamboo coffin built for him by the people there, laid to rest under ash gray skies and a light, mournful rain.[40]

* * *

What Haiti did in 1804 was extraordinary by any measure, and it struck a vital blow in freeing tens of millions of human beings from bondage throughout the hemisphere. But to continuously evoke a glorious, idealized past, as some are wont to do, while failing to hold any present-day actors, Haitian or foreign, to account for their crimes against Haiti and its people does nothing to ameliorate the situation of those forced to endure the reality of the country as it exists today. Quite the opposite, really. When Jean-Claude Duvalier fled in February 1986, a resistance movement already existed in Haiti, and Duvalier's downfall was the moment for these parties to demand and to organize a process of de-Duvalier-ization and accountability. They failed to do that, and they were aided in their failure, time and again, by the brutally cynical *realpolitik* of the international community, especially the United States. If the Duvalierist criminals had been brought to justice for what happened during their three decades in power, the history of Haiti would look very different today. Instead, what has been created is a system where anyone honest is looked upon, at best, as a fool or, at worst, as a threat to be destroyed. Much as the *hounsis* (devotees) in vodou are unable to resist the call of the *lwa* to be ridden, so the Haitian political system remains possessed by corruption, its lure irresistible, with the country's politicians and various foreign actors riding the wave towards calamity. The political dynamic in Haiti today often resembles nothing so much as the scene depicted in Max Frisch's anti-Nazi parable *Biedermann und die Brandstifter* (known in English as *The Fire Raisers*), the theme of which depicts two arsonists who, through a combination of charm and menace, talk their way into homes posing as salesmen and so thoroughly disorient the owners that the latter end up aiding them in affecting the burning down of their own properties and, ultimately, their own deaths. This template more or less sums up the modus operandi approach of Haiti's politicians towards the country's people. The international community, more often than not, seems content to supply the gasoline and the matches.

Today as during its previous eras, Haiti's political dynamic also often remains badly misunderstood in the foreign press. For some who initially became aware of the country during the first flush of its pro-democracy movement in the late

1980s and early 1990s, their views appear cryogenically frozen in time, unable to adapt to and address a changing and more convoluted new reality. Too often Haiti is also reduced, however tangentially, to any way in which it is connected to U.S. *politique du jour*, as if a foreign protagonist could be the only thing to justify interest in the country.[41] Its culture likewise appears to continue to puzzle to the point where, as late as 2016, *The New Yorker* felt comfortable calling Haitian Creole a "guttural ... French patois."[42] As the Syrian political dissident Yassin al-Haj Saleh had observed about his own country, and as Haitians had reiterated to me over the years, "they simply do not see us; it is not about us at all."[43]

More than elections, more than more journalists, more than any new wave of foreign do-gooders washing up on its shores, what Haiti desperately needs, perhaps more than any other single bit of assistance right now, is an equivalent entity to the Comisión Internacional Contra la Impunidad en Guatemala (CICIG), a United Nations-mandated body that has operated in that Central American country since 2007, charged with investigating criminal organizations and exposing their relation to the state. Although Guatemala remains a society deeply riven by corruption, violence and impunity, CICIG has provided the political cover and the direct security assistance to honest Guatemala officials and prosecutors to combat the criminal monarchies that have run the nation for too long, with successes up to and including the arrest of a sitting president and former vice president in late 2015. The creation of such a body and its functioning at a high level would be nothing short of a revolutionary act in Haiti, and perhaps a small gesture of penitence by the international community, after having for so long contributed to the country's suffering.

* * *

A few days after Martelly stepped down, a friend and I went to stay overnight at a little cottage in Belot, located on the slopes of some of the few still-forested mountains above Port-au-Prince. There, peasant farmers still cultivate their land and raise their livestock, not entirely recovered from the dual shocks of the destruction of the Creole pig and the lowering of the tariff on imported rice, but hanging on. Parents walk to church clutching their Bibles, trailed by children so delicate and beautiful in appearance they almost look like dolls, and the intrigues of the capital's politicos below them seem to take place on a different planet. These weren't the ones who made the decisions of the politicians and the foreign actors involved in Haiti. But they are the ones who suffer the consequences. But despite all of this, Haiti has endured. As my friend and I sat watching sunlight fade, eliciting within the clouds drifting in to shelter the mountains a brilliant red hue, we passed a bottle of Barbancourt back and forth, the cool wind rustling the tree branches nearby. The breeze seemed to whisper some lines from more than a decade earlier, written by the poet Jacques Roche, a prose-poem ode to Haiti's vanishing countryside and a legacy of resistance, *Le vent de Maribahoux*:

> No more are the stars pinned by night to the firmament to guide our steps, nor is dawn kindled at night's end. Fate is a puzzle of pieces shredded by shark jaws. Hope flees the nonsense of the madness of crowds and seeks an alternative to prompt forests to emerge, harvests to multiply, drums to beat in concert, songs to burst forth, women to dance, children scattered in rivers to laugh. Until the time of resuscitated dreams returns, let the time come when I, the wind of Maribahoux, become a hurricane to tame hurricanes, an ocean to swallow storms.

The sun set into the valley, and we looked across a Haiti that waits for that time and a Haiti that, despite all the forces arrayed against it, stubbornly survives.

NOTES

PROLOGUE

1   Alexis, Jacques Stéphen (1955) *General Sun, My Brother*. Charlottesville, VA: University Press of Virginia, p. 69.

2   Corvington, Georges (1975) *Port-au-Prince au cours des ans. Vol. 1: La Ville coloniale, 1743–1789*. Montréal, Québec: Les Éditions du CIDIHCA, pp. 85–109.

3   Among some, it is argued that Boukman was in fact a Muslim ("Book Man" signifying the Koran), and the "Bwa Cayman" was in fact "Bwa Kay Imam" (Woods of the House of the Imam).

4   Bell, Madison Smartt (2007) *Toussaint Louverture: A Biography*. New York, NY: Pantheon Books, p. 18.

5   Henl, Robert Debs and Nancy Gordon (1995) *Written in Blood: The Story of the Haitian People*. Lanham, MD: University Press of America, p. 108.

6   Translation of the document by Laurent Dubois and John Garrigus as published in "Slave Revolution in the Caribbean 1789–1804: A Brief History with Documents." The Haitian Declaration of Independence, 1804. Interestingly, the text also went on to caution: "Let us allow our neighbors to breathe in peace; may they live quietly under the laws that they have made for themselves, and let us not, as revolutionary firebrands, declare ourselves the lawgivers of the Caribbean."

7   Henl, Robert Debs and Nancy Gordon (1995) *Written in Blood: The Story of the Haitian People*. Lanham, MD: University Press of America, pp. 119–20.

8   Hunt, Alfred N. (1988) *Haiti's Influence on Antebellum America: Slumbering Volcano in the Caribbean*. Baton Rouge, LA: Louisiana State University Press, p. 132.

9   Daut, Marlene L. (2015) *Tropics of Haiti: Race and the Literary History of the Haitian Revolution in the Atlantic World, 1789–1865*. Liverpool: Liverpool University Press, pp. 426–7.

10 Roberston, David (1999) *Denmark Vesey*. New York, NY: Vintage.

11 Hunt, Alfred N. (1988) *Haiti's Influence on Antebellum America: Slumbering Volcano in the Caribbean*. Baton Rouge, LA: Louisiana State University Press, pp. 46–7.

12 Gaffield, Julia (2015) *Haitian Connections in the Atlantic World: Recognition After Revolution*. Chapel Hill, NC: University of North Carolina Press, pp. 125–7.

13 "Is it time for France to pay its real debt to Haiti?," *The Washington Post*, 13 May 2015.

CHAPTER ONE

1   Henl, Robert Debs and Nancy Gordon (1995) *Written in Blood: The Story of the Haitian People*. Lanham, MD: University Press of America, pp. 189–91.

2 Ibid., p. 192.

3 Gaillard, Roger (1984) *Une modernisation manquée: 1880–1896*. Port-au-Prince, Haiti: Imprimerie Le Natal, pp. 27–39.

4 Henl, Robert Debs and Nancy Gordon (1995) *Written in Blood: The Story of the Haitian People*. Lanham, MD: University Press of America, pp. 309–10.

5 Ibid., p. 348.

6 Ibid., p. 340; also Banque de la République d'Haïti website, http://www.brh.net/ historique.html, accessed 5 May 2016.

7 Marcelin, Frédéric (1904) *L'haleine du centenaire*. Paris: Taillefer, pp. 13–14.

8 Henl, Robert Debs and Nancy Gordon (1995) *Written in Blood: The Story of the Haitian People*. Lanham, MD: University Press of America, pp. 374–83.

9 "Many trials and errors," *The Economist*, 18 February 2012.

10 "Killing Haitian Democracy," *Jacobin*, 22 July 2015.

11 Abbott, Elizabeth (1988) *Haiti: The Duvaliers and Their Legacy*. New York, NY: McGraw-Hill, p. 39.

12 Henl, Robert Debs and Nancy Gordon (1995) *Written in Blood: The Story of the Haitian People*. Lanham, MD: University Press of America, p. 424.

13 Seabrook, William (1929) *The Magic Island*. New York, NY: Paragon House, pp. 145–9.

14 Waugh, Alec (1965) *Love and the Caribbean*. New York, NY: Bantam Books, pp. 119–20.

15 Gaillard, Roger (1982) *Hinche mise en croix*. Port-au-Prince, Haiti: Imprimerie Le Natal, pp. 29–32.

16 United States Congress Senate Committee on Haiti and Santo Domingo (1922) *Hearings before a Select Committee on Haiti and Santo Domingo, Volume 2*.

17 Castor, Suzy (1988) *L'Occupation américaine d'Haïti*. Port-au-Prince, Haiti: Société Haïtienne d'Histoire, pp. 173–5.

18 Smith, Matthew J. (2009) *Red & Black in Haiti: Radicalism, Conflict and Political Change 1934–1957*. Chapel Hill, NC: University of North Carolina Press, p. 2.

19 Parti Communiste Haïtien (1934) *Analyse schématique 32–34*. Port-au-Prince, Haiti: Valcin.

20 Smith, Matthew J. (2009) *Red & Black in Haiti: Radicalism, Conflict and Political Change 1934–1957*. Chapel Hill, NC: University of North Carolina Press, pp. 73–6.

21 Dunham, Katherine (1969) *Island Possessed*. Chicago, IL: University of Chicago Press, p. 56.

22 The author Bernard Diederich's *Bon Papa: Haiti's Golden Years* (Xlibris, 2007) provides an interesting overview of the Magloire years.

23 Diederich, Bernard and Al Burt (1991) *Papa Doc: Haiti and its Dictator*. Maplewood, NJ: Waterfront Press, pp. 115–21.

24 Ibid., p. 112.

25 *Haïti: jamais, jamais plus!: les violations des droits de l'homme à l'époque des Duvalier* (2000) Port-au-Prince, Haiti: Centre de Recherche et de Formation Économique et Sociale pour le Développement, p. 56.

26 Diederich, Bernard and Al Burt (1991) *Papa Doc: Haiti and its Dictator*. Maplewood, NJ: Waterfront Press, p. 202.

27 *Haïti: jamais, jamais plus!: les violations des droits de l'homme à l'époque des Duvalier* (2000) Port-au-Prince, Haiti: Centre de Recherche et de Formation Économique et Sociale pour le Développement, pp. 85–90.

28 Diederich, Bernard and Al Burt (1991) *Papa Doc: Haiti and its Dictator*. Maplewood, NJ: Waterfront Press, pp. 240–2.

29 For the fullest account of the Jeune Haïti invasion, see Prosper Avril's *L'aventure militaire des 13 guérilleros de Jeune Haïti* (L'Imprimeur, 2014).

30 Diederich, Bernard and Al Burt (1991) *Papa Doc: Haiti and its Dictator*. Maplewood, NJ: Waterfront Press, pp. 286–94.

31 Author interview with Sylvie Bajeux, March 2016.

32 Abbott, Elizabeth (1988) *Haiti: The Duvaliers and Their Legacy*. New York, NY: McGraw-Hill, pp. 121–30.

33 For further information, see the website of Haïti lutte contre l'impunité, http://www.haitiluttecontre-impunite.org/.

34 Diederich, Bernard and Al Burt (1991) *Papa Doc: Haiti and its Dictator*. Maplewood, NJ: Waterfront Press, pp. 392–3.

35 "Human rights complaints filed against 'Baby Doc' Duvalier," *The Miami Herald*, 20 January 2011.

36 Abbott, Elizabeth (1988) *Haiti: The Duvaliers and Their Legacy*. New York, NY: McGraw-Hill, pp. 214–16.

37 "2 out of 3 people face hunger as Haiti woes mount," Associated Press, 10 June 2013.

38 "Haiti Ruler Drops 3 Tied To Duvalier," *Philadelphia Inquirer*, 22 March 1986.

39 A good account of this period can be found on pp. 294–332 of Amy Wilentz's 1989 book *The Rainy Season: Haiti Since Duvalier* (Touchstone).

40 "Haiti's Wealthy Elite Turn Blind Eye to Plight of Poor," *The Los Angeles Times*, 29 September 1992.

41 "Haiti Terrorists Form in New Groups," *The New York Times*, 23 September 1988.

42 "Priest's Ouster Silences Haiti's Voice of the Poor," Associated Press, 1 January 1989.

43 Wilentz, Amy (1989) *The Rainy Season: Haiti Since Duvalier*. New York, NY: Touchstone, pp. 360–5.

44 Evans Paul, declaration, Exhibit 1, executed in Haiti on 23 April 1994. Marino Etienne, declaration, Exhibit 3, executed in Paris, France on 10 May 1994.

45 Dupuy, Alex (2006) *The Prophet and Power: Jean-Bertrand Aristide, the International Community, and Haiti*. Lanham, MD: Rowman & Littlefield, p. 89.

46 "The Hope of the Nation's Poor Became One More Autocrat," *The Los Angeles Times*, 1 March 2004.

47 "Murder of the Cathedral," *Chicago Tribune*, 18 January 1991.

48 "Aristide's Offer: A Vision of Democracy," *The New York Times*, 17 September 1994.

49 Transcript of the 27 September 1991 speech by the author.

50 "An Odd Trio Runs Haiti's Armed Forces," *Philadelphia Inquirer*, 18 September 1994.

51   "'93 Report by C.I.A. Tied Haiti Agent to Slaying," *The New York Times*, 13 October 1996.

52   "Still Fragile, Haiti Makes Sales Pitch," *The New York Times*, 5 October 2009.

53   "Aristide returns to acclaim in Haiti," *The Washington Post*, 15 October 1994.

54   "Aristide decides to quit as priest," *The New York Times*, 16 November 1994.

55   "Haitian Cancels Trip," *The South Florida Sun Sentinel*, 6 February 1993.

56   "Aristide Is Forming New Party in Haiti, Undermining Leader," *The New York Times*, 9 February 1997.

57   "Member of Haitian Cabinet Now Suspect in Murder Plot," *The Washington Post*, 4 April 1995.

58   "Killing Wave Threatens Haitian Ties," *The New York Times*, 27 October 1995.

59   "Aristide Dissolves Army that Ousted Him in 1991," *Orlando Sentinel*, 29 April 1995.

60   Author interview with Theodore "Lolo" Beaubrun, Port-au-Prince, April 2004.

61   "The Human Rights Record of the Haitian National Police," Human Rights Watch, 1 January 1997.

62   "Haitian Leader's Angry Words Unnerve Elite and Worry Allies," *The New York Times*, 19 November 1995.

63   "Aristide Urged to Stay in Office for 3 More Years," *The Washington Post*, 25 November 1995.

64   "Préval is Declared Winner of Election," Associated Press, 24 December 1995.

65   "Many in Haiti Are Troubled by Marriage of Aristide," *The New York Times*, 21 January 1996.

66   "Aristide Calls for Donor Compliance on Paris Accord," Inter Press Service, 23 January 1996.

67   "Subsidizing Starvation," *Foreign Policy*, 11 January 2013.

68   "With cheap food imports, Haiti can't feed itself," Associated Press, 20 March 2010.

69   "Ex-leader still enigma as Haitians cast ballots," *St. Petersburg Times*, 7 February 2006.

70   "Pressed by U.S., Haitian President Begins Purge of Guards," *The New York Times*, 16 September 1996.

71   *The Agronomist* (film), directed by Jonathan Demme, 2004.

72   "Aristide in Waiting," *The New York Times*, 5 November 2000.

73   "Does Dany Toussaint Take God's Children for a Bunch of Wild Ducks?," Jean Dominique editorial on Radio Haiti Inter, October 1999.

74   Author interview with Robert Manuel, Guatemala City, September 2003.

75   "Haitian Assembly Candidate Killed, Daughter Wounded as Elections Near," Dow Jones Newswires, 14 April 2000.

76   "Haitian Migration Linked to Violence, Poverty," *The Los Angeles Times*, 29 April 2000.

77   Letter from Leon Manus to Colin Powell, 27 December 2000.

78   Author interviews, Hinche and Papay, January 2001.

79   "Haiti: No Aid Without Accountability," Heritage Foundation, 31 October 2002.

80   "Who killed Jean Dominique?" Reporters Without Borders, 3 April 2001.

81 Ibid.

82 "Ex-Judge: Haitian Leader Blocks Murder Probe," *Newsday*, 27 January 2004.

83 "Is Another Assassination of Jean Dominique about to Take Place?" Radio Haiti Inter Editorial, 3 March 2002.

84 "Government Was Involved in Dominique's Murder," Radio Signal FM, 27 December 2002.

85 The full story of the Cité Soleil armed groups is included in my 2005 book, *Notes from the Last Testament: The Struggle for Haiti* (Seven Stories Press).

86 "Zero tolerance for the media: an enquiry into the murder of journalist Brignol Lindor," Reporters Without Borders, 10 September 2003. Also, author interviews, Petit-Goâve, December 2001.

87 "Haitian Gangs Combat Demonstrators," National Public Radio, All Things Considered, 10 February 2004.

88 "'Militias' might key to Aristide's grip on power," *The Boston Globe*, 19 February 2004.

89 "The Violent Lifeworlds of Young Haitians Gangs as Livelihood in a Port-au-Prince Ghetto," Fafo Research Foundation, March 2012.

90 Author interviews, Cité Soleil, 2001–04.

91 Author interviews, 2001–04.

92 Author interview, Port-au-Prince, January 2016.

93 Author interview, Miami, May 2014.

94 Author interview with Winston Jean-Bart, January 2004.

95 "Le chef d'OP Félix Bien-Aimé toujours porté disparu," Radio Métropole, 23 September 2002.

96 Author interview with Robinson Thomas, Cité Soleil, August 2002.

97 "Beyond the Criminal Acts of December 17, 2001: A personal testimony of Gérard Pierre-Charles," 8 March 2002.

98 "Fugitive leader of Haiti's 'Cannibal Army' found shot to death," Associated Press, 23 September 2003.

99 Author interview with René Civil, Port-au-Prince, June 2002.

100 "Notes from the Last Testament," 1 May 2001, http://windowsonhaiti.com/windowsonhaiti/w01051.shtml.

101 "Gang's raid on Haiti slum kills three, destroys 1,000 homes," Associated Press, 4 November 2001.

102 See "Inter Current Events," Radio Haiti Inter, Port-au-Prince, BBC Monitoring Service, 21 June 2001; and "Is Another Assassination of Jean Dominque about to Take Place?," Michèle Montas Dominique editorial on Radio Haiti Inter, 3 March 2002.

103 "Un ex-maire adjoint de P-au-P se réfugie à l'étranger et fait d'importantes révélations," AlterPresse, 11 August 2003.

104 "Head of U.S. Security Firm That Guarded Aristide Speaks Out," *Democracy Now!*, 2 March 2004.

105 "U.S. allegedly blocked extra bodyguards," *The Miami Herald*, 1 March 2004.

106 United States Department of Justice Foreign Agent Registration Act filings, 2001–04.

107 "Chaos within the PNH: The National Coalition for Haitian Rights," 10 March 2004.

108 "Haiti's ex-chief of police cites corruption," *The Miami Herald*, 28 June 2003.

109 "La lettre de démission de l'ex directeur général de la police, Jean Robert Faveur," 21 June 2003.

110 "Ex-general once ruled Haiti, now is held in jail there," *The Miami Herald*, 31 May 2001.

111 "Coopérative: crise à tiroirs," Haiti Press Network, 18 June 2003.

112 "Assassinat d'une figure de proue dans la lutte pour la promotion de la femme," Radio Métropole, 23 October 2003.

113 "La dernière manif de Maxime Desulmond," AlterPresse, 17 January 2004.

114 "The Human Right to Food in Haiti: Report of an International Fact-finding Mission," Rights & Democracy and Groupe de Recherche et d'Appui au Milieu Rural, 2008.

115 "Planting Now: Agricultural Challenges and Opportunities for Haiti's Reconstruction," Oxfam Briefing Paper #140, October 2010.

116 "Environmental Vulnerability in Haiti: Findings & Recommendations," USAID, April 2007.

117 National Endowment for Democracy, *2000 Annual Report*; data sheet from USAID Mission: Haiti, Program Title: Democracy and Governance.

118 Author interviews, Port-au-Prince, July 2006.

119 Author transcript of remarks, 2003.

120 "The Rise and Fall of Haitian Drug Lord Jacques Ketant," *The Miami New Times*, 27 May 2015.

121 "Drug dealer accuses Aristide," *The Miami Herald*, 26 February 2004; author interviews, Port-au-Prince, 2001–03.

122 "Target of drug probe: Aristide," *The Miami Herald*, 2 July 2006.

123 "Drug dealer accuses Aristide," *The Miami Herald*, 26 February 2004.

124 "Drug probe targets Aristide," *The Miami Herald*, 2 July 2006.

125 "2 More Ex-Haiti Top Cops Charged," *The Sun Sentinel*, 28 May 2004.

126 "Ex-law official in Haiti gets 15 years," *The Miami Herald*, 24 July 2005.

127 "Former Haiti police chief arrested," CNN, 17 May 2004.

128 "Ex-senator in Haiti Faces Drug Charge," *The Sun Sentinel*, 2 June 2004.

129 "Target of drug probe: Aristide," *The Miami Herald*, 2 July 2006.

130 "Drug suspect faces U.S. charges," Associated Press, 11 August 2002.

131 "Bogus dockets shielded informants," *The Miami Herald*, 18 November 2006.

132 "Jury: Haitian smuggled drugs," *The Miami Herald*, 22 July 2005.

133 "Ex-Aristide aide tells of payoffs," *The Miami Herald*, 20 July 2005.

134 "Jury Convicts Haitian Cocaine Trafficker on All Counts," DEA press release, 21 July 2005.

135 "Information on Haiti's drug trade lightens sentence for Aristide aide," *The Miami Herald*, 20 November 2005.

136 "Drug probe targets Aristide," *The Miami Herald*, 2 July 2006.

137 "Ex-security chief: Aristide shielded kingpin," *The Miami Herald*, 21 July 2005.

138 "Haiti's ex-security chief pleads guilty to money laundering," Agence France-Presse, 28 May 2005.

139 "Information on Haiti's drug trade lightens sentence for Aristide aide," *The Miami Herald*, 20 November 2005.

140 "Jury Convicts Haitian Cocaine Trafficker on All Counts," DEA press release, 21 July 2005.

141 "Drug probe targets Aristide," *The Miami Herald*, 2 July 2006.

142 Ibid.

143 Thucydides (1954) *History of the Peloponnesian War*, translation by Rex Warner. New York, NY: Penguin Books, p. 242.

144 "Le fil des événements entourant l'assassinat de Amiot Métayer," AlterPresse, 10 October 2003.

145 "Assassinat de Amiot Métayer, puissant chef d'OP des Gonaïves," Radio Métropole, 23 September 2003.

146 "Haïti: le scandale de trop?," AlterPresse, 25 September 2003.

147 "Manifestations brutalement dispersées par la police aux Gonaïves," AlterPresse, 29 September 2003.

148 "Funérailles de Amiot Métayer, emaillées d'incidents," AlterPresse, 6 October 2003.

149 "Le fil des événements entourant l'assassinat de Amiot Métayer," AlterPresse, 10 October 2003.

150 "Le départ de Aristide à tout prix," AlterPresse, 2 October 2003.

151 "Après la trêve, reviennent les manifestations," AlterPresse, 20 October 2003.

152 Footage of the attack can be seen in the Haitian filmmaker Arnold Antonin's 2004 documentary *GNB Kont Attila*.

153 Press statement of the Fondation Connaissance et Liberté (FOKAL) in regards to the aborted student demonstration of 5 December 2003, released 9 December 2003.

154 "Gangsters Switch Teams, Some Remain Militantly Pro-Aristide," Inter Press Service, 26 November 2003.

155 Author notes.

156 "Requiem pour la Scierie," AlterPresse, 30 April 2004.

157 "At least 41 dead as rebellion pushes through northern Haiti," Agence France-Presse, 9 February 2004.

158 Author interviews, Saint-Marc, February 2004 and June 2009.

159 Author interview with Père Arnal Métayer, Saint-Marc, February 2004.

160 "Town taken from rebels feels heat of reprisal," *The Miami Herald*, 24 February 2004.

161 "Haiti stuck in bog of uprising's bloodshed," *Chicago Tribune*, 17 May 2005.

162 "A Propos du massacre de la Scierie," *Le Nouvelliste*, 17 April 2005.

163 "Requiem pour la Scierie," AlterPresse, 30 April 2004.

164 "La Scierie Genocide," National Coalition for Haitian Rights, 2 April 2004.

165 "Aristide's last days," *St. Petersburg Times*, 28 February 2006.

166 "Jamaica returns arms to S Africa," *Jamaica Observer*, 5 March 2004.

167 "Situation générale des droits humains en Haïti à la veille des elections annoncées pour la fin de l'Année 2005," Réseau National de Défense des Droits Humains, June 2005.

168 Author interview with Luis Moreno, Port-au-Prince, March 2004.

169 See Asger Leth's film *Ghosts of Cité Soleil* (2006).

170 "Aristide and His Bodyguard Describe the U.S. Role in his Ouster," *Democracy Now!*, 16 March 2004.

171 "Head of U.S. Security Firm that Guarded Aristide Speaks Out," *Democracy Now!*, 2 March 2004.

172 "Aristide's last days," *St. Petersburg Times*, 28 February 2006.

173 "Aristide avait 'démissionné' en 2004, dit son ancien Premier ministre," Radio Kiskeya, 6 October 2010.

174 "Yvon Neptune a-t-il vendu la mêche?," *Le Nouvellise*, 12 April 2011.

CHAPTER TWO

1 "What role for the EU? Finding a niche in the Haitian peacebuilding process," Initiative for Peacebuilding and Fundación para las Relaciones Internacionales y el Diálogo Exterior, February 2009.

2 Author interview with Juan Gabriel Valdés, March 2015.

3 "Lettre ouverte au directeur general de la police nationale d'Haïti," National Coalition for Haitian Rights, 10 March 2004.

4 "Youri Latortue Reaches Out," secret U.S. Embassy cable, 27 June 2007.

5 Author interview with Gérard Latortue, Boca Raton, May 2015.

6 "Haiti's president installs new Cabinet," confidential cable from U.S. Embassy, Port-au-Prince, 17 March 2004.

7 Author interview with Juan Gabriel Valdés, March 2015.

8 Author interview with former United Nations official, 2015.

9 Author's observations, Port-au-Prince, May 2005.

10 Author interview with senior MINUSTAH official.

11 "Arrestation de Annette Auguste (So Anne)," Radio Kiskeya, 10 May 2004.

12 "The Release of a Suspected Assassin," National Coalition for Haitian Rights press release, 3 March 2004.

13 "Police recapture two men charged in Jean Dominique murder," Committee to Protect Journalists, 11 August 2004.

14 "Biography of Réginald Boulos," Pan American Development Foundation, http://www.padf.org/Réginald-boulos/, accessed 11 May 2016.

15 "Lavalas Supporter Reveals Palace Involvement in Dominique Murder," Radio Vision 2000, 19 April 2004.

16 "Ex-premier held, suspected in killings," *Chicago Tribune*, 28 June 2004.

17 "Haiti arms row rocks South Africa," BBC, 15 March 2004.

18 "Glossing Over Truth on Aristide Does SA No Favours," *Business Day*, 10 June 2004.

19 "Between Transitional Regime and Permanent Dictatorship," 17 August 2004.

20 "Haiti, U.S. criticize Jamaica over Aristide's return," Associated Press, 15 March 2004.

21 "Haiti rejoins CARICOM," AlterPresse, 24 August 2006.

22 "Caribbean Nations Uneasy About 'Re-engaging' Haiti," Inter Press Service, 7 July 2004.

23 Dumas, Réginald (2008) *An Encounter with Haiti: Notes of a Special Advisor*. Port of Spain, Trinidad: Medianet, p. 18, 21.

24 "One year after Hurricane Jeanne, recovery continues," UNICEF, 18 September 2005.

25 "In Haiti's hour of need," *Jamaica Observer*, 3 October 2004.

26 "Statement by the Hon. Dame Billie A. Miller to the 59th Sessions of the United Nations General Assembly," 27 September 2004.

27 The poem can be found at http://www.haiticulture.ch/haiti_survivre_poeme_jacques_roche.html.

28 "$1 Billion Is Pledged to Help Haiti Rebuild, Topping Request," *The New York Times*, 21 July 2004.

29 "Rebels move out of police station in Haitian town," Associated Press, 22 July 2004.

30 "Les anciens militaires prennent possession de Petit-Goâve," Radio Métropole, 30 August 2004.

31 "Policeman explains reasons behind threat to strike," BBC Monitoring Service, 7 August 2004.

32 "Verdict Rendered in the Antoine Izmery Murder Trial: Chamblain and Joanis Acquitted," National Coalition for Haitian Rights, 27 August 2004.

33 "Procès Chamblain–Joanis: Le Conseil des Sages se prononce," press release by Conseil des Sages, 27 August 2004.

34 Press release from NCHR, CARLI and POHDH, 2 September 2004.

35 "Haitian Police Kill Three Rebels," Reuters, 8 September 2004.

36 "Demobilized soldiers, Lavalas supporters clash in Cap-Haïtien," Radio Galaxie, 9 September 2004.

37 "Un ministre français attaqué," Radio France Internationale, 24 August 2004.

38 Author interview with Juan Gabriel Valdés, March 2015.

CHAPTER THREE

1   "Policemen killed during pro-Aristide demonstration," Associated Press, 30 September 2004.

2   "Lavalas Party Members Arrested at Radio Caraïbes," National Coalition for Haitian Rights, 6 October 2004.

3   "Pro-Aristide Politicians Nabbed in Haiti," Associated Press, 3 October 2004.

4   "Présidence/Parlement: dispute en haut lieu," *Le Nouvelliste*, 15 October 2011.

5   "Lavalas Party Members Arrested at Radio Caraïbes," National Coalition for Haitian Rights, 6 October 2004.

6   "Violences à Port-au-Prince: au moins 20 morts en 6 jours," AlterPresse, 4 October 2004.

7   "Violence racks pro-Aristide slum of Haiti's capital city," Associated Press, 4 October 2004.

8   "Pro-Aristide Politicians Nabbed in Haiti," Associated Press, 3 October 2004.

9   "Concerned at mounting bloodshed in Haiti, UN envoy urges dialogue," UN News Centre, 4 October 2004.

10 "Le gouvernement haïtien réclame la levée de l'embargo sur les armes," Radio Métropole, 6 October 2004.

11 "André Apaid Jr en faveur d'une vaste mobilisation contre la violence," Radio Métropole, 5 October 2004.

12 "Il faut reprendre la mobilisation pacifique, estiment des étudiants," Radio Métropole, 6 October 2004.

13 "Les militaires démobilisés prêts à participer à toute action," Radio Métropole, 9 October 2004.

14 "Pro-Aristide Priest Detained in Haiti," Associated Press, 14 October 2004.

15 "Peacekeepers Battle Gangs in a Ravaged Haiti," National Public Radio, 7 October 2004.

16 "Pro-Aristide Priest Detained in Haiti," Associated Press, 14 October 2004.

17 "Gangsters torch cars, fire in air, in prelude to what many fear will be another violent day in Haiti's capital," Associated Press, 15 October 2004.

18 "Haiti: U.S. lifts 13-Year Arms Embargo," Associated Press, 19 October 2004.

19 "In Bondage to History," NACLA, 9 February 2005.

20 "The Violent Lifeworlds of Young Haitians Gangs as Livelihood in a Port-au-Prince Ghetto," Fafo Research Foundation, March 2012.

21 The entire story is chronicled vividly in Edwidge Danticat's 2007 memoir, *Brother I'm Dying* (Vintage).

22 "A Very Haitian Story," *The New York Times*, 24 November 2004.

23 "Des militaires onusiens de la Minustah attaqués et humiliés par des chimères lavalas," Radio Métropole, 23 November 2004.

24 "Haiti is worse than rock bottom as interim leaders unable to stem poverty, crime," *South Florida Sun-Sentinel*, 4 December 2004.

25 "Anarchy reigns in streets of Haiti," *The Miami Herald*, 29 November 2004.

26 "Rapport sur les evenements survenus au pénitencier national," Réseau National de Défense des Droits Humains, 1 December 2004.

27 "Aristide is no Mandela," *Mail & Guardian* (South Africa), 14 December 2004.

28 "Violence, political feuds cloud Haiti's hopes," *The Boston Globe*, 13 December 2004.

29 "La France est contre le retour d'Aristide en Haïti," Agence France-Presse, 11 November 2004.

30 "Miami Priest: Without Aristide, Peace Unlikely," *South Florida Sun-Sentinel*, 1 February 2005.

31 "Detained enemy of Aristide will not oppose deportation," *The Miami Herald*, 11 January 2005.

32 "Ex-Soldiers Take Over Aristide's Home," Associated Press, 15 December 2004.

33 "Haiti's Transition: Hanging in the Balance," International Crisis Group, 8 February 2005.

34   Interview with CIVPOL official, Haiti, 2005.

35   "Les narcotrafiquants font main basse sur Haïti," *Le Figaro*, 21 December 2004.

36   "Haitian prime minister rejects corruption allegations against cousin," Radio Métropole, 6 January 2005.

37   Author interview with Theodore "Lolo" Beaubrun, Port-au-Prince, April 2004.

38   "Dernières du 6 décembre 2004," Radio Kiskeya, 7 December 2004.

39   "Les militants armés lavalas renouvellent leur allégeance à Aristide à l'occasion des obsèques de Dread Mackenzie," Radio Métropole, 17 December 2004. Also, footage shot by Daniel Morel and Jane Regan at the funeral, viewed by the author.

40   "Two journalists severely beaten in Haiti," Associated Press, 15 January 2005.

41   "Brazil shows backbone in Bel-Air," confidential cable from U.S. Embassy, Port-au-Prince, August 2005.

42   "Undeclared War Escalates in Capital Slum," Inter Press Service, 18 January 2005.

43   "Lancement d'une campagne contre la violence armée," AlterPresse, 17 March 2006.

44   "Haiti's Elections Set for Oct. and Nov," Associated Press, 1 February 2005.

45   "Les duvaliéristes pensent à un retour sur la scène politique," Radio Métropole, 1 February 2005.

46   "Serges Gilles nommé candidat à la présidence de la Fusion des Sociaux-démocrates Haïtiens," Radio Kiskeya, 23 April 2005.

47   "L'inculpé Ronald Dauphin arrêté, un otage libéré," *Le Nouvelliste*, 24 July 2006.

48   "Les chimères lavalas créent la panique à Port-au-Prince," Radio Métropole, 2 February 2005.

49   "Quatre policiers tués dimanche à Port-au-Prince par des hommes armés," Radio Métropole, 7 February 2005.

50   "Les habitants de Village de Dieu vivent dans la crainte d'une nouvelle attaque des chimères lavalas," Raido Métropole, 1 March 2005.

51   "Les habitants de Village de Dieu réclament justice," Radio Métropole, 2 March 2005.

52   "Among Haitians, police are seen as a deadly force," *The Boston Globe*, 27 February 2005.

53   "Haiti's Aristide Says Will Return, Praises UN," Reuters, 9 March 2005.

54   Author interview with Gérard Latortue, Boca Raton, May 2015.

55   "New Truce Quells Gang Violence for Now," confidential cable from U.S. Embassy, Port-au-Prince, 24 July 2006.

56   "Assassinat d'un des principaux chefs de bande de Cité Soleil," Radio Métropole, 31 March 2005.

57   Footage shot by Daniel Morel and Jane Regan at the scene, viewed by the author.

58   Author interviews, Port-au-Prince, May 2005.

59   "UN troops clash with ex-soldiers in Haiti; peacekeeper among 3 killed," Associated Press, 21 March 2005.

60   "Gunmen attack house of Haiti's justice minister, kill policeman," Associated Press, 23 March 2005.

61   Author interview with Juan Gabriel Valdés, March 2015.

62 "As Polls Near, Challenges Pile Up," Inter Press Service, 5 April 2005.

63 "Haitians mark 18th anniversary of constitution with violence," confidential cable from U.S. Embassy, Port-au-Prince, 30 March 2005.

64 Ibid.

65 "As Polls Near, Challenges Pile Up," Inter Press Service, 5 April 2005.

66 "Lavalas torn between boycotting elections and moving forward," confidential cable from U.S. Embassy, Port-au-Prince, 22 March 2003.

67 Author interviews, Port-au-Prince, 2005.

68 "Violences à Port-au-Prince: un ancien zélé partisan d'Aristide passe aux aveux," Radio Métropole, 28 January 2005.

69 "Opération Bagdad: un autre responsable d'OP se démarque," Radio Kiskeya, 15 February 2005.

70 Author interview, Port-au-Prince, January 2016.

71 "HNP Brief on Dread Wilmé Gang Information," confidential cable from U.S. Embassy, Port-au-Prince, 6 July 2005.

72 "The Violent Lifeworlds of Young Haitians Gangs as Livelihood in a Port-au-Prince Ghetto," Fafo Research Foundation, March 2012.

73 "As Polls Near, Challenges Pile Up," Inter Press Service, 5 April 2005.

74 "HNP Brief on Dread Wilmé Gang Information," confidential cable from U.S. Embassy, Port-au-Prince, 6 July 2005.

75 "Le commandant autoproclamé Ravix Rémissainthe tué à Port-au-Prince," 9 April 2005.

76 "Au moins 3 morts, dont Ravix Rémissainthe, lors d'une opération policière," Alter-Presse, 9 April 2005.

77 "4 morts, dont un autre chef de bande, lors d'une opération policière," AlterPresse, 10 April 2005.

78 "Offensive contre les bandits," Radio Kiskeya, 12 April 2005.

79 "Guy Philippe accuse des responsables d'être responsables de la mort de Ravix Rémissainthe," Radio Métropole, 18 April 2005.

80 "For Once, Violence Leaves Greater Sense of Security," Inter Press Service, 11 April 2005.

81 "Nouvelle opération conjointe de la PNH et de la MINUSTAH contre les militaires démoblisés," 25 April 2005.

82 "Les militaires démobilisés du Plateau Central déposent les armes," Radio Métropole, 20 April 2005.

83 "Funérailles samedi d'une ex-otage," Radio Kiskeya, 11 July 2005.

84 "Judicial Police Director Discusses Gangs With DCM," confidential cable from U.S. Embassy, Port-au-Prince, 6 July 2005.

85 "Haiti Ex-Official Charged in Killings," Associated Press, 18 April 2005.

86 "La prison dorée pour l'ancien Premier ministre lavalas Yvon Neptune," Radio Métropole, 26 April 2005.

87 "Unwavering dedication in the face of constant adversity," Réseau National de Défense des Droits Humains, 17 May 2005.

88 Ibid.

89 "NCHR – Haiti Does Not Speak for the National Coalition for Haitian Rights (NCHR) New York," press release, 11 March 2005.

90 "Unwavering dedication in the face of constant adversity," Réseau National de Défense des Droits Humains, 17 May 2005.

91 Ibid.

92 "De l'égalité de tous les citoyens devant la loi," Centre Oecuménique des Droits Humains, 5 May 2005.

93 "Unwavering dedication in the face of constant adversity," Réseau National de Défense des Droits Humains, 17 May 2005.

94 "5 personnes tuées lors d'une manifestation pro Aristide," AlterPresse, 27 April 2005.

95 "Incidents sanglants de Christ Roi," Radio Kiskeya, 28 April 2008.

96 "Gunfire kills five people in demonstration in Haiti," Associated Press, 28 April 2005.

97 "Judicial Police Director Discusses Gangs with DCM," confidential cable from U.S. Embassy, Port-au-Prince, 6 July 2005.

98 "La capitale à nouveau plongée dans le black-out," Radio Métropole, 27 April 2005.

99 "US, France behind black Haiti holocaust," SAPA, 19 April 2005.

100 "Haiti's Aristide Seeks Return to Office," Reuters, 19 April 2005.

101 "Panique et ralentissement des activités à Port-au-Prince," Radio Kiskeya, 16 May 2005.

102 "Le chef de la police d'Haïti dénonce 'l'hypocrisie' de la communauté internationale envers son pays," Radio Métropole, 24 May 2005.

103 "S. Africa's ANC seeks Aristide return to Haiti," Reuters, 13 May 2005.

104 "La police impuissante face la guérilla urbaine à Port-au-Prince," Radio Métropole, 30 May 2005.

105 "Des armes automatiques pour défendre les entreprises," Radio Métropole, 31 May 2005.

106 Confidential cable from U.S. Embassy, Port-au-Prince, 24 July 2006.

107 "L'ancien premier ministre Neptune au cabinet d'instruction de St. Marc," Alter-Presse, 25 May 2005.

108 Statement issued by the Caribbean Community (CARICOM) on the situation of Mr. Yvon Neptune, former prime minister, Haiti, 11 May 2005.

109 Letter calling for the release of Yvon Neptune, 13 May 2005.

110 Letter to Condoleezza Rice from William Delahunt, 16 June 2005.

111 "Lettre adressée Condoleezza Rice," Centre Œcuménique des Droits Humains, 14 June 2005.

112 Letter from Maxine Waters to U.S. President George W. Bush, 13 May 2005.

113 "Haitian Ex-Premier in Gilded Cage as He Awaits Trial That Never Comes," *The Los Angeles Times*, 5 July 2005.

114 Author interview with David Beer, Port-au-Prince, May 2005.

115 "Report: Aristide diverted millions," *The Miami Herald*, 4 August 2005.

116 Author interview with Philippe Lahens, Port-au-Prince, May 2005.

117 "McCain 'Trailblazer' Burned," *The Komisar Scoop*, 11 July 2008.

118 "Haiti Telecom Kickbacks Tarnish Aristide," *CorpWatch*, 29 December 2005.

119 Carrier service agreement between IDT and Telecom, dated 22 October 2003. Copy in possession of the author.

120 "A Lingering Problem for IDT," *Barron's*, 20 September 2010.

121 "Ex-employee who claimed firing over opposition to Haiti bribery settles," *The Komsiar Scoop*, 24 January 2011.

122 Ibid.

123 "Former U.S. Attorney Chris Christie, GOP Candidate for NJ Governor, gets $ from IDT," *The Komisar Scoop*, 22 October 2009.

124 "Haiti Sues to Collect a Phone Bill," *The Wall Street Journal*, 11 November 2005.

125 "Haiti Telecom Kickbacks Tarnish Aristide," *CorpWatch*, 29 December 2005.

126 Jewett IDT Case Exhibit B, 1 December 2006, copy in possession of the author.

127 "Haiti Telecom Kickbacks Tarnish Aristide," *CorpWatch*, 29 December 2005.

128 "Haiti Sues to Collect a Phone Bill," *The Wall Street Journal*, 11 November 2005.

129 "The Haiti File," *The Wall Street Journal*, 12 February 2007.

130 Author interview, August 2015.

131 "Former U.S. Attorney Chris Christie, GOP Candidate for NJ Governor, gets $ from IDT," *The Komisar Scoop*, 22 October 2009.

132 Email to the author, September 2006.

133 "Former U.S. Attorney Chris Christie, GOP Candidate for NJ Governor, gets $ from IDT," *The Komisar Scoop*, 22 October 2009.

134 Personnel announcement, Office of the White House Press Secretary, 31 August 2005.

135 "The Haiti File," *The Wall Street Journal*, 12 February 2007.

136 "Aristide's American Profiteers," *The Wall Street Journal*, 28 July 2008.

137 "Ex-employee who claimed firing over opposition to Haiti bribery settles suit against IDT," *The Komisar Scoop*, 24 January 2011.

138 "Telecoms Exec Receives Longest FCPA Sentence Ever," *The Wall Street Journal*, 26 October 2011.

139 "Former Controller of a Miami-Dade County Telecommunications Company Sentenced to 24 Months in Prison for His Role in Foreign Bribery Scheme," United States Department of Justice, 21 January 2011.

140 Ibid.

141 "Former Haitian Government Official Sentenced to Prison for His Role in Money Laundering Conspiracy Related to Foreign Bribery Scheme," United States Department of Justice, 2 June 2010.

142 "Executive pleads guilty in Haiti telecom case," *The Miami Herald*, 19 February 2010.

143 "Former Haitian Government Official Sentenced to Nine Years in Prison for Role in Scheme to Launder Bribes," United States Department of Justice, 21 May 2012.

144 "Patrick Joseph, Haiti Teleco Defendant, Sentenced to Prison," Anti-Corruption Blog, 11 July 2012.

145 "Miami bribery probe zeroes in on Aristide," *The Miami Herald*, 3 March 2012.

146 Email to the author, February 2004.

147 "Le député Hugues Célestin conteste le choix de Moïse Jean-Charles, accusé de meurtre, comme candidat au Sénat de LESPWA dans le Nord," Radio Kiskeysa, 30 January 2009.

148 "Gérard Le Chevallier, 1953–2010: Chief, Political Affairs and Planning Section (El Salvador)," http://www.un.org/en/memorial/haiti/le_chevallier.shtml, accessed 15 September 2015.

149 "Un consul honoraire de France tué sur fond de violences en Haïti," *Le Monde*, 1 June 2005.

150 "Extradition – Le tueur présumé du diplomate français, Henri-Paul Mourral, écroué," *France Soir*, 7 February 2010.

151 "Situation générale des droits humains en Haïti à la veille des elections annoncées pour la fin de l'année 2005," Réseau National de Défense des Droits Humains, June 2005.

152 "President's chief of staff paints grim security picture," secret cable from U.S. Embassy, Port-au-Prince, 3 June 2005.

153 "Des activistes armés mettent le feu au Marché Tèt Bœuf," Radio Métropole, 1 June 2005.

154 "President's chief of staff paints grim security picture," secret cable from U.S. Embassy, Port-au-Prince, 3 June 2005.

155 "Situation générale des droits humains en Haïti à la veille des elections annoncées pour la fin de l'année 2005," Réseau National de Défense des Droits Humains, June 2005.

156 Confidential cable from U.S. Embassy, Port-au-Prince, 6 June 2005.

157 "Un responsable d'entreprise, Jean-Paul Médina, assassiné à Port-au-Prince," Radio Kiskeya, 9 June 2005.

158 "L'industriel haïtien Charles Henry Becker dans la ligne de mire de la bande à dread Wilmé," Radio Signal FM, 10 June 2005.

159 "Nou pa pral fè kat elektoral pèlen!," leaflet, 27 June 2005, copy in possession of the author.

160 "Décès de Butteur Métayer, dirigeant du Front pour la Reconstruction Nationale (FRN)," Radio Métropole, 9 June 2005.

161 "Ordonnance rendue sur le dossier du massacre de la Scierie," AlterPresse, 17 June 2005.

162 Text of United Nations Resolution strengthening Haiti force, United Nations Security Council, 22 June 2005.

163 "Nouvelle journée de violence à Port-au-Prince," Radio Métropole, 23 June 2005.

164 "Dread Wilmé Killed; PNH More Active," confidential cable from U.S. Embassy, Port-au-Prince, 6 July 2005.

165 "Plusieurs arrestations au cours de nouvelles opérations conjointes de la PNH et de la MINUSTAH dans les zones de tension," Radio Kiskeya, 4 July 2005.

166 "Un bandit lynché par des riverains alors qu'il tentait de kidnapper deux employés d'une Agence de Voyage," Radio Métropole, 29 June 2005.

167 "Attaque contre un sous-commissariat de police," Radio Métropole, 25 June 2005.

168 "Aristide accused of fostering violence," *The Miami Herald*, 24 June 2005.

169 Secret cable from U.S. Embassy, Paris, 1 July 2005.

170 "Réginald Boulos dans la ligne de mire des activistes armés lavalas," Radio Métropole, 30 June 2005.

171 "Haitian business leader criticizes government, cabinet changes," BBC Monitoring Service, 25 June 2005.

172 "U.N. Peacekeepers Kill 6 Gunmen in Haiti," Associated Press, 30 June 2005.

173 "Se Mèt Kò Ki Veye Kò," Plateforme des Organisations Haïtiennes des Droits Humains, 10 December 2005.

174 "Brazil shows backbone in Bel-Air," confidential cable from U.S. Embassy, Port-au-Prince, August 2005.

175 "U.N. Peacekeeping More Assertive, Creating Risk for Civilians," *The Washington Post*, 15 August 2005.

176 "Dread Wilmé et plusieurs de ses lieutenants tués dans des échanges de tirs avec la Minustah," Radio Métropole, 6 July 2005.

177 "Un résident de Cité Soleil dénonce l'exécution de deux de ses enfants par des bandits," Radio Métropole, 6 August 2005.

178 "Se Mèt Kò Ki Veye Kò," Plateforme des Organisations Haïtiennes des Droits Humains, 10 December 2005.

179 "Funérailles symboliques d'un chef de bande," AlterPresse, 11 July 2005.

180 "A man of peace meets a violent end," *St. Petersburg Times*, 26 July 2005.

181 "Affaire Jacques Roche: Le ministère public revient sur d'importantes révélations à l'origine de la condamnation de deux des assassins du journaliste," Radio Kiskeya, 4 September 2007.

182 "A man of peace meets a violent end," *St. Petersburg Times*, 26 July 2005.

183 "Le père Gérard Jean-Juste prêt à appuyer toutes les formes de mobilisation pacifique pour le retour d'Aristide," Radio Kiskeya, 20 July 2005.

184 "Lavalas in damage-control mode," Radio Métropole, 17 July 2005.

185 "Haiti tense as key election approaches," *Chicago Tribune*, 5 August 2005.

186 "Plus de 3 mille personnes émues aux funérailles de Jacques Roche," AlterPresse, 21 July 2005.

187 "Day of Protest Decries Deaths in Haiti," *Democracy Now!*, 21 July 2005.

188 "Interpellation d'un prêtre lavalas à l'occasion des funérailles du journaliste Jacques Roche," AlterPresse, 21 July 2005.

189 "Haitian Priest Assaulted by Mob at Funeral and Arrested for Murder," *Truthout*, 22 July 2005.

190 "La mère du journaliste assassiné Jacques Roche nie tout lien de parenté avec le père Gérard Jean-Juste," Radio Kiskeya, 25 July 2005.

191 "Interpellation d'un prêtre lavalas à l'occasion des funérailles du journaliste Jacques Roche," AlterPresse, 21 July 2005.

192 "Aristide Gangs Alleged to Kill Forty Civilians After U.N. Operation," Radio Métropole, 2 August 2005.

193 "Extraits de l'homélie prononcée par Mgr. Pierre André Dumas, à l'occasion des obsèques du journaliste et poète Jacques Roche," AlterPresse, 22 July 2005.

194 "They Tortured Him Before Shooting Him in the Mouth," 17 July 2005.

195 "Une vie exemplaire, un engagement permanent en faveur des couches les plus vulnérables dans le pays," AlterPresse, 23 July 2005.

196 "Pétition citoyenne pour réclamer la mise en accusation de Jean-Bertrand Aristide et de ses partisans en Haïti," AlterPresse, 26 July 2005.

197 "Une pétition pour demander au gouvernement d'eouvrer à la 'mise en accusation' d'Aristide," AlterPresse, 23 July 2005.

198 "Billet à Jacques Roche," AlterPresse, 21 July 2005.

CHAPTER FOUR

1   "Haiti's government advisory council says Aristide's party should be barred from elections," Associated Press, 17 July 2005.

2   "Rights group accuses gang leader of involvement in Jacques Roche murder," Reporters Without Borders, 22 September 2006.

3   "Le Directeur de la PNH démissionne," Radio Métropole, 18 July 2005.

4   "Mario Andrésol, investi d'un mandat de 3 ans (été 2009) à la tête de la Police Nationale d'Haïti," AlterPresse, 6 July 2006.

5   Author interview with Mario Andrésol, July 2015.

6   "Jacques Roche's kidnapping and death used by 'Council of Wise' as pretext for further criminalizing and slaughtering Lavalas supporters and further disenfranchise the poor masses in Haiti," HLLN statement, 17 July 2005.

7   "North Korea versus the United States: Who are the Demons?," Centre for Research on Globalization, 24 December 2011.

8   "Ottawa's Gaddafi fans find their world crumbling," National Post, 23 August 2011.

9   "Lavalas Party Members Arrested at Radio Caraïbes: Summary Statement of Pierre Espérance, NCHR-Haiti, Director," National Coalition for Haitian Rights, 6 October 2004.

10   "The Politics of Money: Haiti and the Left," Center for Research on Globalization, 24 November 2005.

11   Email sent by Ben Dupuy, 20 July 2006.

12   "Coup d'État or 'Coup de Broom' in Haiti and at WBAI?," Michael Deibert's Haiti blog, 13 May 2009, http://deiberthaiti.blogspot.com/2009/05/coup-detat-or-coup-de-broom-in-haiti.html.

13   U.S. Department of Justice Foreign Agents Registration Act (FARA) filings, 2001–04.

14   "IJDH Board Chair Ira Kurzban interviewed on KPFA re prosecution of Haiti President Aristide," https://youtu.be/uwlN4oHimzI, accessed 16 March 2016.

15   "Put Justice in Haiti on Your Holiday Gift List," http://www.ijdh.org/2010/01/archive/institute-for-justice-democracy-in-haiti-home-241/, accessed 15 March 2017.

16 "Human rights abuse and other criminal violations in Port-au-Prince, Haiti: a random survey of households," *The Lancet*, 31 August 2006.

17 "Debunking the Media's Lies about President Aristide," *Dissident Voice*, 14 March 2004.

18 "Jean Bertrand Aristide: Humanist or Despot?," Pacific News Service, 4 March 2004.

19 "Police use rape to terrorize women and girls in Haiti," *San Francisco Bay View*, 23 December 2005.

20 "Author of Lancet article on Haiti investigated," *The Globe and Mail*, 7 September 2006.

21 "Prestigious medical journal probes allegations of bias," *The Globe and Mail*, 14 October 2006.

22 "Lancet caught up in row over Haiti murders," *The Guardian*, 8 September 2006.

23 "Author of Lancet article on Haiti investigated," *The Globe and Mail*, 7 September 2006.

24 "The Lancet publishes results of inquiry into potential conflict of interest," 5 February 2007, http://ordinary.blogs.com/regret_the_error/2007/02/the_lancet_publ.html, accessed 15 March 2016. A less transparently wrong, though also inaccurate, report was published by the University of Miami School of Law's Center for Human Rights, which claimed that pro-Aristide armed gangs congealed after the president's departure. As it happened, the Center was at the time led by the attorney Irwin Stotzky, who was a longtime board member of the Aristide Foundation for Democracy, had served as an attorney and advisor to Aristide and had long-standing links with Ira Kurzban.

25 "Aristide in Exile," *The Nation*, 1 August 2005.

26 "Mixed U.S. Signals Helped Tilt Haiti Toward Chaos," *The New York Times*, 29 January 2006.

27 "Why they had to crush Aristide," *The Guardian*, 1 March 2004.

28 "Bursting the Dam of Containment," *Dissident Voice*, 21 June 2008.

29 Hallward, Peter (2008) *Damming the Flood: Haiti, Aristide, and the Politics of Containment*. London: Verso, p. 297. In a similar vein, Nicolas Rossier's 2005 film *Aristide and the Endless Revolution*, made by a director who had spent little time in the country, either ignored or dismissed long-standing Haitian organizations that fought and paid dearly for their commitment to democracy and fashioned a hagiography of the president.

30 Mark Weisbrot letter to *The Nation*, January 2006.

31 I myself was personally subjected to a campaign of calumny, harassment and intimidation for my reporting in Haiti, including disruption of my lectures by, among others, Aristide's lawyer Ira Kuzrban (in Miami in 2005), as well as emails sent to me celebrating the death of Jacques Roche (email to the author from Wilbens Charles, 7 December 2005) and photos of corpses sent to my personal email account (email to the author from Jeb Sprague, 22 November 2015).

32 Victor, Gary (2003) *A l'angle des rues parallèles*. La Roque d'Anthéron: Vents d'ailleurs.

33 Trouillot, Lionel (1996) *Rue des pas perdus*. Port-au-Prince: Mémoire.

34 Both songs appeared on the band's 1998 album *Révolution* (Tuff Gong).

35 Trouillot, Lyonel (1998) *Street of Lost Footsteps*. Lincoln, NE: University of Nebraska Press, p. 25.

36 "Multiplication des cas de lynchage de bandits à Port-au-Prince," Radio Métropole, 12 August 2005.

37 "7 présumés activistes armés lavalas lynchés par la population de Bel-Air," Radio Métropole, 11 August 2005.

38 "De nombreuses vies en danger à Cité Soleil, selon un ex-maire adjoint de Delmas," Radio Kiskeya, 10 August 2005.

39 Author interview with MINUSTAH official, 2014.

40 "Insécurité: un quartier de Port-au-Prince vidé de ses habitants," AlterPresse, 3 August 2005.

41 "L'activiste lavalas Paul Raymond et un de ses lieutenants remis aux autorités haïtiennes par le gouvernement dominicain," Radio Kiskeya, 22 July 2005.

42 "La police dominicaine arrête un ex-haut gradé haïtien," Radio Kiskyea, 17 September 2005.

43 "Hundreds of U.N. troops raid slum in Haiti's capital," Associated Press, 8 August 2005.

44 "Haiti's government advisory council says Aristide's party should be barred from elections," Associated Press, 17 July 2005.

45 "Four Alleged Kidnappers Released: RNDDH denounces the offensive decision by the President of the National Association of Haitian Magistrates," Réseau National de Défense des Droits Humains, 5 January 2006.

46 "Arrestation d'un important homme d'affaires en relation avec les cas de kidnapping enregistrés à Port-au-Prince," Radio Kiskeya, 23 August 2005.

47 "L'avocat de l'homme d'affaires Stanley Handal réclame sa libération," Radio Kiskeya, 26 August 2005.

48 "Arrestation de l'inspecteur de police en fuite James Bourdeau," AlterPresse, 16 September 2005.

49 "Affaire BRANDT: Le RNDDH exige l'aboutissement de l'enquête ouverte et le jugement de tous les membres du gang," Réseau National de Défense des Droits Humains, 13 November 2012.

50 "Libération imminente de l'homme d'affaires Stanley Handal et de 3 policiers réputés être ses complices dans des affaires louches," Radio Kiskeya, 19 February 2006.

51 "Un policier, témoin à charge dans une importante affaire de kidnapping, affirme avoir été victime d'un attentat," Radio Kiskeya, 15 January 2006.

52 "Stanley Handal défend son honneur," *Le Matin*, 30 November 2012.

53 "Update of arrests of two top police commanders in connection with Martissant soccer deaths," confidential cable from U.S. Embassy, Port-au-Prince, 30 November 2005.

54 "AVIGES dénonce un plan du gouvernement haïtien et d'un secteur de la Communauté internationale pour libérer l'ex-premier ministre Neptune," Radio Métropole, 12 August 2005.

55 "Le RNDDH fustige le comportement de Juan Gabriel Valdez et de Henry Dorléans dans le dossier de l'ex-premier ministre Neptune," Radio Métropole, 11 August 2005.

56 Author interview with Gérard Latortue, Boca Raton, May 2015.

57 "Des détenus lavalas au cabinet d'instruction," AlterPresse, 3 August 2005.

58 "L'ancien premier ministre lavalas Yvon Neptune et 29 autres personnes doivent être traduits par-devant le tribunal criminel, recommande l'ordonnance de clôture du juge chargé de l'instruction du dossier du Massacre de La Scierie," Radio Kiskeya, 19 September 2009.

59 "Jean-Bertrand Aristide accused of being responsible for the massacre of La Scierie," Radio Métropole, 6 October 2005.

60 "Journée d'effervescence politique et sociale aux Gonaïves," Radio Kiskeya, 26 August 2005.

61 "Rassemblement paysan projeté autour de la politique néo-libérale," AlterPresse, 21 August 2005.

62 "La réforme agraire une urgente nécessité, selon des paysans," AlterPresse, 27 July 2005.

63 "New commander leads Haiti force," BBC, 1 September 2005.

64 "La pacification de Cité Soleil: priorité numéro un du commandant désigné des troupes onusiennes en Haïti," Radio Kiskeya, 27 August 2005.

65 "Les jours du présumé bandit 'Général Toutou' sont comptés, affirme le commandant du contingent brésilien de la Minustah," Radio Métropole, 3 October 2005.

66 Author interview, Port-au-Prince, June 2015.

67 "Anna Ferdinand on Martissant," Michael Deibert's Haiti blog, 18 February 2007, http://deiberthaiti.blogspot.com/2011/07/anna-ferdinand-on-martissant.html, accessed 11 August 2015.

68 "Incident de Martissant: Le RNDDH fait le Pont," Réseau National de Défense des Droits Humains, September 2005.

69 "Alleged attacks by police, gangs investigated in Haiti," *The Miami Herald*, 1 September 2005.

70 "Incident de Martissant: Le RNDDH fait le Pont," Réseau National de Défense des Droits Humains, September 2005.

71 Author interviews, Port-au-Prince, July 2006.

72 Author interview with Mario Andrésol, July 2015.

73 "Situation de terreur à Martissant: la population, déterminée à contrer l'action des bandits, se met à la disposition de la police," Radio Kiskeya, 23 August 2005.

CHAPTER FIVE

1 "How Préval might change Haiti," *The Miami Herald*, 12 February 2006.

2 "Haiti has 18 presidential candidates," Associated Press, 15 September 2005.

3   "Gwoup Refleksyon pou kanpe Fwon Nasyonal Popilè Ayisyen pran pozisyon,"15 January 2004.

4   "Plusieurs milliers de partisans de René Préval dans les rues de Port-au-Prince," Radio Kiskeya, 22 October 2006.

5   Author interview with Juan Gabriel Valdés, March 2015.

6   "Elections: les législatives sont lancées avec la publication de la liste des candidats agréés au Sénat et à la Députation," Radio Kiskeya, 30 September 2005.

7   "Dumarsais Siméus et Samir Mourra sont détenteurs de passeports américain," Radio Métropole, 9 November 2005.

8   "Arrestation d'un lieutenant de feu Dread Wilmé," Radio Kiskeya, 3 October 2005.

9   "Jean Bertrand Aristide sous haute surveillance en Afrique du Sud," Radio Métropole, 28 September 2005.

10   Thomson, Ian (1992) *Bonjour, Blanc: A Journey Through Haiti*. London: Vintage, p. 36.

11   Author interview with Robinson "Labanye" Thomas, Cité Soleil, August 2002.

12   "Pharval Laboratories' CEO Ready to Help in the Investigation about Jean L. Dominique's murder," press release, 28 February 2002.

13   "Des appréhensions concernant la sécurité de la campagne électorale,"AlterPresse, 10 November 2005.

14   "Des milliers de partisans de Préval dans les rues," AlterPresse, 3 November 2005.

15   "René Préval crédité du meilleur score par un sondage Gallup," AlterPresse, 9 December 2005.

16   "Haiti Presidential and Legislative Elections 2006," report by Norwegian Centre for Human Rights (NORDEM), November 2006.

17   "Nouvelle montée de tension à Martissant," AlterPresse, 19 November 2005.

18   "Incendie dévastateur dans un marché populaire du bas de Port-au-Prince," Radio Kiskeya, 16 November 2005.

19   "Le chef de la police judiciaire dénonce la libération par la justice de présumés bandits dangeureux," Radio Métropole, 24 November 2005.

20   "Des policiers sous les verrous, des bandits en liberté," AlterPresse, 23 November 2005.

21   "Update of arrests of two top police commanders in connection with Martissant soccer deaths," confidential cable from U.S. Embassy, Port-au-Prince, 30 November 2005.

22   Ibid.

23   "Incidents meurtriers de Martissant: plusieurs dizaines de manifestants dans les rues pour réclamer la libération des 13 policiers incarcérés et l'arrestation du commandant de la Police Nationale, Mario Andrésol," Radio Kiskeya, 10 November 2005.

24   Author interview with Juan Gabriel Valdés, March 2015.

25   "5 décembre 2003/5 décembre 2005: deux ans après," Radio Métropole, 6 December 2005.

26   "5 décembre 2005: plusieurs dizaines d'étudiants manifestent pour réclamer justice," Radio Métropole, 5 December 2005.

27   "OAS officials abducted in Haiti," BBC, 30 December 2005.

28 "Une intervention de la police haïtienne permet la libération d'un otage belge," Radio Kiskeya, 29 December 2005.

29 "Trois casques bleus de la Minustah ont été blessés par balles," Radio Métropole, 19 December 2006.

30 "Le chef de la MINUSTAH, attribue aux bandits ou aux anciens militaires l'attaque de vendredi dernier contre les casques bleus dans le nord du pays," Radio Métropole, 19 December 2005.

31 "Jordanian UN peacekeeper killed in Haiti," Associated Press, 27 December 2005.

32 "Sécurité: les soldats jordaniens de la Minustah accusés d'incapacité," Radio Métropole, 29 December 2005.

33 "Journée d'accrochages et d'activités mafieuses des bandes armées au nord et au sud de Port-au-Prince," Radio Kiskeya, 12 January 2006.

34 "Mandat d'amener contre 12 individus dans le cadre de l'affaire Mourral," Radio Kiskeya, 23 January 2006.

35 "Gérard Jean-Juste déféré par-devant le Tribunal criminel sans assistance de jury pour 'association de malfaiteurs et détention illégale d'armes à feu'," Radio Kiskeya, 26 January 2006.

36 "Doctor: Jailed Haitian Priest Has Cancer," *Democracy Now*, 30 December 2005.

37 "Imprisoned Jean-Juste rejects deal," *The Miami Herald*, 25 January 2006.

38 "Décès à Miami du père Gérard Jean-Juste," Radio Kiskeya, 27 May 2009.

39 "General brasileiro da ONU é encontrado morto no Haiti," *O Globo*, 7 January 2006.

40 Author interview with Juan Gabriel Valdés, March 2015.

41 Author interview with former United Nations official, 2015.

42 "Brasil acompanhará de perto investigações da morte de general no Haiti," *O Globo*, 8 January 2006.

43 "General Bacellar cometeu suicídio, diz polícia," Reuters, 11 January 2006.

44 Author interview with Juan Gabriel Valdés, March 2015.

45 "General Bacellar cometeu suicídio, diz polícia," Reuters, 11 January 2006.

46 "New Year's message from the President of Haiti 2006," http://haitiaction.net/News/JBA/1_1_6.html, accessed 9 July 2015.

47 "Un chef de gang responsable de kidnapping se déclare favorable au candidat Préval," AlterPresse, 13 January 2006.

48 Radio Métropole broadcast, 13 December 2005.

49 "Haitian presidential hopeful decries gap between rich and poor," Agence France-Presse, 21 January 2006.

50 "Assassinat d'un responsable de la campagne électorale du candidat à la présidence Charles Henry Baker," Radio Métropole, 6 January 2006.

51 "Des installations du parti Lespwa à Saint-Marc incendiées par des individus non identifiés," Radio Métropole, 18 January 2006.

52 "Journée mouvementée pour le candidat René Préval à Ouanaminthe, théâtre d'affrontements entre bandes armées," Radio Kiskeya, 26 January 2006.

53 "Manifestation à Cité Soleil pour réclamer des centres de vote," Radio Métropole, 12 January 2006.

54 "Paris confirme l'enlèvement des trois français dont une religieuse octogénaire à Port-au-Prince," Radio Kiskeya, 27 January 2006.

55 "Two U.N. Peacekeepers Killed in Haiti," Associated Press, 17 January 2006.

56 "Mise à mort du chef de gang Blanc Raymond et représailles de son gang contre les habitants de Nan Palmiste, à Petite-Rivière de l'Artibonite," Radio Kiskeya, 23 January 2006.

57 "Undermining Haiti," *The Nation*, 12 December 2005.

58 "Time to Support Haiti," AlterPresse, 25 April 2006.

59 "Haiti Presidential and Legislative Elections 2006," report by Norwegian Centre for Human Rights (NORDEM), November 2006.

60 "Violence Flares as Top Candidate Slips in Haiti Count," *The New York Times*, 14 February 2006.

61 "Frontrunner Alleges Fraud in Haiti Vote," Associated Press, 14 February 2006.

62 "Les partisans de René Préval attisent la tension à Port-au-Prince," *Le Monde*, 14 February 2006.

63 "One Dead in Pro-Préval Protests in Haiti," Associated Press, 13 February 2006.

64 "Massive protests demand vote results," *The Miami Herald*, 14 February 2006.

65 "Violence Flares as Top Candidate Slips in Haiti Count," *The New York Times*, 14 February 2006.

66 Author interview with Frantz Large, Port-au-Prince, January 2016.

67 "One Dead in Pro-Préval Protests in Haiti," Associated Press, 13 February 2006.

68 "Frontrunner Alleges Fraud in Haiti Vote," Associated Press, 14 February 2006.

69 "Blank Ballots Decide Haiti Election," Associated Press, 16 February 2006.

70 "Haitians Dance for Joy as Préval Is Declared Winner," *The New York Times*, 17 February 2006.

71 "Mirlande Manigat abandonne la course au Sénat de la république," Radio Kiskeya, 21 February 2006.

72 "Préval II: Que la fête aurait été belle," *Le Matin*, 17 February 2006.

73 "Haiti voted for my return," *Mail & Guardian* (South Africa), 24 February 2006.

74 "SA in no hurry to send Aristide back home," *The Independent*, 3 April 2006.

75 "Interview with Haitian President-Elect René Préval: Haiti Has Voted for Change," Radio Havana, 7 March 2006.

76 "The Once and Future President Breaks His Silence," Inter Press Service, 22 February 2006.

77 Author interview with Gérard Latortue, Boca Raton, May 2015.

78 "Haiti's Préval meets Bush at White House," Agence France-Presse, 29 March 2006.

79 "René Préval promet que la Police haïtienne sera une force non politisée," Radio Métropole, 22 March 2006.

80 "Haïti intègrera le programme Pétrocaribe le 15 mai prochain," Radio Métropole, 25 April 2006.

81 "Deux agents de sécurité de l'ambassade américaine tués à Port-au-Prince," Radio Kiskeya, 2 March 2006.

82 "Un 3ème agent haïtien de la sécurité de l'Ambassade des États-Unis tué à Port-au-Prince en moins de 3 mois," Radio Kiskeya, 21 May 2006.

83 "Poursuite de l'enquête sur l'assassinat de quatre policiers haïtiens," Radio Kiskeya, 16 March 2006.

84 "De nouveaux crânes humains découverts à Port-au-Prince," Radio Métropole, 27 March 2006.

85 "Libération d'un ancien directeur de la Police administrative," Radio Métropole, 17 April 2006.

86 "Journée 'positive', mais un mort et plusieurs blessés," AlterPresse, 21 April 2006.

87 "L'UE estime à moins de 15% le taux de participation au scrutin," Radio Métropole, 21 Aprile 2006.

88 "Publication des premiers résultats partiels du second tour des législatives," Radio Métropole, 24 April 2006.

89 "Republique d'Haïti, Resultats Electoraux," Georgetown University, http://pdba. georgetown.edu/Elecdata/Haiti/leg06.html, accessed 24 February 2009.

90 "Haiti's biggest party banned from senate race," Reuters, 17 February 2009.

91 "New Haiti leader seen able to control legislature," Reuters, 26 April 2006.

92 "Lavalas reunification meeting fails," confidential cable from U.S. Embassy, Port-au-Prince, 12 June 2006.

93 "Des partisans d'Aristide annoncent une nouvelle campagne, dès samedi, en faveur de son retour," Radio Kiskeya, 19 April 2006.

94 "Gang kills, burns alleged kidnappers," Associated Press, 3 May 2006.

95 "Insécurité en Haïti: 10 agents de la PNH assassinés," Radio Métropole, 9 June 2006.

96 "Arrestation de l'ancien chef d'organisation populaire René Civil, à la frontière haïtiano-dominicaine," Radio Kiskeya, 13 May 2006.

97 "Agitation à l'audition des inculpés du massacre de La Scierie," Radio Kiskeya, 10 May 2006.

98 "Haiti's president in Ottawa to ask for support," Canadian Press, 1 May 2006.

99 "Haiti gets $48 million boost," Toronto Star, 2 May 2006.

100 "Haiti Legislators Sworn In, Hold Session," Associated Press, 9 May 2006.

101 "Formation des bureaux au Parlement: Eric Jean Jacques est élu à la présidence de la Chambre des Députés," Radio Métropole, 11 May 2006.

102 "La Présidence accorde près de 25.000 dollars à chaque Député pour l'achat de véhicules," Radio Kiskeya, 5 October 2006.

103 "Les partisans et anciens collaborateurs d'Aristide reprennent du service Fidèles," Radio Kiskeya 14 May 2006.

104 "Le président Préval lance un appel à la paix et l'unité entre les haïtiens," Radio Métropole, 14 May 2006.

105 "Préval sworn in, urges era of peace," The Miami Herald, 15 May 2006.

106 "Le Président Préval invite les parlementaires à ratifier son Premier ministre désigné," Radio Kiskeya, 22 May 2006.

107 "L'intégration officielle d'Haïti dans l'accord pétrolier PetroCaribe, premier acte de Préval après son investiture," Radio Kiskeya, 14 May 2006.

CHAPTER SIX

1 Author interview with Edmond Mulet, New York City, June 2014.

2 "Bloc embraces reinstated Haiti," *The Miami Herald*, 4 July 2006.

3 "Assassinat de la veuve de l'ancien Président haïtien, Dumarsais Estimé," Radio Kiskeya, 19 May 2006.

4 "La PNH de nouveau mobilisée contre les bandits en général et les penéurs d'otages en particulier," Radio Kiskeya, 21 June 2006.

5 "La vie du Directeur Central de la Police Judiciaire de la PNH, 'sérieusement menacée' par des secteurs mafieux," Radio Kiskeya, 27 May 2006.

6 "L'ombre de l'État de Droit," Réseau National de Défense des Droits Humains, July 2007.

7 "Lavalas reunification meeting fails," confidential cable from U.S. Embassy, Port-au-Prince, 12 June 2006.

8 "Six morts dans des affrontements entre des bandits et casques bleus de la Minustah à Cité Soleil," Radio Métropole, 8 June 2006.

9 "Le gouvernement Alexis lance des projets sociaux à Cité Soleil," Radio Métropole, 24 June 2006.

10 "Alerte sur la banalisation de la violence armée dans la banlieue sud/sud-est de la capitale," AlterPresse, 22 June 2006.

11 "Plus de 40 personnes auraient été assassinées le week end écoulé à Martissant," Radio Métropole, 11 July 2006.

12 "Plus de 120 blessés par balles soignés par MSF en juillet 2006," AlterPresse, 28 July 2006.

13 "Mario Andrésol, investi d'un mandat de 3 ans (été 2009) à la tête de la Police Nationale d'Haïti," AlterPresse, 6 July 2006.

14 "Nouveau cas d'assassinat dans les rangs de la PNH," Radio Métropole, 3 July 2006.

15 "Ex-cop to head national security," Associated Press, 14 July 2006.

16 "Arrestation de Ronald Dauphin alias Black Ronald," Radio Métropole, 24 July 2006.

17 "Libération de l'ex-ministre lavalas de l'intérieur Jocelerme Privert," Radio Métropole, 19 June 2006.

18 "Haiti Country Summary," Human Rights Watch, January 2007.

19 "Donor nations pledge $750 million for Haiti," Reuters, 26 July 2006.

20 Confidential cable from U.S. Embassy, Port-au-Prince, 2 August 2006.

21 "New Truce Quells Gang Violence for Now," confidential cable from U.S. Embassy, Port-au-Prince, 24 July 2006.

22 "Haiti tells gangs to disarm or face death," Reuters, 10 August 2006.

23 "Deux présumés bandits tués par la police dans le centre commercial de Port-au-Prince," Radio Kiskeya, 1 August 2006.

24 "L'insécurité à Port-au-Prince fait de nouvelles victimes," Radio Métropole, 3 August 2006.

25 "Au moins deux blessés par balle à Port-au-Prince," Radio Kiskeya, 8 August 2006.

26 "Au moins 2 personnes tuées dans de nouvelles violences à Port-au-Prince," Alter-Presse, 9 August 2009.

27 "Gunmen in Haiti kill Italian businessman," Associated Press, 8 August 2006.

28 "Au moins quatre personnes tuées à Port-au-Prince au cours des dernières 24 heures," Radio Kiskeya, 10 August 2006.

29 "Ou le dialogue dans le cadre du DDR, ou la mort, lance René Préval aux groupes armés," Radio Kiskeya, 9 August 2006.

30 "René Préval: les bandits doivent choisir entre la mort ou la remise des armes," Radio Métropole, 9 August 2006.

31 "Haiti tells gangs to disarm or face death," Reuters, 10 August 2006.

32 "Des parlementaires opposés à toute forme de dialogue avec les bandits," Radio Métropole, 8 August 2006.

33 "De nombreux partisans d'Aristide réclament son retour et manifestent pour la première fois contre le Président Préval," Radio Kiskeya, 14 August 2006.

34 "Quatre anciens responsables Lavalas et partisans d'Aristide acquittés dans l'affaire du 5 décembre 2003, l'attaque sanglante contre l'Université d'État," Radio Kiskeya, 14 August 2006.

35 "Les quatre anciens prisonniers Lavalas passent à l'offensive et réclament le retour d'Aristide," Radio Kiskeya, 17 August 2006.

36 "Des étudiants critiquent la libération de trois activistes lavalas impliqués dans l'attaque contre l'Université d'État," Radio Métropole, 17 August 2006.

37 "L'ex-Député Lavalas Nahoun Marcellus de retour après deux années d'exil," Radio Kiskeya, 23 August 2006.

38 "State says Aristide welcome to stay on as 'guest'," Sapa-AP, 16 August 2006.

39 "U.N. renews troops in Haiti for 6 months," Reuters, 15 August 2006.

40 "Des sénateurs réclament la constitution d'une nouvelle force armée," Radio Métropole, 10 August 2006.

41 "Le sénateur Latortue réclame des réformes au sein de la police," Radio Meropole, 1 September 2006.

42 Confidential cable from U.S. Embassy, Port-au-Prince, 20 November 2006.

43 "Libération du Député Rodney Alcide, enlevé vendredi soir," Radio Kiskeya, 26 August 2006.

44 "Deux policiers haïtiens et un civil blessés par balle jeudi dans une attaque aux Gonaïves," Radio Kiskeya, 1 September 2006.

45 "Le juge Claudy Gassant pressenti pour le poste de commissaire du gouvernement près le Tribunal civil de Port-au-Prince," Radio Kiskeya, 18 August 2006.

46 "Arrestation du chef d'OP Lavalas René Civil à bord d'un véhicule vraisemblablement volé en République Dominicaine," Radio Kiskeya, 26 August 2006.

47 "René Civil transféré au Pénitencier National sur ordre du commissaire du gouvernement de Port-au-Prince," Radio Kiskeya, 29 August 2006.

48 "Justice et Paix fait état d'une augmentation de la violence," Radio Métropole, 13 November 2006.

49 "Vague d'attaques criminelles à Port-au-Prince et affrontements meurtriers entre gangs rivaux aux Gonaïves," Radio Kiskeya, 7 September 2006.

50 "Funérailles de Véronique Valmé, une des victimes de l'incident de Pétion-Ville," Radio Kiskeya, 12 September 2006.

51 "L'ex-colonel des FAD'H Guy François abattu par balle à Pétion-Ville," Radio Kiskeya, 14 September 2006.

52 "Une des nombreuses victimes de l'insécurité à Port-au-Prince lutte pour la survie après avoir été atteinte de 8 balles," Radio Kiskeya, 9 September 2006.

53 "Enlèvement du directeur de l'Office National d'Aviation Civile: Jean Lemercque Pierre toujours aux mains de ses ravisseurs," Radio Kiskeya, 13 September 2006.

54 "Arrestation du chef de gang William Baptiste alias Ti Blanc," Radio Kiskeya, 5 April 2007.

55 "Le numéro 3 de la police dénonce le comportement d'un juge d'instruction," Radio Métropole, 13 September 2006.

56 "Haiti Country Summary," Human Rights Watch, January 2007.

57 "Manifestation contre la violence et l'insécurité sévissant dans plusieurs quartiers de la banlieue sud de Port-au-Prince," Radio Kiskeya, 29 September 2006.

58 "Escalade d'enlèvements en Haïti, la police libère deux otages dont une fillette," Radio Kiskeya, 2 October 2006.

59 "U.S. partially lifts arms embargo against Haiti," Associated Press, 10 October 2006.

60 "La mobilisation étudiante contre l'ONU maintenue," Radio Kiskyea, 26 October 2006.

61 "Les duvaliéristes tentent de revenir au devant de la scène politique," AlterPresse, 23 October 2006.

62 "Les OP lavalas annoncent la reprise de l'opération Bagdad," Radio Métropole, 27 October 2006.

63 "Bras de fer entre le gouvernement et les OP lavalas," Radio Métropole, 31 October 2006.

64 "Des bandits sèment la terreur: un mort et plusieurs blessés," Radio Métropole, 3 November 2006.

65 "Confronting the Gangs of Port-au-Prince," United States Institute of Peace, September 2008.

66 "Enlèvement de Fred Joseph, ex-ministre des finances de Préval," Radio Kiskeya, 30 November 2006.

67 "Critiques contre les violences des groupes armés," Radio Métropole, 6 November 2006.

68 Author interview with United Nations official, 2014.

69 "La terreur s'installe à Port-au-Prince, dénonce le RNDDH," AlterPresse, 7 December 2006.

70 "Funérailles du jeune martyr Carl Roobenz Francillon," Radio Kiskeya, 28 November 2006.

71 "La mère de Farah Dessources laisse Haïti en quête d'une terre d'asile," Radio Kiskeya, 27 December 2006.

72 "Manifestation anti gouvernementale à l'occasion des obsèques de Farah Dessources," Radio Métropole, 26 November 2006.

73 "Arrestation de l'un des assassins de Natacha Dessources," Radio Métropole, 30 June 2007.

74 "Arrestation dans la Grand'Anse du redoutable chef de gang Millet Jean Elie," Radio Kiskeya, 30 June 2007.

75 "Arrestation d'un adolescent de 15 ans pour implication présumée dans l'assassinat de la jeune Farah Natacha Kerby Dessources," Radio Kiskeya, 11 January 2008.

76 "Des chefs de gangs, organisateurs de manifestation," Radio Métropole, 14 November 2006.

77 "La terreur s'installe à Port-au-Prince, dénonce le RNDDH," AlterPresse, 7 December 2006.

78 "Reprise des affrontements entre les gangs de Martissant," Radio Métropole, 21 November 2006.

79 "3 morts et 17 blessés par balle dans des incidents entre gangs à Martissant," Radio Kiskeya, 21 November 2006.

80 "Deux fidèles grièvement blessées par balle dans une église à Cité Soleil," Radio Kiskeya, 14 November 2006.

81 "En depit des critiques le chef du gouvernement continue à dialoguer avec les bandits," Radio Métropole, 28 November 2006.

82 "Haitian leader says aid flow is slow," Associated Press, 30 November 2006.

83 "Un commando tue deux personnes dont un enfant à Port-au-Prince," Radio Kiskeya, 2 December 2006.

84 "Evasion spectaculaire au Pénitencier national," Radio Métropole, 4 December 2006.

85 "Confronting the Gangs of Port-au-Prince," United States Institute of Peace, September 2008.

86 "Début timide des opérations de vote," Radio Métropole, 3 December 2006.

87 "Début des municipales et locales en Haïti," Radio Kiskeya, 3 December 2006.

88 "Deux morts et plusieurs blessés à Port-au-Prince et en province," Radio Kiskeya, 3 December 2006.

89 "Le CEP satisfait de l'organisation des élections, mais reconnaît une faible participation," Radio Kiskeya, 4 December 2006.

90 "Résultats Sénatoriales du Nord-Est: la Fusion remporte les deux premiers sièges," Radio Kiskeya, 19 December 2006.

91 "Deux morts et plusieurs blessés à Port-au-Prince et en province," Radio Kiskeya, 3 December 2006.

92 "Quatre personnes assassinées à Port-au-Prince," Radio Kiskeya, 4 December 2006.

93 "Nouveaux affrontements entre les gangs de Martissant, 4 morts," Radio Métropole, 8 December 2006.

94 "Des organisations condamnent les négociations entre le gouvernement et les gangs," Radio Métropole, 13 December 2006.

95 "Haïti s'enfonce un peu plus dans l'horreur," Radio Kiskeya, 12 December 2006.

96 "Deux groupes d'écoliers enlevés à Port-au-Prince," Radio Kiskeya, 13 December 2006.

97 "Haïti de plus en plus déstabilisée par le terrorisme," Radio Kiskeya, 19 December 2006.

98 "Le sénateur Riché explique avoir échappé de justesse à ses ravisseurs," Radio Kiskeya, 16 December 2006.

99 "Des sénateurs réclament de nouvelles dispositions contre l'insécurité," Radio Métropole, 14 December 2006.

100 "Le premier ministre s'engage à combattre l'insécurité," Radio Métropole, 14 December 2006.

101 "Confronting the Gangs of Port-au-Prince," United States Institute of Peace, September 2008.

102 Author interview with MINUSTAH official, June 2013.

103 "Le gouvernement adopte de nouvelles dispositions sécuritaires," Radio Métropole, 21 Deceber 2006.

104 "MINUSTAH Begins Target Operations," confidential cable from U.S. Embassy, Port-au-Prince, 26 December 2006.

105 "9 morts et plus de 30 blessés lors d'affrontement entre des gangs et les forces de l'ONU," Radio Métropole, 22 December 2006.

106 "Accrochage entre les forces de l'ordre et des manifestants," Radio Métropole, 20 December 2006.

107 "'Tout moun jwenn' ('Chacun a eu son lot'), dit Jean Bertrand Aristide en référence au kidnapping: le leader lavalas lance des mots d'ordre et fustige les 'traitres'," Radio Kiskeya, 26 December 2006.

108 "Aristide's SA high life to continue," *The Sunday Independent*, 5 July 2009.

109 "Aristide 'earning his keep'," *News 24* (South Africa), 27 July 2006.

110 "Le parti lavalas impliqué dans le kidnapping selon le sénateur Fortuné," Radio Métropole, 27 December 2006.

111 "Plus de 530 morts de violence armée fin 2006 à Port-au-Prince," AlterPresse, 26 January 2007.

112 "René Préval quitte Les Gonaïves sans avoir achevé son discours," Radio Kiskeya, 1 January 2007.

113 "Les forces de l'ordre poursuivront leur offensive à Cité Soleil," Radio Métropole, 3 January 2007.

114 "La traque des bandits, priorité du chef de l'état," Radio Métropole, 8 January 2007.

115 "Deux policiers blessés par balle lors d'une opération anti-kidnapping," Radio Kiskeya, 8 January 2007.

116 "Deux nouveaux décès dans les rangs de la police haïtienne," Radio Kiskeya, 6 January 2007.

117 "Cambriolage au Parquet: disparition d'une cinquantaine d'armes à feu, de documents et de pièces à conviction constituant 93 dossiers judiciaires," Radio Kiskeya, 1 February 2007.

118 "L'indicateur des droits humains, Numéro 7," Réseau National de Défense des Droits Humains, April 2007.

119 "Des sénateurs ont été soudoyés pour voter une résolution en faveur de la SOCABANK, révèle le sénateur Gabriel Fortuné," Radio Kiskeya, 27 January 2007.

120 "Scandale au Parlement haïtien: le PDG de Haïtel, Franck Ciné, a distribué des pots de vin à des parlementaires, selon le sénateur Gabriel Fortuné," Radio Kiskeya, 29 January 2007.

121 "Enquête sur les pots-de-vin et l'implication de parlementaires dans le trafic illicite des stupéfiants," Radio Kiskeya, 13 February 2007.

122 "Le sénateur Fortuné dénonce des sénateurs corrompus et trafiquants de drogue," Radio Métropole, 16 February 2007.

123 "Scandale de corruption au Parlement: la Fondation Héritage inquiète face au refus des sénateurs d'une investigation plus poussée," Radio Kiskeya, 26 March 2007.

124 "Une nouvelle victime des gangs à Bolosse/Martissant," Radio Kiskeya, 19 January 2007.

125 "In Haiti, photographer gunned down after receiving gang threats," Committee to Protect Journalists, 25 January 2007.

126 "Le gouvernement annonce des opérations contre les gangs de Martissant," Radio Métropole, 23 January 2007.

127 "Des milliers de fans accueillent les champions de la Caraïbe," Radio Kiskeya, 24 January 2007.

128 "Clashes in Haiti leave at least five dead, 12 wounded," Agence France-Presse, 25 January 2007.

129 "4 morts et 6 blessés lors d'une opération musclée de casques bleus à Cité Soleil: un policier national tué par des inconnus armés," AlterPresse, 25 January 2007.

130 "Deux policiers haïtiens assassinés en quelques heures," Radio Kiskeya, 26 January 2007.

131 "US gives Haiti $20 million, seeks longer UN mission," Reuters, 2 February 2007.

132 "La Minustah déloge les membres d'un gang impliqué dans des kidnappings," Radio Métropole, 10 February 2007.

133 "U.N. chases gang chief; 1 killed in slum firefight," The Miami Herald, 10 February 2007.

134 "La résidence d'un chef de gang pillée, des bandits de Cité Soleil sont en cavale," Radio Métropole, 12 February 2007.

135 "Confronting the Gangs of Port-au-Prince," United States Institute of Peace, September 2008.

136 "Le chef de gang Evens: apparemment le plus 'riche' des 'pauvres' de Cité Soleil," Radio Kiskeya, 14 February 2007.

137 "UN peacekeepers turn former gang chief's headquarters into health clinic," UN News Centre, 15 February 2007.

138 "L'étau se resserre sur les bandits de Cité Soleil," Radio Métropole, 21 February 2007.

139 "In Haitian slum, fear recedes slowly," *The Miami Herald*, 20 February 2007.

140 "Les forces de l'ordre lancent une offensive contre les bandits de Martissant," Radio Métropole, 13 February 2007.

141 Letter from Youri Latortue to Jacques Édouard Alexis, 12 February 2007.

142 "Le parti Lavalas prend ses distances vis-à-vis des chefs de gang," Radio Métropole, 16 February 2007.

143 "Peacekeepers seize Haitian leader's home," Associated Press, 21 February 2007.

144 "Bélékou libéré du joug des gangs armés," *Le Nouvelliste*, 23 February 2015.

145 "Une dizaine de kidnappings recensés à Port-au-Prince en trois jours," Radio Kiskeya, 23 February 2007.

146 "Les incidents du Bel-Air ont fait 7 morts et des blessés, selon la police," Radio Kiskeya, 21 March 2007.

147 "Cinq personnes abattues par balle à La Saline," Radio Kiskeya, 23 March 2007.

148 "Venezuelan leader gets hero's welcome in Haiti," Reuters, 13 March 2007.

149 "Arrestation du puissant chef de gang Evens Jeune," Radio Kiskeya, 13 March 2007.

150 "Le Président Préval satisfait de l'arrestation du chef de gang Evens Jeune," Radio Kiskeya, 14 March 2007.

151 "Décès en prison du puissant chef de gang Evens Jeune," Radio Kiskeya, 24 July 2009.

152 "Arrestation de Alain Cadet, alias 'Pinochet', numéro deux du gang de Belony," Radio Kiskeya, 5 April 2007.

153 "Arrestation du chef de gang William Baptiste alias Ti Blanc," Radio Kiskeya, 5 April 2007.

154 "14 ans de prison pour William Baptiste dit Ti Blan," Radio Kiskeya, 23 July 2009.

155 "Lancement officiel du carnaval 2007," Radio Kiskeya, 18 February 2007.

CHAPTER SEVEN

1 "Propos de la première ministre Michèle Pierre-Louis, le 21 mai 2009, à l'occasion de l'investiture au ministère des affaires étrangères de la partie nationale de la Commission mixte haitiano-dominicaine."

2 Price-Mars, Jean (1953) *La République d'Haïti et la République dominicaine: Les aspects divers d'un problème d'histoire, de géographie et d'ethnologie.* Quebec: Classiques des Sciences Sociales, p. 10.

3 Franco, Franklin Pichardo (1997) *Sobre racismo y antihaitianismo y otros ensayos.* Santo Domingo, Dominican Republic: Impresora Vidal, p. 144.

4   Roorda, Eric Paul (1998) *The Dictator Next Door*. Durham, NC: Duke University Press, pp. 21–2.

5   Ibid., p. 131.

6   "The massacre that marked Haiti-Dominican Republic ties," BBC News, 13 October 2012.

7   "I shot the cruellest dictator in the Americas," BBC News, 28 May 2012.

8   "Jose Pena Gomez, 61, Rare Black Dominican Figure, Dies," *The New York Times*, 12 May 1998.

9   "Dominican Republic's outrageously corrupt election," *The Baltimore Sun*, 20 May 1994.

10   "Peña denuncia un frente 'racista' en las elecciones dominicanas," *El País*, 4 June 1996.

11   "Peña Gómez, Balaguer y el racismo," *Hoy*, 2 September 2005.

12   "U.S.-Raised Lawyer to Lead Dominican Republic," *The New York Times*, 2 July 1996.

13   "Haitian cane-cutters struggle," *Christian Science Monitor*, 1 February 2006.

14   "Abuses against Haitian Migrant Workers and Dominico-Haitians in the Dominican Republic," Amnesty International, August 2006.

15   "Film on Plantations Spurs Backlash," Inter Press Service, 4 June 2007.

16   Eduardo Gamarra biography, http://pir.fiu.edu/people/faculty/eduardo-gamarra/, accessed 25 May 2016.

17   Author interview with Javier Hernández, Cap-Haïtien, May 2005.

18   "Thousands of Haitian migrants thrown out of Dominican Republic," Christian Aid, 23 May 2005.

19   "Paysan presque esclave, presque libre," AlterPresse, 30 March 2005.

20   "2,000 Haitians expelled from Dominican Republic: groups," Agence France-Presse, 22 August 2005.

21   "Fernández admet le viol des droits de rapatriés haïtiens par son gouvernement," AlterPresse, 24 June 2005.

22   "Carlos Morales Troncoso, Minister of Foreign Relations Personal Profile," http://www.domrep.org/troncosobio.html, accessed 25 May 2016.

23   "Haitian cane-cutters struggle," *Christian Science Monitor*, 1 February 2006.

24   "In the Kingdom of Big Sugar," *Vanity Fair*, 5 January 2011.

25   Author interview with Father Christopher Hartley, January 2016.

26   Readers should see two excellent 2007 films, director Bill Haney's *The Price of Sugar* and Amy Serrano's *The Sugar Babies* for further information.

27   Author interview, Miami, June 2007.

28   "Hommage au Père Pedro Ruquoy," Groupe d'Appui aux Rapatriés et Réfugiés, 21 November 2005.

29   "Amnesty International Urgent Action 237/05," 12 September 2005.

30   "Cardenal la emprende contra curas extranjeros," *Diario Libre*, 3 November 2005. López Rodríguez also effusively praised Józef Wesołowski, the former Papal Nuncio to the Dominican Republic charged with serious abuse of children who died before he could stand trial. See "Cardenal destaca gestión de nuncio," *La República*, 28 August 2013.

31 "Dominican-Haitian activist Sonia Pierre dies at 48," Associated Press, 4 December 2011.

32 "Décès dimanche matin en République dominicaine de la célèbre militante des droits des dominicains d'origine haïtienne, Sonia Pierre," Radio Kiskeya, 4 December 2011.

33 "Dominican Born Haitian Rights Defender, Sonia Pierre, wins 2006 RFK Human Rights Award," Robert F. Kennedy Memorial, 6 October 2006.

34 "Dominican official blasts U.S. group for awarding rights activist," Associated Press, 21 December 2006.

35 "La République Dominicaine se dit victime d'une campagne de dénigrement pour sa politique vis-à-vis des migrants haïtiens," Radio Kiskeya, 30 March 2007.

36 "A Rights Advocate's Work Divides Dominicans," *The New York Times*, 29 September 2007.

37 "Dominican Government to battle "unjust" campaign on Haitian issue," *Dominican Today*, 27 March 2007.

38 Grupo SID website, http://www.gruposid.com.do, accessed 29 May 2016.

39 "Haitians in the Dominican Republic," confidential U.S. Embassy cable, 18 October 2006.

40 "Champ de Mars (centre de la capitale) devant le Palais National," Radio Kiskeya, 12 December 2005.

41 "At least three Haitians shot during protest of Dominican president's visit," Associated Press, 13 December 2005.

42 "La pression s'accentue sur les étudiants haïtiens en République Dominicaine," Alter-Presse, 16 December 2005.

43 "Plus de 4.000 haïtiens expulsés en trois semaines," Radio Kiskeya, 23 January 2007.

44 Author interview, 2015.

45 "Saisie d'une cargaison d'armes et de munitions à la frontière haïtiano-dominicaine," Radio Métropole, 23 August 2005.

46 "Décès tragique d'un haut fonctionnaire de la justice des Gonaïves," AlterPresse, 24 April 2007.

47 "Le président de la Cour d'Appel des Gonaïves tué dans un accident," Radio Kiskeya, 24 April 2007.

48 "La libération de Amanus Mayette est une décision politique selon Samuel Madistin," Radio Métropole, 27 April 2007.

49 Ibid.

50 "Le RNDDH réclame la poursuite de la procédure judiciaire autour du massacre de la scierie," Radio Mertropole, 3 May 2007.

51 "Massacre de la Scierie: le gouvernement se range du côté des bourreaux," Réseau National de Défense des Droits Humais, 30 April 2007.

52 "Manifestation du RAMICOSM contre la libération de Amanus Mayette," Radio Métropole, 4 May 2007.

53 "Desacord entre le gouvernement et des organisations de Saint-Marc," Radio Métropole, 2 May 2007.

54 "Violente manifestation antigouvernementale aux funérailles du juge Hugues Saint-Pierre," Radio Kiskeya, 7 May 2007.

55 "Lettre ouverte au juge Louis Joinet," from Charliénor Thomson, Coordonnateur, AVIGES, 12 June 2007.

56 "Legal Analysis of Ronald Dauphin Case," Institute for Justice and Democracy in Haiti, 6 June 2009.

57 "EU pledges 233 million euros to Haiti," Reuters, 21 April 2007.

58 "L'Unité de Lutte Contre la Corruption pourrait bientôt être placée sous tutelle du parlement," Radio Kiskeya, 15 May 2007.

59 "La Fondation Héritage pour Haïti n'appuie pas l'idée de la mise sous tutelle du Parlement haïtien de l'Unité de Lutte Contre la Corruption (ULCC)," Radio Kiskeya, 18 May 2007.

60 "René Préval entre en guerre contre la corruption," Radio Kiskeya, 18 May 2007.

61 "Le sénateur Boulos apporte son appui à la lutte contre la corruption," Radio Métropole, 21 May 2007.

62 "L'affaire SOCABANK franchit une nouvelle étape: brève interpellation du PDG de la Haïtel, Franck Ciné," Radio Kiskeya, 14 May 2007.

63 "Hospitalisation de l'homme d'affaires Franck Ciné, incarcéré dans le cadre d'un scandale politico-financier," Radio Kiskeya, 19 June 2007.

64 "Les autorités policières annoncent de nouvelles arrestations de chefs de gang de Martissant," Radio Métropole, 7 May 2007.

65 "Le chef de gang Blade Nasson arrêté à Cité Soleil," Radio Kiskeya, 8 May 2007.

66 "Scènes de joie aux Gonaïves après l'assassinat d'un des principaux chefs de gang locaux, Adecla Saint-Juste," Radio Kiskeya, 20 June 2007.

67 "Le célèbre acteur et publicitaire haïtien François Latour, kidnappé et lâchement exécuté à Port-au-Prince," Radio Kiskeya, 23 May 2007.

68 "Le redoutable chef de gang Junior Acdhély dit 'Yoyo Piman' tué à Cité Soleil," Radio Kiskeya, 12 June 2007.

69 "Arrestation du principal adjoint d'Evens Jeune, Bazile Soifette dit 'Ti Bazile,'" Radio Kiskeya, 9 July 2007.

70 "Le chef de la police déterminé a poursuivre les réformes au sein de l'institution," Radio Métropole, 13 June 2007.

71 "Baisse de la criminalité," AlterPresse, 12 July 2007.

72 "Youri Latortue Reaches Out," secret U.S. Embassy cable, 27 June 2007.

73 "Nouveau raid de la DEA et du BLTS: deux présumés narcotrafiquants arrêtés au Cap-Haïtien," Radio Kiskeya, 22 July 2007.

74 "U.S., Haiti team up on drug raid," *The Miami Herald*, 20 July 2007.

75 "In Haiti, ex-rebel sought by U.S. denies drug ties," Associated Press, 23 July 2007.

76 "Le présumé narcotrafiquant Frantz Cadet arrêté et candidat à l'extradition," Radio Kiskeya, 2 August 2007.

77 "Arrestation de l'homme d'affaires Fritz Brandt et de son fils David Brandt," Radio Kiskaya, 27 July 2007.

78 "La Chambre de Commerce et d'Industrie d'Haïti s'élève contre la 'détention inopportune' et même 'illégale' de certains hommes d'affaires," Radio Kiskeya, 14 August 2007.

79 "Human Rights Indicator Number 8," Réseau National de Défense des Droits Humains, October 2007.

80 "New UN envoy for Haiti in juggle of top posts," Reuters, 27 July 2007.

81 "Mr. Hédi Annabi, 1943–2010 Special Representative to Haiti (Tunisia)," http://www.un.org/en/memorial/haiti/annabi.shtml, accessed 15 September 2015.

82 "Poignant words of UN chief killed in Haiti," Channel 4 News, 14 January 2010.

83 "Secretary-General Appoints Luiz Carlos da Costa of Brazil as Principal Deputy Special Representative for United Nations Stabilization Mission in Haiti," United Nations press release, 10 November 2006.

84 "Au moins 4 ans pour parvenir à une stabilisation d'Haïti, selon le numéro 2 de la MINUSTAH," AlterPresse, 7 July 2007.

85 "UN Chief Backs Haiti Peacekeepers," Associated Press, 2 August 2007.

86 "Des militaires démobilisés réclament dans les rues de Port-au-Prince le rétablissement des FAd'H," Radio Kiskeya, 25 July 2007.

87 "René Préval lance une commission de journalistes chargée d'appuyer les enquêtes sur les cas d'assassinats de journalistes," Radio Kiskeya, 10 August 2007.

88 "Dany Toussaint, au Cabinet d'Instruction, annonce avoir désigné une personne prête à faire des révélations sur l'assassinat de Jean Dominique," Radio Kiskeya, 10 August 2007.

89 "Des secteurs de presse saluent la condamnation de 2 des assassins du journaliste Jacques Roche," AlterPresse, 4 September 2007.

90 "Two gang members get life for journalist's murder, a third is acquitted," Reporters sans Frontières, 11 December 2007.

91 "Le chef de 'Lame Ti Manchèt', Roody Kernisant, se serait suicidé pour éviter d'être appréhendé par une patrouille conjointe de la MINUSTAH et de la PNH," Radio Kiskeya, 11 August 2007.

92 "Le dirigeant Lavalas Lovinsky Pierre-Antoine porté disparu, selon ses proches," Radio Kiskeya, 14 August 2007.

93 "L'ex-responsable de la DCPJ, l'inspecteur général Michael Lucius, blessé par balle," Radio Kiskeya, 26 September 2007.

94 "Une centaine de personnes libérées pour des raisons humanitaires," Radio Métropole, 6 August 2007.

95 "Deux Sénateurs au bureau de Claudy Gassant," Radio Kiskeya, 28 August 2007.

96 "Rencontre sereine entre les sénateurs et le chef du parquet," Radio Métropole, 31 August 2007.

97 "Haiti senators jeopardising stability, says UN envoy," Reuters, 24 August 2007.

98 "Guerre ouverte entre le CEP et le chef du parquet de Port-au-Prince, Claudy Gassant," Radio Kiskeya, 29 September 2007.

99 "Exiled Haitian dictator offers apology," Associated Press, 25 September 2007.

100 "D'importants progrès dans la professionnalisation de la Police nationale, selon la MINUSTAH," AlterPresse, 7 September 2007.

101 "Des sénateurs constatent les conditions infrahumaines de vie au Pénitencier," Radio Métropole, 6 September 2007.

102 "Joseph Lambert rend des secteurs l'ayant accusé de narcotrafic responsables de la mort de son père," Radio Kiskeya, 15 September 2007.

103 "Le sénateur Joseph Lambert contre-attaque," Radio Kiskeya, 26 September 2007.

104 "Le sénateur Fortuné réclame la peine de mort a l'encontre des kidnappeurs," Radio Métropole, 29 November 2007.

105 "Un prévenu réputé dangereux et soupçonné d'implication dans des crimes de sang, libéré pour la seconde fois en moins de 2 mois par le commissaire du gouvernement," Radio Kiskeya, 18 December 2007.

106 "Patrick Jean François, un des lieutenants du chef de gang Amaral Duclona, identifié comme le principal auteur de l'enlèvement du guitariste Claude Marcelin," Radio Kiskeya, 11 February 2008.

107 "Le commissaire Claudy Gassant contraint de libérer un militant de la PAPDA et son épouse peu après avoir ordonné leur interpellation," Radio Kiskeya, 25 November 2007.

108 "Les sanctions contre Gassant et Andrésol sont hypothétiques selon des juristes," Radio Métropole, 24 December 2007.

109 "Il existe un malaise entre le parquet et la police selon le sénateur Fortuné," Radio Métropole, 18 December 2007.

110 "Haiti Makes Real Progress," *Latin American Business Chronicle*, 19 November 2007.

111 "A small success for the UN," *The Economist*, 2 August 2007.

112 "PLANOPA denonse politik ekonomik gouvènman an," Platfòm Nasyonal Òganizasyon Peyizan Ayisyen, 9 August 2007.

113 "Rapport du RNDDH sur les élections sénatoriales partielles," Réseau National de Défense des Droits Humains, June 2009.

114 "Frantz Gérard Verret élu président du Conseil Électoral," Radio Kiskeya, 19 December 2007.

115 Confidential U.S. Embassy cable, 17 March 2008.

116 "Haiti's Préval Seeks to Amend Term Limit," Associated Press, 17 October 2007.

117 "L'ex-Président et leader du RDNP, Leslie Manigat, part à la retraite politique," Radio Kiskeya, 5 August 2007.

118 "Le sénateur Rudolph Boulos, de nationalité américaine?," Radio Kiskeya, 23 October 2007.

119 "René Préval entend s'attaquer au problème de la cherté de la vie," Radio Métropole, 3 January 2008.

120 "204ème anniversaire de l'indépendance: appel à l'unité et à la patience du président René Préval au peuple haïtien," Radio Kiskeya, 2 January 2008.

121 Author interview, June 2015.

122 Author interview with head of foreign mission in Haiti, 2014.

123 Author interview, 2015.

124 "Tournée du Président René Préval dans le Plateau Central," Radio Kiskeya, 21 January 2008.

CHAPTER EIGHT

1 "Kelly Bastien plébiscité, Rudolph Boulos contesté," *Le Nouvelliste*, 19 January 2008.

2 "Gabriel Fortuné critique l'élection de Boulos à la vice présidence du sénat," Radio Métropole, 19 January 2008.

3 Author interview with Rudolph Boulos, Miami, July 2015.

4 "Saendy Aristide, un bébé de six mois, kidnappé et exécuté à l'Arcahaie," Radio Kiskeya, 7 February 2008.

5 "Exécution en plein jour d'un lieutenant présumé d'un puissant chef de gang de La Saline en prison depuis août 2007," Radio Kiskeya, 7 January 2008.

6 Unclassified cable from the U.S. Embassy, Port-au-Prince, 3 April 2008.

7 "Nouvelle opération à Pestel en vue d'appréhender l'ex-chef rebelle anti-Aristide Guy Philippe," Radio Kiskeya, 25 March 2008.

8 "Action commando à Pestel," Radio Kiskeya, 26 March 2008.

9 "Le Parquet de Port-au-Prince 'convoque' le président de la CNDDR, Alix Fils-Aimé," Radio Kiskeya, 27 February 2008.

10 Classified cable from the U.S. Embassy, Port-au-Prince, 13 August 2008.

11 "Statement by RNDDH Executive Director Pierre Espérance on the Nomination of Jean Ostrick Hercule as Director of UCREF," Réseau National de Défense des Droits Humains, 8 March 2008.

12 "Alexis obtient la confiance massive des Députés," Radio Kiskeya, 28 February 2008.

13 "Nouveau bras de fer en vue entre le sénateur Youri Latortue et le ministre des TPTC, Frantz Véréla," Radio Kiskeya, 14 March 2008.

14 "Préval protégé faces S. Fla. financial woes," *The Miami Herald*, 20 October 2010. Célestin purchased the Weston property with one Tania Chihimie, who later said that she took "full responsibility" for it though she could not explain how Célestin had been involved in its purchase.

15 "From faceless to favored for Haiti candidate," *The Miami Herald*, 12 November 2010.

16 "Affaire Boulos/Coup de théâtre: l'élu démissionnaire annonce son 'retour immédiat' au Sénat," Radio Kiskeya, 20 March 2008.

17 "Lettre ouverte de Rudolph Boulos au président du Sénat, Kelly Bastien," 19 March 2008.

18 "Rudolph Boulos, 'Sénateur en exil', décide de saisir la justice internationale," Radio Kiskeya, 24 March 2008.

19 "Altercation entre deux Députés au Parlement: un employé blessé par balle," Radio Kiskeya, 1 April 2008.

20 "4 morts, nouveau bilan des manifestations contre la pauvreté," Radio Métropole, 5 April 2008.

21 "Reprise des manifestations aux Cayes: un mort," Radio Kiskeya, 7 April 2008.

22 "La PNH et la MINUSTAH haussent le ton: les forces de l'ordre riposteront à tout éventuel tir en leur direction," Radio Kiskeya, 7 April 2008.

23 "Le président de la Chambre de Commerce du Sud, l'agronome Pierre Léger, réclame la démission du chef de l'État et du gouvernement," Radio Kiskeya, 6 April 2008.

24 "Des casques bleus de l'ONU dégagent un large périmètre de sécurité aux abords du Palais National," Radio Kiskeya, 8 April 2008.

25 "Vie chère: vive tension à Port-au-Prince," Radio Kiskeya, 7 April 2008.

26 "U.N. Jolted by Attacks on Peacekeepers in Haiti," Inter Press Service, 10 April 2008.

27 "Préval pushed to halt turmoil," *The Miami Herald*, 9 April 2008.

28 Author interviews, June–August 2015.

29 Author interview with former Haitian senator, 2015.

30 "Poursuite des violentes manifestations contre la vie chère," Radio Kiskeya, 9 April 2008.

31 "Plusieurs milliers de personnes participent à une grande manifestation contre la pauvreté," Radio Métropole, 8 April 2008.

32 "18 blessés lors des manifestations contre la pauvreté," Radio Métropole, 9 April 2008.

33 "Nouvelle journée de manifestation anti-gouvernementale," Radio Métropole, 10 April 2008.

34 "Haitian president fails to restore order," Associated Press, 10 April 2008.

35 "President's speech calms Haiti protests, for now," *The Miami Herald*, 9 April 2008.

36 "Le président de la chambre des députés estime que les manifestations sont légitimes," Radio Métropole, 9 April 2008.

37 "16 sénateurs sur 27 somment le premier ministre Jacques Édouard Alexis de se démettre," Radio Kiskeya, 10 April 2008.

38 "Haitian senate confronts prime minister," *The Miami Herald*, 12 April 2008.

39 "Haiti Prime Minister Jacques-Édouard Alexis fired." *The Los Angeles Times*, 13 April 2008.

40 "Menaces de mort contre les 16 sénateurs ayant voté la motion de censure contre Jacques Édouard Alexis," Radio Kiskeya, 14 April 2008.

41 "Haitian prime minister voted out," *The Miami Herald*, 13 April 2008.

42 "Haiti names new PM amid food crisis," Agence France-Presse, 27 April 2008.

43 "Haitian senate ratifies Eric Pierre's PM nomination," Xinhua, 9 May 2008.

44 "Haitian president faces new government setback," Reuters, 12 May 2008.

45 "Les membres de la commission spéciale sont divisés sur le dossier de Robert Manuel," Radio Métropole, 12 June 2008.

46 "Second Haiti PM nominee rejected," Associated Press, 12 June 2008.

47 "U.S. Official Ties Duvalier In-Law to Drug Traffic," *The Los Angeles Times*, 13 June 1986.

48 Author interview with Michèle Duvivier Pierre-Louis, Port-au-Prince, June 2015.

49 "Le Parlement entretient le flou sur le processus de ratification du PM désigné," Radio Kiskeya, 27 June 2008.

50 "Haiti lawmakers ratify 2nd female prime minister," Associated Press, 31 July 2008.

51 Classified cable from the U.S. Embassy, Port-au-Prince, 13 August 2008.
52 "Cité à comparaître au correctionnel, Claudy Gassant repasse à l'offensive," Radio Kiskeya, 8 August 2008.
53 "Haiti's top prosecutor resigns," *The Miami Herald*, 13 August 2008.
54 "Matt Damon, Wyclef Jean visit Haiti city in ruins," Associated Press, 14 September 2008.
55 "UN Security Council extends mission in Haiti," Associated Press, 14 October 2008.
56 "Michèle Pierre-Louis visite Gonaïves, plongée dans la douleur et la désolation," AlterPresse, 15 September 2008.
57 Author interview, June 2015.
58 "Storm-struck Haiti at 'tipping point'," Associated Press, 22 October 2008.
59 "UN Security Council extends mission in Haiti," Associated Press, 14 October 2008.
60 "The Human Right to Food in Haiti: Report of an International Fact-finding Mission," Rights & Democracy and Groupe de Recherche et d'Appui au Milieu Rural, 2008.
61 "Haiti school disaster sparks anger, wider concerns," Associated Press, 9 November 2008.
62 "Un véhicule soupçonné dans l'assassinat de la femme d'un commissaire de police affecté au Sénateur Joseph Lambert, selon son collègue Kelly Bastien," Radio Kiskeya, 1 December 2008.
63 "Confusion autour de l'implication du véhicule du sénateur Lambert dans l'assassinat de Monique Pierre," Radio Métropole, 2 December 2008.
64 Confidential cable from the U.S. Embassy, Port-au-Prince, 12 December 2008.
65 "Monique Pierre avait des relations avec des dealers de drogue selon la police Judiciaire," Radio Métropole, 4 December 2008.
66 "Libéré, l'ex commissaire de police, Ernst Dorfeuille, est acclamé aux Gonaïves," *Le Matin*, 30 May 2011.
67 Confidential cable from the U.S. Embassy, Port-au-Prince, 12 December 2008.
68 "Assassinat d'un policier à Cité Soleil," Radio Métropole, 5 December 2008.
69 "Le retour de l'ex-Président Lavalas réclamé à cor et à cri à l'occasion du 18e anniversaire des élections historiques du 16 décembre 1990," Radio Kiskeya, 16 December 2008.
70 "Arrestation, parmi des manifestants lavalas, de deux présumés bandits réputés dangereux," Radio Kiskeya, 17 December 2008.
71 "Report of the Secretary-General on the United Nations Stabilization Mission in Haiti," 6 March 2009.

CHAPTER NINE

1 "René Préval prévoit une année 2009 difficile," Radio Kiskeya, 3 January 2009.
2 "Anti-corruption campaign bears little fruit," confidential cable from U.S. Embassy, Port-au-Prince, 21 January 2009.
3 "Report of the Secretary-General on the United Nations Stabilization Mission in Haiti," 6 March 2009.

4   "Où est Marcello?," *Le Nouvelliste*, 8 April 2009.
5   "Le responsable de la commission nationale des marchés publics enlevé et séquestré," Radio Kiskeya, 29 January 2009.
6   "Lettre ouverte de la famille Marcello," 5 February 2009.
7   "Fanmi Lavalas fait son entrée dans l'arène," Radio Kiskeya, 29 January 2009.
8   "Deux listes de candidats en compétition au nom du même parti," Radio Kiskeya, 24 January 2009.
9   "Le député Hugues Célestin conteste le choix de Moïse Jean-Charles, accusé de meurtre, comme candidat au Sénat de LESPWA dans le Nord," Radio Kiskeya, 30 January 2009.
10 "Haitian senate candidate a wanted man," *The Miami Herald*, 29 January 2009.
11 "40 barred from Haitian senate race – including Lavalas slate," *The Miami Herald*, 7 February 2009.
12 "Mandat ou non d'Aristide: Lavalas vs Lavalas," Radio Kiskeya, 10 February 2009.
13 "Maryse Narcisse a 48 heures pour présenter au CEP un 'mandat authentique' d'Aristide," Radio Kiskeya, 11 February 2009.
14 "Neuf candidats Lavalas au CEP pour réintégrer le processus électoral," Radio Kiskeya, 12 February 2009.
15 "Le Feuilléton Lavalas entre dans un nouvel épisode," Radio Kiskeya, 13 February 2009.
16 "La liste Lavalas aux sénatoriales définitivement rejetée," Radio Kiskeya, 7 February 2009.
17 Confidential U.S. Embassy cable, 17 March 2008.
18 "Rapport du RNDDH sur les élections sénatoriales partielles," Réseau National de Défense des Droits Humains, June 2009.
19 "Aristide's SA high life to continue," *Sunday Independent*, 5 July 2009.
20 "Le gouvernement défend ses priorités à la Chambre basse," AlterPresse, 15 July 2009.
21 "Haiti: From Natural Catastrophe to Economic Security," Report for the Secretary-General of the United Nations, January 2009.
22 "Ban and Clinton throw spotlight on Haiti," BBC, 10 March 2009.
23 "Questions about his charity may dog Wyclef Jean's presidential bid," Yahoo News, 5 August 2010.
24 "Secretary Clinton: US behind Haiti for long term," Associated Press, 16 April 2009.
25 "Bill Clinton named special envoy to Haiti," *The Miami Herald*, 19 May 2009.
26 "What role for the EU? Finding a niche in the Haitian peacebuilding process," Initiative for Peacebuilding and Fundación para las Relaciones Internacionales y el Diálogo Exterior, February 2009.
27 "Human Rights Indicator Number 14," Réseau National de Défense des Droits Humains, January–March 2009.
28 "Incident violent à la Chambre des Députés," Radio Kiskeya, 17 March 2009.
29 "La Chambre basse présente des excuses publiques au Gouvernement après le grave incident du mardi 17 mars," Radio Kiskeya, 20 March 2009.

30 "Convocation du Directeur de l'ULCC à la Chambre des Députés," Réseau National de Défense des Droits Humains, 30 March 2009.

31 "L'ex-directeur de l'ONA, Sandro Joseph, arrêté et écroué à Port-au-Prince," Radio Kiskeya, 19 March 2009.

32 "Haïti-ONA: 13 millions de gourdes disparues à la direction régionale de Jacmel," Haiti Press Network, 21 September 2011.

33 "Affaire Jean Dominique: les journalistes furieux contre les juges," Radio Kiskeya, 3 April 2009.

34 "Où est Marcello?," *Le Nouvelliste*, 8 April 2009.

35 "Disparition du coordonnateur de la commission nationale des Marchés Publics: 3 mois après, l'enquête avance selon la DCPJ," Radio Métropole, 6 April 2009.

36 "Un conseiller du Président Préval libéré 48 heures après son enlèvement," Radio Kiskeya, 8 April 2008.

37 "Pestel: des unités de la PNH y seraient intervenues," Radio Kiskeya, 11 April 2009.

38 "What role for the EU? Finding a niche in the Haitian peacebuilding process," Initiative for Peacebuilding and Fundación para las Relaciones Internacionales y el Diálogo Exterior, February 2009.

39 "Début très timide des opérations, en dépit de quelques incidents," AlterPresse, 19 April 2009.

40 "Incidents dans le Plateau central," Radio Kiskeya, 9 April 2009.

41 "Des individus armés ferment de nombreux bureaux de vote dans le Bas Plateau Central," Radio Kiskeya, 19 April 2009.

42 "La sénatrice Edmonde Supplice Beauzile et le candidat de son parti, la Fusion, se retranchent dans un hôtel de Mirebalais," Radio Kiskeya, 19 April 2009.

43 "Incident armé dans le Centre: un collaborateur du Député-Candidat Willot Joseph en tue un autre," Radio Kiskeya, 9 May 2009.

44 "Rapport du RNDDH sur les élections sénatoriales partielles," Réseau National de Défense des Droits Humains, June 2009.

45 "Annulation des élections dans le département du Centre," Radio Kiskeya, 19 April 2009.

46 "Deux candidats au Sénat dans le Sud-Est se retirent en raison de la décision unilatérale du CEP de limiter considérablement la représentation de leurs partis dans les bureaux de vote," Radio Kiskeya, 18 April 2009.

47 "La MINUSTAH salue la tenue des élections sénatoriales et déplore les incidents du Plateau Central," AlterPresse, 20 April 2009.

48 "11% de participation aux sénatoriales partielles du 19 avril, selon le CEP," AlterPresse, 24 April 2009.

49 "Rapport du RNDDH sur les élections sénatoriales partielles," Réseau National de Défense des Droits Humains, June 2009.

50 "No winners in 1st round of Haiti senate election," Associated Press, 28 April 2009.

51 "Le BCED déclare Moïse Jean-Charles vainqueur dans le Nord avec 51% des voix," Radio Kiskeya, 6 May 2009.

52 "Some lawmakers allege fraud in Haiti election," Associated Press, 7 May 2009.

53 "Le Vice-président du Sénat réclame officiellement l'arrêt du processus électoral," Radio Kiskeya, 13 May 2009.

54 "Un mort par balle dans le Sud-Est dans un accrochage entre des partisans de 2 candidats rivaux," Radio Kiskeya, 12 June 2009.

55 "Je n'ai jamais été membre d'aucun parti politique, affirme René Préval en visite aux Gonaïves," Radio Kiskeya, 12 May 2009.

56 "Préval, déjà trois ans, mais très peu de résultats," Radio Kiskeya, 14 May 2009.

57 "Haiti Anxiously Awaits Decision on Minimum Wage," confidential cable from U.S. Embassy, Port-au-Prince, 10 June 2009.

58 Ibid.

59 "WikiLeaks Cables: U.S. Companies, Diplomats Fought to Prevent Minimum Wage Increase in Haiti's Textiles Factories," ThinkProgress, 8 June 2011.

60 "Marche dans le Sud-Est en mémoire du ressortissant haïtien décapité à Santo Domingo," AlterPresse, 12 May 2009.

61 "Angry protests in Haiti over slaying of countryman," Associated Press, 8 May 2009.

62 "Funérailles émouvantes de Carlo Mérilus, le supplicié de Santo Domingo," Radio Kiskeya, 16 May 2009.

63 "Michèle Pierre-Louis demande de mettre fin aux abus contre les Haïtiens en territoire voisin," AlterPresse, 25 May 2009.

64 "Santo Domingo critique sévèrement la Première ministre haïtienne," Radio Kiskeya, 24 May 2009.

65 "Dominican soldiers to settle along Haiti border," Associated Press, 30 December 2009.

66 "Assassinat d'un inspecteur de police: aucune arrestation 24 heures après," Radio Kiskeya, 15 May 2009.

67 "Attaque de bandits à Martissant: un inspecteur de police et deux agents blessés par balle," Radio Kiskeya, 14 May 2009.

68 "Présumée tentative de rapt: trois morts à Cité Soleil," Radio Kiskeya, 22 May 2009.

69 "La Première Ministre entend empêcher la résurgence de l'insécurité," Radio Métropole, 25 May 2009.

70 "Report of the Secretary-General on the United Nations Stabilization Mission in Haiti," 6 March 2009.

71 "Importante saisie d'armes et de munitions à Port-au-Prince," Radio Kiskeya, 16 June 2009.

72 "Des centres culturels protestent contre une agression du siège de la FOKAL," AlterPresse, 16 June 2009.

73 "Salaire minimum: un etudiant blesse lors de violentes protestations," Radio Kiskeya, 4 June 2009.

74 "Plusieurs employés de médias victimes d'agressions au cours d'une nouvelle manifestation estudiantine," AlterPresse, 5 June 2009.

75 "Que se passe-t-il à la Faculté des Sciences Humaines de l'UEH?," AlterPresse, 19 March 2007.

76 "Nouvelles protestations étudiantes à Port-au-Prince: un mort par balla," Radio Kiskeya, 10 June 2009.

77 "Manifestation des étudiants; un véhicule de la Minustah incendié," Radio Métropole, 18 June 2009.

78 "Steven Benoît appelle le chef de l'État à engager le dialogue avec les étudiants," Radio Métropole, 19 June 2009.

79 "Le chef de l'État refuse de publier la loi sur le salaire minimum," Radio Métropole, 18 June 2009.

80 "Haiti News – Reportage funérailles Père Jean-Juste," https://youtu.be/vMkOKzY7HWU, accessed 8 September 2015.

81 "Father Jean-Juste's Funeral Mass," https://youtu.be/maRbemWvmyY, accessed 8 September 2015.

82 "Shooting after Father Jean-Juste's Funeral Mass, P-a-P, Haiti … June 19, 2009," https://youtu.be/kF74KU3iFlA, accessed 8 September 2015.

83 "Décès du père Gérard Jean Juste: le sénateur Roudy Hériveaux (Lavalas) rejette les accusations portées contre la journaliste Liliane Pierre-Paul," Radio Kiskeya, 20 June 2009.

84 "Un militant lavalas tué lors des funérailles de Gérard Jean Juste," Radio Métropole, 19 June 2009.

85 "René Préval reconnaît que 'le peuple ne s'est pas mobilisé', lors du second tour," Radio Kiskeya, 21 June 2009.

86 "Au moins deux morts et des blessés: bilan provisoire du second tour des sénatoriales partielles," Radio Kiskeya, 21 June 2009.

87 "Elections: Victoire de Lespwa au second tour des sénatoriales," Radio Kiskeya, 29 June 2009.

88 "Lettre ouverte au Président du Conseil Électoral Provisoire, M. Frantz Gérard Verret," 20 July 2009.

89 "Réponse du Conseil Électoral Provisoire à la lettre ouverte du Vice-président, Monsieur Rodol Pierre en date du 20 juillet 2009," 21 July 2009.

90 Author interview with Michèle Pierre-Louis, Port-au-Prince, June 2009.

91 "South Florida lawmakers call for granting special status to Haiti," *The Miami Herald*, 23 June 2009.

92 "$1.2 billion in debts canceled to help Haiti," Associated Press, 30 June 2009.

93 "Reprise timide des cours dans plusieurs entités, après plusieurs semaines de paralysie," AlterPresse, 1 July 2009.

94 "Les secteurs populaires réaffirment leur position en faveur des 200 gourdes," AlterPresse, 20 July 2009.

95 "Haiti lawmakers OK minimum wage hike after clashes," Associated Press, 4 August 2009.

96 U.S. Embassy cable, 20 August 2009.

97 Author telephone interview with Kenneth H. Merten, June 2015.

98 "Arrestation d'un chef de gang haïtien," AlterPresse, 9 September 2009.

99 "Le chef de gang Amaral Duclona tombe dans l'escarcelle de la police dominicaine," Radio Kiskeya, 9 September 2009.

100 "Incroyables révélations d'Amaral Duclona, chef de gang," *Haiti-Observateur*, 30 September–7 October 2009. Also interview with Ray Baysden, head of MINUSTAH's intelligence center, from Frontline's "The Battle for Haiti," broadcast on 11 June 2011.

101 "Amaral Duclona extradé jeudi soir en France," Radio Kiskeya, 7 January 2010.

102 "Amaral Duclona acquitté en appel," *Le Nouvelliste*, 12 February 2016.

103 "Kouchner: UN should stay in Haiti through election," Associated Press, 18 September 2009.

104 "$258M in Haiti projects announced at Clinton event," Associated Press, 24 September 2009.

105 "Haiti-based WIN Group and Soros Economic Development Fund Announce a $45 Million Commercial Zone in Haiti," Business Wire, 6 October 2009.

106 "WB approves US$24.5 million in grants for economic governance, road rehabilitation," World Bank press release, 8 December 2009.

107 "La route de Fort-Mercredi réhabilitée," AlterPresse, 18 September 2009.

108 "La chaîne américaine Choice Hotels annonce la construction de deux hôtels à Jacmel," Radio Kiskeya, 7 January 2010.

109 "Nouveau mandat d'un an pour la Minustah," AlterPresse, 13 October 2009.

110 "René Préval et José Miguel Insulza proclamés 'héros de l'hémisphère' par la PADF," Radio Kiskeya, 26 October 2009.

111 "Préval justifie la présence des troupes onusiennes par les faiblesses institutionnelles nationales." AlterPresse, 19 October 2009.

112 "Manifestation et contre-manifestation de paysans le 16 octobre," AlterPresse, 16 October 2008.

113 "Gaillot Dorsainvil assure la présidence du CEP," Radio Vision 2000, 29 October 2009.

114 "Haiti's prime minister targeted for ouster by lawmakers," *The Miami Herald*, 27 October 2009.

115 "Michèle Pierre-Louis veut sortir la tête haute," AlterPresse, 27 October 2009.

116 "Haiti's prime minister targeted for ouster by lawmakers," *The Miami Herald*, 27 October 2009.

117 "Interpellation du chef du gouvernement: les sénateurs interpellateurs apparemment 'invariables', en dépit d'une adresse à la nation de Mme Michèle Pierre-Louis," Radio Kiskeya, 27 October 2009.

118 "La Fondation Heritage pour Haiti Attend les Resultats des Verifications des Depenses Effectuees dans le Cadre du Programme d'Urgence Post-Desastre," LFHH press release, 8 December 2009.

119 "Michèle Pierre-Louis veut sortir la tête haute," AlterPresse, 27 October 2009.

120 "Playing politics in Haiti," *The Miami Herald*, 28 October 2009.

121 "Interpellation du chef du gouvernement: les sénateurs interpellateurs apparemment 'invariables', en dépit d'une adresse à la nation de Mme Michèle Pierre-Louis," Radio Kiskeya, 27 October 2009.

122 "Haiti senate ousts Prime Minister Pierre-Louis," Reuters, 30 October 2009.

123 "Le sénateur Joseph Lambert menace de démissionner si la première ministre Michèle Pierre-Louis demeure à son poste après la séance d'interpellation," Radio Kiskeya, 28 October 2009.

124 Author interview with individual present at the meeting, 2015.

125 "Haitian prime minister fired by senate," Associated Press Writer, 30 October 2009.

126 "Haiti senate ousts Prime Minister Pierre-Louis," Reuters, 30 October 2009.

127 "Sénat: la Première ministre Michèle Pierre-Louis destituée comme prévu," Radio Kiskeya, 30 October 2009.

128 "Haitian senate fires prime minister," *The Miami Herald*, 30 October 2009.

129 "Un regroupement paysan met en garde contre des velléités d'un projet antidémocratique," AlterPresse, 4 November 2009.

130 Author interview, June 2015.

131 Author interview, May 2015.

132 Author interview with Michèle Pierre-Louis, Port-au-Prince, June 2015.

133 "Haiti president names new PM," Reuters, 31 October 2009.

134 "Portrait du premier ministre désigné, Jean Max Bellerive," AlterPresse, 3 Noveber 2009.

135 Author interview, June 2015.

136 "Le ministre de la Planification et de la coopération externe, Jean Max Bellerive, désigné premier ministre," Radio Kiskeya, 30 October 2009.

137 "Haiti's new prime minister set for ratification," Reuters, 4 November 2009.

138 "New prime minister confirmed by lawmakers in Haiti," Associated Press, 10 November 2009.

139 "Formation du nouveau gouvernement: onze ministres sur 18 restent en fonction," Radio Kiskeya, 8 November 2009.

140 "Nouvelle échauffourée entre des étudiants protestataires et la police," AlterPresse, 26 November 2009.

141 "Unité: nouvel instrument politique du pouvoir," Radio Kiskeya, 17 November 2009.

142 "Des lavalassiens et la fille de feu Sylvio Claude passent dans les rangs de Inite," Radio Kiskeya, 30 November 2009.

143 "Soixante neuf partis et regroupements inscrits," AlterPresse, 23 November 2009.

144 "Fanmi Lavalas, l'Union et la coalition ESKANP exclus des prochaines élections législatives," Radio Kiskeya, 25 November 2009.

145 Letter from Jean-Bertrand Aristide to Gaillot Dorsainvil, 18 November 2009.

146 "Après le rejet de Famille Lavalas, Aristide critique le CEP," AlterPresse, 25 November 2009.

147 RNDDH press release, 1 December 2009.

148 "Des centaines de sympathisants de Fanmi Lavalas demandent le départ de l'actuel CEP mercredi," AlterPresse, 16 December 2009.

149 "A l'aube d'une année politique cruciale," AlterPresse, 5 January 2010.

150 "Troisième mariage de Préval," AlterPresse, 7 December 2009.

CHAPTER TEN

1 "U.N. Honors the 101 Who Served and Died in Haiti," *The New York Times*, 9 March 2010.

2 "Life in the Ruins," *The Nation*, 9 January 2013.

3 "Heartbreak hotel," *The Palm-Beach Post*, 12 January 2011.

4 "Haiti Emerges from its Shock, and Tears Roll," *The New York Times*, 14 February 2010.

5 "Micha Gaillard, Fought for Democracy," *The Wall Street Journal*, 22 January 2010.

6 "All the symbols of this country are gone," McClatchy-Tribune News Service, 24 January 2010.

7 "Papal nuncio gives dramatic report on Church in Haiti," Catholic News Agency, 14 January 2010.

8 "Structural errors lead to building collapses in Haiti," *Technician*, 7 February 2010.

9 "Philippe Charles Claude Rouzier, 1946–2010," http://www.un.org/en/memorial/haiti/rouzier.shtml, accessed 22 September 2015.

10 "In Memoriam: les disparus du 12 janvier," Radio Kiskeya, 3 February 2010.

11 "Workers struggle to save Haiti history buried in rubble of tax office," *The Los Angeles Times*, 5 February 2010.

12 "Haiti Emerges from its Shock, and Tears Roll," *The New York Times*, 14 February 2010.

13 "In Memoriam: les disparus du 12 janvier," Radio Kiskeya, 3 February 2010.

14 "Emouvante cérémonie en mémoire de huit membres d'une famille cruellement touchée," Radio Kiskeya, 26 February 2010.

15 "Grasses of Ginen," *The Huffington Post*, 25 February 2010.

16 "Haiti president pleads for tents," *The Miami Herald*, 26 January 2010.

17 Ibid.

18 "We have to build better, Haiti premier says," *The Miami Herald*, 26 January 2010.

19 Author interview with Kenneth H. Merten, June 2015.

20 Author interview with Mario Andrésol, July 2015.

21 Author interview with Kenneth H. Merten, June 2015.

22 "Haiti's capital shattered by powerful earthquake," Associated Press, 13 January 2010.

23 "Haiti Chief Says Thousands May Be Dead," *The New York Times*, 14 January 2010.

24 "Quake-stunned Haitians pile bodies by fallen homes," Associated Press, 13 January 2010.

25 "Disorder Adds to Misery in Reeling Haiti; Red Cross Says Death Toll May Be 50,000," *The New York Times*, 15 January 2010.

26 "Panic, looting and triage after major Haiti quake," Associated Press, 13 January 2010.

27 "Haitians Confront Devastation of Quake," *The New York Times*, 14 January 2010.

28 "Disorder Adds to Misery in Reeling Haiti; Red Cross Says Death Toll May Be 50,000," *The New York Times*, 15 January 2010.

29 "Haiti Despairs as Quake Deaths Mount," *The Wall Street Journal*, 14 January 2010.

30 "Haiti Chief Says Thousands May Be Dead," *The New York Times*, 14 January 2010.

31 "Note to Correspondents on the Situation on Haiti from Vicenzo Pugliese, Spokesperson and Chief of Media Relations for MINUSTAH," 13 January 2010.

32 "In Léogane, Miles from the Capital and Waiting for Aid," *The Wall Street Journal*, 17 January 2010.

33 "Miles from capital, Haiti quake ruins coastal city," Associated Press, 18 January 2010.

34 "Before rising again, a need to tear down," *The Miami Herald*, 28 January 2010.

35 "Dysfunctional dam a symbol of Haiti's post-quake problems," *The Miami Herald*, 10 July 2010.

36 "Disorder Adds to Misery in Reeling Haiti; Red Cross Says Death Toll May Be 50,000." *The New York Times*, 15 January 2010.

37 Ibid.

38 "USS Carl Vinson Arrives in Haiti to Support Humanitarian Operations," United States Navy, Story No. NNS100115-03, 15 January 2010.

39 "Struggle to aid Haitians as fears of unrest rise," Associated Press, 15 January 2010.

40 "U.S. Seen Returning to Big Haiti Role," *The New York Times*, 16 January 2010.

41 "Rescuers Race to Find Survivors in Haiti as U.S. Troops Work to Speed Aid Flow," *The New York Times*, 16 January 2010.

42 "Haiti flight logs detail early chaos," Associated Press, 18 February 2010.

43 "After the quake, Haiti and the Dominican Republic have a smoother, but fragile, relationship," *The Miami Herald*, 16 July 2010.

44 "Dominican Ties with Haiti Improve," *The Wall Street Journal*, 18 February 2010.

45 "Time Running Out on Haiti Survivors," *The Wall Street Journal*, 16 January 2010.

46 "The Israeli Field Hospital in Haiti – Ethical Dilemmas in Early Disaster Response," *New England Journal of Medicine*, 18 March 2010.

47 "Amid Earthquake's Ruins, Signs of Revival in Haiti," *The New York Times*, 28 January 2010.

48 "Red Cross Appeals for $100 Million for Haiti," Voice of America, 16 January 2010.

49 "Wyclef Jean's Haiti Relief Tweets Raise $1 Million," ABC News, 14 January 2010.

50 "Unasur to provide $100 million to Haiti," Associated Press, 24 February 2010.

51 "U.S. Marines Land in Villages on Edge of Life and Death," *The New York Times*, 20 January 2010.

52 "UN reinforcements sent in to Haiti to crack down on escaped gang leaders," *The Guardian*, 19 January 2010.

53 "UN's Ban urges desperate Haitians to be patient," Associated Press, 18 January 2010.

54 "Struggle to aid Haitians as fears of unrest rise," Associated Press, 15 January 2010.

55 "Trapped Haitian girl dies despite rescue effort," Associated Press, 14 January 2010.

56 "In Haiti, little separates life and death," Associated Press, 15 January 2010.

57 "Looters roam Port-au-Prince as earthquake death toll estimate climbs," *The Guardian*, 16 January 2010.

58 "Haiti village left to fend for itself after earthquake," by Matthew Price, BBC News, 17 January 2010.

59 "In Léogane, Miles from the Capital and Waiting for Aid," *The Wall Street Journal*, 17 January 2010.

60 "Elderly and abandoned, 85 Haitians await death," Associated Press, 17 January 2010.

61 "Help grows for abandoned elderly Haitians," Associated Press, 24 February 2010.

62 "By the thousands, Haiti returns dead to the earth," Associated Press, 20 January 2010.

63 "Patience Wears Thin as Desperation Grows," *The New York Times*, 15 January 2010.

64 "Looters roam Port-au-Prince as earthquake death toll estimate climbs," *The Guardian*, 16 January 2010.

65 "Haiti Authorities Battle Looters," *The Wall Street Journal*, 17 January 2010.

66 "UN reinforcements sent in to Haiti to crack down on escaped gang leaders," *The Guardian*, 19 January 2010.

67 "More US troops, UN peacekeepers expected for Haiti," Associated Press Writers, 18 January 2010.

68 "Le coup de grâce," Radio Kiskeya, 14 January 2010.

69 Email to author, 16 January 2010.

70 "IMF chief seeks 'Marshall Plan' for ravaged Haiti," Agence France-Presse, 20 January 2010.

71 "Aftershock drives more from Haitian capital," Associated Press, 20 January 2010.

72 "Haiti to resettle 400,000 quake victims to camps," Associated Press, 21 January 2010.

73 "Many flee Haiti capital, govt plans tent cities," Associated Press, 22 January 2010.

74 "Situation Report #13," OCHA, 25 January 2010.

75 "Country Hospitality: Haitian Peasant Organizations Provide Humanitarian Aid," *The Huffington Post*, 24 February 2010.

76 "Many flee Haiti capital, govt plans tent cities," Associated Press, 22 January 2010.

77 MINUSTAH daily briefing, 21 January 2010.

78 "Survivors flee Haiti capital; buried still saved," Associated Press, 22 January 2010.

79 "U.N.: Haiti government calls off search and rescue," Associated Press, 23 January 2010.

80 "French team makes new 'miracle' rescue in Haiti," Associated Press, 28 January 2010.

81 "Full recovery for 'miracle' Haiti quake survivor," Associated Press, 10 January 2011.

82 "Urgent need for tent cities for Haitian refugees," Associated Press, 25 January 2010.

83 "Many flee Haiti capital, govt plans tent cities," Associated Press, 22 January 2010.

84 "Haiti Retracts Death Toll No., Citing Typo," Associated Press, 10 February 2010.

85 "Situation Report #14," OCHA, 27 January 2010.

86 "Piles of the dead finally buried in Titanyen," *The Los Angeles Times*, 1 February 2010.

87 "U.S. troops more than welcome in Haiti," Associated Press, 30 January 2010.

88 "As food distribution improves, Haitians want U.S. to 'take over'," *The Washington Post*, 1 February 2010.

89 "Emergency Doctors Leave Haiti," *The Wall Street Journal*, 24 February 2010.

90 "Survivors flee Haiti capital; buried still saved," Associated Press, 22 January 2010.

91 "Civil–Military Collaboration in the Initial Medical Response to the Earthquake in Haiti," *New England Journal of Medicine*, 11 March 2010.

92 "Cost Dispute Halts Airlift of Injured Haiti Quake Victims," *The New York Times*, 30 January 2010.

93 "U.S. to Resume Airlift of Injured Haitians," *The New York Times*, 1 February 2010.

94 "U.S. Will Reimburse Hospitals that Treat Haitians," *The New York Times*, 2 February 2010.

95 "As Aftershocks Continue, Haiti Ponders Rebuilding," *The New York Times*, 29 January 2010.

96 Ibid.

97 "Situation Report #16," OCHA, 5 February 2010.

98 "A day in the life of a Haiti tent city," *The Los Angeles Times*, 27 January 2010.

99 "Makeshift schools are popping up in tent cities," *The Miami Herald*, 8 February 2010.

100 "Churches rising out of the ruins," *The Miami Herald*, 8 February 2010.

101 "Bill Clinton at Davos: Haiti needs cash, trucks," Associated Press, 28 January 2010.

102 "G7 countries forgive Haiti's debt," Reuters, 6 February 2010.

103 "In Disaster, Tensions Ease Between an Island's Rivals," *The New York Times*, 29 January 2010.

104 "Haiti revival after quake could take generations says UN chief," *The Guardian*, 29 January 2010.

105 MINUSTAH daily press briefing, 27 January 2010.

106 "Before rising again, a need to tear down," *The Miami Herald*, 28 January 2010.

107 "UN: some Haitian hospitals are charging patients," Associated Press, 8 February 2010.

108 "In Quake's Wake, Haiti Faces Leadership Void," *The New York Times*, 1 February 2010.

109 "Haiti food convoy attacked; UN warns of volatility," Associated Press, 2 February 2010.

110 "Consultations initiées au Sénat autour d'un éventuel changement de gouvernement," Radio Kiskeya, 9 February 2010.

111 "Amid Earthquake's Ruins, Signs of Revival in Haiti," *The New York Times*, 28 January 2010.

112 Author interview with Kenneth H. Merten, June 2015.

113 "Haitian Lawmakers Seek to Delay Elections," *The New York Times*, 30 January 2010.

114 "Haiti Is Again a Canvas for Approaches to Aid," *The New York Times*, 31 January 2010.

115 "Haitian president René Préval staring down a crisis," *The Miami Herald*, 1 February 2010.

116 "A Month After the Quake, Haiti Takes Stock," *The New York Times*, 13 February 2010.

117 "Haïti ne périra pas, promet Préval," Agence France-Presse, 12 February 2010.

CHAPTER ELEVEN

1 "Haiti earthquake damage estimated up to $14 billion," *The Washington Post*, 17 February 2010.

2 "Haiti president: 3 years needed to move rubble," Associated Press, 16 February 2010.

3   "Haiti launches into reconstruction," *The Miami Herald*, 13 July 2010.

4   "U.S. paving way to rebuild Haiti," *The Miami Herald*, 11 February 2011.

5   "Canada to build Haitian government base," Associated Press, 15 February 2010.

6   "French leader cancels Haiti debt, announces aid," *The Miami Herald*, 17 February 2010.

7   "2 firms picked for emergency tasks," *The Miami Herald*, 9 February 2010.

8   "Décentraliser, refonder le pays, pas seulement reconstruire …, dixit Préval," Alter-Presse, 24 February 2010.

9   "Haiti Faces Major Food Crisis as Planting Season Nears, UN Says," Bloomberg, 12 February 2010.

10 "More than a million remain with no shelter in Haiti as rains loom," *The Observer*, 14 February 2010.

11 "Tarps, toilets are priorities for quake-hit Haiti-UN," Reuters, 15 February 2010.

12 "Problems linger despite improvement in Haiti aid distribution," *The Miami Herald*, 14 February 2010.

13 Author interview, 5 October 2015.

14 "Delmas mayor tells camp to leave high school or face eviction," *The Miami Herald*, 21 February 2010.

15 "Haiti PM fears government collapse," Associated Press, 18 February 2010.

16 "Haitian gov't to appropriate land for tent camps," Associated Press, 20 February 2010.

17 "In Haiti, the Displaced Are Left Clinging to the Edge," *The New York Times*, 10 July 2010.

18 "Aid group shocked over lack of shelter for Haitians," Reuters, 5 March 2010.

19 Communiqué from GARR, 26 February 2010.

20 "Haiti on edge after steady aftershocks," Associated Press, 23 February 2010.

21 "US reduces troop numbers in Haiti," Agence France-Presse, 13 February 2010.

22 "U.N. Is Faulted as Lacking Coordination of Aid and Security in Haiti," *The New York Times*, 2 March 2010.

23 "Sexual violence in Haitian camps of the displaced, beyond the numbers," Amnesty International, 22 March 2010.

24 "Haiti relief workers try to stem rape in refugee camps," *The Christian Science Monitor*, 5 May 2010.

25 "Le RNDDH présente son troisième rapport sur la situation générale du pays après le séisme du 12 janvier 2010," Réseau National de Défense des Droits Humains, 12 May 2010.

26 "Flights resume to Haiti, reconnecting families," *The Miami Herald*, 19 February 2010.

27 "As Haiti recovers from massive quake, Obama vows support," *The Los Angeles Times*, 10 March 2010.

28 "Groups jockey for role in Haiti revival," *The Miami Herald*, 9 March 2010.

29 "Haiti wants more information on foreign aid." Reuters, 3 March 2010.

30 "Company's Gift to Haiti Stuck in Customs," Today's TMJ4, 9 June 2010.

31 "Aid cargo sits unused in Haitian customs lot," NECN, 15 July 2010.

32 "Haiti and the Voodoo Curse: the cultural roots of the country's endless misery," *The Wall Street Journal*, 5 February 2010.

33 "Pat Robertson says Haiti paying for 'pact to the devil'," CNN, 13 January 2010.

34 "Photojournalism Workshops – Haiti Earthquake Intimate Group Workshop," 6 February 2010, http://www.zoriah.net/blog/2010/02/photojournalism-workshops-haiti-earthquake-intimate-group-workshop.html, accessed 5 October 2015.

35 "Haiti Photo Workshops Face Online Backlash," *Wired*, 9 February 2010.

36 "I'm Gonna Need You to Fight Me on This: How Violent Sex Helped Ease My PTSD," *GOOD*, 29 June 2011.

37 "Female Journalists & Researchers Respond to Haiti PTSD Article," *Jezebel*, 1 July 2011.

38 "EU releases 100 mln euros for Haiti salaries, roads," Reuters, 2 March 2010.

39 "EU to pledge $1.36 billion in Haiti aid," Associated Press, 22 March 2010.

40 "Americas Development Bank Forgives Much of Haiti's Debt," *The New York Times*, 22 March 2010.

41 "IADB commits to Haiti aid, fresh capital," Reuters, 22 March 2010.

42 "Bush, Clinton visit devastated Haitian capital," Associated Press, 22 March 2010.

43 "After U.S. visit, Préval optimistic on direct aid," *The Miami Herald*, 11 March 2010.

44 "Haitian recovery takes root in field of skepticism," Canwest News Service, 13 March 2010.

45 "Haiti reveals ambitious reconstruction plan," Associated Press, 16 March 2010.

46 "Clinton to co-lead Haiti rebuilding authority," Associated Press, 30 March 2010.

47 "Foreign-Led Commission Now Governs Haiti; Voting Membership Determined by Size of Contribution," *Huffington Post*, 13 May 2010.

48 "Donors pledge $9.9 billion for Haiti," Associated Press, 31 March 2010.

49 "U.S. pledges $1.2 billion in aid to Haiti," *The Los Angeles Times*, 1 April 2010.

50 "Clinton asks groups to make Haiti self-sufficient," Associated Press, 25 March 2010.

51 "Bush, Clinton visit devastated Haitian capital," Associated Press, 22 March 2010.

52 "Haiti lawmakers OK Clinton-led rebuilding panel," Associated Press, 16 April 2010.

53 "UN envoy: Haiti should hold presidential election," Associated Press, 4 March 2010.

54 "U.S. to Haiti: Don't delay elections," *The Washington Times*, 10 March 2010.

55 "Haiti's Préval pledges elections for 2010," Agence France-Presse, 13 April 2010.

56 "Haiti able to hold poll by year-end: Bill Clinton," Reuters, 14 April 2010.

57 "Bill Clinton: Haiti's future will be violent if international community doesn't stay involved," Associated Press, 17 April 2010.

58 "Haitian President René Préval asks to remain in office," *The Miami Herald*, 5 May 2010.

59 "Bulldozers start razing Haitian presidential palace," Agence France-Presse, 9 April 2010.

60 "In key step toward normalcy, classes begin in Haiti," *The Miami Herald*, 5 April 2010.

61 "At least a million Haitian earthquake survivors receive emergency shelter – UN," UN News Service, 13 April 2010.

62 "Haiti evacuates quake victims camp, faces critics," Agence France-Presse, 12 April 2010.

63 "Humanitarian Bulletin, Issue # 1," 23 April 2010.

64 "Spotlight falls on Red Cross spending," *The Miami Herald*, 27 April 2010.

65 "Following the Aid Money to Haiti," CBS News, 12 May 2010.

66 "Haitian police break up violent protest at palace," Reuters, 10 May 2010.

67 "Protesters blast Haiti president's quake response," Associated Press, 11 May 2010.

68 "Haiti trade bill heads to Obama for signature," Reuters, 7 May 2010.

69 "Brazil pays first donation into Haiti quake fund," Reuters, 11 May 2010.

70 "World Bank cancels remaining Haiti debt," Reuters, 28 May 2010.

71 "UN, partners gear up to help quake-stricken Haiti hold elections," UN News Centre, 11 May 2010.

72 "Haiti leader vows to step down with 'calm heart'," Associated Press, 18 May 2010.

73 "Lavalas attaque frontalement René Préval," Radio Kiskeya, 7 June 2010.

74 "Une large coalition de l'opposition réclame la démission de René Préval," Radio Kiskeya, 8 July 2010.

75 "Worry, harsh words from U.S. on Haiti recovery," *The Miami Herald*, 21 June 2010.

76 "U.S. Moves to Block Some Funding for Haiti," *The Wall Street Journal*, 10 June 2010.

77 "Schedule elections, U.S. Congress urges Haiti president," *The Miami Herald*, 9 June 2010.

78 "Inside Bill Clinton's New Plan to Fix Haiti," *Esquire*, 8 July 2010.

79 "Commission pledges $20M to help Haitian businesses," *The Miami Herald*, 17 June 2010.

80 "UN head says aid to Haiti slow 6 months after deadly quake, donors should deliver now," BBC, 6 July 2010.

81 "René Préval, farouche défenseur du CEP chargé d'arbitrer les présidentielles," Radio Kiskeya, 30 June 2010.

82 "Préval rejects US advice on presidential election," Associated Press, 30 June 2010.

83 "René Préval pour un troisième mandat mais au poste de premier ministre, avec un président fantoche," Radio Kiskeya, 24 July 2015.

84 "Jacques Édouard Alexis, candidat de l'Unité?," AlterPresse, 27 July 2010.

85 "Wyclef Jean on Bill Clinton and Haiti's New Revolution," *Esquire*, 8 July 2010.

86 "President Wyclef? Ex-Fugee mulling Haiti campaign," Associated Press, 26 July 2010.

87 "Publication de la liste des candidats aux législatives de novembre 2010," AlterPresse, 17 July 2010.

88 "Immense challenge to rebuild Haiti, president tells donors," Agence France-Presse, 2 June 2010.

89 "Haitian farmers protest Monsanto seed donations," Agence France-Presse, 4 June 2010.

90 "Haitian farmers reaping hard times as hunger grows," Agence France-Presse, 19 July 2010.

91 "Haiti still waiting for pledged US aid," Associated Press, 28 September 2010.

92 "A Tremor for Haiti's Aid Industry," *Foreign Policy*, 30 June 2010.

93 "La reconstruction n'est pas viable sans une décentralisation véritable," AlterPresse, 24 July 2010.

94 "300 millions de dollars promis pour le relevement de l'agriculture," AlterPresse, 7 July 2010.

95 "Haiti reconstruction must proceed with all possible speed," *The Washington Post*, 17 July 2010.

96 "Haiti's Homeless: Is 'Transitional' Housing the Solution," *Time*, 16 July 2010.

97 "Déclaration du Service Jésuite aux Réfugiés/Haïti," 12 July 2010.

98 For an excellent primer on *rabòday*, read the journalist Susana Ferreira's "How Disaster and Tragedy Spawned a Radical Music Movement in Haiti," BuzzFeed, 7 July 2015.

99 "Vyolans nan lari zòn metwopolitèn nan," Komisyon Episkopal Nasyonal Jistis ak Lapè, April–June 2010.

100 "Risque de réimplantation des gangs à Cité Soleil," Radio Kiskeya, 27 August 2010.

101 "Police nab 30 in pre-dawn raid on Haiti quake camp," Associated Press, 18 June 2010.

102 "Violentes protestations anti-Préval au Cap, lors d'une inauguration," Radio Kiskeya, 31 July 2010.

103 "Ex-premier could outstrip Wyclef in Haiti election," Associated Press Writer, 4 August 2010.

104 "Singer Wyclef files to run for Haiti's presidency," Associated Press, 5 August 2010.

105 "Questions about his charity may dog Wyclef Jean's presidential bid," Yahoo News, 5 August 2010.

106 "Jude Célestin, directeur général du CNE, désigné candidat à la présidence de la plate-forme électorale de René Préval," Radio Kiskeya, 7 August 2010.

107 "Jacques Édouard Alexis s'en fait pour la démocratie," AlterPresse, 9 August 2010.

108 "Préval laissera un pays 'en feu', en cas de 'coup d'état électoral', avertissent des partisans du candidat Cristalin," Radio Kiskeya, 9 August 2010.

109 "Le candidat Jean-Henry Céant pointe du doigt le chef de l'État," Radio Kiskeya, 24 August 2010.

110 "Le MPP totalement en phase avec les plateformes abstentionnistes," Radio Kiskeya, 17 September 2010.

111 "De graves problèmes pourraient compromettre le scrutin du 28 novembre 2010," Réseau National de Défense des Droits Humains et le Conseil National d'Observation, 27 September 2010.

112 "Wyclef Jean Barred from Haiti Election," *The New York Times*, 20 August 2010.

113 "Keep the Faith," *Huffington Post*, 20 August 2010.

114 "Wyclef Can't Appeal Haiti Poll Exclusion: Council," Reuters, 24 August 2010.

115 "René Préval reçu chez les Manigat," Radio Kiskeya, 28 August 2010.

116 "President René Préval's meetings with candidates puzzle Haitians," *The Miami Herald*, 3 September 2010.

117 "L'OEA et la Caricom soulignent l'insuffisance de transparence dans l'invalidation de certaines candidatures," AlterPresse, 23 August 2010.

118 "Non à la réhabilitation des criminels!," AlterPresse, 27 August 2010.

119 "L'ONU s'inquiète de la sécurité en Haïti à l'approche des élections," Radio Kiskeya, 2 September 2010.

120 "Un fugitif et présumé chef de gang arrêté au ministère des finances," Radio Kiskeya, 6 September 2010.

121 "Affaire Willy Etienne: le ministère des finances nie tout lien avec le chef de gang," Radio Kiskeya, 8 September 2010.

122 "Vaste opération policière dans l'aire de Cité Soleil," Radio Kiskeya, 9 September 2010.

123 "Sept policiers, dont deux femmes, sous les verrous," Radio Kiskeya, 15 September 2010.

124 "Assassinat de l'épouse du directeur départemental de l'ouest de la Police Nationale," Radio Kiskeya, 11 September 2010.

125 "Just 2 percent of quake debris in Haiti cleared," Associated Press, 11 September 2010.

126 "Haiti still waiting for pledged US aid," Associated Press, 28 September 2010.

127 "Another obstacle stalls $1.15B in US aid for Haiti," Associated Press, 4 November 2010.

128 "Haiti: Still Trapped in the Emergency Phase," Refugees International, 6 October 2010.

129 "La IHRC approuve 18 nouveaux projets," AlterPresse, 6 October 2010.

130 "Jacques Édouard Alexis 'se déchaine': 'Préval veut garder le pouvoir, des armes ont été distribuées', dénonce-t-il," Radio Kiskeya, 4 October 2010.

131 "Révélations de Jacques-Édouard Alexis sur le pouvoir: des candidats préoccupés," Radio Kiskeya, 5 October 2010.

132 "La sénatrice du Centre, Edmonde S. Beauzile, dénonce la circulation d'armes illégales dans son département," Radio Kiskeya, 10 October 2010.

133 "Le sénateur de l'Artibonite Youri Latortue dénonce des violations par INITE des règles fixées par le CEP et des actes d'intimidation contre la population," Radio Kiskeya, 11 October 2010.

134 "Le bureau de l'ONI aux Cayes incendié," AlterPresse, 4 October 2010.

135 "Paul Denis proclame la 'victoire' de Jude Célestin à un meeting de INITE," Radio Kiskeya, 7 October 2010.

136 "Un ex-Sénateur s'élève contre le rôle partisan du ministre de la justice dans la campagne électorale," Radio Kiskeya, 8 October 2010.

137 "Jude Célestin s'autoproclame 'Président', au coup d'envoi officiel de sa campagne," Radio Kiskeya, 20 October 2010.

138 "Mandat prorogé par le Conseil de sécurité," AlterPresse, 14 October 2010.

139 "Neuf mois après, les déplacés réclament des logements decents et permanents," AlterPresse, 12 October 2010.

CHAPTER TWELVE

1 "UN to boost Haiti quake relief force," *The Guardian*, 19 January 2010.

2 "Haiti earthquake could trigger possible medical 'perfect storm,'" CNN, 13 January 2010.

3 "Cholera Epidemic: The Haitian Government must determine MINUSTAH's responsibility," Réseau National de Défense des Droits de l'Homme, 3 November 2010.

4 "Haiti Fears Cholera Will Spread in Capital," *The New York Times*, 23 October 2010.

5 "Haiti battles cholera epidemic, nearly 200 dead," Reuters, 22 October 2010.

6 "Cholera in Haiti Matches Strains Seen in South Asia, U.S. Says," Associated Press, 1 November 2010.

7 "Cholera confirmed for resident of Haiti's capital," Associated Press, 9 November 2010.

8 "L'épidémie fait 796 morts, mais le nombre journalier des décès passe de 77 à 66," AlterPresse, 12 November 2010.

9 "Haiti cholera death toll approaches 800 with rapid increase feared," *The Guardian*, 12 November 2010.

10 "Haiti death toll rises to 1,000," *Financial Times*, 14 November 2010.

11 "Haiti cholera reaches Dominican Republic," BBC, 17 November 2010.

12 "Un accès de violence marque cette étape de la campagne électorale," AlterPresse, 28 October 2010.

13 "Distribution d'armes par INITE dans le département du Centre, selon le coordonnateur du MPP/MPNKP, Chavannes Jean-Baptiste," Radio Kiskeya, 1 November 2010.

14 "La POHDH préoccupée par des allégations concernant la distribution intentionnelle d'armes à feu," AlterPresse, 27 October 2010.

15 "Terreur et fraudes électorales programmées, dénonce Mirlande Manigat," Radio Kiskeya, 3 November 2010.

16 "Election keeps tumult coming in Haiti," *The Washington Post*, 19 November 2010.

17 "Des déplacés internes protestent contre leurs conditions dix mois après le séisme dévastateur du 12 janvier," Radio Kiskeya, 12 November 2010.

18 "Des milliers de manifestants dans les rues du Cap-Haïtien (Nord) contre le choléra et la mission des Nations-Unies," Radio Kiskeya, 15 November 2010.

19 "Manifestations contre les casques bleus dans le Nord et le Plateau Central," AlterPresse, 15 November 2010.

20 "Haiti president appeals for calm in cholera riots," Associated Press, 17 November 2010.

21 "Le Représentant Spécial du Secrétaire général des Nations Unies, Edmond Mulet, alarmé par les risques que font courir les manifestations à la population," Radio Kiskeya, 19 November 2010.

22 "Haiti cholera riots lessen, 3rd protester killed," Associated Press, 17 November 2010.

23 "Campaigning in cholera complicates Haiti election," Associated Press, 17 November 2010.

24 "His Music Rules in Haiti," *Miami New Times*, 29 May 1997.

25 Author interview, June 2015.

26 "Crise haïtienne: Mirlande Manigat, arrivée en tête du premier tour, refuse un nouveau comptage des voix," *Le Monde*, 11 December 2010.

27   "Campaign fixer sweetens prospects for Haiti's Michel Martelly," *Toronto Star*, 6 December 2010.

28   "La campagne électorale émaillée d'incidents dans le Sud," AlterPresse, 15 November 2010.

29   "Le syndicaliste Miguel Saint-Louis assassiné à Port-au-Prince," Radio Kiskeya, 16 November 2010.

30   "Graves incidents à Port-au-Prince lors d'une manifestation contre la MINUSTAH et le Gouvernement," Radio Kiskeya, 18 November 2010.

31   "Un meeting de Mirlande Manigat perturbé à Aquin par des partisans armés de INITE," Radio Kiskeya, 22 November 2010.

32   "Fusillade dans la Grand'Anse contre le cortège du candidat à la présidence du parti gouvernemental," Radio Kiskeya, 23 November 2010.

33   "Music turns serious in Sweet Micky's Haiti campaign," *The Miami Herald*, 24 November 2010.

34   "Passe d'armes entre Manigat et le duo Martelly-Céant," Radio Kiskeya, 26 November 2010.

35   "500.000 faux bulletins seraient disponibles pour Jude Célestin, accuse Mirlande Manigat," Radio Kiskeya, 26 November 2010.

36   "Rapport d'enquête sur le climat de violence qui sévit dans les communes de Plaisance et de Borgne," Réseau National de Défense des Droits Humains, March 2011.

37   Author interview with aid worker present in the Artibonite Valley in November 2010, January 2016.

38   "Note de presse," CNO, ISC, RNDDH, CERESS, CONHANE and MOFKA, 26 November 2010.

39   "Where do I vote? Much confusion clouds Haiti polls," Reuters, 26 November 2010.

40   "L'organisation paysanne 'Tèt Kole' ne soutient aucun candidat," AlterPresse, 25 November 2010.

41   "Haitian voters brace for stark choice," Agence France-Presse, 25 November 2010.

42   "Fin de la campagne présidentielle sur fond de polémique et d'incertitudes," Radio Kiskeya, 26 November 2010.

43   "Haiti Election Marred by ID Card Problems," *The New York Times*, 27 November 2010.

44   "Rapport du RNDDH sur les élections présidentielles et législatives du 28 novembre 2010," Réseau National de Défense des Droits Humains, 3 December 2010.

45   "Election in Haiti beset by cholera, confusion," Associated Press, 28 November 2010.

46   "Voting ends in Haiti amid chaos, confusion," *The Miami Herald*, 28 November 2010.

47   Ibid.

48   "Haiti Elections a Shambles," *The Los Angeles Times*, 28 November 2010.

49   "Une odeur de fraude règne en Haïti," *La Presse*, 26 November 2010.

50   "Rapport du RNDDH sur les élections présidentielles et législatives du 28 novembre 2010," Réseau National de Défense des Droits Humains, 3 December 2010.

51   Email to the author, November 2010.

52   Email to the author from witness in Haiti, November 2010.

53   Email to the author from witness in Haiti, November 2010.

54   Author interview with senior United Nations official, June 2014.

55   "Haiti's Doctored Elections, Seen from the Inside," *Dissent Magazine*, 24 February 2014.

56   Author interviews, June 2014 and June 2015.

57   This account of the meeting is a composite of interviews conducted with senior United Nations and United States diplomats and the author's interview with Jean-Max Bellerive in Port-au-Prince, February 2016.

58   "13 candidats à la présidence réclame l'annulation du scrutin," Radio Métropole, 28 November 2010.

59   "Plusieurs milliers de manifestants réclament l'annulation du scrutin," Radio Métropole, 28 November 2010.

60   "Le point sur les élections en Haïti," Radio Kiskeya, 28 November 2010.

61   "Deux morts et plusieurs blessés lors des élections en Haïti," Radio Métropole, 28 November 2010.

62   "Whomever they voted for …," *The Economist*, 9 December 2010.

63   "Les principales villes sont calmes après les manifestations postélectorales," Radio Métropole, 29 November 2010.

64   "Nouvelle situation de tension à Saint-Marc en protestation contre les élections et le président René Préval," Radio Kiskeya, 29 November 2010.

65   "Violentes protestations à St-Marc: la MINUSTAH fait une quinzaine de blessés, dont six par balle," Radio Kiskeya, 29 November 2010.

66   "Des milliers manifestants réclament l'annulation des élections contestées," Radio Métropole, 30 November 2010.

67   "Michel Martelly contre l'annulation des élections," Radio Métropole, 29 November 2010.

68   "Irregularities don't invalidate Haiti poll: observers," Reuters, 29 November 2010.

69   Ibid.

70   "Observers play down fraud in Haiti's election," Associated Press, 29 November 2010.

71   "Silence de l'Exécutif et des observateurs internationaux, préoccupation des Nations Unies," AlterPresse, 28 November 2010.

72   "Rapport du RNDDH sur les élections présidentielles et législatives du 28 novembre 2010," Réseau National de Défense des Droits Humains, 3 December 2010.

73   "Le conseil national d'observation demande une évaluation indépendante du scrutin du 28 novembre," AlterPresse, 6 December 2010.

74   "UN Threatens to Leave Haiti if the Popular Will Is Not Respected," Agence France-Presse, 6 December 2010.

75   "Haiti ruling party acknowledges possible poll defeat," Agence France-Presse, 30 November 2010.

76   "Reprise progressive des activités – Calme apparent," AlterPresse, 30 November 2010.

77   "Je serai présidente, déclare Mirlande Manigat," AlterPresse, 1 December 2010.

78 "Mirlande Manigat en première position, selon le CNO," Haiti Press Network, 6 December 2010.

79 "Haiti awaits presidential results," *The Miami Herald*, 7 December 2010.

80 "Michel Martelly opposé à une 'victoire' de Jude Célestin ou à un second tour avec lui," Radio Kiskeya, 6 December 2010.

81 "Manigat and Célestin appear headed for a runoff for Haitian presidency," *The Miami Herald*, 7 December 2010.

82 "Mirlande Manigat (RDNP) et Jude Célestin (INITE) au second tour de la présidentielle 2010, selon le CEP," Radio Kiskeya, 8 December 2010.

83 "Candidates Face Runoff in Haiti's Troubled Vote," *The New York Times*, 8 December 2010.

84 "Protesters set fire to Haiti candidate HQ," Associated Press, 8 December 2010.

85 "Haiti on edge after disputed poll results," Agence France-Presse, 8 December 2010.

86 "Furious protests greet Haiti election results," Associated Press, 8 December 2010.

87 "Haiti election riot grows, govt party office burns," Associated Press, 8 December 2010.

88 "Haiti protesters rampage against election results," Reuters, 8 December 2010.

89 "Des milliers de personnes rejettent violemment les résultats proclamés par le CEP," AlterPresse, 8 December 2010.

90 "Les Cayes, le chaos absolu," *Le Nouvelliste*, 10 Decembre 2010.

91 "Four dead as Haiti vote protests turn ugly," Agence France-Presse, 9 December 2010.

92 "Réactions aux résultats des élections: quatre morts, le siège de INITE disparaît," Radio Kiskeya, 8 December 2010.

93 "Statement by the Embassy of the United States Following the Publication of Results of the November 28 National Elections by the CEP," 7 December 2010.

94 "Des témoins dénoncent des individus portant le T-shirt du parti officiel INITE," Radio Kiskeya, 9 December 2010.

95 "Haiti officials to re-count disputed election," Associated Press, 9 December 2010.

96 "Officials prepare to review Haiti electoral results," *The Miami Herald*, 10 December 2010.

97 "Haiti recount in disarray," Agence France-Presse, 11 December 2010.

98 "Note de presse d'organismes nationaux d'observation," 10 December 2010.

99 "Jude Célestin conteste les résultats des présidentielles," Radio Kiskeya, 13 December 2010.

100 "Crise haïtienne: Mirlande Manigat, arrivée en tête du premier tour, refuse un nouveau comptage des voix," *Le Monde*, 11 December 2010.

101 "Des Sénateurs, des dirigeants de l'opposition et de la société civile appellent à l'annulation des élections et à la mise en place d'un 'gouvernement de consensus' avant le départ du Président Préval le 7 février 2011," Radio Kiskeya, 22 December 2010.

102 "Haiti election results could be delayed for weeks," Associated Press, 18 December 2010.

103 "Clinton: More expected from Haitian leaders," CNN, 13 December 2010.

104 "Cholera rages in rural Haiti, overwhelming clinics," Associated Press, 3 December 2010.

105 "Haiti cholera came from UN camp: report," Agence France-Presse, 7 December 2010.

106 "Haïti est la preuve de l'échec de l'aide internationale," *Le Temps*, 20 December 2010.

107 "An insider's critique of what went wrong in Haiti," Al Jazeera, 8 January 2011.

108 "OAS Removes Special Representative in Haiti from Post," *Latin American Herald Tribune*, 26 December 2010.

109 "Haïti est à un 'carrefour dangereux', selon René Préval," Radio Kiskeya, 3 January 2011.

110 "Haiti presidential runoff 'impossible' this month," Associated Press, 4 January 2010.

111 "OAS says boot Haiti gov't candidate," Associated Press, 10 January 2011.

112 "3481 haïtiens tués par l'épidémie," AlterPresse, 4 January 2011.

113 "Haiti one year on: suffering, lost opportunities and political paralysis," *The Guardian*, 6 January 2011.

114 "12 January 2011 and Us," AlterPresse, 6 January 2011.

115 "Haiti president unhappily receives election report," Associated Press, 13 January 2011.

116 "Un mort dans des incidents violents ayant suivi la remise du rapport de l'OEA," Radio Kiskeya, 14 January 2011.

117 "Les autorités 'condamnent' les récentes tentatives de trouble," AlterPresse, 15 January 2011.

118 "Dérapages dans plusieurs régions de la zone métropolitaine au lendemain de la soumission du rapport de la Mission d'experts," Réseau National de Défense des Droits Humains, 14 January 2011.

119 "Le CEP reçoit le rapport de l'OEA, mais maintient les résultats contestés du premier tour," Radio Kiskeya, 18 February 2015.

120 "Haiti under US-led pressure over tainted vote," Agence France-Presse, 20 January 2011.

121 "Ex-Dictator Loses Swiss Ruling Over Haitian Cash," *The New York Times*, 24 February 2010.

122 "Ex-Haiti dictator 'Baby Doc' returns to homeland," Agence France-Press, 17 January 2011.

123 "Jean-Claude 'Baby Doc' Duvalier returns to Haiti," *The Guardian*, 17 January 2010.

124 "Baby Doc's back," *The Economist*, 17 January 2011.

125 "Jean-Claude 'Baby Doc' Duvalier returns to Haiti," *The Guardian*, 17 January 2010.

126 "Ex-Haiti dictator 'Baby Doc' returns to homeland," Agence France-Press, 17 January 2011.

127 "Baby Doc's back," *The Economist*, 17 January 2011.

128 "Ex-dictator Jean-Claude 'Baby Doc' Duvalier taken into custody," *The Miami Herald*, 18 January 2011.

129 Author interview, June 2014.

130 Author interview, June 2015.

131 "Quatre anciennes victimes de Duvalier portent plainte," Radio Kiskeya, 19 January 2011.

132 "Un an d'impunité et de mépris des victimes de la dictature," AlterPresse, 20 January 2012.

133 "Duvalier: I have no presidential ambitions," *The Miami Herald*, 20 January 2011.

134 "Baby Doc slips out of Haiti hotel to private home," Associated Press, 20 January 2011.

135 "Texte intégral du discours de Duvalier," 22 January 2011.

136 "With Baby Doc back in Haiti, Aristide calls next," Associated Press, 20 January 2011.

137 "US Discouraging Aristide Return to Haiti," Voice of America, 20 January 2011.

138 "Visite surprise de René Préval à Santo Domingo," Radio Kiskeya, 22 January 2011.

139 "Haiti: Aristide can have passport, hasn't applied," Associated Press, 31 January 2011.

140 "Cuba dément la présence d'Aristide sur son territoire," Radio Kiskeya, 31 January 2011.

141 Author interview with United Nations official, June 2014.

142 "Haiti candidate warns of protests, U.S. pulls visas," Reuters, 21 January 2011.

143 "Washington supprime les visas d'officiels haïtiens et de dirigeants de INITE," Radio Kiskeya, 21 January 2011.

144 "Le retrait de la candidature à la présidence de Jude Célestin évoqué lors d'une réunion de la plateforme officielle INITE," Radio Kiskeya, 23 January 2011.

145 "Haitian presidential candidate Jude Célestin resists pressure to withdraw," *The Miami Herald*, 26 January 2011.

146 "Pas de confirmation officielle du retrait de la candidature de Jude Célestin," Radio Kiskeya, 25 January 2015.

147 "Clinton presses Haiti on elections," *The Washington Post*, 31 January 2011.

148 Author interview with Jean-Max Bellerive, February 2016.

149 Author interview with Jean-Max Bellerive, February 2016.

150 "Manigat et Martelly au second tour, Célestin écarté," AlterPresse, 3 February 2011.

151 "With Subtraction and Addition, Haiti Sets its Presidential Runoff," *The New York Times*, 3 February 2011.

152 "US says 'good day in Haiti' after vote results," Agence France-Presse, 3 February 2011.

153 "Déclaration de Jude Célestin," 3 February 2011.

154 "Position du RNDDH autour des résultats définitifs du premier tour des élections présidentielles et législatives," Réseau National de Défense des Droits Humains, 4 February 2011.

155 Author interview with aid worker present in the Artibonite Valley in November 2010, January 2016.

156 "South Korean garment manufacturer signs deal to build factories," Associated Press, 11 January 2011.

157 "Des milliers de personnes accueillent Duvalier à Léogâne," Radio Kiskeya, 7 February 2011.

158 "Aristide obtient son précieux passeport diplomatique," Radio Kiskeya, 7 February 2011.

159 "Aristide backers march amid talk of Haiti return," Associated Press, 18 February 2011.

160 "Obama has 'deep concerns' over Aristide return," Associated Press, 17 March 2011.

161 "Michel Martelly très satisfait de sa tournée dans le nord et le nord-est," Radio Kiskeya, 21 February 2011.

162 "2 Haiti presidential candidates start campaigns," Associated Press, 17 February 2011.

163 "Poursuite de la campagne de Michel Joseph Martelly (Repons Peyizan) dans la Grand'Anse et le Sud," Radio Kiskeya, 8 March 2011.

164 "Tête-à-Tête entre Leonel Fernàndez et Michel Martelly," Radio Kiskeya, 28 February 2011.

165 "Campaign kicks off for Haiti's presidential run-off," Agence France-Presse, 17 February 2011.

166 "Mirlande Manigat s'offre un meeting à Cité Soleil, malgré un incident ayant fait un mort," Radio Kiskeya, 22 February 2011.

167 "Mirlande Manigat dans un nouveau quartier populaire, Martissant," Radio Kiskeya, 1 March 2011.

168 "Incidents violents lors d'un meeting de Mirlande Manigat au Cap-Haïtien," Radio Kiskeya, 10 March 2011.

169 "Un meeting de Mirlande Manigat à Mirebalais tourne à l'affrontement," Radio Kiskeya, 16 March 2011.

170 "Mirlande Manigat, légèrement choquée lors d'un meeting à Liancourt, dénonce l'apparition d'une milice rose," Radio Kiskeya, 16 March 2011.

171 "Déclaration du Groupe Médialternatif," 11 March 2011.

172 "Three men found dead in Haiti after putting up election posters," Agence France-Presse, 9 March 2011.

173 "Danny Glover in South Africa," *Democracy Now!*, 17 March 2011.

174 "Former President Aristide on his Party's Exclusion from Haiti's Election," *Democracy Now!*, 21 March 2011.

175 "Aristide célèbre 'la fin de l'exil et des coups d'État'," AlterPresse, 18 March 2011.

176 "Ousted Haitian leader Aristide returns from exile," Associated Press, 18 March 2011.

177 "La police tire des gaz lacrymogènes pour frayer un chemin à Aristide," *Le Nouvelliste*, 18 March 2011.

178 "Haitians Go to the Polls to Choose a New President," *The New York Times*, 20 March 2011.

179 "Le candidat Michel Martelly a voté dans une ambiance de rassemblement en sa faveur," AlterPresse, 20 March 2011.

180 "Deux morts et plusieurs blessés par balle dans l'Artibonite et le nord-ouest," Radio Kiskeya, 20 March 2011.

181 "Raid de motards armés: deux morts et plusieurs blessés," Radio Kiskeya, 25 March 2011.

182 "Le staff de Mirlande Manigat soumet au CEP un mémoire contre les 'fraudes' de Michel Martelly," Radio Kiskeya, 28 March 2011.

183 "Haiti postpones preliminary results of runoff vote as count drags on amid fraud allegations," Associated Press, 29 March 2011.

184 "Martelly reportedly wins Haiti election," *The Miami Herald*, 4 April 2011.

185 "Carnival singer tipped to be Haiti's president," Agence France-Presse, 21 March 2011.

186 "Les camps Martelly et Manigat refusent de lâcher prise," Radio Kiksyea, 1 April 2011.

187 "Haiti prepares for Monday's election results," *The Miami Herald*, 3 April 2011.

188 "Les partisans de Michel Martelly célèbrent bruyamment son accession à la présidence," Radio Kiskeya, 4 April 2011.

189 "Les choses vont changer, promet Michel Martelly," Radio Kiskeya, 5 April 2011.

190 "Haiti candidate won't challenge 'Sweet Micky' win," Associated Press, 8 April 2011.

191 "Martelly courts diaspora, pushes education fund to help rebuild Haiti," *The Miami Herald*, 25 April 2011.

192 "Michel Martelly veut créer 'une armée moderne' en Haïti," Agence France-Presse, 22 April 2011.

193 "Préval et Martelly passent en revue les grands dossiers de l'État," Radio Kiskeya, 15 April 2011.

194 "Haiti leader wins ringing endorsement from Clinton," Agence France-Presse, 20 April 2011.

195 "Martelly envisage d'aministier Duvalier et Aristide," Radio Kiskeya, 8 April 2011.

196 "Préval prepares to leave office in Haiti after serving through major disasters," *The Miami Herald*, 11 May 2011.

197 "Haiti delays certification of 19 legislative races," Associated Press, 25 April 2011.

198 "Inite frole la majorité au parlement," AlterPresse, 21 April 2011.

199 "Le coup de massue de Préval/INITE," Radio Kiskeya, 21 April 2011.

200 "Au moins deux morts dans des troubles provoqués par les résultats définitifs," AlterPresse, 21 April 2011.

201 "Des incidents entre rivaux ont fait un mort et d'importants dégâts," Radio Kiskeya, 8 April 2011.

202 "AMARC–ALC condamne l'incendie d'une radio communautaire à Carice," AlterPresse, 26 April 2011.

203 "Note d'Information publiée par Ginette Cherubin," 26 April 2011.

204 "Experts seek annulment of Haiti vote results," Agence France-Presse, 29 April 2011.

205 "Martelly lance un ultimatum au Conseil électoral," Radio Kiskeya, 5 May 2011.

206 "Haiti officials reverse contested vote results," Associated Press, 11 May 2011.

207 "Rodolphe Joazile, sans surprise, président du Sénate," Radio Kiskeya, 29 April 2011.

208 "La 49e législature impose à la nation deux mandats présidentiels consécutifs," Radio Kiskeya, 9 May 2011.

209 "Haitian lawmakers vote to allow dual nationality," Associated Press, 9 May 2011.

210 "Le 'Kase fèy kouvri sa' doit cesser et le règne de l'impunité prendre fin!," Radio Kiskeya, 11 May 2011.

211 "Martelly takes over," *The Economist*, 16 May 2011.

212 "Martelly parle en apôtre du 'changement' à son investiture," Radio Kiskeya, 14 March 2011.

213 "Martelly takes over," *The Economist*, 16 May 2011.

CHAPTER THIRTEEN

1   "Haitians Forced Out of Tents to Homes Just as Precarious," *The New York Times*, 23 April 2011.

2   "Haiti receives less than half of pledges," Agence France-Presse, 23 July 2011.

3   "Final Report of the Independent Panel of Experts on the Cholera Outbreak in Haiti," May 2011.

4   "Haiti cholera outbreak blamed on UN force," Associated Press, 30 June 2011.

5   "Leaked UN report faults sanitation at Haiti bases at time of cholera outbreak," *The Guardian*, 5 April 2016.

6   "Réplique de Michel Martelly au Sénateur du Nord Moïse Jean-Charles," Radio Kiskeya, 27 May 2011.

7   "Haiti clears homeless from stadium parking lot," Associated Press, 16 July 2011.

8   "Plusieurs ex-policiers à la moralité douteuse, se retrouvent aujourd'hui dans l'entourage de Martelly," Réseau National de Défense des Droits Humains, 17 June 2011.

9   "Le chef de la sécurité présidentielle, Carel Alexandre, démis de ses fonctions," Radio Kiskeya, 28 March 2012.

10 "Haïti: 29 millions de gourdes non justifiées," *Le Nouvelliste*, 8 June 2011.

11 "Le monument de Vertières, vandalisé par des marchands de ferraille," AlterPresse, 27 May 2011.

12 "New PM would end Haiti quake panel," Associated Press, 25 May 2011.

13 "L'administration générale des douanes proteste contre la violente irruption d'un groupe de soldats brésiliens de la MINUSTAH à la salle d'arrivée de l'Aéroport international de Port-au-Prince," Radio Kiskeya, 10 June 2010.

14 "Assassinat de Guiteau Toussaint, président du conseil d'administration de la BNC," *Le Nouvelliste*, 12 June 2011.

15 "La faculté d'agronomie en ébullition après l'assassinat du professeur Yves Dorvil," Radio Kiskeya, 30 June 2011.

16 "Des bandits font deux morts à Port-au-Prince," Radio Kiskeya, 4 July 2011.

17 "La candidature de Daniel Rouzier écartée," Radio Kiskeya, 12 June 2011.

18 "Après le rejet de Rouzier, 'le pays ne peut plus attendre', déclare Martelly," AlterPresse, 23 June 2011.

19 "Open letter from Daniel Gérard Rouzier to Haiti," 5 July 2011.

20 "Martelly se rend aux USA et nomme une 'équipe de liaison' avec le Parlement," Radio Kiskeya, 26 June 2011.

21 "Version originale de la résolution anti-Gousse des Sénateurs," 8 July 2011.

22 "Voyage de Martelly en Europe – dix jours de plus sans gouvernement," AlterPresse, 5 July 2011.

23 "16 Sénateurs sur 30 rejettent par anticipation la candidature de Bernard Gousse," Radio Kiskeya, 8 July 2011.

24 "Ratification de Gousse: Martelly veut mettre le Parlement au pas," Radio Kiskeya, 16 July 2011.

25 "Rencontre Martelly/Groupe des 16: toujours pas d'accord," Radio Kiskeya, 21 July 2011.

26 "Haitian leader wants changes in recovery panel," Associated Press, 23 July 2011.

27 "Un nouveau programme de crédit est lancé," AlterPresse, 20 July 2011.

28 "Martelly instaure ses propres règles en matière de liberté de la presse et de démocratie," Radio Kiskeya, 29 July 2011.

29 "Un policier placé en isolement après l'évasion d'un suspect," Radio Kiskeya, 27 July 2011.

30 "C'était une tentative d'assassinat, déclare le président Martelly," *Le Matin*, 26 July 2011.

31 "Un député tué par balle," AlterPresse, 25 July 2011.

32 "Guy Philippe nie toute implication dans la mort du député Dionald Polyte," Radio Kiskeya, 29 July 2011.

33 "Décès aux Cayes (Sud) de l'ex-Directeur central de la police judiciaire (DCPJ), Jean Denis Fortin (41 ans), blessé par balle à Torbeck (Sud)," Radio Kiskeya, 5 September 2011.

34 "Le groupe des 16 impose au Sénat son rejet du choix de Bernard Gousse," Radio Kiskeya, 3 August 2011.

35 "Sénat: Opération Bagdad III," Radio Kiskeya, 6 August 2011.

36 "Offensive du G-16: Michel Martelly doit répondre à dix exigences," Radio Kiskeya, 26 August 2011.

37 "Bill Clinton aide named as Haiti's 3rd pick for PM," Associated Press, 31 August 2011.

38 Email from Cheryl Mills to Hillary Clinton, 20 June 2011.

39 "Haiti MPs finally agree on appointment of new prime minister," *The Guardian*, 25 October 2011.

40 "Un proche zélé du président Martelly agresse un parlementaire," Haiti Press Network, 2 September 2011.

41 "Haiti's quake displaced population makes big drop," Associated Press, 6 September 2011.

42 "Des casques bleus uruguayens accusés de viol sur un haïtien de 18 ans," Radio Kiskeya, 4 September 2011.

43 "Un Jeune de PortSalut violé par des agents de la MINUSTAH: le RNDDH réclame justice pour la victime," Réseau National de Défense des Droits Humains, 5 September 2011.

44 "Preliminary UN probe discards Haiti sex assault," Associated Press, 5 September 2011.

45 "Uruguay to Apologize Over Alleged Rape by U.N. Peacekeepers," Reuters, 6 September 2011.

46 "In Haiti, American ex-priest maintains access to youth," *The Dallas Morning News*, 24 February 2005.

47 "Brazil plans to start removing troops from Haiti," Associated Press, 6 September 2011.

48 "Protesters in Haiti demand ouster of UN troops," Associated Press, 14 September 2011.

49 "Haiti Leader Is Opposed to Reduction of U.N. Force," *The New York Times*, 22 September 2011.

50 "Le président Martelly confirme officiellement disposer d'un plan de rétablissement de l'armée," Radio Kiskeya, 30 September 2011.

51 "Michel Martelly Fignolé un plan de rétablissement de l'armée," AlterPresse, 28 September 2011.

52 "'Une force de répression en plus contre le peuple', selon des secteurs paysan et ouvrier," AlterPresse, 29 September 2011.

53 "Des duvaliéristes interrompent la lecture d'un rapport d'Amnesty International," Radio Kiskeya, 23 September 2011.

54 "Le Président Martelly invite au dialogue ses prédécesseurs Manigat, Aristide, Duvalier, etc ...," Radio Kiskeya, 20 September 2011.

55 "Michel Martelly rencontre Aristide, Duvalier et Avril," Radio Kiskeya, 12 October 2011.

56 "Le Sénat entérine le choix de Garry Conille," Radio Kiskeya, 4 October 2011.

57 "Une 'milice rose' en formation, selon Moïse Jean-Charles," Radio Kiskeya, 6 October 2011.

58 "Haiti confirms new prime minister," *The Miami Herald*, 4 October 2011.

59 "Martelly, vedette de l'entrée en fonction du nouveau gouvernement," Radio Kiskeya, 19 October 2011.

60 "Haiti pres.: Thousands will go to school for free," Associated Press, 3 October 2011.

61 "Michel Martelly menace d'être cynique: quelqu'un qui, au Palais national, s'en prend à la Présidence, peut ne pas pouvoir en sortir, même s'il jouit d'une certaine immunité," Radio Kiskeya, 15 October 2011.

62 "Bras de fer," AlterPresse, 26 October 2011.

63 "Le Député Arnel Bélizaire sur une liste d'évadés de prison recherchés," Radio Kiskeya, 25 October 2011.

64 "Bras de fer," AlterPresse, 26 October 2011.

65 "Arrestation du Député Arnel Bélizaire," Radio Kiskeya, 27 October 2011.

66 "Première nuit en prison pour Bélizaire, des élus dénoncent une 'dictature naissante' de Martelly," Radio Kiskeya, 28 October 2011.

67 "Le parlement passe à l'offensive," AlterPresse, 28 October 2011.

68 "Grève vendredi à l'aéroport de Port-au-Prince contre les brutalités du ministre de l'intérieur," Radio Kiskyea, 29 October 2011.

69 "Haitian lawmaker released from jail amid protests," Associated Press, 28 October 2011.

70 "Martelly tente de calmer le jeu et nie toute responsabilité dans l'affaire Bélizaire," Radio Kiskeya, 3 November 2011.

71 "Ecartelé, le Sénat fait volte-face dans l'interpellation de deux membres du gouvernement reportée au 15 novembre," Radio Kiskeya, 5 November 2011.

72 "Les Présidents des deux chambres déclinent l'offre d'accompagner Michel Martelly à Cuba," AlterPresse, 15 November 2011.

73 "Heureuses retrouvailles entre Michel Martelly et René Préval," Radio Kiskeya, 15 November 2011.

74 "Martelly annonce le rétablissement de l'armée," Radio Kiskeya, 18 November 2011.

75 "Haiti has high hopes for jobs at new industrial park," Reuters, 28 November 2011.

76 "Earthquake Relief Where Haiti Wasn't Broken," *The New York Times*, 5 July 2012.

77 "Digicel Group to Build 173-room Port-au-Prince Hotel to Operate Under Marriott Hotels & Resorts Brand; Will Generate 175 Jobs in Haiti," PR Newswire, 28 November 2011.

78 "Bill Clinton et nous," AlterPresse, 29 December 2011.

79 "Un membre de l'Unité de Sécurité Présidentielle (USP), abattu de plusieurs balles lundi à Port-au-Prince," Radio Kiskeya, 2 November 2011.

80 "Un Inspecteur municipal de police abattu à Santo, en Plaine," Radio Kiskeya, 10 November 2011.

81 "Un policier abattu à Cité Soleil par des inconnus armés," Radio Kisekya, 1 December 2011.

82 "Affrontements entre bandes rivales au Bel-Air," Radio Kiskeya, 6 December 2011.

83 "Un policier tué, son corps brûlé à Port-au-Prince," Radio Kiskyea, 10 December 2011.

84 "Des tirs contre la voiture d'une militante des droits humains font deux blessés," Radio Kiskeya, 27 December 2011.

85 "La police traque les gangs à la veille d'une importante opération," Radio Kiskeya, 15 December 2011.

86 "Des cas de torture policière et l'implication présumée de policiers dans des exécutions sommaires en Haïti, dénoncés par le Haut commissariat de l'ONU aux droits de l'homme et la MINUSTAH," Radio Kiskeya, 29 December 2011.

87 "RNDDH condemns the involvement of MINUSTAH agents in yet another violation of human rights," Réseau National de Défense des Droits Humains, 16 December 2011.

88 "Plus de 6 mille victimes de la violence à Port-au-Prince en 10 ans, selon la Commission épiscopale Justice et Paix," Radio Kiskeya, 26 October 2011.

89 "Aristide's Brain," *London Review of Books*, 8 March 2012.

90 "Commémoration du 16 décembre: Aristide le grand absent, cri de ralliement de son épouse," Radio Kiskeya, 16 December 2011.

91 "Dominican-Haitian activist Sonia Pierre dies at 48," Associated Press, 4 December 2011.

92 "Adieux émouvants de plusieurs centaines de personnes à Sonia Pierre," Radio Kiskeya, 7 December 2011.

93 "Michel Martelly chiffre à 'cent mille dollars' une charge contre la presse," Radio Kiskeya, 30 December 2011.

94 "Le CEP de Gaillot Dorsinvil dissout par arrêté présidentiel," Radio Kiskeya, 30 December 2011.

95 "Haiti panel recommends restoring army," Associated Press, 1 January 2012.

96 "208 e anniversaire de la déclaration d'indépendance nationale," AlterPresse, 2 January 2012.

97 "Haitian military on comeback trail," Reuters, 1 March 2012.

98 "Des ex-militaires présumés occupent un bâtiment ministériel au Cap-Haïtien," Radio Kiskeya, 20 March 2012.

99 "Michel Martelly serait haïtien, américain et italien, selon Moïse Jean-Charles," Radio Kiskeya, 6 January 2012.

100 "Haiti 2 years later: Half a million still in camps," Associated Press, 8 January 2012.

101 "Haiti's Slow Recovery," *The New York Times*, 8 January 2012.

102 "Haitian PM eyes 8% growth in 2012," Agence France-Presse, 8 January 2012.

103 "Martelly préconise la justice sociale et une cohabitation harmonieuse des pouvoirs," Radio Kiskeya, 9 January 2012.

104 "Un an après son retour, le RNDDH s'insurge contre le traitement de faveur octroyé à l'ancien dictateur à vie Jean Claude Duvalier," Réseau National de Défense des Droits Humains, 16 January 2012.

105 "Un an d'impunité et de mépris des victimes de la dictature," AlterPresse, 19 January 2012.

106 "Baby Doc avoids human rights abuse charges in Haiti," Reuters, 30 January 2012.

107 "Haiti president now says no pardon for Duvalier," Associated Press, 27 January 2012.

108 "Déclaration du Collectif contre l'Impunité," 9 March 2012.

109 "Pour lui, pour elles et pour eux, pour tous nos enfants," AlterPresse, 13 February 2012; also see http://www.fordi9.com/Pages/gallery8.html.

110 "Jean-Claude Duvalier se fait discret au lendemain de son étonnant retour," Radio Kiskeya, 17 January 2011.

111 "Que sont devenus les barons de la dictature?," AlterPresse, 6 February 2015.

112 "Dilma Rousseff annonce à Port-au-Prince un désengagement militaire et la fin de l'immigration clandestine," Radio Kiskeya, 1 February 2012.

113 "Martelly insulte des parlementaires chez son Premier ministre," Radio Kiskeya, 2 February 2012.

114 "Martelly défie le Sénat sur sa nationalité et établit un nouveau record d'irrévérence," Radio Kiskeya, 4 February 2012.

115 "Passe d'armes entre Moïse Jean-Charles et Joseph Lambert," Radio Kiskeya, 16 February 2012.

116 "Le sénateur Joseph Lambert viré de son poste de coordonnateur général de INITE," Radio Kiskeya, 3 March 2012.

117 "Haitian Premier Says Loss of Support Led Him to Quit," *The New York Times*, 25 February 2012.

118 "Allocution du Président Martelly," 24 February 2012.

119 "'Nous sommes à quelques mètres du palais national', dixit Moïse Jean-Charles," AlterPresse, 24 February 2012.

120 "Vers une éventuelle convocation de l'ancien président Jean-Bertrand Aristide au Cabinet d'instruction," Radio Kiskeya, 27 February 2012.

121 "Jean-Bertrand Aristide poursuivi en justice pour trafic de drogue et détournement de fonds publics," Radio Kiskeya, 27 February 2012.

122 "Retrait ou dessaisissement dans l'affaire Aristide?," AlterPresse, 28 February 2012.

123 "Des milliers de partisans d'Aristide manifestent contre Martelly," Radio Kiskeya, 29 February 2012.

124 "Martelly fait choix de Laurent Lamothe comme premier ministre," AlterPresse, 1 March 2012.

125 "Haiti's president denies dual citizenship," Associated Press, 8 March 2012.

126 "Four months and $2M US tax dollars later, Haiti's new Parliament building sits unfinished," The Ground Truth Project, 19 March 2012. Also, author interview with United Nations official, June 2014.

127 "Un juge de Paix tué par balle à Port-au-Prince," Radio Kiskeya, 3 March 2012.

128 "Le directeur d'une station de radio, tué par balle," AlterPresse, 5 March 2012.

129 "Le célèbre peintre Burton Chenet tué chez lui, sa femme blessée," Radio Kiskeya, 21 March 2012.

130 "Assassinat de Samba Boukman, ex-chef d'OP Lavalas," Radio Kiskeya, 9 March 2012.

131 "La police lance Dragon 2," AlterPresse, 9 March 2012.

132 "Miami bribery probe zeroes in on Aristide," The Miami Herald, 3 March 2012.

133 "Ex-official slain in Haiti after his son helps," The Miami Herald, 7 March 2012.

134 "Dans l'attente de la demande de levée de l'immunité des sénateurs Lambert et Benoît," AlterPresse, 13 March 2012.

135 "Parade militaire et soutien de nombreux sympathisants aux hommes armés du nord," Radio Kiskeya, 23 March 2012.

136 "Fugitive foe of Aristide backs ex-Haiti president," Associated Press, 29 March 2012.

137 "Le pouvoir durcit le ton et ordonne le recours à la force contre les supposés ex-militaires," Radio Kiskeya, 22 March 2012.

138 "Le chef de la Police Nationale d'Haïti, Mario Andrésol, rejette une proposition du ministre de la justice," Radio Kiskeya, 25 March 2012.

139 Author interview with Mario Andrésol, Port-au-Prince, June 2015.

140 "Plusieurs milliers de lavalassiens réclament la démission du Président Martelly," Radio Kiskeya, 29 March 2012.

141 "Laurent Lamothe l'emporte au Sénat, un vote controversé," Radio Kiskeya, 11 April 2012.

142 "Des hommes armés en uniforme devant la Chambre des Députés," Radio Kiskeya, 17 April 2012.

143 "Haiti lawmakers end 2-month stalemate over prime minister, approve Martelly's nominee," Associated Press, 4 May 2011.

144 "Lamothe forme son cabinet et présente sa politique générale," Radio Kiskeya, 8 May 2012.

145 "La journaliste investigatrice Nuria Piera dénonce des persécutions contre ses sources supposées," Radio Kiskeya, 5 April 2012.

146 "Michel Martelly aurait reçu 2,5 millions dollars d'un Sénateur et entrepreneur dominicain, révèle une enquête journalistique," Radio Kiskeya, 2 April 2012.

147 "Accusations contre Martelly: la Présidence dénonce un 'lynchage médiatique'," Radio Kiskeya, 2 April 2012.

148 "Le RNDDH s'insurge contre les attaques en série d'agents de la PNH," Réseau National de Défense des Droits Humains, May 2012.

149 Ibid.

150 "Un chef de gang assassiné par ses lieutenants," Radio Métropole, 25 July 2014.

151 "En grève contre l'assassinat d'un collègue, des policiers tentent d'agresser un Député dans une station de radio," Radio Kiskeya, 18 April 2012.

152 "Les proches du policier assassiné veulent le jugement du Député incriminé," Radio Kiskeya, 21 April 2012.

153 "Assassinat du citoyen Octanol Derissant: le RNDDH exige le jugement des coupables," Réseau National de Défense des Droits Humains, April 2012.

154 Letter from Réseau National de Défense des Droits Humains to Conseil Supérieur du Pouvoir Judiciaire, 19 November 2012.

155 "Calixte Valentin arrêté pour le meurtre de Fond Parisien," Radio Kiskeya, 20 April 2012.

156 "Enterrement du Policier Walky Calixte 28 Mai 2012," https://www.youtube.com/watch?v=yu_ROV2YK9A, accessed 27 December 2015.

157 "Adieux émouvants à Walky Calixte, le policier assassiné," Radio Kiskeya, 26 May 2012.

CHAPTER FOURTEEN

1 Author interview with Laurent Lamothe, October 2015.

2 "Global leaders call on Haiti's feuding factions to salvage talks, elections," *The Miami Herald*, 21 February 2014.

3 "Lamothe promet la 'rupture' à Washington et se rend aux JO de Londres," Rado Kiskeya, 25 July 2012.

4 "Des fondateurs de la Plateforme INITE, dont l'ex-sénateur Joseph Lambert, proclament sa dissolution," Radio Kiskeya, 7 June 2012.

5 "Le Sénateur Moïse Jean-Charles déclare 'persona non grata' l'ambassadeur vénézuélien à Port-au-Prince," Radio Kiskeya, 14 June 2012.

6 "L'amendement officialisé, la ratification du Premier ministre mystérieusement supprimée," Radio Kiskeya, 21 June 2012.

7 "Furieux contre le pouvoir, des résidents des bidonvilles paralysent la circulation à Pétion-Ville," Radio Kiskeya, 21 June 2012.

8 "Haiti's Gold Rush Promises El Dorado – But for Whom?," Haiti Grassroots Watch, 27 June 2012.

9 "Role of Hillary Clinton's brother in Haiti gold mine raises eyebrows," *The Washington Post*, 20 March 2015.

10 "Le Sénat vote à l'unanimité des membres présents (15 sur 16) une résolution appelant à la cessation de l'exploitation des ressources minières," Radio Kiskeya, 21 February 2013.

11 "En crise depuis plus de deux mois, le Sénat renoue avec les séances," Radio Kiskeya, 18 July 2012.

12 "Le sénateur de l'Ouest, John Joël Joseph, rejette son choix comme membre de la commission bicamérale," Radio Kiskeya, 27 July 2012.

13 "Un deuxième Sénateur refuse de siéger dans la commission bicamérale," Radio Kiskeya, 27 July 2012.

14 "La présidence enfonce le clou: le CEP sera formé avec ou sans le Parlement," Radio Kiskeya, 9 August 2012.

15 "Carnaval des fleurs: controverses et mauvais souvenirs," AlterPresse, 28 July 2012.

16 "Martelly se réjouit du carnaval des fleurs," AlterPresse, 2 August 2012.

17 "Moïse Jean-Charles annonce une mobilisation populaire anti-Martelly," Radio Kiskeya, 2 August 2012.

18 "Le CEP formé sans les représentants du pouvoir législatif," Radio Kiskeya, 15 August 2012.

19 "Timide devant l'offensive du pouvoir, le président du Sénat annonce une possible séance en assemblée nationale ce vendredi," Radio Kiskeya, 16 August 2012.

20 "Sourd aux protestations, Michel Martelly installe son conseil électoral permanent," Radio Kiskeya, 20 August 2012.

21 "La police accusée d'incendie criminel, de répression et de vol à Martissant 23," Radio Kiskeya, 1 August 2012.

22 "La police met à prix la tête des chefs de gang de Martissant," Radio Kiskeya, 7 August 2012.

23 "Rapport d'enquête sur l'éviction des occupants du Parc National La Visite," Réseau National de Défense des Droits Humains, 8 August 2012.

24 "Le CEP formé sans les représentants du pouvoir législatif," Radio Kiskeya, 15 August 2012.

25 "Nouveau DG de la PNH: la POHDH appelle Gotson Aurélus à préserver la neutralité de l'institution," Radio Kiskeya, 17 August 2012.

26 "Les Organisations Haïtiennes de Promotion et de Défense des Droits Humains dénoncent la subordination des Pouvoirs Législatifs et Judiciaires par l'Exécutif," press release, 5 March 2013.

27 "Trente-huit aspirants policiers pistonnés par le palais national, selon le Rnndh," AlterPresse, 19 December 2014.

28 "Avant l'hypothétique séance de vendredi au Parlement, Martelly encore plus inflexible," Radio Kiskeya, 30 August 2012.

29 "Le pouvoir aurait mis à prix la tête de quatre Sénateurs de l'opposition," Radio Kiskeya, 3 October 2012.

30 "Après sa volte-face, Edwin 'Edo' Zenny se dit victime d'un 'lynchage médiatique'," Radio Kiskeya, 10 September 2012.

31 "L'administration Martelly en plein dans un nouveau scandale politico-judiciaire," Radio Kiskeya, 28 September 2012.

32 "Chaude alerte pour Martelly au Cap," Radio Kiskeya, 12 September 2012.

33 "La grève contre l'insécurité largement suivie aux Cayes," Radio Kiskeya, 13 September 2012.

34 "L'opposition à Martelly se durcit au Cap-Haïtien," Radio Kiskeya, 21 September 2012.

35 "Le nord s'apprête à récidiver," Radio Kiskeya, 26 September 2012.

36 "A l'appel de Fanmi Lavalas, plusieurs milliers de personnes marchent contre le gouvernement," AlterPresse, 30 September 2012.

37 "Une soixantaine de Députés forment un nouveau Bloc majoritaire présidentiel," Radio Kiskeya, 16 September 2012.

38 "Des milliers de manifestants pro-Martelly aux Gonaïves," Haiti Press Network, 28 September 2012.

39 "Pour son retour, Michel Martelly prend la tête d'une foule," Radio Kiskeya, 2 October 2012.

40 "La police disperse brutalement une manif contre la visite de Michel Martelly à Petit-Goâve," Radio Kiskeya, 5 October 2012.

41 "En visite au wharf de Jérémie, le chef de l'État tente de mousser sa popularité," Radio Kiskeya, 10 October 2012.

42 "Martelly s'estime à l'abri des coups d'État," AlterPresse, 1 November 2012.

43 "Des milliers de manifestants dans les rues contre Martelly," Radio Kiskeya, 14 October 2012.

44 "Plusieurs milliers d'opposants contestent l'autorité de Martelly au Cap," Radio Kiskeya, 18 October 2012.

45 "The high cost of staying out of politics in Haiti," *The Miami Herald*, 2 November 2012.

46 "Jets de pierres contre la délégation du Premier ministre à Plaine du Nord," Radio Kiskeya, 20 October 2012.

47 "Echec de la séance en assemblée nationale, souci de plus pour le pouvoir," Radio Kiskeya, 15 October 2012.

48 "L'entrepreneur Clifford Brandt arrêté pour kidnapping, deux otages libérés," Radio Kiskeya, 23 October 2012.

49 "Affaire Brandt: le RNDDH exige l'aboutissement de l'enquête ouverte et le jugement de tous les membres du gang," Réseau National de Défense des Droits Humains, 13 November 2012.

50 "Le badge de conseiller présidentiel de Brandt est faux, selon le Palais National," Radio Kiskeya, 15 November 2012.

51 "L'emprisonnement de Brandt, une 'victoire' pour l'État de droit, selon le CSPN," Radio Kiskeya, 30 October 2012.

52 "Où est passé le dossier Clifford Brandt?," AlterPresse, 9 February 2013.

53 "Des milliers de manifestants à Jacmel lancent des pierres sur les autorités après un enlèvement meurtrier," Radio Kiskeya, 19 November 2012.

54 "Audit of USAID's Haiti Recovery Initiative Activities Managed by the Office of Transition Initiatives," Report No. 1-521-12-009-P, Office of Inspector General, 26 September 2012.

55 "Audit: USAID Haiti work not on track," Associated Press, 1 October 2012.

56 "USAID contractor Chemonics cited for numerous mistakes in Haiti," *Global Post*, 5 October 2012.

57 "Audit of USAID's Haiti Recovery Initiative Activities Managed by the Office of Transition Initiatives," Report No. 1-521-12-009-P, Office of Inspector General, 26 September 2012.

58 "In Haiti, Little Can Be Found of a Hip-Hop Artist's Charity," *The New York Times*, 11 October 2012.

59 "La police établit un bilan de quatre morts et nie toute responsabilité," Radio Kiskeya, 3 November 2012.

60 "'Marche pour la paix' à Cité Soleil et Simon-Pelé, champ de bataille des gangs," Radio Kiskeya, 7 November 2012.

61 "Des hommes en cagoule exécutent froidement un inspecteur de police," Radio Kiskeya, 9 November 2012.

62 "Un deuxième policier tué vendredi à Port-au-Prince," Radio Kiskeya, 10 November 2012.

63 "Affaire Brandt: le RNDDH exige l'aboutissement de l'enquête ouverte et le jugement de tous les membres du gang," Réseau National de Défense des Droits Humains, 13 November 2012.

64 "L'ex-Chef de la PNH, Mario Andrésol, dénonce des menaces contre sa personne et des rumeurs sur une investigation dont il serait l'objet," Radio Kiskeya, 13 November 2012.

65 This account is pieced together from author interviews in Port-au-Prince and Cité Soleil, January and February 2016.

66 "Indignation après la libération sans jugement d'un conseiller présidentiel accusé de meurtre," Radio Kiskeya, 10 November 2012.

67 Letter from Réseau National de Défense des Droits Humains to Conseil Supérieur du Pouvoir Judiciaire, 19 November 2012.

68 "Favorables à son départ, plusieurs milliers de personnes condamnent l'absence de Martelly un 18 novembre," Radio Kiskeya, 18 November 2012.

69 "MOPOD: Résolution de la côte des Arcadins," 26 January 2014.

70 Author interview with Mariano Fernández, Port-au-Prince, November 2012.

71 "Me Josué Pierre-Louis objet d'une plainte pour viol," Radio Kiskeya, 29 November 2012.

72 "Pierre-Louis aurait proposé 300 mille dollars et un poste diplomatique à sa victime présumée," Radio Kiskeya, 30 November 2012.

73 "Lettre de 4 organisations et plateforme d'organisations de défense des droits humains aux membres du Conseil Supérieur du Pouvoir Judiciaire," 20 December 2012.

74 "Ses anciens protégés de Lafanmi Se Lavi portent plainte contre Jean-Bertrand Aristide," Radio Kiskeya, 5 December 2012.

75 "Court hearing delayed for former Haitian President Aristide," Agence France-Presse, 3 January 2013.

76 "Jean-Bertrand Aristide et des ex-acteurs de la finance poursuivis en justice pour la faillite des coopératives," Radio Kiskeya, 19 December 2012.

77 "L'ancien président Jean Bertrand Aristide convoqué le 3 janvier 2013 au Parquet," Radio Kiskeya, 13 December 2012.

78 "Court hearing delayed for former Haitian President Aristide,"Agence France-Presse, 3 January 2013.

79 "Huit anciens de Lafanmi Se Lavi relâchés après l'échec d'une demande d'asile aux États-Unis," Radio Kiskeya, 4 January 2013.

80 "Les avocats de l'ancien président Aristide somment commissaire du gouvernement et plaignants," AlterPresse, 7 January 2013.

81 "Mobilisation de lavalas en appui à l'ancien président Aristide invité au Parquet suite à des plaintes," Radio Kiskeya, 9 January 2013.

82 "Aristide auditionné chez lui par le chef du parquet de Port-au-Prince," Radio Kiskeya, 9 January 2013.

83 "Le dossier d'Aristide transféré au cabinet d'instruction?," AlterPresse, 9 January 2013.

84 "L'ex-sénatrice Mirlande Lubéris, proche de Jean-Bertrand Aristide, convoquée au Cabinet d'instruction dans le cadre de l'affaire Jean Dominique," Radio Kiskeya, 6 February 2013.

85 "René Préval a été entendu au cabinet d'instruction," Radio Kiskeya, 7 March 2013.

86 "Martelly to Haitians in South Florida: 'Haiti has changed a lot'," *The Miami Herald*, 10 December 2012.

87 "Haiti to Post Caribbean's Fastest Growth in 2013," *Caribbean Journal*, 13 December 2012.

88 "Three years after Haiti earthquake, loss of hope, desperation," *The Miami Herald*, 8 January 2013.

89 "New hotel offers rare sign of new construction in Haiti," Reuters, 12 December 2012.

90 "Audition à tour de rôle au cabinet d'instruction de Josué Pierre Louis et Marie Danielle Bernardin," AlterPresse, 18 January 2013.

91 "Déclaration de Marie Danielle Bernadin," 28 January 2013.

92 "Nicodème Chéry alias Pè Niko abattu puis décapité à Delmas 2," Radio Television Caraïbes, 19 January 2013.

93 Author interview, Port-au-Prince, March 2014.

94 "Terreur à Delmas 2 et ses environs," AlterPresse, 27 February 2013.

95 "Opl dénonce l'autoritarisme dans la gestion des festivités carnavalesques," AlterPresse, 10 February 2013.

96 "La 'trêve politique' terminée, selon Moïse Jean-Charles qui dénonce la mort d'un anti-Martelly," Radio Kiskeya, 12 February 2013.

97 "Des dizaines de milliers de fêtards investissent les rues du Cap-Haïtien," AlterPresse, 10 February 2013.

98 "American Airlines adds Cap-Haïtien flights from Miami," *The Miami Herald*, 2 October 2014.

99 "Clinton awards more than $700,000 to Haiti farms," Associated Press, 11 March 2013.

100 "Haiti to plant millions of trees to boost forests and help tackle poverty," *The Guardian*, 28 March 2013.

101 The book is *The Democratic Republic of Congo: Between Hope and Despair* (Zed Books, 2013).

102 Author interview with Jean-Max Bellerive, Port-au-Prince, February 2016.

103 Author interview with Laurent Lamothe, Miami, October 2015.

104 "Un 'complot' contre le sommet de la CARICOM a été déjoué, selon le Premier ministre," Radio Kiskeya, 20 February 2014.

105 "Martelly et Lamothe en chemise rouge 'chaviste' à Caracas," Radio Kiskeya, 8 March 2013.

106 "Un véhicule officiel bel et bien impliqué dans le double meurtre spectaculaire du 5 février à Port-au-Prince," Radio Kiskeya, 16 February 2013.

107 "Haiti Gov't Announces Resignation of Employee," Associated Press, 23 February 2013.

108 "Le ministre du Commerce et de l'industrie, Wilson Laleau, proteste contre l'intervention brutale du député Arnel Bélizaire à l'Office des postes," Radio Kiskeya, 9 March 2013.

109 "La Cour d'Appel ordonne que Jean-Claude Duvalier soit contraint à comparaitre par-devant elle," Radio Kiskeya, 22 February 2013.

110 "Une seconde séance fixée à la huitaine, après des heures historiques à la cour d'appel," AlterPresse, 28 February 2013.

111 "Un juge demande la levée de l'immunité de deux Députés," Radio Kiskeya, 21 March 2013.

112 "Report sine die d'une réunion à la Chambre basse autour de la levée de l'immunité de deux députés," Radio Kiskeya, 26 March 2013.

113 "Un policier, témoin oculaire de l'assassinat du policier Walky Calixte en avril 2012 à Port-au-Prince, blessé dans un attentat," Radio Kiskeya, 22 March 2013.

114 "Un ancien collègue du policier Walky Calixte tué, un suspect arrêté," Radio Kiskeya, 2 May 2013.

115 "Retour au calme à Carrefour Feuillés, après un début d'effervescence," AlterPresse, 3 May 2013.

116 "Des bandits armés terrorisent les habitants de Martissant," AlterPresse, 25 March 2013.

117 "La famille du policier Walky Calixte entendue par la commission parlementaire d'enquête sur le dossier," AlterPresse, 28 May 2013.

118 "Les avocats du policier assassiné Walky Calixte demandent la comparution de tous les inculpés dont deux députés," AlterPresse, 21 June 2013.

119 "Vote unanime contre la levée d'immunité de deux députés, inculpés dans l'assassinat de Walky Calixte," AlterPresse, 28 August 2013.

120 "Departing UN official blasts Haiti's rights record," Associated Press, 28 March 2013.

121 "Régine Godefroy, deuxième ministre à quitter le gouvernement en 24 heures," Alter-Presse, 11 April 2013.

122 "Révocation du conseil communal de Cité Soleil: tirs, barricades et deux blesses," Radio Kiskeya, 25 March 2013.

123 "De nouveaux affrontements entre gangs rivaux à Cité Soleil," Radio Kiskeya, 7 May 2013.

124 "Les assassins de Georges Honorat doivent être 'punis avec la dernière rigueur', réagit le premier ministre," AlterPresse, 25 March 2013.

125 "La police nationale s'inquiète de la découverte de plusieurs cadavres dans des coins de la capitale," Le Nouvelliste, 30 May 2013.

126 "Des partisans d'Aristide agitent contre Martelly la menace des 'ghettos'," Radio Kiskeya, 18 April 2013.

127 "Des partisans d'Aristide devant sa résidence quelques heures avant son audition au cabinet d'instruction," AlterPresse, 8 May 2013.

128 "Agression physique contre Radio-Télé Ginen," AlterPresse, 10 May 2013.

129 "AMIH condamne l'agression contre Radio Tele Ginen," Radio Kiskeya, 9 May 2013.

130 "Jean-Bertrand Aristide ressort muet du cabinet d'instruction," Radio Kiskeya, 8 May 2013.

131 "Aristide Répond enfin à l'appel au Parquet," Le Nouvelliste, 8 May 2013, https://youtu.be/D43JAHoYf58, accessed 10 January 2016.

132 "Un vent de divergences dans l'air," AlterPresse, 14 May 2013.

CHAPTER FIFTEEN

1   "Haiti Three Years After the Quake: There's Good News, Too," Time, 12 January 2013.

2   "Haiti hosts 1st conference on mining efforts," Associated Press, 3 June 2013.

3   "Haiti's luxury brand hotel is a showcase for Haitian art," The Miami Herald, 26 December 2013.

4   "In Haiti, at every turn, a new surprise," The Los Angeles Times, 3 February 2013.

5   Author telephone interview with Stéphanie Villedrouin, March 2014.

6   "Deepening relationship between Vietnam and Haiti," Báo Nhân Dân, 29 March 2014.

7   "AED: une première rencontre pour redéfinir l'aide en Haïti," MINUSTAH press release, 13 May 2013.

8   "Feeding Haiti," The Economist, 22 June 2013.

9   "FOKAL and Parc de Martissant: An Urban Success," Haiti Cultural Exchange, 10 December 2013.

10 "Ultimatum d'une semaine des habitants de l'Ile à Vache au gouvernement Lamothe," AlterPresse, 7 January 2014.

11 "Carnival deal for Haiti island hits snag," The Miami Herald, 4 December 2014.

12 "2 out of 3 people face hunger as Haiti woes mount," Associated Press, 10 June 2013.

13 "La Pohdh déplore le manque de volonté du pouvoir pour l'organisation des élections," AlterPresse, 4 June 2013.

14 "L'ambassadeur du Canada à Port-au-Prince tire la sonnette d'alarme sur l'échéance de juillet par rapport à l'objectif d'organiser les élections en 2013," Radio Kiskeya, 10 July 2013.

15 "Temoignages d'un ex-enfant soldat aujourd'hui membre d'un gang arme," as given to Réseau National de Défense des Droits de l'Homme (RNDDH), 23 April 2013.

16 "Contre-attaque de Joseph Lambert après les graves accusations portées contre lui et d'autres personnes, en rapport avec des crimes et le trafic de la drogue," Radio Kiskeya, 9 July 2013.

17 "Le président Martelly dément avoir rencontré le juge Jean Serge Joseph et exercé des pressions sur lui," Radio Kiskeya, 18 July 2013.

18 "L'accusateur de la famille présidentielle, Enold Florestal, arrêté," Radio Kiskeya, 17 August 2013.

19 "Victime d'un harcèlement de l'Exécutif, le juge Jean Serge Joseph succombe à une congestion cérébrale," Radio Kiskeya, 13 July 2013.

20 "La commission d'enquête sénatoriale recommande la mise en accusation du chef de l'État, du Premier ministre et du ministre de la justice," Radio Kiskeya, 8 August 2013.

21 "L'accusateur de la famille présidentielle, Enold Florestal, arrêté," Radio Kiskeya, 17 August 2013.

22 "4 prisonniers politiques libérés en une semaine," Radio Métropole, 18 December 2014.

23 "Le juge Jean Serge Joseph décédé d'une congestion cérébrale, selon le rapport définitif du coroner du Québec, révèle le journal *La Presse*, de Montréal," Radio Kiskeya, 11 March 2014.

24 "Moïse Jean-Charles accusé par un député de vouloir attenter à la vie du chef de l'État, au cours de la tournée de ce dernier dans le Nord," Radio Kiskeya, 23 July 2013.

25 "Martelly en tournée dans le Nord, la tension monte à Plaisance," *Le Nouvelliste*, 22 July 2013.

26 "Michel Martelly accuse Mirlande Manigat de fomenter un coup d'état," Radio Kiskeya, 31 July 2013.

27 "Lettre à la nation Mirlande Manigat Secrétaire Générale du RDNP," 2 August 2013.

28 "Un bras de fer politique dégénère en combat de rue à la Chambre basse," Radio Kiskeya, 7 August 2013.

29 "Michel Martelly jouait mercredi dans un casino, aux Bahamas, selon Levaillant Louis-Jeune qui invite ses pairs à constater la vacance présidentielle," Radio Kiskeya, 21 August 2013.

30 Author interview, Port-au-Prince, March 2014.

31 "L'Organisation du Peuple en Lutte (OPL) et la Fusion des Sociaux Démocrates Haïtiens déclinent l'invitation du chef de l'État à une rencontre autour des élections," Radio Kiskeya, 13 August 2013.

32 "Après deux mois d'atermoiements, l'Exécutif fait enfin le dépôt du projet de loi électorale," Radio Kiskeya, 27 August 2013.

33 "Le président Martelly chez l'OPL," Radio Kiskeya, 13 September 2013.

34 "The Dominican Republic: Becoming a One-Party State?," Center for Strategic and International Studies, November 2013.

35 "Democracy at risk for all Dominicans," *The Miami Herald*, 26 December 2013.

36 "Dominican Ruling Strips Many of Citizenship," Associated Press, 26 September 2013.

37 "Democracy at risk for all Dominicans," *The Miami Herald*, 26 December 2013.

38 "Los parias del Caribe," *El País*, 3 November 2013.

39 "Patriotas extraños," *Acento*, 27 February 2015.

40 "Haitian Leader's Power Grows as Scandals Swirl," *The New York Times*, 16 March 2015.

41 Author interview, Port-au-Prince, January 2016.

42 "Assignation de Radio Kiskeya S.A. et de la Vice-Présidente de son Conseil d'administration, Liliane Pierre-Paul, par le Juge Lamarre Bélizaire," Radio Kiskeya, 16 September 2013.

43 "Le journaliste de Télé Kiskeya, Rodrigue Lalanne, sauvagement agressé par un membre de la sécurité présidentielle," Radio Kiskeya, 1 October 2013.

44 "Libération de l'avocat et militant politique André Michel à l'issue d'une soirée et d'une journée de contestation contre le chef du Parquet, le président Martelly et le gouvernement Lamothe," Radio Kiskeya, 23 October 2013.

45 "Le président du Sénat, Simon Dieuseul Desras, tire à boulets rouges sur le chef de l'État, Michel Martelly," Radio Kiskeya, 25 October 2013.

46 "Plusieurs milliers de manifestants anti-Martelly jeudi à Port-au-Prince," Radio Kiskeya, 7 November 2013.

47 "Une manifestation anti-Martelly violemment dispersée à proximité des ruines du palais national," AlterPresse, 8 November 2013.

48 "Une manifestation anti-gouvernementale dispersée brutalement aux Cayes (Sud) par des pro-Martelly et la police," Radio Kiskeya, 7 December 2013.

49 "Fanmi Lavalas demande au sénateur Moïse Jean-Charles et au député Arnel Bélizaire de cesser de s'exprimer au nom de l'organisation politique," Agence Haïtienne de Presse, 4 December 2013.

50 "The Split in Fanmi Lavalas: How and Why It Came About, and What It Portends," Haïti Liberté, 17 December 2013.

51 Author interview with Moïse Jean-Charles, Port-au-Prince, January 2016.

52 "Le gouvernement accusé d'accaparer les terres agricoles des paysans dans le Nord et le Nord-Est," AlterPresse, 10 December 2013.

53 "Le président de la Chambre des députés favorable à la reprise du dialogue avec l'Exécutif," Radio Kiskeya, 28 December 2013.

54 "Le MOPOD en faveur de la démission du président Martelly et de la tenue d'élections générales anticipées l'année prochaine," Radio Kiskeya, 30 December 2013.

55 "La police est le bras armé du gouvernement, déclare le président Martelly lors de la graduation de la 24ème promotion de la PNH," Radio Kiskeya, 28 December 2013.

56 "Haitian president urges his country to come together,"Agence France-Presse, 1 January 2014.

57 "Evans Paul surfe entre le pardon, l'opposition et le pouvoir," *Le Nouvelliste*, 3 January 2014.

58 "Trois ans après le retour de l'ex-dictateur, les victimes de son régime continuent de crier justice," AlterPresse, 16 January 2014.

59 "La Cour d'appel de Port-au-Prince juge recevables les plaintes pour crimes contre l'humanité et ordonne la reprise de l'instruction," Radio Kiskeya, 20 February 2014.

60 "Les avocats de Duvalier récusent la Cour d'Appel de Port-au-Prince et annoncent un recours en Cassation contre la décision de poursuivre leur client pour crimes contre l'humanité," Radio Kiskeya, 11 March 2014.

61 "Un consensus national minimal pour le relèvement national," 15 January 2014.

62 "Protestations du Ministère de la justice contre l'irruption au Parquet du député Arnel Bélizaire pour libérer des employés de l'ONA," Radio Kiskeya, 26 March 2014.

63 "La majorité présidentielle prend le contrôle du bureau de la Chambre basse," Radio Kiskeya, 15 January 2014.

64 "L'ancien président Aristide aurait ordonné l'assassinat de Jean Dominique," Radio Kiskeya, 17 January 2014.

65 "Affaire Jean Dominique: Sò Anne, Mirlande Libérus et consorts visés," *Le Nouvelliste*, 17 January 2014.

66 "Nine charged in 2000 murder of Haitian journalist Jean Dominique," Agence France-Presse, 18 January 2014.

67 "Pas d'audition ce lundi de Philippe Markenton à la Cour d'Appel," Radio Kiskeya, 23 June 2014.

68 "Nine charged in 2000 murder of Haitian journalist Jean Dominique," Agence France-Presse, 18 January 2014.

69 "Guyler C. Delva vise Aristide, Yvickel Dabrésil menacé," Haiti Press Network, 23 January 2014.

70 "Aristide demeure-t-il un témoin disponible pour la justice?," AlterPresse, 29 January 2014.

71 "Mopod et Lavalas, absents du dialogue, à qui la faute," AlterPresse, 24 January 2014.

72 "Fanmi Lavalas rejoint la table du dialogue," Radio Kiskeya, 27 January 2014.

73 "MOPOD: Résolution de la côte des Arcadins," 26 January 2014.

74 "Dialogue politique: perspectives d'accord sur la reconstitution de l'organisme électoral et l'amendement de la Constitution," Radio Kiskeya, 5 February 2014.

75 "Report 'sine die' de la signature de l'accord d'El Rancho suite au refus du président du Sénat de l'endosser," Radio Kiskeya, 15 February 2014.

76 "Global leaders call on Haiti's feuding factions to salvage talks, elections," *The Miami Herald*, 21 February 2014.

77 "Des leaders politiques, d'anciens officiers de l'armée et une revenante autour de Martelly et Lamothe dans le 'gouvernement d'ouverture'," Radio Kiskeya, 3 April 2014.

78 "Des expulsions violentes se poursuivent à Village Mosaïque," AlterPresse, 3 February 2014.

79 "Des organisations de droits humains accompagnent l'étudiant bastonné par le sénateur Wencesclas Lambert," AlterPresse, 13 March 2014.

80 "Le sénateur Wencesclas Lambert déclaré non coupable dans le dossier l'opposant au citoyen Daniel Théodore," AlterPresse, 3 April 2014.

81 "Le coordonnateur de la POHDH, Daniel Dorsinvil, et son épouse, abattus par balles à Port-au-Prince," AlterPresse, 9 February 2014.

82 "Le principal suspect arrêté en pleine soirée pré-carnavalesque," Radio Kiskeya, 16 February 2014.

83 "Cinq présumés auteurs de l'assassinat des époux Daniel et Girldy Dorsinvil, sous les verrous," Radio Kiskeya, 25 February 2014.

84 "Le meurtre d'un autre chef de gang à Grand Ravine compromet les chances de justice pour les Dorsinvil, selon la Pohdh," AlterPresse, 21 October 2014.

85 "Deux mois après le décès par balles des Dorsainvil, la Pohdh et Mpdp réclament encore justice," AlterPresse, 9 April 2014.

86 "Cinq présumés auteurs de l'assassinat des époux Daniel et Girldy Dorsinvil, sous les verrous," Radio Kiskeya, 25 February 2014.

87 "Le Rnddh appelle au démantèlement définitif du 'gang Galil'," AlterPresse, 19 March 2014.

88 "Libération par le Parquet de l'épouse de 'Sonson La Familia' alors qu'elle était à la disposition du Cabinet d'Instruction," Radio Kiskeya, 30 March 2014.

89 "Le juge d'instruction ne recevra pas Mme 'Sonson La Familia' tant qu'elle ne retourne pas en prison," Radio Kiskeya, 10 April 2014.

90 "Le présumé chef du 'gang Galil' Woodly Ethéart arrêté," AlterPresse, 8 May 2014.

91 "Haitian Leader's Power Grows as Scandals Swirl," The New York Times, 16 March 2015.

92 "L'accord signé, les élections fixées au 26 octobre 2014," Le Nouvelliste, 14 March 2014.

93 "L'accord d'El rancho: l'opposition banalise!," Radio Métropole, 18 March 2014.

94 Ibid.

95 "Les sénateurs Moïse Jean-Charles et Jean-Baptiste Bien-Aimé disent non à l'amendement électoral," Radio Kiskeya, 7 April 2014.

96 "Un silence qui ramène à un triste passé," Radio Kiskeya, 17 March 2014.

97 "Danger of self-censorship after CONATEL warning to radio stations," Reporters Without Borders, 15 April 2014.

98 "L'ANMH rejette le recours systématique à l'autoritarisme par rapport aux pratiques de presse," 14 April 2014.

99 "Amnesty: Haiti human rights activist threatened," Associated Press, 15 April 2014.

100 "Le gouvernement accusé d'être auteur des menaces contre le Rnddh," AlterPresse, 21 April 2014.

101 "De prétendus anciens militaires fondent un parti à tendance macoute et pro-Martelly à Belladère," AlterPresse, 15 April 2014.

102 "L'ex-dictateur Jean-Claude Duvalier inaugure un bureau de son parti à Jacmel," AlterPresse, 23 April 2014.

103 "'Je solliciterai la démission du chef de l'État si des élections ne sont pas organisées cette année', déclare le président du Sénat," Radio Kiskeya, 22 April 2014.

104 "Une manifestation violente pour dénoncer les dérives de Martelly," Le Nouvelliste, 28 April 2014.

105 "Martelly convie une nouvelle fois l'opposition aux élections," AlterPresse, 15 May 2014.

106 "Commémoration des 2 ans de Ti Manman Cheri," Radio Kiskeya, 24 May 2014.

107 "Laurent Lamothe s'assure déjà de l'obtention de la décharge indispensable à sa candidature à la présidence, selon le sénateur Jean Baptiste Bien-Aimé," Radio Kiskeya, 28 May 2014.

108 "L'appareil judiciaire haïtien est transformé en un outil de persécution politique," Réseau National de Défense des Droits Humains, 22 May 2014.

109 "Visite du détenu Rony Timothée à l'Arcahaie," Radio Kiskeya, 22 May 2014.

110 "Le sénateur Moïse Jean-Charles bousculé par un agent pénitentiaire à la prison civile de l'Arcahaie," Radio Kiskeya, 30 May 2014.

111 "L'opposition plus déterminée, la police montre ses muscles," Le Nouvelliste, 10 June 2014.

112 "Jan'l pase'l Pase Manifestasyon," 10 June 2014, https://youtu.be/gsHiHBQKs3w, accessed 31 January 2016.

113 "La Violence du Député Arnel Belizaire," 10 June 2014, https://youtu.be/RKa3r7oz5ww, accessed 31 January 2016.

114 "L'opposition plus déterminée, la police montre ses muscles," Le Nouvelliste, 10 June 2014.

115 "Jan'l pase'l Pase Manifestasyon," 10 June 2014, https://youtu.be/gsHiHBQKs3w, accessed 31 January 2016.

116 "L'opposition plus déterminée, la police montre ses muscles," Le Nouvelliste, 10 June 2014.

117 "Le ministre Phélito Doran 'agresssé' par le député Arnel Bélizaire," Le Nouvelliste, 25 June 2014.

118 "Le Gouvernement condamne énergiquement l'agression de son ministre Phélito Doran par le député Arnel Bélizaire," Radio Kiskeya, 26 June 2014.

119 "Le député Arnel Bélizaire sanctionné par l'Assemblée," Le Nouvelliste, 3 July 2014.

120 "Grève de la faim/Carnaval des Fleurs," Le Nouvelliste, 29 July 2014.

121 "Un chef de gang assassiné par ses lieutenants," Radio Métropole, 25 July 2014.

122 "Mort de Ti Kenken, chef de gang," Le Nouvelliste, 24 July 2014.

123 "Max Mathurin remplace Fritzo Canton à la présidence du CEP," Radio Kiskeya, 21 July 2014.

124 "Le porte-parole du premier ministre qualifie les sénateurs de l'opposition d'ennemis de la démocratie et de kamikazes," Radio Kiskeya, 5 August 2014.

125 "Martelly dénonce un Sénat improductif," Radio Métropole, 22 August 2014.

126 "Menace de démission d'un groupe de sénateurs pro-gouvernementaux," Radio Kiskeya, 27 August 2014.

127 "Paul Denis (INITE) et Vickens Dérilus (PRI) se prononcent contre l'ingérence étrangère dans les affaires du pays," Radio Kiskeya, 31 August 2014.

128 "Des organisations de la société civile appellent l'Exécutif et le Législatif à un nouveau 'round' de négociations en vue d'une solution à la crise pré-électorale," Radio Kiskeya, 2 September 2014.

129 "Maryse Narcisse officiellement désignée candidate à la présidence de Fanmi Lavalas," Radio Kiskeya, 15 July 2014.

130 "Maryse Narcisse imposée à Aristide comme candidate à la présidence par l'Ambassade US et l'USAID, selon le sénateur Moïse Jean-Charles," Radio Kiskeya, 16 July 2014.

131 "Jean-Bertrand Aristide inculpé," *Le Nouvelliste*, 12 August 2014.

132 "Le juge Lamarre Bélizaire 'légalement récusé', selon un des avocats de l'ancien président Aristide," Radio Kiskeya, 17 August 2014.

133 "Jean-Bertrand Aristide mis en résidence surveillée," *Le Nouvelliste*, 9 September 2014.

134 "C'est l'armée dominicaine qui a appréhendé Brandt et deux autres fugitifs en territoire dominicain," Radio Kiskeya, 13 August 2014.

135 "Le Conseil Supérieur de la Police Nationale (CSPN) condamne les violences policières perpétrées récemment par des membres de l'UDMO à Petit-Goâve," Radio Métropole, 23 August 2014.

136 "Cinq personnes abattues à Cité Soleil," Radio Kiskeya, 23 August 2014.

137 "Soutien à Cité Soleil à un présumé chef de groupe armé arrêté par la police," Radio Kiskeya, 6 September 2014.

138 "La Chambre basse vote en faveur de l'application de l'Accord d'El Rancho," Radio Kiskeya, 6 September 2014.

139 "Note de Presse," 9 September 2014.

140 "Haiti's Parliamentary Framework at Risk Unless Political Impasse Resolved," Security Council Meetings Coverage, 11 September 2014.

141 U.S. Congress letter to Simon Dieuseul Desras, 15 September 2014.

142 "Le vice-président du sénat appelle au compromis pour éviter le chaos," AlterPresse, 15 September 2014.

143 "Martelly a quatre sur six," AlterPresse, 3 October 2014.

144 "Aucun policier national, mais des militants lavalas devant la résidence d'Aristide," AlterPresse, 13 September 2014.

145 "Une manifestation du parti Fanmi lavalas, dispersée à coups de gaz lacrymogènes," AlterPresse, 30 September 2014.

146 "Le meurtre d'un autre chef de gang à Grand Ravine compromet les chances de justice pour les Dorsinvil, selon la Pohdh," AlterPresse, 21 October 2014.

147 "Funérailles émouvantes de deux militants politiques du secteur Lavalas récemment assassinés à Port-au-Prince," Radio Kiskeya, 23 October 2014.

148 "Jean-Claude Duvalier Dies at 63; Ruled Haiti in Father's Brutal Fashion," *The New York Times*, 4 October 2014.

CHAPTER SIXTEEN

1   "Le Conseil de sécurité proroge à l'unanimité de ses membres le mandat de la MINUSTAH," Radio Kiskeya, 15 October 2014.

2   "Après l'avortement d'une réunion avec les six partis de l'opposition, Martelly rencontre Préval," AlterPresse, 14 October 2014.

3   "Une manifestation de l'opposition violemment dispersée par la police," AlterPresse, 17 October 2014.

4   "Les militants politiques Rony Timothée et Biron Odigé appréhendés pour incitation à la violence," Radio Kiskeya, 27 October 2014.

5   "Deux opposants politiques rejoignent une quinzaine de manifestants antigouvernementaux en prison," AlterPresse, 27 October 2014.

6   "Malaise entre le gouvernement et sa majorité à la Chambre basse," Radio Kiskeya, 10 November 2014.

7   "Kiko St-Rémy, frère de l'épouse du chef de l'État, présent à la manifestation du 18 novembre de l'opposition pour dénoncer le premier ministre Lamothe," Radio Kiskeya, 18 November 2014.

8   "Démission du premier ministre Laurent Lamothe, du président du CSPJ et de la Cour de Cassation Anel Alexis Joseph, des membres du CEP et libération des prisonniers politiques, aurait recommandé la Commission consultative présidentielle," Radio Kiskeya, 8 December 2014.

9   "Sit-in devant le siège de la Fusion contre l'ingérence américaine," Radio Kiskeya, 3 December 2014.

10 "L'opposition a pu finalement manifester devant le siège de la Présidence à Port-au-Prince," Radio Kiskeya, 5 December 2014.

11 "Des milliers de manifestants ont encore défilé contre le pouvoir au Cap-Haïtien et à Port-au-Prince," AlterPresse, 8 December 2014.

12 "Le Canada critique le comportement d'Arnel Bélizaire," *Le Nouvelliste*, 26 December 2014.

13 "Démission du premier ministre Laurent Lamothe, du président du CSPJ et de la Cour de Cassation Anel Alexis Joseph, des membres du CEP et libération des prisonniers politiques, aurait recommandé la Commission consultative présidentielle," Radio Kiskeya, 8 December 2014.

14 "La marche vers une libération complète des prisonniers d'opinions," AlterPresse, 16 December 2014.

15 "Les frères Florestal finalement libérés," Radio Kiskeya, 20 December 2014.

16 "Haiti's president sacrifices prime minister in bid to reunite country," Reuters, 13 December 2014.

17 "'We did all we could for the country': Haiti PM Laurent Lamothe resigns," *The Miami Herald*, 14 December 2014.

18 Author interview with Laurent Lamothe, October 2015.

19 "Mopod et alliés ne cillent pas et annoncent de nouvelles manifestations," AlterPresse, 16 December 2014.

20 "Lavalas appelle à la poursuite de la mobilisation antigouvernementale Lavalas appelle à la poursuite de la mobilisation antigouvernementale," AlterPresse, 16 December 2014.

21 "Discussions politiques versus manifestations de rues," Radio Kiskeya, 19 December 2014.

22 "Forte augmentation du nombre de décès par balles à P-au-P à la fin de l'année 2014, selon Jilap," AlterPresse, 19 December 2014.

23 "Josseline Pierre, ex-chef de la PNH meurt étranglée," Haiti en Marche, 23 December 2014.

24 "Joceline Pierre assassinée une seconde fois," Le Nouvelliste, 8 January 2015.

25 "Plus de 250 mille armes circulent illégalement en Haïti," Radio Métropole, 21 January 2015.

26 "Elections 2015: une catastrophe annoncée?" AlterPresse, 24 February 2015.

27 "Des chiffres inquiétants, manifestant un désespoir," AlterPresse, 22 December 2014.

28 "Protestations de Radio Kiskeya contre des actes de corruption au Palais National à l'endroit d'un groupe de journalistes," Radio Kiskeya, 26 January 2015.

29 "Agression contre le ministre de l'Agriculture par le beau-frère du président: des sources confirment," Le Nouvelliste, 7 July 2015.

30 "Communiqué officiel de la Présidence," 25 December 2014.

31 "Haiti political veteran nominated as next prime minister," Associated Press, 25 December 2014.

32 "Manifestation: l'opposition en panne de recette," Le Nouvelliste, 26 December 2014.

33 "Evans Paul enfile son costume de rassembleur," Le Nouvelliste, 29 December 2014.

34 "Political accord in Haiti seeks to avert crisis," Reuters, 30 December 2014.

35 "Des avancées dans le processus de résolution de la crise pré-électorale, souligne Sandra Honoré," AlterPresse, 31 December 2014.

36 "Doute sur la tenue de la session extraordinaire du Corps législatif," AlterPresse, 5 January 2015.

37 "De nouveaux pourparlers entre Martelly et une nouvelle commission sénatoriale," AlterPresse, 7 January 2015.

38 "UN Security Council Heading to Haiti to Press for Elections," Associated Press, 5 January 2015.

39 "Plutôt la guerre civile que la négociation!, crie une partie de l'opposition à Port-au-Prince," AlterPresse, 8 January 2015.

40 "Haiti protesters again rally to demand president's departure," Associated Press, 10 January 2015.

41 "Statement of the US Embassy in Haiti on the Political Impasse," 11 January 2015.

42 "Martelly asks Haitians to 'Give the country a chance'," The Miami Herald, 12 January 2015.

43 "23 partis politiques mécontents de la formation du gouvernement," Radio Métropole, 20 January 2015.

44 "Communiqué de presse," 13 January 2015.

45 "Martelly asks Haitians to 'Give the country a chance'," *The Miami Herald*, 12 January 2015.

46 "Une opposition armée dans le Nord?," Radio Kiskeya, 14 January 2015.

47 "Insurrection armée dans le Nord: un mort dans des affrontements avec la police," Radio Métropole, 15 January 2015.

48 "La Plateforme 'Pitit Desalin' très remontée contre l'ambassade américaine," Alter-Presse, 14 January 2015.

49 "La composition du nouveau cabinet ministériel (Officiel)," 19 January 2015.

50 "Communiqué de presse du Rnddh et de la Sofa," 1 March 2015.

51 "Le local du parti Fusion attaqué par des manifestants," Radio Métropole, 19 January 2015.

52 "Assassinat d'un militant de la Fusion à Port-au-Prince," Radio Kiskeya, 1 February 2015.

53 "Une nouvelle manifestation anti-gouvernementale émaillée d'incidents," Radio Métropole, 23 January 2015.

54 "RNDDH condamne les actes de violences perpétrés lors des manifestations de l'opposition," Radio Métropole, 27 January 2015.

55 "Constitution du nouveau Conseil Électoral Provisoire," Radio Kiskeya, 22 January 2015.

56 "Le 'Core Group' salue l'installation du nouveau Premier Ministre, la formation du Gouvernement et la constitution du CEP," Radio Kiskeya, 24 January 2015.

57 "Le RNDDH invite le CEP à une réévaluation des membres des BEC et BED," Radio Métropole, 4 February 2015.

58 "Martelly réitère sa détermination à organiser les élections," Radio Métropole, 26 January 2015.

59 "Des syndicats dénoncent une grève politique," Radio Métropole, 3 February 2015.

60 "Baisse des prix du carburant: l'opposition insatisfaite dénonce l'attitude des syndicats," Radio Métropole, 4 February 2015.

61 "Une grève réussie, mais marquée par des scènes de violences!," Radio Métropole, 3 February 2015.

62 "Les étudiants de l'UEH manifestent violemment contre les prix de l'essence," Radio Métropole, 6 February 2015.

63 "La grève de l'opposition, 'une violence, à la limite, aveugle'," Radio Métropole, 13 February 2015.

64 "Inauguration de divers projets de développement à Léogâne," Radio Métropole, 6 March 2015.

65 "Le barrage hydroélectrique 4 C, un bel exemple de continuité de l'état," Radio Métropole, 10 February 2015.

66 "Le cacao, une des filières d'avenir pour Haïti," AlterPresse, 2 June 2015.

67 "Venezuela satisfied with the management of PetroCaribe Fund," Radio Métropole, 6 May 2015.

68 "Le bilan de la tragédie du Carnaval 2015 s'alourdit," Radio Kiskeya, 18 February 2015.

69 "L'Haïtien retrouvé pendu à Santiago réduit au silence pour une affaire de meurtre?," AlterPresse, 15 February 2015.

70 "Thousands march in Haiti over Dominican racism," *The Miami Herald*, 25 February 2015.

71 "Canciller haitiano dice grupo quemó bandera RD no representa a mayoría de Haití," EFE, 27 February 2015.

72 "Nacionalistas piden muerte de Danilo Medina acusándolo de traidor a la patria," Acento, 27 February 2015.

73 "Oriel Jean tué à Delmas," *Le Nouvelliste*, 2 March 2015.

74 "SOS Journalistes et la CIAPEAJ dénoncent l'assassinat d'un témoin clé dans le dossier Jean Dominique," Radio Métropole, 3 March 2015.

75 "Des révélations posthumes de l'ancien responsable de sécurité d'Aristide sur la mort du journaliste Jean Dominique," AlterPresse, 11 March 2015.

76 "Le gouvernement sollicite l'extradiction de Mirlande Liberus," Radio Métropole, 1 April 2015.

77 "Assassinat d'Oriel Jean: au moins 2 arrestations," Radio Métropole, 25 March 2015.

78 "L'opposition annule la deuxième journée de grève," Radio Métropole, 10 March 2015.

79 "Des dizaines de milliers de personnes ont participé à une marche sportive," Radio Métropole, 16 March 2015.

80 "Communiqué de la présidence en date du dimanche," 15 March 2015.

81 "Le MOPOD se concerte avant de se prononcer sur son éventuelle participation aux élections," Radio Métropole, 18 March 2015.

82 "L'Opposition radicale pourrait participer aux élections," Radio Métropole, 18 March 2015.

83 "OPL, Fusion, INITE, Fanmi Lavalas et UNIR-Haïti en route pour les prochaines élections," Radio Métropole, 20 March 2015.

84 "Le sort des partis inscrits pour prendre part aux scrutins sera connu sous peu," AlterPresse, 24 March 2015.

85 "166 partis politiques agréés par le CEP," Radio Métropole, 2 April 2015.

86 "Environ 60 millions de dollars sont nécessaires pour l'organisation des élections," Radio Métropole, 31 March 2015.

87 "Haïti est relativement stable selon Sandra Honoré," Radio Métropole, 28 March 2015.

88 "Quelles élections pour Haïti en 2015?," AlterPresse, 10 April 2015.

89 "Insuffisance de preuve, motif avancé par la justice pour libérer Woodly Ethéart et Renél Nelfort, accusés de kidnapping," AlterPresse, 18 April 2015.

90 "Appel à manifester contre 'la libération scandaleuse et illégale des présumés criminels du Gang Galil'," AlterPresse, 29 April 2015.

91 "La plupart des candidats sont à la recherche d'un emploi," Radio Métropole, 4 May 2015.

92 "Haiti to redo legislative elections in 25 constituencies," *The Miami Herald*, 20 August 2015.

93 "Elections 2015: le RNDDH questionne la Moralité de certains Candidats," Réseau National de Défense des Droits Humains, 2 June 2015.

94 Author interview, Miami, January 2016.

95 Author interview with Chavannes Jean-Baptiste, Papaye, January 2001.

96 Author interviews, Port-au-Prince, January 2016.

97 "Legal bandits could take charge in Haiti's parliament," *The Miami Herald*, 7 August 2015.

98 "Lamothe écarté des élections par le BCED," Radio Métropole, 3 June 2015.

99 'René Préval accusé de contrôler 3 à 5 conseillers électoraux," Radio Métropole, 17 June 2015.

100 "Le CEP maintient le cap sur les législatives du 9 août," Radio Kiskeya, 30 June 2015.

101 "Des bandits attaquent le commissariat de Cité Soleil," Radio Métropole, 16 June 2015.

102 "Protestations à Cité Soleil après la mort d'un chef de gang dans des affrontements avec des forces de l'ordre," Radio Kiskeya, 18 June 2015.

103 "Recrudescence de l'insécurité à Simon Pelé," Radio Métropole, 30 June 2015.

104 "Une psychose de peur pousse des centaines de migrants haïtiens à retourner au bercail," AlterPresse, 22 June 2015.

105 "Plus de 4 mille migrants haïtiens expulsés de force, en 8 jours, vers le haut Plateau central," AlterPresse, 22 June 2015.

106 "Finalement, Martelly décèle des signes d'une catastrophe humanitaire," AlterPresse, 4 July 2015.

107 "Un enfant décède dans un camp à Anse-à-Pitres suite aux mauvaises conditions de vie," AlterPresse, 10 November 2015.

108 "Fearful, Haitian Migrants Flee Dominican Republic for Camps Along Border," *The New York Times*, 12 December 2015.

109 "Martelly veut créer une nouvelle armée avant la fin de son mandat," Radio Métropole, 24 July 2015.

110 "Plus d'une quinzaine de morts dans de nouvelles violences à Cité Soleil," Radio Métropole, 18 October 2015.

111 "La plateforme Vérité dénonce des attaques systématiques visant ses candidats," Alter-Presse, 24 July 2015.

112 "3 blessés à Petit-Goâve lors des violences électorales," Radio Métropole, 24 July 2015.

113 "Des organisations dénoncent l'incapacité de l'État à établir un climat sécuritaire," AlterPresse 14 July 2015.

114 Author interview, Port-au-Prince, June 2015.

115 "Des dispositions pour faire face à la crise économique," Radio Métropole, 5 June 2015.

116 "Castel alerte sur la détérioration de l'économie," Radio Métropole, 16 July 2015.

117 "PETE PETE'W dixit le président Martelly au champ de Mars," 30 June 2015, https://youtu.be/OCOC_JBtRmo, accessed 1 April 2016.

118 "Prezidan Martelly k'ap joure yon fanm nan vil Miragoane paske li t'ap pwoteste kont li," 30 July 2015, https://www.youtube.com/watch?v=bgdyce_esLg, accessed 18 February 2016.

119 "Martelly's sexist gaffe leads to cracks in Haitian government," *The Miami Herald*, 7 August 2013.

120 "Profonde indignation suite aux agressions verbales et menaces sexuelles de Martelly contre une femme," AlterPresse, 1 August 2015.

121 "La Fusion annonce son départ du gouvernement," Radio Métropole, 5 August 2015.

122 "Démission de Rotchild François Jr," Radio Caraïbes, 15 September 2015.

123 "Vers le lancement d'un programme de financement de véhicule au profit des journaliste," Radio Métropole, 7 November 2015.

124 "Haitian officials to get costly golden parachutes," *The Miami Herald*, 30 October 2015.

125 Mission d'Observation Électorale de l'Union Européenne Haïti 2015 press release, 11 August 2015.

126 "Violences électorales dans le Plateau Central," Radio Métropole, 3 August 2015.

127 "Affrontements violents dans la campagne électorale," Radio Métropole, 4 August 2015.

128 "'Un désastre électoral' et 'une crise post-électorale' se dessinent, avertit le Rnddh," AlterPresse, 7 August 2015.

129 "Une campagne électorale marquée par plusieurs scènes de violences," Radio Métropole, 6 August 2015.

130 "Le CEP maintient le cap sur dimanche pour le premier tour des législatives," Radio Kiskeya, 5 August 2015.

131 "'Un désastre électoral' et 'une crise post-électorale' se dessinent, avertit le Rnddh," AlterPresse, 7 August 2015.

132 "Début timide de la journée électorale législative en Haïti," AlterPresse, 9 August 2015.

133 "Trois centres de vote incendiés à Savanette," AlterPresse, 9 August 2015.

134 "Au moins 3 morts," Radio Métropole, 9 August 2015.

135 "Plusieurs centres de vote saccagés," Radio Métropole, 9 August 2015.

136 "Des coalitions de candidats réclament l'annulation du scrutin," Radio Métropole, 13 August 2015.

137 "Protestations à Belladère et Savanette," AlterPresse, 12 August 2015.

138 "3 candidats arrêtés à Mirebalais," Radio Métropole, 13 August 2015.

139 "8 personnes incarcérées à Jacmel," Radio Métropole, 18 August 2015.

140 "Déjà, 7 journées de protestations à Jacmel – Deux blessés," AlterPresse, 30 August 2015.

141 "Que le CEP se méfie de tous ceux qui lui affirment que tout s'est bien passé!," AlterPresse, 11 August 2015.

142 "Disorder, delays mar Haiti's long-awaited election," Agence France-Presse, 9 August 2015.

143 "Haiti to redo legislative elections in 25 constituencies," *The Miami Herald*, 20 August 2015.

144 Mission d'Observation Électorale de l'Union Européenne Haïti 2015 press release, 11 August 2015.

145 Organization of American States press release, 10 August 2015.

146 "La lutte continue!," *Le National*, 9 August 2015.

147 "Résultats des Sénatoriales du 9 août 2015," Radio Métropole, 21 August 2015.

148 "8 candidats peuvent être élus au premier tour," Radio Métropole, 21 August 2015.

149 "Latortue et Sénatus élus au premier tour pour le Sénat," Radio Métropole, 28 September 2015.

150 "Communiqué de presse #48," Conseil Électoral Provisoire, 17 August 2015.

151 "La Pohdh relève un déséquilibre au niveau des sanctions du Cep," AlterPresse, 25 August 2015.

152 "Haiti to redo legislative elections in 25 constituencies," *The Miami Herald*, 20 August 2015.

153 "Scandaleuse impunité électorale en Haïti," AlterPresse, 26 August 2015.

154 "Les élections sont acceptables selon Pamela White," Radio Métropole, 28 August 2015.

155 "OAS to meet with Haiti officials in support of October vote," Associated Press, 14 September 2015.

156 "Une dizaine d'entités politiques veulent la tête du président du Cep," AlterPresse, 1 September 2015.

157 "Amplification de la grogne contre les élections du 9 août 2015," Radio Kiskeya, 4 September 2015.

158 "Nouvelle manifestation visant à réclamer l'annulation des élections du 9 août," Radio Métropole, 5 September 2015.

159 "Intensification de la mobilisation contre le CEP," Radio Métropole, 11 September 2015.

160 "Fusion et Inité abandonnent le gouvernement," Radio Métropole, 10 September 2015.

161 "L'espace de résistance patriotique appelle à la mobilisation contre les élections du 25 octobre," AlterPresse, 9 October 2015.

162 "Kenneth Merten préoccupé par la crise électorale," Radio Métropole, 25 September 2015.

163 "La circulation rétablie, le 5 septembre 2015, à l'Arcahaie, après une semaine de troubles," AlterPresse, 6 September 2015.

164 "Le gouvernement rencontre des représentants de l'Arcahaie et de Montrouis," Radio Métropole, 12 October 2015.

165 "Intensification des manifestations à Arcahaïe et Fonds des Blancs," Radio Métropole, 16 September 2015.

166 "Martelly annonce le dialogue avec les manifestants de l'Arcahaie," Radio Métropole, 21 September 2015.

167 "Démission de Rotchild François Jr," Radio Caraïbes, 15 September 2015.

168 "Deux policiers abattus par des bandits à Cité Soleil où la tension monte," AlterPresse, 15 September 2015.

169 "Des policiers réclament justice pour leurs collègues," Radio Métropole, 17 October 2015.

170 "Affrontements entre gangs dans le Bas Artibonite," Radio Métropole, 24 September 2015.

171 "Jude Célestin reçoit un appui informel de Vérité," Radio Métropole, 24 September 2015.

172 "Vérité et Inité réunis autour de Jude Célestin," Radio Métropole, 21 October 2015.

173 "L'ancien président Jean-Bertrand Aristide sort de son silence pour préconiser le retour de Fanmi lavalas au palais national," AlterPresse, 2 October 2015.

174 "Le Conseiller électoral Néhémy Joseph a remis ce vendredi sa démission au président de la République Michel Martelly," Radio Métropole, 2 October 2015.

175 "Le secteur vodou exprime sa colère contre Martelly," Radio Métropole, 9 October 2015.

176 "Martelly fait campagne pour Jovenel Moïse," Radio Métropole, 13 October 2015.

177 "Jovenel Moïse appelle ses partisans à un comportement pacifique," Radio Métropole, 23 October 2015.

178 "CIMO dispose d'une nouvelle base," Radio Métropole, 16 October 2015.

179 "Plus d'une quinzaine de morts dans de nouvelles violences à Cité Soleil," Radio Métropole, 18 October 2015.

180 Author interview, Port-au-Prince, January 2016.

181 Author interviews, Cité Soleil, January 2016.

182 "Début des opérations de vote dans le calme," AlterPresse, 25 October 2015.

183 "Taux de participation des électeurs en hausse," Radio Métropole, 25 October 2015.

184 "Retards et irrégularités dans des centres de vote de plusieurs départements," AlterPresse, 25 October 2015.

185 "Trois blessés par balle, neuf arrestations et un centre de vote incendié dans le Sud-Est, selon un bilan partiel," AlterPresse, 26 October 2015.

186 "Pari globalement réussi, malgré des incidents," AlterPresse, 25 October 2015.

187 "Satisfaction générale après les élections pacifiques en Haïti," Agence France-Presse, 25 October 2015.

188 "Polls in landmark Haiti elections close after no big snags," Reuters, 25 October 2015.

189 "Le taux de participation au scrutin est de 30% selon les observateurs," Radio Métropole, 27 October 2015.

190 "Lapeh dénonce des fraudes du PHTK," Radio Métropole, 27 October 2015.

191 "Moïse Jean-Charles se dit 'comfortable' en dépit 'd'irrégularités'," Radio Kiskeya, 27 October 2015.

192 "Moïse Jean-Charles dénonce des fraudes massives," Radio Métropole, 27 October 2015.

193 "Des candidats à la présidence accusent le PHTK de fraude," Radio Métropole, 28 October 2015.

194 "Moïse Jean-Charles confiant de sa victoire," Radio Métropole, 30 October 2015.

195 "In Haiti, tire barricades burn as candidate alleges fraud," Associated Press, 29 October 2015.

196 "Lapeh réclame l'exclusion de Jovenel Moïse du scrutin," Radio Métropole, 3 November 2015.

197 "L'Ocid, soucieux de la transparence dans la phase de tabulation des votes," Alter-Presse, 30 October 2015.

198 "Le candidat du régime, Jovenel Moïse de PHTK, finit en première position," Radio Kiskeya, 5 November 2015.

199 "12 sénateurs élus au deuxième tour des législatives, selon des résultats préliminaires," AlterPresse, 8 November 2015.

200 "PHTK et ses alliés obtiennent la majorité au Parlement," Radio Métropole, 11 November 2015.

201 "Moins d'une vingtaine de députés conserveront leurs sièges," Radio Métropole, 11 November 2015.

202 "Haiti issues preliminary results in parliament vote," *The Miami Herald*, 8 November 2015.

203 "Moïse Jean-Charles appelle à la mobilisation populaire," Radio Métropole, 6 November 2015.

204 "Le parti politique 'Fanmi Lavalas' entre mobilisation et contestation," AlterPresse, 6 November 2015.

205 "Des manifestants dénoncent un coup d'état électoral en faveur de Jovenel Moïse," AlterPresse, 12 November 2015.

206 "Est-ce qu'un Canadien aurait orchestré une fraude électorale massive en Haïti?," Radio Kiskeya, 12 November 2015.

207 "CEP holdout breaks silence as election protests grows in Haiti," *The Miami Herald*, 12 November 2015.

208 Author interviews, Port-au-Prince and Pétionville, January 2016.

209 "Le Cep rejette la proposition de sortie de crise des huit candidats à la présidence," AlterPresse, 17 November 2015.

210 "CEP holdout breaks silence as election protests grows in Haiti," *The Miami Herald*, 12 November 2015.

211 "Moïse Jean-Charles et Steven Benoît blessés lors d'une manifestation," Radio Métropole, 19 November 2015.

212 "Manifestations du 20 novembre 2015: au moins 1 mort et plusieurs blessés," Tele Kiskeya, 12 November 2015, https://youtu.be/Jidd7r1Laxw, accessed 14 January 2016.

213 "Les manifestations deviennent de plus en plus violentes selon le gouvernement," Radio Métropole, 19 November 2015.

214 "Un mort et plusieurs blessés lors d'une manifestation de Fanmi Lavalas," Radio Métropole, 21 November 2015.

215 "L'ouverture officielle de la campagne électorale sur fond de discorde," AlterPresse, 27 November 2015.

216 "Deux victimes, dont un manifestant blessé par balle à la tête, lors de la manifestation du 24 novembre de l'opposition," AlterPresse, 25 November 2015.

217 "Haiti officially declares top 2 winners of presidential race, announcement spurs protest," *The Miami Herald*, 24 November 2015.

218 "Le CEP publie les résultats définitifs, la rue réagit," Radio Kiskeya, 24 November 2015.

219 "Jovenel Moïse, de la banane à la machette ...," AlterPresse, 24 November 2015.

220 "L'ouverture officielle de la campagne électorale sur fond de discorde," AlterPresse, 27 November 2015.

221 "Communiqué du Groupe des 8 candidats à la présidence (G8)," 29 November 2015.

222 Moïse Jean-Charles' Twitter account, @MoïseJC2016, 5 November 2015: "Je ne vx garder avec moi que des braves. Que ceux qui veulent mourir en Hoes libres se rangent autour de moi. Viv yon Ayiti Lib @hpnhaiti." The full phrase of Dessalines was said to be "Je ne veux garder avec moi que des braves. Que ceux qui veulent redevenir des esclaves Français sortent du fort. Que ceux au contraire qui veulent mourir en hommes libres se rangent autour de moi."

CHAPTER SEVENTEEN

1 "Le CEP ne va pas créer une commission de vérification des résultats," Radio Métropole, 1 December 2015.

2 "Le torchon brule entre le CEP et le G 8," Radio Métropole, 1 December 2015.

3 "Le ton monte entre les candidats à la présidence," Radio Métropole, 8 December 2015.

4 "Lapeh de Jude Célestin ira au second tour de la présidentielle sous certaines conditions," AlterPresse, 1 December 2015.

5 "Les membres du G 8 toujours unis," Radio Métropole, 11 December 2015.

6 "Un organisation de la société civile prône le dialogue," Radio Métropole, 2 December 2015.

7 "Le Ministère de la Communication condamne un acte d'intimidation sur les locaux de Radio Kiskeya," Radio Métropole, 2 December 2015.

8 "La première promotion du corps de génie militaire en formation," Radio Métropole, 7 December 2015.

9 "Des enfants soldats existent à Cité soleil selon le maire de cette commune," Radio Métropole, 10 December 2015.

10 "Lettre ouverte au premier ministre Evans Paul et Président du Conseil Supérieur de la Police Nationale (CSPN), en date du 29 janvier 2016," Réseau National de Défense des Droits Humains.

11 "Nouvelle manifestation des lavalassiens à Port-au-Prince," Radio Métropole, 17 December 2015.

12 "L'économie haïtienne affectée par des manifestations en série," Radio Métropole, 17 December 2015.

13 Lakou Lapè press release, 11 December 2015.

14 "Un membre du CEP doute de la crédibilité du scrutin," Radio Métropole, 11 December 2015.

15 "Les conseillers électoraux menacent de démissionner en bloc," Radio Métropole, 14 December 2015.

16 Press release by Association Nationale des Médias Haïtiens, 17 December 2015.

17 "Création d'une commission d'évaluation électorale," Radio Métropole, 18 December 2015.

18 "La CEH soutient la Commission d'évaluation électorale," Radio Métropole, 24 December 2015.

19 "Seul le premier tour de la présidentielle sera évalué, précise la commission d'évaluation électorale," AlterPresse, 28 December 2015.

20 "Haiti PM recommends commission to end election impasse," *The Miami Herald*, 17 December 2015.

21 "Il est difficile de réaliser le scrutin le 27 décembre affirme Evans Paul," Radio Métropole, 18 December 2015.

22 "Haiti officials postpone vote set for this weekend," Associated Press, 21 December 2015.

23 "Le parti Fusion dénonce la création unilatérale de la commission d'évaluation électorale," AlterPresse, 18 December 2015.

24 "Le parti 'Fanmi Lavalas' dénonce les membres de la Commission d'évaluation électorale," AlterPresse, 18 December 2015.

25 "Fanmi Lavalas acceptera le verdict de la commission," Radio Métropole, 22 December 2015.

26 "Fanmi Lavalas annonce la poursuite de la mobilisation," Radio Métropole, 29 December 2015.

27 "Haiti vote was marred by fraud: probe," Agence France-Presse, 3 January 2016.

28 "La commission recommande une enquête approfondie sur les irrégularités graves," AlterPresse, 5 January 2016.

29 "Un membre de la commission d'évaluation électorale recommande un recomptage des procès-verbaux," AlterPresse, 4 January 2016.

30 "Haiti panel says vote irregularities due to incompetence," Associated Press, 4 January 2016.

31 "Jovenel Moïse salue le rapport de la commission," Radio Métropole, 5 January 2016.

32 "Pitit Dessalines soutient que la commission confirme les fraudes massives," Radio Métropole, 5 January 2016.

33 "Fanmi Lavalas rejette le rapport publié par la commission d'évaluation électorale," Radio Métropole, 5 January 2016.

34 "Le G-8 rejette le rapport de la commission et exige une transition," Radio Métropole, 5 January 2016.

35 Communiqué by United Nations in Haiti, 5 January 2015.

36 "Rencontre urgente entre l'exécutif et le Cep – Deuxième tour difficile ou impossible le 17 janvier," AlterPresse, 5 January 2016.

37 "Le président convoque le peuple aux urnes et un conseiller électoral démissionne," AlterPresse, 7 January 2016.

38 "Les sénateurs ne peuvent pas bloquer l'entrée en fonction des nouveaux élus," Radio Métropole, 7 January 2016.

39 Press statement, Bureau of Public Affairs, 7 January 2016.

40 "Message du Président de la république, Michel Joseph Martelly, le mercredi 6 janvier 2016," https://youtu.be/p3lNRCyYnr8, accessed 23 February 2016.

41 "Distribution de certificats de confirmation de victoire aux 'élus' des scrutins législatifs controversés," Radio Kiskeya, 8 January 2016.

42 "La coalition d'observation appelle au sens de responsabilité de l'exécutif et du Cep," 7 January 2016.

43 "Jean-Charles Moïse, Mirlande Manigat, Edmonde Supplice Beauzile et René Civil défendent l'option de la transition," Radio Kiskeya, 10 January 2016.

44 "Validation des pouvoirs et prestation de serment de 92 députés issus des scrutins du 9 août et du 25 octobre 2015," Radio Kiskeya, 10 January 2016.

45 "Aucune majorité évidente à la chambre basse," Radio Métropole, 11 January 2016.

46 "La Droite décroche la présidence de la chambre des députés," Radio Métropole, 14 January 2016.

47 "Les recommandations de la CEEI n'ont pas été respectées," Radio Métropole, 11 January 2016.

48 "Jocelerme Privert remporte la présidence du Sénat face à Youri Latortue présenté comme le candidat à ce poste du pouvoir Tèt Kale," Radio Kiskeya, 14 January 2016.

49 "Adresse aux sociétés civiles des États représentés en Haïti," *Le Nouvelliste*, 18 January 2016.

50 "Jude Célestin annonce qu'il ne participera pas au second tour des élections," Radio Métropole, 16 January 2016.

51 "Haiti presidential candidate won't participate in election,"Agence France-Presse, 19 January 2018.

52 "Le CEP maintient le cap sur le 24 janvier, envers et contre tout," Radio Kiskeya, 18 January 2016.

53 Communiqué from OCID, 20 January 2016.

54 "Le Sénat se prépare à réclamer l'arrêt du processus électoral," Radio Métropole, 19 January 2016.

55 "Seuls 5 conseillers sont impliqués dans le scrutin," Radio Métropole, 19 January 2016.

56 "Haiti police fire tear gas, days before runoff vote," Agence France-Presse, 19 January 2016.

57 "Nou Pap Obeyi 'Netwaye zam nou' nou paka sipòte ankò, Manifestasyon 19 Janvye 2016," https://youtu.be/-240-rsoWVs, accessed 22 January 2016.

58 "Haiti: Influential candidate quits presidential race," Agence France-Presse, 19 January 2016.

59 "La CCI HAITI invite les acteurs politiques à reprendre le dialogue," Radio Métropole, 20 January 2016.

60 "Haiti senate calls for a halt to Sunday presidential runoff," *The Miami Herald*, 20 January 2016.

61 "Des manifestations intensives de l'opposition pour exiger l'annulation du scrutin du 24 janvier," AlterPresse, 21 January 2016.

62 "Haiti plunges on with poll despite opposition boycott," Agence France-Presse, 21 January 2016.

63 "Une école incendiée à Léogane," Radio Métropole, 22 January 2016.

64 "Des manifestants casseurs sont à l'œuvre à Pétion-Ville," Radio Métropole, 22 January 2016.

65 "Un individu battu à mort par des manifestants," Radio Métropole, 22 January 2016.

66 "Le 'restant' du CEP annule le scrutin gouvernemental du 24 janvier officiellement en raison de l'insécurité," Radio Kiskeya, 23 January 2016.

67 "Pierre Manigat Junior abandonne le CEP," Agence France-Presse, 23 January 2016.

68 "Angry Haitians demand president's ouster amid vote delay," Agence France-Presse, 23 January 2016.

69 "L'ADIH condamne les actes de violence perpétrés lors des manifestations," Radio Métropole, 25 January 2016.

70 @sharanyakkn, 8 February 2016.

71 "Les violences ont motivé le report du scrutin affirme une conseillère électorale," Radio Métropole, 28 January 2016.

72 Communiqué from G8, 22 January 2016.

73 Press statement, United States Department of State, 24 January 2016.

74 "Menacée par les sbires du pouvoir, la Radio Télé Kiskeya lance un appel aux secteurs conséquents de la vie nationale," AlterPresse, 26 January 2016.

75 "Ex-Haiti coup leader says to fight 'anarchists' as unrest spreads," Reuters, 24 January 2016.

76 "Calme apparent sur fond de crise, après les manifestations violentes du weekend écoulé," AlterPresse, 25 January 2016.

77 "Tractations autour d'un gouvernement de consensus," Radio Métropole, 25 January 2016.

78 "Exclusive: Short-term interim government likely in Haiti – U.S. official," Reuters, 25 January 2016.

79 "Les acteurs politiques favorables au départ de Martelly le 7 février," Radio Métropole, 27 January 2016.

80 "Des manifestants réclament la tenue du second tour des élections," Radio Métropole, 26 January 2016.

81 "Des manifestants pro-PHTK ont bloqué un pont reliant Limonade à Caracol," Radio Kiskeya, 27 January 2016.

82 "Des milliers de partisans du pouvoir manifestent en faveur de la poursuite du processus électoral," AlterPrese, 29 January 2016.

83 "C'est aux Haïtiens de décider de l'avenir d'Haïti, dixit Celso Amorim de l'Oea," AlterPresse, 26 January 2016.

84 Press communiqué from the G8, 28 January 2016.

85 "Martelly conditionne son départ," Radio Métropole, 29 January 2016.

86 "Des milliers de partisans du pouvoir manifestent en faveur de la poursuite du processus électoral," AlterPresse, 29 January 2016.

87 "Latortue s'attend au départ de Martelly le 7 février," Radio Métropole, 29 January 2016.

88 "Opont démissionne du CEP," Radio Métropole, 29 January 2016.

89 "Les présidents Martelly, Privert et Chancy proposent un calendrier de sortie de crise," *Le Nouvelliste*, 30 January 2016.

90 "Haiti Opposition Alliance Declining to Meet with OAS Mission," Associated Press, 1 February 2016.

91 "Des sénateurs refusent l'intervention de l'OEA," Radio Métropole, 2 February 2016.

92 "La formule de transition proposée par le sénat," AlterPresse, 1 February 2016.

93 Communiqué from the Réseau National de Défense des Droits Humains, 3 February 2016.

94 "La mobilisation des partisans de Jovenel Moïse se poursuit," Radio Métropole, 3 February 2016.

95 "Privert confirme le départ de Martelly au 7 février," Radio Métropole, 3 February 2016.

96 "Privert presse les législateurs à prévenir la vacance présidentielle," Radio Métropole, 5 February 2016.

97 "Martelly dresse un bilan satisfaisant de son administration," Radio Métropole, 5 February 2016.

98 "Martelly lève le doute sur son départ le 7 février," AlterPresse, 4 February 2016.

99 "Problems rampant as Haiti cannot elect a new president,' Al Jazeera, 5 February 2016.

100 "Michel Martelly can't lead Haiti's transition," *The Miami Herald*, 30 January 2016.

101 "After canceling its presidential election, Haiti heads toward chaos," *The Washington Post*, 24 January 2016.

102 "Un défilé inopiné de 'prétendus anciens militaires' armés provoque des échauffourées à Port-au-Prince," AlterPresse, 6 February 2016.

103 "Former Soldiers Clash with Protesters in Haiti; 1 Dead," Associated Press, 5 February 2016.

104 "Yon Milite Atake et Tue Par Manifestan 2/5/2016 Haiti News," https://youtu.be/ ST_hWZeQy4Q, accessed 25 February 2016.

105 "Haiti protesters stone to death ex-fighter as political crisis deepens," Reuters, 5 February 2016.

106 "Haiti leaders move to install provisional government," Associated Press, 6 February 2016.

107 "Haiti reaches accord for caretaker government," *The Miami Herald*, 6 February 2016.

108 "Un accord a été trouvé en Haït," Radio Métropole, 6 February 2016.

109 "Communiqué du groupe des candidats à la présidence engagés dans le processus électoral communément appelé Groupe des 8 (G-8)," 8 February 2016.

110 Trouillot, Lyonel (1998) *Street of Lost Footsteps*. Lincoln, NE: University of Nebraska Press, p. 104.

111 "Haiti's out-going president speaks with Local 10 News' Calvin Hughes," 6 February 2016, http://www.local10.com/news/haitis-out-going-president-speaks-with-local-10-news-calvin-hughes.

112 "Michel Martelly: Discours d'adieu à la Nation, 7 fevrier 2016," https://youtu.be/XtzBPRh4TG8, accessed 21 February 2016.

EPILOGUE

1 "Le nombre de personnes souffrant d'insécurité alimentaire en Haïti a doublé selon le PAM," Radio Métropole, 9 February 2016.

2 "Assassinat d'un membre de PHTK," Bureau de Communication Plateforme PHTK, 9 February 2016.

3 Interview with Jean-Max Bellerive, Port-au-Prince, February 2016.

4 "Lancement du processus d'inscription des candidats à la présidence," Radio Métropole, 11 February 2016.

5 "Jocelerme Privert élu président provisoire d'Haïti par le parlement," AlterPresse, 14 February 2016.

6 "Installation de Jocelerme Privert comme nouveau président Provisoire," Radio Métropole, 14 February 2016.

7 "L'ONU et le Core Group saluent l'élection de Privert," Radio Métropole, 16 February 2016.

8 "'We're back' – Aristide allies toast Haiti's interim president at palace," Reuters, 15 February 2016. The journalist in question was former Martelly government employee Guy Delva.

9 "Moïse Jean-Charles est vigilant face au nouveau président," Radio Métropole, 16 February 2016.

10 "Le G 8 et Pitit Dessalines n'intègreront pas le gouvernement," Radio Métropole, 18 February 2016.

11 "Jovenel Moïse réclame l'application scrupuleuse de l'accord du 06 février," Radio Métropole, 17 February 2016.

12 "Plusieurs organisations sociales dénoncent la prochaine mise en place d'un gouvernement de transition," AlterPresse, 22 February 2016.

13 "Désaccord entre Privert et Paul," Radio Métropole, 24 February 2016.

14 "Un ex ministre révèle l'existence de contrats douteux," Radio Métropole, 11 May 2016.

15 "Privert initie des démarches pour la mise en place d'un nouveau Cep," AlterPresse, 18 February 2016.

16 "Le président intérimaire assure qu'il ne dépassera pas son mandat," Radio Métropole, 22 February 2016.

17 "Privert se présente en rassembleur," Radio Métropole, 22 February 2016.

18 "Installation ce vendredi du premier ministre nommé Fritz Jean," Radio Métropole, 26 February 2016.

19 "Enex Jean-Charles est nommé Premier Ministre," Radio Métropole, 23 March 2016.

20 "Léopold Berlanger à la tête du bureau du nouveau Cep," AlterPresse, 31 March 2016.

21 "Privert se dédouane de toute responsabilité dans le report des elections," Radio Métropole, 12 April 2016.

22 "Privert prêt à lancer la commission," Radio Métropole, 25 April 2016.

23 "Publication du calendrier électoral, entre les 15 et 31 mai, informe Privert," Alter-Presse, 21 April 2016.

24 "Plusieurs milliers de sympathisants du PHTK ont manifesté hier dimanche," Radio Métropole, 25 April 2016.

25 "Privert recommande l'austérité aux ministres," Radio Métropole, 7 April 2016.

26 "Des députés veulent le maintien de Privert au pouvoir," Radio Métropole, 3 May 2016.

27 "Moïse Jean-Charles critique Privert," Radio Métropole, 5 May 2016.

28 "Le Premier Ministre Jean-Charles déclare impossible le respect des dates de l'accord du 6 février," Radio Kiskeya, 12 May 2016.

29 "Installation des membres de la commission de vérification électorale, ce jeudi 28 avril," AlterPresse, 29 April 2016.

30 "Rapport de la Commission Indépendante d'Évaluation et de Vérification Électorale Élections de 2015," 29 May 2016.

31 "Haiti Panel Recommends Throwing Out Results of Disputed Vote," Associated Press, 30 May 2016.

32 "Rapport de la Commission Indépendante d'Évaluation et de Vérification Électorale Élections de 2015," 29 May 2016.

33 Author interview, Port-au-Prince, February 2016.

34 "Michel-Ange Gédéon remplace Godson Orélus à la tête de la PNH," Le Nouvelliste, 8 April 2016.

35 Author interview, May 2016.

36 "Haiti to repeat first round of presidential election in October," Deutsche Welle, 7 June 2016.

37 "U.S. to Haiti: Pay for your own elections," The Miami Herald, 7 June 2016.

38 "Résultats de la Présidentielle," Radio Métropole, 4 January 2017.

39 "As protests erupt over his arrest, Guy Philippe pleads not guilty in Miami," The Miami Herald, 13 January 2017.

40 "L'adieu à René Préval," Le Nouvelliste, 13 March 2017.

41 "Haiti's Michel Martelly: When a Celebrity Becomes President," The Atlantic, 9 February 2016.

42 "Aftershocks," The New Yorker, 1 February 2016.

43 "Syria and the Left," New Politics, Winter 2015.

BIBLIOGRAPHY

Abbott, Elizabeth (1988) *Haiti: The Duvaliers and Their Legacy*. New York, NY: McGraw-Hill.

Alexis, Jacques Stephen (1955) *General Sun, My Brother*. Charlottesville, VA: University Press of Virginia.

Avril, Prosper (2014) *L'aventure militaire des 13 guérilleros de Jeune Haïti*. Port-au-Prince, Haiti: L'Imprimeur.

Beaubrum, Mimerose P. (2013) *Nan Dòmi: An Initiate's Journey Into Haitian Vodou*. San Francisco, CA: City Lights.

Bell, Madison Smartt (2007) *Toussaint Louverture: A Biography*. New York, NY: Pantheon Books.

Blancpain, François (1998) *Louis Borno: Président d'Haïti*. Port-au-Prince, Haiti: Imprimerie Le Natal.

Castor, Suzy (1988) *L'Occupation américaine d'Haïti*. Port-au-Prince, Haiti: Société Haïtienne d'Histoire.

Corvington, Georges (1975) *Port-au-Prince au cours des ans. Vol. 1: La Ville coloniale, 1743–1789*. Montreal: Les Éditions du CIDIHCA.

CRESFED (2000) *Haïti: jamais, jamais plus!: les violations des droits de l'homme à l'époque des Duvalier*. Port-au-Prince, Haiti: Centre de Recherche et de Formation Économique et Sociale pour le Développement (CRESFED).

Cuello, José Israel (1997) *Contratación de mano de obra haitiana destinada a la industria azucarera dominicana, 1952–1986*. Santo Domingo, Dominican Republic: Taller.

Danticat, Edwidge (2007) *Brother I'm Dying*. New York, NY: Vintage.

Daut, Marlene L. (2015) *Tropics of Haiti: Race and the Literary History of the Haitian Revolution in the Atlantic World, 1789–1865*. Liverpool: Liverpool University Press.

Deibert, Michael (2005) *Notes from the Last Testament: The Struggle for Haiti*. New York, NY: Seven Stories Press.

Deren, Maya (1953) *Divine Horsemen: The Living Voodoo Gods on Haiti*. Kingston, NY: McPherson & Company.

Diederich, Bernard (2007) *Bon Papa: Haiti's Golden Years*. Bloomington, IN: Xlibris.

Diederich, Bernard and Al Burt (1991) *Papa Doc: Haiti and its Dictator*. Maplewood, NJ: Waterfront Press.

Dumas, Reginald (2008) *An Encounter with Haiti: Notes of a Special Advisor*. Port of Spain, Trinidad: Medianet.

Dunham, Katherine (1969) *Island Possessed*. Chicago, IL: University of Chicago Press.

Dupuy, Alex (2006) *The Prophet and Power: Jean-Bertrand Aristide, the International Community, and Haiti.* Lanham, MD: Rowman & Littlefield.

Franco, Franklin Pichardo (1997) *Sobre racismo y antihaitianismo y otros ensayos.* Santo Domingo, Dominican Republic: Impresora Vidal.

Gaffield, Julia (2015) *Haitian Connections in the Atlantic World: Recognition After Revolution.* Chapel Hill, NC: University of North Carolina Press.

Gaillard, Roger (1982) *Hinche mise en croix.* Port-au-Prince, Haiti: Imprimerie Le Natal.

Gaillard, Roger (1983) *La guérilla de Batraville: 1919–1934.* Port-au-Prince, Haiti: Imprimerie Le Natal.

Gaillard, Roger (1984) *Une modernisation manquée: 1880–1896.* Port-au-Prince, Haiti: Imprimerie Le Natal.

Gibson, Carrie (2014) *Empire's Crossroads: A New History of the Caribbean.* London: Macmillan.

Henl, Robert Debs and Nancy Gordon (1995) *Written in Blood: The Story of the Haitian People.* Lanham, MD: University Press of America.

Hunt, Alfred N. (1988) *Haiti's Influence on Antebellum America: Slumbering Volcano in the Caribbean.* Baton Rouge, LA: Louisiana State University Press.

Hurbon, Laënnec (1993) *Voodoo: Search for the Spirit.* New York, NY: Harry N. Abrams.

Hurston, Zora Neale (1938) *Tell My Horse: Voodoo and Life in Haiti and Jamaica.* New York, NY: Harper & Row.

Klarreich, Kathie (2005) *Madame Dread: A Tale of Love, Vodou and Civil Strife in Haiti.* New York, NY: Nation Books.

Madiou, Thomas (ed.) (1989) *Histoire d'Haïti: Tome II 1799–1803.* Port-au-Prince, Haiti: Éditions Henri Deschamps.

Métraux, Alfred (1959) *Voodoo in Haiti.* New York, NY: Schocken Books.

MPP (1998) *Bilan 25 An: 1973–1998.* Port-au-Prince, Haiti: Mouvman Peyizan Papay (MPP).

Munro, Martin (2015) *Tropical Apocalypse: Haiti and the Caribbean End Times.* Charlottesville, VA: University Press of Virginia.

Philoctète, René (1989) *Massacre River.* New York, NY: New Directions.

Price-Mars, Jean (1953) *La République d'Haïti et la République dominicaine: Les aspects divers d'un problème d'histoire, de géographie et d'ethnologie.* Chicoutimi, Quebec: Classiques des Sciences Sociales.

Roberston, David (1999) *Denmark Vesey.* New York, NY: Vintage.

Roorda, Eric Paul (1998) *The Dictator Next Door.* Durham, NC: Duke University Press.

Roumain, Jacques (1944) *Masters of the Dew.* Portsmouth, NH: Heinemann.

Seabrook, William (1929) *The Magic Island.* New York, NY: Paragon House.

Smith, Matthew J. (2009) *Red & Black in Haiti: Radicalism, Conflict and Political Change 1934–1957.* Chapel Hill, NC: University of North Carolina Press.

Thoby-Marcelin, Philippe and Pierre Marcelin (1946) *The Beast of the Haitian Hills.* San Francisco, CA: City Lights.

Thomson, Ian (1992) *Bonjour, Blanc: A Journey Through Haiti.* London: Vintage.

Thucydides (1954) *History of the Peloponnesian War*. Translation by Rex Warner. New York, NY: Penguin Books.

Trouillot, Lyonel (1998) *Street of Lost Footsteps*. Lincoln, NE: University of Nebraska Press.

Trouillot, Lyonel (2002) *Children of Heroes*. Lincoln, NE: University of Nebraska Press.

Victor, Gary (2000) *A l'angle des rues parallèles*. Paris: Vents d'Ailleurs.

Waugh, Alec (1965) *Love and the Caribbean*. New York, NY: Bantam Books.

Wilentz, Amy (1989) *The Rainy Season: Haiti Since Duvalier*. New York, NY: Touchstone.

INDEX

Acdhély, Junior "Yoyo Piman", 32, 141
Adrien, Weber, 56
African National Congress (ANC), 66
Agence-France-Presse (AFP), 100
Agrocítricos, 137
Al-Haj Saleh, Yassin, 343
Alcide, Rodney, 119
Aldunate, Eduardo, 100
Alexandre, Boniface, 47-8, 77, 246, 248
Alexandre, Carl, 240, 289
Alexandre, Guy, 220
Alexis, Jacques Édouard, 28, 107, 109, 113, 122, 126-9, 139, 145, 148-52, 180, 209, 211-14, 218, 223
Alexis, Jacques Stéphen, 2, 17, 89
Alexis, Pierre Nord (Tonton Nord), 12, 96
Alexis, Schubert, 121
Allien, Marilyn, 140, 243
Allouard, Philippe, 184, 269
Alphonse, Roberson, 165
Altenor, John, 315
AlterPresse, 85, 301
Amelice, Louis, 133
American Red Cross, 207
Amnesty International, 54, 204, 246, 333
Amorin, Celso, 332
Anacacis, Jean Hector, 103, 105, 144, 177, 214, 237, 318, 320
Andrésol, Mario, 31, 84-85, 90-1, 94, 98, 110-11, 113, 124, 141, 143, 145, 154, 167, 185, 255, 262, 266, 308, 312, 318-19, 326;replaced, 262
Anglade, Georges, 184
Annabi, Hédi, 142, 150, 163, 169, 182, 192; earthquake death of, 183, 197
Annan, Kofi, 46, 114, 116

Anthony, Kenny, 50
Anthony, René Jean, "Grenn Sonnen" 36, 58, 61, 63, 76
antihaitianismo, Dominican Republic ideology, 130
Antoine, Alfredo, 308
Antoine, Lissaint, 133
Antoine, Robert, 73
Antoine, Yvon, 118
Antonin, Arnold, 41
Apaid, Andy, 41, 56, 118
Apollon, Rovelson, 301, 310
Arawak people, 3
Ardouin, Beaubrun, 88
Aris, Patrick, 322
Aristide, Jean-Bertrand, 1, 24, 29, 30-1, 33, 35, 38, 41-2, 46, 58, 66, 68, 71, 87, 92, 94, 100, 150, 152, 174, 180-1, 230, 238, 240, 246, 249, 253-5, 270-1, 275-6, 283-7, 294, 301, 306-7, 316, 319, 325, 337-8; army disbanded, 28; Christmas messages, 125; diplomatic passport, 233; Dominique killing accusation, 306; election anniversary, 157; exile, 43-4; Foundation for Democracy, 38-9, 62, 69, 200, 249, 284; government unravelling, 2; "house arrest", 293; indictment demand, 83; Jamaica stopover, 50; manipulation allegations, 116; 1991 coup against, 26, 153; 1991 coup anniversary, 54, 263; opposition to, 8; overthrow, 47; return demands/mobilization for, 62, 64, 77, 80-1, 118, 208; return of, 234; Salesian order expulsion, 25; security detail of, 48; security detail withdrawal, 295; South Africa lifestyle, 162 South Africa

speech, 61; Tabarre mansion 58; violence responsibility claims, 79
Aristide (née Trouillot), Mildred, 28, 70, 250
Armand, Ducertain, 30
Armée Bouteille, 92
Armée Cannibale, 32, 35, 41, 77, 87, 119
Armée Roche, 92
Arthur, Owen, 51
Artibonite Valley, 7-8, 16, 30, 76, 101, 119, 154, 179, 198, 217, 232, 317; cholera contamination, 239
Association des Industries d'Haïti (ADIH), 8, 166, 330
Association des Journalistes Haïtiens (AJH), 285
Association des Médias Indépendants d'Haiti, 276
Association des Victimes du Génocide de la Scierie (AVIGES), 49, 91, 139, 170
Association Nationale des Magistrats Haïtiens (ANAMAH), 91, 113
Association Nationale des Médias Haïtiens, 287, 322
Association pour la Santé Intégrale de la Famille (APROSIFA), 109
Ateus, Norvella, 300
attache, civilian thugs, 26, 35
Auguste, Anne Marguerite, 143
Auguste, Annette, 35, 49, 118, 161, 250, 284, 308
Augustin, Ricardo, 324
Avril, Prosper, 25, 36, 246, 248, 284
Ayisyen pou Ayiti, 301
Ayiti An Aksyon (AAA), 261, 303, 308, 315, 325
Ayiti Kapab, 60

Badio, Jean-Rémy, 126
Bajeux, Jean-Claude, 8, 22, 25, 82, 164, 171, 228, 244, 289, 296
Bajeux, Sylvie, 8, 21, 164, 171, 289, 296-7
Baker, Charles, 79, 101, 118, 223

Balaguer, Joaquín, 130-1
Bale Wouze, 32, 42, 60, 64, 92, 139, 161
Balthazar, Maxo, 150
Ban Ki-moon, 142, 163, 192, 209, 224
Banque de la Républiqie d'Haïti (BRH), 12, 69, 312, 339
Banque Nationale de Crédit, 240-1
Banque Populaire Haitienne, 241
Baptiste, Fred, 22
Baptiste, William "Ti Blan", 32, 120; arrest of, 128
Barbados, 51
Barbot, Clément, 20, 21
Baron Samedi, 20
Baron, Amélie, 270
Barros, Christían, 302
Barthold, Claude, 195
Bastien, Kelly, 124, 148, 149
Batay Ouvriye, 246
Batraville, Benoît, 16, 217
Batrony, Jean Salim "Johnny", 39
Battle of Vertières, 5, 220, 240, 248, 267-8
Baudin, Ronald, 260
Baussan, Joel, 187, 188
Bautista, Félix, 256
Baz 117, 269, 272, 309
Baz Frustrée, 62
Baz Pilate, 109, 123, 126
Bazile, David, 82
Bazin, Marc, 25, 62, 96
Beaubrun, Chéry, murder conviction, 143
Beaubrun, Theodore "Lolo", 8, 28, 59, 75
Beaubrun, Mimerose, 8
Beaubrun, Mondesir, 27
Beauchard, Esaïe, 317, 321
Beauplan, Evalière, 151, 179, 200
Beauzile, Edmonde Supplice, 151, 179, 208, 213-14, 308, 325
Beer, David, 66,68
Bel-Air district, 19, 45, 56-7, 59, 114; Brazilian UN soldiers in, 79; gang battles, 249
Bellefleur, Yves Michel, killing of, 266

Bellerive, Jean-Max, 180-1, 186, 201, 203, 206, 208, 214, 218, 222-3, 228, 231, 235, 273, 337

Bélizaire, Arnel, 55, 60, 248, 253, 274, 284, 291-3, 299, 308, 311, 315, 337; arrest of, 78, 247

Bélizaire Lamarre, 282, 307

Bennett, Frantz, 153

Bennett, Michéle, 23, 183

Bennett, Rudy, 183

Benoît, François, 21, 144, 340

Benoît, Stephen, 157, 166, 261, 287, 319, 321,

Benoît, Victor, 25, 304

Berlanger, Léopold, 339-40

Bernadin, Marie Danielle, 270, 272

Bernard, Jacques, 102

Berthony, Jolicoeur, 175

Bertin, Mireille Durocher, 27

Best Western hotel brand, 277

Bhatia, Pooja, 170

Biamby, Philippe, 26

Bien-Aimé, Antoine Rodon, 319

Bien-Aimé, Arodon, 218

Bien-Aimé, Félix "Don Féfé", 34, 94

Bien-Aimé, Hugue, 218

Bien-Aimé, Jean-Baptiste, 253, 261, 263, 275, 291, 294, 315, 338

Bien Aimé, Robenson "Ti Ben", 109

Bienvenu, Gilles, 79

Bigaud, Wilson, 190

Bissainthe, Toto, 312

Bissereth, Yvon, 276

Blanc Raymond, 101

Bloncourt, Gérald, 17

Bobo, Rosalvo, 13-14, 16

Bogdanich, Walt, 87

Boisrond-Tonnerre, Louis, 5-7, 35

Bolívar, Simón, 7, 46

Bolous, Rudoplh, 97

Bonaparte, Napoleon, 5

Bonaparte, Pauline, 5, 278

Bonetti, Luis Manuel, 137

Bontemps, Saint-Ange, 21

Borno, Louis, 16, 17

Bosch, Juan, 130-1

Boschwitz, Rudy, 70

Bosco, Jean, 24

Bosquet, Rosalie (Madame Max Adolphe), 21, 213

Bouclier, 308-309

Boukman, 3

Boukman Eksperyans band, 8, 59, 75, 89

Boulbars, El-Ouafi, 93

Boulos, Carlo, 97

Boulos, Réginald, 64, 79, 96-7, 142, 298

Boulos, Rudolph "Rudy", 96, 123, 140, 146, 309; Rudolph, DR exile, 149; Rudolph, US passport of, 148

Boulos, Simel, 96, 97

Bourdeau, James, 91

Bourjolly, Emmanuel Fritz Gérald, 164, 280

Bouterse, Desiré, 237, 280

Boyer, Jean-Pierre, 4, 7, 11

Brandt, Clifford, 266, 269, 291; arrest of, 265

Brandt, David, 142

Brandt, Fritz, 142

Brazil: BNDES, 305; financial aid post-earthquake, 208; Haitian immigration, 252; UN troops, 46

Breton, André, 18

Brice, Manouchka Louis, 213

Brice, Ralph Stanley, 213

Brigade d'Intervention Rapide (BRI), 39

Brigade d'Operation et d'Intervention Départmental (BOID), 310, 322

Briggs & Stratton, 204

Brisson, Richard, 29

Brothers Posse, 80, 272

Brown, Chris, 312

Brown, Sherrod, 65, 67

Brun, Patrick, 114-15, 187

Brunache, Michel, 77, 248, 255, 292

Bruno, Jean Renel (Ti Pay), 212

Brutis, Duly, 305

Bryan, William Jennings, 14

Buissereth, Yvon, 177
Burau des Avocats Internationaux (BAI), 86, 118-19, 140, 267, 271
Bureau du Contentieux Electoral Departemental (BCED), 166
Bush, George W., 64, 72, 104, 207
Butler, Smedley, 14

Cadet, Alain (Pinochet), 80; arrest of, 128
Calderón, Felipe, 219
Calixte, Walky, 257, 274-5, 292, 308; killing of, 256
Cambodia, 142
Camille, Franco, 35, 49, 275, 284, 298, 308, 319
Camille, Ronald, 35
Canaan camp, violent evictions, 286
Canada, 208: International Development Agency (CIDA), 85; Eurasian Minerals, 260; Rights & Democracy group, 155
Cancel, Chrystel, 183
Candelier, Bruno Rosario, 131
Canino González, Pedro Antonio, 260, 305
Cantave, Jules, 331, 335
Cantel, Louis, 1
Cap-Haïtien, 46, 74, 75, 211; Aristide loyalists in, 52; industrial park proposal, 232; Lavalas Shada stringhold, 242
Caperton, William B., 14
Capois, François, 5
Caracol industrial park project, 288-9, 300; farmers dispossessed, 248
Caravane de l'Espoir, 9
CARE, 208
Caribbean Community (CARICOM), 50, 64, 108, 203, 208, 273, 309
CARIFESTA, 313
Carnival Cooperation, Miami, 278
Carrefour, 219; earthquake effects, 191, 192; US quake food aid, 195
Carrington, Edwin, 108
Casséus, Robenson, 120
Castel, Charles, 312
Castor, Suzy, 8, 27, 35, 47, 307

Castro, Fidel, 104
Catholic Church, 283, 285, 322, 324
Cayard, Octave, 22
Cazale, massacre 1969, 22
CBI Sugar Group, 134
Céant, Jean-Henry, 212, 214, 218, 221, 318-19
Cédras, Raoul, 26
Célestin, Fourel, 39, 96
Célestin, Hugues, 161, 213
Célestin, Jude, 149, 159, 176, 178, 198, 202, 212, 214, 218-27, 230-2, 308, 316-21, 340, 328
Centre Ecuménique des Droits Humins (CEDH), 8, 65, 67, 82, 229, 289, 296
Center for Economic and Policy Research (CEPR), 101
Center for Research on Globalization, 85
Center for Strategic and International Studies, 281
Central Africa Republic, 43
Central Romana Corporation, 134
Centrale Autonome Métropolitaine d'Eau Potable (CAMEP), 33
Centre de Recherche et de Formation Économique et Sociale pour la Développement (CRESFED), 8, 35, 307
Centre National des Equipements (CNE), 149, 159-60, 176-8, 198, 202, 211
Centre pour la Libre Enterprise et la Démocratie (CLED), 110
César, Dismy, 62
Chaba Gang, 90
Chamblain, Louis-Jodel, 25-6, 42, 52, 308
Chambre du Commerce et d'Industrie d'Haïti (CCIH), 66, 79, 142
Chancy, Cholzer, 315, 325, 332, 335
Charlegmane, Mano, 322
Charles, Amos, 111
Charles, Carlos Jean, 243
Charles, Destine, 9
Charles, Gervais, 220
Charles, Léon, 47, 64, 84
Charles, Marc Anthony Junior, 256

Chauvet, Ernest, 15

Chauvet, Marie Vieux, 89

Chávez, Hugo, 104, 128, 206; funeral of, 273

Chemonics International, 203; money squandering, 265-6

Chenet, Burton, killing of, 253

Cheramay, Antonio "Don Kato", 80, 314, 318, 332

Chérestal, Jean-Marie, 180

Chérubin, Ginette, 236

Chéry, Cristla, 262, 310-11

Chéry, Nicodéme "Pe Nico", 262, 268-69, 272

Chester, Stanley R., 70

chimere, 32, 53, 56, 61, 67, 325

Choice Hotels, 176

cholera outbreak, 217; aid non-disbursement, 239; death figures, 227; MINUSTAH responsibility, 218, 226

Christian Aid, 133

Christie, Chris, 72

Christophe, Henri, 4-6, 15, 46, 74; suicide, 7

CIA (US Central Intelligence Agency), 26

Cicéron, Johnny, 84

Cicéron, Neroce, 334

Ciné, Franck, 126, 140

Cinergy Telecommunications, 254

Cineus, Elvis, 191

Ciprían, Felipe, 281

Citadel Laferriére, 7

Cité Soleil, 31, 45, 49, 52, 54, 66, 68, 76, 99, 249; armed groups, 33, 53; Bélékou area, 32, 128, 141, 266, 294, 317; BOID raid, 317; Bois-Neuf area, 79; Boston area, 32., 266; Brazilian MINUTO troops in, 249, 326 chimere, 32, 53, 56, 61, 67, 325, 338; Complexe Médico-Sociale, 97; Droulliard section, 316; Jordanian troops in, 77, 101; Konbit Soléy Leve, 215; Lavalas mayor, 233; MINUSTAH-PNH operations, 78,

127, 211; Soleil 19 area, 32; Soleil 21 area, 327; Ti Ayiti section, 141; UNPOL operation, 213

Civil, René, 35, 79, 106, 109, 157, 208, 250, 308, 319, 325; re-arrest, 119

CIVPOL (Civilian Police), 310; UN contingent Haiti, 55, 68

Claude, Marie-Denise, 180

Claude, Sylvio, 180

Clerge, Haryssa Keem, 192

Clérié, Michel, 144, 151

Clinton, Bill, 27, 29, 135, 163, 199, 206-7, 209, 231-2, 244, 248-9; peasant farming destruction role, 273

Clinton Foundation, 245, 247, 249, 272

Clinton Global Initiative, 163, 176, 207, 260

Clinton, Hillary, 163, 177, 207, 226, 230-2, 235, 259, 260, 261

CNN, 187, 206

Coburn, Tom, 213

Coicou, Gessy, 58, 65

Colectif des Notables de Cité Soleil (CONOCS), 65, 67, 211

Collectif Contre l'Impunité, 229, 251, 289

Collier, Paul, 162

Columbus, Hispaniola arrival, 3

Comisión Internacional Contra la Impunidad en Guatemala (CICIG), 343

Commission d'Enquéte, 49

Commission Episcopale Nationale Justice et Paix (JILAP), 119, 125, 211, 262, 301, 310, 328

Commission Independante d'Appui aux Enquetes Relatives aux Assassinats des Journalistes Haitiens (CIAPEAJ), 143, 164, 306

Commission Indépendante d'Evaluation et de Vérification Électorale(CIEVE), 340

Commission Nationale de Désarmement Démantelément et Réinsertion, (CNDDR), 108-9, 124, 148, 167, 254

Commission Nationale des Marchés Publics (CNMP), 160

Comité des Avocats pour le Respect des Libertés Individuelles (CARLI), 52

Compaoré, Blaise, 298

Concannon, Brian, 86, 101, 230

Concern Worldwide (NGO), 169, 269

Conille, Garry, 244-7, 251-3, 257

Conseil des Sages, 47, 52, 84

Conseil Électoral Provisoire (CEP), 30, 60, 95-6, 102-3, 105, 144, 146, 161-2, 177, 180-1, 212-13, 221, 225, 227, 230, 232, 235-6, 261, 263, 270, 272, 278, 285, 292, 299, 304, 307, 309, 313-16, 318, 320-1, 322, 324, 328-30, 332, 339

Conseil Haïtien des Acteurs Non Étatiques (CONHANE), 314, 324, 328

Conseil National d'Observation Électorale (CNO), 212, 224, 314, 324, 328

Conseil National de Gouvernement (CNG), 23-4

Conseil National des Télecommunications (CONATEL), 287-8

Conseil Supérieur du Pouvoir Judiciare, 270

Conseil Superieur de la Police Nationale d'Haïti (CSPN), 42, 116, 294

Consejo Estatal del Azucar, 134

Constant, Bernadin, 288

Constant, Emmanuel "Toto", 26

Convergence Démocratique, 37

Conviction, electoral group, 308

Coordination de l'Aide Externe au Développement (CAED), 278

Coordination des Sociétaires Victimes des Coopératives (CONASOVIC), 36, 271, declaration, 288

Compagnie Haïtienne de Moteurs, 265

"Core Group", 303-4, 324, 338

Coriolan, Anne-Marie, 184

Coriolan, Emmanuel (Dom Laj), 78

Corps d'Intervention et de Maintien de l'Ordre (CIMO), 58, 98, 317, 322

Corvée system, USA restored, 15

Courter, Jim, 70

Creole language, 2, 112, 219, 328, 336, 348

Creole pig, 29; destruction of, 343

Cristalin, Yves, 161, 164, 180, 212

Croix-des-Bouquets prison, 265; prisoner escape, 293

Crowley, P.J., 224, 230

Cuba, 6-7, 60, 103-4, 141-42, 230, 238, 248, 270, 273

Curran, Brian Dean, 37

Da Costa, Luiz Carlos, 142, 145, 183, 192

Da Matta Bacellar, Urano Teixeira, 93, 100

Dabrésil, Yvikel, 271, 284

Damon, Matt, Water.org, 176

Dandin, Marvel, 29, 239

Daniel, Evinx, 281; disappearance of, 282

Daniel, François "Bibi", 143

Dantica, Joseph, 57

Danticat, Edwidge, 57, 129

Daran, Ramy, 35

Darcos, Xavier, 58

Dardompré, Christophe, 252

Dartiguenave, Philippe Sudré, 14, 16

Dauphin, Roland "Black Ronald", 42, 60, 92, 116, 140

Davis, Robert Beale, 13

Delacruz, Francisco, 302

Delahunt, William, 65, 67

Delatour, Calixte, 92

Delatour, Élisabeth Débrousse, 181

Delatour, Leslie, 181

Delatour, Lionel, 110

Délice, Frantz Henry, 276

Délile, Lucmane, 271

Dellums, Ron, 36, 38

Delmas 33, 123

Delpé, Turneb, 264, 267, 291, 304

Delva, Gracia, 234, 314

Delva, Guy, 143, 164, 285, 293, 306

Delva, Réginald, 255, 269, 286

Denis, Paul, 47, 178, 180, 183, 214, 264, 293

Depestre, René, 17, 89

Dérac, Jean Techelet, 200

Deren, Maya, 89
Dérissant, Octanol, 257, 267
Deronceray, Hubert, 184
Desanclos, Jean Simson, 267
Deseme, Willio, 326
Désir, Figaro, 42, 92
Despradel, Consuelo, 135
Desras, Simon Dieuseul, 251, 261-2, 264, 282, 285, 291, 294, 321
Desroches, Rosny, 322-3, 325
Desrosiers, Beckner "Ti Yabout", 59, 90, 99, 143
Dessalines, Casernes, 20, 251
Dessalines, Jean-Jacques, 4-7, 160, 177, 298
Dessources, Farah Natacha Kerbie, 122
Desulmond, Maxime, 37
Deus, Merilus, 30
Development Alternatives Inc, 203
Devla, Zachary, 21
Díaz-Balart, Lincoln, 174
Dienjuste, Arsène, 155
Digicel, 145, 189, 248
Digitek, 69, 254
Diouf, Jacques, 203
Direction Centrale de la Police Judiciaire d'Haïti (DCPJ), 98, 143, 160
Dirección Nacional de Control de Drogas (DNCD), 175-6
displaced people, evictions of, 239
Dixon, Sam, 183
Dlamini-Zuma, Nkosazana, 118
Domi nan Bwa, 33, 143
Dominican Republic, 53, 79, 137, 199, 211, 281; ammunition from, 63; birth of, 7, 129; Haiti earthquake food aid, 188, 195; Haitian expulsions, 133-4, 136, 310; Haitian migrant workers, 129, 132, 135; -Haiti tensions, 167; 1937 pogrom, 17, 132; sugar oligarchy, 134; ultra-nationalists, 305; Universidad Tecnológica de Santiago, 138 USA invasion, 130
Dominique, Jean Léopold, 29, 31, 88, 92, 94, 143, 149, 184, 217, 311; alleged killers,

60; murder of, 49, 89, 112, 119, 164, 244, 270, 275, 284, 306, 308
Dominique, Philippe, 20
Doran, Phélito, 292
Dorcin, Fresner, 302
Doréus, Eloune, 234
Dorfeuille, Ernst Bouquet, 157
Dorléans, Henry, 92
Dorsinivil, Daniel, 286, 292, 295,
Dorsinvil, Gaillot, 177, 225, 235, 250
Dorvil, Yves, killing of, 240
Doyle, Junior (Doy Junior), 292, 295
Dragon, Gilbert, 239
Drouin family, massacre of, 22
drug trafficking, 38-9, 126, 141-2, 145, 157
Duarte, José Napoléon, 75
Duarte, Juan Pablo, 129
Duchemin, Pierre Richard, 102
Duclona, Amaral, 29, 32, 54-5, 62, 76, 80, 99, 101, 124, 127, 141, 145, 175, 215, 266
Duclona. Raymond "Che", 32, 127, 215, 266; killing of, 267
Dudley, Steven, 33
Dumas, Alexandre, 46
Dumas, Pierre André, 82
Dumas, Réginald, 50
Dumas, Thomas-Alexandre, 46
Dumont, Anthony, 150
Dunham, Katherine, 19, 93, 278
Duperval, Jean René, 70, 73
Duperval, Romane, 98
Duplessis, Jerry, 211
Duprat, Yves, 234
Dupuy, Ben, 77, 85
Dupuy, Mario, 92, 256
Durand, Oswald, 88
Duval, Bobby, 228
Duvalier, François, (Papa Doc), 2, 17-18, 20-2, 26, 29, 45, 97, 278, 290, 296; funeral of, 84; 1964 pogrom, 153, 228; prisons of, 21
Duvalier, Jean-Claude, 21-3, 29, 46, 101, 144, 149, 153, 183, 219, 232, 240, 245-6, 268, 274, 283-4, 290, 298, 305, 342;

death of, 296; Léopards battalion, 36; return of, 228-30; reintegration of, 251-2

Duvalier, Simone, 21

Duverger, Yolande, 133

Early, James, 234

earthquake 2010: aid non-dispersed, 195, 210; aid promises, 192, 202; deaths, 183-4, 186, 198; donors conference, 207; farmers ignored, 203; impacts, 190; post disease, 217; prison escape, 213; spontaneous aid, 188

Edmond, Ralph, 170

Édouard, Serge, 39-40

Add entry for:

Efo ak Solidarite pou konstui yon Altenativ Nasyonal Popile (ESKANP), 95, 180

El Azi, Samy, 286

El Roncho Accord, 294

El Salvador, 75

elections: 1957, 20; May 2000, 30; 2005, 60

elections 2010-11: 218, 227; fraud, 222; Lavalas exclusion, 209; run-off violence, 234-5

elections 2015-16: 318; expulsions, 315; independent review, 322; result protests, 320; second round, 317; violence, 314

Elie, Lytz, 184

Elie, Millet Jean "Ti Elie", 122

Elise, Vilaire, 191

elite(s), Haïtian, 174, 177, 202, 219, 240, 259

EnfoFanm, 8, 82, 85

Enock, Lamy, 91

Erilus, Ernst, 90

Espérance, Pierre, 66, 68, 171, 269, 287, 317

Esper, Fahed, 154

Esquenazi, Joel, 72

Esterne, Bruner, 111; murder of, 120

Estimé, Dumarsais, 18-20, 108, 129

Estrella (company), 149

Ethéart, Woodly "Sonson La Familia", 286-7, 307

Etienne, Charles Oscar, 13

Etienne, Darlene, 198

Étienne, Louis "Ti Pa", 96

Etienne, Renan, 98, 105

Étienne, Sauveur Pierre, 202, 308, 318-19

Etienne, Willy, arrest of, 213

European Union, 208, 232; Haiti aid, 140

Eurasina Minerals, 277

Exil, Levoy, 128

Exius, Pierre Francky, 276, 294

Fab, Sandy, 196

Facultédes Sciences Humaines, 168

Fafo Research Foundation, 57

Fanfan, Evel, 301, 328, 330

Fanjul family, 135; Alfonso, 134; Pepe, 134

Fanmi Lavalas, 27, 30, 44, 181, 283, 293, 314, 338; see also Lavalas

Fanon, Frantz, 89

Fareau, Leslie, 62

Farmatrix, 170

Faveur, Jean Robert, 36

Félix, Jean Délouis, 145

Fénel, Mercius "Ti Wilson", 157

Féquière, Patrick, 102

Ferdinand, Anna, 93

Fernández, Leonel, 131-3, 135, 137-8, 166, 209, 211, 233, 237, 256, 281

Fernández Mariano, 240, 268

Feuillé, Jean-Hubert, 28

Feuillé, Yvon, 55, 62, 81, 85, 109, 157, 276

Févry, Osner, 246

Fiaz, Juan, 73

Fignolé, Daniel, 18-19, 45

Fils-Aimé, Alix, 108, 148, 229, 284, 301

Feuillé, Fritzner, 118

Firmin, Anténor, 11, 88

Fisher, Alice, 70, 72

Fleurant, Louisiane Saint, 89

Florestal brothers, 299; Enold, 279

Florida International University, 132, 175, 300

Foley, James, 43, 47, 109
Fondasyon Kole Zépól, 109
Fondasyon Konesans Ak Libéte (FOKAL), 41, 153, 167, 278
Fonds-Verrettes, 1
Food for the Poor, 240
Forces Armées d'Haïti (FADH), 15, 22-4, 26, 29, 52, 63, 120, 143, 257, 271, 288, 334
Forst, Michel, 275
Fort Dimanche Duvalier prison, 21; horrors of, 296
Fort National area, 65, 67
Fortin, Jean Denis, 242
Fortuné, Gabriel, 28, 125-6, 140, 145, 148, 150-1, 214, 263, 298
Fortuné, Lenord "Azor", 128
Fos Lakay-Majik kleng, 327
Fos Patriyotik pou Respe Konstitisyon (FOPARK), 267, 282, 285, 291
Fourcand, Hervé, 308, 314
Fourcand, Jean, 73
François, Guy, 120
François, Hérold Jean, 242
François, Lafortune "kadafi", release of, 145
François, Lavaud, 141
François, Mackendy "Ti Kenken", 256, 262, 286, 292, 295
François, Michel, 26
François, Nixon, 42
François, Patrick, release of, 145
François, Rotchild, 240, 304, 313, 316
François, Saurel, 180
France, 12-13, 175; Haïti debt cancellation, 202
Francillon, Carl Rubens, kidnapping and killing of, 121-2
Francous, Tony, Antonelly, 315
Frankétienne, 89
Frisch, Max, 342
Front de Résistance pour la Libération et la Reconstruction Nationale (FLRN), 42
Front de Résistance des Gonaïves, 41
Front National pour le Changement et la Démocratie (FNCD), 25

Front pour l'Avancement et le Progrès Haïtien (FRAPH), 26, 35, 52, 233, 308
Front pour la Reconstruction Nationale (FRN), 63, 93
Fuller, Anne, 43
Fundación Global Deomocracia y Desarallo, 134
Fusion des Sociaux-Democrates Haïtiens (Fusion), 60 105, 123, 144-5, 148, 173, 180, 213-14, 266, 280, 284, 287, 298, 301, 303, 307, 308, 309, 313, 314, 315, 323; HQ attacked, 304
Fusion Telecom, 71, 72
FXB International, 211

Gabriel, Frantz, 44
Gaddafi, Muammar, 85
Gaillard, Micha, 8, 48, 105, 164, 183
Gamarra, Eduardo, 133
"Gang Galil", 286, 307
Garcia, Marcus, 29, 276
Garcia-Navarro, Lourdes, 56
Gareau, Léonidas, 269
Garry, Jean, 257
Gaspard, Maxo, 318, 324
Gassant, Claudy, 31, 119, 125, 140, 142-5, 148-9, 154, 159, 286-7, 301
Gaudin, Lavarice, 212
Gauthier, Claudel, 252
Gédéon, Michel-Ange, 262, 340
Génélus, Nathaél, 91
Georges, Frantz, 154
Georges, Reynold, 246, 284
Germán Mejía, Mariano, 281
Germain, Gérald, 230
Germany, 12
Gilles, Louis Gérald, 62-3, 85, 109, 161, 263, 291, 308, 323; arrest of, 55
Gilles, Kenol St, 42
Gilles, Serge, 60
Gilmore, Jim, 70
Gilot, Rony, 121, 149
Glencree Centre for Peace and Reconciliation, 169

Global Voice Group, 220, 259

Glover, Danny, 234

Godefroy, Régine, 275

Gonaïves, 5, 50, 146; December 2001 violence, 40; mass demonstrations, 41; New Year messages, 226; 2008 hurricane, 155

Gonsalves, Ralph, 50

Goodman, Amy, 44, 81, 234

Gorton, Slade, 70

Gourgue, Gérard, 24

Gousse, Bernard, 48, 55-6, 61, 63, 92, 241-2

Grand Ravine: gangs, 97, 99, 110-12, 120, 122-23, 126, 256, 262, 274, 286, 292, 295, 311-12, 321

Grande Riviére du Nord, 88

Grande-Saline, water committee, 299, 300

Granderson, Colin, 222, 224

griots, 17

Groupe 77, 267

Groupe d'Appui aux Rapatriés et Réfugiés (GARR), 8, 82, 134, 203

Groupe de Bourdon, 177

Groupe de Travail sur la Compétitivité, 169

Groupe de Recherche et d'Appui au Milieu Rural (GRAMIR), 155

Groupe Haitien d'Etude du Sarcome de Kaposi et des Infections Opportunistes (GHESKIO), 199

Groupement Solidarité, 218

Grupo M, 51

Grupo SID, 137

G7, 199

G8, 319-21, 323, 330-32, 335, 338

Guantanamo Bay Naval Base, Cuba, 142

Guatemala, UN mission, 152

Gué, Jonas, 203, 210

Guendo, Adama, 47

Guistra, Frank, 209

Gumbleton, Thomas, 245

Gustave, Leslie, 62

Habitat for Humanity, 176

Hadden, Gerry, 33

Haïtel, 126

Haiti: Banque Nationale de Crédit, 160; black-mulatto tension, 11 calorie intake deficit, 155; Caribbean Cup victory, 126; CARICOM readmission, 108; Chamber of Commerece, 329; corruption tradition, 159, 160; debt write-offs, 174, 206, 208; Declaration of Independence, 5; deforestation, 156; Democratic Republic tensions, 167; Economic Lift Program (HELP) Act, 208; farmers forcible expulsion, 283; food insecurity, 278, 337; foreign aid withdrawn, 31; France indemnity payments, 7; G7 debt erasure, 199; gendarmerie, see FADH; gold, 260; Jesuit Refugee Service, 210; literature of, 89; living costs rise, 150; minimum wage campaign, 166-8, 172, 175; national identity cards, 75; Parliament dysfunctionality accusation, 303; peasantry free trade devastated, 163, 273; post-earthquake media stereotyping, 205-6; Red Cross, 59, 186, 192; rice harvest, 278; Rights Vision, 87; Senate, 118, 261; State University attack on, 41, 98; Supreme Court, 331; tourism, 277; trade deficit, 312; UNIBANK, 91; US Embassy, 43; US aid suspension call, 226; US occupation, 8, 14, 16, 88; USA embargo, 27

Haitian Hemispheric Opportunity through Partnership, 163

Haitian-American Chamber of Commerce, 37, 55, 100

Haitian-American Convention, 14

Hallward, Peter, 87-8

Handal, Stanley, 91

Harper, Stephen, 106

Harrison, Lawrence, 204

Hartley, Christopher, 135-6

Hériveaux, Rudy, 55, 62, 85, 96, 109, 126-7, 151, 161, 178-9, 250, 285, 287

Henry, Ariel, 47
Hercule, Jean Ostricht, 149
Hernández, Javier, 74
Hertz Cayo, Jean Richard, killing of, 274
Heurtelou, Lucienne, 108
Hillien, Marc Elie Saint, 119
Honorat, Georges, 275
Honoré, Georges, 118
Honoré, Sandra, 279, 302, 307
Human Rights Watch, 43, 116, 204
Hurbon, Laénnec, 8, 175, 289
hurricanes: Jeanne, 50, 56; Matthew, 340; 2008, 154, 155
Hurston, Zora Neale, 89
Hutson, Royce A., 86

Ibero-American Summit, 268
IDT company, 70-2
IJDH, 86, 101, 140, 230, 271/ BAI, 204
Ílende la Tortue, 259
IMF (International Monetary Fund), 174, 197
impunity, 159, 165, 251, 255, 257,290, 296, 300, 330, 340; consequences of, 335; culture of, 296; "trivialization" of, 304
Indiana University, Centre for Philanthropy, 206
Inevil, Alphonse, 70
inflation, 272
INITE, 211, 214, 220-1, 223-5, 232, 234, 236, 242, 245, 252, 256, 259, 293, 301, 303, 307, 315-16, 325; armed supporters, 222; executive board, 230; / Lavalas parliament bloc, 241; weapons allegations, 218
Initiative Citoyenne, 264
Inter-American Commission on Human Rights (IACHR), 137, 149
Inter-American Convention against Corruption, 240
Inter-American Court of Human Rights, 132, 137

Inter-American Development Bank, (IADB), 106, 149, 152, 174, 202, 206, 210, 232
Interim Haiti Recovery Commission (IHRC), 206, 209, 214, 244; creation of, 207; mandate expired, 251
International Organization for Migration (IOM), 94, 109, 199, 245
International Republican Institute (IRI), USA, 37
Isaac, Harold, 197
Israel Defence Forces, 192
Ivers, Louise, 186
Izméry, Antoine, 45, 52, 245

Jacinthe, Sorel, 225, 237, 242, 248, 250, 253, 264
Jackson, Christly, 326
Jacmel, 2, 7, 39, 46-7, 49, 55, 63, 77, 96, 144, 173, 223, 241, 290, 313; kidnappings, 265; 2010 earthquake, 182, 186
Jacques, Pierre Eric Jean, 151
Jamaica, 43; Tacky's Rebellion 1760, 6
Jean, Abdias, 61
Jean, Carvés, 251
Jean, Jean Claude, DR killing of, 305
Jean, Fritz, 339
Jean, Gédéon, 323
Jean,Jude, 116
Jean, Judnel, 123
Jean, Oriel, 31, 34, 39, 49, 119, 284-5, 306
Jean, Rosemond, 36
Jean-Baptiste, Chavannes, 8, 25, 30, 31, 155-156, 165, `80, 212, 218, 308
Jean-Baptiste, Dieugrand, 31
Jean-Baptiste, Eric, 319
Jean-Baptiste, Jean-Claude, 36, 92
Jean-Baptiste, Jean Willy, 261
Jean-Baptiste, Joseph, 63
Jean-Baptiste, M'Zounaya Bellange, 274, 308
Jean-Baptiste, Renaud, 280
Jean-Bart, Winston "Tupac", 32, 34, 53; muder of, 54; funeral, 55

Jean-Charles, Enex, 339; kidnapping of, 165

Jean-Charles, Moïse, 74, 95, 161, 166, 173, 212, 214, 230, 239, 241, 246, 248, 250, 252-3, 260-1, 263, 271, 276, 280, 282-3, 287, 291, 293-5, 299, 301, 303, 308, 318-20, 325, 328, 338-40

Jean-Daniel, Jeudi "Guimy", 31, 49, 60, 284

Jean-Jacques, Eric, 106

Jean-Juste, Gérard, 56, 58, 62, 80-2, 99; funeral, 168

Jean-Louis, Wladimir, 317

Jean-Marie, Marie Carmelle, 275

Jean-Philippe, Jean Baptiste "Samba Boukman", 109, 254, 275

Jean-Pierre, Gabriel, 294

Jean-Rabel: peasant conference, 93 1987 peasant massacre, 210, 295

Jeanty, Jean William, 173, 208, 263, 294, 302

Jeudilien, Joseph, 270

Jeudy, Lesly, 196

Jeudy, Wilson, 203, 239

Jeune Haiti, 21

Jeune, Evens "Ti Kouto", 32, 61-2, 99, 117, 124, 127-28, 141

Jeune, Chevanne, 180

Jeune, Marie-Christine, 28

Jeunesse Pouvoir Populaire, 35

Jevousaime, Marcelin, 274

Jewett, D. Michael, 70-2

Joachim, Nicolson, 327

Joanis, Jackson, 52

Joazile, Jean Rodolphe, 173, 237, 248, 250, 256

Jocelin, Rousse, 98

Jocelyn, Destine, 112

Joinet, Louis, 91, 139-40

Jolicoeur, Aubelin, 59

Jonas, Howard, 70

Joseph, Alby, murder conviction, 143

Joseph, Alix, 141

Joseph, Emanuel, 189

Joseph, François Anick, 263

Joseph, Fred, 121

Joseph, Fritz, 35, 41, 233

Joseph, Jacceus, 318, 322

Joseph, Jean-Serge, death of, 279

Joseph, Jinel, 98

Joseph, John Joël, 166, 173, 212, 214, 230, 241, 252-3, 261, 275, 294

Joseph, Leroy, 42

Joseph, Luc-Eucher, 110, 124, 126, 143

Joseph, Marie Renée, earthquake death, 183

Joseph, Mario, 86, 118-19, 140, 267, 271, 293

Joseph, Néhémy, 316

Joseph, Pastor Enoch, 67-8

Joseph, Patrick, 73-4, 245, 254

Joseph, Ronique, 233

Joseph, Sandro, arrest, 164

Joseph, Vernel, killing of, 73-4, 254

Joseph, Wesley, 289

Joseph, Willot, 31, 218, 221-2, 308, 314, 318

Joseph, Yves Germain, 339

Jude, Paul Fernaud, 267

Jules, Clunie Pierre, 78, 92

Julien, Marie, 111

Jumelle, Clément, 45

Juppé, Alain, 237

Jura, Lucien, 305

Juste, Farah, 250

Kadalie, Rhoda, 50

Kay Fanm, 184, 229

Keane, Katherine, 234

Keen, General Ken, 185

Kemp, Jack, 70

Kennedy, Joseph P. II, 38, 71

Kernisant, Rudy, 143

Ketant, Beaudoin "Jacques", 38

Khodabande, Bahare, 327-28

Killick, Hammerton, 12

Kim Jong-il, 85

Kipman, Igor, 223

Kirkpatrick, Jeane, 70

Klein, Naomi, 87

Kòdinasyon Rezistans Grandans (KOREGA), 95
Kolbe, Athena R. (Lynn Duff), 86-7
Komisyon Fanm Viktim pou Viktim (KOFAVIV), 204
Komité National du Kongrès des Mouvements Démocratiques (KONAKOM), 25, 60
Komité Zafé Elektoral Peyizan pou Eleksyon Pwop (KOZEPEP), 30, 95, 306
Konbit Soléy Leve, 215, 267, 326
konbit, communal work system, 9; Cité Soleil tried, 215
konpa music, 2, 116, 156, 171, 179, 219, 243, 290 332
Kontrapépla, 284, 301, 303, 308
Konvansyon Inite Demokratik(KID), 25, 180, 308, 325; party, 279
Kouchner, Benard, 176
Kovac, Ana, 103
Krome Detention Centrer, Miami Airport, 57
Kucinich, Dennis, 65, 67
Kundera, Milan, 341
Kurtz, Kenneth, 44
Kurzban, Ira, 36, 69, 86, 230, 233-4, 271, 293, 333

La Fondation Héritage pour Haiti (LFHH), 126, 140, 178, 243
La Ruché, 17
La Saline, 45, 55, 167; gang, 148
La Sciere massacre, 42-3, 91-2, 116, 139, 170-1, 212, 325, 338; survivors, 49
La Trinitaria, 129
Labanye, see Thomas, Robinson
Lafanmi Selavi children's home, 33, 69, 87, 270
Lafontant, Roger, 22, 251
Lahens, Philippe, 69
Laïné, Accelesse, 167
Lakou Lapé, 269, 311, 322
Lalanne, Rodrique, assault on, 282

Laleau, Wilson, 322
Lambert brothers, 241, 314; Joseph, 96, 106, 110, 117, 144, 146, 148, 157, 166, 173, 177-78, 180, 211, 214, 224, 236, 247, 252-54, 259, 264, 269, 279-80; Wencesclas, 173, 286, 293
Lambert, Pierre, 144
Lambert, Raymond, 173
Lame Dómi Nan Bwa militia, 221
Lame Ti Manchét, 94, 112, 123, 127, 143
Lamothe, Laurent, 220, 247, 250, 253, 255-7, 259, 264-5, 273, 277-9, 285, 287, 291-2, 294, 300, 302, 305, 309, 312; resignation of, 299, 301
Langlois, Cardinal Chibly, 285, 287, 307
Laraque, Yvondrouin, Louis, 22
Laréche, Girldy, 286, 292
Large, Frantz, 102, 191
Latham & Watkins, 71, 72
Latibonit Ann Aksyon party (LAA), 105 61, 92, 214, 315
Latortue, Gérard, 47-51, 82, 92, 103-4
Latortue, Youri, 48, 51-2, 59, 61-2, 105, 118, 126-7, 141, 144, 146, 149-51, 155, 179, 223, 280, 308, 325, 331-2; accusations against, 119
Latour, François, killing of, 141
Laurent, Marguerite, 85
Lauture, Claude Bernard, 176
Lavalas, 31, 47-9, 55, 63, 75, 81, 84, 96, 105, 110, 121, 146, 157, 161, 166, 177-8, 180, 209, 212, 249, 255, 263, 276, 285, 287, 291, 301-2, 307, 308-9, 315, 319, 322-3, 327; activists killed, 295, factions, 62, 143; split in, 161
Lavelanet, Lesly, 69, 254
Lavni, 234
Le Chevallier, Gérard, 75-6, 175; earthquake death, 183
Le Matin, 51, 80, 103, 142, 150
Le Moniteur, 285
Le Nouvelliste, 15, 59, 165, 301-2, 328
Léger, Félix, 247-8
Léger, Gilbert, 91

Lény, Fredd'Herck, 108
Léogâne, 194; earthquake effects, 182, 186, 192-3
Leahy, Patrick, 208, 226
Leblanc, Camille, 209, 271, 309
Leclerc, Charles, 5
Leconte, Cincinnatus, 12
Lee, Barbara, 65, 67
Leger, Nathan, 194
Léger, Pierre, 122, 150
Leonard, Hermione, 34, 39, 49
Lerer, Jack, 71
Les Cayes, 11; demonstration killings, 150; election intimidation, 222; general strike, 263; prison killings, 208
Lescot, Élie, 18-20; overthrow, 17
Lespwa, political platform, 95-6, 101, 103, 105-6, 119, 144, 148, 161, 165, 173, 177-8, 181, 184, 259
Leth, Asger, 33
Lewinsky, Monica, 135
Lewis, Arthur, 205
Libérus, Mirlande, 62, 271, 284-85, 306
Ligonde, François-Wolff, 25
Ligouri, Chiara, 333
Ligue Alternative pour le Progrès et l'Émancipation Haïtienne (LAPEH), 234, 309, 316-20
Ligue Haïtienne des Droits Humains, 24
Limonade, 161, 211; electricity, 300
Lindor, Brignol, 33, 92, 221; murder of, 143
López Rodríguez, Nicolas de Jesús Cardenal, 136
Lochard, Carlo, 47, 94, 98, 105, 112, 184
Lochard, Jean-René, 280
"looting", earthquake stereotypes, 206
Lorquet, Jojo, 331
Louidor, Shiller, 308
Louis, Armand, 325
Louis, Clunie Pierre, 64
Louis, Pére Jean Pierre, 153
Louis, Phozer, 327
Louis, Renan Jean, 59

Louis, Sedwán, 134
Louis-Jeune, Levaillant, 164, 180, 225, 251, 280
Louissant, Jean-Claude, 164, 284
Louverture, Toussaint, 4-6, 283
Lowry, Malcolm, 89
Luc, Wench, 62
Lucien, Jean Nesly, 36, 39
Lucius, Michael, 98, 108, 120, 144
Lugar, Richard, 209
Lula da Silva, Luiz Inácio, 46
Lumarque, Jackie, 309, 316
Lusk, Ron, 92
Lustin Junior, Murray, 184
Lynch, Marika, 43

MacKenzie, Dread, 59
Madiou, Thomas, 88
Madistin, Samuel, 78, 139, 267, 308, 319, 321
Magaña, Alvaro, 75
Magloire, Danielle, 47, 251
Magloire, Nicole, 229
Magloire, Paul, 19, 32
Magloire, René, 139, 143, 154
Malary, Guy, 45
Malpasse boder zone, 257
Malraux, André, 89
Man Medya Pou Akyson Kominoté, 63
Mangonés, Lorraine, 278
Manigat, Leslie, 24, 47, 96, 97, 146, 213, 246
Manigat, Mirlande, 102-4, 146, 200, 212-14, 218, 220-6, 231-5, 246, 256, 267, 280, 291, 315, 325, 330
Manuel, Robert "Bob", 30, 95-6, 152-3,
Manus, Leon, 30
Marcadieu, Luther King, 152
Marcelin, Frédéric, 12
Marcelin, Magalie, 184
Marcelin, Pierre, 45
Marcello, Robert, 160-1, 176; disappearance of, 165
Marcello, Rose, 160

Marcellus, Camille, 36, 41, 90
Marcellus, Nawoon, 36, 75, 79, 118, 161-62, 222, 308, 314, 318
Marchaterre, US killings 1929, 16
Marclein, Marie Nic, 143
Markington, Philippe, 285
Marriott Hotels brand, 248
Mars, Jean-Price, 129, 312
Mars, Louis-Henri, 169-70, 269, 311-12
Martelly, Michel("Sweet Micky"/Tét Kale), 128, 171, 212, 219-24, 231, 232, 233, 235, 237, 239-44, 246-7, 249, 250, 251, 252-3, 255, 261-3, 267, 268, 269-71, 275, 277-8, 280-1, 289, 291, 293-4, 298, 300-5, 307, 309, 312, 314, 317, 319-20, 322, 324-5, 328-32, 334-40, 343; advisory council, 299; anti-gay slogans at, 292; demonstrations against, 264; erratic behaviour, 316; inauguration, 257; -Lamothe government, 258; new military plans, 321; reforestation project, 273; resignation calls, 283-4
Martelly, Olivier, 279, 312
Martelly, Sophia, 240, 274, 279, 308
Martial, Beneche, 172
Martissant, 93, 97, 99, 111, 113, 115, 123, 125-6, 150, 233, 262; Baz Pilate gang, 109; Cité l'Eternal area, 167; Descartes quarter, 143; football killings, 98, 105; gangs, 274; massacre, 120
Marx, Gary, 43
Mathelier, Jacques, 157, 161
Mathurin, Max, 105, 123, 144, 146, 292
Mattar, Julien, 191
Mayard, Max, killing of, 28
Mayard-Paul, Constantin, 220
Mayard-Paul, Gregory, 219
Mayard-Paul, Thierry, 164, 219, 247-8, 253, 256
Mayette, Amanus, 32, 42, 64, 92, 118, 161; freeing of, 139
Mbeki, Thabo, 43. 49-50, 116
McClelland, Mac, 205-6
McLarty, Thomas 'Mack', 71

Médecins sans Frontière (MSF), 76, 110, 187, 203-4, 218, 225; Carrefour, 191; Cité Soleil hospital, 59
Medika, Mamba, 210
Medina, Danilo, 281
Médina, Jean-Paul, 77
Méndez, Noemí, 135
Méril, Jean Clédor, 120
Mérilus, Carlo, Santo Domingo beheading, 166
Métayer, Amiot 'Cubaine', 32, 34, 40
Métayer, Buteur, 41, 56, 58, 77-8
Métayer, Pére Arnal, 43
Métro Sécurité, 154
Meek, Kendrick, 174
Mejía, Hipólito, 132
Mengual, Yolette, 330
Mercier, Isidore, 150
Mercier, Jean-Richard, 35
Merlet, Myriam, 184
Merten, Kenneth H., 175, 182, 185, 200, 222-3, 230-1, 244, 253, 315, 331
Messdaieu, Luc, 35
Mevs family, 176
Miami, 272; Federal Detention Centre, 39
Michel, André, 267, 275, 282, 319
Michel, Riquet, 183
Michelet, Louis, 184
Milfirt, Ann Valerie Timothee, 241
Miller, Zoriah, 205-6
Millien, Dymsley "Ti Lou", 31, 49, 60, 94, 112, 284, 311
Mills, Cheryl, 231, 261
MINUSTAH (Mission des Nations Unies pour la Stabilisation en Haiti), 47, 49, 52-3, 56-8, 61, 63-4, 66, 68, 74-7, 79, 81, 90, 93, 96, 99-101, 108-9, 113-14, 118, 120-5, 127-8, 138, 142-4, 150, 155-7, 165, 167-9, 175, 177, 186, 189, 192, 197, 200, 204, 246, 264, 268, 279, 289, 291, 302, 307, 309-10; attacks on, 223; Brazilian troops, 240; Canadian troops, 299; cholera outbreak responsibility, 217, 226, 239; departure demands, 328; mandate

extensions, 78, 176, 214, 298; hostility to, 243; HQ earthquake collapse, 182; Martissant operations, 126; Petit-Goave base attacked, 151; reputation deterioration, 245

Miot, Serge, 183, 197, 200

Môle Saint Nicolas, 295, 296

Mobilisation pour le Progrés de Haïti, 212

Moïse, Claude, 103

Moïse, Jovenel, 308, 317-21, 323, 328, 333-4, 337-8, 340; 2017 inauguration, 341

Moliere, Dickinson, 189

Momplaisir, René, 212, 230

Monfrére, Ducken "Ti Blan", 304

Monsanto, GM maize seeds donation move protests, 210

Montas, Michéle, 29, 31, 83, 229, 284

Moreno, Luis, 43-4

Morette, Lucknel, 288

Morin, Jean Wilner, 274

Moscoso, Michael "Didi", 191

Mourra, Samir, 96, 212

Mourral, Paul-Henri, 76, 99, 176

Mouvement Chrétien pour une Nouvelle Haïti (MOCHRENA), 30, 35, 101, 166

Mouvement Patriotique de l'Opposition Démocratique (MOPOD), 267, 280, 282-3, 285, 287, 291, 303-4, 307-8

Mouvement de Liberté, d'Egalité des Haïtiens et de la Fraternité, 291

Mouvement de Revendications des Paysans de l'Artibonite (MOREPLA), 93

Mouvement des Ouvriers et Paysans (MOP), 18-19

Mouvement pour la Reconstruction Nationale (MRN), 56

Mouvement pour l'Instauration de la Democratie en Haiti (MIDH), 25, 62

Mouvman Gran Béle, 282

Mouvman Peyizan Nasyonal Kongre Papay (MPNKP), 8, 155, 179

Mouvman Peyizan Papay (MPP), 8, 155, 198, 212

El Movimiento de Mujeres Dominico-Haitianas (MUDHA), 136

Mulet, Edmond, 108, 112-13, 116, 124-5, 128, 142, 144, 169, 197, 199, 207-8, 218, 222-4, 240

Mulrean, Peter, 315

Mulus, Pierre Richard, 145

Muselier, Renaud, 52

Myrthil, Nanoune, 35, 49

Najman, Charles, 33

Namphy, Henri, 23-4; overthrow of, 25

Narcisse, Marc Ariel, 171

Narcisse, Maryse, 161-2, 180, 200, 208, 250, 282-3, 285, 293, 301, 308, 316, 318-19, 323, 340

NATCOM, 277

National Coalition for Haitian Rights (NCHR), 43, 47, 52, 85

National Credit Bank, Haiti, 225

National Democratic Institute (NDI), USA, 37, 75

National Public Radio, 56

Nau, Jacky, 239

négritude, 17, 88

Nelfort, Renél, "Le Recif", 286, 307

Nelson, Jean Lipléte, killing of, 253

Nelson, Roro, 245, 331

Neptune, Marilise, 184

Neptune, Mireille, 184

Neptune Olivier, 184

Neptune, Yvon, 31, 42, 44, 49, 60, 64-5, 67, 91-2, 106, 116, 161, 180, 212-13, 223

Nerée, Pastor Luc, 23

Newlink, 132

Newmont Mining, 260, 277

Nicolas, Augudson "General Toutou", 59, 93, 105

Noël, Jean Yves, 149

Noel André Jean, 123

noirisme, 17, 20

Nordberg, Jenny, 87

Noriega, Roger, 78

Normandin, Paul, 279

Novaes Miranda, André Luis, 93
Numa, Marcel, 22
Numa Valéry, 143

O'Neil, Daniel, 188
Obama, Barak, 187, 204, 208, 211, 233
Obin, Philomé, 190
Observatoire Citoyen pour
    l'Institutionnalisation de la Démocratie
    (OCID), 318, 328-9
Occénat, Zacharie (Barthold), 213
Occilius, Johnny, 35
Octave Cayard mutiny, 84
Odigé, Biron, 42, 92, 298-99
Office National d'Assurance-vieillesse
    (ONA), 164
Opération Pa Ka Tan-n, 121
Operation Baghdad, 56, 62, 82, 90, 103,
    121, 167, 169, 241-2
Operation Thunder, 79
Operation Uphold Democracy,
    US-launched, 27
Opont, Pierre-Louis, 146, 209, 304, 307,
    315, 318, 321, 324, 330, 332
Orcel, Emmanuel, 251
Orélus, Godson, 262, 301
Óganizasyon Politik Lavalas (OPL), 27,
    47, 105, 166, 173, 178, 180, 280, 284, 301,
    307-9
Organisme de Developpement de
    l'Artibonite (ODVA), 177, 221
Organization of American States
    (OAS), 40, 91, 99, 208, 222-3, 293,
    315; -CARICOM election observers,
    213, 224, 236 election observers, 226;
    election fraud conclusions 2010-11, 227;
    Haiti observer missions, 332, 335 , 91,
    99, 208, 222-3, 293, 315; election fraud
    conclusions 2010-11, 227
Oxygéne, David, 291

Pan American Development Foundation
    (PADF), 177, 188
Pandor, Naledi, 125

Parlementaires pour la Stabilité et le
    Progés, 284
Parsley Massacre, 133
Parti Haitien Tét Kale (PHTK), 262,
    307-8, 312-15, 317-19, 321, 325, 331-3, 337,
    339
Parti Communiste Haïtien (PCH), 16, 18
Parti de la Rénovation Nationale (PRN),
    288
Parti Démocrate-Chrétien Haïtien
    (PDCH), 30
Parti Louvri Baryé (PLB), 95
Parti National Démocratique Progressiste
    d'Haiti (PNDPH), 264, 267
Parti Nationaliste Progressiste et
    Révolutionnaire Haïtien (PANPRA), 60
Parti Populaire National (PPN), 77, 85,
    275
Parti Unité Nationale (PUN), 144, 290
Partido de la Liberación (PLD), 131-2, 281
Partido Reformista Social Cristiano
    (PRSC), 130
Partido Revolucionario Dominicano
    (PRD), 130-1
Partners in Health, 186
Pascak-Trouillot, Ertha, 25
Pascal, Anthony (Konpé Filo), 29, 322
Pasquet, Alix, 20, 23
Patterson, P.J., 43, 50
Paul, Dieuseul, 59, 89
Paul, Evans, 25, 27, 62, 96, 105, 118, 264,
    279, 284, 302, 304, 308, 313, 322-3, 329,
    332, 335, 339
Paul, Odonel, 40, 41
Pax Christi, 245
PDNA, reconstruction plan, 206
Pénitencier National, 57, 119, 122, 142, 164,
    184; attack on, 60; conditions, 144; 2005
    jailbreak, 116
Peck, Raoul, 58, 89
Peintures Caraïbes, 300
Peña Gómez, José Francisco, 131
Penn, Roudy Stanley, 324
Perpignan, Henri, 20

Péralte, Charlemagne, 15-16, 217
Péralte family, 13
Pérez Paul, Judge Jean, 91, 99, 105
Pérez, Antonio, 73
Pétion, Alexandre, 3-7, 298
Pétionville, 20-1, 45, 119, 154, 168, 172, 242;
    earthquake 2010 effects, 189; prison,
    49; school collapse deaths, 156; 2016
    demonstrations, 329
peasant conferences, foreign press ignored,
    210
Petit, Jonas, 62, 92
Petit-Frere, James, 32, 53-4, 60, 169
Petit-Goâve, 194; earthquake deaths, 186;
    police station, 61; 2010 earthquake, 182;
    UDMO forces killing, 294
PetroCaribe, 104, 107, 128, 260, 273, 339;
    Haiti projects, 305
Phebé, Marc Arthur, 265
Phelps, Anthony, 89
Philippe, Guy, 35, 37, 42, 56, 60, 63, 93,
    96, 142, 148, 150, 161, 165, 239, 242, 255,
    308, 318, 331; extradition of, 341
Philippe, Jean Reynold, 275
Philocrète, René, 129
Piera, Nuria, 256
Pierre, Monique (Antoine)), 157
Pierre, Avile, 111
Pierre, Belony, 124, 128
Pierre, Ericq, 152, 227, 249
Pierre, Gotson, 181, 233, 307
Pierre, Joceline, killing of, 301
Pierre, Ricard, 166, 173
Pierre, Rodol, 146, 173
Pierre, Sonia, 136, 137; death of, 250
Pierre, Wesley Jimmy, 196
Pierre, Wilkens "Chien Chaud", 111-12, 122
Pierre, Worky, 139
Pierre-Antoine, Lovinsky, 109, 118,
    disappearance of, 143
Pierre-Charles, Gérard, 8, 27, 35, 47
Pierre-Louis, Johnny "Ti Bazil", 127
Pierre-Louis, Josué, 244, 247-8, 262-3,
    272, 304; rape accusation, 270

Pierre-Louis, Michéle, 153-5, 158-9, 163,
    164, 167, 173-4, 177-80, 194, 278
Pierre-Louis, Pére Jean, 30
Pierre-Paul, Liliane, 29, 168, 197, 282,
    331, 333
Pinochet, Augusto, 47
Pitit Desalin, 303-4, 307-9, 314, 318-19,
    323-4, 330, 338; Delmas HQ, 306;
    Platfòm, 301
Plaine du Nord, 4, 280
Plaisance, 280
Platforme des Organisations Haïtiennes
    de Défense des Droits Humains
    (POHDH), 52, 64, 262, 286, 292,
    295, 328
Plate-forme des Secteurs Motives pour
    l'Avancement de Grand Ravine
    (PLASMAGRA), 327
Plateforme Haïtienne de Plaidoyer pour
    un Développement Alternatif (PAPDA),
    8, 51, 82, 99, 145
Plate-forme Nationale des Organisations
    Paysannes Haïtiens(PLANOPA), 93, 309
Platinum Sound, 211
Plum, Marc, earthquake death, 183
Police Nationale d'Haïti (PNH), 28, 36,
    38, 47, 49, 51, 56-8, 61, 68, 76, 78, 82, 85,
    90, 92, 98, 106, 112-13, 116, 120-1, 128,
    138, 143, 150, 156-7, 167, 193, 195, 208,
    213, 228, 235, 247, 257, 266, 269, 301,
    309, 321, 340-1; apolitical development,
    262; BLTS, 148; Brigade d'Intervention
    Rapide, 38; Dragon 2 operation, 254;
    purge announcement, 124; officers
    killed, 249; 20th anniversary, 141; Unité
    Départmentale d'Ordre (UDMO), 262
Polycarpe, Wesner, 294, 315
Polynice, Edmond, 13
Polyte, Dional, killing of, 242
Pompée, Pierre, 241
Port-au-Prince, 2, 15, 47, 57; police killed
    2012, 256; 1770 earthquake, 3; 2010
    earthquake, 182; US Embassy, 303;
    Wharf Jérémie area, 264

Post Chabert, USA plantation complex, 15
Post Disaster Needs Assessment (PDNA), 204
Poujol Oriol, Paulette, 89
Power, Samantha, 294
Pradel, Rosemond, 144
Pras Michel, 235
Prélus, Godson, 340
Pressoir, Cyril, 190
Présengloir, Deshommeboul, 118
Préval, René, 25-6, 28-31, 35, 48, 66, 68, 95-7, 100-04, 107, 110, 113-14, 116, 118, 121, 123-5, 128, 132-3, 138-40, 142-3, 147, 148-51, 154, 156, 158-60, 163-6, 168-9, 173, 177-9, 180-3, 185-6, 197, 200-2, 204, 206-9, 211-13, 218, 220-7, 229-33, 235-8, 246, 248-9, 255, 262, 271, 282, 298, 301, 306-7, 309-10, 325, 339; CEP dissolution, 146; death of, 341; Marmelade burial, 342; 'self-marassa', 152; 2006 inauguration, 106, 108
Previllon, Yonel, 337
Price-Mars, Jean, 17, 88, 169;
Prío Socarrás, Carlos, 238
Privert, Jocelerme, 34, 49, 60, 64-5, 67, 92, 116, 161, 332-3, 325, 335-6, 338-41
Program for the Eradication of Porcine Swine Fever and Development of Pig-Raising (PEPADEP), 23
Prophète, Hilaire, 121
Pryam, Riccardo "Kiki", 157
Pugliese, Vicenzo, 218

Quigley, Bill, 81
Quisqueya Store, 69
Quisqueya University, 192

Rabb, Clinton, 183
Raboteau: slum, 32, 41; trial 2000, 86
racism, US in Haiti, 14-15
Radio Boukman, 253
Radio Caraïbes, 55, 256, 306
Radio Echo 2000, 143
Radio Enriquillo, 136

Radio France Internationale, 153, 331
Radio Haiti Inter, 29, 30, 35, 97, 322
Radio Ibo, 143, 242
Radio Kiskeya, 81, 94, 101, 120, 123, 126, 168, 197, 212, 250, 253, 270, 282, 292, 321, 331
Radio Métropole, 56, 62, 79, 82, 90, 98, 100, 111, 123, 140-1, 151, 183, 321, 324, 330
Radio Signal FM, 31, 52
Radio Solidarité, 143, 180
Radio Vision 2000, 49, 79, 142, 143
Radio-Telé Ginen, 246, 276
Rangel, Charles, 65, 67
Rapwoche political party, 314
Rassamblement des Militants Conséquents de Saint-Marc (RAMICOSM), 42, 170
Rasanbleman Medya Pou Akyson Kominoté, 63, 201
Rassemblement des Democrates Nationaux Progressistes (RDNP), 24, 146, 212, 220, 235, 267, 280
Rasin music, 2
Ravix, Rémissainthe, 37, 47, 51-2, 56, 58, 63, 76
Raymond, Paul, 35, 79, 90, 118, 250
Agricole du Bas-Aritbonite, 93
refugees, DR Haitians, 310
Refugees International, 204, 214
Registre, Jean-Reginald, 67-8
Releco, 254
Renaud, Lener, 321
Renmen Ayiti, 212, 309, 314-15
Renois, Clarens, 228
Reseau des Associations Cooperatives du Commerce et de Production Agricole du Bas-Artibonite (RACPABA), 93
Réseau National de Défense des Droits Humains (RNDDH), 64, 66, 68, 91-2, 139, 149, 165, 171, 181, 204, 212, 224, 227, 229, 232, 239, 245, 251, 262, 267, 269-70, 279, 286-7, 302, 304, 307, 313-14, 317, 323-4, 328, 333
Reuters, 2, 105, 143, 200

Ribeiro Periera, Agusto Heleno, 93
rice, tariff lowering, consequences, 29, 37, 343
Rice, Condoleeza, 65, 67, 96, 103
Rice, Susan, 228
Richard, Jean Frantz, 184
Riché, Andrys, 105, 124, 166, 178-9, 261, 294, 324
Rigaud, André, 4-5
Riobé, Hector, 21
Rivera, Sandra Liliana, 183
Robert F. Kennedy Human Rights Award, 137
Robertson, Pat, 205
Robillard, Louino, 216, 267, 326
Robinson, Randall, 38
Robinson, Thos, 111
Roc, Nancy, 43, 50, 82
Rochambeau, Jean-Baptiste, 5
Roche, Jacques, 51, 84, 88, 99; murder of, 80-1, 83, 99, 213; murder convictions, 143
Roche, Madame Victor, 81
Rodham, Tony, 260
Rodriguez, Carlos, 72
Roitberg, Sergio, 132
Romage, Milien, 29, 31
Romain, Franck, 252
Romeo, Francesca, 243
Roosevelt, Frankin, 130
Ros-Lehtinen, Ileana, 174
Rosen, Marvin, 71
Rosenberg, Norman, 70
Rosier, Claude, 229
Roumain, Jacques, 1, 16, 88
Rousseau, Elise, 1
Route Nationale 1, 46, 170; blocking attempts, 151
Rouzier, Daniel Gérard, 198, 240-1
Rouzier, Philippe, 184
Roy, Véronique, 121
Ruelle Vaillant massacre, 102, 330
Ruquoy, Pierre, 136
Russef, Dilma, 252
Russell, John H., 15

Saieh, Issa L., 59
Saint Martin area, 90, 169-70, 262, 268, 272, 311
Saint-Fleur, Almétis Junior, 317
Saint-Jean, Franck, 145
Saint-Juste, Newton Louis, 253, 267, 271, 285-6
Saint-Louis de Gonzague school, 203, 219, 259
Saint-Marc massacre, 42-3, 64-7, 78, 92, 139-40, 170
Saint-Pierre, Hugues, 138-9
Saint-Rémy, Pierre Léon, 240
Saint-Rémy Charles "Kiko", 281, 286, 298, 302
Saint-Vil, Bernard, 31
Saintil, Napela, 109, 120
Saintilus, Hervé, 98
Salellas, Angela, 299
Salomon, Jean Marie, 281
Salomon, Lysius, 11
Salvation Army, 186
Sam, Guillaume, 14
Sam, Tirésias Simon, 13
Sam, Vilbrun Guillaume, killing of, 13
Samedi, Jean-Marie, 62, 105, 118
Sanders, Ronald, 332, 335
Sanderson, Janet, 109, 116, 175
Sanon, Jean Renél, 263, 269, 280-1, 285
Sanon, Sherlson, 279
Sansaricq family, massacre of, 22
Sant Kominote Altènatif Ak Lapé (SAKALA), 215
Santana, Pedro, 130
Santo Domingo, 22, 37; invasion fails, 11
Sarkozy, Nicolas, 202
Sassine, Jean-Philippe, 57
Schultz, Debbie Wasserman, 174
Sea-A Trading Co. Ltd, 232, 289, 300
Seabrook, William, 15
Seitenfus, Ricardo, 222-3, 226
Séjour, Rodriguez, 256, 274-5
Selavi, Lafanmi, 34

self-organized camps, post 2010 earthquake, 204
Sénatus, Jean Renél, 315; ousting of, 263
Service Jésuite aux Migrants, Ouanaminthe, 133
Sévére, Harold, 49, 284
Shah, Rajiv, 210, 213
Shannon, Thomas, 116
Siméus, Dumarsais, 96-7
Simidor, Daniel, 86
Simon Pelé, 32, 115, 120, 128, 266, 309
Simon, Woodly, 234
Skytel, 71
Slavant, Guitz "Guy" Adrien Salvant, 75
Slavick, William, 245
Slim, Carlos, 209
Smailes, Alex, 42
Smarth, Rosny, 28, 152
Smith, Matthew, 16, 175
Smithsonian Institution, 234
Société Caribéene de Banque SA (SOCABANK), 126, 140
Societé Haitiano-Américaine de Développement Agricole (SHADA), 17
Societé Nationale des Parcs Industriels (SONAPI), 288
Soifette, Bazile "Ti Bazile", 141
Sola, Antonio, 219, 220
Solidarite Fanm Ayisyèn (SOFA), 8, 184, 270, 304, 324
Solino district, 59, 90, 93, 119
Soros, George: Economic Development Fund, 176; Open Society Institute, 153
Soulouque, Faustin, 11
South Africa: Aristide in, 43; University, 125; USA pressure on, 79
squatters, post-earthquake nevictions, 262
St. Gilles, Kenol, 171
Stanford-Columbia University medical relief team, 199
Stapleton, Craig, 79
Steele Foundation, 36, 44
Storm TV, 331
Stotzky, Irwin P., 38

Strauss-Kahn, Dominique, 197
Suffrad, Charles, 30, 95-6, 164
Supplice, Daniel, 164, 219, 247
Supplice, Edmonde, 323
Switzerland, Departmwent of Foreign Affairs, 228

T-Vice band, 154
Tét Kale, 295
Tét Kole Ti Peyizan, peasant group, 198, 221, 246
Teleco, 33, 70-4, 77, 277
Telemax, 211
tent camps, post-earthquake, 243, 251
Terra Telecommunications Corp., 72-3
The Lancet, 86, 87
Thélusma, Sonny "Ti Sonny", 270
Therassan, Rudy, 39
Thermilus, Frantz, 165
Thimoléon, Jacques Stevenson, 284
Thoby-Marcelin, Philippe, 45, 89
Tholbert Alexis, Jean, 283
Thomas, Robinson "Labanye", 32, 41, 53, 61, 64, 66, 68, 76
Thomson, Charliénor, 91, 139, 170
Thomson, Ian, 97
Ti Bois, 99, 110-12, 122, 148, 262, 310-11
Ti Jackson, 215
Ti Kominote Legliz group (TKL), 35, 90
Ti Soldats, 25
Timothée, Rony, 285, 291, 298-9, 319
Tontons Macoutes, 20-24, 34, 261; creation of, 20; dissolution, 24
Torchon, Jean "Blade Nasson", 32, 140, 215
Toussaint, Dany, 143
Toussaint, Guiteau, 240
TransAfrica, 38
transitional government 2016 call for, 325
Treaty of Amiens, 5
Treaty of Ryswick, 3
Troncoso, Carlos Morales, 134, 137
Trouillot, Jean-Claude, 30

Trouillot, Lyonel, 89, 287, 328, 335
Trujillo, Rafael, 130, 133
Tufankjian, Scout, 190
Turner, Nat, 6
Tutu, Desmond, 102

UN (United Nations), 127, 162, 212,
    324; Centers for Disease Control
    and Prevention, 239; Collier report,
    232; Convention against Corruption,
    240; Department of Peacekeeping
    Operations, 77; Development Program,
    47; Food and Agriculture Organisation,
    203; MINUSTAH, see above; Office
    for Project Services, 319; Office for the
    Coordination of Humanitarian Affairs
    (OCHA), 200; Office on Drugs and
    Crime, 165; Police (UNPOL), 168. 213;
    Security Council, 150, 192, 228, 236, 298,
    304; Special Rapporteur for Human
    Rights in Haiti, 91; UNESCO, 58;
    UNICEF, 210;
Unión de Naciones Suramericanas
    (UNASUR), 192
Union de Citoyens Haïtiens Democrates
    pour le Developpement et l'Education
    (UCADDE), 165
Union Patriotique, 16
Uniplex Telecom Technologies, 73, 254
Unité Centrale de Renseignements
    Financiers (UCREF), 49, 69, 126, 149,
    253
Unité Départementale de Maintien
    d'Ordre (UDMO), 286, 292, 294, 322
Unité de Lutte Contre la Corruption
    (ULCC), 126, 140, 146, 164, 240
Unité de Sécurité de la Garde du Palais
    Nationale (USGPN), 42, 295
United Fruit, 18
Université d'État d'Haiti (UEH), 56; anti-
    MINUSTAH protests, 120; earthquake
    deaths, 184
Université de Port-au-Prince, earthquake
    2010 impact, 196

Uruguay, MINUSTAH troops, 245
USA (United States of America), 12, 19,
    261; Centre for Disease Control and
    Prevention, 218; confused Haiti policy,
    208; Department of Health and Human
    Services, 199; Department of Homeland
    Security, 58; Drug Enforcement Agency,
    38, 141, 148; earthquake actions, 187;
    Federal Communications Commission,
    72; Haiti Embassy attacked, 225;
    Haiti occupation, 8, 14; occupied Post
    Chabert prison, 248; Haiti trade ban,
    7; Haitian army attraction, 24; media
    cliches, 333; 1915 troops, 13; post-
    earthquake troops, 199, 204; realpolitik,
    342; State Department, 224, 330;
    troops food aid, 195; undocumented
    Haitians, 174; USAID, see below; War of
    Independence, 4
USAID, 37, 109, 176, 183, 202-3, 293; aid
    non-distributed, 213; Haiti mission, 205;
    Project Winner, 210
USS Carl Vinson, 187

Valdés, Juan Gabriel, 46-8, 53, 55, 61, 77,
    81, 91, 99, 108, 113
Valentin, Calixte, 241, 257, 267, 275, 308
Valenzuela, Andrea, 183
Valmé, Véronique, 120
Vargas Llosa, Mario, 281
Vazquez-Boidard, Manuel, 186
VCS Mining, 260
Venezuela, 26, 104, 107, 128, 141, 206, 260,
    273, 277, 301, 305, 339
Véréla, Frantz, 149
Verette, Donelus, 190
Vericain, Paul, 20
Verité, 309, 313-14, 316, 325
Vernet, Pierre, 184
Verret, Frantz, 146, 162, 173
Vesey, Denmark, 6
Veye Yo, 267
Viard, Angelo, 260
Vicini Burgos, Juan Bautista, 132

Vicini family, DR, 132, 135
Victor, Gary, 89
Victor, Guy, 314
Viergelin, Carline, 330
Vietnam, 277, 278
Viettel telecom, 277
Vieux, Max Édouard, 288
Villedrouin family, massacre of, 22
Villedrouin, Stéphanie, 247, 250, 256, 277, 286
Vincent, Jean Marie, 92
Vincent, Sténio, 16-18, 130
Viv Ansanm, 211
VJLS Computer Services, 69
Volcy, Assad, 154, 230, 282, 298, 301
Voltaire, Leslie, 47, 212, 214
Voordouw, Jan, 290
Vorbe, Joel Édourad "Pacha", 250
Voss, Ron, 245
Vodou, 2-3, 11, 17, 20-21, 35, 45, 205, 243, 280, 295, 316, 330, 342
Vwadèzil, 210

Wadestrandt, Jacques, 21-2
Waller, Littleton, 14
Wallis, Hilary, 299
Walsh, Amber, 269
Washington Post, 334

Waters, Maxine, 38, 64-5, 67
Waugh, Alec, 15
Weisbrot, Mark, 88, 101
Werleigh, Claudette, 154
White, Pamela, 298, 304, 315
Wilbert, Jacques Jean, 165, 184
Wilmé, Emmanuel "Dread Wilmé", 32, 41, 54-5, 60-62, 76-80, 96
Wilson, Destiné, 62
Wilson, Innocent, 192
Wilson, Woodrow, 14
WIN group, Haiti, 176
World Bank, 155, 174, 176, 206, 208, 277; emergency grant from, 151; structural adjustment policies, 28
World Economic Forum, Davos, 199
World Food Programme, 337
Wyclef Jean, 163, 192, 209, 211-12, 219, 233, 266

Yéle Haiti Foundation, 163, 192, 211, 266

Zamor, Oreste, 13
Zenny, Edwin, 225, 263, 279, 302
zinglin (armed partisans), 11
Zoellick, Robert, 155
Zounon, Carl Lubin, 120